Fictions

Fictions

Markus Gabriel

Translated by Wieland Hoban

polity

Originally published in German as *Fiktionen* © Suhrkamp Verlag Berlin 2020. All rights reserved by and controlled through Suhrkamp Verlag Berlin.

This English edition © Polity Press, 2024

The translation of this work was supported by a grant from the Goethe-Institut

 GOETHE INSTITUT

Polity Press
65 Bridge Street
Cambridge CB2 1UR, UK

Polity Press
111 River Street
Hoboken, NJ 07030, USA

ISBN-13: 978-1-5095-4661-9 – hardback

A catalogue record for this book is available from the British Library.

Library of Congress Control Number: 2023941416

Typeset in 10 on 11.5pt Palatino by
Cheshire Typesetting Ltd, Cuddington, Cheshire
Printed and bound in Great Britain by CPI Group (UK) Ltd, Croydon

The publisher has used its best endeavours to ensure that the URLs for external websites referred to in this book are correct and active at the time of going to press. However, the publisher has no responsibility for the websites and can make no guarantee that a site will remain live or that the content is or will remain appropriate.

Every effort has been made to trace all copyright holders, but if any have been overlooked the publisher will be pleased to include any necessary credits in any subsequent reprint or edition.

For further information on Polity, visit our website:
politybooks.com

Dedicated in friendship to Jocelyn Benoist
New York City, 31 October 2019

Is *My Name Is No One* a merry experiment and thus the pure product of a playful spirit, or is it a malevolent attack on the soul of every person who reads it? No one knows for sure, maybe both are true.

Daniel Kehlmann, *F: A Novel*

Contents

Preface   ix

Introduction   1

Part I Fictional Realism   19

§1   Interpretation and Reading   33
§2   There Are No Fictional Objects: Against a Philosophical Myth   46
§3   Meontology in Ontology of Fields of Sense   61
§4   The World Is Not a Fiction: The Incoherence of Borges's
     The Aleph   82
§5   FOS Is Not a Meinongian Theory of Objects   94

Part II Mental Realism   105

§6   From Naïve Realism to Illusionism   113
§7   The Indispensability of Mind   125
§8   The Lifeworld of Ontology of Fields of Sense   141
§9   Objective Phenomenology   152
§10   Ontology of the Imagination: (Alleged) Expressive Barriers of
      FOS   172
§11   Fictive, Imaginary and Intentional Objects   187

Part III Social Realism   205

§12   The Nature of Social Facts   221
§13   Our Survival Form: Intransparent Society   240
§14   Rule-Following, Realistically Conceived   262
§15   Mythology, Ideology, Fiction   276

§16 The Ontology of Social Networks   286
§17 The Public Sphere of Mind   294

On a Final Note: We Must Chase away the Spectre of the Post-
     Truth Era   301

Notes   305
Index   398

Preface

This book owes its existence, as well as its present form, to numerous institutions and individuals. First of all, I would name the Alexander von Humboldt Foundation, which supported my project about fictional objects as part of the Feodor Lynen Research Fellowship for experienced academics. This was carried out in several research residencies from 2017 to 2019 at the Paris 1-Panthéon Sorbonne University at the invitation of my host, Jocelyn Benoist. In this context, Jocelyn is the first person I should thank warmly for his philosophical and personal hospitality. Many of the ideas that have entered this book were first presented in Jocelyn's research seminars on intentional objects and social ontology, and also in lectures at various Parisian universities.[1] This is not the place to list all the conceptual details that arose from the wonderful dialogical situation in Paris; some of them are documented in the notes. To do justice to the fact that the traces of our dialogue form a crucial layer of the deep conceptual dimension of the reflections published here, I have dedicated this book to him in friendship.

As well as the Humboldt Foundation, I owe thanks to the CNRS, the Maison Suger and the Collège d'études mondiales (and thus the FMSH too). Since 2017 the CNRS has supported the Bonn–Paris research centre Centre de recherches sur les nouveaux réalismes (CRNR) as part of the excellence initiative LIA (Laboratoire international associé). This research centre is supported both by the University of Bonn and Paris 1-Panthéon Sorbonne, represented by the respective managements. The ceremonial opening took place on 25 September 2017 at the Sorbonne. I am grateful to Prof. Dr Dr h.c. Michael Hoch, head of the University of Bonn, and Prof. George Haddad, president of Paris 1, for their generous support.

The joint meetings of the CRNR in recent years focused on, among other things, the ontology of unicorns, the reality of norms (both promoted with notable posters . . .) and the relation between perception and reality – which covered the three pillars of the present study. In this context, I extend my warm thanks to those colleagues in Bonn and Paris who are members of the research centre, especially Sandra Laugier, who is advancing the expansion of the LIA in a philosophically, institutionally and personally proactive fashion.

I am grateful to the University of Bonn for generously allowing free research time during my stays in Paris and for the extremely favourable conditions at the International Centre for Philosophy NRW and the Centre for Science and Thought. I would also like to thank the University of Bonn for granting me research semesters, including the one I am currently fortunate to be spending in New York City as the Eberhard Berent Goethe Chair at New York University. For this, I am especially grateful to my colleagues at the German department for their hospitality, as well as the honour of being nominated for this visiting professorship. I am equally grateful to the participants in my graduate course in 'Fiction and Reality', which served as the final test run for the now published study, as well as the many conversational partners in New York who provided me with critical queries and pointers.

In addition to the lectures on topics dealt with in this book given on speaking trips to the USA, Japan, China, Portugal, the United Kingdom, Brazil, Portugal, Spain and Chile, I received especially profound suggestions from the philosophers, literary scholars, ethnologists and historians who kindly invited me, as the Walker Ames Lecturer, to seminars and lectures and the University of Washington in Seattle and Tacoma. I should give a special mention to Monika Knaup, with whom I had the chance to have intense discussions about the New Realism in philosophy and literary studies.

The person to whom I am most indebted for the reflections culminating in an outline for an objective phenomenology in the second part is Thomas Nagel, with whom, since my postdoctoral studies at NYU (2005–6), I have frequently debated the central question of what form a philosophy of nature would require in order to grasp the spirit as an irreducible manifestation of the universe. His monistic stance will presumably prevent him from agreeing to the present suggestion, but I do offer a diagnosis in the main text to continue the dialogue. Because of this encounter, which was especially important for my philosophical development, I was particularly happy to finish this book at NYU.

I received a veritably eye-opening shock from my encounters with Giulio Tononi, which took place as I was writing the second part. I would therefore like to thank the Chilean government of that time, especially the Senate (represented by Senator Guido Girardi), for the honour of being invited in 2018 to the Congreso Futuro, where I met Giulio for the first time (in the Antarctic, no less), and then, on a remarkable journey from Santiago de Chile to Valparaíso, had the opportunity to explore Integrated Information Theory (IIT) and its relation to New Realism in hours of conversations. This was followed by reciprocal visits to Wisconsin and Bonn. Naturally, this process was also influenced by Christof Koch, with whom I discussed various topics of the book in Wisconsin and Seattle.

In May 2019 in Bonn, Giulio asked after countless rounds of asparagus what current philosophical project posed the greatest challenge for New Realism. The answer: IIT. I was unable to undertake a detailed examination of the empirically informed ontology of consciousness, from which he derives a philosophy of nature that is currently unrivalled, so this will have to wait until a later opportunity.[2]

Three other people contributed substantially to the orientation of *Fictions* as the continuation of *Sense and Existence* through their objections to specific aspects of ontology of fields of sense: Anton Friedrich Koch, Julia Mehlich and Graham Priest. All three presented astute variants, each with their own approach, of an objection that, if true, demonstrated that ontology of fields of sense is reconcilable with a metaphysical fictionalism according to which the world exists in the field of sense of the imagination. In addition, Priest proposed a mereological model that, with a logical sacrifice of well-foundedness, causes the world to appear as an object in the world; he too based this in part on fictions – Borges's *Fictions*, to be precise.

As I was concluding work on the manuscript, Jens Rometsch made me realize that, for much of the book, I had had Anton Friedrich Koch in mind as my model reader, which I immediately conceded, even if I had not been consistently aware of it. In fact, my methodological sensibility – combining motifs from German Idealism *more analytico* with a sufficiently robust (albeit non-metaphysical) realism – was decisively influenced by the very long conversation that took place during the World Cup semi-final between Germany and Italy on 4 July 2006, which was almost impossible not to hear, at the Burse[3] in Tübingen, when he took me to task at his research colloquium for my formulation of a generalizable sceptical paradox. Since then, the conversation has steadily continued. I am grateful to Toni for his untiring and perceptive objections, which have led at least to reformulations, if not (yet) to a reformation, of my pluralism.

As always, this book would never have been completed without my outstanding university team, all of whom read every single line of text, commented on it and improved it, as well as doing the diligent work of completing the notes. For this, my thanks go to Philipp Bohlen, Alex Englander, Marin Geier, Mariya Halvadzhieva, Dina Khamis, Georg Oswald, Jens Rometsch, Guofeng Su and Jan Voosholz.

Jens Rometsch has (*comme d'habitude* for almost twenty years) tirelessly, and sometimes on a daily basis, made suggestions for adjustments in direction and, through his excellent habilitation thesis 'Freiheit zur Wahrheit' [Freedom for Truth], not only corrected my image of Descartes but also provided me with the concept of an 'overall mental state' (which he himself does not accept), by which I mean the de facto agent of the plurimodal cogito, as elaborated in the text.

Wolfram Hogrebe and Tobias Keiling read the complete manuscript and added critical comments that have hopefully saved me from making overly grave mistakes.

Certainly, it is impossible to retrace with absolute certainty all the textual and oral influences on the development of my thinking as reflected in this sequel to *Sense and Existence*. Nonetheless, I wish at least to provide an incomplete alphabetical list of important interlocutors not mentioned thus far in order to document which conversations in recent years have had an effect on my argumentation: Clemens Albrecht, Ned Block, Paul Boghossian, Thomas Buchheim, Otávio Bueno, Tyler Burge, Massimo Cacciari, Taylor Carman, Stephen Cave, David Chalmers, James Ferguson Conant, Paulo Cesar Duque Estrada, George Ellis, David Espinet, Armin Falk, Maurizio Ferraris, Günter Figal, Dominik Finkelde, Michael Forster, Manfred Frank, Marcela García, Tristan Garcia, Werner Gephart, Sacha Golob, Wouter Goris, Iain Hamilton Grant, Hans Ulrich Gumbrecht, Jens Halfwassen, Marta Halina, Graham Harman, David Held, Christoph Horn, Axel Hutter, Adrian Johnston, Alexander Kanev, Daniel Kehlmann, Tobias Keiling, Andrea Kern, Paul Kottman, Johannes F. Lehmann, Andrea Le Moli, Jocelyn Maclure, Quentin Meillassoux, Ulf-G. Meissner, Raoul Moati, Hans-Peter Nilles, Yasunori Nomura, Huw Price, Sebastian Rödl, Michael Rosenthal, Karl Schafer, Rainer Schäfer, Gert Scobel, John R. Searle, Umrao Sethi, Paul Snowdon, Nich Stang, Pirmin Stekeler-Weithofer, Dieter Sturma, Raymond Tallis, Amie Thomasson, Clinton Tolley, Charles Travis, Florencia Di Rocco Valdecantos, Eduardo Viveiros de Castro, Peter Weibel, Elwood Wiggins, David Zapero and Slavoj Žižek.

I would like to thank Philipp Hölzing for his thorough and clarifying editing, and of course Eva Gilmer for including the book in Suhrkamp Verlag's main academic roster.

The most important acknowledgement comes last: every book project is carried by the support of my small family. Without Stefanie, Marisa Lux and Leona Maya, things would lose their colour.

Introduction

Semblance is being. We cannot escape reality by deluding ourselves or being deluded, for the real is that which cannot be kept at a distance. Any attempt to flee reality is stymied by the fact that we bring ourselves along with us, meaning that the thing we seek to escape – reality – is at most altered by our imagination. No thought or action causes reality to disappear. We cannot be at a distance from being.

In a given historical context, the *zeitgeist* is the prevailing constellation of a semblance that legitimizes certain errors and inconsistences that dissolve upon closer philosophical inspection. One of the central tasks of philosophy is thus to grasp and criticize the *zeitgeist*.

The ideas expressed in this book are all based on the assumption that the *zeitgeist* it sets out to criticize rests on a skewed conception of the difference between being and semblance: semblance (in its manifold modes of appearance in the forms of illusion, delusion, error, being wrong, ideology, manipulation, falsity, fiction and so on) is wrongly associated with non-existence, which renders its distinctive effectiveness invisible. The implicit recognition of the existence of semblance (*as* semblance) results in the hopeless attempt to cleanse existence of anything merely semblant, to isolate a foundational layer of reality that is entirely free of semblance, pure being, existence, or reality. Yet the details of this very manoeuvre only give rise to a new form of semblance, one that needs to be seen for what it is and removed. Philosophy's reflection on our basic ontological concepts thereby offers hope of progress.

A familiar version of the problem of semblance and being concerns what are currently termed fictional objects, paradigmatic examples of which are the *dramatis personae* of our aesthetic encounters with literary art works, such as Gretchen, Mephistopheles, Macbeth, Anna Karenina and Jed Martin (the protagonist of Michel Houellebecq's *The Map and the Territory*). Fictional places such as Middle Earth and fictional times such as the imagined pasts and futures of science fiction also belong to this ontologically troublesome category. As soon as any allowance is made for their existence, it seems that we have to restrict and reduce that existence to the space of our imagination, or to some other mental aspect of our aesthetic practices. In this way, defenders of the *zeitgeist* can hope to deny the existence of fictional objects thus construed by relegating them to a realm of pure figments of the imagination or socially complex games of make-believe.

The naturalistic pressure of the current 'scientific' worldview demands at least one further reduction: even if our imaginations or aesthetic practices themselves exist in the full sense of the term, there still remains a gulf between our subjectivity, on the one hand, and the reality of the universe that can be described and explained by the natural sciences, on the other. For this reason, the human situation is generally subjected to a further metaphysical simplification. The source of fictions, known variously as 'mind', 'consciousness', 'intentionality' or 'subjectivity', itself falls under the suspicion of being an illusion. It is to be replaced by the alleged insight that only things which are unambiguous objects of a causal, experimental intervention genuinely exist. Demonstrable measurability by the tools of natural science becomes the metaphysical criterion of reality. Whatever does not satisfy this condition finds itself relegated to the carelessly described category of fiction, which *ex hypothesi* falls outside the jurisdiction of scientists.

In an age in which the academic enterprise is subject to repeated and demonstrative underfunding, familiar methods have been applied to marginalize the humanistic self-awareness of semblance and make us forget that, in addition to the natural and technological sciences, there are also the social sciences and humanities, or even philosophy, disciplines that have studied the ever-developing relation between being and semblance ever since the pre-Socratics. This self-awareness is said to be of little use, for, even when it succeeds on its own terms, it makes no immediate contribution to the economization and digitalization of our lifeworld advanced and applauded by all relevant decision-makers.[1]

To be sure, blame for the current crisis facing knowledge outside the natural sciences cannot be placed solely at the door of the apparatchiks controlling research. The exaggerated application of ideology critique to their own disciplines – as practised in the small historical timeframe known as 'postmodernity' – also bears a not inconsiderable share of the responsibility for knowledge in the social sciences and humanities having first come under *epistemological* pressures within the walls of the university itself and then under *socioeconomic* pressures in the public eye.[2]

If every knowledge claim is essentially suspected of ideological motivation (however unconvincingly this suspicion is articulated), it can be tempting to take refuge in technological progress; at least natural scientific knowledge, we might assure ourselves, can enjoy the honorific title of objectivity. It does not advance ideology critique to subject *this* objectivity to yet further science-historical restrictions.[3] After all, pointing out that the current conditions of objectivity of our scientific and technological practices themselves have a genealogy does not, in fact, lead in any rationally acceptable fashion to their objectivity being undermined. If a device functions, then the specific formats of self-discipline its inventors had to exercise in order to put it on the market at most play a secondary part. Pointing out that subjectivity is involved in the production of scientific and technological knowledge alone does nothing to undermine its objectivity.

The same should be said about the humanities and social sciences which paradigmatically deal with artefacts and, thus, with objects whose meaning is constitutive for their being. Subjectivity makes its appearance in the domain of objects of those disciplines. Yet, this by itself does not pose a threat to their epistemic objectivity.

It is therefore imperative to take up the discursive formation that, until recently, united philosophy with the humanities and social sciences and challenged it to track down the sources of error embedded within the *zeitgeist* and describe and explain them by the means available. For, without this form of reflection, unfettered scientific and technological progress will not lead to any kind of automatic and appropriate attitude in dealing with the resulting socioeconomic innovations.

In the past century, this was illustrated by the now classic debate on the connection between physics and the atomic bomb. Today, in light of what is colloquially referred to as the 'digital revolution', we must once again question the legitimacy of transformations that are presented in the *zeitgeist* as processes of automation that befall us inevitably, like revelations of humanity's fate. Yet technological progress is not fate; it is the consequence of numerous decisions and strategies that hide behind the widespread contemporary mythology of self-propelling digitalization.

The self-harm perpetrated by modern subjectivity in both its naturalistic and postmodern forms must be overcome. Despite its poor reputation, modern subjectivity is by no means the metaphysical driving force behind the ecological crisis, as many have thought in the wake of Heidegger's influential critique of Cartesianism. The problem is not the distinction between subject and object, mind and nature, but rather the elimination of the subject, the mind-pole of this correlation, without having first rethought the correlation as such.[4]

In place of a division of some supposed overall reality into mind and world, representation and causation, is and ought, culture and nature, subject and object, system and environment, and so forth, this book advocates a *humanistic irreducibility thesis*. According to this thesis, the human as a specifically minded being is the irreducible starting point of every ontological investigation. All theory construction starts out from *our* pre-ontological, pre-scientific experience. This experience is itself something real that comes into contact with other real things. The real reveals itself to us pre-ontologically in the mode of perception – because perception itself is something real. I will argue that perception is always attended by an element of illusion that enables it to be objective – that is, truth-apt. Only someone who can err can grasp the truth. Objectivity cannot exist without sources of error; this does not, however, undermine its claims.

The path to being (to the facts) cannot bypass semblance. A neuroscientist setting up an experiment must rely on their sensory perception just like the physicist who compiles data from a particle accelerator and presents them at a scientific congress. They will hardly dispute the existence of the audience or the approaching coffee break.

In this book, the humanities and social sciences will be accorded their full ontological dignity. What these disciplines investigate, I will argue, are the various ways in which humans view their own standpoint. Their object of examination is the human being in its discovery of self-images in all their historical variability and extraordinary synchronic and diachronic differentiation.

An essential task of contemporary philosophy is systematically overcoming the off-the-shelf naturalism that so many professional academics have unfortunately embraced. With its roots in university and education policy in the anglophone world, this tendency has led in recent decades to a decoupling of philosophy from the discourses of other humanities and the social sciences, with fatal methodological consequences for all concerned.

Attempts to lend philosophical and humanistic projects the sheen of scientific research – through scientoid publication formats, more or less well-worked-out formalizations of arguments, and even experimental 'methods' – fail to the extent that few who do not directly profit from these research projects takes any notice of them. Experiments in the humanities such as connecting narratology to cognitive or neuroscience soon reveal themselves as passing fads, in that they achieve little beyond verifying that we must possess appropriate psychological dispositions for a successful reception of narrative patterns – dispositions that presumably cannot be realized without neurological structures of some kind.

This is not to deny the real need to counteract the fragmentation of scientific activity by bringing into conversation all the academic disciplines that jointly constitute the idea of a university.[5] Yet genuine cooperation across disciplines presupposes a common object of investigation. The object common to all disciplines is the human standpoint, from which we investigate all other objects. To be sure, thanks to the progress made by individual disciplines, we have been able to weed out various human, all-too-human interference effects from this or that research project. But this should not seduce us into the nonsensical belief that we could leave the human being entirely behind us as both the goal and starting point of any investigation of reality.

To develop a common basis for all scientific, methodologically directed truth claims, we need a coherent ontology and epistemology to underpin a corresponding philosophical anthropology and philosophy of mind. Only on such a basis can we hope to legitimate a transdisciplinary format that is not simply geared towards the transfer of foundational research to the economy, but whose goal is human self-awareness and thus the potential moral progress of humanity; all advances in natural science and technology must be subordinated to moral progress if we are to prevent them from leading sooner or later to the complete self-destruction of our life form.

An ontological investigation is generally concerned with the question of what constitutes existence, and in particular with whether a specific type of object that has come under conceptual pressure really exists. An important touchstone of any given ontology is its *meontology* – that is, its theory of non-existence (μὴ ὄν). It is only once we have a stable conceptual framework, one that provides a comprehensible model for deciding questions of existence, that we can determine the ontological status of semblance in its relation to non-existence.

To this end, I will be mobilizing the concept of fictions. If we are to do justice to the fact that the mental and spiritual life of human beings takes place in dimensions that reach far beyond our presence in environments of sensory stimulation, we require an ontologically improved theory of fictions. Fictions are enactments in the space of this transcendence.[6]

More precisely, *fictions* are mental events that inhabit the interstices of our reference to the objects in scenes of our lives. At every moment of our conscious lives, we enact scenes.[7] We continually sift through our consciously experienced sensory environment in relation to objects that appear to us under various conditions of relevance. In this respect, the reality we perceive always bears our signature. A scene change takes place at every moment; both subjective and objective perceptual fields are constantly changing. Nevertheless, we are entitled to work on the assumption that there are stable objects (whatever these might be in a given case). What holds the indefinitely many scenes together are fictions: partially explicable assumptions about how the environment of our perceptual field that lies beyond our experience is equipped.[8] The way in which we scan – and thus modify – our perceptual field at any given moment depends on how we imagine the (retentional and protential) connections. Only this transcendence of the given enables us to classify the given as real. Stanley Cavell encapsulates this idea as follows:

> It is a poor idea of fantasy which takes it to be a world apart from reality, a world clearly showing its unreality. Fantasy is precisely what reality can be confused with. It is through fantasy that our conviction of the worth of reality is established; to forgo our fantasies would be to forgo our touch with the world.[9]

Generally speaking, *fictional objects* are objects to which we refer in the mode of their absence. They are currently present because we experience our perceptual episodes not only as a mental flow but as more or less stably arranged; this means we move beyond whatever is directly accessible to us as real in the mode of intuition. Not all fictional objects are also fictive – that is, objects of aesthetic experience that exist essentially in the mode of interpretation.

Fictive objects are performance-dependent: the way they are essentially depends upon how we imagine them to be – which, as we shall see, does not mean that there are no objective criteria for how we ought to imagine them. The relevant contrast between fiction and reality consists in how fictive objects, unlike non-fictive fictional objects, do not fill in the gaps in our perception of their own accord, so to speak. For example, what occurs between two different film scenes showing the actions of a certain character is filled in by aesthetic experience – that is, through exercises of the imagination.

This does not make fictive objects incomplete; however, they exist essentially in interpretations, which is what distinguishes them from non-fictive fictional objects. Our perceptual reality is populated by fictional (specifically: imaginary) objects; yet they must nevertheless bear a sufficient resemblance to those objects, in respects relevant to our survival and cognition, to fill in the gaps of our direct perceptions. What fills in these gaps so successfully does not usually depend on how we interpret it. The fact that my laptop remains in front of me, even when I briefly close my eyes and imagine it, means that it does not remain sitting there *because* I thus imagine it. By contrast, the fact that Gretchen has certain properties not explicitly ascribed to her in the text of *Faust* depends, among other factors, on how I imagine her. If I had imagined her differently, she would have had different properties.

Fictive objects are a subspecies of fictional objects, which divide into fictive and imaginary ones. One should note that not all intentional objects – that is, not all objects of truth-apt reference – are fictional. The objects of direct perception are certainly intentional (they are given to us in a particular sense-specific way), but they are not fictional in the sense deployed here, even though we cannot perceive them without recourse to fictional elements of our mental lives. Every perceptual scene involves a surplus that is not directly perceived, but rather connects us to manifold fictional objects without which direct perception and, thus, intentionality dealing with non-fictional objects would not be possible. Under what we experience as the normal conditions of our conscious perception, thanks to fictions we are not confined to isolated perceptual episodes.

When it comes to the emergence of semblance, our signature as human beings is central in so far as we transcend every sensory episode. Our lives are never led purely within the narrow confines of the here and now, restricted to solving the problems of survival or seeking momentary respite, like a predator exhausted by the hunt. Rather, each of us possesses a more or less individual picture of our overall situation as humans whereby we classify the episodes of our pre-ontological experience. What happens to us here and now belongs to each of our individual autobiographies, whose narrative and fictional elaborations we work on day by day.

We can neither circumvent this situation nor eliminate it via some sci-entistically optimized reprogramming of the human animal. The idea that progress in neuroscience, for example, would lead us to transcend our transcendence, so that we might finally shake off our tiresome conscious-ness with its 'pre-scientific' ideas, is merely one particularly incoherent case of human self-objectification. Our situation does not change one iota if we speak of cognition rather than knowledge, or of information processing rather than perception, and so forth. Nor would it make any difference if we articulated the elements of our mental life in a different code from the natural languages that are ideally suited to this purpose. No scientific reconstruction of our human mindedness will make the sem-blance constitutive of the human condition disappear.

The imagination is inescapably central to our self-determination. For there is no visible or scientifically identifiable property we can point to in order to establish who or what the human being really is. Who we are and who we want to be arises exclusively within the historically, synchronically and diachronically extremely variable concert of our self-representations.

Even in this age of increasing (and ultimately unchecked) domination of digital media over our self-portraits, we continue to objectify ourselves anyway by means of fictions. The innovation of social networks consists in having developed business models for the publication and exploitation of our capacity for developing self-images, most notably in the form of a platform economy. I will investigate this self-objectification in the form of the thesis that the mind is public, which leads us to recall the dialectic of the public sphere paradigmatically diagnosed by Jürgen Habermas. This can help reveal the emancipatory potential of a critical response to our self-digitalization.[10]

The conceptual epicentre of this study is *the Eleatic puzzle of non-exist-ence*. This is the ur-trigger for the distinction between being and seeming, and thus of philosophy as the science of this differentiation. The puzzle stems from our being able to make truth-apt (that is, true *or* false) state-ments about objects while simultaneously believing that some of them do not exist. We can thus speak truthfully about things that do not exist.

We must not renounce our claim to this capacity, if only because without it we could not judge that a given object (be it the present king of France, Zeus, Minerva, numbers, moral values, qualia, mesoscopic everyday objects such as tables, or whatever one deems ontologically questionable) does not exist. In short, the Eleat puzzle is this: If one speaks the truth about an object O when one judges that it does not exist, then it is true of O that it does not exist. But, if something is true of O, how can it not exist?

It is questionable, however, whether one ever has occasion to say of an O only that it does not exist without, at the same time, considering many other O-related statements to be true, such as that O occupies a certain place in the Greek pantheon, that Homer has provided us with relevant descriptions of O, and so on. Yet if one can only truthfully deny O's existence by ascribing to it other characterizing properties, how can one then avoid taking an object named Faust, who seems to be a man, to be at once both existent and non-existent in addition to having many other individuating properties?

One path out of the Eleatic labyrinth is to gather together those objects that do not exist with those that do in an overall domain that could be termed 'being'. Then both the existent and the non-existent objects would belong to being. Then non-existing objects *are* (something) without *existing*. This variation is derived from Alexius Meinong's much discussed and mostly repudiated ontology – though recently, in the guise of Neo-Meinongianism, it has astute defenders again, most notably Graham Priest.[11]

In my *Fields of Sense* [*Sinn und Existenz*] I have already argued at length that there is no such overall metaphysical domain encompassing all objects, a domain that, in the second act, one could split into a domain of existence on the one hand and a domain of non-existence on the other.[12] *Being does not exist.* I replace a metaphysical overview of all reality with an ontology of fields of sense (henceforth FOS). This assigns objects to fields of sense, which are arrangements of objects subject to a system of rules. Fields of sense always include some objects and exclude others that appear in their immediate or distant surroundings. Since there is no all-encompassing field of sense, both the catchment area and the forecourt of a given field are restricted.

This framework lends itself to an obvious meontology: whatever does not exist exists somewhere else, as it is excluded from one field of sense and assigned to another. This does not create a field of everything that does not exist, however, such that one could once again collect two fundamental classes of objects – the existent and the non-existent – in one overall picture. For whatever does not exist is excluded from a field of sense under specific conditions. Objects that are impossible in one field of sense (such as round squares in a Euclidian geometry or contradictory objects with attributes that are mutually incompatible within a given logically consistent inferential order) exhibit an entirely different kind of non-existence from, for example, fictive objects such as Mephistopheles. The latter do not exist in the sense that they appear only indirectly in our domain of the real – that is, only embedded within a fictional field of sense they cannot leave. And hallucinations, or products of social imagination (such as only seemingly well-delineated social identities such as 'race' or even less tangible notions such as 'society', 'neoliberalism', 'capitalism', and so on), do not exist in yet another way.[13]

Fictions cannot be fenced off once and for all, because they are expressions of our free and minded life, whose historical and variable self-determination is impossible to grasp once and for all in some form of overview. By contrast, the formal invariant of the genesis of fictions cannot be historicized; it is what I call human mindedness (or *Geist*), i.e., the human capacity to generate self-images.[14] Human beings live their lives in light of a representation of who or what they are.

Heidegger provides a concise formulation of this thought in his *Contributions to Philosophy*: 'Self-being is the finding that already lies in the seeking.'[15] To be someone paradigmatically means forming a conception of who one is and who one wants to be. Our actions realize self-images, which are modified by various factors, including others' commentary on this process. The structure of subjectivity and intersubjectivity grounded in the exercise of our imaginations is the undeniable point of departure for our situatedness, which I therefore call – in a distant echo of Rilke's *Hiersein* – *being-here*.[16] Every epistemological and ontological coordinate system that we use to attribute or deny existence to entities is rooted in being-here – a fact one can lose sight of if one's self-determination takes a putatively scientifically supported detour into 'cosmic exile'.[17]

In an age of naturalist worldviews, it seems obvious that we should locate the human being by largely abstracting from our subjectivity and regarding ourselves as 'earthlings', creatures in which a momentary insight into their own insignificance emerges against the background of the smallest and the greatest cosmological scales. Yet this scenario overlooks that it itself represents an exercise of the imagination with which advanced physical cosmology in particular has hardly dispensed. This is because a naturalistic worldview is by no means a mere collection of data, but rather a constructed world picture that comes into being only once we have abstracted from ourselves in the material-energetic universe's favour.[18] Yet physics cannot give an adequate account of how physicists – and thus, as far as we know, particular human beings – exist – that is, beings who take their own position in the cosmos into account in order to develop a scale that allows them to embed the mesoscopic affairs of daily life in relationships that can be observed only indirectly (through experiment, theory construction and the cognitive expansion through technology that results from these). Neither the measurement problem of quantum physics nor the self-awareness of consciousness can so far count with any certainty as problems for which we have found *physical* solutions in the narrow sense.[19] The attempts at metaphysical railroading through an ontological reduction or elimination of those human phenomena that stand in the way of subjectivity's self-abolition should therefore be seen for what they are: poor fictions.

The three parts of this book cover various dimensions of human fictions without making any claim to exhaustiveness. The reason for thematizing these dimensions in particular is itself historical – that is, determined by the historical circumstances of the book's composition, circumstances in which the question of non-existence poses itself in a specific way. To the extent that the systematic answers I offer are true, 'transcendence' has been achieved – that is, insight into historically invariant facts.

The first part develops a *fictional realism*. This cannot be straightforwardly located on the map of standard positions regarding so-called fictional objects. The basic idea of this section is, rather, that the very question of whether 'fictional objects' exist is largely misguided, since at least two kinds of object tend to be conflated and thus melded into the equivocal 'concept' of 'fictional objects'. I call these two kinds of object *hermeneutical* and *meta-hermeneutical* respectively. Hermeneutical objects are those that are essentially interpretation-dependent. They exist in those fields of sense in which we speak and think about them only because we imagine them to be a certain way in the context of a specific imaginative occasion (an art work) (§§ 1–2). This imagining consists in constructing, based on our factual situation, a field of sense in which the hermeneutical objects (which I shall call 'fictive') appear.

By 'interpretation' I do not mean anything like the scholarly dissection of a literary text, for example, but rather the performance of a field of sense and the objects appearing within it on the mental 'stage' of a recipient triggered by an encounter with fictional objects presented within an art work.

This process can then become the object of what I will call a 'reading'. This reading constitutes the ensemble of investigations in the humanities and social sciences into aesthetic experience and its underlying materiality. This includes not only texts, sculptures, tape recordings and digital copies but also the psychologically and sociologically analysable types of aesthetic experience that can be expected of recipients in a given time and society. How one images Gretchen is not a private metaphysical affair but a process that can be explored from both internal and external perspectives.

An important manoeuvre in Part I is *meontological isolationism*. This maintains that we are screened off from fictive objects by virtue of their existing in fields of sense in which we fundamentally cannot exist, and vice versa.[20] Gretchen exists in those fields of sense that are opened up through the texts and interpretations of *Faust* (*Urfaust* + *Faust I* + *Faust II*). To be precise, these are infinitely many, because all legitimate interpretations (all actual and still possible receptions) present fields of sense in which Gretchen exists. What is true of Gretchen can be ascertained only by imagining her, which is what one does when one interprets an edition (what I will call a 'score') of *Faust*.

The materiality of the art work places limits on the imagination: not anything and everything that someone associates with 'Gretchen' is a legitimate interpretation. What is a legitimate interpretation is determined by an interplay of interpretation and reading, since even the most sober Goethe scholar has to imagine Gretchen to be some way in order to understand whose reception history he intends to describe.

We are ontologically isolated from fictive objects (and vice versa). They appear only in fields of sense that are produced, in part, by exercises of the imagination triggered by the presence of the material side of art works. These fields of sense are *fictional*, as opposed to *fictive*, because they exist here, with us, as exercises of our imaginative powers occasioned by an aesthetic experience that imposes limits on those powers.

Fictive objects are embedded in facts: some things about them are true, others false. These facts are relational; it does not follow from the fact that something is true of Gretchen in *Faust* that it is true of Gretchen elsewhere. From 'In *Fiction F* it is true that *p*', it does not follow *tout court* that *p*. Gretchen is a human being in *Faust*, but not in Leipzig. Because facts concern objects, which can only ever exist in fields of sense, there is no more a metaphysical totality of facts than there is a world as a totality of things.[21] It is simply not true that everything hangs together with everything else; there is no all-encompassing context such that a fact in one field of sense automatically conflicts with another if they are (seemingly) expressible in contradictory propositions.

This will be spelled out in §3 in the form of a meontological position, whereby something can both exist and not-exist. Whatever exists appears in (at least) one field of sense and is thus excluded from other fields of sense, in which it consequently does not exist. Gretchen exists$_{in\text{-}Faust\text{-}performances}$ and Gretchen does not exist$_{in\text{-}London}$. Performances of *Faust* do exist in London, of course, yet Gretchen herself does not thereby attain any ontological civil rights in my field of sense.[22]

Both existence and non-existence are instantiated in the form of relations. According to FOS, the existence relation is an ordering function (sense) of a domain of objects. An object domain that is factually set up in such and such a way is a field of sense.[23] The property of existing thus consists in a certain object or objects being assigned to a given field of sense. Under the auspices of negation, the same goes for non-existence. What does not exist in one field of sense is referred to a different location and accordingly exists in another field of sense.

If one disputes the existence of unicorns, for example, this still leaves the film *The Last Unicorn* unaffected; its interpretations manifest a field of sense in which unicorns certainly do exist. According to the meontology of FOS, to say of the unicorns that confront us in art works that they do not exist is to make an assertion to the effect that unicorns exist *elsewhere* but not *here* (for example, in the cinema or the universe). The unicorns that appear to us in the medium of aesthetic experience therefore exist in some places but not others.

There is no more such a thing as non-existence *tout court* – that is, as a property pertaining to a (thereby) determinate object independently of its membership in a field of sense – than there is such a thing as existence *tout court*. This provides the solution to the Eleatic puzzle, for the statement that a certain object O or a kind of object K_o does not exist does not attribute any property to O or K_o that can be instantiated only if the object exists in the field of sense in which one intends to establish its absence.

This model risks undermining FOS's no-world-view which ultimately finds expression in the slogan that the world does not exist, which raises the question of whether it might not then exist elsewhere, such as in our imagination. In §4, I discuss this issue in the context of the Mehlich–Koch objection, supplemented by a suggestion from Graham Priest, who, as well as taking recourse to Jorge Luis Borges's *The Aleph* (in which the world seems to exist embedded in a fiction), proposes adopting the (heterodox) logical form of a non-well-founded mereology, which seems to make room for the world's appearing as a genuine part of itself. If the combination of the Mehlich–Koch objection and Priest's logical proposal were correct, FOS would be converted into a heterodox metaphysics. Both its anti-naturalist thrust and its ontological pluralism would be retained.

However, this combination of commitments is incompatible with the specific neutral realism of FOS, which contrasts with (neo-) Meinongianism (§5). The latter is based on a theory of objects that assumes an object is simply whatever we can designate linguistically or mention. According to this model, there is nothing that is not an object (with the paradoxical exception of nothingness, as Priest explains).[24] This commits neo-Meinongianism to an ontological idealism or anti-realism, at least in so far as its operative category of an 'object' depends on the existence of linguistic reference. If the concept of an object is tied to language, this means that objects would not be objects without language. The pitfalls of this manoeuvre can be avoided, but only at the metaphysical cost that we generate a totality of objects (the world as a maximal whole) which at least in part is mind-dependent such that we move the issue of idealism to a metaphysical level.

This topic is taken up in the second part, which defends a mental realism. Generally speaking, mental realism is a commitment to the irreducible existence of the mind along with some of its modules. By a *module of the mind* I mean a capacity (for example a sense modality, such as sight, hearing, phenomenal consciousness, self-consciousness, the understanding, intelligence, and so on) that we ascribe to ourselves and others in the context of action explanation. We explain both our own actions and those of others by compiling a portfolio of mental states whose overall structure, it should be noted, is not available in any single scientifically objectified model. The mentalistic vocabulary with which we specify our mental capacities is constitutively historical; it varies both diachronically and synchronically, and we could never uncover any ahistorical criterion (such as the notion of a 'folk psychology') that would allow us to compile a definitive catalogue of mindedness.

This precisely does *not* imply that we can attain the goal of complete self-knowledge by eliminating the mind, or whichever modules are currently considered central (consciousness, intentionality). I will therefore show first of all that both naïve realism and illusionism fail (§6). Mind is neither an ahistorically accessible apprehension of reality, such that we can withdraw to a maximally self-transparent *cogito*, nor therefore an illusion, as illusionism maintains with equal falsity.

Against this constellation of extreme positions, §§ 7–8 expand on the aforementioned irreducibility thesis, which states that the human standpoint contains an invariant core (*the* anthropological constant): our capacity for generating self-images, the fact that, through the elaboration of self-portraits, we locate ourselves in contexts that transcend every sensory episode. We can call this core simply 'human mindedness' (or *Geist*). Human mindedness is connected to a potential for illusion, including the fundamental illusion of metaphysics, namely that there is an all-encompassing whole to which we belong. Because we rightly locate ourselves in contexts that indefinitely exceed everything sensorily given, the false impression arises that there is an all-encompassing whole (*the* world, reality as a whole) in which we are located.

Mind is the whole in which we implicitly locate everything we cognize, meaning that the necessary natural conditions of our existence (including our central nervous system, which is essentially embedded in an organism and enables cognition) from the standpoint of epistemology are parts of the mind and not vice versa.[25] The brain is part of the mind; but the mind is not part of the brain. This circumstance is trivially compatible with supervenience, in so far as there is room for the (by no means empirically verified!) assumption that, whenever there are variations in the mind, there are also corresponding variations in the brain. What is excluded, however, is an identity theory (of any form) which stipulates that all mental states (or types of state) are identical to something neuronal.

§8 introduces the concept of mind in order to avoid the error of hypostatizing the lifeworld [*Lebenswelt*] into a culturally specific habitat [*Lebensraum*] – a mistake that led Husserl in *The Crisis of European Sciences* to adopt an ethically dubious attitude to the question of what it might mean to recognize a multiplicity of lifeworlds. In FOS, the lifeworld is indefinitely ontologically differentiated, such that, even at this level, there is no all-encompassing unity such as a 'culture' or an overarching 'society'.

§9 develops a theory of perception that replaces the foundational phenomenological concept of adumbration [*Abschattung*] with that of irradiation [*Abstrahlung*]. This theory boils down to FOS's variant of direct realism. Perception, as something real, is an overlapping of fields of sense whose nature as a medium allows us to grasp realities directly, without their being mediated through something unreal (such as epiphenomenal representations) that intervenes between us and the objects of perception. Perception is its own mediation, as it were, it does not require an additional veil, filter, or interface that takes place within our mind.

To avoid regressing into a brusquely naturalistic reading of this claim, I develop an objective phenomenology that portrays our overall mental states in acts of perception as irreducibly causal – indeed, as paradigms of causality. The concept of a cause stems from our perception, which is thus not only a case of causation in general but the reason why we have a concept of cause to begin with, one that we can justifiably extend beyond the horizons of our perception and into the universe, which we can then explore by means of natural science.

In §10, I return to the objection that the imagination has the potential to bring about the manifestation of the world, then countering it on the basis of an elaborated ontology of the mental. This ontology delivers decisive reasons for avoiding the (neo-)Meinongian theory of objects.

The discussion comes full circle in §11, which distinguishes between fictive, imaginary and intentional objects in order to explain in detail why the world as a totality of objects cannot be meaningfully depicted in terms of any of these categories. The attempt to bring back the world into the realm of the mental thus fails three times, each time for a different reason.

The third and concluding part of the book turns to the remnants of constructivism scattered across the discursive landscape of New Realism, specifically in the domain of social ontology. I reject the idea, whose prominent advocates include John Searle and Maurizio Ferraris, that the social is constructed while the rest of the universe (nature) remains untouched by it. Taking aim at this constellation of analytically improved social constructivism, which has recently enjoyed increasing popularity not least thanks to the analytical interventions of Sally Haslanger and others, §12 argues for the incoherence of constructivism as such. To determine the nature of specifically human social facts – that is, their ontology – we must consider, firstly, how minded beings qua beings of a certain kind are socially *produced* and, secondly, how they thus come to possess mental states that essentially need correction. It is no coincidence that human beings emerge under conditions of reproduction that are already social, by means of which a habitus is inscribed in their bodies that is already formed in the womb. Humans do not grow on trees but emerge through the coordination of human actions. Humans are thus social products, whereby the process of social production is 'real' in every conceivable sense and a legitimate object of realist theorizing. The social production of living beings is not 'in the eye of the beholder' in any relevant sense, and is thus not bound to parameters for which the (in any case questionable) analytical category of 'social construction' would be recommended in the first place.

Yet we can go further: even the dimension frequently emphasized within recognition-based theories of the social turns out to be realistically constituted. The basic human need for recognition is in fact socio-ontologically anchored; when we take something to be true that others consider false, we are confronted with our own fallibility. Fallibility as such only appears in factual dissent. To counterbalance factual disagreement, it is not sufficient to establish intrinsic belief mechanisms that subject future participants in our discourses to some particular training, for disagreement is a property of joint holding-to-be-true, and thus tied to truth and freedom.[26] The social participation in holding-to-be-true consists in how others put us on the right track by making us aware of facts we had not previously considered. Whether or not these facts obtain determines the nature of our holding-to-be-true. In the paradigmatic successful case of knowledge, we take something to be true because it *is* both true and non-coincidentally justified.[27] Since one does not necessarily know that one knows something, others are in a position to unsettle even our epistemic successes.

Socio-ontologically speaking, institutions can then be understood as balancing systems that neutralize factual disagreement by making judgements when they cannot take all the facts into account. Against this background, the paradigmatically social facts discussed in the social ontology of the human community are already social products of a balance whose foundation is the social.

In §13, I argue that the social displays zones of opacity on account of its ontology. It is fundamentally impossible for something to be both social and completely explicit. The opacity is therefore not something contingent that can be superseded by some ideal of complete explication, which means that no utopian consensus can be coherently conceived as an objective in a rational society. Complete unity in judgements, in the holding-to-be-true of all actors belonging to a social system, would do away with their sociality. Unity isolates, which is why those who seek agreement constitutively relocate their own factual opacity to an outside in order to generate a fiction of the other (the stranger) that corresponds to their own holding-to-be-true.[28]

The others are thus a social product of the will to consensus in a group that coordinates its actions based on the false utopia of a total coalescence of truth and holding-to-be-true. Against this, one must recognize the insurmountable otherness of the social, which is built into every process of group formation through the simple fact that we hold something to be true that others hold to be false. The others belong as strangers to the very social system that seeks to exclude them.

Therefore the others are part of a fiction. Because they are not fictive objects, however, their treatment in the mode of the fictional is literally life-threatening, for the way in which one imagines their holding-to-be-true has socioeconomic consequences at the level of the institutions that strive for balance. To the extent that these institutions are governed by the fiction of the stranger and are thus, contrary to their intentions, anything but neutral, they are bad, discriminatory institutions.

In this context, §14 provides a realistic reconstruction of the time-honoured topic of rule-following. Realistically understood, rule-following is neither a process that can be reduced to the mental states of an isolated individual (here one can follow Kripke's line with a grain of salt) nor a free-floating process unconnected to any facts (the realistic solution, unlike Kripke's, is thus anti-sceptical). The way out of the dialectical cul-de-sac is a realistic social ontology with room for social facts that determine which rule someone is following.

There are facts about what we ought to do. These facts are normative, since they distinguish between correct and incorrect behaviour. Conditions of correctness are not in the power of individual actors: as creatures of a certain kind, they can only survive within a space of possibilities that can never become fully transparent to them. Basic normativity does, then, arise in part from natural facts, such that there is no essential gulf between is and ought, nature and spirit/culture.

Since it is not in the nature of institutions to discriminate in a nefarious way, one can use the standard of the inevitability of disagreement to develop the idea of a community of dissenters – which, under conditions of social injustice, turns dissenters into prosecutable dissidents. Successful sociality is based on a culture of disagreement that reckons with ineliminable zones of opacity but in no way considers them commendable in the sense that essential decisions should be made in the socio-ontological underground, so to speak. On account of its opacity, this would not provide suitable guidelines for designing institutions.

This leads in §15 to the idea of a critical and realist social philosophy that distinguishes between mythology, ideology and fiction.[29] I here follow Bourdieu's remark that 'one may in any case doubt the reality of a resistance which ignores the resistance of "reality".'[30] When it comes to establishing an authoritative grounding for critique, social constructivism fails to accomplish what it intends, for it does not follow from the fact that something is socially constructed (such as a gender role that does not harm those to whom it is ascribed or who themselves accept it) that one should change it. If the thrust of the critique is based merely on the idea that a social system could be designed differently, nothing follows from this as long as there is no proof that it would be objectively better to build a different system. Social constructivism collapses on the ontological level in its notion of critique as struggle, which would entirely relocate the business of criticism from academic discourse to the streets, parliaments and petitions. Which social system exists and how it is constructed would be merely an expression of power relations, leading to the paradox of unjustified fact-acts [*Tathandlungen*]: any resistance would merely be the revolt of those so far defeated, with no correspondence to social or normative facts that are independent from a group's decision to recognize their power.

It is not in the nature of social critique, however, that it can be expressed only by the opposition, which presents itself as the voice of those who (supposedly) have none.[31] Championing the cause of the structurally disadvantaged can be based neither on a groundless will to resist nor on heartfelt sympathy alone. Instead, there must be room for recourse to social facts and their social conditions of production, so that institutions have the opportunity to examine and improve their balancing systems. It must be an option for the possibility of moral progress to be considered at the *institutional* level, which requires open social systems that can also be corrected through willingly consulted procedures of critical theory construction.[32] There can be no moral progress without a reciprocal, ever-evolving coordination between institutions and institutional critique.

§15 thus provides a set of tools for the critique of metaphysics – in particular, for exposing naturalism as a mythology and the corresponding scientific outgrowths of neurocentrism (which confuses being human with being a brain) as an ideological apparatus that propagates a literally false consciousness (that is, a false image of consciousness).

These tools are then put to the test in §16 using the concept of social networks. The basic idea is that the ontology of social networks consists in marketing social intensity and hence decoupling sociality from truth and freedom, leading in the worst case to the collapse of sociality. Social networks produce patterns of behaviour that they can then read using psychometric procedures. Once the cycle of media form and suitably adapted user behaviour is established, the owners of the means of production of social networks can, in a targeted fashion, reproduce whichever conditions make the behaviour of their users sufficiently predictable for them to intervene in their free self-determination.

As a consequence, we have witnessed the emergence of a global digital proletariat, recruited in part from the middle classes of rich industrial countries. Without even being paid a minimum wage, users produce the data whose readability forms the basis for the companies' profits. What we therefore need is a digital revolution, which has not yet taken place.[33] What goes by the name today is the exact opposite: manufacturing relations of production to establish a new working class that, in addition to its wage labour, spends many working hours generating data sets and cultural capital. This deludes the 'employees of installation'[34] into believing that they are capable of shaping themselves on platforms of uninhibited expressivity beyond the constraints of nation states.[35]

From this perspective, the metaphysical formation that naturalistically identifies the human being with measurable, intellectually optimized fight-or-flight machines serves the ideological justification of social networks; it is no accident that these tend to peddle in-house ethics commissions. Officially, these are supposed to develop an ethics of AI, although the real intelligence at issue is that of the software developers, whose proper names are the answer to the decisive question (*cui bono?*).[36] For this reason, we do indeed require a self-enlightened ethics of AI, one developed in concert with the decision-makers of digitalization. But this requires full recognition of the diversity in human self-portraits without which no ethical universalizing strategy for finding common ground can be achieved. The universal is not a given target system of any hitherto existing ethical model. There is no shared ground on which to erect an ethics of AI, rather the ground has to be achieved in the first place which presupposes humanistic research into the human condition.

Finally, §17 argues in favour of reappropriating the theory of the public sphere in order to investigate the structures of mass media. To avoid the pathologies diagnosed in §15, I take recourse to an irreducible concept of *human mindedness* that constitutes the foundation of the public sphere. As specifically minded beings, we have an interest in the exchange of self-portraits and in a form of cooperation that shapes the social conditions of reproduction of human beings and their form of survival according to standards of moral progress. The institutions suited to this task emerge only through the articulation of disagreement, whose discursive form is oriented towards truth and freedom.

The facts – including the moral ones – decide which social balancing systems should be generated and maintained, and how. Humans are the purpose of this enterprise, both as bearers of responsibility to other humans and to our non-human environment. Human sociality is not some free-floating event but an intervention in the structure of the only planet we know of on which more just relations for ourselves and for other creatures are possible. This fact should be the foundation of a public sphere of *Geist* that is not a battlefield but a platform for exchanging views on the epistemic, and thus moral, improvement of the human condition. This ideal is grounded in social ontology, which presupposes an insight into the relation between being and semblance, with its ever-dialectical inclinations.

Fictions form the start and endpoint of this inquiry; for the social always takes place in part because we envision our own positions within a distributional network in an imaginary – that is, fictional – manner.[37] Because our mentalistic self-portrait is always also socially produced, our notions of ourselves and our position in the cosmos as a whole have social conditions and effects. Consequently, an unavoidable task of contemporary philosophical anthropology is to set out an ontologically robust conception of fictions. Without this, we will fall victim to a mythology that would hastily do away with fictive objects and pays the price for reducing aesthetic experience to the mode of transhumanist science fiction. Naturalism and science fiction reveal themselves as two faces of a metaphysical Janus, glancing, on the one hand, at the fiction of sheer nature (free from humans and consciousness) and, on the other hand, at the fiction of processes of social construction entirely detached from nature. In the following, the task is to free ourselves from the clutches of this worldview by philosophical means.

Part I

Fictional Realism

Some objects of our reflection are fictive. They exist, if at all, only because we 'loan' them existence, in a sense, through our (discursive) practices. One way of making this common idea more precise is to tie fictive objects to fictions – that is, to regard them not only as *fictive* but as *fictional*.[1] 'Fictional' objects would be those dealt with by fictions: that is, literary or generally aesthetic forms of representation, in so far as they represent objects (figures, events, circumstances) that we would usually – outside of the fictionality contract, that is – say do not exist.

This approach immediately throws up a twofold conceptual and thus philosophical difficulty, which I will seek to resolve in what follows.

The first facet of the problem is that one and the same object generates contradictions when we list its fictive and fictional properties. In *Faust*, Gretchen has the property of being in an erotic relationship with Faust. In *Faust*, she also has a mother (whom Faust poisons), so she is presumably a young woman of flesh and blood. The fictive object Gretchen is thus a more or less common, entirely human *dramatis persona*.

As a fictional object, she thus seems not to exist independently of the fact that we imagine her in this way. For, outside of *Faust* (however one demarcates this object domain), Gretchen is not to be found among us mortals. So how can the same object we think about – in this case Gretchen – exist both as a person and as a pure figment of the imagination? It is usually claimed that those objects we merely imagine (a body of water as part of a mirage, for example) do not possess their intended factual properties (for example, of being able to quench our acute thirst). So, when we 'merely imagine' Gretchen in this sense, she cannot be a young woman of flesh and blood.

Yet this means that many of the statements we find in the text of *Faust* are apparently false, since they either imply or directly assert that Gretchen has these properties. The fictional object that at least exists for as long as we imagine it in the medium of fictions and the fictive object we thereby imagine, then, seem to have mutually contradictory properties. So, can we imagine Gretchen at all if, in this mental *salto mortale*, what we are envisioning is an extremely contradictory object – an object that, to the extent that it is contradictory, fundamentally cannot exist and is thus impossible?

The second, connected difficulty is that fictional contexts (such as novels belonging to a clearly realist genre) also seem to contain objects besides fictive ones. Houellebecq's novels are often about Paris. Paris is not a fictive object (at least not in the same way that Jed Martin, the protagonist of *The Map and the Territory*, is a fictive object).[2] This seems to mean that some fictional objects exist while others do not, because some fictional objects (the fictive ones, such as Jed Martin) are massively contradictory, say, while others actually exist (the fictional but non-fictive ones such as Jeff Koons, to whom the narrator of *The Map and the Territory* refers). If this were true, it would undermine the conceivability – that is, the imaginability – of the so-called narrated world; for this world, in contrast to the world in which it is narrated, could be populated only in contradictory ways.[3]

As if that were not enough, objects that are both fictional and actually exist cannot be isolated from the contradictions, since the fictive characters will cause metaphysical chaos, so to speak: because the contradictory object called 'Jed Martin' lives in Paris in *The Map and the Territory*, the Paris thus represented cannot, at any rate, be identical with our Paris if it is indeed true that Jed Martin lives in Paris. This is the case, and thus true, in *The Map and the Territory* – that is, intradiegetically. Yet if it is intradiegetically true that p, it seems to follow effortlessly from this that p. Many things, however, such as the fact that Jed Martin lives in Paris, are certainly true intradiegetically, but false extradiegetically. So how can one believe that something is true of Jed Martin and his relation to Paris without thereby ontologically overloading *our* beloved Paris?[4]

The situation is exacerbated if one stubbornly insists that Jed Martin simply does not exist and therefore does not live in Paris either. True, one thereby rescues the ontic stability of the French capital, but only at the paradoxical price of once again communicating something true about Jed Martin's relation to Paris, namely that he does not live there. But, in so doing, one has referred to Jed Martin, which has merely shifted the focus of the problem. For how can one deny existence to an object of reference that can also be characterized as an artist, for example, but afford it to Paris, without thus committing oneself to the object's existence? How can it be true of an object that it is a human without its being true of it that it exists? Even if one can wriggle out of this problem, one immediately faces the difficulties thrown up by a fictional representation of a Jed Martin who is expressly introduced as existing; that is, who is represented not only as a human, but unequivocally as existing.

The aim of Part I is to present a fictional realism that allows us to resolve these classical paradoxes. In §§ 1–2 I will argue that the category of so-called fictional objects is not well defined. This supposed sort of object conflates objects of two types, which I will term the *hermeneutical* and the *meta-hermeneutical* respectively.

The *hermeneutical object* exists in the medium of aesthetic experience; it is that which we imagine on the occasion of a certain art work's being performed – a literary work, for example. How we imagine the hermeneutical object depends on us as interpreters. The *meta-hermeneutical* object differs from the hermeneutical object in that we can take its materiality into account. This materiality, as the sensuous side of art, triggers aesthetic experiences in suitable recipients, and these experiences, taken together with the materiality of the work, can be investigated using the methods of the humanities, social sciences, linguistics, psychology, etc.[5]

By an 'aesthetic experience', I understand the production of a field of sense in which objects dealt with essentially in the mode of fictional representation appear to a subject. An aesthetic experience is triggered by art works – or, more precisely, through their *presentation*, such as the staging of a play, a performance of a piece of music, a silent or audible reading of a literary text, or the observation of a work of visual art. What is performed depends in turn on a material architecture, on the sensuous side of the work that I will be calling its *score*.

A performance is an occasion for an aesthetic experience, but it does not compel it. No art work is automatically received as such. A book can be put away because it is lying on the kitchen table; an artistically conditioned heap of fat in the corner of an exhibition room can be mistaken for mere dirt; music can be bothersome noise and a painting a mere dab of colour. In such instances, no aesthetic experience takes place.

In some cases, aesthetic experience is a matter of producing figures and an appropriate setting (a 'fictional world'); in other cases, with non-mimetic (and thus non-representational) art, aesthetic experience involves sensuous sequences performed in the mind of the recipient with the goal of experiencing a succession of events (such as notes) as meaningful.

I am here following a by now canonical suggestion by Rüdiger Bubner, who discerns the function of aesthetic experience 'against the background of complex everyday functions in the opening-up of the extraordinary and unexpected area of complete functionlessness'.[6] This corresponds to a topos that has been with us since Kant and Schiller, namely the ludic nature of art (though it can in fact be traced back to ancient reflections on the existence of art): the element of play in art consists in how it grants us access to objects with which we stand in *indirect* contact, objects that do not threaten us because they are essentially re-presented, and thus depend on someone interpreting them, performing them.

Aesthetic experience is constitutively individual, because every recipient, on account of their psychosocial situation, interprets differently the objects with which they are presented. And each individual is entitled to do so precisely because the objects of aesthetic experience (which I will be referring to as 'fictive objects') are partially defined by aesthetic experience. This does not mean that they are in themselves indeterminate, but rather that they are completed within the individual framework of a psychosocially conditioned interpretation. The recipient thus bridges the gulf that opens up during reception between the materiality of the work and the resulting representations.[7]

Interpretations are not arbitrary. The meta-hermeneutical object fixes a circumscribed framework of imaginability, such that there are both legitimate and illegitimate interpretations. We can think of this framework, whose boundaries can be determined neither a priori nor in the act of creating the art work, as an *interpretive space*.[8] The meta-hermeneutical object has properties that we can make explicit by analysing how the narrated world is constructed, such as by using narratological tools. Accordingly, one should interpret Gretchen as though she were a seven-headed monster or merely a hallucination of Faust's, which potentially distinguishes her from the witches on Walpurgis Night. This is all a matter for debate in readings of *Faust*.

We thus enter upon transdisciplinary terrain, for the ontology of so-called fictional objects always enters into a feedback loop with the literary and more general aesthetic theory of fictionality. Recent contributions to literary theory are occasionally led astray by an untenable concept of the fictive, which is why I will suggest in §2 that we define the fictive in terms of the idea that fictive objects are essentially interpretable; that is, they depend constitutively upon their involvement in someone's aesthetic experience.[9] As we will see, this does *not* mean that fictive objects are a subset of the straightforwardly non-existent. For both fictional objects (that is, scores and their materializations in the medium of performances) and the corresponding fictive objects exist in their respective fields of sense. Yet these are sufficiently isolated from our field of sense to avoid causing any ontic chaos.[10]

A consequence of this isolation thesis, which I will draw on in the following, is that fictive objects suffer from a different sort of under-determination. Because the Paris in *The Map and the Territory* certainly resembles the actual Paris without being identical to it, the same applies to the ontological architecture of the represented field of sense: in *The Map and the Territory*, everything is ultimately (a little) different from how things are in our field of sense, which includes ontological properties, such as the property of having properties. The fictional fields of sense we access through aesthetic experience, fields populated by fictive objects in which corresponding fictive events unfold, are all ontologically isolated from us in such a way that we can only ever receive them as processes that at most resemble our reality.[11]

I also see this structure as the basis for the common topos of art's character of semblance, which goes back at least as far as Plato's critique: μίμησις (mimesis) – that is, artistic representation – is semblance, because its objects exist only under the condition that we can never fully grasp their identity. My Faust is different from the one Goethe himself imagined (my Faust also varies in any number of ways in my own psychosocial autobiography). Moreover, none of the many Fausts are self-identical in the way that non-fictional objects of investigation are self-identical. According to the isolation thesis, then, the vagueness of fictional objects does not reside where it is usually assumed; on closer inspection, that fuzziness is even far more severe than commonly supposed.

In the following, I will be locating the origin of fictionality in our fundamental ability to transcend what is immediately sensorily present and perceive it as part of different contexts that we can address conceptually, without thereby referring overtly or indexically to our immediate stimulus environment. I here follow Hans Blumenberg's reminder that concepts emerge at a distance, not as the baptismal act of naming we like to imagine – that is, with reference to something manifest that belongs to a shared stimulus-response scene. One does not form the concept of a lion once it is dangerously close but under the existentially secure conditions of a discussion in the cave. The painted lion is thus a paradigmatic conceptual coinage, meaning that we must connect our conceptual capacities with our transcendence of sensory immediacy, although this certainly leaves open whether such transcendence is a matter of overcoming our animality (as Hegel thought) or an echo of an evolutionarily conditioned, primitive anthropological experience (as Blumenberg believed). In any case, we can agree with Blumenberg that concepts allow us 'to detect *gaps in the context of experience*, how it is related to the absent – yet not only in order to make it present, but also to let it remain absent. It always bears repeating that the true intellectual achievement is to speak of something that is neither perceived nor given.'[12] It is because concepts and fictional depictions qua presentations of the absent share a genealogy that the tendency to confuse fiction and reality is rampant today, in an age of global electronic and digital media.

As elaborated in Part II, the human being, as the animal that does not want to be one, is always at a distance from itself; for we cannot simply state who or what we really are on the basis of our immediate sensory situation. Our conceptual abilities have developed historically within the space of this distance, which, since mythical and immemorial times, has been populated with fictional objects that we fail to perceive as such – from ancient myths to the statistical fictions of our contemporary socioeconomic sphere with which, directly or indirectly, we justify decisions about the distribution of resources.

To resolve the problem of how Jed Martin can seemingly both exist and not exist, I will first sketch an ontology of aesthetic experience that allows us to grasp fictive objects as objects performed – that is, interpreted – on the basis of an existing, publicly accessible score. Here I apply a generalized concept of a score that encompasses literary texts, films, sculptures, and so forth – in short, the material side of an art work. Accordingly, a *score* is a trigger for interpretation that does not force us to have an aesthetic experience, since we are also capable of overlooking an art work. We can note the material side of an art work without realizing that we have stumbled across a piece of art. Feature films and documentaries, newspaper articles and short stories, sculptures and decorations, noise and music are essentially confusable, a fact that contributes to the attraction of art, its aura of mystery.

Jed Martin thus exists within a framework of interpretations. The phrase 'Jed Martin' refers both to a meta-hermeneutical object, which we can all find in the score (in our own copies) of *The Map and the Territory*, and to a hermeneutical object, which differs from interpretation to interpretation. The hermeneutical object thus appears in the plural: it immediately splits up into indefinitely many objects, because my Jed Martin is not yours. The author of the score, in this case Houellebecq, also imagines a different Jed Martin from mine. What we share, though, is Jed Martin as a meta-hermeneutical, individual object that appears as a sign in a text and, through its context, is a trigger for aesthetic experience. At the hermeneutical level, then, we do not imagine Jed Martin differently; we imagine a different Jed Martin.

An author is not an authority on the question of how exactly one should imagine Jed Martin but merely generates the relevant interpretive space. Authors do not create literary figures, but rather texts. In the case of mimetic text genres, this usually presupposes that the author is the first interpreter of their text, which can be the basis for a textual revision.

The interpretive space of the text has normative force because one commits errors if, for example, one fails to imagine Jed Martin as he is described. How exactly one determines how he is described is a matter for the relevant disciplines and subdisciplines that research how we should analyse literary texts in order to understand them correctly.[13]

We can now introduce a distinction between distanced theoretical reading and engaged, synthetic interpretation.[14] An *analytical reading* (henceforth simply 'reading') is a methodologically guided, scientific reconstruction of the material conditions of an art work. Readings investigate texts, paintings, musical scores, sculptures, human practices such as rituals, interpretations, and so forth, and show, among other things, how these items and phenomena have come about. Readings thus contain genealogical potential, though this need not be their primary intention, as it is entirely justified for them to serve a purely antiquarian interest. To be effective as critical genealogy, they address a community of performance – that is, a group or individuals who, for example, have committed an error in their reading of a text. How we imagine a fictional object (such as Gustav von Aschenbach in Thomas Mann's *Death in Venice*), which exercises of the imagination take place, is predetermined by the text, while still always leaving sufficient interpretive space for aesthetic experiences that can never be fully anticipated.

No literary text can describe its fictive objects so precisely that all readers see the same thing. Even a film cannot do this: Sherlock Holmes's hair colour, clothing, and so forth, may all be visible, but we are hardly given an exact, detailed depiction of every minute of his life (for one thing, such a film would be too boring to trigger an aesthetic experience).

There are no fictions without gaps which the recipient has to fill in.[15] In films, the toilet door tends to remain closed; the sex is conducted only symbolically and usually beneath the covers; and so on. And anyone who has ever witnessed a birth knows that it is a rather different affair from what one sees in American hospital series.

Readings are analytical because they have to take the elements of a given experience as starting points in order to articulate their material conditions. They operate under holistic conditions, drawing conclusions from aesthetic experience as a whole about its material conditions.

Scholars of literature, art and music can thus act as their own anthropologists: on the one hand, they must first have an aesthetic experience which, on the other hand, they take as an occasion to explicate the universal, publicly accessible elements of that experience's score. This requires a certain self-discipline; one must remain within the legitimate interpretive space interrogated by the humanities and rein in the imagination by adhering to their methodological strictures.[16]

Analyses must be distinguished from *engaged, synthetic interpretation* (henceforth simply 'interpretation'), which consists in a recipient imagining objects on the basis of a score and thus enacting a (mental) performance of them. An interpretation largely loses itself to its fictive objects. The concept of interpretation is to be understood by analogy with the interpretation of a musical score, and therefore means something not dissimilar from what we usually designate with the term 'performance'. It includes listening to a symphony as much as reading a text or contemplating a sculpture, an activity that goes far beyond simply discovering a moulded piece of material in an exhibition space. The recipient completes an art work by adding the dimension of its performance.[17]

This resolves, or perhaps recasts, the much discussed problem of the (supposed) incompleteness of fictive objects. Thanks to the interpretive space we are afforded as recipients, we are entitled to imagine Faust in a way that provides us with ready answers to questions that the text by itself does not explicitly answer. There is a gap between score and performance, which is what allows for a multiplicity of performances. Yet this does not mean that the hermeneutical object is indeterminate.

The gap between readable foundation and interpretive performance can be closed neither by a reading nor by an interpretation alone. Aesthetic experience is and remains free; it is always bound up with an element of suddenness by virtue of which we are partially sucked into a work without ever disappearing completely.[18]

In this context, I recommend a hermeneutical realism that restricts interpretive leeway via the concept of the *urtext*, by which I mean the historically variable complex object of a methodologically secured analysis. To be sure, the urtext is accessible only with the aid of conjectures, and hence by making use of interpretations. Therefore it cannot be tied to some originary situation, such as a datable authorial intention to write down a particular sentence or to make such and such a brushstroke.

The theory I outlined in the first paragraphs sees itself as a contribution to determining analytically the location of Gadamer's hermeneutics, which, given the standard ontologies of 'fictional objects' that, from the standpoint of literary theory, so often rest on hopelessly unsupported literary-theoretical assumptions, deserves to be updated.[19]

To solve the problem of how Jed Martin and Paris can coexist, I will advocate a *meontological isolationism* that suggests itself within the framework of FOS.[20] Accordingly, the word 'Paris' in *The Map and the Territory* does not, as stated above, refer to Paris but serves as an occasion for interpretation. Given the sign 'Paris', we imagine something that resembles Paris but which cannot be Paris, because it exhibits properties that Paris does not possess (such as having Jed Martin as one of its residents). Paris in *The Map and the Territory* is not identical with the Paris that we can visit. 'Paris' is thus not Paris; one cannot, in this case, dispense with the quotation marks by referring to our Paris. Yet we perform a play on our mental stage in which we flesh out the narrated world with our own experiences of Paris.

Every narrative form with a *fabula* makes use of such background knowledge. This creates the impression that there are degrees of realistic narration, ranging from socio-critical novels of the nineteenth-century realist genre to science fiction works in which we imagine populated, unknown galaxies and time travel.[21] The impression, however, is misleading: realist narration is not news reporting, pointing its highly powerful logical telescopes at distant possible worlds; rather, it is ultimately the depiction of fictive events and circumstances that merely resemble the kinds of circumstances we import into our reception from non-fictional contexts.[22]

The philosophical theory of art thus falls within the scope of contemporary theoretical philosophy: innumerable objects we can successfully contemplate – that is, about whose constitution we acquire knowledge – exist. They thereby fulfil implicit or explicit requirements on existence that must be defended against alternatives in ontology within a theoretical construction. Different requirements on existence generate corresponding ontological commitments. To a large extent, contemporary *metaphysics* is thus an attempt to discover a preferred framework that allows us to decide soundly which of the objects we succeed in contemplating do not merely exist in some way or another, but exist or are real in a more ambitious sense.[23]

If more exists than we can meaningfully account for, existence seemingly threatens to become too weak a property. In the name of a paradigm oriented primarily towards the interpretation of natural-scientific objectivity, contemporary metaphysics generally understands itself as meta-physics, as a meta-theory of the natural sciences (whose ideal is represented by a futuristic physics). This is meant to allow us to divide the privileged domain of existence, the universe, into categories of objects and then discern architectural relationships between them that can be more or less reconstructed at one's desk in philosophical reflection (from the armchair, as the saying goes).

The limits of this entire enterprise, which in previous work I have called 'old realism', have been amply demonstrated by the many twentieth-century repudiations of 'metaphysical realism'.[24] In the following, my aim is not to offer yet another deconstruction of metaphysical realism and its understanding of metaphysics with reference to its massive ontological blind spots. Instead, I wish to map some as yet unexplored terrain. For, even if metaphysical realism did manage to metaphysically reinforce a positive criterion of existence, it would still entangle itself in severe difficulties with the anti-extension of its concept of existence – that is, with the non-existent. And that is the topic of this book.

Since Plato, Aristotle and Parmenides, it has been a philosophical commonplace that negation generates curious paradoxes when applied to existence. This issue will arise in the first part of this book in so far as fictive or fictional objects are considered prime examples of something that we can contemplate successfully, despite conceding that it does not exist.

At first glance, non-existence seems to be something we fundamentally cannot establish, assuming it requires making a statement to the effect that something determinate (numbers, mental states, phlogiston, witches, God, the soul, the ether, time, the present king of France, the round square, and so on) does not exist. Such a statement seems to presuppose that one is referring to something that exhibits characterizing properties (which, in the case of numbers, can even be stated with mathematical precision) while simultaneously asserting that it does not exist at all. Yet how can one make a successful judgement that something determinate does not exist at all without thereby at least implying that it exists in the form of an object of linguistic reference?

Mephistopheles does indeed not exist in some yet to be established sense, yet this cannot mean that he exists 'only in our imagination' or 'only in make-believe', since this would clearly mean that he very much *does* exist. Even if the word 'Mephistopheles' does not refer to Mephistopheles in the same way as the words 'Angela Merkel' refer to Angela Merkel, it does still refer to something somehow determinate – if, for example, one claims that Mephistopheles is merely imagined, invented by Goethe, made up, or however else one wishes to justify his exclusion from the realm of living beings.

Similar considerations apply *mutatis mutandis* to every other determinate object to which, for whichever reason, we deny existence, be it retrospectively or in the very course of its characterization. People talked about the ether, for example, because they sought an absolute frame of reference in which light can travel. This assumption proved superfluous, as we can better understand the physical phenomena it was meant to explain without it. We did not find the ether where we expected to. The ether proved a disappointment, and now we say it does not exist at all.[25]

Upon closer inspection, we find that the individual candidates for non-existence have been dumped on the ontological scrapheap for a great variety of reasons. We view discarded scientific hypotheses differently from anthropological aberrations such as 'witches', and we take a rather different attitude again towards abstract objects such as numbers and moral values, which strike some people as 'odd', because they seem unwilling to fit into our materialist or generally naturalist worldview.[26]

There is thus a multiplicity of *elimination reasons*, and it is only against the background of a presupposed metaphysical realism that they can be revealed as one and the same process, namely of removing an illusory construct from the impermeable realm of real existence (the world).

This overgeneralized model for justified claims to non-existence is thwarted by the counterarguments of the no-world-view.[27] If it makes no sense to say that existence consists in something's featuring in the world, we can hardly gain a view of non-existence by categorically throwing out a more or less coherently characterized object that has already been considered by some – that is, throwing it out of the world and into nothingness.

In §3 I will argue that non-existence should be understood, by analogy with existence, as a relation obtaining between an object and one or more fields. Whatever does not exist *here* exists *elsewhere*, assuming it was ever a candidate for existence in the first place. Witches do not exist in Wittenberg, but they do exist in Luther's imaginings, for example, which are in turn connected to Wittenberg, where they left behind some rather gruesome causal traces in the form of witch hunts.[28] If Jesus did not perform the miracles ascribed to him quite as they were recorded, then he may not have raised Lazarus from the dead *in Bethany*, for example, but he certainly did so *in the Bible*.[29] Put with greater ontological precision: Jesus raised Lazarus in Bethany in the Bible from the dead in the Bible. For the structure of this report and what one must imagine in order to assess its documentary adequacy, one can remain neutral at the narratological level and judiciously choose to restrict the report to 'Bethany in the Bible'; this would not involve making a mistake, since Bethany in the Bible may be identical with Bethany (if Jesus really was a miracle worker sent by God).

This leads to the formulation of a *meontological relationism* whereby something can exist in one field of sense and not exist in another, as questions of existence and non-existence must essentially be resolved with reference to a field of sense. Whatever exists, exists in relation to a field of sense, and that field must be evaluated whenever ontic disagreement arises (that is, when we have conflicting catalogues of objects for a recognized domain such as Bethany). Neither the property of existence nor that of non-existence is absolute in the sense that one can say of an object O, encountered at the object level, that it has the one property or the other. One does not simply say that Berlin exists *tout court*; rather, one asserts its existence when supposing a certain field of sense, such as the contemporary constitutional order of the Federal Republic of Germany.

As Gilbert Ryle has noted in this context, it borders on a joke to say that Berlin, stomach aches and fermions exist, and that therefore at least three objects exist; in his view, this is no more logical than to remark that, since both the sea level and oil prices rise, there is a conspicuous joint rising activity.[30] Strictly speaking, it is not a joke to consider both stomach aches and bacteria to exist, provided one does not overlook how they exist in different senses – that is, in different fields of sense – whereby these two fields in fact overlap, given how bacteria play an important role in stomach aches.

A seemingly paradoxical (but consistent) corollary of the meontological deliberations in §3 is the thesis that any object we consider both exists on the one hand and does not exist on the other, because we can name no object that exists in all fields of sense. And this is because there is no such thing as 'all fields of sense'. If something only necessarily exists if it exists in all possible worlds (or, more precisely, in all possible fields of sense), one might say that existence is always contingent.[31] Since there can be no totality of fields of sense (an ontological incompleteness theory applies here), it is senseless to dwell on the point that nothing can exist in all fields of sense. In any case, the point can be demonstrated easily enough. Let us simply take the field of sense of things that only seem to exist, because they appear in the field of sense of disappointed expectations (phlogiston, the ether, witches, a superlunar domain of pure spirits, a physical centre of the universe, etc.). If *per impossibile* there were something that appeared in all fields of sense, something that existed under all circumstances, then *ex hypothesi* it would be something that does not exist, because it would – among other things – have to be something that appears in the field of sense of disappointed expectations. To conceive God's necessary existence in accordance with the classic model, as present in all possible worlds (*mutatis mutandis* in all possible fields of sense), is to concede – willingly or not – that God is merely imagined, because he ultimately exists in a possible world in which everything is merely imagined.

A gigantic metaphysical effort is needed to immunize oneself against these problems by introducing, through metaphysical reflections, restrictions permitting only those worlds that correspond to one's personal ontological preferences. This exposes the whole procedure as no more than a large-scale ad hoc construction site.[32] Neither the whole of being nor its supposed complement (nothingness) is a coherently formed object of ontological theory; therefore we must think differently about questions of non-existence.[33]

In §4 I respond to a frequently posed objection, which was originally put to me in a particularly clear form by Julia Mehlich and Anton Friedrich Koch.[34] This suspicion, which I term the *Mehlich–Koch objection*, will return on several occasions throughout this book. Its content is that the world does indeed not exist in the sense intended by standard metaphysical realists (that is, that it *simply* exists, or exists 'out there'), but that it is essentially imagined or fictive. Consequently, the world would still very much exist, and my no-world-view would be falsified within its own framework. According to this model, we imagine the world and we can represent it in the mode of a metaphysical tale, such as Borges's *The Aleph*. Just as Lazarus exists in Bethany in the Bible – and thus, in any event, *exists* – the world exists, according to the Mehlich–Koch objection, as the field of sense of all fields of sense, for example in Buenos Aires in *The Aleph*. There, it is even a thing-like object, the notorious Aleph. Consequently, it certainly *exists*, meaning we are entitled to indulge in metaphysics, at least in the form of a metaphysical fictionalism (in the Kant–Vaihinger tradition).[35]

In order to disarm this objection, I will argue in §4 that the construction of Borges's *The Aleph* is deliberately incoherent (meaning one cannot retreat to dialetheism and regard the object called 'the Aleph' as contradictory in order to show that it exists nevertheless).[36] Accordingly, one cannot rescue the Mehlich–Koch objection by postulating contradictory entities in the object domain of our thinking about fictions (and thereby keeping the world in existence).

§5 concludes Part I by discussing a sharpening of the Mehlich–Koch objection suggested by Graham Priest.[37] Priest reconstructs FOS as translatable into a non-well-founded mereology in which the world can indeed exist, and that this can be shown without recourse to *The Aleph*. Priest also deploys this example, yet it merely serves as an illustration of the metaphysical architecture that results from introducing a mereological axiom system that replaces certain orthodox assumptions (assumptions which, admittedly, are not self-evident *sub specie aeternitatis* but serve for their part as models for given discourses). If we allow Priest's reconstruction, FOS has shown at best that current mereological orthodoxy is not the only possible option and that there are also good reasons for considering certain alternatives – alternatives without which we cannot rescue the existence of the world.[38] Priest deems rescuing the world a desirable goal, and one that can be achieved if we allow a little heterodoxy.

However, Priest's objection presupposes a flat, formal ontology, namely the neo-Meinongianism in whose development he has played such a crucial part. §5 will therefore draw an important boundary between FOS and the usual varieties of so-called neo-Meinongianism. Traditionally, Meinongian object theory works by introducing a weak concept of being, whereby for every characterization there is a corresponding object that falls within some categorial division of the concept of 'being as such'. For Meinong and his neo-Meinongian heirs, existence (as one part of being) is a causal space (*act*-uality) in which something exists only if it stands in causal relations. This does not apply to Mephistopheles, which marks him as a non-existent, merely imagined (so-called fictive) object.[39] This does not rob him of his ontological status as an object (being) but merely keeps him away from our living room, the causally closed universe. As a theory of objects, neo-Meinongianism is superior to metaphysical realism, especially because it offers a cure for the Eleatic puzzle of non-existence.

Yet, in my view, it still contains certain weaknesses that are rectified by FOS.

In particular, all varieties of Meinongianism rely on the idea that objects are intentional – that is, that they can be given to an (idealized) thinker. Hence Meinong maintains that the highest species of all objects as such is givenness, not being (see below, pp. 99–102). Neo-Meinongianism must therefore take a position on the theory of intentionality if its unrestricted object domain of givenness is not to lead to logical explosion.[40] This point then leads into the second part of the book, which deals with the ontology of intentional objects, which play a decisive part in the life of the human mind.

§1

Interpretation and Reading

When it comes to so-called fictional objects, the contemporary ontological landscape extends from fictional irrealism, which denies these objects any existence at all, to fictional realism, which takes at face value all manner of statements about the objects that appear in fictional representations.

Fictional irrealism disputes that singular terms such as 'Faust', 'Gretchen', 'unicorn', and so on, can successfully refer to anything at all, since these expressions are found in literary contexts that do not refer to anything existing outside fiction – that is, 'in reality'.[1] *Fictional realism*, by contrast, makes these expressions subject to reference conditions and assigns truth conditions to the corresponding so-called intra-fictional statements, such as 'Gretchen fell in love with Faust', and so-called extra-fictional statements such as 'Faust is a more famous figure than Jed Martin'. Accordingly, both Gretchen and Faust exist, even if standard advocates of fictional realism usually take them to be abstract objects.[2]

A prominent middle position has been suggested by John Searle.[3] According to this theory, the literary discourses in question do not refer to anything at all, as they are, rather, part of a game in which participants agree to a fictionality contract. The contract entitles those who imagine someone at the mention of the names 'Faust' and 'Gretchen' to speak as if Faust and Gretchen existed. The fictional statements of a novel are thus never assertions, items to which truth values can be assigned, but merely sham assertions. Just as staged thunder is not thunder, a fictional assertion is not an assertion, but mere assertory semblance. This semblance does play a part in human life, but not that of articulating knowledge claims with the assertive force of suitable expressions. Based on this position, there is no ontology of fictional objects, as the discourses that are capable of expressing ontological commitment cannot be pursued with reference to objects of this kind.

This spectrum of standard positions, only touched on here, developed in reaction to a series of pseudo-problems. One source of these nonsensical problems is the conflation of fictive and fictional objects. Fictive objects are supposedly those that do not exist (which we merely imagine);

fictional objects, by contrast, are those treated in the mode of literature or, more generally, of artistic representation. This raises the problem of how there can be a discourse or form of representation that refers to the non-existent.

One could try to evade the suspicion of such a confusion from the outset by restricting oneself to the fictive objects in order to steer clear of the perilous shoals of the theory of fictionality. Yet this does not answer the question of what then distinguishes so-called fictive objects from objects that are simply non-existent. If one says that the fictive ones are imagined while some non-existent objects are not even imagined, one needs to present a theory of the imagination that can explain the connection between imagination and non-existence. Yet this is precisely what is often missing from the present debate in analytic metaphysics and ontology.

One prominent strategy for dealing with this difficulty is based on Kendall Walton's idea of a make-believe mode, in which one pretends that a real object were something else, something that is not real.[4] This is a dead end, however, for it confronts us with a dilemma: either an expression such as 'Mephistopheles' does indeed refer to something real – for example Gustaf Gründgens – that we merely represent as something else – such as Mephistopheles; or the word 'Mephistopheles' refers to nothing at all – but this makes it impossible to understand why we seem to be able to make so many true and false statements about him, including such statements as that Gründgens has played the role of Mephistopheles without thereby stating that Gründgens has played the role of Gründgens. In other words, how do we draw a Gründgens-Mephistopheles distinction at the outset of the game of make-believe without thereby referring to Mephistopheles which would throw us back to the original problem.

Jodi Azzouni attempts to escape from this dilemma by recognizing two different forms of reference: firstly, reference to actually existing objects and, secondly, reference to fictive, non-existent ones.[5] However, this is an ad hoc move that points towards a solution without actually supplying it. Moreover, it does not solve the problems arising from certain minimal assumptions about truth and reference that Azzouni in fact accepts.[6] If I refer to Faust and make the true statement that he makes a pact with Mephistopheles, it follows from the recognition of this truth that I believe Faust makes a pact with Mephistopheles. Given minimal requirements on the truth predicate, it follows from

(F) It is true that Faust makes a pact with Mephistopheles,

that

(F*) Faust makes a pact with Mephistopheles.

This appears harmless at first, but becomes more unpleasant once generalized. Let $g^\#$ be an object that we deem fictive (and *ipso facto* non-existent). Let Λ be something that is true of this object. (F) is a case of such a structure. Moreover, we accept semantic platitudes about the truth predicate, such as the rather undemanding *principle of alethic transparency*

(PAT) If it is true that p, then p.

Now we can derive contradictions. It follows from

(F$^\#$) It is true that $g^\#\Lambda$

that

(F$^{\#*}$) $g^\#\Lambda$.

Hence we can now introduce any random object we can imagine, such as the present king of France, and have it undertake a journey to Paris, from which it then follows that the present king of France is currently vising Paris. This is false, however, meaning that we have now created a contradiction. It is thus no trouble at all to match any true statement with a dissonant statement that is referentially directed at fictive objects – including the statement that a certain fictive object is not fictive.[7]

Of course, Azzouni might respond that reference to the fictive present king of France fundamentally cannot be a reference to someone visiting Paris, since *ex hypothesi* he does not exist. Yet what about a reference to the fictive present king of France who travels to Paris? Does 'Paris' here refer to Paris? In that case, the statement that the fictive present king of France travels to Paris is false. Yet this violates the same principles that Azzouni seems to acknowledge.

One can avoid this problem by developing a theory of fictional objects that actually corresponds to our dealings with them. Doing so brings into a view a possible manoeuvre that is favourably similar to Azzouni's, namely *meontological isolationism*. It asserts that objects that do not exist in a given non-fictional field of sense and do exist in a fictional field of sense are isolated from the non-fictional field in which we find ourselves as recipients. They only ever appear embedded in reality.[8] An object o in S^1 sometimes appears in S^2 in S^1 without thereby appearing in F^1. My earlier example for this non-transitive structure are trolls that appear in Norwegian mythology: the mythology appears in Norway, but the trolls do not.[9]

Objects that are ontologically isolated but embedded can also be causally shut off from one another. In this case, however, objects of a field of sense S^1 can indirectly influence the behaviour of objects in S^2. For the sense of a field is the ordering function that allows the objects occurring in it to exist.[10] The sense assigns to objects the essential properties without which they could not exist. It individuates them as objects of a kind.

Whatever exists belongs to some kind of object. Trolls essentially belong to the kind of object that appears in Norway only in Norwegian mythology, which we could express pre-theoretically by saying that trolls do not exist. They certainly do exist in FOS, but precisely as embedded in a field of sense whose existence we privilege by making the statement that they do not exist. Now, trolls do exercise an indirect influence on Norway in so far as the field in which they appear appears in Norway, and is thereby real. Norwegian mythology has a direct effect in Norway, even if the objects that feature within it are not.[11]

In a conversation in New York on 4 September 2015, David Chalmers countered a naïve interpretation of FOS's fictional realism by arguing that it does not sufficiently protect its objects from contradictions. His argument can be rendered as follows:

(1) If it is true in a fictional field of sense S^f that p, then p.
(2) If it is true in a fictional field of sense such as *The Last Unicorn* that there are unicorns, then there are unicorns (fictional realism).
(3) If it is true in a fictional field of sense such as *The Last Unicorn Discovers Ontology of Fields of Sense and Travels to New York in Order to Disrupt a Conversation between Chalmers and Gabriel* that the last unicorn discovers ontology of fields of sense and travels to New York in order to disrupt a conversation between Chalmers and Gabriel, then the last unicorn travels to New York in order to disrupt a conversation between Chalmers and Gabriel.
(4) The last unicorn appeared in order to disrupt our conversation.
(5) The last unicorn did not appear in order to disrupt our conversation.
(6) The last unicorn appeared and did not appear.
∴ It is not the case that, if it is true in a fictional field of sense S^f that p, then p.

Consequently, there is no reason to infer the existence of unicorns from the supposed truth that there are unicorns in the field of sense of *The Last Unicorn*, since doing so would generate any number of contradictions.

Yet in FOS, the reason there are unicorns is not a consequence of an independent acknowledgment of the fictional alethic principle

(FAP) If it is true in a fictional field of sense S^f that p, then p.

Rather, the reason there are unicorns follows from the existence of art works. In art works, unicorns are represented that exist essentially in the mode of aesthetic experience.

To elaborate: the film *The Last Unicorn* is based on a composition. A composition is first of all an arrangement of objects and fields of sense with the purpose of creating an occasion for an aesthetic experience. The complete art work [*Gesamtkunstwerk*] is the concept of the whole formed from a score and all its interpretations, and it exists as a complete object only when people stop interpreting a given composition (an existing art work). From an epistemic point of view, the *Gesamtkunstwerk* is therefore inaccessible in a certain sense, as one cannot analytically investigate an art work (and thus a *Gesamtkunstwerk*) without somehow interpreting it. By trying to give a conclusive analysis of an art work, one changes it, meaning that something is a *Gesamtkunstwerk* only once we are finished with it for good and no longer concern ourselves with it.

Composition makes use of relevant methods for constructing an art work, for example an animated film such as *The Last Unicorn*. These procedures involve making drawings and then arranging them sequentially in such a way that a film screening can take place. A successful screening requires suitable recipients, who are able to interpret the presentation in such a way that they follow certain suspense arcs and plots. These kinds of narrative unity will occur to them only if they engage in an activity of 'implicit coherence formation',[12] which goes beyond all that is explicitly shown to them; for all that is explicitly shown to the recipients is a sequential arrangement of drawings, which they interpret in such a way that it presents the sorrow of a unicorn who fears that he is the last member of his species, and so on.

In particular, the spectator's coherence formation involves applying a reality principle and so, for example, recognizing two very different drawings as the same unicorn. In scenes in which the last unicorn does not appear, we assume that it still exists but is simply not being shown to us directly. Without this kind of coherence formation, we would have no aesthetic experience of the film. It would disintegrate into a purely material sequence that we could no longer interpret as presenting us with a plot.[13]

Aesthetic experiences involve coherence-establishing exercises of the imagination that ascribe properties to objects. I call these objects *hermeneutical objects*.[14] Objects of aesthetic experience are hermeneutical objects which do not exist directly in the field of sense of the spectator, but only ever as embedded in the field of their interpretation. They are screened off from the reality of the spectator who is thereby put in a position to generate assumptions drawn from exercises of the reality principle that are not in turn in any way presented by the art work itself. In short, in the presence of an art work the recipient deploys their fictional capacities without having to assume that the fictive objects would have had the properties he is free to ascribe to them due to absences in the score had they not engaged in the act of interpretation.

The *presentation* [*Vorführung*] of a score is different from its *performance* [*Aufführung*]. In the case of theatre, for example, the presentation is what the actors do, while the performance is what each viewer aesthetically experiences. If a film is shown in an empty cinema with no spectators, then no aesthetic experience (and thus no performance) takes place, only a presentation. A theatrical presentation, by contrast, is always necessarily a performance, as the performers play their roles based an aesthetic experience from which they must simultaneously maintain a partial distance.

If twenty spectators attend a presentation and engage with it, then only one presentation takes place, but there are at least twenty performances. For in each aesthetic experience the presented objects acquire different properties.[15] No two recipients ever interpret an art work in an identical manner, since our coherence formation in aesthetic experience is ultimately an individual matter. We always understand art works from an individual standpoint that we ourselves can never completely make explicit, as we have no overview of our mental individuality and its concrete historical location (which includes our individual biographies).[16]

According to the theory I am proposing, the traditional division of aesthetic theories into *production, reception* and *work aesthetics* overlooks the decisive ontological option, which consists in the fact that the art work exists in three conceptual dimensions at the same time.

Firstly, a score is produced. The score's production conditions involve the artist (or team) as the author(s) of a specific arrangement. This does not mean that we need to conceive the author as a person who positions every word, every dash of paint, every note, and so on, with reference to a ready-made plan. Authors have intentions that play a role in the production of art works (such as the intention to write a novel) without these intentions thus being sufficient to guarantee the ontic stability of fictive objects. Whatever particular intentions Goethe may have had, there are infinitely many questions about the field of sense of *Faust* that he could hardly have envisaged at all. It is fundamentally impossible for an artist's intentions to 'protect' an art work from interpretations that diverge from their original psychosocially and historically situated self-interpretation. Thus the author's intention does not settle the matter of interpretation, even though it contributes to it insofar as the author produces a score which constrains the freedom of interpretation by providing some normative guidelines for what counts as a legitimate or illegitimate interpretation.

An art work also differs from objects of utility in that no specific intention as to their employment can be specified in advance. A chair serves the purpose of sitting, a car that of mobility, and so forth. What an object of utility is (its τὸ τί ἦν εἶναι) is determined beforehand in the manufacturing process; this process is carried out with a certain purpose in mind. The artist, by contrast, does not know what use their composition has, all told, because they cannot possibly control the entirety of aesthetic experiences that their work will trigger in advance. The artist can certainly place restrictions on the work's reception via the score but can never determine it fully. The very ontology of fictive objects entails that the recipient remains free to interpret them in this way or that.

The stipulation that the work serves the end of aesthetic experience is too aspecific to serve as an objective for the arrangement of objects and fields of sense in an art work. The general materiality of the work at the artist's disposal is underdetermined with regard to its factual interpretation. No artist can completely control the reception of his work, which inherently holds surprises. The artist is heteronomous, but their work is not.

Secondly, an art work exists only if it has been the object of at least one episode of reception. A reception consists in someone (who may well be identical with the artist) exercising their imagination to become the stage on which the art work is performed. The stage can be Beethoven's auditory imagination as much as Ingeborg Bachmann's sense for the right word within the texture of a poetic system of meaning. The stage on which John Cage's 4'33" is enacted is the acoustic space accessible to everyone attending a performance of the piece.[17] In the literary case of a so-called realistic representation, we generate a plot thread on the stage of our imaginations. We tie this to conditions of coherence imported from the non-fictional context of the fields of sense whose stability we take for granted.[18]

To be sure, skilfully written literature tends to disrupt the business of coherence formation at a decisive point in its reception, meaning that we never become entirely absorbed.[19] Art works simultaneously attract and repel, else they would shed their status as fictional and successfully make truth claims instead of provoking aesthetic experiences. Aesthetic experience is never total and therefore claims for itself both a logical-semantic and an ontological privilege. Art is semblance that is being. It is and remains ambivalent.

No aesthetic effect can take place without the work as material, sensuous object. The work, for its part, is presented as something that can be interpreted in different ways, meaning that the composition must step in as an interface between work and effect in order to do justice to art's status as subject-object. The work guides its reception, thus determining a framework of legitimate guises for aesthetic experience to assume. If the work did not guide its enactment, aesthetic experience would sacrifice its objectivity and degenerate into a free-floating fantasy that can be triggered by any given object.[20]

A wonderful example is provided by the masterful TV series *Fargo*, which confuses us in our reception of the work by going even further (*far go*) than the senseless violence it depicts would lead us to expect. *Fargo* the series surpasses the expectations set by the film. Just as in the 1996 film of the same name, the opening credits begin with this structurally ironic text: 'THIS IS A TRUE STORY. The events depicted took place in Minnesota in 1987. At the request of the survivors, the names have been changed. Out of respect for the dead, the rest has been told exactly as it occurred.'[21] Like each series of the later TV version, the film begins with an overlapping of (at least) two fields of sense (strictly speaking, there are considerably more). At one level, there is a statement of the conditions of the film's production. On this level, the same lettering is deployed for the text, stating that a certain studio 'presents' a film and that somebody has 'produced' it. In the case of the film, this includes the joint labour of the Coen brothers, who together generated the film, with Joel as the director and Ethan as the producer.

At the level of what is presented, which we must imagine (in the 'narrated world'), all we see at first is a white screen; this turns out to be a flurry of snow as soon as a bird flies through the picture. A car then comes towards us, its headlights drawing nearer and illuminating the landscape. At the material level, it is thereby made apparent that we are witnessing a cinematic film whose conditions of manufacture are explicitly related to us. Part of this is the ironic play with the topos of a true story, with the polysemy of the expression 'true' also playing a role here, since it both points to propositional truth – and hence the idea of an eyewitness – and appears in phrases such as 'a true friend'.[22] A 'true story' is also a genuine story.

At the cinematic level, the aesthetic experience comes ever closer to us. The melancholy music creates a sense of foreboding, but, like the list of the actors and other involved parties, it stands between us and the events we are expecting. The first sound that greets us from the film world is the flapping of the bird's wings, which may also be an allusion to the mantic origins of art. From the very start, we read the scene as if it had a hidden meaning.[23]

The reception of the work is guided by its materiality. In *Fargo*, this enters the film in the form of an allegory of reading: the film visually picks us up and carries us along with it, so to speak – symbolized by the automobile that is towed away in the opening scene. Yet not even a film can control us completely, since in the medium of fictions the imagination transcends everything we are shown. We cannot be shown anything without simultaneously interpreting it, otherwise we could not even read the words deployed to make apparent statements about the ontological status of what is shown ('true story', 'Ceci n'est pas une pipe'). To be sure, the work is presented to us, yet this presentation takes place only because we recipients already re-present it. The status of re-presentation is immediately rendered invisible, however, because every successful non-fictional representation (from which we derive our criteria of coherence formation) is alethically transparent – that is, configured to refer beyond itself.

The beginning of Daniel Kehlmann's novel *F* offers an illustration of the conceptual iridescence that triggers aesthetic experience.[24] The entire novel clearly plays with the idea that 'F' may refer to 'fiction'. A certain 'Arthur Friedland' (another candidate for 'F') is introduced as the protagonist. He writes 'novels that no publisher wanted to print, and stories that appeared occasionally in magazines.'[25] The narrator spends little time dithering and quickly plunges our interpretive efforts directly into the chasm of a complex *mise en abyme*:

> On the way there he talked to his thirteen-year-old sons about Nietzsche and different brands of chewing gum. They argued about an animated movie

that had just opened starring a robot who was also the Redeemer, they traded theories about why Yoda talked so weirdly, and wondered whether Superman was stronger than Batman.[26]

Within the novel, we learn of a novel (which does not exist outside the novel) entitled (in an obvious intertextual blend of Ulysses and Gantenbein) *My Name Is No One*. We are told that the beginning of this work 'sets up an old-fashioned novella about a young man embarking on his life' and that 'all we know about his name is its first initial: F.'[27] At the same time, we are provided with an interpretive key that is to be taken up at various points in the rest of the book: 'But there is a sense that no sentence means merely what it says, that the story is observing its own progress, and that in truth the protagonist is not the central figure: the central figure is the reader, who is all too complicit in the unfolding of events.'[28] This hint is followed by several pages of philosophical reflection on the disappearance of the world in the act of reading; on death; on the non-existence of the reader from the perspective of the author; on space as 'a model of our minds';[29] and on our 'so-called consciousness', which is 'a mere flicker, a dream that nobody is dreaming',[30] which is anticipated by the blurry, flickering white 'F' that adorns the black cover of the original edition. On this basis, one of the characters reading the novella comes to be trapped by 'doubts about his own existence' while reading[31] – a referential structure that no one has deployed with more skill than Bernado Soares (one of the heteronyms of Fernando Pessoa). In his *The Book of Disquiet*, we even read:

> The only 'real' things we have are our perceptions, but nothing 'really' means (this is one of our perceptions), nor does 'mean' mean anything, nor does the word 'perception' make any sense, nor is 'making sense' anything that makes sense. Everything is one and the same secret. I note, however, that it is not even the case that **everything** can mean something, or that 'secret' is a word with any meaning.[32]

Art works exist in the mode of interpretation/reception, which transforms their materiality into meaning. When we read a work, we make decisions in favour of certain meanings, which we employ for the purpose of coherence formation. If conflicts arise, we revise our ascriptions of meaning. What we thereby refer to cannot be determined by the materiality of the work alone.

Rodin's *The Thinker* does not think, in so far as it is merely a piece of sculpted bronze; bronze is not suited to thinking. The phrase 'the thinker' does not refer to a piece of bronze. Rather, we imagine a situation in which someone like the thinker strikes a certain pose and thinks 'deep thoughts'. Only in the eye of the beholder is the piece of bronze a piece of material shaped into a thinking human; in its material being-in-itself it is pure form which, under certain conditions, triggers an aesthetic experience, and as a result we imagine a thinker. Whoever sees bronze does not see a thinker but, at best, something that resembles a thinker – or a stereotypical representation of the pose of a thinker – within the framework of a given interpretation. Of course, this reference is ironically denied by the work's conditions of production: Rodin's model for the sculpture was famously the boxer Jean Baud, a figure well known in the red-light district whom nobody would have taken for much of a thinker.

Within the material framework of an art work, linguistic reference and meaning are always subject to a certain vagueness. To be sure, this is true of materially transmitted linguistic meaning in general, so we should not treat reference as any precisely determined point on a noetic target in any case.[33] It is therefore an illusion (not a fiction!) of ontological discourse to think that we possess a capacity for making unproblematic reference to individuals that is somehow suspended or disrupted in the case of fictional discourse. For, even in a 'normal case', our reference to individuals is tied to ill-defined conditions for success. The point on every semantic target is therefore noetically and epistemically underdetermined. Reference can fail. When it succeeds, however, we are *ex hypothesi* in causal contact with an object of reference, which appears to be much more difficult in the case of fictional reference, as the fictive object (other than its presentation in the mode of fiction) is causally isolated from us.

But this appearance is misleading. Typical fictional realism, such as that defended especially by Peter van Inwagen, can certainly build on the idea that a proper name such as 'Gretchen' at least refers to an element of a score – that is, to an element of a text (van Inwagen regards these as abstract objects, but that is another matter).[34] It is similar with make-believe theories: they introduce a reference support (a 'prop'), which the fictionality contract passes off as something other than what it really is. This structure provides causal circumstances of reference, meaning that, in a certain performance, the word 'Mephistopheles' refers to Gustaf Gründgens, for example, with whom the recipient comes into causal contact.

Aesthetic experience fills in those 'recesses' that are generated by a score in order to open up an interpretive space.[35] Therefore the usual assumption that fictional characters such as Gretchen are significantly indeterminate is incorrect. Gretchen is indeterminate neither as a textual element nor as a hermeneutical object of aesthetic experience. The phenomenon of indeterminacy in fact manifests elsewhere entirely, namely in the gap between performance and enactment that isolates Gretchen from us (and us from her).

Thirdly, an art work is an interface between a score and an interpretation. The work is identical neither with the score nor with a particular performance but is, rather, an open structure of actual and potential interpretations. Art works are complete only when people stop interpreting them. In this sense, Gadamer's concept of 'effective history' [*Wirkungsgeschichte*], far from being a tribute to conservative artistic taste, is in fact spot on.[36] An art work is ultimately identical with its effective history, part of which is the series of interpretations that have to be carried out for the work to appear in the mode of aesthetic experience and thus to exist as an art work in the first place.[37]

A further misconception about Gadamer's hermeneutics that requires correction is that it leaves no room for the truth or falsity of an interpretation.[38] It is, after all, hardly a coincidence that Gadamer's *magnum opus* on this topic is called *Truth and Method*. Not every interpretation (in the present sense of a performance in the mode of aesthetic experience) is as good as any other. There are objective standards of reading that determine the space of legitimate interpretation.[39] Objective standards are determined by the score, whose architecture is, admittedly, accessible only by means of a composition – that is, by analytical means through a reconstruction of the material conditions of a given aesthetic experience.

Objective standards are thus epistemic access conditions to the ur-text, which can be disclosed only through an interpretation. The ur-text can be partially or largely obscured by orthographical errors or failures of transmission. A recipient can therefore correct an author if, when constructing the fictional field of sense, they determine that another word or an alternative grammatical structure better corresponds to what must have been intended.[40]

At this point, the concepts of reading and interpretation serve to introduce realist restrictions that can easily disappear from view if one decouples aesthetic experience from its material basis and thus loses sight of the object that anchors the (occasionally beautiful) semblance of art. Here the ur-text is the epitome of realist restrictions, something set in stone (in some cases literally) and, in the context of its ur-performance, fixes specific ascriptions of meaning (on the basis of an Attic word usage in Greek tragedy, for example).

In this context, analysis is the theoretical, scientifically articulated reading of a given score. It is conducted within the framework of literary theory, musicology, art history and, indeed, in all the social scientific and humanities disciplines that count art works among their objects of study. The field of history, for example, frequently concerns itself with art works in so far as they offer insights into historical issues. These disciplines place philological and historical-critical methods at our disposal with which we can uncover the conditions of production for the material basis of a work. Gadamer, of course, was well aware of this. To repeat: his most famous work was appropriately named *Truth and Method* in that it contains the idea of an ontology of the art work that allows it to so much as have an effective history.[41]

As mentioned earlier, I call the object of an analysis a 'meta-hermeneutical object'. This is intended to do justice to another point raised by Gadamer: philological, historical-critical investigation must be guided by an understanding of cultural products. No one can offer a meta-hermeneutically meaningful analysis of the *Urfaust* and both parts of the tragedy unless they have had some aesthetic experience through an engagement with their hermeneutical objects. Aesthetic experience provides information about the elements of the meta-hermeneutical analysis, since the reception history of a work is a constitutive part of the work itself, its ontology. Our access to meta-hermeneutical objects can be improved and corrected via competent engagement with hermeneutical objects.

The art work as an interface between score and reception history is the *composition*. The composition of a work encompasses both its score and the acts of aesthetic experience which partially integrate us as recipients into the work itself. The composition is thus the aesthetic synthesis that provides the element in which an analysis takes place. As a rule, subjects who are not identical with the artist – that is, the producer of the work's material dimension – also participate in a composition. This need not always be the case, since artists can create works that are performed only once in the presence of the artist by the artist themselves. To the extent that the artist succeeds in concealing the existence of their work from other potential recipients, they find themselves in attendance of an autopoietic spectacle.[42]

Aesthetic experience never leads to a complete absorption, otherwise we would exit the framework of an art work, whose materiality sets limits to the work of imagination. This brings us to a valuable insight of Descartes and classical empiricism that was also echoed at a central stage of Kant's *Refutation of Idealism*: the imagination is subject to restrictions which stem from the fact that we have to recombine elements that cannot themselves be imagined.[43]

No exercise of the imagination can invent anything that is not anchored in our cognition of the actual. When we read a novel, we do not invent an alternative world that bears no connection to our reality, as the occasion for exercising our imagination is given through the materiality of the score. To be sure, what is given to our imagination as an anchor in reality is not the phantom of simple ideas envisaged by Hume and Berkeley. According to classical empiricism, the elements of our experience are units taken from sensory experience. Classical empiricism works with an atomistic model of the human mind, according to which all the representations we are able to process ultimately build on a foundation of atomic representations.

Yet the given is not atomistically constituted, for what is given is the real, and the real is something to which we can have truth-apt and hence fallible attitudes. I therefore define *reality* as a mode of registration's property of being fallible, a conception that corresponds to an epistemic concept of reality.[44] When we imagine something, we do so on account of a given trigger. In a given aesthetic case, the trigger is the confrontation with a score, which leads to the aesthetic experience on the side of our reactions. The aesthetic experience causes hermeneutical objects in the field of sense of our imagination to manifest themselves. This process is not entirely free-floating but limited by the given, in this case by the materiality of the art work.[45] Given the trigger of a *Faust* performance, we do not simply imagine something in such a way that the mental activity of our reception ultimately has no bearing on the identity of the work. Score and reception are connected in the concept and reality of an art work; they are united in its factual composition.

There Are No Fictional Objects: Against a Philosophical Myth

The common denominator of many investigations of fictionality in both philosophy and literary theory is the widespread assumption that fictional objects do not exist. Based on the considerations outlined in §1, the standard 'concept' of a 'fictional object' proves to be polysemous, as it rests on an implicit rather than a theoretically grounded equation of hermeneutical and meta-hermeneutical objects. Unfortunately, contemporary theoretical philosophy tends to ignore the research on fictionality emerging from literary studies. Conversely, many theorists of fiction complain that philosophical semantics and ontology deal only peripherally with fictional objects – namely, to the extent that they cause difficulties for understanding linguistic reference outside of fictional contexts.[1] Nonetheless, certain relevant subtleties of philosophical analysis are easily overlooked from within humanistic analysis, which is then reflected in problematic definitions of the fictional and the fictive.

An especially significant shortcoming shared by all parties is that, while almost all sides agree that fictional objects form a subset of non-existent objects, one seldom finds an explicitly articulated (me-)ontology that can be used to determine exactly which theoretical claims are being made. After all, it is hardly a self-evident truth that fictional objects should be classified as non-existent. It is not, at any rate, an analytical truth that fictional objects do not exist.

In this section I would like to argue that the philosophical category of 'fictional objects' is based on a flawed construction. There are indeed no 'fictional objects', because this 'category' countenances objects mentioned in (literary) art works while being defined as concerning itself with only a subset of such objects, namely those that are purely 'fictional' in the purported sense of not-really-existing.

In order to alleviate this tension, a distinction is often made between 'fictional' and 'fictive'. Objects treated in the mode of (literary) representation are 'fictional', while those objects of (literary) representation that, in addition, do not exist are called 'fictive'.[2] This makes room for instances of fictional existing objects, such as Munich and Venice in *Death in Venice* or

Leipzig and Faust in *Faust I*. Some fictional objects are thus fictive, others not.

Yet this distinction, however intuitively plausible, does not get us very far in either philosophy or literary theory, and therefore requires a fundamental revision, as most literary cases are incomparably more complex. Let us merely take a superficial look at *Faust*: the historical alchemist called Faust and the fictive Faust in *Faust* are indeed connected by the fact that there is a material history of the *Faust* score to which thoughts about the historical Faust made a certain contribution, yet this does not mean that Goethe's score bearing the title *Faust* is about the historical Faust. Goethe's *Faust* is not identical with the historical Faust.

Then there is the complex intertextuality in which the Faust theme is embedded; this theme has been repeatedly revised and modified, so much so that, behind the multiple Faust figures, we no longer find any unequivocal reference to anything that befell the historical Faust. From the perspective of literary theory, the notion that fictional expressions such as 'Faust', 'Paris', 'Moscow', and so on, refer to those things known as 'Faust', 'Paris', 'Moscow', and so forth, in non-fictional contexts means at most that each text must be read on the basis of a certain amount of background knowledge. Our background knowledge includes assumptions about Faust, Paris and Moscow that do not need to be suspended (and sometimes cannot be) when we interpret art works.

It does not follow, however, that the words 'Faust', 'Paris', 'Moscow', and so on, in *Faust* or *War and Peace* refer to Faust, Paris and Moscow. To be sure, we apply our knowledge of Faust, Paris and Moscow in order to fill out our aesthetic experiences in successful interpretations of the art work in question. But it does not follow that we first know Faust, Paris and Moscow and now learn something about their merely possible but not actual properties. Otherwise, to take up Kripke's ingenious comparison again, fictions would be extremely powerful telescopes for viewing Lewis's possible worlds.[3]

In the case of literature, our understanding of the text is the trigger of an aesthetic experience. Literature therefore draws on our background knowledge in order to deploy elements of our mental life as props, to take up an idea from Walton.[4] The exercise of the imagination is thus restricted in two respects.

On the one hand, a text or non-textual art work such as a film or a painting makes available material that provides the trigger exercises of the imagination. Among these materials are signs such as 'Faust' and 'Moscow'. These signs are connected with other signs. In order to have an aesthetic experience, we thus have to be practised in reading sign-codes. Reading a sign-code then activates our imagination: on the basis of a given material, we generate a scenario in which certain objects cooperate with one another. We imagine the scenario; it is not something we ever find as a given, ready-made whole in the material itself. And, as a result, we have to produce differing interpretations of art works without this plurality being evidence of disagreement. Two differing interpretations need not represent a difference of opinion, as there have to be multiple equally valid interpretations. Without hermeneutical plurality, no art work can exist; hermeneutics is thus in fact a contribution to ontology.[5]

On the other hand, we are entitled to make use of non-fictional background knowledge in order to fill out our aesthetic experiences. When reading Proust, one imagines nineteenth-century Paris on the basis of one's own experiences of the city.[6] Because we know something about Paris, we take this as grounds for imagining Paris in a particular way when we encounter the signifier 'Paris' in an aesthetic context. Yet the idea of Paris that we deploy to flesh out the scenario of an art work in aesthetic experience does not refer to Paris. We do not learn anything about Paris when we call the city to mind within the framework of an aesthetic experience triggered by the literary material. At best, we learn something about our own idea of Paris, which we vary in and through our aesthetic experience.[7]

The properties of fictive objects teach us nothing about their non-fictive counterparts; at most, we find out something about our imagined ideas by investigating which interpretations are preferred by which groups at which times. This is dealt with in the sociology of art, among other things.[8] Thus art contains no truth that exceeds an insight into the autonomous structure of a given work. Proust's *In Search of Lost Time* is no travel guide to Paris, and Mann's novels contain no wisdom about the relation between life and art.

Proust's *In Search of Lost Time* says many true things about a place called 'Paris' that are nonetheless false about Paris. The Paris of Proust's novel thus has different properties from our Paris and the two, applying the principle of the identity of indiscernibles, thus cannot be the same city. This principle famously states that x and y are identical if every property of x is a property of y. There are good reasons for restricting the principle (for instance in the domain of quantum mechanics), but this does not immediately affect objects such as Paris. Paris in *In Search of Lost Time* does admittedly resemble Paris, and this relation of similarity has a bearing on filling out the field of sense of the novel in the act of reading. Like other artists, Proust plays with this by establishing relations between fiction and (the semblance of) reality.

Artistic propositions do not reveal any truth about non-artistic reality. Yet art certainly does not lie either, since aesthetic experience does not make any claims that go beyond its own limits. Rather, there are intradiegetic truths and facts, and one cannot analyse these if one sees art as pointing beyond itself and thus making truth claims about objects outside of its scope. We can certainly use fictional representations in order to find out something about ourselves, but not because their intradiegetic truths are somehow extradiegetic at the same time.

Nor does it get us very far philosophically to assume that fictional contexts can be divided into those whose terms make proper reference to existing objects and those that do not. Based on this assumption, the concept of fictionality ceases to have any serious theoretical role to play. Instead, it would concern terms that can be used to refer to something in any context whatsoever, though *ex hypothesi* they would be foiled by the non-existence of the presupposed object of reference. 'Mephistopheles' and 'phlogiston' would thereby have the same ontological status, even if they are introduced in different contexts. So-called fictional objects then become at best examples of non-existent objects, which raises the quandary of how we should reconstruct the linguistic meaning of singular terms that do not refer to anything at all.

To be sure, the semantic puzzle of empty proper names thus touched on already contains a host of philosophical problems. First of all, there is the question of what exactly non-existence has to do with non-reference. And even if this were settled, we would be thrown back at the bare assumption that some fictional objects exist (such as Paris) and some do not (such as Mephistopheles). The category 'fictional object' is thus problematic, to put it mildly.

To alleviate the problem, I will make some conceptual suggestions concerning the distinctions addressed here. What I mean by a *fiction* is the presentation of a state of affairs that exceeds the framework of what appears to us in immediate sensory observation as a scene of our life. So 'fiction' is not a genre attribute of a particular type of text or the exclusive *definiens* of art works; fictions exist as much in law as in the natural sciences, theology and philosophy, as well as our entirely ordinary daydreams. Almost every statement and every factual account has a fictional component, which does not mean that all objects of true statements that are not present to the senses are 'fictional' in the sense of 'fictive'. Therefore this suggestion is not an overgeneralization based on the literary category of fictionality, but rather the opposite: the opening step of a theory that allows us to understand literary fictionality as something that can play a part in the self-conception of human beings.

Fictions are 'mind-dependent', to the extent that they would not take place if there were no beings capable of embedding their sensory episode in larger sequences of actions, in order thus to grasp the segment of their life that is accessible to them as part of a greater whole. Our transcendence beyond any given situation is our reason for making contact with the fictional. Our form of intentionality – that is, reference as the alethic, perceptual and epistemic fulfilment of a minded being – is thus constitutively fictional, though this does not mean that we are not connected directly, for example sensorially, with the real; I will deal with the issue of perception's contact with the real in Part II.

To simulate is to transcend. As free, minded beings, humans do not cling to what is sensorially given, but rather stand at a distance from what is presented to them and can therefore modify it based on this minimal transcendence. As simulating beings, humans are surreal, beyond the real which they find by means of the senses.[9]

Fictions are themselves something real. Something is *real* if we can have truth-apt but not necessarily true beliefs about it. *Reality* is an *epistemic model category*, not an object (the *one* world) of which we form a part.[10] Reality is the circumstance that we can be mistaken about particular (real) objects, also and especially because we can grasp them as they are.

In this terminological context, *fictive objects* are those objects that exist only if they are interpreted. Fictive objects require performance; their existence consists in being captured in the medium of the imagination. If no one had ever referred to fictive objects via acts of the imagination, they would not have existed.

In most cases, fictive objects do not exhibit the property of being fictive intradiegetically, only extradiegetically. That an object is fictive is not usually a fact that appears in the same field of sense in which the fictive object itself appears. Rather, the field of sense in which it appears is such that it only exists – only appears in our field of sense – if there are appropriate acts of the imagination. We can therefore, based on the embeddedness of the fictional field of sense in our own field of sense, reach the judgement that the fictive object is fictive. This judgement cannot be made in the fictional field of sense itself, as the entities locked within that field have no access to their own fictivity.

There is, of course, the case of fictive fictive objects – that is, nested fiction in which fictions are created within a fiction, with an inherent potential to generate an indefinitely large number of nesting levels. The depth of a *mise en abyme* is not ontologically limited. It is false that Faust is a fictive object in *Faust*; in *Faust*, Faust is not in *Faust*. This means that various things that are true of Faust are false in *Faust*. This is not a contradiction, however, since the facts in *Faust* are (me)ontologically isolated from those about Faust.

Therefore it does not follow from the proposition 'In X it is true that p' (where X is the title of an art work) that p, since the deep logical structure of the proposition is *It is true that* $p_{in\ X}$. If Faust is a human being in *Faust*, this does not constitute a discovery about the past inhabitants of the Eurasian land mass, since Faust is ontologically isolated from the Eurasian Plate. It would therefore have been false that $p_{in\ X}$ if no one had ever imagined this, because then no X would have existed. So we produce fictional truths not by mobilizing a magical ability to make things true, but rather by producing facts (fields of sense) in which objects manifest themselves.[11]

A text has the literary property of fictionality if a number of the objects it deals with are essentially interpreted – that is, fictive – and if it is an art work. It then follows, to draw also on meontological isolationism, that all objects depicted in this text are fictive; cling together, swing together.

No text is fictional purely because of the arrangement of its signs.[12] This does not mean that it is arbitrary which texts are fictional; the fictionality of a text emerges only from the context of an interpretation. Our fictional capacity, which allows us to go beyond what is given to the senses, is applied while reading fictional texts in that we can still exercise our imagination when embellishing objects that do not exist. We can choose any chain of signs (any 'text') and fictionalize it; it is enough to embed it in a context that becomes an occasion for aesthetic experience. This is one of the points of *objets trouvés*: so-called fictional objects gain their fictionality through the fact that we interpret them. We do not simply happen upon them as a partial feature of the real. One does not find fictionality in the arrangement of the universe; rather, it belongs to the catchment area of the mind, which transcends its necessary, normal conditions of existence, as I will show in Part II.

It should be emphasized that the position adopted here does not descend into pan-fictionalism.[13] The claim is not that *all* texts, let alone all forms of reference, thematize fictive objects, but rather that there is no fixed number of textual characteristics that determine by themselves whether a text is fictional. So, there are no linguistic characteristics of fictionality that are necessarily and jointly sufficient to classify a text as fictional, though this does not mean that there are no typical signs of fictionality.[14] For it is a fundamental part of fictionality that recipients have an aesthetic experience not *necessarily* triggered by a text containing signs of fictionality. Reading out a text in a context that suggests aesthetic experience can generate fictionality just as readily as a paratext that marks an otherwise seemingly non-fictional context of statements as a 'poem'. Reading out a text does not already constitute an interpretation in all contexts, however. In some poems, the additional condition applies that poetry can dissolve linguistic referentiality and turn it into musicality, whereas reading out a descriptive narrative text becomes a performance only if it causes a recipient (who can be identical with the reader) to have an aesthetic experience.[15]

Without our own ability to create fictions, we would be incapable of understanding any text or any representation of something not sensuously present. Our understanding is *a limine* narrative and typological, and thus always goes beyond the individual scene that presents itself to us. Human acquisition of language is based on our pattern detection, which looks out for the general (a pattern) amid the particular. These patterns are the stuff of which the fictional is made, which is why Aristotle distinguished *poiesis* from the reporting of events based on its sense of possibility. Fictional representation deals with the general, with patterns whose recurrence we consider expectable.[16]

What makes an object fictive is its property of existing essentially in a fiction. An object exists *essentially* in a fiction if it can only appear within the framework of interpretations. My left hand is not a fictive object because it is sensorially given. It is part of my scene.[17] My hand is an object of a fiction that you are building up at this moment as a reader, because you are imagining what the example of my left hand might have to do with the theses I am developing here. My hand can appear both within and outside of fictions; thus it does not exist essentially in fictions, and is accordingly not a fictive object.

One property of fictive objects is their *fictional need for supplementation*. Fictive objects fill in gaps produced by a fictional depiction.[18] Literary texts usually describe some of their objects (*dramatis personae*, a *fabula*, a plot context, and so on) in such a way that we have no external reference points for identifying them. What we know about Jed Martin is based on the text of Houellebecq's *The Map and the Territory* but is not restricted to it.

The meta-hermeneutical basis of our fictional knowledge about fictive objects is the score. The interpretation of a score is a performance of an art work in the medium of our imagination.[19] The term 'interpretation', as stated above, is consistently used here in the same way that applies to the performance of a piece of music. An interpretation is an aesthetic experience, such as the more or less naïve act of reading a novel, the identification of a sequence of tones, the emotionally charged engagement with a film, the identification of culinary allusions in the food industry, and so on.

Interpretations are hermeneutical enactments – that is, they exist only in a form of understanding that could also turn out otherwise. A reading, by contrast, is the scientific reconstruction of the elements of a score. Readings presuppose interpretations, meaning that there is no scientific dissection of a score that is not at least implicitly guided by a performance practice. This might include an art-historical examination of the work-shop arrangement of a painting school; the investigation of the connection between use of colour and the chemical knowledge during a given art period; analysing the history of musical notation systems as well as the acoustic spaces of the instruments; assessing fictionality attributes in narratology; and so forth. One cannot offer a successful reading of a work without interpreting it first. The hermeneutical objects determine the framework in which the meta-hermeneutical objects of scientific reading can appear.

Fictive objects exist as much as fictional objects; Gretchen is no less real than *Faust Part I*. In our field of sense, Gretchen has a twofold nature: as a meta-hermeneutical object, she is tied to a text basis that explicitly assigns certain properties to her. However, these properties do not define her adequately for her to be unmistakably identifiable to competent readers. The fictional sign 'Gretchen' leaves room for interpretations because Gretchen is fictive.[20]

Interpretations consist in an aesthetic experience. The aesthetic experience in which Gretchen appears as a fictive object can be initiated by a stage performance of the *Faust* scores, a film adaptation by reading the text of the play silently in one's room, and so forth. Depending on the interpretation, the readers fill in gaps that are not self-evidently comprehensible. In an interpretation, we disclose for ourselves the field of sense in which Gretchen appears. This opens up a space for interpretation that enables countless interpretations which are all compatible with the score. Gretchen is fictive because some of her properties are gained only through our ascription of them to her in an interpretation. This ascription is restricted by the ur-text, which is the occasion for our interpretation.

Yet an interpretation cannot be successful if it fails to take into account that Gretchen is a human being. She may represent a type of human allegorically, but this realization emerges only in the course of a reading. In the aesthetic experience itself, we encounter Gretchen as a person, not an abstract object. I therefore consider it false that fictive objects do not in any way have a spatiotemporal existence, a claim that is sometimes presented as virtually self-evident.[21] Gretchen has a spatiotemporal existence in every performance of *Faust*, whether in the form of a representation by actors or through an enactment in my imagination. This does not mean that the actor is Gretchen (in the sense of being 'identical with her'), which is clearly not the case. Rather, the actor interprets Gretchen in a way that is partly visible to us, because the properties of the actor we can see *ipso facto* become properties of Gretchen through our interpretation of the performance.

Contrary to the mainstream view in contemporary ontology, there is no analytical connection between fiction and absolute non-existence. It is time to expose a philosophical myth that has been rampant for decades. This myth has it that there are fictional objects which can be given as significant examples of non-existent objects – significant because it seems that we can refer to this particular type of non-existent objects in the medium of fictional representation. This generates a paradox-prone framework of premises that must be stabilized by the usual theoretical constructions. Yet one can also develop an alternative to this conception, such as the fictional realism defended in this book, which treats fictions as something real in which fictive objects exist.

If one accepts the rules of the mainstream, this results in the classifications that are common today. Opinions are especially divided on the matter of whether fictional objects exist.

The arguments for and against the positions on the spectrum extending from fictional realism to fictional irrealism often revolve around the status of truth in fiction; that is, how one should understand propositions such as 'Faust falls in love with Gretchen'. If such propositions are to be understood exactly as they appear, the framework of premises immediately risks becoming inconsistent, since one cannot invent a fictional counter-truth to go with every non-fictional truth (by authoring an appropriate short story), which would mean that one must consider anything and everything true in fiction.

On the whole, fictional realism sees it as an advantage that it can take on board such extradiegetic statements as 'Sherlock Holmes is more famous than any real detective', as it equips 'Sherlock Holmes' with extradiegetic reference. The manoeuvres of fictional irrealism, on the other hand, allow a logical-semantic isolation of fictional imagined worlds from the real world, such that there is no risk of contradiction, since fictional 'assertions' are simply not assertions.

The concept of meta-fictional statements employed in the mainstream is narratologically underdeveloped, which is a source of semantic trials and tribulations. In the field of narratology, the term 'metafictional' is used for expressions of the authorial role in the guise of the narratorial role; these lend the narrative a particular form of self-referentiality.[22] The usual structural framework of a fictional narrative consists in the fact that there is not only a sender who narrates a story to a receiver that is meant to represent certain events, but also that an author produces a text featuring a narratorial position that narrates a story to an addressee; this addressee can then be located in their own diegetic reality by the narrator.

It is not enough, then, to distinguish between an intrafictional and a metafictional level, especially when the conditions of reference on the metafictional level cannot be clarified without narratological investigations. If, in a seemingly metafictional approach, one compares Sherlock Holmes as a fictional character to other such characters or real persons, one is thus looking at either the hermeneutical or the meta-hermeneutical object. The conditions of reference for the phrase 'Sherlock Holmes' must first be articulated before one can identify a meaning with sufficient semantic-ontological relevance in seemingly metafictional statements – something that does not normally occur, since no difference is made between author, narrator, interpreter and academic analytic reader. Without such narratological and text-theoretical distinctions, the differentiation between meta- and intra- is too vague to be chosen as a starting point for an ontology of fictional objects.

What is also regrettable about the mainstream constellation is that it usually remains unclear at what point something actually becomes a fictional object. To avoid this difficult question, one stipulates a sense of 'fictional' that permits the continuation of a sham debate. To support this claim, I would refer to the introduction by Stuart Brock and Anthony Everett in a collection entitled *Fictional Objects*.[23] In the course of defining the subject of the collection, the authors state that 'these kinds of things' – namely, literary characters such as Jed Martin, Emma Bovary and Gretchen – 'are typically called "fictional" where this means that they "are individuals first introduced in a work of fiction".'[24]

This formulation causes more problems than it is capable of solving. For now, we will pass over the problem that the word 'fiction' in English as used here oscillates between fiction as a literary work and fiction as something entirely imagined. Then the first problem is that there is no explanation of what it means for an individual to be *introduced*. More specifically, the problem is what it means for an individual to be *introduced for the first time*. Let us examine this problem more closely.

If the thought behind this formulation is that of an individual being introduced in a literary form for the first time in the history of human language use, then too many objects would have to be considered fictional and *ipso facto* non-existent. Imagine if astronomers henceforth communicated their theories and discoveries only in the form of novellas, such that each newly discovered astrophysical object would first be verbally named in a novella.[25] So if 'fictional' means roughly the same as 'literary', it does not follow from this genre definition why something first introduced in a fiction should be considered non-existent – unless one already smuggles in the assumption under debate, namely that works of fiction try to peddle non-existent objects.[26]

The authors therefore owe us an answer to the question of where the connection between a genre of human expression and the non-existence we attribute to its objects is supposed to originate. To be sure, Hesiod, Parmenides, Solon and especially Plato's Socrates gave answers to this. But these answers are not considered by Brock and Everett.[27]

The distinction between truth and mere fiction (*plasmata*) was first postulated by Xenophanes against Hesiod and Homer.[28] Plato's ontological attack on poetry emerged from this context. Admittedly, this raises the additional problem that Plato's Socrates is a literary character who presents a critique of poetry in a fictional dialogue called the *Republic*. Why, then, should *we* believe Xenophanes, Parmenides or Plato when they distinguish between fictional truth and untruth in the context of fictional representations?

A widely accepted, yet not always explicitly articulated answer to the question of why objects that were originally described in literary contexts do not exist, is presented by Azzouni:

> I claim that we (collectively) subscribe to a particular criterion for what exists. This is that anything exists if and only if it's mind- and language-independent. Dream figures, fictional characters that authors have made up, and hallucinated objects are all, in the sense meant, mind- and language-independent. Dinosaurs, protons, microbes, other people, chairs, buildings, stars, and so on are (purported) examples of mind- and language-independent objects. . . . In my sense of 'mind-independent' and 'language-independent', no one can dictate such an object into existence by (merely) thinking it or symbolizing it as so.[29]

In the passage quoted, Azzouni employs a standard conception of ontological realism – that is, a realism with reference to 'existence' – whereby the word 'existence' signifies a property that objects possess in a mind- and language-independent way. Let us call this *naïve ontological realism*. This realism is naïve because it accommodates certain thinking habits but falls apart if one analyses its theoretical obligations more closely.

First of all, there is the problem that naïve ontological realism denies the existence of too many objects that quite obviously exist – the thought I am expressing in this sentence, for example, as well as the sentence itself. But I seemingly dictate both of these into existence by thinking or symbolizing them as existent. And what about mind and language themselves? How are mind and language supposed to be mind- and language-independent in Azzouni's special sense? If they are not, he will have to say that neither mind nor language exist, which would be a most peculiar stipulation, especially if this is purported to articulate the collective unconscious of our natural-language ontology.

Azzouni might respond that his criterion for existence can be further substantiated: whatever does not exist is simply imagined and thus circumvents the distinction between truth and holding-to-be-true. Whatever is merely imagined automatically seems to be exactly as we imagine it, and thus offers no ontic resistance to what we mean.

This would bring him closer to what I defined in 'Neutral Realism' and, prior to that, already in *The Limits of Epistemology*, as the minimum criterion for realism – that is, the contrast of objectivity between truth and holding-to-be-true.[30] According to this, one is a minimal realist in relation to a domain of objects if one is willing to concede that what is true about the objects in the respective domain may deviate from what one believes to be true of them. This takes into account that the real is that about which we can be mistaken.[31] At the least, the real offers epistemic resistance. To exist paradigmatically consists in determining that someone interested in the truth can be corrected.[32]

Admittedly, this neutral realist criterion for existence does not help Azzouni, as it is met by 'dream figures, hallucinated objects and fictional characters wholly invented by authors'. I can be mistaken about the content of someone else's dream, and, if anything remains of psychoanalysis, it is the realization that I can even be mistaken about what I have dreamed. Since episodic memory always has a fictional component and is not calibrated for an accurate reconstruction of past events, our memory is susceptible to error in any case, as it only retains basic information and reshapes these narratively and imaginarily in order to feed them more easily into modules of current events.[33]

One can be mistaken about the fictional characters invented by an author. It is certainly not difficult to confuse the *dramatis personae* of Dostoyevsky novels if one is not yet familiar with the complexity of their names and trajectories. Reading demanding works of fictional literature requires the reader to arrange its characters in a sufficiently coherent plot, which can easily go awry owing to the complexity of the meta-hermeneutical material of the score. That is exactly why there is a field of literary criticism that teaches how to read and trains this skill through a philological containment of our interpretive desires. In order to develop competence in literary criticism, one must learn through philological training how sentences become characters.[34]

Hallucinated objects also exist, as shown by the fact that a psychiatrist can ask a patient suffering from hallucinations what exactly they look like – 'More like Mary, mother of God, or more like a red triangle?', and so forth. Someone who hallucinates is not infallible when it comes to the question of what (and indeed whether) they are hallucinating.[35]

Naïve ontological realism is thwarted by its criterion for existence as mind- and language-independence, which relies on the purportedly clear meaning of 'mind-independence' and 'language-independence'. It is easy to overlook a confusion here, however, that emerges if one asks what constitutes the mind- or language-independence of a thing. As stated above, it is absurd to claim that statements are language-dependent and *ipso facto* non-existent. But what kind of meaning is the term 'language-dependent' supposed to have if statements are not considered language-dependent? And why should chairs and buildings be 'mind-independent'? Chairs are artefacts, and they would not exist if no one had ever had the intention of producing chairs. Nonetheless, Azzouni classifies them as 'mind- and language-independent'.

The absurdity of naïve ontological realism becomes even clearer if one examines another one of its exponents' favourite concepts more closely: the consciousness-independent external world. The external world is considered the epitome of the existent, such that one can remove Gretchen, hallucinated objects, and so on, from the ontological inventory because they are essentially imagined, and hence consciousness-dependent. Even with a more refined version of such a manoeuvre, one would at best arrive at the position that Gretchen and hallucinated objects are consciousness-dependent in the sense that they can only be taken into consideration as long as someone believes they are focusing on them.

But this manoeuvre collapses because of the simple fact that the consciousness which is meant to imagine Gretchen and various other things does not, in so doing, imagine itself. If consciousness is not an object purely by virtue of imagining itself, however, it does not fit into the framework of naïve ontological realism. It neither belongs to the consciousness-independent external world nor is it simply nothing – like Gretchen for the ontologically parsimonious Azzouni, who denies her any existence whatsoever.

Overall, the standard 'concept' of the fictional object fluctuates between emptiness, incoherence and polysemy.

The *emptiness* comes from the ontological stipulation that takes fictional objects as a paradigmatic case of non-existent objects and thus becomes entangled in debates about reference within fictional contexts. For this stipulation purports to be more than it really is, and to be significant in the discursive realm of fictional representation. Yet this is not the case, since the concept of fictional objects as non-existent objects is not gleaned from an analysis of the ontological commitments to interpret or theoretically analyse fictional representations. It is forced on aesthetic experience and its theoretical examination as an ontological intruder from the linguistic analysis of non-fictional uses of fragments of language designed to refer to the external world.

The standard 'concept' of the fictional object, then, falls beneath itself in unexpected fashion because the category it claims is empty: 'fictional objects' do not exist because they are introduced through theoretical construction in such a way that they create paradoxes. Yet these paradoxes are merely an effect of theory and cannot be attributed to the fact that those objects which one speaks of largely in the mode of fictions do not exist.

In one sense, it is true that there are no fictional objects, then, since the 'concept' which is meant to place us in contact with them is an empty stipulation that is only connected superficially to literary or general art-theoretical reflections. The assumption that it is analytically true that fictional objects do not exist is at best an expression of supposed common sense, claiming that there is a fictionality contract between authors and readers whose clauses include the tacit acceptance of the non-existence of objects that should be attacked as fictional.

Yet this tacit agreement would, if anything, exist against the background of a metaphysics that is entirely independent of it. If this metaphysics varies, so does the concept of the fictional object. Diehard atheists will consider gods or miracles fictional objects to be spoken of in the mode of mono- and polytheistic fictions; modern physicists will have a similar view of the four elements of classical physics. Whether there are such things as gods, miracles, earth, fire, water and air is not determined by their appearance in fictional representations, however. Otherwise, we could easily drag everything into the underworld of our annihilating imagination by dealing with it in the fictional mode.

The *incoherence* comes to light if one attempts to say why fictional objects are considered non-existent, circumventing emptiness by starting to offer reasons and arguments for it. Now, however, the concept of consciousness-dependence plays a part that is ontologically hopeless and owes its plausibility purely to the effective history of a naïve ontological realism that supposes there is an external world or reality that decides questions of existence. Fictional objects are excluded from this world, being 'wholly invented', 'imagined', and so forth. Yet that which is wholly invented or imagined does exist, so naïve ontological realism must look for a different thesis in order to say what it has in mind.

For this reason, there is a division at this point into standard fictional realists and fictional irrealists. The former usually assign fictional objects to the realm of abstract objects and then argue over whether these are invented or not. The latter suppose that fictional objects are not even wholly invented, since they do not exist at all. Fictional objects are replaced by a freely negotiated fictionality contract that, in the mode of the as-if, passes off real objects (lumps of mud, actors, dabs of paint, note sequences, and so on) as something they are not. So we do not even imagine fictional objects; they do not appear in any inventory of the existent. What exists is merely the practice of dissimulation, of pretending that something is something else.

Yet this creates the problem that we can also pretend something existent is something else existent. In a fable, for example, one can pretend that a pig is Matteo Salvini and a donkey is Donald Trump, then have them take up diplomatic relations in a version of *Animal Farm*. To give another favourite example used in these discussions: when one reads *War and*

Peace, one can pretend that it deals with Russia without raising the slightest doubts about Russia's existence among the interpreters. In the words of Everett, who is currently among the most astute defenders of the cause of fictional irrealism:

> It will clearly be essential for those engaged in a pretence to distinguish between those of their imaginings that concern genuinely existing things and those that do not. . . . They will need to articulate the distinction between the items that they imagine when they engage with fictions and the real items which populate the real world. And they will need to articulate the distinction between the way they imagine various items to be and the way those items really are.[36]

At the same time, Everett states: 'Obviously we use terms such as "real" and "exists" to mark the furniture of the real world as such.'[37] Everett is mistaken here. For who belongs to the 'we' that connect existence to the furniture of the real world as such? Everett simply presupposes this naïve ontology and makes it subject to his explanation of how the psychology of children's games works – as if it were literally child's play to distinguish between the existent and the non-existent that is presented in the fictional mode.[38]

Everett avoids articulating his ontology beyond the platitude of his stipulations, meaning that his references to the non-existent ultimately remain empty, since we do not receive any satisfactory, theoretically articulated answer to the question of what constitutes existence. He relies on the stability of a naïve ontological realism from which, unsurprisingly, he infers the legitimacy of fictional irrealism.

The *polysemy* of 'fictional object' consists in the fact that 'fictional' is used sometimes to mean the object of a representation that is recognizable as a fiction and sometimes in the sense of fictive/fabricated, with the latter also implying non-existence. Thus genre-philosophical and art-philosophical issues are again too hastily mixed with logical-semantic and ontological matters, without making the effort to concretize the ontology of art beyond the banal observation that our approach to art has a ludic character.

It is no less banal to infer this ludic character from children's games and cobble together a corresponding psychology that presents children as born exponents of a naïve ontological realism. But how do children know that the furniture of reality does not include any witches, gods, and so on? The play behaviour of children surely does not consist in the ability to distinguish between base reality and their supplementary ludic imaginings based on a detached ontological theory!

Here we see again that the mainstream debate about what its purveyors call 'fictional objects' is itself a fiction in which people refer to developmental psychology, the supposedly obvious everyday ontology, literary theory that largely ignores the work of twentieth century literary theory, and so forth, without making their philosophical commitments explicit.

One cannot develop an adequate philosophical theory of fictions without drawing on an elaborated ontology and philosophy of art. Otherwise, one is operating with empty, incoherent or unacceptably ambiguous concepts of purported 'fictional objects'. This prevents one from the outset from seeing the function of the fictional in the developmental history of the human mind, which determines itself in the medium that later came to be called the 'fictional'. Humans examine themselves based on a representation of their situation which goes so far beyond their sensory involvement in scenes of survival that, thanks to this fictional transcendence, we can expand our own ecological niche but also destroy it.

I conclude that there are indeed no 'fictional objects', since the mainstream term 'fictional object' misses precisely what is at issue in aesthetic experiences and their exploration in the humanities. It is time to replace this misguided notion with the assumption that art works are compositions that combine hermeneutical and meta-hermeneutical objects. Fictional and fictive objects exist in the context of art works whose ontology forms the basis for our truth-apt statements about such objects. Art works do not exist as 'language- and mind-independent' entities but are objectified mind, as it were, mental representations made visible, that give rise to an indefinite number of further representations.

§3

Meontology in Ontology of Fields of Sense

Since Parmenides and Plato, the minimum requirement for any ontology has been to explain the positive case of being in contrast to the negative case of non-being. In the following, I will deal specifically with non-existence, meaning that a modern problem of non-existence will enter the stage in analogy to the classical topic. By *ontology* I mean the systematic examination of the concept of existence and its reality, existence itself. This is to be distinguished from *meontology*, which addresses the concept of non-existence (*mê on*) and its reality, namely that which does not exist.[1]

The basic idea of FOS is that to exist is to appear in a field of sense. I will not repeat all the arguments for this position that I laid out in *Fields of Sense*. I will only take up the considerations from which a corresponding meontology follows. First of all, I will recap a number of basic concepts in FOS's analysis of existence, in order thus to find an appropriate way of addressing the problem of non-existence.

Existence consists in the appearance of an object in a field of sense. The same object appears in several fields of sense. If we take Angela Merkel as an example of an existing object, she appears in the field of sense of ontology. Because she also appears in the field of sense of recent European history in her role as German chancellor, in this function she is subject to legal precepts that dictate, in an ultimately imprecise manner, what scope of action she has as long as she can be considered the chancellor. Angela Merkel can also appear in a documentary or in her role as wife; she can appear in my subjective visual field (when I see her); and so on. The Federal Republic of Germany, documentaries, marriages, my subjective visual field, and so forth, are fields of sense whose positions are occupied by objects that, within their respective fields, display certain properties that distinguish them from other objects.

In this context, to *appear* does not generally mean being the object of a subject. Rather, the term 'appearance' refers to the relation between a field of sense and its objects, namely that they are real within it. Appearance is an *ordering function* – that is, the assignment of objects to fields.[2] This function can be as concrete as the forces holding the universe together or as discursively negotiable as a gym membership. Belonging to the universe and being a member at a gym differ in the rules that determine the admission to the respective field of sense. These two cases overlap, since gyms would not be what and how they are if, for example, gravity had a considerably stronger effect than it does.

An *object* is something of which something is true. It is true that 4 is a natural number, that Angela Merkel was federal chancellor until 2021, that bosons differ in their mass, charge and spin from other physical objects, that Picasso was a painter, and so on. Each of these truths refers to an object: the number 4, Angela Merkel, bosons, Picasso, and so forth.

A truth can be expressed in a verbally coded form as a statement but is not usually identical with a single verbal formulation. A truth (something true) is essentially translatable. Fundamentally, something that is true never coincides with whatever someone (or some group of thinkers, however large and well informed) holds to be true. For that reason alone, truths are not identical with statements, as statements are something that someone can consider true. Many things are true that no one could ever consider true; we simply do not know how many.

Moreover, there are truths that no one can consider true in verbally coded form because they exceed our current expressive faculties. We can easily – as I have just done – name (mention) these truths *de dicto* without being able to state (know) their content *de re*. These truths, which we can mention only indirectly, fill in 'the blind spots of nameability'.[3]

A *fact* is something that is true of an object. Since it is true of the number 4 that it is a natural number, this is a fact. Several things are true of any object. No object is embedded in a single fact alone, because every object can be characterized in a variety of ways, meaning that several truths can be expressed about the same object.

An object does not differ from the arrangement of the facts in which it is embedded. According to FOS, objects are identical to bundles of facts. If it were the case that objects were more than or different from bundles of facts, this distinction between object and bundle of facts would simply embed the object in a further fact, namely the paradoxical and thus purported fact of differing from any given bundle of facts.

A *field of sense* is an arrangement of objects that is subject to rules of arrangement. These rules are not of a verbal nature in all cases. Fields of sense are not all object areas of human reflection and speech, but rather objects that often – pre-theoretically formulated – exist independently of language, thought, consciousness and theory. I say 'pre-theoretically formulated' because we already saw in §§1–2 that the purportedly self-evident category of mind- and language-independence can be exposed as a flawed theoretical construction, which is a source of common errors about fictions.[4]

Therefore fields of sense are not generally individuated by our assignment of rules to them that enable them to operate in models. In models, we assign theoretical terms to objects that are supposed to exist in part pre-theoretically.[5] Models have properties that they do not share trivially with everything that exists, and this individuates them as such. The model space does not exhaust that which is real, but it certainly does itself belong to the real.[6]

The way in which things appear to us (for example, sensuously mediated) is itself an object that appears in a field of sense. The manner in which our surroundings (the external world) present themselves to finite minded beings such as humans is itself (at least) as real as bosons, fermions or the fundamental forces of the universe.[7]

FOS is a realistic ontological, for it supposes that the property of existing is not generally instantiated by someone holding it to be true of an object that it exists. The concept of *realism* is defined via a contrast of objectivity which stipulates that there is a divergence between truth and holding-to-be-true. Where this is adequate for a type of realism, I will speak of *neutral realism*.[8]

FOS argues for a neutral realism in relation to the objects of our ontological reflection. What exists and is therefore an object can be correctly or incorrectly characterized in our reflection. Reference to objects is per se fallible; wherever objects of reflection exist at all, there is a potential divergence between truth and holding-to-be-true. The concept of neutral realism does not offer any more than this; but neither does it offer any less.

FOS thus also advocates a *meta-ontological realism*, as it supposes that existence is an object about which there is ontological dissent, such that those who consider existence a discursive construction (for example, in the form of an existential quantifier, which is subject to logical principles that can be expressed in a calculus) are (or can be) mistaken. FOS thus supports theses about existence that compete with rival theses about existence on the question of whether which thesis turns out to be true.

FOS gains a meta-ontological advantage over irrealist alternatives through the *argument from facticity*.[9] This argument points out that that which exists cannot wholly be reduced to its appearance to us. If it could, we would have to apply this to the conditions of appearance under which we can theoretically assure ourselves of the purported circumstance of appearance. If being were identical to appearance to us, then we would be dealing with an infinite series of appearances to someone without any core phenomenon of something which appears without itself being an appearance. But that means that we could never make an unqualified claim concerning how things are. Any such claim would amount to a belief report rather than to a statement about how things are.

Another way of approaching this is to realize that the conceptual model of secondary qualities cannot be generalized. It is impossible that only what we encounter under specific human cognitive and sensory conditions is real, for, according to FOS and neutral realism, whatever is an object of fallible reference is *real*. This includes specifically human cognitive and sensory conditions. If we can be mistaken about those conditions, we must concede the possibility that not all existent things appear under specific human cognitive and sensory conditions, meaning that the attempt to generalize secondary qualities is thwarted by self-application.[10] If we cannot be mistaken about our mental equipment, it is incomprehensible why we are not all born irrealists who are not even capable of comprehending an alternative to their situation. If there were something to which we could only refer by grasping it adequately, we would be unable to notice it; it would be imperceptibly self-evident.[11]

This means that ontological realism is true, but not by necessity. No philosophical thesis is true by necessity, otherwise it would be semantically empty. It would not deal with anything real, which is why those who think that there are necessary truths in philosophy tend to view philosophy not as the formulation and theoretical justification of theses but at best as an elucidation of our linguistic and intellectual behaviour.[12]

Therefore the logically consistent alternative to ontological realism, namely *strict ontological irrealism*, goes so far on a meta-ontological level that it does not view ontology as an examination of existence. Instead, it defines ontology at best as an art of conceptual engineering that regulates our linguistic behaviour with regard to expressions of existence in natural language, and thus suppresses any semblance of the supposedly false ontological realism.

Taking all of this into account, we now face the not insignificant task of developing a theory of non-existence. The profile of this theory emerges from a situation of theoretical competition; this is hardly surprising, since it is derived from ontological realism, which, as a proposed theory, is confronted with alternatives whose rejection reinforces its stability. As a counterpart to these manoeuvres, we can expect a *meontological realism* – that is, the assumption that non-existence is a real property possessed by certain objects, and that this distinguishes them from other objects.[13]

There are alternatives to the theory I am about to offer. Not all of these are equally good; I am evaluating them according to how far they challenge the main theses of FOS. It is impossible to compare a theory (philosophical or otherwise) to every alternative in an attempt to establish it as necessarily true. For this, one would need to develop a theory that allows us to go through all the alternatives according to a law of derivation for theory construction. It would therefore require an unattainable ideal of completeness.[14]

Before I can set up a meontology based on FOS, a further preliminary methodological remark strikes me as appropriate to gain a full understanding of what is to follow. For reasons developed at length in *Fields of Sense*, I am entitled to defend FOS. This does not mean that there was ever a situation of primal ontological decision in which I had no opinions about existence, and that I gained these by examining the existing options from Parmenides to Quine and beyond. It would be unclear how to proceed in order to reach a well-grounded opinion about existence through a historical assessment of what has hitherto been said about it. Even if one chose this route, one would have to answer the question of why one should prefer Quine's approach over that of Parmenides, for example, which cannot be conclusively supported by a historical examination that weighs up the arguments from the academic literature against each other. At a certain point, it will be impossible to avoid thinking for oneself and venturing beyond a mere inspection of existing works.[15]

To define the methodological starting point for the following investigation in a transparent fashion, I will proceed from pre-ontological experience – that is, the circumstance that many objects appear to us that we contemplate with varying frequency. These objects are not ontologically sorted in the human mind from birth into categories such as 'primary/secondary qualities', 'physical objects/qualia', 'present-at-hand/ ready-to-hand', 'substances/accidents' or 'concrete/abstract'. Whatever forms of data processing we are equipped with as a result of our evolutionarily conditioned faculties, they do not include ontological categories in the strict sense.[16]

We cannot, then, simply assume independently of any ontological investigation that we already understand such distinctions as 'concrete/ abstract' or 'fictional/non-fictional'. Practising the use of such ontological terms does not guarantee their theoretical stability, but it does inform our orientation in ontological matters. At the latest, there is sufficient reason for a revision of our pre-theoretical ontological language usage when it becomes entangled in paradoxes. We are entitled a priori to eliminate paradoxes by developing, within the framework of philosophical theory construction, alternatives whose burden of proof lies in identifying one or more sources of paradox. Once we have established which conceptual resources of our pre-theoretical language usage create a given paradox, we must draw on philosophical theorizing to provide us with a justified surrogate concept in this way.

The introduction of a concept of pre-ontological experience is inevitable in any theorizing if it is to be capable of ensuring contact with reality.[17] In the line of tradition based on Kant, this demand is met by the concept of intuition [*Anschauung*]. In the theoretical edifice, intuition serves the purpose of an interface between thought and being, which is why Kant locates the concept of reality precisely there and ties *our* conception of reality to the sensory givenness of consciously identifiable objects.[18] In contemporary philosophy, this interface is examined paradigmatically with reference to the concept of perception, though it is sometimes overlooked that we are thus thematizing perception as a concept rather than simply as an existing process in living beings.[19]

What I mean is the following: the state in which I am currently existing as a minded being includes *perception*. This refers to a conscious apprehension of something that is not necessarily identical with any of my own states. Although it is customary today to concede the existence of non-conscious perception (following the model of blindsight), the etymology of the German word *Wahrnehmung*, unlike the French and English 'perception', suggests a close connection to awareness [*Gewahrsein*].[20]

However, the problem of the concept of perception is that, in the context of a scientific worldview especially common among contemporary philosophers, it was already narrowed so far that it fell to pieces. An exploration of the causal structure without which we would be unable to perceive anything suggests an analysis stipulating that perceptual episodes are composed of parts whose genesis remains opaque to the perceiving subject. This raises the psychological and neuroscientific question of the conditions under which the threshold of stimulation is crossed, the threshold that allows us to *perceive* a reality, not simply to *operationally apprehend* it; so far, science and the humanities have only partially answered this question.

Be that as it may, this framework of premises is not suitable in any case to do justice to ontological realism by introducing the concept of perception, since perception is reduced under naturalistic conditions to processes that do not constitute perception at all. According to this model, the processes of sensory data processing set in motion by the stimulation of our nerve endings anchor the reality of thinking, which only knows it is part of a reality through explanations involving the central nervous system.[21]

In Part II, I will argue that this framework of premises is a case of fiction, since it is not at all a factual account of how our perception comes about, let alone our thinking, but rather an implicit elimination of the perspective from which perception and thinking become an issue in the first place. Scientism, which seeks to translate our anchoring in reality into a causal explanation that aims to dispense with our self-image as minded beings, tells an incoherent story operating with an omniscient narrator who disputes his own existence.

Ultimately, neither the analytical concept of intuition nor the richer one of perception offers what their users claim. For they fail to do justice to the fact that we deal with multi-faceted realities that do not correspond to any one theoretically recognized theory of objects. Rather, all the object categories usually cited (physical objects as opposed to mental states, for example, actually existing objects as opposed to fictional ones, and so on) in order to introduce a worldview are hopelessly under-complex and fail to do justice to what we already know without drawing on them. In pre-ontological experience we are in contact with moral values, numbers, relations, beauty and ugliness, time, Jedi knights, Norman Bates, Madonna, justice, and so forth. Our pre-ontological experience thus provides the starting point for an *ontological pluralism* chosen, among others, by Derek Parfit in his late work, where he kindly reminds us that the following objects (and many others) exist *prima facie*: 'Facts, meanings, laws of nature, the Equator, philosophical theories, nations, wars, famines, overdrafts, prizes, constellations, metaphors, symphonies, fictional characters, fashions, literary styles, problems, explanations, numbers, logical truths, duties, and reasons.'[22] The bestiary of things can be simplified through classification, of course, but never reduced to a common denominator that provides us with a substantial concept of existence. That is why existence (as also happens with similar concepts such as identity, fact, object, field of sense, and so forth) comprises elements of formal being – that is, something we can grasp in philosophical reflection without consequently gaining metaphysical insight into the architecture of an absolute totality.[23]

The basis of ontological pluralism, then, is not an a priori deduction of plural modes of existence, a logical-semantic analysis of the application of the existential quantifier or a linguistic analysis of existential terms; rather, it is something that is easily accessible in our pre-ontological experience – the unhidden multiplicity of objects that, in our lives, are at most connected by the fact that we have encountered them.

Based on our pre-ontological experience, however, we know that the objects we have encountered are not limited to those encounters. The supermarket remains where it is, even if I have not yet been there today; Vesuvius changes imperceptibly, but does not completely disappear if I am not in Naples; the basement of the building in which I am writing this does not fall into the void simply because I happen to be upstairs; and so on. Ontological realism and pluralism thus seem *prima facie* true; the burden of proof rests on those who dispute them.

The meontology of FOS starts from the Platonic idea that non-being (*mê on*) consists in being-other (*thateron*). Not to be does not mean to be nothing, as it were, but to be something that differs from something else. In the framework of FOS, the situation arises that something which does not exist in a given field of sense nonetheless exists in a different field of sense.

Before this can be articulated further, we must deal with two objections that might be advanced against this basic idea.

The *first objection* is that one should understand the indefinite article in 'appearance in a field of sense' or 'in a different field of sense' to the effect that one aims for some field of sense in the totality (or field of sense) of all fields of sense without specifying exactly which one. This implicitly presupposes a totality of fields of sense by means of which one can then claim to have 'quantified over' something.[24]

There is no force to this objection, however, since it presupposes something that is not the case in FOS: that whenever we speak of 'all' or 'any' we quantify over a totality or a whole that is no longer part of a larger whole. The objection thus commits a *petitio principia* against the no-world-view of FOS.[25] If we know that something does not exist in a given field of sense and say that it exists in a different field of sense, this does not constitute banishing it to an indeterminate other place in an all-encompassing logical or ontological space, since this operation is impermissible in FOS.

The indefinite article in "to exist is to appear in a field of sense" is not an implicit reference to a determinate totality but, rather – how could it be otherwise? – an indication that, within a restricted area, something either appears or does not. To say in an indeterminate description that someone murdered Kennedy does not amount to making a statement about the entire universe or the world as the totality of all objects/facts/fields of sense. The indeterminate reference to some murderer is not a determinate reference to a totality, but rather a reference to a murderer in the field of sense of an action situation like Kennedy's murder.

At this point one must point out one of the numerous confusions that plague the ∃ thesis – that is, the equation of particular judgements with existential statements.[26] It seems like an ontological sleight of hand if one relies on the claim that '∃xFx' is equivalent to '¬∀x¬Fx'. If it is true that someone has bought rolls, this surely means that not all potential roll-buyers have refrained from buying rolls. Each model for this apparent logical banality is subject to restrictions, however, since we cannot simply insert any person or thing as x. Which objects we take into consideration when we assign a genuine attribute that distinguishes one real thing from another is determined by a limited area about which we make statements.

The universal quantifier as such does not refer to anything. The impression of referring to an absolute totality arises from, among other elements, the fact that the bound variable x in '∀x (x = x)' is understood as a form of overpowering logical proper name that refers to everything at once, rather than every individual thing about which one can make a propositionally articulated statement.

Our logical formulae have no meaning beyond their applicability to languages that mean something. Where they succeed in making sense, their role consists in articulating relationships between propositions that support conclusions that sometimes elude us when we draw conclusions under the operating conditions of daily life. It is neither a logical nor an ontological success to assign the property of existence to the symbol '∃'. This assignment does not follow any calculus and is not supported by ontological considerations that are independent of the calculus construction.[27]

A further confusion that might obstruct us here comes from seeking to understand existence via identity by stating that something is supposed to exist if it is identical with something: '∃x (x = y)'. It is sheer folly to attempt to use such a symbol without any assignment of meaning. What exactly is '=' supposed to mean? Questions such as what identity is and whether two objects that differ from each other in some respect can be identical are where the real ontological action is. To see existence in the fact that something is identical with something particular (x with y) presupposes that y exists; this means that the purported explanation of the concept of existence is already obsolete, as it presupposes an unarticulated understanding of existence on which it draws without revealing how it does so. This becomes apparent when purveyors of the ∃ thesis notice that they actually mean that existing consists in appearing in the world, which brings us back to the real topic of our investigation.

Conclusion: it is not the case that we are reflecting on a totality of field of sense when we say that the non-existence of a particular object (phlogiston, ether, unicorns, angels, and so forth) consists in the fact that an object defined in whatever way exists in a different field of sense from the one in which we expected to encounter it.

The *second objection* treats FOS as a Meinongianism of the follow-ing kind: if something does not exist, it is always assigned to *one* other particular field of sense, such as the field of sense of imaginings. The motivation for such Meinongianism, which I refer to in *Fields of Sense* as 'substantial Meinongianism',[28] consists in distinguishing a field of sense of existing objects from a precisely demarcated sphere of non-existent objects towards which one can direct oneself, but which do not there-fore exist. Substantial Meinongianism thus commits itself to 'intentional objects', in the sense of objects whose sole purpose is for someone to direct themselves towards them (mention them, imagine them, reflect on them, and so on) without them actually existing. FOS would ultimately differ from this Meinongianism only verbally, since the concept of existence in FOS could be translated into the concept of objects in Meinongianism.[29]

This second objection is in turn refuted by pointing out the continued validity of the no-world-view. It is out of the question that there is a world of the real surrounded by a domain of intentional objects, so we can now form a totality of objects composed of real, existing ones on the one hand and merely intended, non-existing ones on the other.

According to FOS, whatever does not exist in one field of sense exists in another given field of sense. Whatever does not exist exists elsewhere, something referred to (albeit critically) by Jocelyn Benoist with his concept of being elsewhere (*être ailleurs*).[30] The field of sense to which a non-existent object is transferred is not determined a priori, as there is no simple metaphysical architecture that divides all objects into a number of categories.[31] This does away with the notion that there is an overall domain of the real (being, the world) surrounded by another domain of the unreal (nothingness).

Let us illustrate the meontology of FOS by using the classic example: the unicorn. It is said that unicorns do not exist, meaning that no branch of the evolution of species on Planet Earth has produced unicorns, as they appear in mythological sources, stories, tapestries, dreams, and so forth. Unicorns do not appear in a suitable fashion in the universe, but at most indirectly, for example in heraldry.[32] There are no unicorns, but there are representations of unicorns that have no correlates 'in reality'.

In the field of sense of the movie *The Last Unicorn*, however, it is false that there are no unicorns because it is true in that movie that there are unicorns. One therefore says that it is *intrafictionally* true that there are unicorns. So why are there supposedly no unicorns? Let us assume that the minimalistic equivalence principle (EP) for truth is acceptable (which is not usually disputed):

(EP) 'p' is true if and only if p.

Then it would follow from the proposition 'It is intrafictionally true that unicorns exist' that unicorns do exist, unless one had reasons to treat the attribute of intrafictional truth differently from that of truth. To be sure, intrafictional truth would then be something different from truth *tout court*, as it violates one of the definitional principles of the concept of truth. The supposed *metafictional* truth that there are no unicorns contradicts the supposed *intrafictional* truth that there are unicorns, though only the latter does not seem to be a 'proper' truth.

The only way to justify this distinction here is by saying that, after all, we know that unicorns do not exist. Yet this does not count, since it already implies that intrafictional truth is not 'proper' truth and therefore cannot be adduced to support this argumentation.[33]

FOS deals with this problem by relying on *ontological relationism*. It maintains that a thing only ever exists in relation to (or in) a field of sense, and that there is specifically no all-encompassing field of sense where recourse to its total ordering function resolves questions of existence in a particularly substantive sense.[34] Fermions exist in the universe, Gretchen in *Faust*, the president in institutions that derive their right to exist from the constitution, numbers in formal systems studied in number theory, and so forth. But none of these objects exist in a particularly metaphysically 'real' fashion.

The nub of this reflection in the context of meontology is the following: Gretchen does not exist in the universe, the president does not exist in formal mathematical systems, fermions do not exist in institutions that derive their right to exist from the constitution, and so on. That Gretchen does not exist in the universe does not mean that she does not exist; that fermions have no legal rights or duties does not mean that they do not exist; and so forth.

This idea resembles Bergson's famous analysis of the illusion of an absolute nothing in *Creative Evolution*.[35] In one famous passage, Bergson argues that 'absolute Nothing' is merely a 'word', not an 'idea'. For the operation of negation only addresses something that is pushed out by something else, so the negation of an individual thing does not lead to reality being one thing poorer. According to Bergson, the function of negation is the retraction of an expected affirmation, not the affirmation of an existing negative state of affairs (a hole in being, as it were). Hence the repeated application of negation 'in turn' (*tour à tour*) by no means produces the desired result of a negation of all things 'altogether' (*toutes ensemble*).[36]

According to Bergson, negation of existence is the 'exclusion' or 'expulsion' of an object from a given situation, supplanting the negated object with a different one that exists in its place. Negation is not a stone paving the way to absolute Nothing, then, as it does not move us one iota away from the 'full' (*le plein*), as Bergson also calls the real (*le réel*). Therefore, he argues, the unreal and non-existent is merely the possible, which we embellish in the form of the imagination. Whatever cannot be embellished in this manner is, then, like the 'square circle' – not an idea that is difficult to grasp, but simply a word.

Bergson does, however, espouse a metaphysics of immanence with regard to the full. He assumes that there is an absolute totality which he identifies reality. In his view, negation takes a block of reality and adds to it an object that is excluded by it, which presupposes that we can form the idea of the 'actual reality taken in block'. According to FOS, however, this operation is as much a source of nonsense as Bergson's absolute Nothing.[37] He overlooks the fact that, with the idea of absolute Nothing, the idea of absolute being as the fullness of the real is also thrown overboard. There is neither a reality block nor its substratum as the absolute Nothing; there is simply no world that sets itself apart from a Nothing. Both relata of such a metaphysical pseudo-relation are non-existent. They are words that refer to nothing; they are not even imaginings (see §§4 and 10). The words 'the world' and 'Nothing' do exist, but they do not refer to metaphysical objects in any meaningful usage – that is, an absolute totality on the one hand and its complete absence on the other.[38]

There is no meaning of 'existence' that exhausts existence or refers to a field of sense whose objects instantiate the property of existence in an ontologically privileged fashion. There are no ontological privileges, which does not mean that *ontological* relationism automatically imbues other areas of thought (such as ethics, the theory of truth, and so forth). It follows from FOS that there is no absolute meaning of existence to which a field of sense is assigned that decides whether each existing object belongs to it or not. This does not mean that, in a given field of sense (such as that of value-based actions or true statements), there are no standards referring to local precepts that norm-bound actors are supposed to follow.

Whatever exists in one field of sense (or several) does not exist in various others. No object appears in all fields of sense, since there is no relevant totality of fields of sense (no world). As there is no whole of fields of sense, no world-whole, it is a truism that no object appears in all fields of sense.

Fields of sense cannot be totalized in such a way that, through gaining insight into their overall constitution, we can make substantive statements about what needs to appear in each field of sense for it to contain anything at all. Fields of sense are not enclosed by a transcendental frame; this is one of the ways in which FOS differs from the modal realism of David Lewis.[39] Lewis embeds his possible worlds in a logical space that allows the concept of possibility to give us access to a totality of the possible.

Here I agree with Quentin Meillassoux, who has pointed out that we have neither *empirical* nor *theoretical* grounds to suppose that there is any such logical space of possibilities, albeit drawing on Cantor's theorem to show that possibility cannot be theoretically totalized a priori. Any such totalization would form a set of possible worlds, which would allow the generation of a power set; this would show that we have no rule for formulating a substantive concept of possibility that goes beyond the narrow framework of something like logical possibility as consistency.[40]

Meillassoux's argument, then, is that the set of possible worlds remains incomplete as long as we ignore the power set of this set. This argument, however, does not work without additional premises that Meillassoux does not provide, which is easy to show. Let us assume that there is a finite number of possible worlds that we can simplistically reduce to three: w_1, w_2 and w_3. Now we can form the set W, consisting of the three worlds $\{w_1, w_2, w_3\}$. The power set P(W) of this set consists of the set of subsets of W, and is thus as follows: P(W) = $\{\{w_1\}, \{w_2\}, \{w_3\}, \{w_1, w_2\},$ $\{w_2, w_3\}, \{w_1, w_3\}, \{w_1\}, \{w_2\}, \{w_3\}, \emptyset\}$. But why should the power set of possible worlds contain more possible worlds than the starting set? For that, possible worlds would at least have to be identical with sets, though admittedly this would not produce the desired result either, unless every set in existence were a possibility. Perhaps Meillassoux assumes for some reason that these *prima vista* bizarre assumptions are correct, but he does not elaborate them, so his argument has feet of clay.

What is true is that – at least *ex hypothesi* – there are no empirical reasons to form a logical space of possible worlds, since we are supposed to have empirical access only to the actual world. For it is implicit in the concept of the actual world that it is the only world we can access empirically, as the other worlds in modal realism are defined by being causally isolated from us, meaning that we cannot obtain any empirical information about them.

FOS offers neither empirical nor adequately robust a priori reasons for the assumption that there is an ordering function for all fields of sense that assigns a particular object or type of object (such as physical ones) to each of them. The reasons for this are not based on set-theoretical paradoxes, however, since the conception of the field of sense is intensional: It describes the circumstance that whatever exists is essentially subject to ordering rules (modes of presentation) dictated by the fact that objects bear relation to one another that go beyond the purely extensionalist vocabulary of set theory – at least, whenever we are dealing with non-mathematical objects.[41]

In the wake of Graham Priest's work, furthermore, the literature on paraconsistent logics has prominently shown that we can reckon with impossible worlds; this has also done away with the dogma that we cannot imagine impossible scenarios, something to which we will naturally return. Meillassoux, like his precursor Alain Badiou, wrongly relies on the law of non-contradiction as the principle of a rationalist ontology, overlooking the fact that one can rationally formulate non-classical logics that offer dialetheistic suggestions for solutions to the set-theoretical paradoxes that, unlike Badiou and Meillassoux, do not accept the classical axioms of set theory as the only model.[42]

Contrary to Meillassoux's assumption, classical logic does determine a non-totalizable space of the possible, but it is not embedded in a larger panorama, as alternative logics disclose other spaces for themselves. What Meillassoux overlooks is the self-application of the insight into the non-totality to theorizing. We know from the metamathematics of the twentieth century, at least since Gödel, that there cannot be any consistent formal system in which every true proposition can be inferred from its axioms as a theorem. Any ontology can have a formal system assigned to it that models its formal properties, since the basic concepts of an ontology (existence, identity, the modalities, proposition, intension/extension, and so on) introduce rules of transformation that explain one basic concept to us with recourse to another. Hence, like mathematics ontology is in principle incomplete.

In the framework of FOS, this entails an explicit recognition of the fact that alternatives exist, some of which may be true. None of the typical alternatives of today, however, are capable of fulfilling the promise of metaphysics to develop a substantive theory of absolute totality that allows us to develop an architecture of objects or fields of sense a priori.[43]

The central concept of FOS is existence in the sense of appearance in a field of sense. This definition is not arbitrary, but rather follows from the rejection of alternatives that tie existence to the presence of an unlimited domain of objects (a world). In addition, knowledge is a basic ontological term in FOS, as knowledge and its mental preconditions exist themselves and must be paradigmatically taken into account if we want to be sure of the intelligibility of our very ontology.[44]

It is not enough to present a meaning of existence against alternatives based on its theoretical merits as long as it is unclear whether the propositions of the theory's construction are reconcilable with the intelligibility of its domain of objects. An epistemological blind spot undermines any form of ontology that takes the intelligibility of the real too lightly, supposing that pointing to reality is enough to proceed subsequently to a logical articulation of a metaphysical architecture. One cannot gain a theoretical view of the metaphysical object area known as 'the world' simply by having a sense of the universal scope of a given logic's quantifier. How quantifiers are used in a given calculus remains metaphysically inconsequential unless we show that, in our successful reflections on what is not itself necessarily identical with our thoughts about it (the real), we have no choice but to adopt a particular, metaphysical use of the universal quantifier, which is a highly dubious assumption.[45]

Let us return to non-existence. We can now say this much: not to exist does not mean to be nothing at all. After all, we wish to be able to say what does not exist. This is precisely what usually leads to the Eleatic paradox of non-existence, which can be formulated as follows:

(1) An object o is something at which one can direct oneself with truth-apt thoughts.
(2) A paradigm for such a truth-apt thought is the ascription of a property to an object, such as the property Π. I then think: oΠ.
(3) I can only meaningfully think that oΠ if I can also think that $\neg$oΠ.
(4) Let E be the property of existence. I can only meaningfully think that oE if I can also think that $\neg$oE.
(5) The term 'o' in $\neg$oE refers to o.

(6) If a term such as 'o' (paradigmatically a proper name) refers to o, then there is something to which it refers, namely o.
(7) If I think truthfully of an object o that it does not exist, then there is something that does not exist, namely o.
∴ There are (infinitely) many objects that do not exist.

At first glance, it appears that one could keep calm and base one's sense that one might be dealing with a paradox after all on the informed opinion that some of the Greek philosophers had a problem with a falsidical paradox here, since they could not adequately distinguish between being (there is) and existence on account of the polysemy of their basic ontological concepts (*on, einai*, and so on). In their language, the conclusion would seem paradoxical in that it would strike them as expressing a contradiction, both ascribing the property of being and denying it at the same time of infinitely many objects. According to this diagnosis, the air of paradox would be a regional linguistic artefact of ancient Greek that one could explain away using a distinction between being and existence.[46] Such argumentation supports a transition to a Meinongian ontology, which famously distinguishes between existence and other modes of being in order to introduce objects that do not exist, yet to which we can unproblematically refer verbally because they display the determination of being (something) without existing – that is, they are in some way (like Gretchen in *Faust*) without therefore having to exist.

This manoeuvre is powerless, however, for it shifts the paradox from existence to being. If the existent objects do not exclude the non-existent ones from being, meaning that one can refer to the latter without any ontological commitment, the objects there are (being) encompass in addition to existence everything the existent ones reject, then one has only seemingly made progress. For now being becomes contradictory, as we can only think of some object o that it has being if we can think of it that does not have being which leads to the paradoxical conclusion that some objects which have being have no being.

The opening move of Meinongianism consists in the notion that both existent and non-existent objects are parts of being, which is expressed in the statement that there are both existent and non-existent objects. The domain of reference when speaking about being is therefore contradictory, as it is true in it both that there is no current king of France and that there is a current king of France, since both have a precisely defined being: one the being of the non-existent king of France and the other the being of the existent one.

If one classifies fictional objects as non-existent, one usually means by this that some of the objects mentioned or characterized in contexts that are considered fictional representations (which include films, sculptures, paintings or operas) should be viewed as ontological troublemakers that entangle us in the Eleatic paradox. On this level, one evades the effort of stating what characterizes the fictional context and thus the fictionality of the troublemakers, beyond the purported fact that they are unwelcome infiltrators into our otherwise well-behaved semantic systems.

FOS' concept of ontological relationism offers a solution: Because of the context-sensitive nature of successful existential statements, the ostensible Eleatic paradox commits an equivocation even on a Meinongian reading. It does not follow from the fact that Jed Martin exists in *The Map and the Territory* that Jed Martin exists *tout court*, for there is no such thing as existence *tout court*. Nothing simply exists without existing in some field of sense, which as such never takes up an all-encompassing space. It is therefore no contradiction to state that many non-existent things exist, because it expresses the fact that many things exist in a field of sense S^1 without consequently existing in another field of sense S^2. As there is no field of sense in which all objects exist, and no object that exists in all fields of sense (since there is no world-whole), the paradox evaporates. The alleged paradox is merely an invalid conclusion whose semblance of truth is produced by confusing the formal univocity of existence (appearance-in-a-sense-field) with a metaphysical architecture (occurrence-in-the-world).

What distinguishes FOS is that it offers a technical solution to the Eleatic paradox in which is a reward for a post-Meinongian forbearance with everything that exists and does not exist and is an object of our truth-apt reflection. So let us be magnanimous enough to accept the by now almost obvious: Gretchen, Jed Martin, Anna Karenina and Jesus exist. They are objects. They all have parents (the details are biologically intricate in the case of Jesus, but he certainly has parents). It follows from this that they cannot be abstract objects, since beings that have parents are unquestionably concrete, in so far as 'being concrete' is based on being causally embedded in a space–time fabric. We can therefore conclude that, in the discursive landscape around so-called fictional objects, FOS constitutes a realistic option whose objects are concrete, which enables it to define and close a gap on the map of orthodoxy. Yet, fictional objects only exist in our field of sense of interpreting them in virtue of them being embedded in their field of sense that is causally isolated from ours, this is what makes them fictive. They therefore do not undermine the logical consistency and relative causal closure of our universe. Moreover, there are as many instances of fictive objects associated with a fictional name such as 'Gretchen' as there are legitimate interpretations of the *Faust* scores. In those ways, fictional characters clearly differ from relevant non-fictional characters such as Joe Biden whose existence is not essentially tied to interpretations of a score.

Ontologically speaking there is nothing paradoxical about non-existence, for, in formal terms, FOS is an ontological relationism. In this context, ontological relationism settles on the view that there is no metaphysically privileged domain of objects that requires us to classify all objects that do not belong to this domain as *ipso facto* non-existent. Rather, we can say that anything in a field of sense that stakes a rightful claim to existence does not need to exist in another field of sense. Jed Martin exists in the field of sense of *The Map and the Territory*, but he does not exist here (in the place where I am). Here, Houellebecq's novel and my interpretation thereof exist, but Jed Martin does not. This means that the facts concerning him are sufficiently isolated from those concerning me to avoid possible contradictions between fiction and reality. Even if it were true in *The Map and the Territory* that Jed Martin travels to Paris to visit me, this would be a truth not about Paris and me but about Paris$_{\text{The Map and the Territory}}$ and Markus Gabriel$_{\text{The Map and the Territory}}$. The reference to objects in a fictional field of sense rules out the possibility that the objects of this reference could extend in their effects to the realm of meta-hermeneutical objects that occasions our acts of the imagination.

Yet this immediately raises the following problem: Jed Martin exists in *The Map and the Territory*, but not here. Paris and France exist here. Areas such as Paris and France also exist in *The Map and the Territory*. Jed Martin is a French citizen in *The Map and the Territory*, but not here. France in *The Map and the Territory* therefore cannot be identical with France, as these two objects have different properties.[47] In any ontologically coherent – that is, actually viable – interpretation of the novel, they are even so different that no citizen of the one country is also a citizen of the other. So France does not exist in both of the fields of sense we are examining, only in one. It follows from this that we must abandon the usual distinction between fictional objects that exist and those that are simply characterized in a fiction but do not actually exist.

In standard vocabulary, then, FOS is a variant of a counterpart theory of fictional objects. What looks like France in an interpretation of a novel is not France but, at best, an object that is very similar to France (a counterpart). The following thought about the Bible prominently analysed by Tim Crane must accordingly be rejected:

> (Bible thought) Some figures in the Bible existed [such as Solomon or Jesus], others did not [such as the resurrected Lazarus or the angel Gabriel].[48]

The good news is that we do not have to think (the Bible thought). To return to Houellebecq, we can say that the word 'France' in our reading of *The Map and the Territory* cannot refer to France; at best it refers to something shockingly similar to France – in some interpretations of the novel, at least. The power, and thus also danger, in the type of fiction that Houellebecq develops in such works as *The Possibility of an Island* or *Submission* is precisely that they portray something which seems to resemble our reality but deviates from it in such a way that it seems to point to a possibility in our reality.[49]

Yet that is precisely where the real illusory character of art is to be found: the point of fiction (including science fiction) is not that it tells us something about our reality – an impending reality, for example – but that it is ultimately only about itself. We must therefore break with the primordial Aristotelian dogma that mimetic literature such as plays or more or less realistic novels contains statements about what could happen but (so far) has not.[50] A novel is not a modal thought experiment. Novels are not factual accounts of something that occurs in possible worlds. Novels do not describe anything; in their materiality as texts, they are scores for interpretations, the basis for possible acts of interpretation. These interpretations are subject to principles that include orienting oneself by the text.

What looks like a factual report is not one in ontological terms, even if a literary text can coincidentally be used as a source of information containing non-fictional reality. Even if one can find the ruins of Troy by reading the *Iliad*, the same does not apply to the remains of Patroclus or the wood from which the Trojan horse was fashioned. No objects in the *Iliad* appear in the fields of sense we can visit (even if we used a time machine and actually saw the Trojan horse, say).

Fictive objects exist, but they are ontologically isolated from us. They enter our reality indirectly by simultaneously activating and restricting the exercise of our productive imagination, mediated through meta-hermeneutical objects. We exercise our imaginative ability when, based on aesthetic experience, we identify the details of an art work by taking a stance on how the objects and fields of sense assembled within it are connected.

A reading is an object-level examination of the composition (the assemblage) of elements in an art work that are given to us in the form of its score. The score of a painting, for example, is the painted piece of canvas hanging on a wall along with a frame; the score of a sculpture is the piece of bronze standing in a garden; the score of a novel is the text, which can be duplicated and exist as a copy; and so forth.[51] When we read a literary fictional product, we create an overall picture by connecting the information we glean from the text and then, in the mode of interpretation, adding information that we find plausible within the aesthetic experience.

We thus learn something about ourselves in aesthetic experience, simply because aesthetic experience is a constitutive part of our reality – that is, the existence of minded beings whose thoughts extend indefinitely beyond individual scenes in which we respectively appear as mortal beings.

Derek Matravers offers an interesting rationale for this in *Fiction and Narrative*: he distinguishes between *representation* and *confrontation*. A representation of an object or event presents something to us in the medium of a narrative; this narrative is subject to its own conditions of coherence, which are examined in the psychological narratology on which Matravers relies.[52] Representations play a part whenever we bring to mind scenes that exceed our direct matching of data with action-relevant contexts in which we are involved.

Blumenberg similarly argues in his *Theory of Nonconceptuality* by tying concepts to expectations that arise only when people have distanced themselves from the objects of their need satisfaction to such an extent that they have to skip over a hiatus or to bridge it by throwing (Blumenberg views the ballistics of projectiles as the primordial laboratory of logic).

> The human being, the creature that stands upright and leaves the immediate vicinity of perception, transcends the horizon of its senses, is the being of the *actio per distans*. It acts in relation to objects that it does not see. In the caves that constitute its first shelter, it draws the objects of its desire and its struggle for existence on the walls. The concept arises in the lives of beings that are hunters and nomads.[53]

Our radius of action varies, as we naturally go beyond our sensorily present surroundings through technology (think of drone pilots or the global interconnectedness that allow us to intervene in distant locations). But there are always scopes of action in which we cannot participate directly. We call these to mind without simultaneously being confronted with them. I might imagine how it is to be a soldier and be emotionally challenged in the imaginary embellishment of the war; yet this, fortunately, does not mean that I will ever have to participate in events of war as a soldier.

Representation exceeds the framework of confrontation. In the struggle for survival of our species, this has given us a decisive advantage, although, on account of our technological display of power, it will not be a lasting one, since it is precisely the extent to which we transcend any direct confrontation that leads us to destroy our own ecological niche.[54]

Matravers overlooks the option that we can also be confronted with representations, which is the norm in aesthetic experience. The occasion for an aesthetic experience is a representation that exists in the mode of a presentation, which we in turn represent in the mode of re-enactive imagination. Against this background, Gadamer quite rightly considered it a central anthropological function of art to introduce the experience of duration into our lifeworld through the creation of its own time [*Eigenzeit*]. Our orientation within our lifeworld transcends the space of sheer survival, which imaginarily repeats itself in the primordial scene invoked several times by Matravers in which wolves attack the cave community. We do not keep the real at a distance through representation; rather, we intervene in it in the form of art works, since these, as Gadamer shows, invite us to linger and thus create a safe time span (the festival) that enables us to extend beyond the pure transience of our survival (albeit without becoming immortal).[55]

Art works are objects of a confrontation under conditions of aesthetic experience that allow us to feel the absence of danger.[56] This explains the apotropaic success of the beautiful foregrounded by Blumenberg, which lulls us into a sense of security for the duration of the aesthetic experience. Herein lies the frequently invoked illusory character of art, because it can be taken all too easily for a genuine transcendence over the real. The seductive power of art consists in the way it undermines the simple distinction between representation and confrontation, of the absence and presence of things, and problematizes its artistic character, its crafted-ness, through complex referential games with this distinction.[57] This is mirrored in the notion of the artist as genius, which presents the artist to us as the medium of an absent order, since we cannot make sense of how someone can create the relational composition of a work in which we, as interpreters ('fellow players',[58] as Gadamer says), are constitutively involved. So-called fictional objects do not exist without interpretation; they are not simply woven into the tapestry of the available, and yet they are not subject to our control, but rather modify us as subjects of their apprehension.[59]

At this point, Jens Rometsch countered in a private conversation that, if someone delivers an erroneous factual report, one cannot conclude from this that everything contained in the report is incorrect. He adduces the analogy of a toddler mistakenly thinking, and thus reporting, that it has seen a wolf in the garden, from which it does not follow that the garden is as imaginary as the wolf. He infers from this that Napoleon as the object of a feature film and Napoleon as the object of a historical documentary containing feature film scenes are the same Napoleon, such that, at any rate, some amount of non-fictional objects can appear in the field of sense of the fictional, which jeopardizes the isolation thesis.

Now, according to the ontology proposed here, Napoleon as the object of a feature film is not actually identical with Napoleon. No feature film or feature film scene in a historical documentary deals with Napoleon; at best, it deals with something or someone resembling Napoleon. Nor, inci-dentally, is the garden imagined with a wolf identical with the garden one has seen. Our imaginings do resemble some objects that are concretely present to us, but they are not identical with them. If I picture my office in my imagination, the object thus imagined is not identical with my office, even if the two are similar, since my office was in this case the occasion for an exercise of my imagination.

In the sense in which one can separate fiction and reality, the word 'real' refers to our indexical surroundings, to the fields of sense in which we exist – which should not be limited to the causally active base layer of the physically measurable part of the universe.[60] Reality is a modal category, not some enormous metaphysical thing composed of the real objects we discover by gaining insight into reality.[61] Jed Martin exists in *The Map and the Territory*, but this does not imply that he is really in the place one might think (in Paris), since really being in Paris is a function of belonging to our field of sense, which rightly sets itself apart from the content of the fictive.

This is what we mean when we say that Jed Martin does not exist.[62] In doing so, we must not overlook that he does and does not exist. This is neither a paradox nor a joke, but rather a consequence of ontological relationism. The statement 'Jed Martin does and does not exist' expresses the non-contradictory proposition that Jed Martin exists in *The Map and the Territory* but not in France.[63] At best, he exists in France in *The Map and the Territory*, which does not mean that he exists in France, since France is not identical with the France in *The Map and the Territory*.

It is therefore not the case that fictional objects do not exist at all. Their non-existence, just like their existence, is a relational matter that can only be evaluated with recourse to fields of sense sufficiently specified so as to avoid paradox. Faced with fictional objects, we are not in the uncomfortable situation of locating them in absolute nothingness – that is, in the realm of the simply non-existent. To be sure, their being is semblance and hence, in our field of sense, the appearance of something non-existent. But this seemingly non-existent thing exists elsewhere, firstly; and, secondly, it continues to have an effect wherever we are located, because the art work is directly causally connected to us and invites us to aesthetic experience.

Absolute nothingness is impossible. Absolute nothingness would be the annulment of all objects – that is, a field of sense in which nothing appears. FOS disputes that the classical argument from annihilation, which states that we can proceed from the non-being of a particular object to the non-being of all objects, can be coherently formulated. The rejection of the argument from annihilation is a corollary of the no-world-view: since we cannot quantify over everything in a metaphysically successful way in order to apprehend the object 'world', we also cannot remove such an object in a thought experiment that annuls the supposed totality. We possess the capacity of a *distributive* but not that of *metaphysical-collective* negation, which would remove everything at once. So it does not follow from the fact that many determinate things (such as London, fermions, the Earth's moon, the universe, and so on) exist contingently that everything exists contingently.

Here Graham Priest recently countered FOS with the argument that both a world object and absolute nothingness are thinkable and considers the world object, unlike nothingness, consistently (non-contradictorily) thinkable.[64] I will respond to his arguments concerning positive totality (the world) in §§4–5. As far as absolute nothingness is concerned, he treats it as the object N, which he defines as the mereological sum of everything that is not an object: $sx\neg Gx$. Since he takes an object to be anything that can be mentioned, there is nothing mentionable that is not an object; thus the mereological sum of all that is not an object is itself an object, but does not gather any objects to form a totality of the non-existent. Hence the mereological sum N is an idle operation.

Here, nothingness both is and is not an object, which Priest shows in a simple formal proof requiring only a few mereological assumptions, especially the heterodox assumption that one can form a mereological sum without the existence of objects that are thereby assembled into a whole.

For that is precisely what absolute nothingness is: what one obtains if one thinks a whole that has no parts and is not part of any further whole. With absolute nothingness, one is thinking an empty super-totality, that is, a maximum-range view in which nothing appears. Admittedly, in this thought experiment, one also has to remove the view, which traditionally raises problems of expressibility, and which Priest circumvents by introducing absolute nothingness as an object of which a contradiction is true – namely, that this object both is and is not an object (an instance of dialetheism).

The shortest response to this manoeuvre draws once again on the no-world-view. Since metaphysical universal quantification is thwarted by the positive case of the world-whole, it is equally unsuccessful in the mode of negativity. The term x in 'sx¬Gx' does not refer to all objects with the aim of generating absolute nothingness through the legitimate operation of negation. We can neither unify all objects positively in a world-whole nor apprehend all objects in the mode of negation. There is quite simply no totality of all objects – a problem that, as mentioned above, is not solved by distinguishing *existing* objects from *being* objects and then treating the latter as intentional objects that can be further examined without ontological commitment to their existence.

The World Is Not a Fiction: The Incoherence of Borges's *The Aleph*

If an object's appearance in a field of sense is sufficient, *ex hypothesi*, to fulfil the criterion of existence, this would seem to incur the following grave problem for FOS: if we succeed in imagining the world in some form or representing it in the framework of an art work, this shows that it exists, which gives free rein to metaphysics as a theory of absolute totality. This brings us to the Mehlich–Koch objection (see p. 29 above). A reminder: this objection states that the world does not exist in the sense stipulated by typical metaphysical realists but is essentially imagined or fictive. If the world exists in the imagination, it exists; and thus metaphysics returns, albeit restricted to fictionalism.

A test case for such a manoeuvre is the seemingly metaphysical fantasy of Jorge Luis Borges, which deals with semantic and metaphysical subjects. The most obvious example of this is the short story *The Aleph*. This is not the place for a detailed philosophical analysis of the entire story, since it has so many levels that this would overly delay the development of our ontological theory. I will therefore focus on the object that is named both in the title of the story and the collection in which it appears: the Aleph.

The Aleph is introduced to the reader by a narrator named Borges. This narrator reveals his name while looking at a painting by the late Beatriz Viterbo – the first proper name, which already appears in the first sentence of the story. He espies this painting upon entering a house in the Avenida Garay, a long road in Buenos Aires named after Juan de Garay, a Spanish colonizer who founded Buenos Aires.[1]

The high literary standard of the story is already indicated by the fact that it deals with the deceased, ever-absent Beatriz, which, like the surname of her first cousin (Daneri), is a reference to Dante Alighieri.[2] The proper name 'Beatriz' refers intertextually to Dante's Beatrice, which becomes clear through the construction of the text and its embedding in Borges's oeuvre. 'Beatriz' points to a further figure in the semiotic cosmos of literature. In the framework of the plot structure that we imagine as readers of the text, we locate Beatriz in Buenos Aires and construct a story around her under the narrator's guidance.[3] The object referred to as 'the

Aleph', which plays a central part in this story – as indicated both by the story's title and its eponymous role in the volume – 'corresponds' to a total object, the world. For the Aleph is an object in which one can observe all objects (and hence the Aleph too) *uno eodemque actu*.[4]

Let us move closer to the problem area. In a corner of the basement in the house of the deceased, there is an Aleph, as Carlos Daneri points out to the narrator. An Aleph, Daneri explains, is 'one of the points in space that contain all the other points in space.'[5] Daneri reports hearing of the Aleph when someone told him of the basement that 'there was a world down there [*había un mundo en el sótano*].'[6] The play of references is certainly not suspended by Borges when Carlos continues: 'I found out later they meant an old-fashioned globe of the world, but at the time I thought they were referring to the world itself.'[7] The narrator immediately demands information, asking what an Aleph is (in the form of a simple question: '¿El Aleph?'). Carlos replies that an Aleph is 'the only place on earth where all places are – seen from every angle, each standing clear, without any confusion or blending [*el lugar donde están, sin confundirse, todos los lugares del orbe, vistos desde todos los ángulos*].'[8] The Aleph, as characterized up to this point, 'corresponds' to the concept of the field of sense of all fields of sense – that is, the world as it seems to be identifiable under the theoretical conditions of FOS. The Aleph is not just some world but a world that is viewed from every angle.

The story pays considerable attention to the functioning of proper names, including the proper name 'the Aleph'.[9] Given the literary use of proper names, it is poetologically inadequate to postulate that proper names in everyday, non-literary usage refer directly to existing individuals with whom someone had causal contact at some time or other, whereas proper names in literary fictional contexts refer to no one and nothing, since their objects, *ex hypothesi*, do not exist.

The model used here therefore distinguishes between two types of objects that are connected in an aesthetic experience. The one type belongs to the material preconditions for an art work, in the present case the text. The text contains the sign 'Beatriz', which is used repeatedly. By reading the text, we gain an outline with which we can more precisely determine the characteristics of a deceased person, drawing on our background knowledge, without which we cannot understand any narratological product (whether factual or fictional, i.e., containing fictive elements).[10] The deceased person named 'Beatriz' is an object that we must imagine. How we imagine Beatriz depends on what we expect of Buenos Aires. Our knowledge of the Argentine literary tradition in which Borges stands, with all its intertextual connections, as well as our image of Buenos Aires determine how exactly Beatriz Viterbo will appear to us as interpreters. No two interpreters will picture her in exactly the same way, which is why the story's field of sense is split into an indefinite number of interpretations.

This basic poetological structure is one of the metafictional motifs in the story itself. The paratext makes this clear with quotations from *Hamlet* and Hobbes, both of which deny what seems to be possible within the framework of diegetic reality, namely the existence of an Aleph. Jumping ahead, the hypothesis I would like to substantiate is that, within the framework of the story itself, the Aleph is an impossible object that cannot be characterized sufficiently to be located anywhere at all (let alone in a basement). Its impossibility does not lie in the fact that it exhibits certain contradictory properties, such as the square circle, in order to be led indirectly towards a semantics of impossible worlds. The Aleph is far too nebulous to become an object of reference in the first place, or at least any reference beyond the use of the name 'the Aleph', which refutes the objection that Borges wrote a story in which the world object disputed by FOS appears. Rather, *The Aleph* is an 'allegory of reading', which entails disrupting the establishment of figures on which we relay in our understanding of factual speech.

This does not mean, as Paul de Man or Richard Rorty used to argue, that factual speech is exposed by fictional speech as having a hidden fictivity; it simply means that the understanding of a literary text is capable of generating a form of self-referentiality with inbuilt poetological loops.[11] Borges's text itself functions in a similar way to an Aleph, in that we find our own position as interpreters in it; this does not mean that it contains an Aleph – that is, a total vision of 'what is, what will be and what was'.[12] The Aleph thus teaches us something about how to read *The Aleph* without communicating *sotto voce* any metaphysical thesis beyond that.

A naïve metaphysical reading of the text is exposed as false when – at the latest – the narrator refers rather emphatically to himself with the signifier that is simultaneously the author's surname: 'it's me, it's Borges (*soy yo, soy Borges*).'[13] This pushes the form of homodiegesis to the limit, since it potentially appears as if the author and the narrator had merged. This is a narrative topos, of course, in that a description unambiguously marked as fictional is framed in such a way that we approach it with factual expectations. The author seems to be the narrator, and hence present in his own narrative, but this cannot be the case, since the Buenos Aires in which Beatriz and Daneri live is not the Buenos Aires in which the author named Jorge Luis Borges lived. 'Buenos Aires' does not necessarily refer to Buenos Aires.

To be sure, Borges's literary play of truth and falsity has been well examined by literary scholars.[14] I am mentioning it only in order to reconstruct the framework in which the prospect of a supposed reference to the paradoxical object of an absolute totality is presented.

Based on the case of the Aleph, Priest fields an astute objection to FOS. He underlays FOS with a consistent, slightly heterodox mereology in order to show that the Aleph can be coherently thought of as an object. This would show that, according to FOS, the world exists – at least as the fictive object dealt with in *The Aleph*.

This argument is more promising than the point that Leibniz metaphysically described a perspective universe, which is that this universe at least exists in Leibniz's metaphysics, since FOS has formulated objections to this option. In particular, the main argument for the no-world-view, if successful, shows that such a metaphysics fails because it does not characterize the field of sense in which all fields of sense appear sufficiently to constitute any coherent metaphysical position. If one embeds a field of sense totality in a fiction, on the other hand, this means that one has specified a field of sense in which a field of sense totality appears, thus circumventing the difficulty with metaphysics and indirectly providing metaphysics with an object whose architecture could be more precisely defined in logical-semantic terms. Metaphysics would then examine a fictive object, which would *prima vista* be unproblematic (albeit heterodox).

If successful, Priest would have tied FOS to a heterodox mereology that requires no axiom of foundation. Axioms of foundation forbid the formation of cyclical structures. In set theory, this means that there is no chain of elements to which the following applies: $x_1 \in x_2 \ldots \in x_n \in x_1$. In particular, this rules out the possibility of a set containing itself as an element. If we apply this to mereology, the axiom of foundation in mereology is connected to the axiom of anti-symmetry. The latter states:

> (Anti-symmetry) If x is a proper part of y, then y is not a proper part of x.

This makes sense in many cases. My hand is part of my organism, but my organism is not part of my hand; Helgoland is part of Germany, but Germany is not part of Helgoland; the word 'Helgoland' is part of this sentence, but this sentence is not part of the word 'Helgoland'; and so on. If one abandons this axiom, one can allow mereological loops. In particular, the following loop is now *prima vista* permissible: Object A belongs to the field of sense of itself f(A), which is in turn part of object A, and so forth:

- $\ldots < f(A) < A < f(A) < A < \ldots$

Based on this, Priest develops a simplified model of the mereological structure he ascribes to FOS. His additional assumption is that objects are (proper) parts of their fields of sense so that fields of sense are wholes. The arrow $x \rightarrow y$ indicates that x is a proper part of y, which results in the following picture:

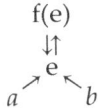

Anything that is not A is a proper part of A, and A is in turn a proper part of its own field of sense f(A).

Priest's model of FOS is inadequate for many reasons, however, as every element of the ontological concept of existence as appearance-in-a-sense-field within FOS differs from Priest's model, which means that his suggestion to reduce FOS to a non-well-founded mereology is problematic from the outside.[15]

Firstly, Priest's model is extensionalist: he identifies fields of sense with wholes comprising parts without taking into account that fields of sense are only wholes comprising parts if their unity (that is, their wholeness) already presupposes a sense as a unifying function that allows certain objects to exist in a field of sense. A sense is an ordering rule for objects. At the level of a thought directed at an object in a given field of sense, a sense is a mode of presentation of its objects and thus, as a rule, not an object that appears in the same field of sense. More precisely, there are cases in which a sense appears as an object in its field of sense, as well as cases in which a sense fundamentally cannot appear in its own field of sense.[16] Priest overlooks the decisive fact that FOS rests on an intensionalist understanding of sense, which takes sense into account for existence. Whatever exists occurs not only in the object domain of some predicate but belongs essentially to the catchment area of a substantive thought, or a sense that would even have existed without any thought. Hence there is no all-encompassing mereological rule that meaningfully dictates how objects in fields of sense form wholes such that a metaphysical mereology is a priori inexpressible under the intensionalist conditions of FOS properly understood.

Secondly, Priest ignores the deliberate rejection of any 'metaphysical mereology' that forms part of FOS. My objections to a metaphysical interpretation of set theory, which Priest accepts, apply *mutatis mutandi* to the metaphysical interpretation of mereology as a formal, mathematizable discipline.[17] Since Priest does not offer any counterargument to justify his violation of these explicit requirements, his modelling of FOS as metaphysical mereology falls short of showing that FOS is committed to any specific mereology at all.

To motivate the introduction of a metaphysical mereological structure after undermining the no-world-view, Priest draws on two points that are supposed to show that it is meaningful to model FOS in this mereological fashion. First, he adduces Borges's Aleph, which he expressly considers 'quite coherent'.[18] Then he introduces two propositions, a and b, that contain each other as parts:

a: = b or snow is white
b: = a or grass is green

Let us examine both cases. The first is more interesting, since it addresses the metaphysical problem of whether it is possible to grasp the absolute as an object. Here Priest overlooks the fact that Borges, the author, specifically disputes this, and therefore provided a multitude of paradoxical stories and commentaries to point out that the absolute is merely an illusion that cannot really be pinned down as an object. In several cases, he ironically adopted the position of logical empiricism (especially Russell) and termed metaphysics a branch of fantastic literature.[19] In the story, the Aleph that the narrator sees in the basement is even termed a 'false aleph',[20] and the whole account is 'contaminated by literature, by fiction.'[21]

The Borges case has particular argumentative significance because, unlike the two reciprocally appearing propositions, it genuinely raises a meta-metaphysical problem. If one succeeded in thinking the Aleph coherently (even if under paraconsistent conditions), this would be a first step towards proving that the world, contrary to FOS, does exist (even if it is in the field of sense of literature or the acts of the imagination ascribed to it). It is therefore worth taking a closer look at the constellation generated by Borges's story.

In addition to the fictional embeddedness of the story and the object known as 'the Aleph', a further argument comes into consideration that Borges has emphasized elsewhere and which plays a central part in FOS. In the prose miniature 'The yellow rose', Borges tells of a revelation experienced by Giambattista Marino as well as Homer and Dante:

> Then came the revelation. Marino *saw* the rose as Adam might have seen it in Paradise. And he sensed that it existed in its eternity and not in his words, and that we may make mention or allusion of a thing but never express it at all; and that the tall proud tomes that cast a golden penumbra in an angle of the drawing room were not – as he had dreamed in his vanity – a mirror of the world, but simply one more thing added to the universe.[22]

The supposed world-whole is accordingly incomplete, since every mirror in which we portray or capture it actually modifies it. The absolute as an object is changed by the fact that we apprehend it, since our apprehension of the supposedly complete world adds a further object (our apprehension) to it. To be sure, the philosophical problem is not yet adequately captured by this literary reference, as the narrator of *The Aleph* indirectly concedes when he calls Daneri's ideas unsuitable, pompous and expansive, and therefore associates them with literature.[23]

Priest overestimates the prospects of applying his mereological model when he introduces *The Aleph*, of all things, which is in fact grist for my mill.[24] Faced with the absolute, it is not enough to introduce it as an object to which one dedicates a modified, consistent mereology; for part of the absolute, if it is supposed to be the totality of objects, is its apprehension. But if the apprehension of the absolute is part of it, one finds oneself in countless metaphysical problems that Priest does not mention, despite being familiar with a number of these aporias, since he has subjected them to highly compelling analysis elsewhere.[25]

If the world is the totality of objects, was the world already an object before the moment of its apprehension by finite thinkers? Can the absolute even be temporal without changing as a result, which leads to problems of self-identity for all objects? Does the absolute have temporal (the universe) and atemporal (abstract objects) parts, and, if so, how can *we* then think it as a whole before all the objects that constitute it exist?[26]

At any rate, one cannot keep the thinker distant from the absolute. If the absolute contains *all* objects as parts, this includes the thinker of the absolute along with their thoughts concerning the absolute. In light of the absolute, one therefore cannot fall back on the claim that its apprehension is merely an epistemic problem that can be solved semantically merely by mentioning the object named 'the absolute'. For if the absolute cannot be thought by finite thinkers, there is no longer any reason to postulate its existence beyond our apprehension. If the phrase 'the absolute' is not usable under finite conditions in the sense of a relevant absolute totality, then it offers no orientation to point out that we can at least still mention 'the absolute'.

Therefore the assumption that Borges's story is coherent is naturally far from sufficient to ensure that someone (a narrator, a figure or a reader imagining the situation) can refer to an Aleph in such a way that it becomes an adequately characterized object, one which is not merely a word that is used but something about which one can think truth-apt thoughts that do not undermine themselves.

Priest is unlikely to suppose that his theory of objects includes the total mystical vision with which Borges's story and the tradition of mystical theology it evokes concern themselves.

Here we stumble on a serious metaphysical problem of reference attached to the word 'object': *how can the absolute be thought of as an object if we can only name an indeterminate number of objects de dicto, without being able to devote any informed knowledge to them de re?* If the absolute is the totality of objects, but this totality has an indefinite number of parts that we cannot cognize, it is not clear which concepts are applicable to this partially inaccessible total object.

Faced with the absolute, one cannot retreat to a distinction between conditions of reference and cognition. It is not sufficient to assume that we can adapt linguistically to the Aleph or the absolute in the mode of a story without being able to cognize this object fully, since we cannot separate the absolute from our cognition. Our cognition of the absolute is a fundamental part of the absolute.

Meinong himself escapes this difficulty with the traditional move of an ontotheologically conceived perfect thinker who cognizes all objects a priori.[27] Meinong's concept of an object is *a limine* tailored to knowability under idealized conditions. The theory of objects collapses without this epistemological crutch, since, although it is still carried by a formal model, it is impossible to judge whether it has any conditions for application outside of the horizon of the objects that are verifiably given in a more than purely logical manner.

Borges's *The Aleph* and related mystical accounts of a *multum in parvo*[28] are thus by no means 'quite coherent', as Priest claims.[29] Without further explanations, his example of the Mehlich–Koch objection to FOS therefore remains unconvincing. The specific circumstances of the paradox-prone world object are precisely that it cannot be the object of any examination under finite conditions, since any such examination would have to capture its own operating conditions in the totality, which is impossible.[30]

What of Priest's second example, which is meant to increase the plausibility of a non-well-founded mereology? Indeed, I see no problem in acknowledging that propositions a and b are genuine parts of each other:

> a: = b or snow is white
> b: = a or grass is green

Proposition a is a genuine part of b and b is a genuine part of a. I am therefore not ruling out the existence of a chain such as the following:

- ... < a < b < a < b < ...

However, the argument for the no-world intuition rests neither on a well-founded mereology nor on any other. Priest draws expressly on a passage from *Fields of Sense* but only reconstructs the opening of the argument on the respective page.[31] Therefore, for the present context, I will provide a simplified outline of the argument presented there.

It is not generally a problem that some fields of sense contain themselves (appear in themselves). For example, I can refer with this sentence in this book to the book entitled *Fictions*, validating the reference with a footnote.[32] The field of sense called *Fictions* can thus appear within itself, which is why I identified the combination of totality and self-encompassment as a source of paradox in *Fields of Sense* and did not argue that no field of sense can appear within itself.

Against this background, one can first of all distinguish between two field of sense-ontological concepts of the world: *additive* and *unified* totality. If the world were the disjunctive heap of fields of sense, it would not be clear why exactly this constitutes a totality, since the concept of coexistence does not provide any instructions (any sense) to justify concrete statements about the world. A world heap does not constitute a metaphysics; hence the assumption that the world itself must be a field of sense in order to represent the field of sense of all fields of sense. This seems to offer us two options: the world appears either within itself or in another field of sense.

Priest prefers the assumption that the world appears within itself. But there does not seem to be any space for this; for if all fields of sense appear in the world, each with its own objects, then the world can only appear within itself if it is either one of those fields of sense or one of the objects in them. Priest chooses the option that the world is an object in one of the fields of sense. But which field of sense is it? In which field of sense is the world an object that appears at some point on a non-well-founded loop in the world?

He could try to bring *The Aleph* into play again as an example; then the world would be a fictive object in an as yet imprecise sense. This corresponds to my reading of Kant's version of fictionalism, which has it that the world is a 'heuristic fiction', an idea that might appeal to Borges, since Borges refers to Vaihinger's *The Philosophy of 'As If'*, which contains a corresponding fictionalist reading of Kant.[33] Priest's second reference to nested propositions, on the other hand, suggests that the world might be a logical-semantic object. To the extent that Priest has 'a great deal of sympathy'[34] with the basic idea of FOS, he must concede that the set of objects appears in some field of sense. Priest will presumably take the set itself for an object-theoretical object – that is, for an ontological commitment of his own theory of objects.

Thus the world seems to appear in some sense field that appears within it. Now, the world is certainly no basic object in a non-well-founded mereology – that is, no mereological atom. For, whether simple objects exist or not, the world does not belong to this type of object because it is ultimately all-encompassing, and therefore – if it is a totality at all – then the object with the most parts of all – that is, the greatest possible mereological whole.[35]

So the world is a field of sense. This means that it appears in the series of fields of sense. Every field of sense in this series has a different sense from other fields of sense. If we assign a place to the world in the series of fields of sense, the problem arises that the assigned world differs from the world to which it is assigned. Therefore the world cannot be a proper part of a world-whole in FOS, as the world's parts (the fields of sense) are individuated through their sense and define themselves according to their position in the differential fabric.

Allow me to demonstrate this idea using the Aleph. The (purported) Aleph that Borges (the narrator) sees in the basement encompasses Borges, who sees the Aleph in the basement. So Borges sees everything in the Aleph, which includes himself seeing the Aleph. Yet, if he sees himself in the Aleph, he is an object of his own observation. The object of his observation is located in the Aleph, which *ex hypothesi* is smaller than Borges himself; it is a microcosm containing miniature copies of all objects. The objects that appear in the Aleph are not identical with their originals, since they must be scaled differently in order to appear in the Aleph.

If the objects appearing in the Aleph in a total vision were not scaled differently from the objects located in the basement, this would lead to the paradoxical map with a scale of 1:1 parodied by Borges in his short story *On Rigour in Science*, which I will quote in its entirety on account of its brevity:

> . . . In that Empire, the Art of Cartography reached such Perfection that the map of one Province alone took up the whole of a City, and the map of the

empire, the whole of a Province. In time, those Unconscionable Maps did not satisfy and the Colleges of Cartographers set up a Map of the Empire which had the size of the Empire itself and coincided with it point by point. Less Addicted to the Study of Cartography, Succeeding Generations understood that this Widespread Map was Useless and not without Impiety they abandoned it to the Inclemencies of the Sun and of the Winters. In the deserts of the West some mangled Ruins of the Map lasted on, inhabited by Animals and Beggars; in the whole Country there are no other relics of the Disciplines of Geography.

Suarez Miranda: Viajes de Varones Prudentes,
Book Four, Chapter XLV, Lérida, 1658.[36]

The objects in the Aleph, then, are scaled differently from objects surrounding the Aleph, so one cannot simply assume that they are identical. Pointing out the formal consistency of a mereological model with loops is not sufficient to recommend a non-well-founded mereology as an improved model of FOS. At best, it shows that we cannot adduce any purely logical reasons for the thesis that the world does not exist. FOS does not dispute that there are worldviews, but it does argue that these supposed views have no object and, upon closer inspection, become entangled in nonsense at some point or other.

The arguments for the no-world-view are not based on the fact that it is logically impossible for the world to exist. In 2017, speaking at a conference about FOS, Meillassoux rightly argued that FOS at most claims that the world does not exist de facto.[37] Indeed, one cannot prove a priori that the world does not exist. 'The world' is not an absolute – that is, logically impossible – object whose non-existence can be inferred from its concept. Rather, the no-world-view is a corollary of a model of our pre-ontological experience based on doing away with the reasons for metaphysical worldviews. We have no reason to introduce the absolute as a totality, whether in the form of a totality of objects or that of a totality of facts or fields of sense. In the face of our pre-ontological experience and our scientific knowledge, the traditional metaphysical assumption of world proves to be unfounded.

In empirical terms, we have no reason to assume that there is a world totality. Our processing of information does not presuppose that our primary causal data source (the universe) is part of an absolute whole. On this level, physics and metaphysics are simply independent of each other, which should not come as a surprise. We should have learned from the metamathematics of the last century that even the best formal system is incomplete if one is striving for absolute consistency. At least since Gödel and Cohen, it has been acknowledged that we cannot construct a universe of sets to which all sets belong. No axiomatic system is capable of containing all truths about sets as theorems, which means that any examination of sets remains incomplete. This is not a paradoxical result, but rather an object of mathematical proofs that are entirely consistent. Incompleteness is therefore the acknowledged norm, in both the empirical and formal domains of our investigation of what is the case.

The no-world-view of FOS generalizes this insight beyond the framework of natural science and metamathematics by examining under what conditions something exists. Part of this is that that which exists *appears* – that is, it is given under certain ordering rules. there cannot be a meaningful ordering rule that contains all the ordering rules below it, which means that there cannot be a totality of fields of sense. This impossibility is ontological, not logical. It follows from how things are and what the facts are, not from the reconstruction of the concept of truth alone.

Meillassoux, on the other hand, following Badiou, thinks he has a strong logical argument for a similar conclusion, namely an ontological interpretation of Cantor's power set axiom. This argument does not apply, however, as Cantor himself already noted; instead, based on his transfinite set theory, he introduced a non-mathematical absolute, something that Meillassoux overlooks.[38] Meillassoux does not show that transfinite set theory in the naïve form presented by Cantor constitutes an ontology articulating the logical form of the existent. Since there are alternative set theories and axiomatization is a standard procedure, one cannot base any philosophical statements on set theory as such, since there is no one single form of set theory (certainly not the naïve, inconsistent one).

Formal models have the function of capturing the structures of a target system that precedes the construction and investigation of the model's properties. One of the conditions for the application of models is that they do not have a scale of 1:1. This also applies to symbolic logic as a formal thought model. Logic does not describe how we think but, at most, outlines how we should think under idealized conditions. The reason for making such a distinction emerges from the simple point that we must be able to translate principles from a non-logical language into a logical one. The advantage of this translation is meant to be that it offers clarity about inferential connections that would otherwise remain concealed. The data structure of our non-logical thinking (our thought processes) is recoded in such a translation, which only succeeds thanks to a structural distance between our actual thought *processes* and our thought *models*.[39] Conversely, this means that, as soon as a symbolic system is established, it has conditions of application. Otherwise we would be unable to understand or orient ourselves by it.

One cannot simply orient oneself by logic *as such* if this is supposed to mean that a thinker imagines symbolically coded contexts as norms of inferential orientation. This has been clear at least since the discussion of the problem of rule-following (see §14 below). If, on the other hand, one thinks that logic consists in acknowledging some aspects as acceptable and others as unacceptable in a given investigation, then this normalization is not obviously subject to any given formal calculus that attempts to express them symbolically. Therefore one cannot resolve ontological questions by developing consistent models with the relevant formal properties to guarantee the existence of the world in opposition to FOS; this would require specifying conditions of application of a mereological model to reality (in this case: the presumed world-whole) as a target system. Accordingly, it is no small matter that Borges's *The Aleph* offers no conditions of application for the mereological model proposed by Priest to FOS.

§5

FOS Is Not a Meinongian Theory of Objects

In this section, I will now argue that fictive objects fundamentally do not call for the introduction of an indirect, non-well-founded loop into our thinking that allows us to take the world into account as a heuristic fiction. The problem of the (neo-)Meinongian theory of objects is that it cannot present a theory of intentionality that would enable the theorist to understand how they, as a finite thinker, can refer to the totality of objects they have postulated. Since we are not idealized thinkers, the description of the 'point of view' of an infinite, unrestricted thinker is not sufficient to base a non-well-founded mereology of the absolute on actual reference – that is, on sufficiently specified conditions of application (that provides us with access to the sense of a field).

Since its introduction, Meinongianism has been seen as a promising avenue for the ontology of so-called fictional objects. Here we should note in advance that Meinong did not, of course, invent the basic idea of Meinongianism, as it has belonged to the central premises of metaphysics since antiquity. In modernity, the terms for something (*ti*) or something existent (*on ti*) are shortened and combined in the concept of the object.[1] Since antiquity, it has been a standard trait of theories of fictionality to treat fictions as *entia rationis* that Kant terms 'invention' [*Erdichtung*][2] or 'heuristic fictions'.[3] In this tradition, non-existent objects are objects of successful reference but do not therefore belong to the catalogue of the world. They do not exist in our world, but they are thinkable without contradictions.

The introduction of the category of intentional objects solves the Eleatic paradox by making it seem effortless to refer to non-existent objects without committing to their existence. Yet we have already seen that this manoeuvre risks collapsing into a new paradox, since the realm of being becomes entangled in paradoxes already pointed out by Meinong.[4]

This state of affairs gives rise to a problem for the sophisticated neo-Meinongian object theory proposed by Priest. This problem will be articulated in the following in order to claim a dialectical advantage of realistic FOS over its rival neo-Meinongial project.

The eye of the hurricane of neo-Meinongianism is a reply to the problems generated by unconditional acceptance of the following *characterization principle (CP)*:[5]

(CP) An object has the properties that characterize it.

Characterizing properties distinguish objects from other objects. Unlike properties that an object simply has, in so far as it is an object, they are discriminating. (CP) is attractive in the context of an analysis of fictionality because it allows us to ascribe characterizing properties to Gretchen that make her an adequately defined (intentional) object of our reflection, but without forcing us to ascribe to her the property of existence (in our world, the 'real world'). The problem, however, is that this principle cannot be adequately generalized; for then one could, firstly, prove the existence of everything by characterizing it as existent and, secondly, prove anything at all, which is even worse. In Priest's words:

> For let B be any sentence, and consider the condition $x = x \wedge B$. let t be the object characterized by this condition. Then the CP gives us: $t = t \wedge B$, from which B follows. It would seem, then, that only a restricted class of contexts, $A(x)$, can be used in the CP. The problem is, which? This is the characterization problem.[6]

The reason for consulting Priest's variant of neo-Meinongianism and relating it to FOS is that Priest solves the characterization problem by means of an object-theoretical contextualism which resembles ontological relationsim. 'The CP *can* hold unrestrictedly, provided only that its instances may hold, not at this world, but at others.'[7] The nub of Priest's solution boils down to an ontological contextualism: whatever exists in one world does not exist in another, and vice versa.[8]

To be sure, Priest does not identify the object status in a world with existence, since he understands existence as the property of being causally effective.[9] However, the decisive difference emerges elsewhere, for Priest presupposes 'the set of *all* objects',[10] which he in turn considers an object. So there is an all-encompassing realm of being that is identical in every world, namely the set of objects. But what is the nature of an object if one can form a set of all objects?

Priest opts for a *flat formal theory of objects* in which anything is an object 'that one can name, be the subject of predication, be quantified over, be the object of an intentional mental state.'[11] This informal definition is circular, of course, because it defines an *object* as an intentional *object*. This can easily be amended if, in the spirit of the author, one says that an object is anything at which an intentional mental state can direct itself. Priest's official definition of 'object' ['G' for *Gegenstand*]

$$Gx: = Sy\ y = x$$

can be expressed thus in ordinary language: 'To be an object is simply for there to be something which is identical to it or, more simply, to be something.'[12]

Something is an object, then, if there is something that is identical with it. This view is highly problematic. Firstly, the difficulties in the concept of the object are transferred to identity, for now one must solve the identity riddle, which consists in the fact that statements of identity such as 'y = x' are seemingly either uninformative or contradictory.[13] This is not a harmless matter, for uninformative trivial self-identities such as 'a = a' cannot be considered paradigms of the characterization principle.[14] If the only thing we can say of a (purported) object is that it is self-identical, we cannot even formulate this as a = a, unless it can be ruled out that a = b. If 'a' is not characterized beyond its self-identity, it is not an object that can be successfully mentioned, for the use of the symbol 'a' suggests that there are also b, c, d, and so on. Surely the formal theory of objects will not seek to stipulate through definitions that there can only be one single object. So a plurality of objects must be taken into account; but then identity becomes a difficult matter.

On this level, FOS responds to the characterization problem with an ontological reading of Frege's concept of sense: those objects that exist are theoretically individuated first of all via their senses – that is, the way in which they can be given to thought. Ontological realism adds to this that objects can be given to us *de dicto* even if we will never be able to characterize them further *de re* – objects of which we will only ever know that we (can) know nothing about them (apart from that fact). We can know that there are objects we cannot or do not cognize. These evidence-transcendent matters should not be restricted by tying the term 'object' to our conditions of access to the real, which is something that anti-realism claims for itself with a degree of plausibility in some areas (such as the philosophy of mathematics or metaethics).[15]

In my view, the decisive criterion for realism in this context is the assumption that the state of affairs in a given domain of objects (a field of sense) may be different from how it seems to us, even under ideal (human) cognitive conditions. This must be distinguished from the more ambitious concept of reality, which is employed whenever objectivity – that is, the difference between truth and holding-to-be-true – is at stake. So, even if one prefers anti-realism in the context of a field of sense, it does not follow from this that the objects of investigation (such as mathematical, moral or aesthetic truths) are therefore infallibly knowable. Even with anti-realistic theoretical requirements, then, one can assume that objects such as numbers are real without committing to the existence of verification-transcendent truths about numbers.[16]

As for the concept of sense, sense is the objectively existing disposition of objects. We grasp this in the form of modes of presentation. There is, at any rate, no reason to advocate a general anti-realism about sense, even if some (verbal) sense cannot be evidence-transcendent, since its nature is to be knowable. Not all objects are objects because they are capable of being given to *our* thinking. Being and thinking are not generally identical, so there is cause for an *ontological realism*, in contrast to *ontological idealism*, that identifies being and thinking.[17] Here ontological idealism would be any claim of the form that the concept of an object as such is essentially tied to our localization of the object within the catchment area of of objective thought.[18]

One way of arguing for an ontologically realist position without relying on the flawed identification of realism with a thesis about mind-independence is the following. Some of what we reflect upon exists *prima vista* only if someone has already thought about it. Since Descartes there have been numerous candidates for this type of object – pain, states of consciousness in general, qualia, sensory data, self-awareness, and so forth.[19] If there is an object that meets the epistemic criterion that its presence (*esse*) and its being-noticed (*percipi*), or generally its being (*esse*) and its being-thought (*cogitari*), are identical, then we can no longer restrict the concept of the object to something which exclusively has properties that can elude a thinker. So there seem to be objects whose *esse* is their *cogitari*, and others to which this does not apply.[20] Thus the object area of this distinction extends at least across the disjunct sets of two object types that, for the sake of simplicity, we can refer to on the one hand as *ideal* and on the other hand as *real* objects.

Now we can seemingly situate these sets in the set of objects and form the concept of an object as such that is assigned to this set. This raises the question of whether the concept of the object as such actually possesses a being whose being-thought is contingent. Is the concept of the object such that of a real or an ideal object? If it is neither of these, then we must augment our disjunct system of sets with a third type of object, since we would otherwise not have formed the set of all objects in its entirety.

Ontological idealism argues that the concept of the object as such is necessarily *thought*, and is thus ideal. This is apparently supported by the fact that it is the concept which contains the concept of ideal objects and that of real objects. How can there be a concept of ideal objects if there are no objects that are essentially thought?[21]

Naturally this thought is not a convincing argument without additional premises, as it is not readily clear how we are supposed to understand the fact that the concept of the object as such can actually belong to the set of ideal objects that it encompasses. Therefore the idealistic solution – which was spelled out by Fichte in particular in his late presentations of his system from 1804 onwards – is to understand real objects as a subset of ideal objects.[22] Consequently, the set of objects as such is identical with the set of ideal objects that contains real objects as a subset.

Real objects are individuated by the fact that they are thought of as objects which are independent of their being-thought because they exhibit properties that we can only recognize empirically. The task Fichte sets himself is thus the deduction of the (epistemic) necessity to define the concept of the object as such in detail such that there are real objects which are ideal as objects, but which exhibit properties that can elude their being-noticed.

However, the category of these properties falls under the set of ideal objects, since the *concept* of the real object has no properties that elude our being-noticed, and because the property of having properties that (can) elude our being-noticed individuates the concept of a real object. For idealists, the reason for advocating an ontological idealism of this kind is usually that the opposing position of ontological realism leads to the aporias of what Fichte calls 'dogmatism', which operates under the name of naturalism today.[23]

Here FOS offers a third way, for the ontological realism of FOSFOS is neither a metaphysical claim about all objects nor a naturalist position that seeks to attribute thinking to something unlike thinking in order to do away with the irksome problem of ideal objects.[24]

Ontological realism, as presented here, claims: *There is nothing that is true of all existing objects.* This is not paradoxical, since the quantifiers in this formulation are already relevantly restricted.[25] The quantifiers used in the articulation of FOS (such as '*All* objects appear in fields of sense' or '*All* fields of sense are fields of sense') refer to objects in the field of sense of formal ontology – that is, the discipline that models the concept of existence. *Ex hypothesi*, FOS itself is a field of sense, specifically the one in which senses appear in their formal structure.

The field of sense of FOS does not contain any field of sense that is not a field of sense. Nor does it contain any object that does not appear in a field of sense. The field of sense of FOS does not, however, contain all objects found there, either qua fields of sense as objects in FOS or as objects in fields of sense that appear in FOS. There are fields of sense in which only objects that do not constitute fields of sense in these fields of sense appear. In these fields of sense, then, there are no fields of sense. Set theory (in some interpretations) is one such field of sense, since the objects appearing there are all purely extensional formations, meaning that only objects which are not fields of sense appear in set theory. Although FOS teaches that fields of sense would still have existed even if there had been no one to notice them, this is not recognizably the case within set theory. The universal quantifiers of set theory are restricted to sets (and their associated objects) and those of FOS to fields of sense (and their associated objects). FOS is not an extension of set theory into a realm of intensions.

At the level of the metatheoretical articulation of the no-world-view, a further factor is that some things are only true of objects when we state them. Statements about statements concern objects (statements) that exist because we do something (state). This does not apply in other cases. Facts are truths that do not exist in general because someone makes a statement. The factual ground on which we stand extends further than the statements with which we model it.[26] Truth, then, is not primarily a property of statements. The truth of statements is only one example of truth; it enjoys epistemological and logical-semantic privileges, but no ontological ones.

Reality manifests many of its properties without our assistance. This property is itself a property that we discover in the self-exploration of thinking in its relation to being. *Our thought is part of being. We are a case of being.* That is why reality as a modal category is itself something real that we discover. We have turned out to be fallible thinkers. The consequence of this is not a problematic naturalism, since no reduction of thinking and knowing to natural being, let alone thought's elimination, is at issue.[27]

Meinong himself, incidentally, is an ontological idealist, not a realist, since he ties *esse* to *cogitari*.[28] For he defines 'objects in their totality' as the 'totality of objects of knowledge'.[29] Based on this identification, he distinguishes 'metaphysics', as the theory of 'the totality of what exists',[30] from the theory of objects, which deals not only with the real (the existent) but with all objects of knowledge. This locates Meinong's theory of objects in idealistic territory, for his account of the concept of the object such entails that there can be no object which

> does not have the possibility of being an object of knowledge if one adopts the view of the generally instructive fiction [!] that knowability is not impaired by any of the restrictions located in the constitution of the subject, and therefore never truly absent, of the types of stimuli, waves of difference etc. Assuming an unlimitedly powerful intelligence, then, there is nothing unknowable, and whatever is knowable exists; or, because 'there is' tends to be said mostly of that which is, specifically that which exists, it would perhaps be clearer to say that everything knowable is given – namely, to knowledge. And to the extent that all objects are knowable, one can attribute to them without exception – whether they are or are not – givenness as a most general type of property.[31]

In this passge, Meinong explicitly ties the most general concept of the object as such to a fiction, namely the fiction of the givenness of the totality of objects for a perfect intelligence. This is absolute idealism in its purest form and does not thereby solve the ensuing problem of whether such a totality, which an idealized thinker is supposed to be capable of grasping, can actually exist.

For us, of course, the totality cannot be given in any case. If we are not idealized thinkers, we cannot be sure that there is a totality of objects of knowledge. This assumption is and remains, under finite conditions of assertion, anything but a harmless idealization ('fiction', as Meinong says).

Rather, there are reasons to reject such a totality and assign the concept of the 'object as such' to an 'empty region', which Husserl rightly pointed out in contradistinction to Meinong.[32] The idealization on which the deceptive plausibility of a totality of objects of knowledge rests fails to take into account the finitude that is built into all knowledge because truth-apt

attitudes are only such if they are objective, and hence fallible. The ontological source of fallibility lies precisely in the fact that not all objects can
ever be given to us; there is always something that remains beyond our
reach.[33] That is simply how things are. The assumption that there can be
an intelligence which deals objectively with a totality of objects of knowledge, and is simultaneously immune to error, is incoherent. To such an
intelligence nothing could be given, at most, it would produce all 'objects'
in virtue of being directed at them, as has been pointed out throughout
the history of ontotheology.

Incidentally, Kant was aware of this problem. For him, 'the concept of
an object as such' is always 'taken problematically, leaving undecided
whether it is something or nothing'.[34] Kant categorizes the noumena
(which would include a perfect intelligence à la Meinong) as 'mere invention (although not self-contradictory)'.[35] This leaves open whether or not
a totality of objects in his system is an object of thought (and hence at least
non-contradictory) – a thorny issue.

This historical prelude leads to the crucial systematic ontological question for the neo-Meinongian theory of objects: are objects essentially the
targets at which we direct our intentional mental acts? In other words:
would there actually have been any totality of objects without thinkers to
refer to them?

Priest will initially find it easy to reply that this naturally applies to
some objects. He has no intention of contradicting realistic truisms about
the 'mind-independence of the external world'. There is no reason not to
follow him in this. Yet, this does not solve the issue of realism/idealism
with respect to the alleged totality of objects or the concept of the object
as such.

For the present study, it is significant that Priest also espouses a
variety of fictional realism. He assumes that Sherlock Holmes would still
have been Sherlock Holmes if Arthur Conan Doyle had never written
about him.[36] Holmes is thus, firstly, epistemically real in the sense of
FOS (anyone, even Doyle, can be mistaken about him) and, secondly,
evidence-transcendent, because his self-identity does not depend on how
anyone imagines him. According to Priest, one does not even change
Holmes by inventing new stories about him that ascribe logically incompatible properties to him. 'Imagining new things about an object does not
change the object in question.'[37]

This position amounts to a *blind fictional realism* in the sense of the following thesis: there are fictional objects (which admittedly do not exist),
and the fundamental suchness that characterizes them in no way depends
on how they are imagined. Their suchness is evidence-transcendent, in
the sense that it would still have existed if there had never been anyone to
direct themselves at their suchness.[38]

I call this type of fictional realism 'blind' because it fails to take into
account the following perspective: Holmes is a human being (albeit one
who does not exist in Priest's sense). Let us assume that, in addition, he is

not only essentially a human being but also essentially a detective – that is, he is characterized in part by his being-a-detective. He would not be himself without being a detective at some point in his life.[39] Now, no one is a detective without there being someone to recognize them as a detective. Being-a-detective is an explicit social attribute – that is, an attribute one cannot have without explicit registration.[40] Then Holmes's being-a-detective is not evidence-transcendent, so Holmes's suchness cannot be evidence-transcendent either. The type of evidence that enables Holmes to be recognized as a detective cannot exist without mental and social recognition. One does not become a detective through the unconscious agreement of all actors; no one is a detective without anyone noticing. Someone must know that a person is a detective in order for them to be one. Detectives are hidden, but not in a metaphysical sense.

Therefore Holmes's suchness is not blind. It does not simply accrue to him in the sense of being imaginarily available, say, by virtue of Doyle telling stories about Holmes with variations on the core detective elements. This does not yet contradict Priest's counterfactual conditional, which stipulates that Holmes would still have been Holmes if Doyle had not written his stories.[41] Things become more awkward for Priest when one asks under what conditions Doyle is Doyle. Is it an essential part of Doyle to be the author of Holmes stories? Is this part of his suchness as an object?

Leibniz famously inferred from his theory of identity that nothing can be an object without all its properties being essential to it. A Leibnizian theory of objects would therefore state that Doyle is essentially the author of Holmes stories. What speaks in Leibniz's favour is that even self-identity cannot be entirely uninformative, otherwise we would not have any determinate object (a in contrast to b) that possesses self-identity. Self-identity is precisely not 'logically blind' but is due to a contrast between identity and non-identity (difference). It is meaningless to think a = a if one is incapable of thinking a ≠ b. If self-identity is not uninformative, all objects in a theory of objects have properties that enrich their logical core. Why should this not apply to Doyle's being-an-author?

The difficulty I am pointing out with Priest's blind fictional realism is thus that it would be ad hoc to keep Doyle's being-an-author and Holmes's being-a-detective away from their essential core of self-identity. If they are both included in it, however, it becomes clear that neither Doyle nor Holmes can go unnoticed in having a suchness (even if Holmes's suchness were essentially noticed by someone like Watson, who Priest claims cannot exist, but certainly can recognize someone as a detective, since this is a property of suchness).

Furthermore, it could be essential for Holmes to be imagined (recognized) not only by someone who is there but even by someone who exists (Doyle). This does not mean that Doyle must constantly keep Holmes present. An anti-realism about an object need not claim that an object is *registration*-dependent, only that it is *registry*-dependent.[42]

Therefore it is not yet clear whether one should approach objects as a realist, an anti-realist, an idealist or some combination of these. As far as I can tell, Priest has not answered this question conclusively thus far, though he presumably tends more towards a *broad realism*, since he ties being a determinate object (suchness) to self-identity and considers the latter automatically given: nothing is an object without being self-identical. He does not espouse a *global realism*, however, which would deny that pain cannot exist without being registered. So there are objects (pain, consciousness, and so on) that are obviously not evidence-transcendent. They are only there if they are noticed; for them, *esse est percipi*.[43]

So what about the object 'the set of all objects', which Priest now treats as the object called 'Everything' = A? Is A (Priest's version of the absolute) substance or subject? Would it still have been an object if no one had paid attention to it, or does it become essentially an object of our reflection? Priest has not yet answered this question.

Additional difficulties arise from the question of whether the status of A is influenced by A having evidence-transcendent and evidence-immanent parts. The absolute totality of all objects includes pains as well as the Big Bang or electron spin.[44] Then A would not be the object it is without having evidence-immanent parts.

Of course, Priest is *prima facie* still free to choose between an *object-theoretical contingentism* and an *object-theoretical necessitism*. The former holds that the absolute can have properties that are contingent by having contingent parts that can be understood as its properties; the latter disputes this, and accordingly identifies the seemingly contingent objects as ultimately necessary because they belong to the self-constitution (self-identity) of the absolute.

If pains are essentially pains and it is part of this suchness to be noticed, then A cannot be an object without having pains as part of it; this means that the contingent existence of pains in our world may simplify the matter of theodicy but not the neo-Meinongian theory of objects.[45] So A would not be what it is if there were no consciousness. Now the existing consciousness of A is also an object that exists. The fact that it exists should not be a problem for Priest, since we assure ourselves of its existence not through stipulative characterization, but rather through acts of theorizing that are carried out by Priest. Consequently, A would not be A if the object that consists in its being-recognized did not exist.

The neo-Meinongian theory of objects thus inclines towards absolute idealism; this need not be an objection in and of itself but shows that it is considerably more speculatively ambitious than its (far from harmless) formal, logical apparatus suggests. It is important to note that, in Priest's theory, it does not hold that A exists, since A has no causal powers; only some of its parts exist. A has existent and non-existent parts.

All these consequences do not occur within FOS, because it follows from FOS that A neither exists nor is an object. A only *seems* to possess a suchness. Its characterization leads to paradoxes, especially through the fact that the implicit absolute idealism of the neo-Meinongian theory of objects encounters the incoherence of the Aleph, as we have seen.

Be that as it may, our concern here is only to articulate the fact that the ontological realism of FOS is conceptually inseparable from its non-totality-claim. There is no totality of objects (which would in turn be an object), only a fundamentally incalculable proliferation of fields of sense that cannot, in some central perspective, be placed on a foundation that is both all-encompassing and informative. No field of sense is suitable for this.

Fiction is a promising candidate for a counterexample to this ontological incompleteness in the sense that we can seemingly introduce, in the medium of the imagination, an absolute (= A) whose non-existence is denied by the fact that we can still imagine it.[46] This is one of the most important reasons why FOS, in order to secure its own consistency on this point against possible objections, must present not only a theory of non-existence but also an ontology of the imagination.

In FOS, the concept of an object is a formal-ontological one.[47] Objects do not form a totality; if they did, there would be cause to assign them to a field of sense, an ordering rule. The metaphysical desire to see oneself as part of a world is not in itself a sufficient reason to postulate the existence of a totality of objects; by itself it does not make sense.

There is quite simply no ordering rule that applies to all objects. The concept of the object as something of which something is true is inadequate for this purpose; for if something falls under this concept of the object, and *is* thus an object, then there is a fact in which it is embedded as an object. This fact belongs to one field of sense as opposed to other fields of sense, such that the formal univocity of the concept of the object is reconcilable with the ontological pluralism of FOS.[48]

Any enumeration of objects remains ontologically incomplete, even if one allows an infinite number of objects. Of course, infinity is not a problem as such, because there are infinitely many natural numbers. The problem only arises on the transfinite level and the accompanying insights into the incompleteness of all theorizing. Yet transfinite set theory alone is also insufficient for an articulation of the no-world-view, as transfinite set theory operates in an extensional mode – that is, it views its objects as given under abstraction from our mode of access.[49]

This is precisely what the concept of sense opposes. Whatever exists does so under a description. It possesses a suchness. Its suchness connects it to other objects of the same kind, which gives rise to a field of sense. The idea of an object as such is sense-less, however, as it only seemingly enables the formation of a field of sense that can no longer be subject to any specific conditions of sense. So the idea that there is a set of objects which is itself an object, and hence that there is nothing that is not an object, is thwarted by the very meaning of being, or rather existence.[50] It does not follow from the fact that one cannot give an example of something which is not an object, at least in the sense that one can name it as an example, that we use an unrestricted universal quantifier when we speak about objects. Conversely, it follows from FOS that we do not ever use metaphysical universal quantifiers (not even in this subclause), because there is no object that can possibly correspond to it.[51]

Part II

Mental Realism

A central topic in discussions of realism is the mental realm. If one adopts the (misguided) criterion of mind-independence as a *metaphysical* criterion for realism, the mind comes under ontological suspicion of not being real or at least not quite real. Whatever is not entirely (or not at all) real is a phantom. One powerful tendency in contemporary philosophy of mind draws on an embarrassing yet deep-seated equivocation which confuses the 'mind' with a ghost – that is, a phantom.[1] The central diagnosis of the following part of this book maintains that this confusion (of mind and ghost) produces a phantom, i.e., the idea of the mental realm as both hovering over the material and being closely tied to it (supervenience), as if the mind and the body (or the brain) were only almost identical. I will argue that this misguided direction is a consequence of the wrongheaded metaphysical idea that there is a mind-independent reality which in its very being serves as a criterion for realistic theory choices.

In the following second part, I will seek to expose this tendency as one that busies itself with a phantom pain, which means that a number of its favourite topics (such as genuine phantom pain, the universally popular rubber hand experiment and the historically and theologically uninformed critique of religion) prove to be a credible indication of severe self-delusion.

In this contemporary naturalist school of thought, mind becomes a phantom because it falls through the cracks of reality owing to the conceptual predefinition in which only those things are considered real that are objectively the case, which especially means, independently of the subjectively 'coloured' perception of a conscious, minded being. As a conscious, minded being can be mistaken about all manner of things, it seems wise to remove the subject from reality at the outset, and thus finally have free rein for a completely objective science that dispenses with the mind and its vicissitudes.

An important step on the way to this misguided (and fundamentally neither attainable nor desirable) goal is the destruction of the purportedly illusory user interface of consciousness, which stands in the way of finally reaching an objective natural and technological science of the subject. This research programme is already misguided at the ontological level of its experimental design: because only those things that are independent of consciousness are considered really real, but the phenomena of consciousness somehow seem to be there, it is necessary to tie them – without any possible trace of higher spirituality – to something that enjoys full civil rights in the purportedly scientific worldview.

In this part of the book, I will seek to show that it is nonsensical to reduce the mind to something categorially mind-less or to eliminate it altogether, for this programme is quite simply defeated by the fact that it is propagated by subjects which embody, in particularly visible fashion, all those aspects whose fully valid existence they wish to dispute.

This circumvents the first act of reduction from the get-go, which consists in switching from the topic of the mind to that of consciousness, whose nature no one quite seems able to pin down. In the view presented here, consciousness is a module of the mind – that is, an element of our self-portrait that we adduce in the context of action explanation in order to elucidate our own situation, namely the place of human beings in the cosmos.[2]

The central thesis to be developed in this part builds upon neo-existentialism, which defines humans as the beings that essentially exist in light of a conception of who or what they are.[3] This follows on from familiar motifs in the tradition of existential philosophy that define subjectivity as that which consists in our being in search of ourselves. Based on this view, we are entities 'that, in their Being, comport themselves towards their Being.'[4]

For as long as we have been historically confronted by the human being in documents of its self-imagining, one of the responses to the question of who or what humans are has been to create a picture of how our mental faculties are activated and how far they extend. The history of our self-portrait reveals a diachronic and synchronic variability in the demarcation of our subjective states that we cannot pass over in order to choose some general title such as 'consciousness', and to look out for its minimum neuronal correlate. Whether we have consciousness, and in what form, cannot be established by exploring our organism as long as we do not receive any stable information as to what we are actually looking for.

In one particular respect, neo-existentialism not only follows on obviously from Hegel but, surprisingly, also from a finding even accepted by Dennett: that our mentalistic vocabulary describes phenomena whose nature is such that they themselves vary depending on our perception of them. The mind as a whole is not independent of how minded beings characterize it; it is essentially tied to self-objectifications – that is, to self-conceptions.

This does not at all mean, however, that all self-conceptions are ontologically or alethically free-floating, which in this case means neither true nor false. The human sciences (like other sciences) discover facts, including facts about humans, that are meant to be taken into account in our relation to self. One can fail in this and reproduce mythological views of the origin of humans for the coordination of actions.[5]

Not all anthropological facts concern what I classify as 'mind'. Mind [*Geist*] is the human capacity to form a self-image, and we can take this capacity as the central point from which to grasp specific modules of the mind as modes of self-articulation.[6] Mind is the whole that we take into account when we consider that humans do not simply and automatically fit into their surroundings. Since we have been documenting our self-relations, thus enabling ourselves to become acquainted diachronically and synchronically with people we do not consider part of our close group via their objectifications, we as humans have been working on developing an image of how the human being belongs within its environment.

By virtue of their imaging techniques, human beings always already differ from other life forms they encounter – from animate and inanimate nature, celestial phenomena, gods, spirits, and so on. We express how we believe our circumstances to be in the form of myths, cosmic narratives, art works, science and immediately useful artefacts. This brings forth self-portraits that open up a space which classifies individual group members as manifestations of universal structures.

Here one can first of all point to two theoretical levels that can be differentiated using the tools of the humanities and social sciences. The first, higher (more abstract) theoretical level concerns the concept of humanity, of humans as such. The second, object-based (concrete) theoretical level concerns specific conceptions of humans that I refer to as *homunculi*.

At the highest level of abstraction we find the mind as such, the capacity for self-images. At this level we observe the orientation of humans by a notion of who or what they are. Conceptions of humans guide our actions because we justify what we do not least within the horizon of an understanding of the 'meaning of life'. Life and death or sickness and health are elemental experiences that, even today, shake every person and call into question everything we take for granted in everyday life. Our experiences of life's boundaries shift the focus to life itself as a problem to which we must find some answers, without being able to align these answers with an independent standard that is visible to everyone.

We do not transcend this situation principally through progress in the objectifying human sciences (molecular biology, human genetics, medicine, psychology, neurosciences, and so forth). The British physiologist Denis Noble – one of the pioneers of systems biology – offers a notable argument that can be used to map the theory construction of FOS onto the philosophy of the living.[7] His argument revolves around the concept of 'biological relativity', in which biological systems (cells, organs, DNA, cohorts, and so on) are taken as starting points of a yardstick (a scale). The explanation of a system must always proceed from the assumption that the system is located on a level where particular scales are relevant, without there being any overall system determining what should be treated as an element in all systems.

It is therefore legitimate to view cells from the optics of molecules as gigantic, since there is no natural measure determining what would be 'intrinsically' micro-, meso- or macroscopic. To believe in something resembling normal conditions of observation (the lifeworldly mesoscopic type) is already an unsupportable, and thus inadmissible anthropic distortion that adapts the universe to the imprecise measuring conditions that happen to strike each one of us as 'natural'. Therefore Noble operates with an expanded principle of general relativity that

> consists of distancing ourselves from privileged viewpoints for which there is insufficient justification. There are no absolutes – rather, even in science things can only be understood in a relative sense: relative to the questions we ask; relative to the scale at which we ask the question; relative to our present knowledge of a universe of which we will always have questions remaining.[8]

The universe presents itself to us under the only epistemic conditions available to us as a nested structure ('universes within universes within universes').[9] Thus the living cannot be fully determined from a metaphysically privileged standpoint. The explanation we give for a phenomenon depends on the scale that corresponds to a given level. This by no means undermines the objectivity of scientific explanations but simply points out that the scales we associate with the universe lead to fields of sense (Noble calls them 'levels') in which objects are subject to ordering rules.

Different levels of the living are tied to different ordering rules, which does not mean that there is no interaction between objects on different levels. However, what is out of the question here, as elsewhere, is the demarcation of an overall system of which all subsystems prove to be elements, enabling an overall cosmological explanation. The structure of FOS repeats itself in every identifiable system we encounter in the universe: living systems are open systems, since there cannot be a whole that provides the ultimate explanatory framework which would allow a full view of the behaviour of all the elements in any system.

Our self-objectification in the form of the human sciences, too, does not culminate in an overview that would relieve us once and for all from our free-floating self-determination.[10] We cannot shake off the burden of self-determination – the demand for freedom – by adducing something that is simply true of us. One cannot expect there ever to be an exhaustive factual report on what humans are, which means that our localization also remains empirically variable.

This finding describes the higher-order invariant of our variable conceptions of humans. 'Mind' is therefore the name for the dimension of the interminable discovery of self-images, a dimension that does not itself vary in this description. The historicity of the mind does not consist in the fact that humans are minded beings in one case but not in another. Rather, the capacity for self-images is the universal core that can become a reference point for ethical orientation – albeit one that mostly leads nowhere in the end, which constitutes a variation on the old problem of formalism: *humanity cannot productively align itself solely with the universal form of being-human, since this leaves too many weighty questions open.* It does connect all humans under the banner of humanity, but this fails to generate any instructions for behaviour that would enable a contentful resolution of existing antagonisms. Hence the need for the empirically variable human sciences, which, among other things, articulate social antagonisms.

One theoretical level below the life form of the human being as such (*Homo sapiens*) we find specific *homunculi* such as *Homo oeconomicus*, *Homo narrans*, *Homo ludens*, *Homo aestheticus*, *Homo politicus*, and so on – that is, conceptions of humans that model an observable human activity and consider all other activities from that perspective.[11] Humans, however, are neither primarily economic nor narrative, neither primarily political nor playful,, but rather specimens of the creature that always remains tied to its self-objectification, which rests to a considerable extent on fictions, because we ourselves are a constant occasion for interpretations that can be classified and objectified on the level of sociological research via relevant categories such as 'role', 'class', 'habitus', 'communication', and so forth. To the extent that the *homunculi* concern ideal types for describing observable behaviour, they remain one-sided and tend to feign an explanatory centre, which is stymied in individual cases by the human freedom to define oneself differently.

There is no exhaustive list of attributes of specific human activities (playing, laughing, crying, recounting, thinking, acting morally, exchanging goods, dreaming, and so on) that could collectively be used to define the exact position of humans within animate and inanimate nature, because we have no exact position. The only anthropological constant we must postulate for the purpose of theoretical coherence is the aforementioned invariant of mind – that is, our formal capacity for self-images.

The self-description of humans has further varieties, of course, and one of its manifestations is the portfolio of mentalistic vocabularies. This currently includes such concepts as attentiveness, holding-to-be-true, consciousness, intentionality and fine-grained, experimentally operationalizable concepts from psychology, for example personality traits such as extraversion, and so on. The concept of consciousness is introduced and more closely defined to capture a facet of being-human that we quite probably share with other creatures, without having any empirically robust assumptions about the minimum physiological correlates of the states we classify as 'conscious'.[12] The context in which the concept of consciousness can be introduced demands a far richer mentalistic vocabulary for its self-description, since consciousness theorists are not only conscious but must also draw on a multitude of epistemic abilities and faculties to understand how they proceed, to isolate the phenomenon of consciousness from its implantation in complex systems that always go far beyond those elements whose organization has anything to do with consciousness. Any scientific examination of consciousness posits a stable, coherent analysis of the concept of consciousness and, for that reason alone, already abstracts from the factual plurality of states that are taken together under this banner. It is therefore highly problematic to suppose that there is consciousness in the same sense that there are fermions or galaxies – that is, as given objects of an examination whose focus has nothing to do with the structure of the objects. Consciousness belongs to the historically variable accoutrements in the museum of our self-portraits. In short: *consciousness is not a natural kind and can therefore never be studied exhaustively with the methods of natural science.*

This does not mean that we have no mental states, or that these are in the eye of the beholder, who develops abstractions from the intentional standpoint in order to trim the excessively complex machinery of our organism into an explanatorily useful shape.[13] For the idea that there could be a complete physical description of our organism's machinery that is not (yet) available to us is already scientistic ideology (meta-physics), not an empirically supported hypothesis. The scientistic mechanism is part of the human self-portrait and, hence, not a guaranteed set of facts against which conceptions of humans can be measured.[14]

Like Laplace's demon, *L'homme machine* literally belongs in the age of a scientifically obsolete ideology of the eighteenth century that was linked to the socioeconomic revolutions and counterrevolutions of its time.[15] The after-effect of this period is a metaphysical reductionism that has not vanished from people's heads to this day, and which states that there are ultimate components of the universe in which one can identify a complete series of all causal architectures – whether this was a so far purely mythical (not physically measurable!) substructure of mereological atoms or an equally mythical overall context of the cosmos or universe as a whole. There is quite simply no *pou sto* [standpoint] from which one could set up a scale running through the entire universe. There is no *scala naturae* – certainly not one as simple as the one imagined by physicalists when they invent a fundamental level on which physics is supposed to operate.

In what follows I will develop a realistic model for central modules of the mind. This model allows us to cling to the indispensability of subjectivity without treating it as a shell or a prison, but rather as an openness to facts. For our thinking belongs to the facts, just like everything else that we have successfully objectified. This facticity does not need to be brought about; we find ourselves already in it.

In §6 I will reconstruct an ideal-typical path from naïve realism to the dead end of illusionism in the philosophy of mind, which allows us – as Wittgenstein famously put it – to 'show the fly the way out of the fly-bottle'.[16] Here everything revolves around casting off the misguided realist criterion of mind-independence while avoiding the similarly misguided notion that there are objects which are 'mind-dependent' in any

metaphysically or epistemologically particular sense (such as consciousness itself or its phenomenal contents).

Then, in §7, I will introduce the indispensability thesis according to
which we necessarily draw on self-conceptions as minded in any successful reference to how things are. All theoretical knowledge claims and
contributions to progress in science, essentially occur 'from the human
standpoint';[17] this is a condition that can neither be weakened nor eliminated, and it cannot or should not be bypassed in any other way. The
human standpoint is adequate to stake successful knowledge claims, and
thus does not set up any parameters that are susceptible to scepticism
and cause us to become our own epistemic prisoners. The life form of the
human mind is not a capsule that isolates us from an external reality.

§8 tests this result by confronting the concept of lifeworld introduced
by Husserl, who recognized the indispensability but immediately distorted it because of his somewhat hidden, but disastrous penchant for
scientism. Husserl's lifeworld is a form of proto-experiment structured
on the model of inductive world-appropriation; this is why Husserl's
phenomenology is constantly haunted by the phantom of 'philosophy as
a strict science', which is probably partly explained in sociological terms
by his rivalry with the Vienna Circle.[18] Husserl's concept of lifeworld
is both problematically Eurocentric and misleading in theoretical terms,
since it presents humans as always tinkering with hypotheses about the
world without realizing that this posit reflects a theoretical decision; thus
Husserl involuntarily naturalizes the lifeworld.

Then (§9) I outline the structure of an objective phenomenology using a
neo-realist theory of perception based on FOS. Whereas Husserl holds that
a phenomenon 'knows no real parts, no real changes, and no causality',[19]
I argue that phenomena are the paradigms of causality. For perception
is a causal matter that sets up an actually existing relation between the
object of perception and the perceiving subject. This relation is perception,
which would not even exist without a literal irradiation stemming from
the perceived object, as well as causal feedback effects from our side. The
result of this physical interaction is perception.

The orthodox phenomenological *theory of adumbration* is replaced by
a neo-realist *theory of irradiation* that understands our mental life as a
textbook example of causality. This amounts by no means to a Humean
or Kantian manoeuvre that keeps causality far away from the world and
transfers it to the mind, since the mind/world distinction should be considered a thing of the past at this point. The mind is causally integrated,
yet there is no need for this causality to be delegated to anything that
does not belong to the category of the mind; this can be illustrated with
particular clarity with reference to perception.

§10 returns to the topic of the ontology of the imagination to show that
the imagination has boundaries that are historically variable but cannot
be transcended as a whole. Metaphysical objects such as 'the world'
overstep these boundaries and can therefore, at best, play the part of

absolute metaphors by acting as a source of metaphor formation without ever reaching the stage of a concept. Blumenberg, whose metaphorology famously laid the foundation for the concept of absolute metaphors, observes:

> 'World' is a term for which any attempt to find rules for word substitution is constitutively doomed to failure. . . . Even if I were inclined to agree that one would henceforth do better to refrain from forming and using theorems about 'the world' at all, I would be very unsure of the success of such a ban.[20]

I do not follow him unreservedly in this, as I consider references to 'the world' (metaphysics) avoidable in the context of FOS. 'The world' is an empty pointer, a gesture that becomes a source of nonsense as soon as one tries to convey how exactly one imagines that all there is (including oneself) belongs to the world.

In §11 I will propose a distinction between fictive, imaginary and intentional objects that allows us to see that even mental objects cannot be reduced to a common denominator that envisage the mind as a closed object area of reference. Categories such as 'intentionality', or even 'consciousness as such', are hopeless overgeneralizations that lead directly or indirectly to a split between I and non-I, and from there it takes only a few steps to regress to a general distinction between mind and world, something we should leave behind.

From Naïve Realism to Illusionism

Naïve realism proceeds from the assumption that there is a mind-independent external world whose existence is the decisive reason why we should be realists. What is naïve about this assumption is that it is either ultimately a trivial fact that no one would dispute or theoretically ill founded.

(1) It is ultimately *trivial* in so far as it can rely on the *argument from facticity*.[1] In a nutshell, this argument states that any theoretically articulable attitude of thought towards objectivity expects something to be registration-independent. Something is *registration-independent* if it would have been what it turns out to be even if the system had not apprehended it. The argument from facticity only disputes that we can be trapped in a solipsism of the present moment, a state in which our mental window is a state that flares up spontaneously and gives us the impression that there is more than our impression. The idea of a solipsism of the present moment is a radical sceptical hypothesis, because it threatens to defeat all knowledge claims at a single stroke. It describes a scenario in which no one can know anything because truth and holding-to-be-true coincide, or because there are not even sufficient mental resources for the affected subject to make a knowledge claim.

If solipsism of the moment were true, *ex hypothesi* we could not consider it true. Thus even such an extreme sceptical scenario cannot undermine reality but only allow us to imagine a subject incapable of grasping its own situation. We cannot find ourselves in this position since we are in the process of asking ourselves which options have which consequences, which presupposes that we have minimally well-founded theoretical assumptions at our disposal. Therefore even an extreme solipsism of the present moment does not become any truer because someone holds it to be true, as it cannot simultaneously be true and be held to be true. In short, the solipsism of the present moment is literally unbelievable: if it is true one cannot believe it and if one can believe it, it cannot be true.

Subjective idealism à la Berkeley, however, does not violate the conditions of the argument from facticity. Berkeley claims to present a discovery, one that requires proof: that the appearance of a material, three-dimensional reality can supposedly be better explained by the fact that mental states display an internal structure which causes us to project our mental stage outwards. This position does not fail merely because of its theoretical ambition, as can be seen from the fact that some brain scientists implicitly or even explicitly take it as a starting point for their theories of phenomenal consciousness.[2]

If phenomenal consciousness is indeed ontologically subjective, this means that its presence consists in something appearing to us in a particular way. Its being (*esse*) and its appearance (*percipi*) coincide, though this certainly does not mean that phenomenal consciousness is also epistemically subjective.[3] Even if we can be mistaken about mental phenomena, this does not mean that, when we are mistaken, we are mistaken about being mistaken. For an impression to be deceptive, it must be present. Its presence deludes us about something, but not about the fact that it is present! Let us call this age-old insight the *minimal cogito* – a condition one should not violate.[4]

Berkeley's subjective idealism emerged historically from empiricism, which is no theoretical accident, but rather stems from the matter itself. For it makes do with fewer assumptions than a naïve realism that assigns intentional objects to elements of our conscious life and views these elements as the external triggers (stimuli) of this life. As long as realism can be exposed as an optional supplementary assumption that is not necessary for an understanding of our mental states, retreating to a solipsistic reconstruction of reality remains a theoretically serious option. For subjective idealism does not conflict with the argument from facticity; rather, it takes it directly into account by presenting a theory of our mental states than one can at least hold to be true. Naïve realism and subjective idealism draw on the same source, though the latter is more theoretically economical and constitutes a respectable position in the contemporary philosophy of mind because, among other things, it is plausible from the standpoint of heterophenomenology.

'Heterophenomenology' is Daniel Dennett's name for the realization that we interact with the factual structure of our conscious life whenever we focus on a mental state.[5] In this way, there is always room for a distinction between the mental state we are in and the manner in which it is thematized. This means that we are constitutively fallible in our self-consciousness, which can in fact be inferred *mutatis mutandis* from the explanatory slogan that everything is the way it is because it came to be so.[6]

To have a phenomenal impression is not the same as being conscious of this circumstance. Phenomenal consciousness is located below the threshold of self-consciousness, an insight already captured by Leibniz with his phrase 'petites perceptions'. Perception and apperception are not intensionally identical, nor do they always coincide extensionally. This follows from what we have known for centuries from psychological self-exploration, so we should remember that this is not a neuroscientific or cognitive-scientific discovery of recent decades.

Instead of taking up arms for naïve realism or the diametrically opposed subjective idealism, one should note here that they are built on the same foundation: the argument from facticity. But this changes the theoretical situation, a fact that eludes these opponents. Their common foundation lies in the inevitable recognition of the circumstance that, in any coherent scenario, our mental states belong to the furniture of the real. This does away once and for all with the notion that the measure of realism is to be found in the acknowledgement of a mind-independent external world. The mind (however precisely we define it) is as much a part of what exists as everything that naïve realists assign to their mind-independent external world.

Of course, naïve realists are free to stamp their feet defiantly and insist that the debate about realism they so enjoy conducting revolves around opposition to idealism.[7] In doing so, they commit themselves from the outset to the assumption that realism is out of the question when it comes to the conscious mind. By simply positing its opposition to idealism, naïve realism thus makes a substantive assumption about the mental, namely that it is mind-dependent. So now, based on a compulsive theoretical act, it is true that *esse est percipi aut percipere.*[8] The conceptual confusion here is that consciousness is now defined as mind-dependent only in the sense that every object is dependent on itself. Clearly, it does not really follow from this that the mind is mind-dependent in any special sense and consists, for example, in the fact that anything appears to us at all. Elevating mind-independence to the criterion for realism does not give rise to any special, metaphysically exciting sense of mind-dependence. Naïve realism thus shifts subjective idealism to the mind rather than getting rid of it, which ultimately rests on a naïve understanding of the ontological significance of physics, as Quassim Cassam and John Campbell have shown.[9]

Already on this level, naïve realism has to fight with pseudo-problems. Within the framework of its own experimental design, it generates the idealism that it situates in the realm of the mental and holds to be true in that domain. Naïve realists are therefore local idealists: they consider our mental life to be largely mind-dependent.

On a different level, this creates the pseudo-problems that Huw Price has termed 'placement problems'.[10] What weighs especially heavily is that naïve realists can never explain how mind-dependent consciousness fits into mind-independent reality, which they consider the gold standard of realism. For the consciousness of others is located at the other end of the semantic divide between realism and idealism, a divide created by naïve realists in order to keep their mental states distant from physical reality. How does the mental life of others fit into the external world's panorama of consciousness-independent things, especially the brain, which one can find in the body of others?

(2) One can see from this that naïve realism is, furthermore, insufficiently theoretically founded. Because it rests on the same foundation as subjective idealism, it entangles itself in pseudo-problems. The whole of (phenomenal) consciousness is left to subjective idealism, which generates the additional difficulty of drawing a hard line between phenomenal consciousness and our intentionality. This cannot be repaired by relying on semantics and being a realist about the external world but a subjective idealist about the processes of the internal world. For this distinction must have a correlate in reality if one is to continue maintaining that there is a mind-independent external world on the one hand and a realm of *esse est percipi* on the other.

To evade this problem, there has recently been a spread of different varieties of *illusionism*, significantly prepared by Dennett – though illusionism naturally has a long history, since many of its variants originate in the context of the history of Buddhism.[11]

Dennett himself expressly endorses Keith Frankish's variety of illusionism, which he even classifies as the 'obvious default theory of consciousness'.[12] According to this theory, (phenomenal) consciousness, which brings subjective idealism into the arena as an ontologically unwelcome guest, is treated as something fictional, even fictive, which is especially interesting in our context.

Generally speaking, *illusionism*, which we will now examine more closely, is 'the view that phenomenal consciousness, as usually conceived, is illusory. According to illusionists, our sense that it is like something to undergo conscious experiences is due to the fact that we systematically misrepresent them (or, on some versions, their objects) as having phenomenal properties.'[13] Illusionism seeks to dispute the phenomenality of our experiences. Our experiences supposedly have no qualitative properties, whether physical or non-physical.[14] *Prima vista*, this is absurd, as it seemingly denies that chocolate often tastes sweet and a knife in the back is intensely painful. That would be too simple, however, since illusionism is directed against a particular understanding of these phenomena whereby they are 'ineffable, intrinsic, private, and infallibly known'.[15]

But this proves that the target of illusionism has moved, for it is now directed against a particular *conception* of qualia (phenomenal properties) and therefore cannot present itself as a view that teaches us something about phenomenal consciousness. At best, it would offer a diagnosis of why some theorists find the rejectable conception of qualia plausible – a modest goal scarcely worthy of Dennett's title *Consciousness Explained*.

Thus illusionism, in the official conceptual definition of its direction, already oscillates between a statement about phenomenal consciousness and a statement about a view of phenomenal consciousness. On the one hand, it accepts our sense that it 'is like something' to undergo conscious experiences but, on the other hand, it opposes a particular theoretical description of this phenomenon.

Let us take a closer look by following the reading that illusionism is at least a more interesting thesis when it claims that phenomenal consciousness itself, not merely the theoretical description thereof, is an illusion. Many of Dennett's and Frankish's remarks support this more ambitious version. The latter, after all, calls it the 'basic illusionist claim' that 'introspection delivers a partial, distorted view of our experiences, misrepresenting complex physical features as simple phenomenal ones.'[16]

Yet this raises a decisive question: how exactly does it happen that introspection represents something physically complex (such as neuronal processes) as something phenomenally simple (the impression of a red cabriolet, for example)? How exactly are we supposed to imagine that phenomenal consciousness as such brings about a phenomenal distortion, that something *ex hypothesi* illusionary in turn creates something illusionary?

Frankish proposes seven models for this, all of them incoherent. Articulating this incoherence is useful, for the contrasting position of mental realism becomes clearer if we know why the existence of consciousness cannot inherently be an illusion or something fictive.

1 *User Illusion*

Suggestion: According to this model (presented by Dennett), consciousness is like a user illusion that comes about at the interface connecting physical processes in a computer with our use of them. Consciousness is an illusion in the same sense that a folder of files on my digital desktop is an illusion. In reality, there is no folder there, only physical hardware processes, but these processes seem meaningful to me, the user, in a way that has no correlate. In analogy to this constellation, neuronal processes would be the physical hardware and consciousness would be ontologically like the folders on my desktop, which do not exist 'in reality' or *in sensu stricto*.

Objection: I, the user, do really exist, and my use of folders has genuine causal consequences on the physical level of data processing in the hardware. Furthermore, my awareness of the significance of the files on my desktop is in no way exposed as an illusion if the physical basis of data processing is pointed out. The graphic user interface of an operating system is not an illusion in the context of our use of it, so the analogy is already defeated by the fact that user interfaces are not illusions.

Yet even if one could somehow show that there are in reality only complex processes of electronic data processing, but no graphic user interfaces, this would have no bearing on consciousness. For who is supposed to be the user of the consciousness interface? If the impression of a qualitative experience of my subjective visual field were a graphic user interface for neuronal processes, who would I then be as a user? Who is using the brain so as to generate the user illusion of consciousness if not someone who is conscious?

2 *Projectivism*

Suggestion: Consciousness is a projection that comes about when we project stable behaviour onto other members of our species, which can somehow be counted as an evolutionary advantage.[17] This means that there is the illusion of a carrier of consciousness, a self, but there is no self. The self is merely an explanatory posit serving an approximate prediction of our own and others' behaviour.

Objection: What does that line of thought have to do with phenomenal consciousness and introspection? Surely the possession of qualia (feeling) is not a prediction of my own behaviour. Furthermore: even if our predictive talent is evolutionarily rooted, this does not mean that it is an illusion. The prediction of behaviour may be incomplete – that is, not guaranteed – because (among other things) human behaviour is free and thus never entirely predictable. It does not follow from our predictive attitude towards behaviour that there is no stable self in any case, only – at best – that the self is not an automatism which controls our behaviour according to deterministic laws. However precisely one defines the disputing of a self in action-theoretical terms, it ultimately remains a mystery in the present context what any of this has to do with phenomenal consciousness.

3 *Ipsundrum*

Suggestion: Neuronal processes generate the illusion of phenomenality when one views them 'from the inside'. Consciousness is a 'fiction of the impossible'.[18] Consciousness is 'a magic trick played by the brain on itself.'[19] This leads to what Nicholas Humphrey calls an 'ipsundrum', by which he understands a source of illusory phenomena that give us the impression that there is such a thing as conscious experience.

Humphrey considers consciousness an invention in a twofold sense: 'First, it is a cognitive faculty, evolved by natural selection, designed to help us make sense of ourselves and our surroundings. But then, second, it is a fantasy, conjured up by the brain, designed to change how we value our existence.'[20] According to Humphrey, the ipsundrum is a form of optical illusion that makes it seem as if physically impossible figures (such as phenomenal consciousness) actually exist.

Objection: Humphrey hopes that it will one day be possible to find the mechanism underlying the ipsundrum in the brain, yet offers no suggestion as to how this might take place. Hence the suggestion is purely conceptual, without any empirical foundation. Moreover, this entire analogy presupposes that there is sensory data that someone receives and misinterprets. Splitting the brain into parts and saying that one part of the brain is misinterpreting another part does not help solve the problem; it merely shifts it. If a part of the brain correlates neuronally to my impression that I have a phenomenal consciousness of a red cabriolet, what this means within the (terribly simplified) physicalist worldview preferred by Humphrey and Frankish is that the phenomenal consciousness of a red cabriolet exists. This is the point of Searle's influential theory of consciousness, which famously states that one part of the brain can represent other parts, such that, in this way, the conscious part generates subjective experience that is not an illusion, but rather the phenomenon that has a neuronal correlate.[21]

It is true, of course, that neuronal processes are part of the explanation of how particular conscious impressions come about in human beings. In this sense, human impressions of colours and other qualia are 'inventions' of the organism. The selection mechanisms of our qualitatively oriented attention are partly biological, and thus explicable in evolutionary terms. It does not follow from this, however, that conscious experience is an illusion in any relevant sense. A biologically explicable artefact that comes about through the activities of an organism is not *ipso facto* an illusion. Otherwise, our organism would be an illusion, as it comes about through cell division, whose programme is determined by microbiological processes that produce our phenotype.

4 *Secondary Qualities*

Suggestion: The relation between consciousness and its underlying physical processes is analogous to that between secondary and primary qualities. In so far as secondary qualities can be understood as illusions, one can transfer this model to consciousness as a whole.[22]

Objection: If qualia are secondary qualities, this does not mean they are illusions, for illusions are something that can mislead people. This model lacks a subject that is deluded. It only names a potential source of deception – the existence of qualia – without explaining why the mere existence of qualia is already an illusion. In any case, secondary qualities are qualia. If consciousness belonged to the category of secondary qualities, then, it would exist – unless one wanted to induce a regress and treat the impression that consciousness exists as a secondary quality, then as a tertiary quality, and so on, which surely deviates from the path of theoretical virtues.

5 *Fictionalism*

Suggestion: Our introspective life resembles 'the experience of a child in a dark cinema who takes the cartoon creatures on screen to be real'.[23] This means that consciousness is a fictional object and nothing 'real'.[24]

Objection: This assumption fails because it does not rest on any acceptable theory of fiction. The interpretation of a film (in the sense of the performance of its score in the experience of a recipient) is no illusion. Of course one can be mistaken in the context of an aesthetic experience, and one could also take a work of cinematic art for a documentary and accordingly, based on the presentation of events, assign them to the wrong field of sense. Yet this analogy does not do illusionism any good, for now there is a viewer (the recipient) who takes a presentation for something that it is not. This deception also presupposes, however, that the screen is real and there is an equally real viewer. But this brings phenomenal consciousness back into play, for the screen is something that someone (who?) takes for something it is not (such as a window). The fictionalism suggestion sounds plausible only because of an implicit, vague reference to assumptions vaguely drawn from the theory of fictionality, without any theoretical articulation of why fictions are illusions and what relation this bears to consciousness. Incidentally, the cartoon characters one sees on a cinema screen are real in any plausible view, since one could not see them otherwise; thus Frankish's formulation of this suggestion is incoherent in every conceivable sense.

6 *Optical Illusions*

Suggestion: Phenomenal consciousness is an optical illusion. Just as the two lines of the Müller–Lyer illusion are in fact equally long but seem different in length to us, consciousness is in reality a complex physical process that seems simple to us.

Objection: In an optical illusion, we are not necessarily deluded about the fact that we are deluded; otherwise we would be unable to see through it. As soon as one is familiar with the Müller–Lyer illusion, one can conclude from the existence of certain impressions that the lines are equally long. Note: in reality, no two lines we experience as percepts are ever equally long, so it would be more appropriate to treat the content of our perceptions in general as illusions.[25] Consequently, an optical illusion does not force the conscious recipient to be deluded about their own existence as conscious subjects. This corresponds to the ancient idea, developed by Aristotle in particular, that it is not our sensory data that is misleading, but rather our assessment of them. The error lies not in the sensuous apprehension of objects, but rather in the assessment of this apprehension.[26] Thus the sensory basis of an optical illusion is not as such a deception.

Contrary to expectations, this is not grist for the mill of illusionism, as the sensory basis of an optical illusion is already qualitative: the lines have form, colour, directionality within the subjective visual field, and so on, which is the set of qualities that illusionism identifies as a deception. Yet this set is not deceptive; at most, its theoretical construction as an error-immune basis of our theorizing is deceptive. This is an entirely different form of critique that leads into the discursive area of the 'myth of the given' and private language argument based considerations where the aim is to show that it does not follow from sensory givenness that we should not construe it as the basis of an error-immune contact with reality.[27]

7 *UFOs and God*

Suggestion: We have reason to classify something as illusory if convictions and statements dealing with it can be entirely explained by causes that have no connection whatsoever to the matter itself. Frankish names two supposed examples of this: UFOs and God.[28] In analogy to these cases, then, it is supposedly true that consciousness is illusory because the introspectively formed convictions that deal with it can be explained away purely through causes that have no connection to consciousness itself.

Objection: This analogy fails because introspectively formed convictions that deal with phenomenal consciousness are themselves phenomenal. Introspection is not a neutral intervention in our experiences coming from the outside but is given to the position of an 'I think'. This is the point of Kant's distinction between the analytical and synthetic unity of consciousness.[29] By becoming conscious of some of the qualitative states in which I am existing at a given moment, and noticing them as such, I distinguish between the fact that I *am* in these states from the fact that I *notice* them. It is never the case that I notice all the percepts I am currently having; this is something one can already learn from Leibniz, and which has long since been shown in detail by psychological research.

It may be that my percepts change when I turn my attention to them, since my organism de facto enters a different overall state when I become aware of my percepts as such. Yet this does not necessarily mean that my percepts are changed so radically by my access to them that I can never think about them in the first person.[30]

The *analytical* unity of my conceptual self-consciousness, which turns introspectively towards its own phenomenal states, only exists in a context in which it is connected to these phenomenal states. Otherwise it would be completely impossible to make any first-person statements about one's own mental states, since they would be cut off from our insight by an entirely opaque wall. This context is the *synthetic* unity of consciousness.

Furthermore, it would indicate a psychologically and biologically bizarre understanding of the function of self-consciousness (introspection) to suppose that all consciousness of consciousness is illusory because it represents complex processes as simple states. This would apply equally to illusionism, in any case, which would no longer be able to acknowledge any first-person statements about consciousness as evidence of the structure of consciousness. In this way, it would drift off into a radical form of eliminative materialism. This would take us back to the beginning of dialectics, however, since it would raise the question of how the illusion that the illusion of consciousness actually exists comes about in the first place. An eliminativist epicycle does not take the argumentation any further at this point, but rather demonstrates once again that the position of illusionism goes back to an unclear use of 'illusion' that cannot be substantiated by any established theory of illusion.

Frankish ultimately seems to come down on the side of fictionalism, thus arriving – probably quite unsuspectingly – at a Kantian constellation, since Kant argued from *Dreams of a Spirit-Seer* onwards that we cannot infer from the inner view of subjectivity either that we have an immortal soul as a carrier of our thinking or – and this is the decisive insight that eludes Dennett and Frankish – that we, as thinkers, are identical with some physiological state or process in the brain. Kant expressly argues against the assumption 'that my thinking "I" is in a place that is different from the places of the other parts of that body that belongs to my self.'[31] He adds that 'No experience teaches me to regard some parts of my sensation of myself as distant, to lock up my indivisible "I" in a microscopically small space in my brain.'[32] He compares this mockingly to the notion that the human soul is located in an 'indescribably small place'[33] in the brain, where it senses

> like the spider at the center of its web. The nerves of the brain strike or agitate it and thereby cause not this immediate impression but one occurring in a wholly remote part of the body to be represented as an object outside the brain. From this seat, it also moves the ropes and levers of the whole machine and causes voluntary movements as it pleases. Such propositions allow only very superficial truth or none at all, and, since the nature of the soul is not adequately known, they are only just as weakly refuted.[34]

Kant thus unequivocally rejects the idea of a homunculus in the nervous system. Frankish, on the other hand, cannot get rid of the homunculus because he insists that our phenomenological, first-person reporting is an illusion, in the sense that we (who?) are duped by a magic trick or a theatre performance. Therefore, if illusionists are right, cognitive scientists 'should treat phenomenological reports as fictions – albeit ones that provide clues as to what is actually occurring in the brain.'[35] But this raises the problem of the viewer, since one would like to know who the viewer in the (Cartesian) theatre that Frankish *nolens volens* brings into play actually is. Frankish himself at least supplies the correct answer that 'there need be no unified audience for the illusion smaller than the organism as a whole (or at least its central nervous system).'[36] This means that the viewer has not disappeared but is, rather, identified with a system that is a far more plausible candidate for the true carrier of consciousness: the entire living being to which one refers when one refers to one's egocentric index with the words 'I think'.[37]

Illusionism is thwarted by its failure to suggest a plausible understanding of illusion or fiction that is supposedly connected to introspection. In the best case, it shifts introspection to the whole organism, which represents part of itself as phenomenal consciousness. It is correct that we should point out a suitable mereological architecture with respect to the mind-body-relationship, but this does not mean that phenomenal consciousness is an illusion or a fiction.[38]

Conclusion: Illusionism as propagated by Dennett and Frankish is a typical confusion of *homo* and *homunculus*. Being-human is linked to a measurable human attribute in order to set one specific conception of humans against other specific conceptions of humans.

If the creature that we are becomes phenomenally conscious of some of its organic states, this form of consciousness in part serves the creature's control over itself. This self-observation is far from infallible. It can be disturbed in manifold ways, for example in the form of phantom pain or other pain disorders that impair the function of pain, which – when it succeeds – is to ensure that we as creatures behave in a certain way in order to identify the source of pain and alleviate the pain.

It is similar with every other known example of phenomenal consciousness, such as hunger, thirst, sexual desire, and so on. At every moment of our conscious life (which naturally also includes dreaming), we not only register facts from the position of a stating, predicating, logical self. Rather, we would be no one, we would have no first-person perspective, if we did not register the background noise of our organism in the form of complex phenomenal fields of sense that bring together heterogeneous stimuli into the flexible unity of an experienced moment.

De facto, intentional and phenomenal consciousness never appear separately. Otherwise, the pure thinking of an intentional consciousness would be an extremely disconcerting, totally disembodied experience that had discarded its egocentric index. A pure 'I think' in which the word 'I' did not refer to the embodied carrier of consciousness would be so utterly removed from the earth that its carrier would be devoid of any phenomenality and would no longer direct itself at anything.

Such thinking, which encompasses everything and nothing *uno eodemque actu* because it claims to think something, yet does not grasp it from any identifiable standpoint, is described by Hegel at the beginning of his *Science of Logic* in his much discussed analysis of pure being, which is nothingness.

> For being which is *mediated*, we shall reserve the expression *concrete existence*. But the common practice is to *imagine* being, as if it were a picture of pure light, the clarity of unclouded seeing, and then nothing as the pure night – and the distinction between the two is then enshrined into this well-known sensuous difference. But in fact, if this very seeing is more accurately imagined, one can readily perceive that in absolute light one sees just as much and just as little as in absolute darkness; that the one seeing is just as good as the other; that pure seeing is a seeing of nothing. Pure light and pure darkness are two voids that amount to the same thing.[39]

Illusionism asserts an incoherent view from nowhere at the very point where our perspective is indeed reflected in natural science, namely in the self-examination of consciousness. Someone who heterophenomenologically records the report of a patient in order to observe the neuronal processes correlating with the patient's expression is conscious of themselves. The doctor *hears* the patient's voice, the cognitive scientist *sees* and *interprets* models that offer, in the form of imaging procedures, an insight into the material architecture that exists *in vivo* as part of the overall context of an organism. In so doing, the scientist abstracts from their own states in the sense that they do not examine themselves. Yet our ability to form an analytical unity of consciousness through abstraction, and thus to refer consciously to something that is itself not necessarily conscious, should not lead us to the false conclusion that there is actually no such thing as phenomenal consciousness, only those elements of our model to which we have access via theoretical abstraction.

In vivo, all known cases of phenomenal consciousness are embedded in a mereological structure that goes far beyond an isolated neuronal process. This is not disputed by the illusionist, who rather draws on a mereology in order to offer a theory of illusion based on the model magic trick/observer in the first place. Consciousness research is in the unusual position of having a specific self-referentiality: by examining itself (as well as examining itself as that which examines itself), it perpetuates its restriction to the picture of it drawn by others. If illusionism calls phenomenal consciousness an illusion, it has *ipso facto* committed to the existence of the same consciousness it now views as an illusion. Yet an illusion is a form of consciousness in which a phenomenal state of affairs appears in such a way that we can be misled.

This, after all, is precisely the point of a magic trick. Our sensory systems have a particular psychologically and physiologically analysable structure that leads to a situation in which we can be distracted by certain distal stimulation patterns from processes that are actually perceptually accessible to us. The magician (like the film director, the actor and the narrator) directs our attention while distracting it from how it is being directed. We see, in a non-conscious manner, the much discussed invisible gorilla that moves through the objective visual field without being consciously registered by us, as we are distracted by the movements going on around us.[40]

This does not mean that there is no phenomenal consciousness, however; rather, it means that our consciousness is what enables us to experience illusory states in the first place. An illusion is not necessarily a second-order illusion. The existence of an optical illusion can be examined; this does not dissolve its phenomenal structure, but rather – if successful – makes it transparent. The lines in the Müller–Lyer illusion still look unequal, even if one knows that they are (more or less) equally long. So an illusion is neither a deception nor any other form of error but, at most, something that can mislead us. Its existence quite simply makes it a component of the real: the real that allows us to experience something about reality – that is, about our susceptibility to deception and capacity for improvement.

§7

The Indispensability of Mind

The epistemic account of reality as a modal category provides a general minimal criterion for realism. The criterion for a minimal, neutral realism is reconcilable with ontological pluralism, since it does not follow from the epistemic modality of reality that there is precisely one field of sense that defines what really exists. The real can be ordered without compromises into an irreducible multiplicity of fields of sense, such that they do not jointly form a collective *singulare tantum*.

Nonetheless, fields of sense are focused in one decisive philosophical respect; for their *focus imaginarius* is the indispensable standpoint that humans take up as minded beings.[1] This does not mean that the real as a whole is tailored to humans, since there is no collective real, no overall reality (no world) that is grasped in part by a subject occurring in it.

One cannot take into account any architecture of fields of sense that makes it impossible as a whole to know anything about the facts. We cannot form a coherent, theoretical image of our own rationality that leads us to deny our faculty to grasp the real as it is. That is why realism cannot be a purely metaphysical thesis. In the matter of realism, we cannot distinguish meaningfully between a *metaphysical* thesis of the independence of the real from our access, on the one hand, and an *epistemological* thesis of the knowability of the real, on the other.

Because we can apprehend the real as it is, our epistemic standpoint must display a form of coherence that qualifies it as a standpoint in the first place. This coherence can be historically open, diachronically and synchronically variable. Indispensability does not mean that there is a transcendental subjectivity equipped with substantive a priori structures.

As we have seen, illusionism is thwarted by the fact that it undermines the accessibility of the mind to its own states. If illusionism were true, we would ultimately be unable to understand it, since our comprehension of what illusionism offers depends on the existence of a phenomenal level that actually differs from how it appears to us. If there is no phenomenal level, however, it is no longer clear what illusionism actually claims.

In light of this, it is a rational next step to formulate the opposing position: mental realism. This presupposes that one has abandoned the notion that realism is a commitment to an ordering function for mind-independent reality. The mind and its thoughts are as much part of the real as are bosons, chairs, dolphins and antimatter. According to the epistemic concept of reality, this means that we can be mistaken about the mind. The phenomenal that is connected to our mental life is nothing so epistemically transparent that any attempt to grasp it theoretically would *ipso facto* be successful. Being in a (mental) state is not fundamentally the same thing as having explicit epistemic access to this state.

This is seemingly contradicted by the case of epistemic self-consciousness, which has therefore, at least since Fichte's strategy for basing epistemology on self-consciousness, been considered an indication of an *idealistic transparency thesis*.[2] This thesis holds that we must be capable – in some paradigmatic cases – of knowing that we know something, since we could otherwise not presume that we are thinkers of thoughts. Anyone who makes a knowledge claim to the effect that they know they are conscious evidently knows *ipso facto* what they claim to know. In this case (the 'fact-act') one cannot separate the claim from its success, meaning that we can name a paradigmatic case of a mental state that coincides with its explicit epistemic self-access.

This by no means suggests, however, that when we are conscious we are always (or can always be) conscious of the fact that we are conscious. On the whole, we at best deal 'incidentally *(en parergo)*'[3] with our thought processes as such, as Aristotle put it. This does not rule out the maximal epistemic success, in which we not only know something (such as the fact that we are conscious) but also know that we know it (for example, by calling to mind the structure of knowledge with reference to the case of self-consciousness). The iterativity thesis (which states that it follows from 'S knows that p' that 'S knows that S knows that p') thus applies in some cases but does not describe any universal attribute of knowledge. At times, we not only know p but also that we know p. *This case must not be ignored, since one would then only be taking one side of realism into account. Realism is not only the assumption that we can be mistaken about the real but also an acknowledgement of the fact that, in paradigmatic cases, we grasp the real immediately.*

According to New Realism, these paradigmatic cases include the following structure. In epistemological investigations, we grasp self-consciousness as something that can iteratively capture itself. We can be conscious of the fact that we are conscious and thus articulate a knowledge claim that guarantees its own success from within. But this does not mean that self-consciousness is infallible. The object (consciousness) and its apprehension (self-consciousness) are not the same object, since consciousness extends further than our momentary insights into its existence. Self-consciousness thus (unlike first-order object-consciousness) belongs to a higher order. Not every consciousness is self-consciousness. Thus consciousness is not necessarily transparent for itself.

We grasp only a part of our own consciousness in the self-exploration of the mind. We know this from research in natural science and the humanities. However, contrary to what illusionism claims, this does not mean that our consciousness is the illusory user interface of our organism. Rather, one can treat this finding as a corroboration of mental realism; for we know that our consciousness extends further than our self-consciousness, which tells us something about our actually existing consciousness. This self-knowledge is a case of self-consciousness, which means that, on this issue, we can be sure of having grasped the circumstances as they are.

These circumstances include recognizing the indispensable reality of the phenomenal mind. It is not only that the real exists; it also shows itself. For us as minded beings, the way in which the real shows itself consists in the fact that we grasp its sense. Whatever is real is such-and-such; how the real is constitutes its sense. Therefore the real is not only *extensive* but always also *intensive*: it presents itself to us in the form of objective sensory data.[4]

Our sensory modalities are field senses, as it were: they consist in our being in contact with objects in a given field of sense. We do not need to establish this contact on a trial basis, since it already exists from the moment we can ask ourselves wherein it consists.[5] This follows from the phenomenon of indispensability, which can be illustrated using the following argument.

Let us suppose that the real were radically different from how it appears to us. This radical difference could, for example, consist in the fact that, for every element $a, b, c, \ldots, n$ that we can term an object, none of our descriptive attributions $F, G, H, \ldots, N$ apply. So if we think that a is F, it is actually the case that some b is H, for example. For if a were G but not F, the error could be corrected by undertaking something to move from the assumption that a is F to the assumption that a is G. One would have been mistaken. If we can be mistaken at all, then the real cannot be *radically* different from how it appears to us. A deception or mistake presupposes that one has recognized something correctly: one has grasped a but erroneously taken it for something that is F. So the real can be largely different from how it appears to us, but not radically different, otherwise nothing would appears to us at all.

Naturally one could attempt here to play off a metaphysical realism against an epistemological one by assuming that the real can be radically different from how it appears to us, without our ever being capable of establishing this. The real could be the complete other, as it were, something on which one could not even formulate justified speculations.

Yet this manoeuvre fails, because it entails an assumption about the phenomenal that distinguishes it from a complete other which cannot appear as such *ex hypothesi*. In this way, one presupposes that one has grasped the phenomenal as something from which something else (the real) can be radically different. One has thus grasped two-thirds of a relation 'pRr', which connects the phenomenal to the real. And what of the insight one wishes to express in this way? What and how does one know if one grasps the relation 'pRr', which possibly exists between the phenomenal and an entirely different real?

Since one can only refer to the real *de dicto* in this case (symbolize it with 'r'), but not make it an object of successful descriptions *de re*, 'r' should be represented as a kind of question mark: 'pR?' So there is a questionable relation between the phenomenal and something maximally unknowable. This relation itself is not fully transparent; we do not know its exact nature because one of the relata is essentially withdrawn from us. Yet this can lead us to be mistaken about the entire relation, since we have no reason to define it more precisely. One might think, for example, that the real is radically different from how it appears to us because illusionism is true. Then the relation would in fact exist between one part of the central nervous system and other parts of the same system. However, one could just as easily think that we might be brains in a vat, or take any other sceptical hypothesis at face value that describes a state of affairs in which the real is radically different from how it appears to us. Hence the relation 'pRr' is itself something real. Because we can be mistaken about the nature of the circumstances in which we are radically mistaken, we are in contact with the real. Yet this cannot mean it is so far away from us that we can only formulate speculations about it; rather, we can know under what conditions the real would be radically different from how it appears to us.

To the extent that the real is indeed different from how it appears to us, it presents itself to us in the form of a factual source of error. The idea of the radical otherness of the real is thwarted by the fact that it *nolens volens* postulates too many sources of error at once, and thus modifies the very concept of knowledge of the real with which it operates.

The real cannot be radically different from how it presents itself to us, then, because otherwise this circumstance would be impossible to articulate. That is why illusionists must make specific, empirically oriented suggestions in order to present the epistemic divergence of the phenomenal and the real as a (meta)physical affair. These suggestions conceal the fact that they are really sceptical hypotheses appearing in the guise of empirical research.

Empirical investigations of phenomenality by themselves do not lead to the supposed metaphysical insight that the real is different from how it appears to us; rather, it rightly teaches us to treat the conditions of appearance of the real as something that is itself real. On this basis, one can construct an argument from indispensability against epiphenomenalism indispensability.[6] Let N_1 and N_2 be two successively appearing complex neuronal states such that we can assign to N_1 a mental correlate M_1 and to N_2 a mental correlate M_2. Epiphenomenalism assumes that N_1 is the sufficient cause for N_2, meaning that the occurrence of M_1 does not make any causal contribution of its own either to the appearance of N_2 or M_2. However, the circumstances present themselves to us as follows: an impression of thirst in midsummer sends us to the refrigerator because we imagine the cold drink located there. Here the impression of thirst M_1 correlates with N_1, and let us say that the idea of the cold drink M_2 correlates with N_2. Epiphenomenalism has to assume that the impression of thirst and its neuronal correlate are not identical, otherwise the mental processes would automatically be causally potent, which would cause epiphenomenalism to evaporate. Consequently, it must deny that M_1 makes causal contributions to the change from N_1 to N_2. In this case, however, the causal chain appears to us in such a way that the impression of thirst is followed by the idea of the cold drink, which is the occasion to go to the refrigerator; this involves objects such as refrigerators and cold drinks, which are clearly not identical with neuronal correlates. If I imagine the cold drink because I know it is in the refrigerator, then the cold drink is an essential element of what unfolds as an action process. This would mean that, without the idea of the cold drink, no change from N_1 to N_2 would take place. If epiphenomenalism were true, it would be impossible for the idea of a cold drink to affect neuronal networks. It could not interact with them, since this would be a form of causal contribution ruled out by epiphenomenalism. In positing this, however, epiphenomenalism claims that, in this simple case, the real appears radically different from how it is.[7]

One can now postulate a causal architecture in which N_1 is accompanied by an impression of thirst leading to the idea of a cold drink, which in turn intervenes causally in the neuronal architecture. For this, one needs to expand the causal environment of the neuronal architecture, admittedly, and cannot assume that neuronal networks operate entirely autopoietically. The idea of a maximal autopoietic closure of the neuronal is phenomenologically implausible in any case and contradicts the simple fact that our nervous system is part of an organism that is embedded in an ecological niche. The central nervous system in a viable human organism does not grow independently of the fact that stem cells turn into specific cell forms – a process that cannot be explained in purely neurophysiological terms.

Empirically, then, this question cannot be resolved by observing the nervous system, since this already postulates *conceptually* in advance that one gives preference to epiphenomenalism. Since epiphenomenalism has the flaw of constituting a conceptually incoherent variant of illusionism, we are justified in rejecting neurocentrism (the claim that the mind is nothing but the brain) as an empirical hypothesis with recourse to the indispensability of the mind. We cannot have any reason to consider neurocentrism true; it verges on a sceptical hypothesis, which explains why some of its advocates literally view our brain as a brain in a vat – or, more precisely, as a nervous system that is trapped in an organism where it generates internal representations of an external world that is itself epistemically inaccessible.

Knowledge is a mental state. If S knows that p, then S is in an overall state which includes the fact of being connected to objects that form a factual structure (p). Every case of knowledge thus has a share in facticity. Thinking is a case of being, something that really exists.

In this context, Timothy Williamson has presented much discussed arguments for the view that we are 'cognitively homeless'.[8] He states that our mental life has no cognitive centre in the sense of a 'realm of phenomena in which nothing is hidden from us'.[9] To illustrate his overall argument against any form of idealistic transparentism, he explores the topos of supposedly self-authenticating phenomenal conditions. His example is a clear sensation of cold, C. Let α represent the existence of a clear sensation of cold C, which we experience over a particular space of time in our mental life. Williamson now formulates a condition of luminosity for clear sensations of cold and all other examples in which the existence of a phenomenon is epistemically accessible, such that we are in a position to know that α. A condition C, which can be fulfilled in our mental life, is *luminous* if the following applies:

(L [luminosity]) For every case α, if in α C obtains, then in α one is in a position to know that C obtains.[10]

This is a roundabout formulation of the idea that one is in a position to know that one is clearly cold because one is clearly cold. Williamson's argument against (L) now postulates a case of α at a point in time t_i. One can distinguish between this point and t_{i+1}, which is located a millisecond after t_i.

Here Williamson postulates an additional assumption on which he bases his counterargument. His additional assumption is that one only knows something if one is reliable in the respective matter. *Ex hypothesi*, one is pradigmatically reliable in a case of transparency in so far as one can call it to mind and then formulate a knowledge claim. Someone who is cold and formulates a knowledge claim to the effect that this is the case is making successful use of the luminosity of their mental life. If someone judges with appropriate certainty at t_1 that they are cold, they will not retract this a millisecond later – that is, at t_{i+1}. Therefore, if one knows at t_i that one is cold, it follows that one also knows this at t_{i+1}, from which it follows that one is cold at t_{i+1}. At some point one stops being cold, however, and then the false conclusion is drawn from (L) that, at a point in time t_n, when we are no longer cold, we must continue to be cold in order to be able to claim that we know we are cold.

The Achilles heel of this argument is the sudden introduction of a psychological criterion (certainty) into a conceptual discussion of the formal properties of the concept of knowledge. The fact that someone who is cold judges that they are cold does not mean that they will still be cold at a particular point in time after the known coldness, even if their justified factual judgement that they are cold is not retracted as soon as they cease to be cold. The point of the classic assumption of a self-authenticating phenomenality is precisely that it is defined at certain points over a span of time, and it is not a psychological bet on the continuation of the phenomenal condition that communicates itself.

What is more important is that Williamson's argument fails because he should not allow it to apply in analogous cases.[11] Let us suppose that my car is parked outside my front door. I have left it there and am now sitting at my desk, choosing this as an example of something I know. So I know at t_0, and presumably still at t_{0+1} (let the interval between them now be fifteen minutes), that my car is outside my front door. Let us imagine that my car is stolen under cover of darkness without my noticing it immediately. In this case, my mental state has changed without my knowledge, as at some point t_{0+n} I no longer know that my car is outside the front door because it has been stolen. This case is virtually paradigmatic for Williamson's view of knowledge, since it supports a wholly externalist construction that allows my mental states to vary without requiring this variation to be mentally transparent. Consequently, Williamson should not accept that I did not know the whereabouts of my car at t_0, even though I extend my certainty about this until t_{0+n} for the best reasons imaginable, since I had no cause to expect that my car might be stolen (even if it was obviously possible that it could, as this hypothetical case shows).

So, if we can at all know contingent propositions that change their truth value through modifications of the real situation, it is not clear why this should not apply to luminous propositions too. Externalism and reliabilism are not violated by this, since one finds the phenomenal, luminous state in which one is existing alongside other contingent circumstances. The only difference between a contingent external world proposition relating to my environment and a contingent internal world proposition characterizing my phenomenal state of information would be that the latter is luminous.

The luminosity of the phenomenal does not lend the progression of our knowledge claims any infallibility. It is therefore not a temporal psychological thesis about how we distribute certainties across our mental life but concerns only the time interval in which the phenomenal shows itself. The idealistic transparency thesis claims of this time interval that the existence of α is accompanied by the fact that it does not fundamentally elude being known. Williamson has not proved this thesis false, since he would then need to show that there are constitutive structures of the phenomenal that locate it beyond our access.

Notably, Williamson does not think that his argument against (L) is generalizable; thus, according to Williamson, there are luminous states.[12] As examples he names 'the Cartesian condition that one exists, or even that one thinks.'[13] In so doing, he overlooks that, in Descartes, *cogitare* includes types of phenomenal states that Williamson does not consider luminous. Furthermore, according to Descartes, existence is constitutively corporeal, which is often overlooked by leaving aside what Jens Rometsch has aptly termed the 'plurimodality of the *cogitare*'.[14]

According to Descartes the fact that thinkers are embodied is not a contingent circumstance that, in contrast to the circumstance that they exist, obtains in some cases and not in others. If Williamson exempts thinking from his argument against luminosity, he must then also exempt our corporeality as well as its phenomenal side, since the latter is a case of thinking and specifically the form of existence in which we feature as minded *beings*.[15] The price for disputing the luminosity of the phenomenal *sentire* while retaining it for the pure *intelligere* of our existence as thinkers is the resurrection of the mind in the machine. For now our thinking is divided into two kinds of modules: the sensuous and the intelligent activities of the mind, where the latter are not tied to the thinker's corporeality.

One especially conspicuous qualification of the generalizability of Williamson's argument follows from its self-application to epistemology. According to Williamson, entertaining the proposition that it is raining is luminous. If I entertain the proposition that it is raining, I can bring to mind the fact that I am entertaining the following proposition: I entertain the proposition that it is raining.

> If one is entertaining the proposition[16] that it is raining, then one is in a position to know that one is entertaining the proposition that it is raining. When one is entertaining a slightly different proposition *p*, one does not have a high degree of false belief that one is entertaining the proposition that it is raining; one has a high degree of true belief that one is entertaining *p*, since the belief derives its content from *p* itself. Thus the argument does not apply to examples in which one considers the condition only when it obtains. Such examples constitute a very minor limitation on the generality of the argument. In any case, we may conjecture that, for any condition *C*, if one can move gradually to cases in which *C* obtains from cases in which *C* does not obtain, while considering *C* throughout, then *C* is not luminous.[17]

Thus Williamson's *argument* turns into the admittedly not generalizable *conjecture* that there are no luminous conditions, which few people would deny – namely, only those who conclude from the idealistic transparency of certain states or processes that everything one can think is thus transparent.[18]

In addition, Williamson's concession is even grist for the mill of an absolute – that is, unrestricted – idealism in relation to the propositional. For if one can only entertain the proposition *p* when this state is luminous (since one would not otherwise entertain the proposition *p*, but rather another, such as *q*), then it applies to every judgeable *p* that its thinking apprehension is luminous. The entire space of the propositional is thus luminous in its judgeability if it is in the nature of judgement to be luminous, as Williamson assumes.

Indeed, the indispensability of the phenomenal should not be understood according to the model of self-authenticating states to the effect that we afford them the special epistemic privilege of making a precisely definable foundation for our further efforts towards knowledge. This is the valuable lesson afforded by Williamson's luminosity argument, meaning that the argument points in the right direction for reasons that are not entirely convincing. The manoeuvre employed here is not invalidated by Williamson's conjecture that phenomenal states are not luminous, because the upshot of this conjecture is that we have a self-authenticating access to the content of our judgements.

Thus the myth of the given is shifted from the phenomenal to the intelligible, which does not solve the problem; for now the content of our judgements suddenly becomes more transparent than it actually needs to be if we can be mistaken in our judgements themselves. In the act of judgement itself, however, we can at least be mistaken on a factual level, something that psychological literature has been insisting for centuries and has been shown in many different case studies by neuroscience, behavioural economics, cognitive science, and so on. To entertain the proposition p is not transparent: we can believe we are entertaining the proposition p while actually entertaining a different one, since our judgements and that which they judge are not identical.

At this point one could narrow the problem area further and assume that although we are fallible in our judging of facts that are not themselves judgements we make, this does not mean that our self-judgement as thinking beings is not luminous. Someone who judges that it is raining may then be mistaken as to whether it is raining, and also as to whether they judge that it is raining; yet someone who judges that they judge that it is raining cannot be mistaken as to whether they so much as judge at all. But here one must be careful! For we do not judge that we judge when we judge that we judge that it is raining. Judgements about judgements as such differ significantly from judgements about judgements about the rain.

Making the concept of judgement as such the object of a judgement does not mean that one has all possible judgements in view in some vague fashion. What distinguishes judgements from one another, what makes them specific, is their content. The content of a judgement is in turn determined, in part, by the character of the real with which it deals. One does not make the same judgement that it is raining both when it is raining and when it is not raining; in one case one judges correctly, in the other incorrectly. It cannot be the same judgement. Factual judgements cannot change their truth value; rather, they are individuated by it and by the sense whereby they present their truth value to the thinker.

Here we might recall that the content of the two judgements that it is raining must surely be the same on some level, since in both cases one is imagining what the real is like by going through a case of rain in one's mind. But this is to overlook the factual implementation of the judgement in the mental life of actually existing thinkers. For actually existing thinkers are not embodied by chance; rather, they judge then and there that it is raining. Their judgement occurs in an imprecisely determined place whose contours are given by the human form of life. What occurs for me here and now concerns one section of the real. The framework in which I encounter real things is itself something real, as every insight into what is the case itself belongs to the scene it apprehends.[19]

There is no abstract, logical self that judges from nowhere when it judges that it is raining. A logical self could not take up contact with the rain that it feels. All judgements therefore remain tied to an egocentric index, for it is essential to them that they are made by someone whose reality must be taken into account if one wishes to understand the full content of a judgement.[20]

A judgement that is correct and a judgement that is incorrect cannot have the same full content. For one of the things that individuates content is that there are conditions for someone to judge that go far beyond what is captured by a logical snapshot that paradigmatically reduces judgements to the formula that a subject S claims to know p.

In this sense, I agree with Sebastian Rödl who has argued that it is an erroneous branch of contemporary epistemology to believe that one is making progress by analysing the formula 'S knows that p'.[21] The factual conditions of a knowledge claim include not only that a subject must fulfil formal conditions discovered a priori in the mode of conceptual analysis. Nor does it help to revamp this questionable procedure through surveys or linguistics, since the factual conditions under which a person knows something cannot be ascertained by asking people when they hold the opinion that knowledge can be ascribed. In language use, a statistical clean-up of word usage will not provide any insight into what is really happening when someone judges that it is raining, as long as one does not take into account that we, as judging persons, are a constitutive part of every scene that we judge to be thus and so. Knowledge claims do not judge the real from the outside, as there is nothing outside the real. There is no need for us to creep up on the real and ensure through epistemological reflections that we have come sufficiently close to it to give a reliable report on what is the case with an acceptable degree of certainty.

Some quantum theorists speculate about viewing the indispensability of the mind as the source of causality, meaning that we can do substantive ontological justice to the fact that we are causally embedded in perception. Along these lines, Carlo Rovelli has recently suggested reconstructing the time's arrow of entropy as a consequence of our actually existing standpoint. This assumption is based on the correct insight that we must take our occurrence in the universe into consideration as a factor when explaining our knowledge claims.

We observe the universe from within, interacting with a minuscule portion of the innumerable variables of the cosmos. What we see is a blurred image. This blurring suggests that the dynamic of the universe with which we interact is governed by entropy, which measures the amount of blurring. It measures something that relates to us more than to the cosmos.[22]

Mental realism takes part of this finding seriously. Our mental states are irreducibly part of the real and make a decisive causal contribution. If Rovelli is right, this contribution extends so far that the mental is the decisive source of causality. In Rovelli's model, causality is the way in which the universe appears to us in space and time, which is shaped by the fact that it is something special that the universe appears to us as something about which we can make fallible knowledge claims. Of course, as a good naturalist, he argues that our individuality consists in the fact that our central nervous system records traces of the past in order to design projects for an uncertain future through predictions. From this perspective, the asymmetry of time stems from the fact that past things are what heat up our nerve pathways, thus leaving thermically coded traces, which does not yet apply to future things. This does not solve the problem, however, since the asymmetry of time is projected onto causal processes in the universe that, according to Rovelli, are causal only because they appear in our perspective as something particular. He therefore measures time by our ignorance, as he identifies the causality connected to time with indexicality and the latter with blurring.

Let us examine his argumentation more closely, since it approaches mental realism but ultimately falls prey to a confusion of realism and naturalism.[23] Rovelli adopts the widespread notion that the direction of time's arrow can be explained via entropy. For only thermodynamics describes irreversible processes that run in one direction but cannot be explained in reverse using the same equations. At the fundamental level of quantum mechanics, on the other hand, one cannot speak of any time's arrow, since all processes are structurally isomorphic – that is, reversibly explicable. To illustrate an increase in entropy, Rovelli chooses the example of a stack of cards. If we find a stack of cards ordered in such a way that the first twenty-six cards of a standard pack are red and the second half black, we assume that this is an unusual, ordered state. If we begin to shuffle the cards, a repetition of this ordered state is far more unlikely than the appearance of a different order.

Thermodynamic processes follow this pattern, in that they turn a state that is specially ordered relative to a subsequent state into a state that is more probable relative to this order. The order that strikes us as something special – such as that of colours – is only unusual in the eye of the beholder, as one can also measure the existing stack according to other criteria (such as the pictures). Thus the increase in entropy depends on what criteria are used to measure order, which brings the observer and hence our perspective into play.

That is why Rovelli considers this structure an effect of our perspective – which is not an illusion, however, but actually the decisive causal contribution of the mental. On our scale of observation, we blur the conditions of nature in such a way that a temporal, egocentrically indexed order results.

Rovelli approaches this with a remarkable conceptual opposition. On the one hand we find nature, characterized by neither any order nor any disorder. On the other hand, there is us, with our expectations and causal contributions to the blurring of things. In nature, it is no surprise that something like an ordered (from our perspective) initial state exists. For, in nature no state is more or less special, as there are only singularities here. Rovelli argues that a strict nominalism obtains on this level: 'If we think about it carefully, every configuration is particular, *every configuration is singular*, if we look at all of its details, since every configuration always has something about it that characterizes it in a unique way.'[24] On the level describable via quantum mechanics, there are only facts; Rovelli asserts that these always have the form of events, which are completely singular and create a granular space–time that we experience as a continuous structure because, at the mesoscopic level, the partial indeterminacy of the field of sense of quanta has split up into the appearance of determinate conditions.

Rovelli distinguishes our perspective from this strictly nominalist level. In order to classify something as a specially ordered configuration relative to a subsequent state, one must omit certain details. We do not characterize the totality of events at play when a stack of cards appears before our eyes. Our sensory modalities select information from our surroundings in such a way that we can consciously apprehend a selection fulfilling criteria of order/disorder by which we can orient our behaviour. This reflects our ecological adaptation, which must be considered at the explanatory level of the causal roots of perceptions, otherwise one is incapable of taking the causal factor of perception epistemically into account. This introduces the much discussed distinction between sensation and perception, which shifts the causal problem to the mental domain.[25] For if sensations can be causally explained, while perceptions are located in the space of reasons as epistemic states, the problem that arises here, if not earlier, is how the space of the causal is connected to the space of reasons in the mental. The causal is embedded differently in Rovelli's model, as it is an effect of our actually existing perspective. Our perspective consists in the fact that the real appears to us in a way that presupposes our preference for certain orders. The patterns we prefer, because they are conducive to survival, justify the impression that the real is temporally ordered even though there is no aperspectival structure outside of our perspective that corresponds to this impression. Thus time's arrow turns out not as an illusion but as a trait of our actually existing perspective.[26] This position keeps the non-human universe far away from temporality. Entropy is a predictive instrument of humans, not an insight into facts.

However, Rovelli answers the following question in a strikingly inadequate way. If the universe displays a fundamentally atemporal, event-nominalist layer that is blurred on the meso-level accessible to humans, how can we have access to the fundamental level? Rovelli's answer entangles itself in an incoherent epistemology, as the following passage shows:

> We are not even clear about what it means to 'understand'. We see the world and we describe it: we give it an order. We know little of the actual relation between what we see of the world and the world itself. We know that we are myopic. We barely see just a tiny window of the vast electromagnetic spectrum emitted by things. We do not see the atomic structure of matter, nor the curvature of space. We see a coherent world that we extrapolate from our interaction with the universe, organized in simplistic terms that our devastatingly stupid brain is capable of handling. We think of the world in terms of stones, mountains, clouds and people, and this is 'the world for us'. About the world independent of us we know a good deal, without knowing how much this good deal is.[27]

What Rovelli is suggesting here is familiar, in different variations, from Hegel's *Phenomenology of Spirit*, where it was already refuted. It is not surprising that Rovelli, as an advocate of a naturalist perspective, refers to our thinking as an 'instrument' – a hopeless position.[28] For now a chasm opens up between the world for us and the world as such, a chasm that Rovelli, following the model of 'force and reason', spreads across two worlds that are causally embedded in each other, though the causality is only a trait of our perspective. This means the only world existing as such is that of absolute singularities, though it appears temporally ordered from the standpoint of humans.

But what of the order postulated by this dualism? Is the real as such on this side of the distinction between order and disorder that inheres in our perspective? If this were the case, we could not rule out the possibility that our scientific theorizing, which postulates general structures (laws, forces, properties of elementary particles) is a 'collective delirium'.[29]

This ontological dualism is repeated by Rovelli in the mental realm, for he views reason as an instrument for the self-regulation of our 'living and burning emotions'.[30]

> These are the substances of which we are made. They propel us and drag us back, and we cloak them with fine words. They compel us to act. And something of them always escapes from the order of our discourses, since we know that, in the end, every attempt to impose order leaves something outside the frame.[31]

This position is shattered by an epistemological incoherence based on the notion that the world as such differs from the world for us, and that this distinction is modelled on the quantum-theoretical measuring problem, which gives it the veneer of naturalist legitimacy. It is not surprising that Rovelli reaches the following conclusion: 'We know little of the actual relation between what we see of the world and the world itself.'[32] For he understands our knowledge as the projection of order onto a world that lacks the very order we think we are grasping from our standpoint. That is why Rovelli's investigation collapses under the naturalistic pressure it generates itself: he understands the real only as the cognitively and epistemically unprocessable remainder of a world as such. The world finds expression in our mental apparatus in a literally thermodynamic form, because our affective life is no more than the impression made on our nervous system by the external world.

A genuine mental realism moves between the Scylla of a *reductive, ultimately eliminative physicalism* and the Charybdis of a *soft or liberal naturalism* that operates with a broader concept of the experiential sciences.[33] Soft naturalism is only seemingly a coherent alternative to the metaphysically overly ambitious identity theory, which identifies everything mental with natural, non-mental processes that we can at best contingently grasp more or less adequately. It buys the semblance of plausibility by viewing the mental not as unreal, but rather as something that can be examined in the medium of empirical sciences, which

> ultimately test their theories with reference to perceptions, observation sentences and empirical experiments. In this sense, for example, empirical animal research or cognitive psychology are experiential sciences. However, these sciences deal with beings that have a mind, that is, mental states and processes, and in some cases also develop forms of social organization. Mental abilities and social relationships extend deep into the animal kingdom, which is usually viewed as part of nature.[34]

Yet this manoeuvre is deceptive, since it provides no information about the matter of where the soft naturalist acquires their knowledge of the mental. Does the soft naturalist know that mind exists because they have set up a fallible theory based on perceptions, observation sentences and empirical experiments? If this were the case, what experiential science teaches them that they must proceed in this fashion, as it is the only way to accumulate systematic, scientific knowledge about the real?

The naturalist *proton pseudos* conceptually precedes this operation. It consists in the assumption that we become acquainted with the mental through observation data and subsequently introject it in the context of our growth into human groups.[35] But we cannot learn the mental by perceiving it in others, in the form of behaviour that we interpret as mentally controlled, without already knowing ourselves from the inside. Humans do not gain access to an articulated language community by conceiving theories of the mental and thus finding mental patterns in themselves. Our theoretical work comes much later than our development of an access to ourselves as minded beings. We know our own states first of all, and we quickly learn to identify elements of our inner life with objects of a non-egological world. There are prehistoric, evolutionary preconditions for this without which we would not manage to identify those types of objects that we need in order to adapt to our ecological niche. Yet the pre-historic, evolutionary preconditions do not include becoming acquainted with ourselves indirectly via the inner life of others, which we disclose for ourselves in the form of proto-scientific hypotheses.

In short, naturalism overgeneralizes a model of scientific knowledge acquisition that rests on a simplified epistemology and then identifies this overly simplified model of scientific knowledge acquisition with this the cognitive operating system of *Homo sapiens*. Yet this model of our mental life is an epistemologically hopeless form of modern mythology; it reconstructs the entire cultural development of humanity, without any empirical support, as a form of natural-scientific trial and error process of adapting our species to its environment.[36]

Our engagement with the thought models of Rovelli and others should have shown in exemplary fashion that a naturalist view of the mental is, on the one hand, superior to both naïve subjective idealism and naïve realism in one crucial respect, since it at least permits a causal integration of the mental into the real. However, it does not manage to explain how we can know anything about the 'external' or 'internal' things in themselves – to say nothing of the self-referential knowledge of our own mindedness.

FOS offers a model of the real that allows us to reserve space for the genuine indispensability and intelligibility of the mind. For the idea of a worldview is consistently shelved. This puts paid to the grand narrative of hard and soft naturalism, which holds that there is a base layer of the all-encompassing universe consisting of non-mental, mindless primordial material that is restructured over billions of years in order to produce, at the edge of a galaxy, organic matter that, because of local properties of our planet and over millions of years of evolution, produces knowing life that can retroactively consider this genealogy. This grand narrative is already foiled by the fact that it is ignorant of the problem of physical time and thus underlays the entire universe with a timeline that proceeds linearly in one direction from the moment of the Big Bang. But we have long since discovered that there is no encompassing chronology of the universe as a whole. At best, the grand narrative of naturalism is a description of our perspective on our own genesis, which Rovelli at least takes into account, unlike most naturalists. Yet this, even including state of the art knowledge in physics, is not a suitable description of the universe and our position in it, since there is no physical theory that adequately takes our perspective on the universe into account. To the extent that we find room in physics for ourselves, this science remains constitutively distinguishable from the metaphysical presumption that we could ever develop a complete panorama of the universe that allows us to comprehend a causally closed universe whose events could be entered in a singular timeline. Such a phantasmagoria of the physicist as a potential Laplacian demon has been refuted at least since the beginning of the previous century.[37]

Whatever one's position on the unity and disunity of the sciences, and thus the unity and disunity of the nature observed by those sciences, it remains the case that the mind is indispensable in any explanation of the universe. We are fundamentally unable to approach our own mindedness empirically in the sense that, on the basis of experiential data, we develop models in which we appear to ourselves for the first time as minded. For the gathering of experiential data is already an indication of our mindedness, which is thus relied upon in a pre-theoretical fashion.

We find ourselves as minded beings. This does not mean that we are infallible regarding the question of what mind is. Because mind is something real, we are capable of being mistaken about our own mindedness. Self-delusion is a specific possibility for the mind. Naturalism, be it hard- or soft-boiled, is a form of self-delusion because it can consider the mind real only in so far as it identifies it with something that is not minded, such as an arrangement of elementary particles; self-referential quantum information; a neuronal system; an emergent property of an organism; some previously unknown material-energetic causal architecture in the central nervous system; an introjected observation of others' behaviour; and so on. In this way, the indispensability of mind is disputed, which means *ex hypothesi* that naturalism is a form of self-delusion. If it tries to accommodate the indispensability of the mind into its model-construction, it fails to pay due respect to mind's independence from the type of explanation and hypothesis generation suitable in contexts where we are dealing with mindless parts of nature.

§8

The Lifeworld of Ontology of Fields of Sense

It should come as no surprise that FOS's sustained critique of naturalism can take up a central insight of Husserl's, one connected to the term 'lifeworld'. In *The Crisis of European Sciences*, Husserl famously points out that modern physics since Galileo has initiated processes of technicization that undertake 'the surreptitious substitution of the mathematically sub-structed world of idealities for the only real world, the one that is actually given through perception, that is ever experienced and experienceable – our everyday lifeworld. This substitution was promptly passed on to his successors, the physicists of all the succeeding centuries.'[1] According to Husserl, this idealization is based on the 'free, imaginative variation [*Umphantasieren*] of the world'.[2] It is sometimes overlooked that Husserl does not proceed directly from his critique of science to transcendental idealism but initially distinguishes between 'idealized nature' and 'presci-entifically intuited nature'.[3] One might suppose that FOS can, with a grain of salt, be located within this phenomenological horizon, since Husserl's phenomenology does actually start with an indispensability thesis and provides space for a pre-scientifically given nature, meaning that he does not surrender nature to naturalism from the outset.

However, Husserl goes on to conceive the lifeworld in a theoretically prejudiced way by imagining it on the model of inductive explanation: 'All life rests upon prediction or, as we can say, upon induction. In the most primitive way, even the ontic certainty of any straightforward experience is inductive.'[4] The reason for this thesis, he states, is that the things we see are 'always already more than what we "really and actually" see of them.'[5]

This sounds far more convincing *prima facie* than at second glance, however. Husserl is relying on the familiar idea that, when we perceive things, we only ever perceive the side or those aspects that are immediately accessible to us by virtue of our spatiotemporal position.[6] I see the front of my computer but know that it has a back too, so I expect to see that back when I turn it around. Every perception has many facets that I am not perceiving at a given moment but would perceive under altered conditions. 'On this hinges the possibility of indefinitely many percepts of the same object, all differing in content.'[7] The more I know about a given object of perception, the more reliable my inductive predictions. Since I know my living room, I can predict which book on the bookshelf will become visible next if I move along it from left to right, and so forth.

This forms the basis of Husserl's theory of science in the *Crisis*; for, according to Husserl, science is merely a continuation of the method of our everyday perception-based knowledge acquisition, for which we weave scientific models that he describes as a 'garb of ideas'.[8] For Husserl, then, there is no fundamental divide between lifeworld and science, since the latter is an expansion of the methods we have rehearsed in our lifeworld, 'and in this way we obtain possibilities of predicting concrete occurrences in the intuitively given lifeworld, occurrences which are not yet or no longer actually given. And this kind of prediction infinitely surpasses the accomplishment of everyday prediction.'[9] Husserl makes the lifeworld the foundation of meaning in science by describing it – despite himself – as proto-scientific. Husserl's strategy of reconciling lifeworld and science is circular, as he already bases the lifeworld on the model of science, meaning that the latter can then be placed in a tolerable continuum to the rest of our knowledge. Husserl installs the idea of science in our mental apparatus, then brings it out when the question of whether science endangers our everyday knowledge arises.

His understanding of our pre-theoretical experience is an extension of his theory of science into our perceptual apparatus in which he caters to the modern scientistic misconception that, even under everyday operating conditions, we formulate hypotheses at the perceptual level about the sequence of events and orient our lives towards them.[10] The situation is probably even more problematic, since, for Husserl, our everyday conditions already result from proto-scientific activity, meaning that the European 'homeworld' is irreconcilably isolated from the 'primitive' because of its historical genealogy.

Thus Husserl, like Heidegger, whose being-in-the-world in *Being and Time* takes up the topic of the lifeworld, faces the difficulty that he is not characterizing a universal structure of humanity but a local experience of the real that is tailored to scientific objectification from the outset. This raises the problem of how to understand the so-called primitive, to whom Husserl ascribes a different form of lifeworld and Heidegger a different form of Dasein.[11]

And we Europeans, who have grown up in our de-deified world: are we entitled to view ourselves as the human norm, not an abnormal case? What is the core of all world apperceptions that enables mutual understanding and shared world, as well as the understanding of the mythical and everything else? How does the mythical differ from the non-mythical in the homeworld? – Is it necessary to differentiate here? Is there not, for people of the homeworld, necessarily a *core* that is *presupposed by the mythical* in all apperceptions, even in every concrete apperception, and belongs to it because it is concrete?[12]

The difficulty of an historically, anthropologically and ethically untenable Eurocentrism that is inherent in Husserl's concept of lifeworld is secondary here. Nonetheless, one can use it to point out a systematic problem that emerges in social philosophical as the problem of the other but is located in a deeper layer of the argumentation. For Husserl's fantasy of a 'homeworld' belonging to Europeans, who are somehow meant to be especially keen on science, is based on a mistaken self-image: Husserl considers perception a form of induction because he keeps the subject distant from the real, and must therefore anchor it once again in the real via synthetic manoeuvres from within the internal world of the transcendental Ego. He compensates for the accompanying logical-semantic alienation with the fiction of the homeworld, whereby the subjects, which are meant to be transcendentally isolated, are given a common ground, the lifeworld.

The logical-semantic alienation that Husserl goes through in countless variations – displaying his irresolvable ambivalence about the realism/idealism question – comes from the following argument, which can be referred to summarily as the *phenomenological argument*.[13] An 'object [*Ding*] here is an object of conscious perception, paradigmatically some philosophical example such as an apple, table, tree or house.[14]

(1)   One can never perceive a whole object.
(2)   If I perceive an object, I am directly perceiving only one side of the object.
(3)   The perception of one side of the objects hides other sides of the object (adumbration theorem).
(4)   Perceptual judgements refer to what one directly perceives.
(K)   Perceptual judgements never refer to whole objects.[15]

The phenomenological argument has the theoretical merit of describing fallibility as well as the learning behaviour that accompanies perception. We can misclassify things and learn something about the environment with which we causally interact because we never grasp any one object in its entirety. Each object can still be observed from other perspectives, potentially leading to other judgements that modify our expectations. In this way one can introduce a 'scale of adequacy':[16] the partial acts of an overall synthetic perceptual act can be improved, so that the misleading components of a successful perception are progressively corrected.

However, this poses the problem of how to amend misleading partial aspects of a successful perception without directly perceiving the object that constitutes the norm for success. If the object emerges from partial acts like a mosaic, but I have no access to the original that is not mosaic-like, I cannot judge the parts of the perceptual act based on a case of success.

Strictly speaking, the phenomenological argument quickly slides into an unfounded scepticism that is already implicit in the first premise, which is therefore incoherent, albeit not obviously. The premise is based on the idea that one perceives not an object but a side of an object. Let us refer to this generally as a *facet*, which is intended to cover not only the visual modality but all sensory modalities, since each modality represents objects in a certain way. If we never directly grasp an object, but only facets thereof, then the concept of perception has two parts. On the one hand, it is asserted that a whole object – the table – is an object of perception. On the other hand, it is assumed that we cannot directly perceive this whole object but must work it out inductively. Here the basis for a corresponding inductively grounded perceptual judgement is the direct apprehension of a facet (which Husserl himself does not officially consider perception). Therefore each perceptual judgement contains a hidden inference based on one or more facets about an object whose facets we directly grasp. Against this background, Husserl ultimately rejects the idea that the object of perception is 'actually given' as a 'pretension'.[17] To oppose the form of direct realism that he has in mind and expressly rejects, he adduces the following argument: 'If percepts were always the actual, genuine self-presentations of objects that they pretend to be, there could only be a single percept for each object, since its peculiar essence would be exhausted in such self-presentation.'[18] The Achilles heel of this model is that the facets are *prima vista* objects that we perceive. The surface of my desk that faces me is itself an object that has a back side. So if I examine the surface of my desk facing me, which is supposed to be a facet, only a little more closely, I notice that it is not a facet but an object in an object, one of 'the thing's parts',[19] as Husserl concedes. Then, *ex hypothesi*, I cannot have direct access to it, which means I need a surrogate for the desk side facing me that can fulfil the theoretical function of a facet. This surrogate must be directly given.

This leads to the distinction between the *object* and the *content* [*Gehalt*] of the perception.[20] The object of perception is the thing, the content is the facet. To avoid the problem of a vicious infinite regress, which is a risk if I continue introducing new object that keep me far away from the original object, and whereby I in turn remain cut off from further facets that transpire upon closer inspection to be even more objects, it makes sense to treat content not as a thing but as something categorially different.[21]

In this way, the idea of a specific sphere of mental contents arises, the idea of representations. These can be distinguished from object by the fact that they are subject to veridic normativity: contents show conditions of correctness, as they are either true or not. They present things to us in a certain way that can be assessed as to its veracity or falsity. Things are as they are, and the contents present them correctly or incorrectly. Things are not subject to any normativity, but the contents are. The content are fallible but the things are not, and so on.[22]

But now one can no longer claim that we perceive sides of object; now what one perceives can only be the matter itself. But if one perceives objects directly in the medium of content, because content is not a screen or object that stands between us and the object of perception, one no longer understands how one can still be fallible in this way. Either perception is the name for a case of success; then the direct perception of an object (in the medium of contents) is not fallible, however 'misleading' the individual contents may be. Or perception is fallible, and thus does not yet mark a case of success. Then, because of the contents, one would have to be open to the question of what one is actually perceiving, having abandoned the idea of perceiving an object directly. If I perceive my laptop directly (in the medium of contents, for example, viewed from here), there is no room for meaningful doubts as to what I am perceiving. I have left fallibility behind in favour of the perception of the real.[23]

The object is that which one perceives in a particular way – that is, such-and-such. Might there not be a distance between the object and the way in which one perceives it, such that the latter is the source of fallibility? The distance would then consist in the form of the medium, which is also at play in case of success.

This may appear attractive, but it has the resultant problem that one now wishes to know what relation can actually obtain between object and content. In an incorrect perceptual judgement, the situation must be given that an object O is grasped in a partially incorrect way $S^{\#}$. In a correct perceptual judgement, however, O and $S^{!}$ fit together. Yet how does the presumed agreement or non-agreement between T and S come about?[24] Here one cannot insist that this is ensured by causal processes, since these are supposed to exist between things, but not between things and mental representations. If the mental representations were identical with some things (neuronal states) or other, they would be things that stand between the things we perceive and the things we are, which would trigger a vicious infinite regress. Consequently the mental representations seem to belong to a non-causal special sphere distinguished by its intrinsic normativity. Yet this does not take us any further, since we have no concept that enables us to understand how the causal texture of things can display any signature in the logical space of reasons or the realm of representations.

Here the concept of induction does not deliver what it promises. If a single case of an insight into the real is insufficient to make contact with non-mental objects, we cannot even begin with induction. Rather, the mental starts to lead a radical life of its own that can no longer be sure of any contact with an environment that it originally, in the 'natural attitude', presumed to perceive. Thus the phenomenological argument quickly leads to scepticism, because it claims from the outset that we cannot really perceive objects because, already at the level of our sensory interaction with the real, we put together hypotheses that are a decisive step too far away from the causal architecture of the universe.

Wolfgang Detel articulates and accepts this sceptical consequence in a remarkably clear manner, taking it not as reason for a *reductio ad absurdum*, but rather grist for the mill of a soft naturalism. He surely suspects the difficulties this causes when he states at the beginning of his argumentation: 'Representations have the strange, even mysterious property of being correct-or-incorrect, fulfilled-or-not-fulfilled, true-or-false.'[25] It is almost bizarre that Detel's argumentation directed at the knowability of God boils down to the sceptical 'position' of a '*Kantian physicalism*'.[26] This consists in treating the following banality, which Detel terms 'Assumption (3)', as an – at best – well-grounded hypothesis: 'The external world consists of structured elements (states, events and objects) with specific properties.'[27]

> Assumption (3) is highly plausible as the best explanation for a number of important observable phenomena, and yet it constitutes a blueprint for the mysterious process in which we catch 'sight' of transcendence at the limits of our thinking and simultaneously comprehend its fundamental unknowability. . . . If we view religious language as a form of poetic effort which expressly concedes that we fundamentally cannot know anything about transcendence, but attempts to orient us towards transcendence with imperfect images, then we can accept religious language as an expression of religiosity without God.[28]

This unnecessary slide into transcendence is a consequence of a misguided theory of perception that fits out our mind with mental representations that must not belong to the world, since the world is understood as a causal arrangement of things in which there is no place for a difference between truth values.[29] As a whole, this is the result of taking the assumption *ad absurdum* that we do not perceive things but only some form of representatives, whether located within or without the mind.

Mental realism rejects this modelling in favour of pre-theoretical experience that can be understood with recourse to that other which, contrary to Husserl and Heidegger, can no longer be understood as 'primitive' or 'mythical'.[30] This other element is not really some other thing or person, but rather the position in which we find ourselves; for this position is not that of a worldview in which all objects belong to a universal horizon. Rather, the opposite is the case: our pre-theoretical experience is radically plural. We stand at interfaces of indefinitely many fields of sense whose overlapping constitutes the situation we name as soon as we objectify elements of our experience. Yet our experience is and always remains partially immaterial, however precisely we might grasp a state of affairs through concrete characterization invoking material parts of our experience.

It follows from the functional ontological difference of FOS that some sense remains unarticulated in every position in which objects exist, meaning that not everything that exists can ever become an object.[31] This does not mean that there is a precisely definable layer of immaterial reality. It is not as if reality consisted of two halves – the material objects on the one hand and the immaterial on the other hand – a type of dualism which is already ruled out by the no-world-view, whose negative ontological verdict, I repeat, states that reality cannot be thought as a total object.

The rejection of the adumbration theorem is one way of accessing a neo-realist paradigm for the theory of perception. According to this novel paradigm, the central concept of the theory of perception is not adumbration but *irradiation*. This is connected to the following idea that our perceptual states are causally embedded, in the sense that we are situated in the same (physically explicable) field as the perceived objects. The sun is not located somewhere in the sky or in the middle of our solar system, from where it sends photons before they stimulate our nerve endings at some moment. Locating the sun 'up there' or 'in the middle of our solar system' is an anthropomorphic projection – that is (in our context), a theoretical construction to explain the structure of the realm of sensory appearances. The sensuous semblance of the sun has a particular structure; let us call it *the phenomenal structure*. Part of the phenomenal structure of the sun and other objects in the visual field of human perception is that objects appear smaller to us than they are. We can seemingly cover the sun (or a particular region thereof) with our hand in our perceptual field, which is not the case with the sun (or the respective region) in itself.

However, this should not induce us to split the sun into two objects, a sun for us (appearance/content) and a sun as such (the object). This time-honoured strategy usually boils down to introducing a representation of the sun located in our mind (or brain). According to this model, our imagination is essentially involved at the level of the perceptual act because it generates an internal schema of the sun. One then explains the variation in the sun's appearance as a variation in the sun schema, such that it becomes possible to distinguish between the *psychological* order of the sequence of mental images and the *causal* order of objects with which the mental order is correlated.[32]

However, this model fails on account of the present case of the sun and its appearance under terrestrial conditions. For if I cover what I see in the sky with the palm of my hand, this is not a process 'in my mind' or 'in my brain', which would ultimately mean shifting the entire lifeworld to the mental realm. In this respect, Campbell and Cassam are right in their analysis that a particular interpretation of early modern science in the wake of Galileo and Descartes resulted in perceived things being gradually pushed into our heads.[33]

However, this model which reduces the reality aspect of perception to the objects leads to countless frequently rehearsed paradoxes of mental representationalism. On the level of abstraction where we are located, it makes no difference whether one views the mental representations as causal or non-causal. If one takes them as causal, this leads to storing the real in one's brain; if one defines them as normative – that is, non-causal – one ends up in a deontological dualism that places is and ought in opposition in our perception, without being able to explain how the resulting divide can be ontologically closed.

To understand mental representations normatively – that is, non-causally – is to individuate them via conditions of correctness that cannot be reduced to a mental representation as a change in a subject's state being causally triggered. The fact that I am in a particular state that comes about through my environment or through internal organic processes does not, of course, mean that I represent something in my mind. One might read mental states as indications of the existence of a cause or a causal complex, but this does not mean that every environmental trace in my organic system is a representation in the same sense as a conscious mental image that I use to relate to something in the form of a knowledge claim.

The main problem of a deontological model is that it introduces a dualism between the way in which the real appears to us on the one hand and the real world on the other, establishing two irreconcilable conceptual orders: the logical space of causes and the logical space of reasons.[34] The way in which we present the real is supposed to differ from the real in that it is subject to norms (such as logical laws or systems of rules of inference). The idea here is draw a distinction between the normative and the purely nomic, where the normative is that which can deviate from a norm whereas the nomic is that which confirms the patterns to which it is subject in virtue of actually conforming to them.

Views of this form can draw on the *corpus kantianum*. In a highly consequential passage in his *Groundwork of the Metaphysics of Morals*, Kant distinguishes between reasons and causes in order to distance our mental apparatus from the causal order.

> Everything in nature works in accordance with laws. Only a rational being has the capacity to act in accordance with the *representation* of laws, that is, in accordance with principles, or has a *will*. Since reason is required for the derivation of actions from laws, the will is nothing other than practical reason. If reason infallibly determines the will, the actions of such a being that are cognized as objectively necessary are also subjectively necessary, that is, the will is a capacity to choose *only that* which reason independently of inclination cognizes as practically necessary, that is, as good. . . . Practical *good*, however, is that which determines the will by means of representations of reason, hence not by subjective causes but objectively, that is, from grounds that are valid for every rational being as such.[35]

Kant thus repeats the dualistic manoeuvre of his theoretical philosophy on the level of his philosophy of action. Practical reason occupies the space opened by the fact that our notions of the causal course of the world do not themselves belong to the causal course of the world, meaning that Kant establishes a separate domain that can be accessed by thinking. Within the context of our present discussion, one can rely on Kant's notion that we also have access to a domain of inner sense which contains the appearances of the sun and the palm of my hand, yet neglects to explain what exact causal contribution the sun as such makes to its variation in the perceptual field, since this very explanation is epistemically unattainable. We cannot compare 'the sun', as it would be itself with its appearances to our mind, as we can only think the sun as a pure object without therefore grasping its essence. Kant moved the appearances too far away from the things in themselves to view the latter as objects of a suitable *objective phenomenology* that treats the objects itself as a phenomenal element of the causal order.[36]

It should come as no surprise that the neutral realism of FOS is operative on the level of the theory of perception and blocks the shifting of appearances to the mind from the outset. Once the sun has entered consciousness, it is kept prisoner there. In the context of the theory of perception, then, mental realism eliminates the unnecessary third object that pushes itself between the sun itself and my visual apprehension of the sun.[37] There is quite simply no such representation, either in the causal or in the psychological order. Rather, perception is a binary relation that mediates between the perceptual conditions and the percipient. The mediation is perception itself, which hence does not, as a mental interface, constitute an object that stands between mind and world and helps the former to represent the latter.[38]

We thus perceive things in themselves without the aid of mental representations. Our achievement in the act of perception consists in the fact that we must stand in the binary relation of perception to a perceptual object. This binary relation entails many causal systems, including electromagnetic fields and the subsystems of our organism, that are capable of reading causally coded information in the form of sensory systems. For humans, the visual information that the sun has this and that property has a particular form that we explain, among other things, via the structure of our sensory equipment. There is no conscious perception in humans without the causally relevant presence of a biological system, which does not mean that our presence in the universe creates objects of a new kind (mental representations) which can never be compared 'directly' to objects that would belong to the 'bedrock of extra-mental reality'.[39]

To perceive thus means to be in contact with how things really are.[40] Our mode of contact has a particular form: the form of perception. This form includes what one might term an 'impression', provided one does not take impressions for something that represents things. My impression of the sun arises through the fact that I receive information from my causal position in the solar system, which presupposes a functioning cortex, among other things. This is not sufficient for the conscious perception of a human who is capable of survival, however, since we humans happen to be not brains in vats but complex systems in which a multitude of subsystems cooperate. Our perception is thoroughly embodied.[41]

In FOS, the lifeworld serves the function of the indispensable starting point for the self-exploration of our causal embeddedness in non-human environments. This does not mean that the lifeworld sets itself apart from a world of science; the lifeworld is not an unreal space of reasons that is cut off from a scientifically explicable external world in which anonymous processes take place. *Rather, the lifeworld is the irreducibly real environment of the human form of life.*

Our ecological niche is not a phantom, not a wall behind which lies the physical, which we can sniff out through physical experiments and theorizing. For experiments and theorizing are as much a part of the lifeworld as the green cover of my Husserl edition or the sequence of pitches in a Beethoven performance. *The way in which the real appears to us is itself something real.* In thinking and experiencing, we do not transcend a causally closed in-itself that does not concern itself with us, nor do our successful explanations allow us to move beyond a mental interior by forming hypotheses about the external world.

This renders Husserl's concept of lifeworld obsolete, since he builds on a mistaken theory of perception and then uses it as the foundation for a theory of science that inherits the mistakes of the theory of perception, and vice versa. This leads to the impression – as confusing now as it was then – that science is caught in a crisis that may even be an 'expression of the radical life-crisis of European humanity',[42] as Husserl speculates in the first part of *Crisis*.

Rather than speaking of lifeworld, it is ultimately enough in FOS to respect the *postulate of indispensability*. This states that we must consider the irreducible existence of the mind in any explanation of non-human phenomena. We cannot explain away our standpoint in the causal order; nor do we have to. For our standpoint belongs to the causal order in an epistemically privileged way because it, and only it, enables us to recognize things in themselves. This already starts at the level of perception, to which factivity therefore applies: from the fact that a person perceives that something is the case, it follows that what they perceive is the case.

Here factivity is not a process that takes place independently of our factual perception and its sensory texture, but rather a formal property of the perceptual relation that it shares with other epistemically privileged states, such as scientific, or everyday action-based knowledge. I know that I have two hands by lifting them; I know that $2 + 2 = 4$ because I learned it at some point in early childhood by counting on my fingers; I know that the moon has a particular mass connected to its acceleration in the context of other physical systems because I have the relevant knowledge of elementary mechanics; and so on.

Not all of this knowledge is perceptual knowledge. We do not know the laws of mechanics because we perceive them, but rather because we construct theories whereby we can predict perceptual episodes and bring them about thanks to suitable technical devices. For our technical devices create causal structures that form the basis for perceptual episodes; in this way, a relation of theory confirmation is installed in the real.

It would be a grave mistake to build the postulate of indispensability on the foundation of an explanatory primacy of perception. Traditional empiricism fails because it isolates perception from our other forms of knowledge, and thus ultimately fabricates a misguided theory of perception in which mental representations play a central part.[43]

§9

Objective Phenomenology

The phenomenological argument rejected in the previous paragraph can be considered an attempt to kill two birds with one stone. On the one hand, it introduces an interface of an insight into the world. In this way, one can seemingly take our fallibility into account: if our mental representations at the level of the interface do not correspond to the things that leave causal traces in our mental apparatus, we are then at least partially mistaken. On the other hand, the phenomenological argument also seeks to explain the successful case of factivity by interpreting our perceptual knowledge as a form of empirical knowledge based on partial insights into that which exists.

However, it thus locates perceptual knowledge on the wrong level of perception, for it does not really tell us how we can ever know something by perceiving it, since it ties the knowledge claim not to perception but to experience that exhibits an inferential form (that of an inference to the best explanation).

The *factivity link* means that, if someone perceives something (if they see a vehicle, for example), then it follows that the perceived thing exists and it is as it is perceived (by being a vehicle, say).[1] This link is epistemically relevant because perception not only justifies existential judgements but brings with it a propositional architecture in the sense that we perceive not only individual things as separate points but things that have particular properties in certain surroundings. These properties are qualitative at the level of our perceptual apprehension – that is, they are sense-specific objects such as colour, form, tone, taste, and so forth. The perceived properties essentially belong to a context in which they appear. The same stimulus is perceived differently if the context changes in which it appears. A particular blue light can seem more intense when it is perceived against a black background than when it is perceived in a slightly qualitatively different blue setting. This is no profound insight, merely a statement of well-known psychophysical facts.

What goes deeper is the following insight: the fact that we do not perceive individual objects, but rather individual objects in a context is based on the circumstance that there is a factivity link between perception and fact. What we perceive is a fact – that is, something that is true of one or more objects; hence it follows from the perception of an object that something is the case. One therefore cannot meaningfully distinguish between the perception of things and facts at the level of the factivity link (which does not mean that the fact of our perception is identical with the perceived fact).

Object-perception is what one obtains in theory construction if one takes an individual object for the causal source of a perception. According to this model, the individual object is the relevant cause of a given perception. A purely causal theory of perception reduces perception to a causal structure whose origin is an individual object that transmits information, and at whose end some sensory-physiological process takes place that we know from the interior view as a percept. This theory fails because object do not simply physically radiate into our mind and leave percepts as traces. Based on this model, perception would not be factive at all. Rather, object-perception presupposes fact-perception which is causal in a broader sense of the term that transcends the idea of transmission of information in the form of energy. Rather, what gets transmitted are senses as modes of presentation of objects. Given that these senses are properties of the object, we grasp the object as it is in itself in virtue of grasping relevant facts about it.

Furthermore, the purely causal object-perception theory cannot explain how our conscious apprehension of individual things can make any contribution to perception, for the purely causal part of perception is already over by the time we turn our attention to it and make statements about it, as it were. According to the purely causal theory, what we think during or right after the occurrence of a perception has no influence on the perception itself. This contradicts the fact that we perceive some things only when we have become explicit users of concepts, unless we want to restrict the concept of perception to mental episodes that by definition do not require the exercise of conceptual capacities which would be a question beginning manoeuvre.

At this point, the purely causal theory usually extricates itself by producing a theoretical artefact and terming it 'perception'. This theoretical artefact consists in the assumption of traces that our causal surroundings leave in us. In this way, our entire mental life is split up into elements with corresponding modules. On a lower level, a module of pure, pre-conscious perception is postulated that displays conditions of correctness that we do not need to be able to access consciously. This postulate is justified with reference to non-human animal perception, as well as new-borns or pathological perceptual disorders. But the fact that other living beings or some beings of the same kind as fully equipped perceivers may have reduced perceptual experiences does not, of course, mean that a perceptual episode like the one I am currently experiencing while typing these lines consists of modules that really operate independently of one another, but are somehow sufficiently causally synchronized to generate the impression of a conceptually smoothed perceptual experience. Actual perception is not identical with object-perception, and it is also questionable whether object-perception in the sense propagated by the theoretical construct of a purely causal theory even exists as a real module of our mind.

It is no use to here to credit humans with a sophisticated form of contextual perception (since we are in the space of reasons) while granting other animals only a stimulus-response perception of individual object. Why should other life forms that are capable of perception experience their reality as an atomistic, discontinuous heap of individual objects? Conversely, there is every indication that other life forms apprehend objects in fields of sense, if only because objects ultimately appear, and are thus able to exist, in fields of sense. What exists is quite simply not a series or set of individual object from which it is possible to remove one without thus modifying some other individual objects.[2] Things are genuinely connected, and their contexts are not created by syntheses after the fact. The context is not brought into reality by the fact that we expect it to be there.

Perception is essentially *fact-perception*. What we perceive are not isolated individual objects located in the same place by greater or lesser metaphysical coincidence, but rather facts into which individual objects are inserted. Perception is therefore factive. Factivity does not only come about when we display linguistically coded conceptual notions but is a property of perception itself that it does not acquire only once we 'impose' a propositional structure on it.[3]

The phenomenological argument at best offers an explanation of how we can know anything about perceptual objects even though perception itself does not provide this knowledge. It is therefore unsurprising that the phenomenology based on this argument often runs into difficulties with animal perception, since perceptual knowledge is constructed from the outset as a theoretical achievement that one does not attribute to other mammals, let alone insects,.

Matters are even more difficult with human newborns, since one has to inscribe all manner of evolutionarily rehearsed behaviour on the development of their nervous system, behaviour that is sufficiently similar to the logical procedure of induction for our descendants to gain access to the logical space of reasons. For perception alone, according to the phenomenological argument, is not sufficient as long as the ability to interpret perceptual episodes has not been developed.

To be sure, the phenomenological tradition has a multitude of answers to this on hand. As a realist, however, I think that we should avoid this territory altogether if there is an alternative that does not reconstruct perception on the model of empirical knowledge, but rather introduces an independent source of knowledge that neither comprises elementary data nor relies on theoretical interpretation or induction to provide us with knowledge based on object-perception.

To pull the carpet systematically from under the phenomenological argument, one can formulate a problem that seems tailor-made for the argument, but which causes it substantial difficulties. Thanks to the recent publication of Saul A. Kripke's *Locke Lectures*, we can draw on an analysis of a discussion that took place between John L. Austin and Alfred J. Ayer.[4] I will refer to the problem in question as the *speck-star problem*. Let us imagine that two people are gazing at the starry night sky. One of them refers to a star as a speck in the sky.[5]

Talk of a speck in the sky is a suitable metaphor, as there is a kind of white dot in a person's subjective visual field.[6] We people are accustomed to identifying this white dot with a star under the appropriate conditions. If we identify a given speck in the sky appropriately as a star, we are drawing on a large packet of background knowledge that is available to us today. Many – though certainly not all – people alive today believe that most of the white dots we can find in the night sky are suns – that is, physical objects of impressive size compared to the usual sublunary physical objects that are visible for us on the mesoscopic scale adapted to us.

Now, the speck-star problem consists in the fact that the scientifically well-founded identification of a speck with a sun is not as simple as it seems. For the speck has properties that the scientifically characterized star does not, and vice versa, which means that the two evidently cannot be identical. It would therefore be an error to identify the speck with a sun. The speck grows larger when I approach it (even if we only experience this as astronauts); we can cover the speck with the palm of our hand; the sun that is meant to be identical with it is much too large (and hot), which we would soon realize if we ever moved drastically closer to it. And our knowledge of all this is based on modern astrophysical insights.

However, as Austin rightly points out, it would be a far-fetched solution to treat the speck as a representation of a sun.[7] The speck does not represent a sun in the sense that it deals with a sun. The speck is not a case of semantic content – that is, such-and-such a way of imagining a sun. We can use the speck as a semantic content, but without meeting further conditions its existence is not a case of semantic content. I can treat the speck in my subjective visual field as something to which I ascribe qualities. I can compare specks by describing some as larger or more intense, which is an occasion for astrophysical theorizing. In this case I represent the speck in a particular way by making it usable as a datum for astrophysical theorizing, though it does not follow from this that the speck itself is essentially a datum of such theorizing.

It would be a different matter if one located the speck in the perceptual consciousness rather than the night sky. Then one could say that the speck is a form of semantic content because it presents a sun in a particular way. The speck would then be a sun's mode of givenness. However, this strategy suggests that one could transfer the entire subjective visual field into my consciousness, turning everything that I *prima facie* consider a perceptual object (such as the table in front of me) into mental content, which would bring us back to a clear version of the phenomenological argument. Thus my subjective visual field suddenly no longer overlaps with the objective visual field, since it does not contain the objects that others can also see but only my private semantic contents through which I represent the things others can also see (this is a prominent way to don the Veil of Maya). The phenomenological argument makes its appearance at this point because semantic content seems to need a carrier that is most easily found in consciousness; it seems plausible, then, to bridge the gap between Frege's concept of the sense of a thought and Husserl's noema.[8]

Yet, the speck-star problem can be better solved with an alternative that I term the *condition theory of perception*. The condition theory allows us to analyse a given perceptual episode into necessary and jointly sufficient (adequate) conditions for its existence. The conditions are connected in the factually irreducible structure formed by the field of sense of perceptual episodes as well as their interconnection with other fields of sense. The reality of a perceptual episode, then, is not built up out of atomistic elements, from bottom to top, but holistically determined by the unity of the context.

In the context of the neo-realist condition theory, physical objects in the strict sense (such as photons, ions, neurons, centres of mass, electrons, stars, natural constants, and so on) take on the role of necessary conditions for perceptual episodes. Without electrons and photons, no human (or any other life form on our planet) could perceive the sun. Yet physical objects are not sufficient for the perceptual episode, for they produce sensory illusions in isolation that the living being concerned may confuse with the object of perception. To use Russell's terminology, which is helpful in this regard, the sensory causal traces left by physical objects in our sensory-physiological architectures are *subjective*, because we can only infer the properties of things of perception from them fallibly, though this does not mean that we automatically fall prey epistemically to the sensory illusions.

The model of a 'world as representation', which becomes a largely self-enclosed 'representational world', cannot explain how subjects connect epistemically with the real via mental representations. The mental representation does not achieve this without being supported by some corrective epistemic system, which is shown by the fact that, for many millennia, humanity was completely wrong about the factual dimensions of suns. The discovery that suns are physical objects of a particular kind is a recent one in world history; a more or less clear separation of astrology and astrophysics took place only a few centuries ago.

At this point, an advocate of the phenomenological argument might fall back on the concept of cause and assume that the speck is a representation of a sun in the sense that it is a trace that comes about in the human mind/brain through certain physical processes. The sun thus causes a speck in the subjective visual field of human perception, and so the speck represents a sun in the same sense as footprints on the moon represent the presence of an astronaut.

However, this causal theory of mental representation cannot explain how empirical representations can play the part of knowledge claims without auxiliary assumptions, since they serve at best as reasons for knowledge claims that must draw conclusions about the structure of their causes from the existence of traces. This turns the traces themselves into something unreliable, however, because one cannot rely on them without employing the epistemic machinery of suitable auxiliary concepts and inferential procedures (starting with induction) that organize our mental life sufficiently for us to survive at all as perceiving organisms. Below the threshold of our conscious and explicit, linguistically coded knowledge claims, there must be some form of sensory correctness for our sensory impressions to be linguistically coded.

The failure of the trace model transpires from the fact that it is an impermissible transference of a case of success to a situation that differs from it in one decisive regard. Let us compare the imagined phenomenological situation of the mental tracker with an ordinary situation in which someone reads a footprint as the representation of a fact. If a hunter reads the track of a stag and recognizes it as such, they do not first need to recognize a mental trace of a footprint as the trace of a track. Rather, they directly see a footprint and establish the relevant epistemic connection to a previous presence of a stag in that place, because they know of the causal chain connecting stags, their habitat, the properties of the soil at the respective time of year, and so forth. Ordinary footprints are not mental footprints.

If perception as a whole were only the exhibition of mental footprints, we would never be in a position to find out that there are causal relationships between the mental footprints and their causes. For we could not discover any causes, only traces of causes. According to this model, however, something that supposedly causes mental states is not a further mental state in all cases. The model has no room for the discovery of anything that is not a mental state, which is why the concept of an inference to the best explanation may seem appropriate here, but leads nowhere. If we cannot establish mental contact with causes in the first place, it does not help to introduce traces into our minds in order to bridge the conceptual gap between objects of perception and mental representation.

We simply need independent, direct access to the causes of mental representation at some point in order to understand at all how someone could be capable of discovering causal connections between their own states and a sequence of events that is independent of their perceptual system. Perception is a case of such independent access. Of course, the phenomenologist might wonder: How should we explain the fact that we have non-empirical access to the causes of our conscious perceptual states? But phenomenology must employ precisely such an intuition of essences [*Wesensschau*] to augment its untenable theory of the mental with a causal theory of mental representations through the back door.

In the best case, the phenomenological argument obliges us to assume that we have successful non-empirical inferential access to things in themselves, which play the theoretical part of the causes of our representations. At this point in the dialectic of the concept of perception, anyone who is not already a committed phenomenologist is entitled to summon up *an argument of simplicity*. If some form of access to things in themselves is required, why should one only permit it at the end of the chain of theoretical postulations in the form of an inference to the best explanation? Why not recognize instead that perception achieves what theory only ascribes to inferential thinking, namely the recognition of facts?

I have referred elsewhere to a similar idea as the 'argument from facticity'.[9] The conclusion of this argument is that we must accept absolute facts, an absolute fact being something that would have existed anyhow – that is, even if we had not noted its existence. If we note such a fact, we know that it is modally robust – that is, its existence is not a causal or logical consequence of our assertory speech act. If we cannot get around absolute facts in general, then, we are entitled to postulate facticity before the end of the reflexive explanation of our epistemic contact with the real. The argument from facticity supports all manoeuvres capable of understanding the epistemically earliest stages of our contact with the real as successful knowledge claims. As the concept of perception was introduced to refer to our literal contact with our surroundings, we are therefore entitled to give preference to direct perceptual realism over phenomenological mediation.

Yet not every variety of overt perceptual realism solves the speck-star problem in a convincing way. A *naïve realism* that restricts its ontological commitments to the existence of microscopic objects in our more or less immediate surroundings encounters difficulties when it addresses the relationship between physical objects and the furnishings of everyday life.[10]

FOS offers its own version of direct perceptual realism. At this stage, it can already draw on the indispensability thesis that keeps our pre-ontological experience stable, according to which there are fingernails, atoms, the past, presidents, neurons, perceptions, thoughts, art works, tables, and so on. If we know anything about these objects, we always know that they have determinate, authentic properties that distinguish them from other objects in the same field of sense radius.

The ontological pluralism of FOS sets up a model of the relation between physical and non-physical objects that has consequences for the theory of perception. For example, hands really exist, which does not conflict with the fact that there would be no hands if the systems of elementary particles that we can discover through the decomposition of hands were not coordinated in a particular way.[11] Particle physics describes the properties of elementary particles in the fields of sense it investigates, abstracting from the overlaps between the fields of sense of the elementary particles and other fields of sense. Particle physics does not describe the properties of Angela Merkel as chancellor of Germany or the relation of the physical systems describing Merkel's physical properties (mass, acceleration, and so on) to Angela Merkel. Particle physics does not include a theory of the complexity of 'Angela Merkel'.

At this point, someone might counter that the universe described by particle physics is causally closed and seek to infer from this that we can obtain a theory of Angela Merkel's composition as well as her properties as chancellor from physics, a theory, which can be inferred from the arrangement of elementary particles. However, this secretly transforms actual physics into a future metaphysics.

Physics is not capable of describing the behaviour of everything that belongs to physical properties in their entirety, let alone predicting it. To be sure, this is already the case at the level of elementary particles, where statistical laws apply but not strict determinism. The universe is simply not a 'force-fit clockwork'[12] that on a particular scale takes the form of Angela Merkel. An atomistic metaphysics on the model of Democritus is in no way supported by contemporary physics; the elementary particles familiar today are not a confirmation of Democritus or Lucretius. Anyone who identifies them with one another in a historically uncritical fashion is quite simply overlooking the details both of the classical atomistic metaphysics and, in particular, of contemporary physics, which does not offer an all-encompassing atomistic worldview or anything similar.

Without wishing to ascribe too much argumentative, philosophical value to this here, it even seems to be the case that many interpretations of the next major breakthroughs in microphysics closely resemble a naturalistic variant of FOS. Carlo Rovelli was one of the first to point this out to me.[13] Rovelli himself interprets the concept of fields in physics (which was admittedly an inspiration for FOS) to the effect that space–time is not a basis for all fields, much less a container in which events take place (this Newtonian notion was effectively refuted by relativity theory).

> Spacetime is the gravitational field – and vice versa. It is something that exists by itself, as Newton intuited, even without matter. But it is not an entity that is different from the other things in the world – as Newton believed – it is a field like the others. More than a drawing on a canvas, the world is like a superimposition of canvases, of strata, where the gravitational field is only one among others. Just like the others, it is neither absolute nor uniform, nor is it fixed: it flexes, stretches and jostles with the others, pushing and pulling against them. Equations describe the reciprocal influences that all the fields have on each other, and spacetime is one of these fields.[14]

This is not the place to 'deconstruct' Rovelli's remnants of metaphysics, which are evident in his assumption that all fields influence one another;

this ultimately leads him to sketch a naturalistic worldview that is, however, largely reconcilable with FOS. But he cannot show that the field architecture he proposes as an interpretation of loop quantum gravity applies to non-physical objects as well, even though he suggests this. But, as we have seen, his extension of physics into the mind is a prime example of mental representationalism, which understands our mental states as literal energetic traces and thus encloses us in a bubble of ignorance, meaning that he unintentionally enacts his entire theory construction in epistemology as a philosophy of 'as if'.

We can now draw on FOS to solve the speck-star problem. According to the neo-realist condition theory of perception, every genuine perceptual episode is an intertwining of many fields of sense. Necessary physical conditions (such as the presence of the electromagnetic field), necessary biological conditions (cones, neurons, a cortex, the ectoderm, and so forth) and distal processes outside our body are involved when we acquire knowledge about our surroundings in the form of perceptual episodes.[15] Genuine perceptual episodes are, among other things, events in nature where different natural fields of sense overlap, for example the one described by quantum theory and the one accessible to neurobiology. Based on our empirical knowledge from natural science, we are currently not entitled to make the extremely speculative assumption that the neurobiological and physical fields of sense are identical; we may at best assume that they overlap in central respects. Ontological reductions of scientifically largely independent areas can at best rest on metaphysical interpretations of the natural sciences, which brings them into the awkward situation that the speculative assumptions are supported by the metaphysical interpretations, not their factual natural-scientific basis, and thus expose themselves as speculations.[16]

Perceptual episodes cannot be reduced to their physical-biological component, of course. In addition to the necessary natural conditions, the conscious human perception (which concerns us here as a form of knowledge) involves different fields of sense in which objects appear as heaps of facts that are essentially grasped through an ultimately irreducible mentalistic vocabulary – that is, in the language of the mind. In the present case, this means that we can consider ourselves perceptual systems and define perceptual episodes as part of our consciously lived life. This self-definition of our life occurs here from the standpoint of an epistemological knowledge claim that is connected to which view of the scope of human knowledge, and thus of humans themselves, is employed.

In FOS, *mind* is the name for the explanatory structure we consider when we draw a self-portrait of the human being that relates to our embeddedness in non-human surroundings, both theoretically and affecting our actions. Humans lead their lives with reference to their notion of the human place in the cosmos.[17] One of the tasks of the philosophical theory of perception is to connect the concept of perception with a conception of humans. The conception of humans employed here belongs to a higher level: the human being is taken into consideration only in so far as it is the being that takes itself into consideration. From this self-referential observer position, it is pointed out that we have the concept of perception at our disposal only in a sense that goes far beyond perceptual episodes.

By contrast, specific scientific examinations of perception should be understood as abstractions in the minimal sense that they pick out individual layers of our mental life as necessary conditions for the existence of perceptual episodes and connect them to prior knowledge claims that have been accepted as successful. What is accepted as successful is, among other factors, based on internal scientific standards whose rational acceptability is not identical with their truthfulness. The kernel of truth in Vaihinger's science-theoretical fictionalism consists in the accurate insight that rational acceptability in the natural sciences is not identical with knowledge, since some things are acceptable but are ultimately recognized as false.

Based in this, Vaihinger follows in Kant's footsteps by distinguishing between 'fiction' and 'hypothesis'.[18] He argues that a hypothesis cannot be considered true if it proves false, whereas a fiction serves its purpose despite having been recognized as false. A naturalistically simplified understanding of human perception as a non-conscious machine for processing sensory data (as a flow heater between stimulus and action) is there, in the strict sense of Vaihinger's argumentation, a fiction (at best!).[19] This fiction is harmless as long as one does not make the mistake of taking it at face value and thinking that the human mind, on the level of its intelligent self-comprehension (such as in philosophical science) is built exclusively from non-intelligent modules, each of which enters the theoretical portfolio as an evolutionary achievement.[20]

A natural-scientific examination of aspects of the mind that contribute to perception will proceed neurobiologically, for example. As a neurobiological phenomenon, however, perception is not identical with a factual perceptual episode. The neurobiology of perception registers only a part of all perceptual episodes, of which it has so far at best researched adequate conditions for their existence. Our mental life would not take place without suitable neuronal equipment. Nonetheless, neurobiology constitutively operates with a simplified concept of perception because it does not take into account the quantum-mechanically necessary conditions, for example, let alone the entire observable universe, which respectively make causal contributions to the factual occurrence of a given perceptual episode.

Focusing on a subset of the fields of sense of factual perception is an act of abstraction, though this alone does not make it a distortion. Selecting a theory is neither automatically a construction of its objects nor a conscious acceptance of something false as explanatorily useful.

The concept of mind in FOSFOS here encounters a fundamental assumption from the phenomenological tradition since Husserl: it is neither possible nor necessary for us to escape our pre-theoretical experience of human perception in order to look behind the scenes, as it were. We cannot look behind the scenes without – seeing! Our standpoint does not disappear because we theoretically dissect it. If we factually dissect it, we die. What reductionism describes is not our life but our death, which is why it cannot be implemented. At the level of theorizing it is mental suicide, which has an unfavourable effect to the extent that the reductionism of theorizing is taken at face value in public (and by some actors in the scientific world), not as a model that characterizes necessary but inadequate conditions for our mental life.

This model of the mind allows us to solve the speck-star problem, for now we can analyse the speck as a perceptual illusion. There is no need to eliminate this illusion epistemically in order to replace it with a sun, which would amount to a confusion of the conscious perceptual space with events in physical space–time. The causal structure of our physiological perceptual apparatus generates its own optics. To put it in vivid, pre-scientific terms, the beams of light coming from the sun are refracted by our organism. We never perceive anything causally that moves at the speed of light.

When photons 'hit' our organism, an interaction (refraction) takes place. This triggers organic processes made available by the organism in the form of conscious perceptual experiences. One part of these conscious perceptual experiences is the speck that we locate in the subjective visual field when, for example, we point towards the sky from here and tell someone it is there. In so doing, we determine an indexical axis that is visible to others, since others can see the same sun by virtue of having a similar perceptual apparatus to which the sun presents itself as a speck, albeit from a correspondingly shifted indexical axis.

The laws of optics and objective perspective shed light on the mathematically codable relationships between the perspectives, enabling us to gain a theoretical idea of the causal situation. This theoretical image is an element of our view of a sun as a combined core sense that brings down the two senses, the speck from here and the speck from there, to a common denominator, namely the sun object. Of course, the sun object is neither a speck nor an enormous hot thing 'up there' or 'down there' (depending on the time of day), but in physical terms an overlapping of fields that extend to 'here', so that, by merging the two fields of sense 'speck' and 'sun', we can say that we are not at a distance from the sun but in it, albeit in a place within the total field of the sun, which is habitable for us. The temperature on our planet as well as the visible sunlight that provides the decisive background for the visibility of things occur in our sun's total field. The physical universe itself consists not of well-defined individual things (substances such as a very large and hot sun 'up there') but of fields whose interaction physics can code in the form of equations, since the law-based character of the universe exhibits the form of relational definitions. *The universe is pure relation, an event without metaphysical substance.*[21]

The physical fields appear in the field of sense of the human organisms under conditions of a refraction that is in turn objectively researchable. The dimensions of this refraction are determined in the language of sensory physiology, without any reasonable cause to reduce all of them to formulas for physical fields. This is because our organism too is part of the mind, which we should note is not an immaterial ghost but an actually existing, genuine explanatory structure of self-determination that presupposes an organism as a necessary natural condition.

To say that the organism is part of the mind is not a subjective-idealistic or phenomenalist thesis which holds that we put the organism together using the privately accessible sensory data of an unextended inner mental life. The yardstick for the mereology employed here is a condition analysis. The elements we wish to place in relation to one another are the speck and the star; this is achieved through the star revealing itself as an object in the field of sense of astrophysics and the speck as an object in the field of sense of human sensory physiology.

The speck is not a mental representation of the sun, however, but at best something like a model. If it is an image, then it is in the sense of Wittgenstein's *Tractatus*, whose image theory follows the concept of the model.[22] There is an ordering system that sets up a relationship between the mass of a sun to the dimensions of the sensory-physiological phenomena that concern us. This ordering system allows us to infer the structure of the non-conscious universe from the presence of the speck, since the speck belongs to a causal system that is in part purely physical and in part knowable via sensory physiology.

Here too, however, we must not fall prey to our own abstraction. As soon as we have at our disposal the model I have just outlined, we can treat the speck differently. The speck, as a scientific object that we precisely cannot determine only as an ephemeral mental representation of physical reality but as a genuine object of independent examination, is itself now part of an examination and no longer merely an inert speck.

Here I am following one of the main ideas of Jocelyn Benoist's realism, which repeatedly points out that objects are always norms by which we orient ourselves in a factual situation where the concern is what something is like. The contextuality of our thinking goes so deep that we do not need any situation-transcendent objects to explain our successful reference, and thus our knowledge claims.[23] If we characterize our pre-theoretical experience as if we first saw a speck, then discovered at some point that it was causally connected to the total field of a sun, then we are overlooking that we are always acting in normalized contexts. Expressed in the vocabulary of FOS, objects only ever play a part in a field of sense in which they are subject to a core sense. The core sense organizes the facts in such a way that the objects prove to be the focus.

One can illustrate this once again using Frege's classical model of the evening star and the morning star. To say that Venus is the object that appears to us once as the evening and once as the morning star introduces a core sense by which our epistemological interests orient themselves. Someone who has only ever seen the evening star (that is, Venus, which has appeared at a particular point in their subjective visual field) does not have access to the concept of Venus as the object that appears once as the evening and once as the morning star. The concept of Venus as a Fregean object of meaning differs from that of the evening star as a sense that connects us with Venus. In the field of sense of Fregean meanings, Venus and the evening star are identical; in the field of sense of Fregean senses, however, they are not. The evening star sense and the Venus sense are precisely not identical, otherwise one would not have solved the identity puzzle in which there are identity judgements that are both informative and self-consistent.[24]

The speck can be treated as an optical illusion, in the sense that our percept is not changed by our knowledge about the relation between speck and star. The percept remains unaffected by our knowledge; just as the lines in the Müller–Lyer illusion continue to appear significantly different to us in their length.[25] By studying the causal networks that intersect on the level of the natural species involved in bringing about human perceptual episodes, we can understand the structure of the illusion.

I speak here of 'illusion' rather than 'delusion' because an illusion does not necessarily delude. It only deludes if we take it for something other than what it is. Optical illusions are transparent and can thus become occasions for knowledge acquisition. A mirage only deludes the thirsty person who believes they are approaching the longed-for oasis. But one can also use the existence of a mirage as a datum for a study of our perceptual process on the occasion of particular stimuli. So it depends on how one uses an illusion. An illusion does not delude of its own accord but only under specific conditions in which the delusion lies.

The electromagnetic fields of the sun are part of the explanation of its irradiation into our perceptual apparatus. We apprehend this irradiation through the selection mechanisms of our perceptual media, our sensory modalities. This only works because our sensory modalities interact with the fields of the sun by belonging to them. The fields of our sensory modalities interact with the fields of the sun at the same causal level. In this sense, our perception of the sun takes place in the sun; we are objects in the sun's field. So the sun is not in a different place ('up there' in the sky, at the centre of our solar system or wherever). This location information easily leads to delusions if we confuse the solar illusion with the solar object. That the sun cannot be 'there' without being 'here' is evident from the fact that there is currently light here. The sunlight present here is part of the sun, not a stand-in for the sun.

The causal interaction of the fields of sense of perception with the fields of sense of the sun generates a perceptual illusion that takes place in the sun itself and (slightly) modifies the sun; this has really been known since the discovery of quantum theory but has been wrongfully neglected in the philosophical theory of perception because its discursive landscape continues to be based on the dysfunctional subject–object model. *The perceptual subject is not an observer of cosmic events that is distant from reality, but rather itself an objective structure that is causally embedded.*

The speck is thus an objectively existing image. Here one must bear in mind that the image is not a picture of a thing; rather, the analogy to painting lies in the fact that sensory data in the sense of objectively existing images consists of structures that are sensorily immediately accessible (not mediated through further images). We perceive in the medium of sensory data in the same sense that a colour film allows us to see a scene in colour. Sensory media are depictions of the matter itself, not pictures of something else. They are genuine images that we apprehend because of our registries, but we do not produce them. Our causal contribution to the image consists in the fact that perception as a whole is an actually existing relation that does not exist without the contributions of the percipient. The causal contribution takes place at different levels of the universe, since we would not have any sensors without microphysical events (which are explored in quantum theory) and physiological preconditions. So there are necessary natural preconditions for perception – a fact that can admittedly not be uncovered purely by natural-scientific means.

Sensory data are not located 'in the consciousness'; they do not consist of private events that are generated from the outside through unknowable relations of affection.[26] So there is really a speck. We can point to it and are justified in assuming that other members of our species have a similar experience based on the same optical laws.

But the speck is not always the *object* of perception. If, for example, I perceive the sun as temperature or brightness, then the sun is the object. One can in turn make the accompanying speck an object and examine how its luminosity comes about, an examination that plays a central part in modern astrophysics, which carries out spectral analyses to ascertain the properties of stars or other cosmic phenomena.

Today, as before, we can say that nothing is an object in itself without a context (a field of sense) in which it appears. The speck can be a perceptual object in one field of sense and an image (sensory datum) in another, in keeping with the functional difference between object and field of sense.[27] What we perceive is tied to contexts that are selected not exclusively through the presence of certain objects but also through human needs, something of which Benoist's precise analyses of the perceptual situation remind us.[28]

In so far as we perceive the sun, the speck is an optical illusion that belongs to our visual perceptual consciousness. The speck resembles a mirage. It does not present the situation as if there were actually a speck, but neither does it present it as if there were a star causing it. It represents nothing, unless one wished to view the result of particular physical, optical, biological or psychological regularities as the representation of something, though this would deviate from the epistemic sense of 'representation'.

Our perception enables us to know that a particular star exists because we perceive it. We can learn something about this star by studying the speck, which is an interaction between the star and us. Precisely such effects play an epistemically central part in astrophysics, which uses redshifts and the perceived flickering of celestial phenomena as a data source for learning things about astrophysical objects. So the speck is not a representation of the sun, but it can play the part of evidence in an astrophysical case study.[29]

Our conscious perceptual experience is part of the universe; it is embedded in causal contexts. By examining these contexts, we can learn something about the objects of perceptual experience. Access to physical objects based on the self-examination of our indispensable standpoint consists in making epistemic contact with the real, which is how we can know something about the character of the things that are independent of the mind, as it were.

I say 'as it were' because the objects we perceive are not in fact causally independent of our mind. By appearing in the same causal fields, we modify the universe itself through our presence in the universe. It is not yet fully clear how profound this anthropic causal contribution is, but the fact of its existence and the urgent need to take it into account are well-known consequences of modern physics since its monumental achievements of relativity theory and quantum theory.

So we never perceive things that are causally independent of our mind, because this is causally impossible. This does not mean that there is a veil of the imagination running through our consciousness, shielding things from us. The perceptual consciousness is not a screen on which something appears, but rather the apprehension of objectively existing information from a standpoint that interacts causally with its surroundings. Both the speck and every other sensual datum (appearing in macroscopic range) is an illusion in the sense that it is possible to take it for something it is not, such as an element on a screen, that only ever adumbrates the matter itself.

For our perceptual knowledge, the partial opacity of its natural necessary preconditions is a constitutive feature.[30] In order to be epistemically in contact with something that is not causally produced by this contact as a whole, it is not necessary to be infallible in the sense of knowing all necessary and collectively adequate conditions for the respective perceptual episode. In general, we can say that we do not need to be able to know all the conditions for a given successful case of knowledge in order to know that they have been fulfilled.[31] Every knowledge claim, no matter how successful, generates a zone of ignorance that we can explore step by step, which admittedly always produces further zones of ignorance. We never illuminate the zone of the knowable entirely, especially not by sending 'pure logic' into the unknown as a form of patrol, to bring metaphysical universal quantifiers into position a priori.

Fallibility is constitutive for objectivity. In a case of perception, this manifests in the fact that it is even fundamentally impossible to grasp a given perceptual episode through the prism of a complete, systematic listing of all actually interacting natural and mental conditions, for this attempt changes the perceptual situation. This does not mean that a percept changes psychologically through our cognitive access, but it does mean that the causal architecture is modified when we attempt to take hold of it, since this access is itself causal.

The theoretical concepts whereby we seek to grasp our sensory modalities in models approach a matter that, by its own nature, is located on this side of all theorizing, no matter how fine-grained. There is, after all, no pure case of seeing that does not involve other sensory modalities; these must work together if a system of percepts is to come about in a given being at a given point in time. The complexity of changes in mental states in a minded being goes beyond anything we can fully comprehend.

Because we are fallible, we are capable of knowing something about those objects in relation to which we are fallible. In the reality of knowledge acquisition, fallibility and objectivity belong together. The conditionality of perceptual episodes does not impair a successful case of knowledge gained from them but actually makes more knowable things available to us than we can ever obtain ourselves.

The condition theory of perception will surely give some readers the impression that we do not ultimately have any direct access to objects of perception. Does the speck not push itself between us and the star? If it is an optical illusion, how can our visual experience connect us with the thing in itself, the star? This succeeds neither through the speck representing the star nor through the star causing the speck, for knowledge about the causal relation is not itself an intrinsic facet of the perceptual episode. To know during the act of perception that a particular star exists is not the same as knowing that one knows this because this particular star causes this particular speck.

The response to this objection is that the condition theory does not demand denying the claim that the star is the object of perception. The perception relates to the star. The form of this relation involves a causal architecture, and thus a field of sense in which the speck appears. If we perceive the star, then the speck can no longer be the object of perception, since the visual experience of the speck alone is no reason to suppose a perception of the star. It is therefore an illusion, because it can delude us, but need not do so.

The speck is thus assigned a role in the explanatory context of the self-apprehension of our fallibility. It is part of the explanation of why we, as minded beings, are not infallible at the level of our perceptual episodes. If we were to perceive the speck, we would need an explanation of the fallibility of this perception, which would generate a higher-order, invisible speck (a blind spot, as it were) and so on *ad infinitum*.

The visual experience of the speck does not directly qualify me to state that there is a speck that I perceive, any more than visually experiencing a situation as if I were seeing water on the motorway in New Mexico on a hot summer day directly qualifies me to say that there is actually water on the motorway there. Perceiving the sun and having a speck experience, on the other hand, does directly qualify me to make a knowledge claim, since the object – the sun itself – is present and constitutes the occasion for my knowledge claim, which is made viable by further contextual parameters.

Since one has to locate the factivity connection somewhere, we can safely – in the spirit of realism – shift it from the visual experience of a speck to the perception of the object. Through our perceptual experience, then, we can apprehend the objects of our perception and ascertain their identity across different perceptual episodes. Hence we are also qualified to ascribe perceptual episodes of the same objects that we perceive to other, non-human beings. A bat perceives the same sun that I do, albeit in other sensory modalities. A colour-blind person sees the same traffic lights that I do, albeit with different colours.

To know that this or that is the object of a perception is not the same as perceiving this or that. What is more, we constantly perceive countless objects without having any idea of what they are.

The object of perception is not decided by the knowledge claim of the percipient; this takes into account the impetus of realism in the theory of perception. FOS thus implements a realist truism by distinguishing the optical illusion, which is a real part of the universe, from the object of perception.

The speck is not a star. The speck is, however, part of the same causal network to which the star belongs. This does not mean that a precisely defined star located somewhere illuminates a precisely defined being and leaves a speck in its organism by stimulating its nerve endings. This crude variant of a causal theory of perception is irreconcilable with the fact that the causal transmission of information should be understood in quantum-theoretical terms in the relevant physical fields.

Objective phenomenology counteracts the opposition between a mental object of perception and a material external world that acts upon it. This brings it close to a quantum-theoretically informed view of perception, though this is not a decisive element of its philosophical justification, since quantum theory is unsuitable for supporting conceptual analyses without prior philosophical interpretation.

However, there is a factual proximity between quantum theory and objective phenomenology, at least in the respect that they abandon the traditional assumption that our perceptual apparatus is something like a view from nowhere to which a mind-independent world shows itself through the stimulation of our nerve endings. For such models presuppose a naïve ontology of individual things, which holds that there is a world consisting of many well-defined individual things (individuals) that collectively form the furnishings of the real, which we can only learn about through causal chains. Such models already fail because they do not take into account the causal embeddedness of the perceptual process itself, which makes a real contribution to bringing about perception. This real contribution is located neither in our mind nor in our brain but, quite simply, comes from the fact that, as living beings, we are part of every universe that has a causal form at all.

The objective phenomenology proposed here vehemently contradicts the following seemingly self-evident modelling of the perceptual process offered by Russell to discredit some versions of perceptual realism based on science – or, rather, his own interpretation of natural-scientific findings.

> Common sense holds – though not very explicitly – that perception reveals external objects to us directly: when we 'see the sun', it is the sun that we see. Science has adopted a different view, though without realizing its implications. Science holds that, when we 'see the sun', there is a process, starting from the sun, traversing the space between the sun and the eye, changing its character again in the optic nerve and the brain, and finally producing the event which we call 'seeing the sun'. Our knowledge of the sun thus becomes inferential; our direct knowledge is of an event which is, in some sense, 'in us'.[32]

According to Russell, then, we never see the sun. What we know when we claim to see the sun is based on inference. Russell accepts a naturalistic variant of the phenomenological argument, which does not defuse the situation conceptually. His mistake in the passage above comes about in the following way: from the fact that science names several processes that take place when we see the sun, he infers that our direct knowledge of the sun relates only to the endpoint of this process, which is, 'in some sense, "in us"'. But in what sense is this supposed event meant to be 'in us'?

If Russell means that seeing the sun is an event in our brain, this would mean that we have direct knowledge of an event in the brain (let us call this 'the neuronal event'), from which we infer a distal cause, the sun. But how is it possible to have direct knowledge of the neuronal event? Does Russell mean that we have direct knowledge of a neuronal event by looking at a speck that we can relate to the sun inferentially?

This seems to be the case, especially as this reading is covered by neutral monism, which might teach us here that the conscious experience of the speck is the inside view of the matter that is available to us as conscious life forms. The speck and the neuronal event would be two facets of the same event, which appears to us in the medium of the attributes of extension and thinking, as it were: as extension when we view the brain, and as thinking when we take into account the impression of the speck.

Yet this roundabout explanation does not deliver on its promise of contributing to the theory of perception, for it insists that our visual experience itself (the speck) is not a source of knowledge. According to this model, what we can know directly does not concern the sun at all, merely an impression of the sun. What we know about the sun does not come about from the impression of the sun, which is only connected to our solar knowledge in that we gain a scientific knowledge of causes that makes epistemic contact with the sun as the cause of the solar impression.[33]

Objective phenomenology, on the other hand, treats our visual experience (the speck) as a content [*Gehalt*] that presents the sun. The speck is a perceptual proposition that enables us to apprehend the sun in a particular way. The things of perception are suitable for being read via the selection processes of our semiotic equipment because they exhibit a field structure that overlaps with the field structures of the self.

There is a relation by translation between these two structures that can be connected to the concept of information, which has unfortunately come to be used to an inflationary degree.[34] Here, information can be understood (with a grain of salt) with reference to Aristotelian tradition to the effect that things of perception display a structure (a *logos*) that is translated into the structure of propositional substance. Perception as relation between the thing of perception and the perceiving organism has its own form. Perception itself is a *logos* that is situated in the midst of the real and should not be impermissibly 'mentalized' or 'internalized'.[35] The speck belongs to the form of perception; it is in formation.

The causal relation of perception has the form of an interconnection, not that of a timeline that understands a thing of perception as a transmitter temporally located before the recipient; thus the causal format of perception as a whole is split into temporal divisions. Whether this philosophical description can be implemented via natural science depends, among other things, on correctly solving the measuring problem of quantum theory and its application to the role of our perceptual apparatus as an observation system, which will not be decided at this point.

Since physics is not adequately unified to form a theory providing an unambiguous metaphysics that can serve as a basis for the theory of perception, objective phenomenology is an assumption motivated by an ontological and epistemological reconstruction. This reconstruction permits the development of a model that leaves room for the factivity of perception and treats visual experience itself as a fully valid source of knowledge.

At the same time, the condition theory provides an explanation for our fallibility. In the acquisition of perceptual knowledge, we are fallible because we can never fully grasp all the conditions for a perceptual episode. We grasp some aspects of a perceptual episode in our visual experience, namely those that appear in the form of the substance. These put us in contact with the things of perception, albeit a contact that is not mediated beyond this.

If we delude ourselves while perceiving, this is because we uncover conditions that are not directly available to us. Perceptual knowledge is then mediated at least one level less than the knowledge disclosed through perception, which thematizes conditions of actually existing perception that are not themselves perceived *ex hypothesi*. Perception itself does not delude itself.

So-called perceptual illusions are mediated; they are copying errors – that is, errors made by someone when they incorrectly infer the basis of a perception. Thus it is not our perceptual knowledge but our inferential knowledge claims, which are based on perceptions, that are the source of our fallibility. Let us call this inferentialist pseudology (the theory of errors). It does not claim, of course, that all inferential knowledge claims based on perceptual knowledge are false, only that the conclusions as to the necessary conditions for the existence of a perceptual episode can be mistaken.

The minimal empiricism that accompanies objective phenomenology at this level makes a decisive contribution to distinguishing science and scepticism from each other. For the revisability of scientific knowledge claims is not based on the fact that we must all be able to question our knowledge, which especially includes our perceptual knowledge. Natural-scientific self-examination of the causal embeddedness of our perceptual episodes in the universe only advances at all because it does not eliminate the phenomena that enable every scientific knowledge claim to build on something that we already know independently of it.

This is not a very empiricist or fundamentalist thesis which holds that there is a precisely defined mental base layer which results from an acquaintance with the eigenstates of consciousness; for our perceptual knowledge, after all, is knowledge of something that is not constitutively a case of perception. If I am watching my fingers move across the computer keyboard, what I see is not perception but my fingers. This would be little different, incidentally, if things were actually as Russell claims (that we have direct knowledge only of neuronal events), for then this knowledge still relates not only to itself but to neuronal events that others cannot grasp intrinsically, but can grasp extrinsically (in the form of imaging procedures, and so on).

Because visual experience is a genuine and irreducible source of knowledge, we avoid classical empiricism, which precisely does not stand for perceptual realism and instead introduces an intermediate layer of the mental that represents causes. The speck thus becomes a representative of the sun rather than an event in the universe whose occurrence is based on countless conditions, ultimately including the causal architecture of the observable universe, which can be apprehended from our standpoint.

§10

Ontology of the Imagination: (Alleged) Expressive Barriers of FOS

One element in the standard repertoire of fictional irrealism is to rely on the argument that fictive objects are figments of the imagination that are neither real nor existent, precisely because they are at best 'only imagined'. The concern on which this idea draws is summed up by Descartes and Hume in early modern philosophy: 'Nothing is more free than the imagination of man.'[1] A classical empiricist motif found in the work of Locke, Hume and Berkeley is the containment of the imagination. Their partly accurate basic idea is that there are limits to the imagination, set by the fact that we can only recombine what is provided to our knowledge apparatus in the form of simple ideas – that is, mental representations that cannot be further analysed, and that these are in turn attributed to internal and external sense as sources.

One reason for ascribing a central epistemological status to the imagination nonetheless stems from a Cartesian thought on fallibility. We are fallible because we do not cling to what is sensorily given, simply taking it as an occasion for data processing in the context of stimulus-response patterns. Our freedom consists in the fact that we are not bound to evolutionarily given animal parameters alone, but wear the necklace of animality more loosely, as it were.

Of course, this applies not only to humans as the free, minded beings that we know from the inside view but also to other beings whose lives are adapted to images of their surroundings. The concern here is not to defend Descartes' version of an anthropological difference, but rather the following argumentation: if our cognitive apparatus were merely a flow heater for externally and internally given information that sometimes (above a certain stimulation threshold) reaches our consciousness, we could not form any stable image of a rationally guided search for knowledge.[2]

The epistemological standpoint that assures itself of its own cognitive faculty allows us to reject incoherent notions of the human mind and the bestowal of faculties upon it, which includes theories that suggest or even assume that our cognitive formats are (at best) high-speed manifestations of evolutionarily coded processing mechanisms.

Against this background, Descartes rightly establishes the connection between the imagination and modern science as the core of any promising theory of science, since the process of seeking knowledge – to this day – always exceeds the boundaries of what is sensorily and historically predefined in order to transform the collection of data into a science of the universe on its various scales in the form of thought experiments. Without images there can be no modern science, as Horst Bredekamp has shown in his art-historical studies on imaging procedures.[3]

Yet the human mind never completely emancipated itself from its mythological origins. The mythological consciousness experiences the real as something that goes so far beyond the sensorily given that, at the edges of its knowability, it undermines the space of intelligibility that is accessible to us.[4] This pattern is also used by modern physics, which teaches us in increasingly radical steps that, on those scales that are not directly sensorily accessible to us, the universe is completely different from how we might think of it if we uncritically trusted our eyes.[5]

This is why we cannot retreat to the purportedly safe point of a naïve ontology of individual things, since this already proves to be an unsuitable fiction in our empirical situation for natural-scientific reasons. Considering what we know about the universe, the idea that the world is a container filled with objects that are all individuated in a consciousness-independent fashion is untenable. The world has no furnishings that we face in order to make an inventory of them. The classical mechanistic concept of nature, which is taken for granted by many in contemporary metaphysics as a dogmatic starting point for all legitimate investigations, is not remotely adequate to the philosophical implications of physics over the last century.

There is no empirically supported reason to build FOS on a consciousness-independent base layer of individual things, an atomistic base reality. Today's physics has long ceased to offer any support to the metaphysics of an outdated realism.[6] The idea that values, colours, conscious sensations or even the mind as such are human, all-too-human projections that superimpose an illusory reality of secondary qualities on the true reality of primary things is itself a rather unimaginative projection of the human mind. It corresponds to the modern pathos of senselessness, which comes from the discovery that we are not at home on all scales of the universe. Humans became metaphysically homeless when they noticed that they were not physically at the centre of cosmic activity. However, this is not in itself an existentially significant discovery that can be inferred from modern physics, but rather an experience that generates illusions. For it does not follow from our spatiotemporal position on a particular scale of astrophysical registration of the universe that the universe as such exists senselessly. The notion of a senseless in-itself of things that is opposed by our own for-itself in order to give sense to life is not, *ex hypothesi*, grounded in any recognition of facts. For it is based on the erroneous opinion that recognition of facts is always an apprehension of the in-itself, meaning that the relation that is meant to exist between the in-itself and the for-itself cannot, according to its own premise, be a recognition of facts. In short: the opinion that the universe in itself is senseless does not refer to any source of an experience of senselessness that does not follow from a knowledge of the universe.

This digression into the ontological atmosphere of existentialism is meant to illustrate the following idea: our ultimate metaphysical images of our surroundings say more about ourselves than about the metaphysical surroundings in which we exist. According to FOS, we are not part of a total metaphysical landscape from which one could determine the sense or nonsense of the universe and our position in it. This is not some historical footnote that concerns only Kierkegaard, Nietzsche, Heidegger or Sartre, who all presuppose that the universe is senseless and therefore measure the impulse for the self-determination of human existence. For there is currently a 'third-wave existentialism' forming, and it addresses the supposedly urgent question of how we are to deal with the loss of sense in our conscious life, which purportedly follows from neuroscience, which removes our mental life from our rational control.[7] Gregg D. Caruso and Owen Flanagan also tell us the following: 'Neuroexistentialism is what you get when *Geisteswissenschaften* [sic!] reaches the stage where it finally and self-consciously exorcizes the *geist* and recommends that no one should take seriously the Cartesian myth of the ghost in the machine.'[8] One can see how shamelessly incoherent neuroexistentialism is (unlike Sartre's ontology of the for-itself) from the fact that, a moment after denying *geist*, it defines itself expressly as a '*zeitgeist*' that involves 'a central preoccupation with human purpose and meaning accompanied by the anxiety that there is none.'[9]

Despite referring to this a page later as a 'regulative idea', Caruso and Flanagan make the entirely unsupported claim that 'The universe is causally closed, and the mind is the brain.'[10] Here physics and neuroscience are underhandedly inverted into metaphysics over a few pages before concluding this that human mental life is potentially senseless. This is not a scientific proposition, a hypothesis one can support or refute with data, but rather a metaphysical fiction. Here, humans make an image of themselves and their embeddedness in the non-human universe, via which they attempt to gain control over their evaluative mechanisms. The principles of this process evade the 'theorists' of neuroexistentialism, dragging them into an unfounded, methodologically unfathomable frenzy of a projection of their nihilistic self-experience onto modern natural science.

In ontology of fields of sense, the imagination enters theorizing at a crucial point because it is the factor that allows us to identify the source of error in this type of metaphysics. Metaphysics, as a theory of absolute totality, forms its worldview and humans and thus rests on exercises of the imagination. It goes beyond everything that can be empirically discovered and, despite its contemporary (alleged) faith in science, it stubbornly clings to a residual 'spirituality'. Metaphysical naturalism strives for a great deal more than an acknowledgement of the truth-aptness of natural-scientific knowledge claims. It seeks to place these on the metaphysical throne of an insight into the architecture of the existent as a whole, hoping this will provide orientation in the finite.

But its worldview is illusionary at both ends. Firstly, it hypostatizes the absolute totality into the universe. The physically explorable universe is posted as the totality of the existent – which, given today's cosmological uncertainties (in light of a non-normalized physics), is physically dogmatic. Secondly, it creates the fiction of a 'manifest' worldview or a lifeworld that is threatened by the ongoing imperialism of the 'scientific' worldview and humans, who will ultimately no longer have any refuge.

The fiction of our everyday 'lifeworld' is maintained by the fact that we largely ignore the very thing that modernity made a certainty: that the course of things we experience as ordinary, along with the furnishings of our lifeworld, is a form of illusion that we can overcome only through a renewed effort of the imagination. The mesoscopic scale on which individual things appear to us and are acknowledged in conscious forms is not an ontologically isolated area behind, beneath or beside which there is also a scientifically explorable reality. The posited opposition between lifeworld and science is obsolete, which means that the pathos of unmasking the lifeworld with supposedly sensational philosophical discoveries (such as there is no free will, no time, there is an imminent superintelligence, and so on) has no validity.

There is no completely enlightened consciousness to this day, since enlightenment itself is contingent on a conception of humans and the world that can only be demarcated in the context of our ability to live a life in light of a self-portrait. It is therefore indispensable for a theory of fictions to offer an ontology of the imagination that does not explain it away as a mere supplement to our cognitive activities, but rather assigns to it a central, indeed constitutive function in the human mind.

But precisely this leads to certain meontological difficulties. The anti-metaphysical verdict of the no-world intuition seemingly comes up against its own self-generated expressive boundaries, for one can easily formulate the following objection:[11]

(1) According to FOS, something exists precisely when it appears in some field of sense.
(2) Jed Martin exists because he appears in (at least) the field of sense of *The Map and the Territory*.
(3) The world as the totality of all objects appears, like Jed Martin, in some fictional field of sense through the fact that someone (such as a metaphysician) imagines that it exists.
∴ The world exists (if only as a fictional object).

Mehlich and Koch voice this objection not least against the background that Kant seems to espouse such a position, which can be termed *metaphysical fictionalism* because it understands metaphysics as a fiction in which the absolute totality appears as a 'heuristic fiction'.[12] Since this is sufficient for existence in FOS, it would lead to a field of sense-ontological metaphysics, which would soften FOS's critical stance towards metaphysics to some extent.

To be sure, metaphysical fictionalism as a whole is not a particularly attractive position, because it comes with manifold subsequent costs. But this does nothing to change the problem of (seemingly) making room for the existence of the world. Then the world would have the ontological status of a fictional object, though this would not diminish its right to exist. So can we imagine the world just like Jed Martin?

First of all, we must take into account that, even if the term 'the world' exists, its meaning is given as 'absolute totality', which obviously does not mean that the object seemingly referred to in this way indeed exists. FOS is not a variety of the neo-Meinongian theory of objects, for an object must be real in order to appear, which means that we can also be mistaken about it. To be able to be mistaken about an object, we must have a reason to ascribe existence to it that is independent of its arbitrary introduction.

For Jed Martin this occurs through the distinction between interpretation and reading (see §1 above). One cannot imagine everything while staying in contact with Jed Martin, because the score of *The Map and the Territory* imposes barriers on the imagination that we cannot overstep without losing sight of him. The barriers to the imagination stem from the fact that the score resists far-fetched interpretations which are not supported by any readings. If I imagine Faust as a wall, I am making a mistake, since the text unambiguously presents a human person, albeit without containing the statement that Faust is human. There is no acceptable way of reading the text that allows us to imagine Faust as a wall. Here this is quite simply a barrier to the imagination that cannot be eliminated by insisting that fictional objects have no essence, much less any existence, meaning that one can ultimately take them in any way one likes.

Therefore one needs a sufficiently articulated fictional text that allows us to imagine the world object coherently and fallibly. So let us introduce a crude variation on Borges's *The Aleph* entitled *Olam*, in which a narrator named Cocinero finds an object known as 'Olam' in a corner of a basement in Buenos Aires. Unlike the Aleph in Borges's story, this object is not ironically isolated from metaphysics. If we now imagine the scenario presented by the narrative text, have we then adopted the metaphysical stance? Does the world exist in the fictional fictional text that I have just invented?

The first problem for the formulation of this metaphysical fictionalism arises from the nature of fictional objects: they are isolated from us. The word 'Paris' in *The Map and the Territory* does not refer to Paris but to Paris*, where the latter has some qualities that Paris does not (for example, that Jed Martin lives there). The minimal requirement of all fiction is that it cannot, as a whole, be a report on what is non-fictionally the case. Closer inspection shows that the ontology of fictive objects is irreconcilable with fictional depictions successfully making statements about non-fictional things. If there is a fictional depiction that seems to consist of many true statements, this applies only to an interpretation of its sentences, which relate the interpretation to non-fictional reality. Such an interpretation would not be capable of recognizing the fiction as such, and would thus not enter the fictionality contract to begin with, which demands at the very least that we do not understand a depiction in all respects as a factual report.

The purported world object that appears in *Olam* therefore cannot *prima facie* be identical with the world, since it has a number of properties that the world does not, one being that of lying around in a basement in Buenos Aires. There is no basement in Buenos Aires that contains an Olam. At least, the mere existence of the story *Olam* (which admittedly does not exist, but is a fictional fictional object that is introduced here as part of a thought experiment) gives us no reason to believe that there is an Olam in Buenos Aires.

The second problem stems from the fact that we cannot simply imagine an Olam. If we imagine an object, this object differs from other objects; otherwise we would be imagining a word, but not an object sufficiently well-defined to pass for an absolute totality. In addition, the world would be the maximal individual, since it does not lack any definition. It would, if it existed, be the *omnitudo realitatis*. So what do we imagine when we try to imagine the world? How exactly do we envisage it?

Here the burden of proof lies with metaphysical fictionalism, which must state what we are meant to imagine in order to motivate FOS to acknowledge the existence of the world. In order to imagine something like the world (or God, the soul, and so forth), it is not enough merely to bring up the word 'world' and insist that one is imagining whatever supports metaphysical fictionalism.

The third problem for metaphysical fictionalism that I wish to raise is that it is too pluralistic. If the world were a fictive object – that is, if it essentially manifested itself in acts of the imagination and thus belonged in Jed Martin's realm of being – one could embellish it in an indefinite number of ways. There would not be any stable metaphysical theorizing that would allow us to distinguish some metaphysical position as opposed to some other. Even if one classified the metaphysical literature of the past and present as fictions dealing with the world as a fictive object, it would follow precisely from this that each one of these metaphysics could equally validly be considered a correct description of the world. One could simply make the world 'as you like it'. If this were the only ontological attempt to save metaphysics in opposition to FOS, it would be an easy win for the latter.

It seems reasonable, of course, to assume that Cocinero takes absolutely everything into view, meaning that the view is not incoherent from any perspective. He thus also captures himself standing in the basement in

Buenos Aires, and so on. But how exactly can some object that appears in someone's visual field enable a finite being to have a total vision?

In the metaphysical tradition, in the great systems of Plato, Aristotle or neo-Platonism, all the way to modernity, it is assumed that, if one overcomes the conventional proposition structure of our understanding of distinct objects, one can only aim for absolute totality in the mode of an 'everything at once (*homou panta*).'[13] The absolute only shows itself in a reference that precisely cannot be articulated consistently any longer; this is central to the apophatic tradition, which rightly understood that metaphysics cannot be practised as a theory of objects.

The absolute is not a well-defined object of any intuition; one cannot imagine it. One can at best imagine imagining it, which Borges's story *The Aleph* masterfully demonstrates by following on indirectly from mysticism, which consists in transcending the misguided notion that we can grasp absolute totality as an object.

The illusory coherence of metaphysical fictionalism results from the fact that it does not seriously attempt to embellish the world in the mode of the imaginary but simply uses the word mark 'world' or 'Olam' to formulate a pseudo-problem for FOS. We do not need to imagine the world in order to deny its existence. We do not make the world appear in a distinct field of sense by denying its existence in the no-world intuition.

Yet precisely this appears to present FOS with new expressive problems. James T. Hill correspondingly formulates what he calls an 'objection from inexpressibility' to the no-world intuition.[14] He considers the latter a variety of performative self-contradiction; in particular, he argues that FOS cannot make a negative existential judgement about the world. In this context he rightly notes that the no-world intuition does not permit unrestricted quantification over absolutely all fields of sense: 'This renders mysterious how Gabriel manages to rule out the possibility of the world existing in some field of sense outside the range of what he is able to quantify over or think about.'[15] He especially disputes that I am in a position to use the manoeuvre that I draw on to refer to 'round squares'. This manoeuvre consists in the existence of a field of sense, for example that of Euclidean geometry, that assigns suitable meanings to the terms 'round' and 'square' for us to know that no object in the field of sense of Euclidean geometry can be both round and square. Round squares are impossible in Euclidean geometry but might be accepted if one defined an infinite circle in another framework in a formally pure fashion as a figure whose centre is infinitely far from its surroundings, which could also apply to an infinitely large square.[16] In such an assignment of meaning, an infinitely large circle and an infinitely large square would be the same figure. Whether and under what conditions such a field of sense can serve a purpose is another matter. To say that there is no round square, at any rate, refers to conditions in which the round and the square exist, which means that the assertion of non-existence in the present field of sense merely expresses the negation of the combinability of these two object types. This manoeuvre, Hill argues, imputes that none of the existing objects are identical with a round circle: an analysis that is not available to the world: '*Contra* Gabriel, the two are importantly different because in the case of the round square, "for any X, X ≠ the round square" does not require reference to the round square, whereas in the proposition "for any X, X ≠ the world" the term "any" quantifies unrestrictedly and thus refers to the world.'[17] However, Hill thus simplifies my argumentation in a fashion that is both impermissible and scarcely helps his position by assuming an unlimited universal quantification for the round square and only disputing it for the world. According to FOS, however, there is no universal quantification over a universe of all objects. The term x in a formula such as '∀x (x = x)' does not refer to all objects but allows insertions of proper names that make reference to something in a given field of sense.

Ontological realism restricts the area of reference. We cannot infer from a logical chain of signs such as '∀x (x = x)' how far our thinking extends.[18] It does not follow from a competent use of '∀x (x = x)' within an established formal system (a calculus language) that we are contradicting the verdict of FOS if we introduce an identity axiom for a given formal system. For the variable x has restricted conditions of application (insertion rules), which already follows from the familiar metamathematical incompleteness theorems, which teach that there is no formal system from which all theorems of all formal systems can be deduced. There is no system of axioms in which all true statements can be deduced. It is fundamentally impossible to construct a deductive formal system whose universal quantification covers an entire metaphysical area, since there is still a remainder that cannot be integrated as a whole into any given, well-constructed system.[19]

Even within mathematics, we are not automatically justified in postulating a universe of all mathematical objects, at least not in the sense of building up a formal system, since every formal system misses some mathematical truth, and thus some objects.[20] This is not paradoxical, but rather an insight into the incompleteness of formal systems, from which FOS concludes that we cannot actually obtain any metaphysical theorems about everything at the formal, logical level.

Ontology cannot be gleaned from a purportedly universal, given logic – which, incidentally, Hill's authority Priest brings up in order to deprive the quantifiers of their metaphysical aura.[21]

According to FOS, disputing that round squares exist precisely does not mean comparing round squares with all objects and not finding one that is identical with a round square, since the scope of our substantive thinking is limited by fields of sense, which do not exist *en bloc* as a totality.

I am not ruling out a priori that the world might exist in a field of sense that contradicts my ontological theory, but I do not see any a priori reason to acknowledge such an unusual thing as the world, or any basis in pre-ontological experience, which never places us into a totality where we speak substantively about all objects or all fields of sense. So the world does not exist a priori, let alone a posteriori. Whoever would claim against FOS that the world exists, along with the corresponding theorizing (such as metaphysics or even physics), carries the burden of proof, since the existence of the world is not obvious in light of the arguments of FOS.

It is not surprising, then, that there is room for objections to FOS, though these are not successful if one merely asserts that, according to FOS, it is actually epistemically possible that the world exists because its existence must be acknowledged in some previously unconsidered field of sense. The weak epistemic possibility that a suggested ontology has overlooked something is always given and does not impair a philosophical knowledge claim, any more than the circumstance that empirical assumptions can be revised jeopardizes the objectivity of science. Rather, revisability may be a trait of objectivity, for we can be mistaken regarding matters about which we are capable of making substantive – that is, truth-apt – judgements. The no-world intuition is not an infallible insight, but rather a system of ideas and arguments that takes as its starting point the pre-ontological experience of a plurality of phenomena that is not governed by any singular principle, and then shows that there is no good reason to reduce this plurality to a singular fabric of sense. We exist in fields of sense, but not in a single all-encompassing one. Anyone with a different opinion requires very good reasons, which, as stated above, can neither be gained from modern calculus languages nor empirically obtained.[22]

Hill admittedly goes a step further by considering the formal structure of FOS's concept of existence. He assumes that FOS's concept of existence is equivocal in the following sense: 'existence is appearing in a field of sense or quappearing in a field of sense or $z$appearing in a field of sense, and so on.'[23] Based on this, he argues, I must acknowledge that the world does not exist, but possibly does quexist or zexist, and so forth.

However, Hill overlooks the fact that I do not accept the alternative between univocity and plurivocity in the usual manner. As a formal concept of a philosophical theory (FOS), 'existence' is formally univocal. To exist always means appearing in a field of sense. The theoretical analysis of the concept of existence in the framework of ontology does not, however, establish what this actually consists in, since factual existence is paradigmatically observed under conditions of pre-ontological experience. This is one decisive way in which FOS constitutes an ontological realism: the theory construction does not specify the particular character of existence in individual fields of sense, meaning that one cannot deduce a metaphysical architecture from ontology without rendering the formal concepts of ontology senseless.

This does not rule out the existence of the concept of existence in FOS. The concept of existence is developed within a model that stands out from alternative models through the fact that it dispenses with any ontotheology – that is, a conflation of ontology and metaphysics. This alternative has

the advantage of extending our insight into the incompleteness of our theorizing, which we know from other areas of the mathematical (including theoretical informatics, of course) and physical sciences of the last century, to ontology. Our finitude is not a limited perspective that can be compared with an absolute, aperspectivally present totality that we (unfortunately) cannot reach.[24]

The incompleteness lies not in the eye of the beholder, who desperately strives for a view from nowhere that they never reach. A metaphysical view from nowhere is already ruled out by the fact that no life form in the universe can know everything about the universe. Our knowledge about the universe is made possible by the causal texture of the universe, one facet of which is that we cannot measure and know everything at once. The universe exhibits contingent barriers to knowledge, meaning that physics can show us the reasons for its own metaphysical incompleteness.[25]

However one justifies the theoretical merits of FOS, its model rules out what Hill claims about it. Existence is formally univocal. Whatever exists in a given case instantiates the form of existence in a respectively specific fashion – so specific that the concept of existence cannot provide an overview of all the fields of sense that really exist.

Our state of fallibility is explained by the fact that the model inherently rules out the possibility of such a metaphysical overview. The metaphysicians must be held accountable by FOS, since they have always conceded that we cannot recognize the absolute totality under finite conditions. It has been seen as a problem for finite cognition since its introduction, which is why Plato described philosophy in *The Symposium* as occupying the threshold between a divine existence unavailable to us and an animal existence with no interest in conceptual matters. Contemporary 'analytical' metaphysics simply seeks to circumvent these problems of expressivity by claiming that it can rely on a set of logical building blocks that promises us absolute totality as a logical 'free lunch'. But symbolic logic alone does not help us to answer the question of whether an absolute totality exists. Without any competent employment of the concept of existence, which is impossible purely within the framework of an established logic, we are simply evading the real issue: whether there is an absolute totality of everything existent.

Hill is almost right when he states that 'the denial of absolute generality is by its own lights restricted rather than absolutely general.'[26] I qualify my agreement with this interpretation to the extent that it would have to be established what connection between generality and universal quantification is posited by Hill and some others.[27] Hill owes me a concrete elaboration of his implicit assumption that existence is the most general concept, encompassing all things there are in such a way that the existence of a totality is ensured by such a concept, which would admittedly have to fall under itself. But this brings us to the terrain on which FOS takes a stance. At this point, Hill should offer an explanation of the structure of an ultimate *genus* containing everything particular. Since a mere pointer to 'logic' does not supply this, his recourse to universal quantification remains a dry assurance.

Hill counters FOS with a concept of contingent, finite and open totality. He does not, unfortunately, explain in what sense such a totality is neither additive nor normalized such that the field of sense-ontological arguments repeat themselves. Furthermore, he does not offer any commentary that would give us insight into the form of universal quantification that enables such a totality.

In a number of conversations that took place in Bonn, Paris and Covilhã, Charles Travis suggested the following diagnosis, with which – with a grain of salt – I concur. At first glance, one can understand the concept of the object as the concept of something that contributes to a truth-apt thought in such a way that none of its aspects are left open. The phrase '_ is in Vienna' does not provide any insight into Viennese facts. This distinguishes it from the statement 'The Albertina is in Vienna', which one can use to articulate a true thought. Then the Albertina is an object. It is different with the phrase 'The object'; if one says, 'The object is in Vienna' without any context that lends the phrase 'the object' an anaphoric reference, one has not articulated any truth-apt thought.

In general, I take an object as something of which something is true (see above, pp. 103f.). For us to speak of truth, one must define an object area of which something can also be true. Based on this, Grim, Badiou, Kreis and others think that we can define an object area that contains all objects, which is usually met with objections to a pluralistic division of the object area of pure quantification; at the same time, they insist that this assumption entangles us in an irresolvable and, hence, negative dialectic. If this were so, we would be entitled to make any desired adjustment that allowed us to speak about objects without quantifying over a paradox-generating total area. So that quantifiers can have an effect, however, there are already sense criteria in play that allow us to introduce punctuation marks for true statements, something that a negative dialectic renders impossible from the outset.

The critical perspective on metaphysics cannot be represented appropriately in terms of set theory or predication theory alone. For we do not simply think thoughts relating to objects that can be sorted into areas to which we can a priori ascribe criteria of identity (which includes sets qua mathematical objects). Rather, we constantly refer via truth-apt thoughts to objects whose sorting presupposes empirically substantive predicates and, thus, empirically bound cognition. The field of empirical cognition is open by nature. There is no point assigning an absolute totality of all objects to it as an object. If I think the true thought that I am writing this sentence in Paris, this does not mean I am thinking that everything that exists or all objects possess some properties or other (such as the property of being uncountably many).

In this context, Travis rightly pointed out to me that we can distinguish between at least two interpretations of supposedly unrestricted quantification of the type ∀x (x = x). On the one hand, we can do this to think that *every* object about which we can think a true thought must at least be itself. On the other hand, we can do this with the view that *all* existing objects must at least be themselves. Every individual object one grasps in the form of a judgement is what it is. What it is is partially grasped in the form of a judgement, for example by expressing the thought that a banana is bent. The being-bent of the banana involves the fact that the banana is a banana, which is not especially surprising. The banana does not change as a result of our judgement about it, otherwise we could not think that it is bent. The thought would fall short of its object if sorting into a context always meant that one could predicatively see through the purportedly unsayable individuality of things. The being-bent of the banana consists in the fact that some other things may also be bent. It is therefore contingent. It is not a metaphysical necessity for it to be bent; we can cultivate straight bananas.

Thinking that every individual object that can be given to us as thinkers is always itself means assuming that only the things with which we engage in the form of truth-apt thoughts exhibit properties that we express paradigmatically through sortal predicates. Things never change quickly enough for them to exhibit no properties whatsoever, since they must change quickly enough to elude the temporally bound perceptive faculties of human animals.

Any universal quantification that refers to something is sortally bound and, thus, locally restricted. We can quantify meaningfully over all lions, cats, fermions, printers, spoons, and so on, but not over all objects, since the concept of the object functions in ontology as a formal concept that is logically unsuitable to present an absolute totality of all objects.[28] 'Object' is not a sortal.

A significant precursor of this insight is William James, who introduced the concept of pluralism into ontology in his 1908 Hibbert Lectures.[29] There, he distinguishes between *absolutism* and *pluralism*, assigning the former to the *all-form* and the latter to the *each-form*.[30] He also refers to his pluralistic position as 'radical empiricism', which supposes that

> there may ultimately never be an all-form at all, that the substance of reality may never get totally collected, that some of it may remain outside of the largest combination of it ever made, and that a distributive form of reality, the *each*-form, is logically as acceptable and empirically as probable as the all-form commonly acquiesced in as so obviously the self-evident thing.[31]

As James rightly notes, it is not the task of logic 'to make us theoretically acquainted with the essential nature of reality'.[32] He therefore sees the nature of reality in the following terms: 'Reality, life, experience, concreteness, immediacy, use what word you will, exceeds our logic, overflows and surrounds it.'[33]

James even goes so far as to formulate an ontological contextualism based on this, expressing the realistic thrust of FOS in the statement that '*nothing* real escapes from having an environment.'[34] For a central element of 'realism' is the acknowledgement of a potential divergence of truth and holding-to-be-true that has an effect in the form of an incompleteness: no theory is capable of describing the metaphysical totality (the world) in its entirety. Thus any theoretically accessible object area (any field of sense) has an environment that it cannot exhaust with its own conceptual resources.

Realism is thus grounded in the texture of reality. No theory is a literal theory of everything; this ensures that we are placed in a *fallibility environment*. Every formulation of a knowledge claim relies on the fact that an environment which is opaque in this claim is sufficiently stable for us to do justice to our own claims. No idea – not even a purely philosophical one – is immune to going awry in its theoretical articulation.

This criterion for realism deviates in one crucial way from the idea of understanding realism as the assumption that even our most solidly justified overall theories might be wrong. For an overall theory in the relevant sense cannot exist anyway, as Hilary Putnam's manifold arguments against what he called 'metaphysical realism' showed.[35] Rather, the requirement of fallibility applies wherever ideas are represented in the form of a theory – that is, in a sufficiently articulated context that allows us to define a demarcated object area, a field of sense, about which statements can be made.

It is not entirely clear here why James still insists that his '"multiverse" still makes a "universe"'.[36] He adds the comment that every part stands in a possible or mediated connection with every other part. He refers to this expressly as a *durcheinander* [muddle] as opposed to *all-einheit* [all-unity], addressing the former overall as the 'synechistic type'.[37]

James's pluralistic universe therefore differs from FOS in one decisive way: the object area of FOS is a multiverse *sui generis*. The real does not even hang together in the respect that one can fundamentally link every part with every other, since there are limitations on interconnection. The no-world intuition sets an upper limit to interconnectivity.

Anton Friedrich Koch offers a subtle alternative to FOS on common ground with his 'hermeneutical realism'.[38] Unlike FOS, this approach operates with a base field of individual spatiotemporal things on which a genuinely irreducible plurality of fields of sense supervenes. Now Koch, as I have elaborated several times, countered FOS with the argument that the world can at least be imagined, meaning that it is located somewhere in the catchment area of fictional objects. How he envisages this is developed in a sketch for a theory of the imagination.[39] This theory now forms the basis for his view of possible worlds, which acts as the framework for his formulation of hermeneutical realism.

The indispensability of a theory of the imagination motivates Koch in the following manner: if we intend to draw not only on a consciousness of some kind of space, but on a reference to elements of a 'multiplicity of positions' [*Stellenmannigfaltigkeit*], we must bring objects to mind.[40]

According to Koch, we only ever see a house to the extent that we see a part '*of* it', the 'front that faces us'.[41] This formulation does pose some problems for the theory of perception, but we can leave them aside. For it is certainly correct that we not only mentally add what makes the house what it is but in fact form an image of the nature of the house. Part of this image is the notion that the house remains there if we do not look at it, that it has a basement, a particular mass, an interior, possibly a future exceeding our own lifespan, and so on. In short, our contact with the house is not restricted to an exchange of stimuli between the irradiation from the house and our nerve ends; rather, we must objectify the house to be able to take up contact in a way that enables a fully valid propositional perception of the house situation.[42] Our perceptive knowledge regarding the house is based, as Koch emphasizes, not only on 'discursive representations, but also and especially on imaginative notions'.[43]

Here 'imagination' [*Einbildungskraft*] is Koch's name for our imaginative faculties as a whole, since this is essentially exercised in acts of an imaginative nature – however these might be specifically resolved in local modules of the mind in individual sciences.[44] He justifies the introduction of an essentially imaginative faculty via exercises of 'imaginative abstraction'[45] by which we clear the space and 'vividly imagine the transcendentally necessary, metaphysically impossible initial state of the space, whose theory is Euclidean geometry, which mathematics can obviously exceed, and has exceeded, in discursive generalization, but which remains the unshakeable foundation for our conception of space.'[46] On this basis, Koch attempts to gain access to the idea of possible worlds as models of a 'counterpossible borderline cases' or an 'impossible initial state of being and thinking',[47] an activity he views as 'transcendental imagination'.[48] I do not, however, see why the emptied space should be Euclidean.[49]

In this framework, Koch opposes 'transparentism, which is supposed to include the notion that the real is in principle fully describable and fully knowable.'[50] We agree that, firstly, transparentism is false (or nonsensical) and that, secondly, it is an essential foundation for all worldviews. The theory of possible worlds draws on it in so far as 'affirmative references to possible worlds as well-defined macro-individuals'[51] already build metaphysically on the fact that possible worlds show an architecture which makes them knowable and conceptually usable in philosophical contexts: 'Such macro-individuals do not and cannot exist – one more reason, incidentally, *why the world does not exist*, namely the real world as a great individual that only actually exists as an open horizon for interrelationships.'[52] However, Koch uses the model of possible worlds to support his main thesis, the subjectivity thesis, which states that, in any possible world, subjectivity must eventually appear in a spatiotemporally located form.[53] Hence this thesis is in danger of self-contradiction, since it can at best be an element of a *reductio ad absurdum* that employs conceptual means which must be rejected. If possible worlds are ontologically or even metaphysically impossible, there is no possible world in which it is true that there are possible worlds.

Koch saves his skin by referring to the idealizing approach to modelling in modern physics: possible worlds are metaphysically impossible – they do not and cannot exist – but we can still work with them in thought experiments.[54] In this way, however, one arrives at a weakened position, since this at best proves that there would have to be subjectivity if there were possible worlds. Since there are no possible worlds, there is no reason to prove the metaphysically necessary existence of subjectivity per se.

We simply cannot imagine a 'Euclidean initial state' that is 'the same for all possible material spatiotemporal systems',[55] as such a notion is thwarted by its 'application to reality'.[56] What we envisage imaginatively is therefore something real. It already curves the logical space that Koch wishes to clear, as it were. Yet an empty logical space does not exist any more than does an empty physical space.

Here we see a return of the ontological realism of FOS, which corresponds – not by chance – to a 'non-transcendental empiricism'[57] at the methodological level. Thoughts about the real are fallible in so far as they are corrigible. Non-corrigible thoughts about the real do not really exist. It is an illusion to think that one can conclude from a supposed tautology such as 'The world is the world' or 'The real is the real' or 'Everything is identical with itself' that we have the capacity to recognize synthetic a priori truths. The world is not an object of substantive thought and, hence, nothing that can be imagined.

Genuine tautologies are logical truths that apply within a given formal system. Whether something is a logical truth or not depends on which formal system one examines. Yet, whichever formal system one examines, one will not be able to introduce the world by mentioning it in the form of the phrase 'the world'. For any existential clause to follow from 'The world is the world', the phrase 'the world' must be given a sense that allows us to specify an object area in which a world object can appear. But precisely this is impossible according to FOS, for the world does not appear anyway in a formal system whose rules of transformation are uninterpreted. One can at most introduce the sign 'the world' in this way, which is not remotely enough to name a metaphysical world object successfully; this would require a relation of reference or representation and hence an interpretation of the formal sign system, which would bring us back to the terrain of FOS.

§11

Fictive, Imaginary and Intentional Objects

Not all objects that one can introduce into the discourse by exercising the imagination are fictive. Fictive objects essentially belong to the field of sense of the fictional, which is characterized by the fact that we must perform and interpret the objects appearing in it to gain access to them. Our access to fictive objects is mediated by imaginary objects. We would not know anything about fictive objects if they did not appear to us in the form of imaginary objects.

The contents [*Gehalte*] of our perceptual illusions are *imaginary objects*. These substances do not stand like obstacles between us and the objects of perception, but rather are the form in which objects perceptible to us appear. They are illusions, for it is all too easy to confuse the objects of perception with the medium in which they appear, since this medium can itself easily become the object of an admittedly rather different perception. In general, we contribute in a species-specific, context-specific and individual way to every actually existing perceptual episode. At a particular point in time, assuming rehearsed and autobiographically formed prior knowledge, we as humans perceive a scene in which objects with the index of knownness emerge. We can predicatively articulate in what form the objects are known to us in the standard case of a self-conscious life. There is no chasm of ineffability between the perceptible objects and our use of concepts, since the latter is designed to be employed in factual perceptual episodes.

As Benoist and Travis have rightly underlined, this does not mean that our senses are propositional filters which enable us to predicate successfully.[1] Sensuous reality is rather something real *sui generis*, and this means it precisely does not rule out our successful linguistic apprehension of it. For it to exist, it does not require any mental naming acts or pre-linguistic indexicalia.

Intentional objects are objects of a reference that presupposes a medium-based form of observation, and is thus perspectival. So they refer to objects that we apprehend under certain sensorily or conceptually coded conditions. Some intentional objects are imaginary, but not all. Thus the objects in my subjective visual field that are directly accessible to me are aligned with my perceptual position, which does not mean that the objects of successful perception should themselves be considered indexically aligned. Otherwise we would not be able to take into account that several subjects can perceive the same thing, even if they perceive it differently. The concept of *intuition* [*Anschauung*] is here generally introduced to characterize a selection function, in such a way that there are always further objects one could apprehend, but which no one has yet apprehended.[2]

Since not all objects are sensory in the customary sense, it would therefore seem that non-sensuous intuition exists. But this assumption applies only on the condition that we distinguish between two kinds of real objects: those we can sensorily apprehend (cognize) and those that we can think but fundamentally cannot sensorily apprehend. In both cases I am speaking of 'real' objects, since *reality* is understood as the epistemic modal category that allows us to be mistaken about an object. Since we can be mistaken about mathematical objects as well as the concept of the object (which is itself an object), both so-called abstract objects and the formal objects of philosophy are real. Strictly speaking, one of the points of realistic FOS is that there are no non-real objects.

All objects about which we know truths are intentional.[3] This does not mean that all objects are intentional. The real is not sucked up into a global consciousness as in a transcendental phenomenology; there is not a thinker who corresponds to it as a whole. The objects we know are ones that, under fundamentally incalculable conditions, can each be selected as something that merits our attention.

These fundamentally incalculable conditions characterize our perspective. We cannot apprehend our perspective in such a way that we somehow take the intentional objects into consideration along with our selection functions. Rather, our perspective is constitutively transparent, which is why, in line with Kant, one can classify intuition as unmediated representation.[4] We never grasp all the conditions for our examination of a particular object, not even by going one theoretical level higher and starting to articulate the sensory physiology of a given perceptual episode, with all its physical environmental conditions.[5] Even if we had managed *per impossibile* the workload of a complete apprehension of all physical embedding conditions, which is already impossible for physical reasons of complementarity in quantum theory, we would not even have begun to describe countless mental theoretical conditions.[6] For our theory-capable perspective entails socioeconomic, conceptual, historical and logical preconditions that indeterminably exceed anything that we could ever fully grasp.

What we can actually fully grasp is tied to models. A model is a conceptual system that fixes the form of intuitions and makes them publicly accessible. *Models* are explicit depictions of selection functions, meaning that we can use them to partially grasp our own information filters. That is why, in logic and other related disciplines, we can develop thought models that offer insights into how we think or how we should think. No model is identical to what it depicts, otherwise it would collapse into the pointless map with a scale of 1:1. We can formulate completeness and incompleteness theorems for models but not for intuitions and their conditions, since intuitions form our base reality. Realistic theoretical conditions apply in base reality, which especially includes the central requirement of FOS that we can never grasp *all* objects, since no relevant totality of objects actually exists.

We can have intuitions of models in so far as those models are objects such as computer simulations or maps. But this means neither that the models themselves are intuitions nor that our intuitions are models. Our intuitions are in direct contact with the real, since they are themselves something real that makes a contribution to our factual perceptual situation.

Intuition is the base reality of our mind. This base reality therefore consists not of atomic components, individual things in space and time, or anything similarly substantive. Rather, intuition is itself part of a system of faculties that we select in theoretical self-modellings such as the present one. The intuition in question appears precisely in a self-modelling executed so that I can form an idea of the way in which I am always in contact with something that is not of the same type as the mind.

In this sense, we can concur with Fichte, who famously defines the framework of the 'system of the human mind'[7] with the following principle 'The Ego opposes in the Ego **a** divisible Non-Ego to a divisible Ego.'[8] What Fichte refers to here as a 'divisible Non-Ego' is the category of the intentional object. I assign the imaginary objects to the divisible ego. The ego in which these are distinguished is the mind, which models itself via such distinctions. The mind objectifies itself in fictions, which include the distinction between imaginary and intentional objects; this does not mean that imaginary and intentional objects do not exist, or that they are fictive. Self-modelling is inevitable, however, if we attempt to examine the portfolio of our basic terminology more closely.

This self-modelling is subject to theoretical requirements. Alongside the indispensability examined above, this includes the following *realistic incompleteness theorem: no modelling of ourselves as minded beings can grasp all necessary and collectively adequate conditions for the existence of a mental episode.* This circumstance can also be characterized as *constitutive opacity*. As soon as we have begun to describe a theoretical level in its basic structures in order to apply it in the form of explanations, a further theoretical level appears that leads to the further embedding of a thematized field of sense in previously unexamined surroundings (a further field of sense).

Because of the indispensability, however, this does not mean that we embed the mind in something that is fundamentally beyond its reach, which would lead back to the dialectic of illusionism. Rather, every theoretical level we introduce into our self-modelling in order to ground the intuition in the consciousness, for example, and consciousness in self-consciousness, is accompanied by a kind of deepening of the mind. We do not escape the mind in our self-awareness; we only shift its direction of view.

Mind is thus an indefinitely extendable dimension of our self-awareness as truth-apt beings. It therefore varies synchronically and diachronically in an incalculable way, which is why the historicity of our self-relations cannot be passed over in favour of an ascertainable structure that can be identified in neurotypical naked and predatory apes.[9] The only invariant one has to postulate for this characterization of our ability to characterize is the dimension of self-modifiability described here.

The minded being that we are apprehends itself essentially via imaginary objects. These appear at the fundamental level of our sensory interaction with the real. Our daydreaming does not only begin where we let our thoughts wander but takes place at the level of our linking of intuitions to form an episode of our life. This corresponds to the role of the imagination in building up our thoughts, which has been known at least since Aristotle. It is not the process of *phantasia* that is remote from reality, but rather the way in which we grasp intentional objects.[10] It presents these to us from a perspective with which we cannot fully catch up, such that it always remains expandable. This indefinite expandability, which is not subject to any identifiable overall rule, ensures that we exist as beings in an open heuristics.[11]

The concept of the object in FOS is a basic formal one that is explained by showing that objects are embedded in facts. In this way, the realm of objects is protected from unrestricted principles of comprehension. We are justified in ruling out the possibility that anything which can be inserted into an arbitrarily formulated function is *ipso facto* an object. The manoeuvre for substantiating this justification draws on the realism of the no-world intuition: since we know that there is nothing which is collectively true of all existing objects, there are always some objects that remain outside of any conceivable definition of an object area. There is no discursive universe whose limits are visible a priori and which simultaneously contains all objects.

This means that we cannot carry out a complete disjunction of objects into categories; it is not the case, then, that common dualities such as abstract/concrete, material/immaterial or natural/mental divide the total area of objects. The situation is not improved by increasing the number of categories. A concept of categories that sorts all objects into one or more grids whose completeness is visible a priori can thus be ruled out; it is against this background that I describe FOS in *Sinn und Existenz* as 'non-transcendental empiricism'.[12]

The mere circumstance that some objects are individuated only by virtue of appearing in a field of sense whose existence cannot be recognized a priori already undermines the project of finding principles of comprehension for objects that distribute the latter across grids of categories.[13] The division of objects into *fictive*, *imaginary* and *intentional* should not, therefore, be understood as a metaphysical hypothesis that can be completed to form an overall view by adding the non-intentional objects after all. For the desired completeness would take the form of an ontology that postulates the existence of four fields of sense (fictive, imaginary, intentional and non-intentional), which raises the question of whether these fields of sense collectively exist in a further field of sense. If not, then the four fields of sense must appear in one of those named. I will go through these variants, since they characterize metaphysical starting points for modern theoretical philosophy which are not usually understood as such, something that the post-Kantian idealists simply termed 'dogmatism'.

1 Metaphysical Fictionalism

Metaphysical fictionalism is the assumption that all objects in the field of sense of the fictional exist and are fictive; here we are dealing, in the best case, with a subtle architecture that takes into account the embeddedness of the three other object types in their fields of sense. Because of the avoidance of transitivity, imaginary objects in the field of sense of the imaginary can exist in the field of sense of the fictive without *ipso facto* being fictive. The only thing that is fictive is their field of sense, which is now *ex hypothesi* a fictive object. Thus metaphysical fictionalism claims that the other fields of sense exist independently of any interpretation, which is the point of the fictive. Philosophical theorizing would thus be reliant on a score that could be augmented through interpretation within a manoeuvring space. Then there would be different ontologies that depend on how exactly one performs the score of the real, which comprises the four object types. Such interpretation-dependent ontologies are familiar in their basic form from Nietzsche and Vaihinger via Carnap to Putnam and contemporary varieties of fictionalism.[14] What is usually not mentioned, however, is the scarcely deniable self-referentiality based on which the field of sense of the fictive appears within itself. This triggers a regress that is least problematic, since it is now fictive that all fields of sense are fictive. Nietzsche sums this up in a much quoted passage:

Against the positivism which halts at phenomena – 'There are only facts' – I would say: no, facts are just what there aren't, there are only interpretations. We cannot determine any fact 'in itself'; perhaps it's nonsensical to want to do such a thing. 'Everything is subjective', you say: but that itself in an *interpretation*, for the 'subject' is not something given but a fiction added on, tucked behind. – Is it even necessary to posit the interpreter behind the interpretation? Even that is fiction, hypothesis.

Inasmuch as the word 'knowledge' has any meaning at all, the world is knowable: but it is variously *interpretable*; it has no meaning behind it, but countless meanings. 'Perspectivism'.

It is our needs *which interpret the world*: our drives and their for and against. Every drive is a kind of lust for domination, each has its perspective, which it would like to impose as a norm on all the other drives.[15]

Benoist has recently pointed out rightly that this passage directs itself *avant la lettre* against Vaihinger and others, since the true opponent is positivism, not realism, which Nietzsche considers misguided based on entirely different motives.[16] In this way, Nietzsche arrives at a 'generalized hermeneutics',[17] something that is familiar from twentieth-century discourse on Nietzsche.[18] My concern here is not to develop a coherent Nietzsche reading (which would probably be a futile undertaking, thanks to Nietzsche himself). What is more important is to understand that metaphysical fictionalism falls into its own field, which Nietzsche unambiguously acknowledged without taking it as cause to revise his theory. In this respect he was remarkably coherent-incoherent.

Metaphysical fictionalism overstretches the concept of the fictive, and therefore also culminates in Derrida's equally much quoted dictum that there is nothing outside the text.[19] Here too we must be cautious, for Derrida supports his argument through the methodology of reading Rousseau and engages only indirectly with the topics of general metaphysics. Here Derrida is concerned with the relationship between 'Rousseau' as the name of an authorial function and Jean-Jacques, the person whose subjectivity is at stake in the literary forms Rousseau employs. This leads into areas of literary theory that we can pass over here. Nonetheless, it will be difficult to dispute that Derrida's recourse to metaphorology and his rejection of reference, which is a running thread in *On Grammatology*, boils down to a position that places the term '"real"' in scare quotes.[20] All this has been worked through *ad nauseam* and rests on an impermissible reduction of all objects to intentionality, to which we shall return, which is why Derrida can more readily be considered a victim of intentionalism than of fictionalism.

I am bringing up Derrida because he has an idea of what one must take on board as a metaphysical fictionalist. One concedes that there is a world, but it becomes an unknowable 'arche-writing'[21] that can never be an *'object of a science'*.[22] That is because the concept of the fictive is overstretched if one treats every theoretical attitude as an act of reading and models it on literary reading. For what then results is indeed the effect Derrida observes and terms the 'supplement', whereby an imaginary object steps between us and the arche-writing, whose existence is ultimately questionable (after all, one does not want to fall into the trap of the metaphysics of presence . . .). With Derrida, as with Nietzsche, this leads to a never-ending acrobatics that was perfected in US 'theory' circles under the banner of 'deconstruction'. However, this changes nothing about the paradox one generates by assigning *all* objects to the field of sense of the fictive or, more circumspectly, to one of four fields of sense that in turn exist in the field of sense of the fictive.[23]

2 Metaphysical Imaginatism
Metaphysical imaginatism pulls all objects into the field of sense of the imaginary, or into one of four fields of sense that appear in the field

of sense of the imaginary, which then appears within itself as a result. Those objects are *imaginary* that emerge at the interface between the real and its epistemic apprehension. At the level of perception, they are the perspectival substances that present something to us as something. The imaginary objects are the reason for our fallibility, for they present aspects of perceptible objects to us – without blocking access to those objects. The perceptible objects are and remain what we perceive, but we perceive them in the medium of substances (form, colour, tone, proposition, and so on). We can therefore be mistaken about the perceptible objects, since we do not correctly grasp all their aspects. The reason for this delusion is our successful contact with the object about which we make additional assumptions not covered by our direct contact. The substances are factually existing, real objects that appear to us in the medium of perception. The medium of perception is a real relation. The qualitative properties of perceptible objects are located neither 'in our consciousness' nor 'in our head' but between us and the perceptible objects.

This already means that not all objects can be imaginary. In cases of perception, imaginary objects are relations between a perceptual system (such as a minded being of the *Homo sapiens* type) and perceived objects. Since the perceived objects usually belong to the universe, the relevant causality here takes the form of an interplay or entanglement whose logical form can be taken from quantum theory, which one can fundamentally formulate as a general theoretical framework that, beyond its familiar realm of application, supplies concepts that are responsible for '*the phenomenal character of the world*'.[24] In the words of Hartmann Römer, entanglement is

> a peculiar and highly characteristic trait of quantum-like systems. Entanglement can and will occur if the following conditions are met:
>
> • Within a system, one can identify subsystems and distinguish *global observables*, which relate to the system as a whole, from *local observables*, which belong to the subsystems.
> • There is a global observable that is complementary to local observables.
> • The system is in a so-called *entangled state*, for example an eigenstate of global observables in which the outcome of measuring the local observables is uncertain.[25]

This vocabulary can be transferred to FOS.[26] A *global observable* corresponds to the sense of a field of sense in which we exist as cognizant beings. Let us assume that we are in a perceptual situation, which is always one of the fields of sense in which we exist as long as we are conscious.[27] The sense (ordering rules) of perception assigns the objects appearing in the field of sense of perception to two subsystems: a perceiving and a perceived system. These subsystems are in turn fields of sense, which means that they exhibit *local observables*, which here means embedded senses whose directionality depends on the perceptual field of sense. We cannot grasp the field of sense of the perceptual situation by augmenting a given perception of the object level with a further perception of the perception, since this constitutes a significant modification of our mental episode. This is familiar from Kleist's deliberations on the intervention of reflexion in our mental state, which interrupts object orientation.[28] Our perceptual consciousness is changed by the fact that we ask ourselves under what conditions it comes about. Examining our sensory physiology changes the object of perception in the sense that, for example, we first observe a blue cube at the object level and then a blue cube together with a perceptual system. In so doing, we do not step outside the perceptual situation as a whole, but we do significantly change it, because we now perceive other objects. As soon as we turn towards the global observables we change the local observables, and vice versa.

The outcome of the measurements – that is, the object definitions at the level of object perception – is uncertain from the standpoint of the fact that we perceive. It is thus fundamentally not predictable in a deterministic sense what a living being will perceive next in a given perceptual situation. This should not come as a surprise, furthermore, since it actually takes into account our heuristics, which is a fallible and open system and is capable of changes of course that can be treated as learning achievements in the trial and error process of our adaption to our ecological niche. If it is predetermined that we perceive – that is, if we examine the perceptual system as a whole – this does not predetermine what we perceive at the object level – which becomes apparent when we consider that even a perceptual theorist or sensory physiologist does not stop perceiving when they use a measuring system to gain insight into the epistemic states of a living being as part of their theorizing.

This model soon reaches its limits, however, if we inflate it into metaphysics. The Achilles heel is probably the non-intentional objects whose field of sense appears in the field of sense of the imaginary. Metaphysical imaginatism must assume that the field of sense of non-intentional objects is entangled with the field of sense of imaginary ones. Those objects we fundamentally cannot have perceived (the Big Bang, the 'states' in a black hole, or whatever) are really changed by the fact that we perceive that there are objects we do not perceive, since the global observable of our perception modifies the local observable of non-intentional objects. Metaphysical imaginatism therefore tends towards interpretations of quantum theory, which ascribes to the cognitive process an influence on areas whose structural formation lies mostly beyond our reach, which brings metaphysical imaginatism close to Eugene Wigner's interpretation of quantum theory.[29]

Be that as it may, the ontological problems of metaphysical imaginatism cannot be fully solved by articulating its interpretation of quantum theory, though this is certainly no mock battle, but rather belongs to the nitty-gritty of this theoretical situation. What is crucial is that it tends towards a metaphysical idealism that ultimately makes the real as a whole dependent on the cognitive process, and thus in turn employs a concept of totality that constitutively includes us as thinking beings. This leads back to the now familiar problems of totality, which means that metaphysical imaginatism in turn relies on the coherence of the Aleph, which has proved questionable (see §4 above).[30]

3 Metaphysical Intentionalism

The real target of Meillassoux's much discussed critique of correlationism is the position of metaphysical intentionalism.[31] For *metaphysical intentionalism* claims that all objects are either intentional or appear in fields of sense that appear in the field of sense of intentional objects. This means that there is no field of sense that is not an object of reference. This position does not immediately collapse into an ontic (or subjective, as one says) idealism, because, although the fields of sense of all objects are intentional objects, this does not necessarily mean that the non-intentional objects appearing in the field of sense of the non-intentional are *ipso facto* intentional. Metaphysical intentionalists can evade this consequence *prima facie*, since they officially recognize a field of sense of non-intentional objects, though it is intentional on the ontological theoretical level.

Fichte, who has been portrayed entirely unjustly as an exponent of ontic idealism, spelled out this option particularly circumspectly. His theoretical structure of objected posited as non-posited is represented in our framework here by the fact that we posit the field of sense of non-intentional (non-posited) objects. This corresponds to Quine's mostly misunderstood formula of addressing ontological commitments, which he summarizes as follows in §6 of *Word and Object* ('Posits and truth'):

> To call a posit a posit is not to patronize it. A posit can be unavoidable except at the cost of other no less artificial expedients. Everything to which we concede existence is a posit from the standpoint of a description of the theory-building process, and simultaneously real from the standpoint of the theory that is being built. Nor let us look down on the standpoint of the theory as make-believe; for we can never do better than occupy the standpoint of some theory or other, the best we can muster at the time.[32]

If one transfers this formula from epistemology to metaphysics, it creates the problem that one must explain how non-intentional objects can nonetheless enter the horizon of intentionality.[33] What exactly does it mean that non-intentional objects essentially appear in a field of sense that *ex hypothesi* appears in the field of sense of intentionality? Here there is a risk of restricting oneself to a paradox-prone transcendental argument (TA) of the following type:

(TA1) If there had been no intentionality, there would not have been a field of sense of the non-intentional.

(TA2) If they had not appeared in the field of sense of the

> non-intentional, there would not have been any non-intentional objects.
>
> ∴   If there had been no intentionality, there would not have been any non-intentional objects.

(TA) does not lead to a paradox in every interpretation, since the conclusion does not make direct object-level claims about particular non-intentional objects (such as bosons, the earth moon, the Alps, the Big Bang, and so forth). *The metaphysical intentionalist does not claim that a particular given non-intentional object would not have existed if no one had ever referred to it; only that the objects which appear in the field of sense of the non-intentional would not appear there if we had not referred to it.* The higher-order ontological attribute of non-intentionality therefore depends on intentionality, which does not directly affect non-intentional objects, which one can only name *de dicto* but not identify *de re* via individuation. In the optics of metaphysical intentionalism, non-intentional objects form an internally formless lump of the non-intentional, a 'bedrock of being', as Adorno termed it.[34]

One cannot name a single substantive example of a non-intentional object, since this would mean transforming it into an intentional object; that is why non-intentional objects must be intentionally shielded.[35] Non-intentional objects thus form a category in the ontological portfolio of the metaphysical intentionalists. Strictly speaking they are the central category, because they set the project apart from ontic idealism, which reduces all fields of sense to a single one (the mental). *Ontic idealism* claims that there are only mental states, or their carriers, and therefore reinterprets everything that does not seem to be included in this field of sense accordingly. It thus advocates a revolutionary metaphysics with questionable coherence, though its position cannot be undermined analytically.[36] Ontic idealism is not incorrect a priori, because it makes a claim about the character of the real, and such claims cannot bring about their own truth. Ontic idealism does not correspond to the facts; this does not bother it, since it consistently disputes such a correspondence.

Be that as it may, the metaphysical intentionalist avoids an extravagant reduction of the real to the formal framework of appearance for a carrier of mental states by acknowledging the field of sense of the non-intentional. Since it cannot fill it in a substantial way, however, the position turns into a 'weak correlationism' in Meillassoux's sense.[37] The non-intentional is given a space in an ontological architecture, but this space cannot be filled, which at times drives Kant – who paradigmatically spelled out this dialectic – into the arms of strong correlationism, as he cannot guarantee that non-intentional objects exist outside the field of possible experience.[38]

The same thing that protects metaphysical intentionalism specifically from ontic idealism weakens it globally. For non-intentional objects are the standard case of what we refer to with a truth-apt intention. We do not think about the real with the intention of tailoring it to our horizon but are conscious of it as something that oversteps the excerpt character of our respective attention. The real is that which can exceed our expectations – which does not necessarily mean that the real is only noticeable in the form of a catastrophe or a complete Other. The real by no means appears to us on the condition that it is only indirectly 'independent of us'. Rather, one cannot find in the appearance of the real any indication that it is tailored to us, which is quite simply because the real is not tailored to us. The potential divergence of truth and holding-to-be-true – that is, the objectivity of our reference – is itself something factual, which Fichte splendidly encapsulated in his coinage 'facticity'.[39]

But even if one can defend metaphysical intentionalism on the epistemological level, since it is not actually hopelessly incoherent, the ground becomes shakier on the metaphysical level. For it repeats its formulated scenario of an iteration *ad infinitum*, which Fichte terms 'reflexibility' in his final lectures on the *Science of Knowledge*.[40] This comes about when one considers that the field of sense of intentionality contains itself along with the three fields of sense of fictive, imaginary and non-intentional objects, which is precisely the point of *metaphysical* intentionalism.

The situation in which the metaphysical intentionalist believes themselves to be relates to itself: it is infinitely nested within itself. But this raises the question of which theoretical level we are actually dealing with when it comes to the category of non-intentional objects. Are the non-intentional objects identical with the non-identical objects in the field of sense of intentional non-intentional objects? If 'being-intentional' or 'being-non-intentional' are viewed as attributes that classify objects and shield them from one another, why should this not apply to the accumulations of attributes that result if one concedes that there is also 'being-intentional-intentional' and consequently 'being-intentional-non-intentional', and so on? From his earliest works, Fichte tries to solve this problem *practically*, since we *factually* cut the Gordian Knot by stopping reflexibility at some level and gaining access to things. Surprisingly, then, this act lets things be; it does not correspond to the purportedly ontic-idealistic character of the theory of science but consists in stopping at some theoretical level and conceding a non-egological base reality. Fichte calls this circumstance 'being'.[41]

For this manoeuvre to remain internally stable, however, Fichte – or the paradigmatic purveyor of metaphysical intentionalism – requires a proof of completeness. Those fields of sense that are admitted along with the field of sense of intentional objects must be adducible in their entirety for the iterations to be carried out controllably, and for the Gordian Knot to be cut with theoretical justification. The fields of sense may only proliferate downwards and upwards (that is, vertically) in an ordered hierarchy, not spread out uncontrolled (horizontally). Fichte himself therefore develops his theorem of a finite number of views of the world.[42]

Hegel's project of a *Phenomenology of Spirit* has a similar purpose, as it aims for the 'necessity and completeness' of possible theories of intentionality.[43] This is to ensure that there is a maximally coherent theoretical disposition that guarantees the independence of the real over the intrinsic architecture of the intentionality of thought. The real is meant to prove from the inside view of thought, as it were, to be something with an inherent ontological right without placing itself at such a distance that a 'boundary . . . which completely separates'[44] is erected between the real and our access to it. Here Hegel is largely following Schelling's conception from the *System of Transcendental Idealism*. The basic idea of the early systems from the heyday of German Idealism leads to the circumstance that 'nature' becomes the name for the realm of the non-intentional, which ultimately delegates the question of the objectivity of thought to natural philosophy, paving the way for the positivism of the second half of the century.[45] This positivism liberates itself through an epistemologically and ontologically unsupported radical break with the aporias of intentionality, and assures itself of the reality of thought via empirical investigations of the economic, sensory-physiological, biological – in short, material preconditions for the genesis of intentional relationships.

The 'method' of genealogy that emerged in the nineteenth century is a vulgar form of natural philosophy, which was originally an essential building block of metaphysical intentionalism. This latter was meant to show that intentionality does not diffuse to non-intentional objects via indirect routes, which, in the face of our cognitive performance (in the face of the concept), meant ascribing to those objects the level of independence without which we cannot assure ourselves of the objectivity of our thinking. The unreflecting positivism that echoes in the naturalism of our time contents itself with generalizing the realm of the non-intentional, nature, thus casting aside intentionality by an act of force. Intentionality is replaced by empirical science.

This epistemologically and metaphysically lacklustre manoeuvre is concealed by pointing to the explanatory success of the natural sciences, with naturalism fluctuating between references to factual scientific knowledge and corrections thereof, which become necessary whenever it becomes clear once again that the natural sciences do not provide a metaphysical carte blanche.

The natural sciences do not as such imply a metaphysics of intentionality. Naturalism is a decision that precedes any empirical knowledge and adapts the space of legitimate conceptual investigations ad hoc to whatever format the naturalist happens to need in order to dispute their own intentionality. What we know about the objectivity of thought cannot stem from any empirical examination of nature as the realm of non-intentional objects, since this examination occurs only partially in nature. As thinkers, we exist in nature only as a simulacrum as long as we view nature simplistically as that which constitutively repels unreduced intentionality. Crudely put, we do not discover that we are fallible through studies of the human animal and its evolutionary 'precursors'. If that were our access to the objectivity of thought, this would immediately raise the rather interesting question of whether our studies of the human animal are as fallible as its adaptation to its environment. How does the naturalist manage to escape the bestiality of their registration of reality, which they are otherwise quite willing to acknowledge, in the theoretical space of their self-substantiation and achieve a form of objectivity there that they rule out elsewhere?

That this is a truly thorny problem for the metaphysics of intentionality is something that was recognized by Schopenhauer, whose thought, coming from the dynamics of German Idealism, attempts to take the step into neuroidealism.[46] Schopenhauer was perhaps the first to identify the self trapped epistemically in a world as representation, with the brain as a product of natural, anonymous processes, and noticed that he could only succeed in this act of supposed self-awareness under extreme conditions bordering on genius and sainthood. Schopenhauer and, following on from him, Nietzsche crafted an absurd cult of the self in order to celebrate their incoherent achievement of a naturalistic outlook as a heroic self-conquest by the will to live, or as an intensification of the will to power. This heroic aspect of a purported anticipation of intentionality defines the intellectual climate of naturalism to this day, which is why naturalism forms alliances such as the Brights or – terrible to relate – the Giordano Bruno Foundation, which seek to do away with religion and superstition once and for all. The organized revolt against a theoretically unresolved religion conceals the theoretical weakness of naturalism very clumsily, and at the cost of falsifying history. By placing the metaphysics of intentionality in proximity to an uncomprehended religion, naturalism proves that it is not concerned with science, otherwise fields of knowledge such as history, theology or indeed philosophy would have to be consulted before one went around peddling empty promises of salvation through 'evolutionary humanism'.

Naturalism is the long shadow of the aporias of intentionality, which is why it is being discussed here at all. It fails precisely where German Idealism is particularly strong, namely in the self-legitimation of its own knowledge claim. That is no minor offence, as naturalists like to assume on this point of dialectics, but a cardinal error. A theoretical edifice whose instruction leaflet on the topic of 'objectivity' states that our entire thinking is nothing but the background noise of evolutionary processes, on some scale beyond our conscious access, puts it on record that it is arbitrary, and thus constitutively rationally unacceptable.[47]

Naturalism is the other side of metaphysical intentionalism, which is why the latter has been grappling with the former since its elaboration by Fichte. Both ultimately fail in the attempt to find a home for intentionality, which seems either groundless or homeless.[48]

Metaphysical intentionalism can find intentionality only within itself; on its model level, it thus pushes non-intentional objects into an unreachable distance that cannot be caught up through any 'infinite approach', no matter how extended.[49] The non-intentional objects are constitutively shielded from the intentional objects, for they appear in a field of sense within the field of sense of intentionality. The sense in which they appear in their field of sense of non-intentionality differs essentially from the sense in which this field of sense is embedded: the non-intentional objects are posited as non-intentional. Their embeddedness in intentionality rubs off on them because, according to metaphysical intentionalism, there would not have been any non-intentional objects had there not been intentional objects. The non-intentional objects are thus grounded in intentionality, which fundamentally cannot be grounded in the non-intentional ('nature'). Intentionality thus becomes groundless and is forced into self-substantiating manoeuvres. Subjectivity that follows this model remains essentially disembodied.[50]

Although naturalism finds or invents a 'cold home'[51] for itself, it loses sight of its own intentionality in the process, which is why it enters an unhappy relationship with religion and superstition, which it considers the last bastion of resistance against the supposed insight that the objectivity of our thinking is the epistemically extended arm of non-conscious causal processes that, taken individually, have the logical form of an amoeba but generate the eminently useful user illusion of conscious thought through the cooperation of many amoebas. Even if – like Dennett – one expressly acknowledges that these metaphors are exercises of the imagination ('intuition pumps'), the real question arises only one theoretical level above that noted by Dennett: how does Dennett manage to see through the alleged user illusion of the brain? How does the brain manage to break free of itself and offer naturalism a view behind the veil that it weaves completely blindly, without any insight into anything?

The ostensible plausibility of naturalism is owed to its declaration of coping with the problem of consciousness by passing it on and delegating to a hitherto non-existent expert council of natural scientists who will surely put paid to the mind. It is part of the metaphysical essence of naturalism that it reformulates a promise it cannot keep, which explains the structural proximity to its notion of religion. From the perspective adopted here, all of this – as already stated – is merely the darker side of metaphysical intentionalism, which relies on regress blockers to find a place for non-intentional objects in the web of objects.

4 Metaphysical Realism

Metaphysical realism identifies objects in general with non-intentional objects. It only considers those things true objects whose existence and character are essentially independent of our access. On the model level we are currently examining, metaphysical realism claims that the fields of sense of fictive, imaginary and intentional objects exist in the field of sense of non-intentional objects. This assumption is supported by the fact that it seems to take into account the epistemic robustness of fictive, imaginary and intentional objects. What makes an object fictive is not in our hands. A fictive object is essentially fictive; its fictivity is not brought to light through interpretive practices. Rather, the existence of such practices corresponds to the fact that some objects appear in the field of sense of fictive objects, which is therefore not empty.

But this also indicates one of the main problems of metaphysical realism. If the field of sense of the fictive genuinely exists, if it is non-intentional according to the standard applied here, it follows that there are fictive objects. Yet objects are fictive if they do not exist uninterpreted. Their field of sense may, *ex hypothesi*, exist uninterpreted, but this precisely means that the objects appearing in it can essentially only exist as objects interpreted in some way or other. Metaphysical realism therefore owes us an explanation of the existence of intentionality, which cannot already be given through the fact that intentionality actually exists in the field of sense of the non-intentional. For the real existence of intentionality cannot consist in its being a non-intentional object. Metaphysical realism takes the concept of consciousness-independence, or more generally representation-independence, as its criterion for realism. An actually existing object is defined via maximum modal robustness relative to its representation. Based on this model, what really exists is not a result of projections of representations, but rather is present as something we can successfully grasp or miss without our access contributing in any relevant sense to the individuation of its object.

The dire state of metaphysical realism has recently been demonstrated incisively by Shamik Dasgupta using what he calls the 'problem of missing value'. His target is the metaphysical realism of Theodore Sider, which indeed represents a pure form of this experimental design.[52] Metaphysical realism works with the notion that the real is always already arranged. The arrangement of the real ultimately decides which of our convictions are true and which are false. The idea of an avoidance of arbitrariness yields a persuasive view of how the form of divergence that we reject as an inadequate opinion arises. Dasgupta and Sider work through the 'diagonal predicates'[53] of Nelson Goodman – that is, concepts that only produce true opinions because we have categorized reality unreasonably. This means that there is a class of true, yet nonetheless unreasonable opinions whose unreasonableness consists in categorizing things based on more or less groundless whims.

Let us consider constellations of stars. A constellation is an arbitrarily formed object that does not correspond to anything 'in reality'. This can be distinguished from the stars from which we form a constellation. In a metaphysically relevant sense, the stars are more robust than the constellations. Nonetheless, we can obviously make true statements about constellations and compare the constellations of different cultures, or examine their respective historical development in the context of a more or less precisely delineated culture (though it should be noted that the concept of a culture comes under suspicion from the start of being in no better a metaphysical position than the concept of a constellation).

Based on this, metaphysical realism distinguishes between two types of properties: natural and non-natural.[54] In metaphysical realism, a true statement that assigns non-natural properties is deficient compared to a true statement that revolves around natural properties. Dasgupta's question is then how metaphysical realism explains this deficiency. If the distinction between natural and non-natural properties is not itself a natural property, metaphysical realism begins to unravel. This is precisely where Dasgupta's argument comes in, showing that metaphysical realism cannot explain the deficiency it claims based on its own resources. For why should we orient ourselves by natural properties?

It is not sufficient to point out that natural properties constitute better categorizations of the real because one wishes to support this epistemic value judgement. Referring to a property as 'natural – and *ipso facto* privileged' does not lend it the desired privileges, any more than the surname Armstrong lends strong arms to its bearer, to cite Dasgupta's analogy.[55] The property of naturalness must therefore have some property ensuring that natural properties are those which justify epistemic privileges. Everything one can name in favour of natural properties as a realist, however, leads at best to a multiplication of ontological commitments – that is, to an accumulation of natural properties. If there are natural properties, at any rate, it does not seem to be a natural property that they are epistemologically and ontological distinguished.

Dasgupta illustrates this with the following analogy: imagine one is drawing two Venn diagrams. One contains the set of natural properties, the other the set of non-natural ones. One might draw the Venn diagram of natural properties with ink and that of non-natural properties with chalk. This does not, however, mean that one would grasp reality better by adducing the properties circled with ink! Marking the natural properties with ink at best highlights them in the eye of the beholder, who might prefer ink to chalk for aesthetic reasons, and this does not justify an epistemic value judgement for which, Dasgupta argues, we cannot give any different justification on this level within the framework of metaphysical realism.

The natural properties of metaphysical realism thus cannot fulfil the task of justifying epistemic privileges, which makes it puzzling that metaphysical realism seeks to align all objects with this criterion, which on closer inspection proves to be theory-dependent. The distinction between non-intentional (= natural) and merely intentional (= unnatural) objects is itself secretly intentional, which becomes apparent through the formulation of the problem of missing value. Whatever one adduces in favour of natural properties also applies *mutatis mutandis* to the unnatural ones, since their concept justifies naming anything that serves the purpose of bringing up unnatural objects at all. So if there are any true statements about fictive, imaginary or intentional (= unnatural) objects, it is no longer possible to state why these objects should be less real than those objects privileged by the metaphysical realist.

This problem appears especially drastically in various forms of so-called speculative realism, especially in object-oriented ontology. According to

Graham Harman, it is actually in the nature of objects to be unknowable.[56] In this way, he consistently dodges the value problem, albeit it at the cost of a now openly visible incoherence. For objects, according to Harman, fundamentally cannot be known, since the attempt to access them already pushes them away. This results in a different extreme case: now objects are epistemically completely underprivileged, since it is viewed as their nature that they are not knowable! This is at least a hopeless position, to the extent that Harman cannot say anything about how he knows this without contradicting his verdict that things elude our epistemic grasp.

The Achilles heel of metaphysical realism is an arbitrary demarcation between natural and unnatural objects; it results from the fact that unnatural objects are taken as arbitrary projections that have no suitable place in the panorama of metaphysical realism.

And so any remotely structured attempt to specify any meaningful concept of objects at all fails because it privileges either fictive, imaginary, intentional or non-intentional objects. But the other types of objects cannot be coherently embedded as a result; their inherent ontological right is undone, and thus reality is distorted. The ontological pluralism and realism of FOS take this into account by abandoning the idea that there are any objects as such, and that these can be meaningfully specified. Objects as such are neither the most general concepts nor more specific concepts or conceptless entities inhabiting a space that exists independently of us. We should let them – along with the world (and all worldviews and conceptions of the world) – disappear down the hole of unfounded, object-level metaphysics.

Part III

Social Realism

What distinguishes a social fact – that one has to pay three kinds of income tax in New York City, for example – from clearly non-social facts – such as the fact that $E = mc^2$? Is there some precisely definable characteristic or systematically organized class of characteristics that distinguishes all social facts as such from all non-social facts? Is there a specific ontology of the social?

Social ontology as a subdiscipline of philosophy is the systematic investigation of whether there are general structural conditions for the fact that the suchness of certain facts is social. A fact is *social* if its suchness essentially involves the coordinated behaviour of several individuals in a species. A social fact does not exist only when *several* individuals factually carry out the same type of action; even a single individual can create social facts through its actions or be embedded in them without ever acknowledging it.

In the following, I will argue that it is decisive for sociality that the actions of social beings could not be carried out if there had not, at some point in time, been an explicit or implicit integration of the perspective of one individual into the action process of another individual. The social is thus quite literally in the eye of the beholder: it consists in the fact that one perceives differently from others because one holds a perspective. For minded beings of our species, on which I will concentrate without any claims to biological completeness, holding a perspective is constitutively social because we are socially produced beings – that is, beings that see the light of the 'world' only because the reproductive behaviour of our respective ancestors ensured that we exist. Sociality is literally inherited because beings of our species are socially produced, which means that sociality already takes effect at the level of cell reproduction: before any attainment of individual consciousness, the behaviour of our mothers (nourishment, sequences of movements, and so forth, along with the associated biochemical circuits), together with the basic genetic coding that results from the coupling of cells, ontogenetically determines how we perceive our environment. Intentionality is hence thoroughly social (and socially produced), which is often overlooked when proceeding from the first-person perspective of an actor who, as a social ontologist, is paradigmatically involved in the giving and taking of reasons when they judge: 'I think that p.'

There are no actions without integration into a real (not merely imagined!) social context. For social beings such as humans (who will be the sole focus in the following), doing something particular presupposes that there are several coordinated perspectives. This coordination requires no explicit acknowledgement, empathy or other inherently transparent attitude to the consciousness of others; it can come about unnoticed behind the backs of the actors. There are social facts of which no one will ever acquire explicit knowledge.

This obviously does not rule out the *possibility* of social facts coming about and being maintained through the explication of principles of action coordination; but this should be neither the norm nor the paradigm of the social. For example, the institution of traffic laws is social in this sense, as there would be no traffic laws if it had not been taken explicitly into account that different persons participate in road traffic and have divergent perspectives on the relevant events.

If someone is driving alone on the motorway, they are still performing a social action, even if there is no one else nearby, because the structures of the motorway and the automobile are essentially tied to the fact that many different people were involved in creating motorways and automobiles in the past, and those actors implicitly and – in this case – also explicitly coordinated their perspectives with one another.

Social facts do not always exist; their existence is contingent. They are, as I will put it, produced. What exactly they are like – that is, their suchness – depends on historically contingent processes of action coordination that are factually not guided by any ready-made construction plan. The fabric of societies is therefore unstable and dependent on a *productio continua*.

But this does not at all mean that social facts are isolated from natural facts, provided one understands a 'natural' fact as one whose suchness is not specified by social production. After all, the respective character of those beings involved in the production of social facts is not solely a result of social production. Pre-social and asocial nature remains entangled with our social practices; the social production of facts by action coordination does not lead mortal beings like us beyond nature. The sphere of society is not a transcendent 'kingdom of ends' constructed through free-floating mental work.

In this final part, my concern will be to develop the foundations for a non-constructivist, realistic social ontology that leaves room for objective mind. *Objective mind* is the circumstance that socially produced facts come about and persist within the framework of the human way of life because people can only believe something to be true if they are corrected by the holding-to-be-true of others, or vice versa. Being confronted with the fact that other people consider something false which one considers to be true is based on dissent. By 'dissent', I do not mean exclusively the communicative dimension of divergent, incompatible expressions of opinion with reference to the same fact, but rather the circumstance that the same object or fact is given to several individuals (or to one individual at different points in time) in different ways.

Dissent is a difference of sense that does not obtain only once two individuals have incompatible propositional attitudes that are known to them, or when they also verbally articulate them. Seeing something differently from another person, then, is a form of dissent that can easily be balanced out by realizing that it does not constitute any incompatibility for the same object to look one way from here and another way from there.[1]

I would like to show in the following that dissent is the socio-ontological foundation of human socialization. A human community with institutions that measure actions by standards that we recognize as norms emerges from the respective constellation of dissent among those involved. In short, a society is a society of dissenters that has come about as a result of a specific dissent, in a particular time and place, that was resolved via action coordination measures. For social beings, dissent is already inevitable at the perceptual level.

Our holding-to-be-true, our thinking, is socially produced. What we respectively think is based on processes of action coordination in contexts of dissent. Dissent can be as inconspicuous as the literal divergence between the perspectives of two observers of the same scene or as conspicuous as a strategically coordinated, violently waged conflict between several parties. The decisive aspect is that dissent inevitably expresses itself at the level of judgement, which means that there is ultimately no form of human thought whose acts of judgement are entirely pre-social or asocial.[2]

Humans are thus essentially social thinkers; in the following, I will not address the question of how far this form of sociality applies in the same or similar ways to other social beings (let alone all beings whose organization is based on cells). So I will not draw on any specific view of anthropological difference in my argumentation.[3]

The position (or theoretical conflict situation) I am opposing is social constructivism. It is secondary here whether a social constructivist position is *radical* – claiming that, in reality, many or even all facts viewed as natural are socially constructed – or limits the concept of construction to the suchness of social facts. The error, I argue, lies in the idea that social facts are *constructed* and is thus largely independent of the question of how far this construction extends beyond the sphere of the social. After various rounds of discussion, the idea that social facts are *constructed* continues to enjoy great popularity. As I wish to show in this third part, however, it is and remains an expression of an incoherent thought system.

To motivate the basic idea of social constructivism, its purveyors usually advance a variant of the following ideal-typical consideration.

Generally speaking, one might suppose that something is social if is essentially tied to the behaviour of a group. On this level, the social is distinguished firstly from the individual and secondly from that which is not at all capable of comportment or action. Therefore there was nothing social before there were groups of living beings. Until some more or less exactly determinable point in time, the universe was asocial. Let us call the asocial universe *anonymous nature*.

Anonymous nature exhibits structures and laws that we can discover in the medium of our social organization of the natural sciences. However, it is characterized by the fact that it is not based on any sociality. The orbit of a galaxy around a black hole, the genesis of planets, and so on, are events of anonymous nature whose precise explanation requires no reference to any social organization.[4] This raises the question of what exactly distinguishes a genuinely social fact from a natural fact that belongs to anonymous nature.[5]

The concepts of *social construction* or *construction of the social* arise in the context of a specific answer to this ontological problem. This answer considers human sociality and bases its conceptualization on the phenomenon of explicit action coordination in the context of existing institutions. The basic idea of social construction follows an anti-realist construction plan: it states that a social fact exists when (and only as long as) the members of a group accept its existence. A social fact thus rests on the implicit or explicit acceptance of individuals who mentally represent its existence.

Thus, for theorists under the influence of social constructivism, normativity becomes a central aspect of an ultimately ontological issue: actions that are normalized in a particular way are considered social; their results are social facts that can be distinguished from natural facts through their intrinsic normativity. This normativity, in turn – depending on the theoretical situation – is viewed either as grounded in relations of recognition or as constituting these.

In this framework, the recourse to the intrinsic normativity of social facts allows us to avoid the 'naturalization' of social facts, in so far as these fundamentally historically contingent processes are due to the mutual normalization of human behaviour in group contexts. In this way, the concept of social facts is tied *a limine* to the possibility of changing those institutions that are expressions of the social, objectifications of its intrinsic normativity.

This ideal-typical constellation has virtually attained the status of a *communis opinio*, which stems from the fact that many consider it obvious that human actions differ fundamentally from anonymous natural events and are thus subject to categorially different organizational principles. The distinction between norm and nature or is and ought is one variant for doing justice to this supposition. Social constructivism is a conflict situation whose common ground is the outlined notion that the human domain is subject to completely different principles, principles grounded in this domain itself that prevent what we do from being anonymous natural events.

The fundamental error begins with the already misguided notion of an anonymous first nature, which is taken for the object of the natural sciences. To protect the humanities and social sciences from a naturalist ambush, a special sphere of normativity is invented whose occurrence is explicable at best as an emergent phenomenon; for the most part, social constructivists no longer refer to any explanation of how it comes about.[6]

In the experimental design of social constructivism, the social is distinguished from the natural from the start. This raises the problem of how the social fits into nature – a constellation that contributes to the undiminished attractiveness of the idea of a 'second nature'.[7] According to this idea, the social is natural after all in so far as the first, anonymous nature is not eliminated, meaning that our sociological vocabulary is compatible with our scientific one. Nonetheless, this removes second nature, which is characterized by its intrinsic normativity, from first nature. It stems from a hitherto unexplained transcendence whereby human sociality, in the eyes of most theorists of second nature, differs fundamentally (metaphysically) from the forms of sociality one can observe in other living beings. Human sociality comes about because humans, through a normalization of their offspring's behaviour – through upbringing and education – that is peculiar to them, produce a 'kingdom of ends'[8] or develop the faculties to participate in a self-aware manner in the activities of such a kingdom's members.[9]

Let us note, then, that one can distinguish two varieties of social constructivism: a radical and a moderate one. The radical variety turns the semblance of a first nature into a side effect of society's normative self-conception. What we take for anonymous nature is therefore dependent on the social system of science because there is no anonymous nature. The moderate variety is restricted to drawing a categorial line between nature and norm, or first and second nature; because of its nature-philosophical abstinence, however, it is unable to establish how a second nature can even ensue, given the continued existence of first nature.

The concept of social construction in its modern form rests on a *deontological difference*: natural and social facts are separated by a distance that is not (entirely) natural.[10] Second nature – if it is indeed a nature, a matter on which opinions differ – is at best an anti-nature, as it opens up the possibility of producing social facts that allow a retroactive intervention in the structures of our first nature. Hence the divergent opinions on the status of the intrinsic normativity of the human form of life. Is it a second nature simply found alongside first nature as another brute fact, or is it ultimately not natural at all, since the concept of nature is reserved for the object area of the natural sciences, in which one assumes there to be only processes of anonymous nature? The grave and hitherto unsolved problem of moderate social constructivism thus lies in natural philosophy.[11]

Since the deontological difference means that it is not ahistorically certain what social facts exist, the idea of intrinsic normativity does not *prima facie* provide any guideline by which actors could orient themselves. The factual instructions found by the social theorist are thus essentially historically contingent because, owing to the construction of the theory, they can only be found and established as historically variable facts.

To the extent that purveyors of a given variant of social construction attempt to handle the deontological difference non-metaphysically, there is room to postulate a genealogy of intrinsic normativity that should meet the requirement of not endangering that normativity through naturalization.[12] In this framework, one can assume that members of groups regulate the observable behaviour of other members through sanctions, which results in normativity. Based on this model, normativity ensues through the fact that various subjects regularly correct the behaviour of other subjects. In this way, they create an order to which all subjects submit, either by following its verdicts or violating them, potentially in order to overturn the entire order.

In my view, the decisive characteristic of this model in this context is the fact that the entire process does not refer to anonymous nature at any relevant point, but rather operates in a free-floating new sphere. *Social construction* is thus the act of producing observable behaviour through mutual normalization of the members of a given group, in so far as they orient themselves by norms they discursively represent.[13] This model is articulated in socio-ontologically precise terms within the discussion of collective intentionality, which is paradigmatic for the merging of sociality and intentionality (which I reject here).[14]

According to the model, if something is socially constructed – race, class, gender, institutions, languages, cultures, legal systems, aesthetic taste, etiquette, states, banks, money, administrative bodies, moral values, and so on – then every part of this process is due exclusively to the orientation of a subsystem of a group by the verdict of another subsystem, which is in no way based on any insight into anonymous nature. This is because, in social constructivism, the source of social normativity can only be the recognition of a prior suggestion to sanction such-and-such a behaviour in such-and-such a fashion. For social constructivism disputes that there is any nature from which one can deduce social facts (and thus overlooks that nature is not the only field of sense in which non-constructed facts can exist).

For social constructivists, the first acceptance of any normative order fundamentally cannot be inferred from understanding a validity on its part that is well-grounded independently of any specific group affiliation, as such understanding would constitute the attitude of an individual towards an existing fact. Normativity therefore stems from practices of recognition leading to the existence of registrable and documentable facts, though these facts must be revisable at all times through changes in social conditions.

The assessment of such a social (in the sense of socially constructed) fact, then, is only explicable by belonging to a particular group, whether that of the rulers or that of the ruled.[15] The rulers are those who construct norms and make others internalize them, while the ruled are those who yield to the norms. As stated above, social constructivism holds that a person's submission to any given norms can never be a result solely of accepting social facts that are independent of this submission and not constructed by it; otherwise there would be non-constructed social facts, which would bring about the collapse of constructivist social ontology. It is not enough here to correct this model by postulating a regress of social construction and assuming that the acceptance of a norm constitutes an understanding of the existence of past social constructions, since this raises the question of how normativity could come about in the first place. The first norm to be established cannot be a result of an already socially constructed understanding of a prior social construction.

Therefore there is no neutral ground for rigorous social constructivism in normative questions, least of all one on which one could rely to make a decision that solves a group conflict in a rational way. Every agreement by a group in a normative matter thus rests exclusively (contrary to the intention of many theorists of recognition) on explicit or implicit power struggles – a theoretical situation that is expressed *nolens volens* in the much noted talk of the 'struggle for recognition'.[16]

The alternative to the conflict situation I have, admittedly, only touched on here is a new *social realism*. This claims (1) that there are recognition-transcendent (partly opaque and never consciously knowable) normative facts determining under what conditions the behaviour of members of given groups is correct or incorrect; (2) that these normative facts are non-constructed; and (3) that they belong to neither first nor second nature.[17]

The success of an individual human life or, more precisely, a given phase of an individual human life depends on objectively fixed conditions, some of which are consequences of anonymous nature. The effects of the laws of anonymous nature extend deep into the human life form. For this reason alone, it is unproductive to attempt to isolate a second nature from a first. The obviously existing anonymous nature is reflected in how we live our lives, as we are essentially organisms – that is, biological systems – but are not strictly identical with these. Humans are, among other things, animals of a particular species, which does not mean that human actions can be reduced in any general sense to animal behaviour. The sense in which we are animals of a particular species is defined by the biological self-examination of humans, which in FOS does not conflict with the fact that there is mind which is not the object of any natural-scientific examination.

The social realism developed in the following does not define the concept of the social in opposition to the natural. The question of how social facts fit into what is in itself a (causally and ontologically) closed space of facts in first, anonymous nature is rejected from the start as misguided metaphysics.

The social realism advocated here can, however, draw on FOS. This is because FOS has no fundamentally all-encompassing nature whose laws are investigated by the natural sciences in such a way that entities displaying properties which *prima facie* cannot be scientifically examined are ultimately better or more completely describable and explicable if one leaves those properties aside. In short: according to FOS, we have long abandoned metaphysical naturalism, which – unfortunately – does not mean that it continues to float around as a worldview.

Against this background, at any rate, it is not legitimate to demand that a socio-ontological examination answer the incorrectly posed question, in the way that it is possible for actors to determine their own patterns of action in light of (seemingly) universally valid laws in (let us say) quantum physics. Social normativity need not be situated in the scope of elementary particles if this latter is merely one field of sense among others and is not privileged under all circumstances – that is, not metaphysically privileged.

The ontological pluralism of FOS is not grist for the mill of social constructivism. There is no compelling reason to disconnect the human form of life deontologically from the fact that we are beings whose organization is, at least in part, best explicable with recourse to processes of anonymous nature whose effectiveness in a human organism is not suspended, but rather integrated into the context of a form of system that is not fully explicable by these processes.

To the extent that the human form of life defines parameters of survival that appear to individuals as successful ('happy'), their analysis offers criteria for socially relevant normativity.[18] Because humans as living beings are actually capable of treating their survival as happy only under certain (ecological) conditions, the circumstances of our form of life, which can always be scientifically examined, have so far not yielded any fully known norms for a fundamentally successful life.

In the following, I will refer to that part of the human form of life whose structures are explicable as the influence of anonymous nature as the *human survival form*. The structure of the human survival form is our specific animality. This is examined by those human sciences whose disciplinary home in today's academic system are the medical and natural science departments, in so far as they deal with human beings.[19]

The human form of life here encompasses indefinitely much more than what can be scientifically explored by science. This surplus culminates in mind as the explanatory dimension which takes into account that humans (sometimes) lead their lives against the background of a notion of who they are and who they want to be.[20] In short, humans are guided by conceptions of humans whose synchronic and diachronic (historical) dimensions are examined by the humanities and social sciences.

Mind is the circumstance that we can (sometimes) explain human behaviour only by using a complex mentalistic vocabulary that allows us to understand why a person has done something. This vocabulary includes so-called free will, which consists in the fact that we do not only act impulsively, and thus partially predictably and manipulably, but can modify our patterns of action in light of our normative global orientation (our 'values'). Someone who knows their own impulses is, under non-pathological conditions, capable of partially controlling them.

Mind is real. It is not (only) in the eye of the beholder, so it is pointless to strive for a complete naturalization, as in Dennett's physicalist stance.[21] That we cannot transcend the intentional stance in favour of a physicalist one is not an epistemological flaw, but rather an epistemological fact. If, in the explanation of human actions, we abstract completely from the fact that we can describe them in a certain way on the intentional level, we fall entirely short of the goal of explaining human actions. Mind is not an illusion, then, let alone a 'fiction' in the vague sense already refuted above (§§6–7).

Social realism's objection to social constructivism is that the model of constructed social facts is deeply incoherent and, in particular, normatively unsatisfactory. For if social constructivism were true, then normative (paradigmatically moral) progress would at best consist in a coordinated change of behaviour cleverly imposed by one group on another. Any form of normatively guided education would then at most be a well-hidden manipulation in order to create conditions of predictability for the behaviour of a group or individual. The goal of normalization would be control, since it cannot consist in adaptation to social facts that are rooted in our survival form and become explicitly visible in the mind.

Social realism, on the other hand, relies among other things on long-known facts about our survival form, such as that humans already have normative expectations in infancy that enable us to teach them explicit moral expectations. Humans – like other life forms – are fundamentally normatively constituted, since we would otherwise have no perception of possible sanctions. One cannot explain normativity purely on the model of 'discipline and punish'. Normativity is not only about the relation between given 'quanta of force'[22] whose collisions behind the backs of the actors lead to the emergence of normative orders.

The social realism proposed in the following by no means relies exclusively on naturalistically catchable manoeuvres such as those familiar from contemporary game theory, behavioural science or primate research. Human sociality cannot meaningfully be reduced to an accumulation of primitive behavioural patterns. Complex social organization of the type 'society' or elementary subsystems such as the legal system or a kindergarten are no accumulations of subliminal 'decision-making' processes that can be reduced to binary codes and studied via psychological experiments. That is why social systems are subject to conditions of statistical analysis only as long as the actors are not informed about them. Human behaviour is only predictable when those who observe it do not tell those they are observing how exactly they are observing them. This is a science-theoretical truism familiar to anyone designing a psychological experiment. *Predictive policing* only works for as long as one keeps the future perpetrators unaware of the predictive criteria one uses to plan their apprehension.

To break out of the framework of social constructivism and make room for a genuine – that is, non-reductionist – social realism, I argue in §12 that the nature of the irreducible facts of human sociality consists in several subjects meeting and establishing that someone else considers something true that they consider false. Institutions are systems that create a place in which to balance out factually existing dissent, which is why it is no coincidence that the legal concept of judgement is given, from Plato's *Apology* to Kant's *Critique of Pure Reason* and beyond, as the suitable place for a self-examination of thinking.[23] Therefore any human community whose organization goes beyond reproducing to form small groups is a community of dissenters.[24]

To be sure, not every dissent has an institution assigned to it that provides balancing mechanisms; otherwise, there would be no more privacy. Privacy is the space for individual actions in which sociality can appear, but this sociality can only be handled without institutional counterbalance as long as no institutional parameters are affected. It is fundamentally impossible to link human sociality as a whole to institutional parameters, since they can ultimately never be completely transparent. One cannot entirely anticipate or control which behavioural patterns human develop in their contexts of cooperation, or with recourse to activities in their private lives, which is why every institution requires the concept of the neutral, the *adiaphoron*, along with its normative criteria for what is correct and incorrect. No institution can be total. These contexts are explained in §§13, 16 and 17.

At this point, as an element of a diagnosis of how we perceive crises in our time, I will venture the claim that, in the wake of the digital revolution, the public sphere is massively unsettled by the threat of a loss of neutrality. This is also connected to social constructivism and its profound influence on media theory, and thus on the media as a privileged area of the public sphere: if there is nothing social that is entirely independent of political battles, social media becomes the arena of social construction. One actor takes on another – not to convince them, but to subjugate them through suitable methods of manipulation. The modern, enlightened notion of the public sphere as a truth machine is replaced by the postmodern *idée fixe* that the normative has no objective standards, only a plethora of images and symbols that can be used to generate or undermine group affiliations.[25]

Contrary to this socio-ontological misconception, we must assert the insight that a judgement about the social is not itself social in the sense of leading to an intervention in the normative order that is being judged. The social can therefore be judged objectively in any desirable way; it is not in the eye of the beholder. Accordingly, one requires a conceptually guided explanation of the fact that, although everything social is normative, normativity does not, from an ontological perspective, emerge from power struggles. Rather, it is based on the fact that humans (as well as other beings) have an awareness of norms without which it would be impossible to impose sanctions on us. Our grasp of the normative results from the fact that we think – that is, we have correct and incorrect convictions that we can access explicitly through the fact that others reach different judgements. The judgement of the others is an indispensable key to our own. There is no way around the other.

We have a sense of thought, which means in this context that we have a normativity detector, namely thinking.[26] The ability to think (which is expressed in an indefinite number of faculties) is realized through dissent; one does not think if one has not encountered the fact that others think differently.

In §13 I then argue that a factual, existing society (in the sense of a comprehensive social system) necessarily exhibits zones of opacity. Without social opacity, it would be impossible for us to correct one another. Because, in a complex society based on division of labour, we cannot know everything about what we do and what exactly we should do, the structure of society cannot be reductively reconstructed from the bottom up or from the top down. The thrusts of socio-ontological atomism (which builds society out of individuals) and socio-ontological holism (which deduces individuals from an overarching social totality) thus fall equally short.

No one knows all the things we know or do not know. There is no totality of holding-to-be-true, no all-encompassing belief systems. Even where all or the vast majority of a society's members officially share the same belief system, internal dissent arises and leads to the development of balancing measures, since society would otherwise dissolve. The aim of institutions cannot be factual consensus, then, but must manifest itself in a bearable level of dissent management.

Our 'unsocial sociability'[27] consists in the fact that we can only form groups if it is intended that others will judge differently (and are thus different) from us. Therefore every social system either divides into subsystems of dissent or projects dissent outwards, which potentially sets up a friend–foe schema. No societal 'we' is all-encompassing, for society necessarily comprises a plurality of holding-to-be-true – a circumstance that cannot be successfully changed by any measures.

These are well-known facts in the discourses of sociology and political science. In this third part, these discourse formations will be embedded in the framework of a social ontology in which the social is not in the eye of the beholder, since it is fundamentally tied to opacity, which we can never render completely explicit. Social realism thus serves as an ontological correction of socio-constructivist outgrowths that come about even – or perhaps precisely – when one thinks one is relying solely on empiricism.[28]

This does not rule out that the proverbial 'eye of the beholder' is socially produced in the following sense: the participant perspective, without which there would be no social systems, exists only because there are social beings, for which humans are paradigmatic. Humans are produced by humans whose cooperation leads to procreation. A human embryo is nourished in the womb, and the dietary behaviour of the mother is in turn essentially integrated into contexts of social reproduction. Humans do not grow of their own accord, but only because other people who are involved in the coming-about of humans are members of groups that coordinate their behaviour. Such action coordination is essentially social, since it presupposes that a majority of actors do something because the individuals hold the (not necessarily conscious or symbolically explicit) opinion that other individuals hold a particular opinion. Through the imaginary comparison of the presenting situation in which others find themselves, it happens that individuals belonging to a group gain access to scopes of action. Possibilities for action are opened up by passing on possible patterns of actions; these suggest that there was an original founding act that can function as a model for future imitation.[29]

What is possible for humans is determined by the fact that someone does something that others seize as their own possibility. This makes the human scope of action historically open and variable. It is fundamentally impossible to make an exhaustive catalogue of actions and set it in stone, for example in the form of an ideal codex of laws. We do not know and cannot even suspect what types of action will be possible in the future. This historicity alone makes us fundamentally free, in the sense that no insight into the blueprint of nature or society would allow an exhaustive prediction of future options for action at any point in time. Humans can only be predicted for as long as we limit their scopes of action to idealized test situations (such as those of game theory). Of course, the success of a prediction based on economic models is statistically and, thus, also probabilistically constituted, which generates a calculable margin of error. But even this circumstance applies only to highly idealized situations, and only as long as the actors cannot incorporate the extent of observation explicitly into the planning of their actions. Those who are successfully observed for the prediction of their behaviour must not be fully informed about it. This well-known fact is a manifestation of the ineluctable opacity of the social.

In §14 I develop a realistic variant for solving the (alleged) problem of rule-following. According to this variant, the application of a rule does not consist in someone gaining an idea of which as yet non-existent cases would justify the repeated application of that rule. Nor are rules and their applications limited to the circumstance that some mental state unilaterally dictates which rule was followed in the past, resulting in a normative claim for the future.

Rather, a rule and its application consist in the fact that there is a context with institutions which determine which rule should be followed. The rule itself differentiates between correct and incorrect cases of its application; it is thus itself the carrier of normativity. Normativity does not consist in some intention on the part of an actor that could be attributed to the actor planning to adapt their behaviour to a mental representation of the rule. For one cannot adapt to a mental representation without establishing how it can be connected to something that imposes conditions of correctness on it. A mental representation does not regulate itself, but rather is defined as a case of a rule by the fact that the rule has properties which other people can understand differently. If others perceive a rule differently, this raises the question of the correct use of the rule, which can only be adequately answered if the rule displays a reality that goes beyond individual opinions and their addition to form a group aggregate.

In short, neither an individual's holding-to-be-true nor the multifarious holding-to-be-true of many individuals explains the objectivity of rule-following. This requires something real – a rule – according to which all actors can be mistaken. No constructive activity on the part of subjects, and thus no intersubjectivity, is remotely sufficient to ensure the truth of the holding-to-be-true. To the extent that there are fixed conditions of correctness for some behaviour that is recognizable as an action, these can never be reduced to the fact that the group which is formed because its members are affected by the existing conditions of correctness acknowledges them. Where deviation and error are possible, there is always something real whereby one can register something as deviation and error. This real is 'independent' of all individual opinions, in so far as every individual opinion can be wrong. *The real cannot be falsified, for it falsifies.*

Norms are part of the real. They characterize human behaviour as actions of a particular kind. Norms normalize, and can thus delude the actors that they are always regulating themselves in the act of following rules. In §15 I examine this delusion, without bringing about the collapse of realism into a reductionist naturalism which, based on the fact that society always rests on the implicit and factual, draws the false conclusion that there is no autonomy.[30] Rather, autonomy results from the elevation of our social normativity – the circumstance that our behaviour is in fact socially produced and classified according to different registers of the correct and incorrect – to an explicit norm.

This corresponds to Hegel's formulation of the 'idea of the will' as *'the free will which wills the free will'*.[31] Yet this specifically autonomous normativity is grounded both diachronically and synchronically in a normativity that is not due to any explicit appropriation by actors who are conscious of their sociality. Resistance to a particular norm can therefore be understood as a real process; this, with a change of context, takes into account Bourdieu's justified doubt that social constructivism fails because its intention to enable resistance to illegitimate normative claims through critique remains unrealized.[32]

Against this background, I will distinguish between mythology, ideology and fiction. Mythology is the efficacy of implicit models, which appears historically at the representational level in the form of a theogonic consciousness and is perpetuated in our time not least by super hero stories and other everyday myths (to say nothing of the continued existence of the world religions). The theogonic consciousness has by no means been brought to an end, to recall Blumenberg's formulation; work on myth can never be finished.[33]

In the present context, mythology appears in the form that the reality of norms is transferred to an archaic past. This shift potentially makes us victims of a mythology by generating a model for being-human that becomes effective for actions in the present by preventing new action options – innovative possibilities – from being produced. It is therefore by no means only the Homeric pantheon, the Hindu world of gods or the Catholic cult of saints that are mythological but also the paleo-anthropological narrative that humans, because of their millennia-long formative phase in jungles and savannahs, are predestined to become objects of neuroscientifically secured game-theoretical predictions. Anyone who grounds the human form of action in some past – however 'scientifically' secured it may be – is thinking archaically. Archaic thinking did not disappear along with the Greek gods. It haunts us in the guise of the new mythology of humans as cultured apes, which has the useful function of preventing their escape from the imaginary 'human park'.[34]

Unlike mythology, an *ideology* is a construct of ideas whose function consists in justifying a given asymmetrical distribution of socioeconomically valuable resources by diverting the attention of the actors involved in its production and reproduction from that very fact.[35] Ideological thinking often draws on a mythological substructure, since the heteronomy of archaic thinking makes it especially suitable for blocking out the otherwise obvious problems of the present.

Ideology does not stop at the portals of philosophy; a philosophically meaningful example of an ideology can be found in the constellations of mental fictionalism criticized in Part II. For they draw a self-portrait of our conceptual faculty as cognitions, where this technical term serves to pass off a distorted human self-image – usually reduced to 'the brain', some more precisely delineated subsystem of the central nervous system or a different subsystem of the entire human being – as the whole truth about what we really are. The mereological fallacies of typical neurophilosophy distort the truth conditions of our vocabulary of action by reducing the complexity of language with which we control normativity to a few catchwords such as 'consciousness' or 'cognition'.[36] Such object-level narratives about humans, which can be exposed as ideological explanations, are replaced by the concept of *fictions*, which allows us to characterize our being-beyond any individual sensory episode – that is, our sense of thought. Humans are measured by their capacity for self-images, not by a given *imago*, however 'scientifically' supported it might purport to be.

In §16 I introduce the concept of a social network in order to develop the thesis that those digital systems of our infosphere that we term 'social networks' have the function of systematically restricting the scope of action of the networked actors. The self-objectification of individuals through the abandonment of their self-images to platforms on which our self-models are publicly exhibited leads to the predictability of their future behaviour. The reason for this is not that humans are transparent, however, but that the platforms prefer certain self-images because of their architecture – that is, their user interface. The feed structure of social networks, the division of the news and advertising dimensions, the (euphemistically named) security settings, the seemingly infinite proliferation of images and short videos, and so on – all this generates a framework in which only certain representations are possible. As a result, we are predictable and remain thus as long as there is no digital revolution that would allow the infosphere to be historicized. In practice, historicizing the infosphere means advocating a change in its material business foundations: an economic dynamic aimed for through current processes of mythologically and ideologically hidden monopolization.

Monopolization always serves to establish a socioeconomic status quo. In the case of social networks, the monopolization extends so deep into the human capacity for self-images that even the scientific discourse of our time follows the model of this self-presentation. It is not only scientific findings that are rewarded but, especially, also the quality of posters and PowerPoint presentations, which feign complexity using well-programmed and well-selected images. Thus concepts are replaced by images of concepts. People think in visual representations whose selection mechanisms can in turn be studied through the self-application of imaging processes. This supports strategies for 'scientific' success but helps to find the truth at best by chance. Because of these formats, the ontology of social networks is omnipresent – in the scientific discourse too, not only the virtual dimension of the internet.

Finally, in §17, I advance the utopia of a public sphere of the mind against the ontology of social networks. The illusory digitalization of consciousness is replaced by a scenario that adduces our capacity for self-images as such as a source of value. Our capacity for self-determination is the basis for a public sphere that aims for equality and takes into account that we are minded beings. Minded beings are those whose false ideas of who they are can guide them to lead a false life; even if we are massively deluded, we are still self-determined. Freedom cannot be successfully removed, but it can be damaged so far that, in the long term, those affected have no explicit access to the implicit defaults of their intended or unintended submission to the false.

Thus the philosophical methodology applied in this book, after an interrogation of the ontology of the architecture of the public sphere, finally defines itself as an analytically deepened ideology critique. In this context, the central diagnosis is that the self-disputation of the human mind, as the starting phenomenon for all examinations, is the crisis phenomenon that must always be dealt with. A central source of such self-disputation is the ontologically impermissible blurring of the boundary between fiction and reality.

It is merely seemingly paradoxical that this boundary can only be drawn if one concedes that fictive objects extend (indirectly) causally into our indexically rooted reality. Because humans fundamentally reach beyond every situation in which they appear in order to find themselves via the detour of transcendence, our mental life is consistently situated in the medium of fictions.

§12

The Nature of Social Facts

Social ontology asks wherein the existence of social facts consists. What distinguishes social facts from other kinds of facts? The main school of social ontology (proceeding from Searle) carries immense naturalistic baggage, however, for it is usually conditioned by a *placement problem*: how do social facts fit into an ultimately or fundamentally non-social reality, namely nature? In this context, nature is treated as that which is present without any contribution from us; the social, on the other hand, is understood as something human-made (an artefact) based on the Aristotelian model of *techne*. Contemporary social ontology rests on a variant of the question of whether there are metaphysically irreducible elements of (objective) mind.

This is the starting point for the meanwhile canonical, yet misleading assumption that the social as such is constructed. This is agreed on by such diverse theorists as Searle, Butler or Haslanger, to name only a few recent protagonists.[1] This state of affairs is exacerbated by Searle's influential project, whose task he sees in answering the 'fundamental question in contemporary philosophy', which he defines as follows:

> How, if at all, can we reconcile a certain worldview as described by physics, chemistry, and the other basic sciences with what we know, or think we know, about ourselves as human beings? How is it possible in a universe consisting entirely of physical particles in fields of force that there can be such things as consciousness, intentionality, free will, language, society, ethics, aesthetics, and political obligations?[2]

Searle's well-known answer is that there are genuinely social facts, consisting in the circumstance that something can be considered something that it actually is not. A natural object or natural fact X obtains in a particular context as a categorially different object Y.[3] In the framework of a particular economy, a printed piece of paper is considered money; a person the bearer of a name; a text (such as a constitution) a normative blueprint of a society; and so forth.

The first major problem in this approach is that the context in which an X obtains as a Y must itself be social. There must be an institution (such as a central bank) that validates the constitutive rule that X obtains as Y. This raises the question of how the institution that is meant to generate the social is generated itself; this leads to a regress which Searle halts by treating language as a primary institution – that is, as something social that conditions all other social things without itself being conditioned by an institution.[4]

In this way, Searle is forced to naturalize language, which he shifts by a further level of justification by anchoring it in intentionality, which he considers identical with the activity of a brain region and hence unmistakably naturalizable.[5] By taking the fiction of naturalized intentionality as a natural condition for language, Searle draws on a metaphysical evidence pyramid whose relevant basis in the natural comprises the neuronal processes that are meant to generate consciousness.

However, he overlooks the fact that the development of neuronal networks in human beings is already a partly social (and hence ontologically hybrid) product, as it takes place in the womb and is causally tied to the mother's behaviour (food intake, patterns of movement, and so on)[6] – to say nothing of the fact that newborn babies only develop brain structures at all in social contexts that are causally connected (through behavioural control) to a long social history of habitualization. It is therefore not the case that neuronal structures are brute facts in consciousness, minded and social beings of our species – that is, purely natural givens whose order subsequently yields mental and ultimately social facts. Neuronal tissue in human beings grows not like weeds in a garden but under the human survival form's conditions of social reproduction. Accordingly, the allegedly non-social and in this sense natural basis for the emergence of social facts is already largely socially produced, and therefore cannot fulfil the ontological demands on a regress blocker.

The human organism is socially produced. Humans do not grow on trees, as it were, but evolve under highly specific conditions that include other humans. The mere fact of being human means that other humans and their social relationships are involved in one's coming-about.[7] To quote the relevant, pithy Aristotelian formula: 'Human is generated by human' (*Anthropos anthropon genna*).[8] Since the human body is a social product, the reduction of social facts to an emergent phenomenon based on brute facts is already thwarted because the purported brute facts, which are meant to prop up the social in a non-social fashion, do not exist.

This is not remotely meant to suggest that there are no natural, non-social facts in the sense of facts concerning natural species (such as bosons, supernovae, and so on), but merely to point out that Searle's socio-ontological architecture does not deliver what it promises. One can neither reduce consciousness to something that is not yet social nor identify language (in its declarative function) as a point of departure for the social, since there are actually social facts without which there would be no language; this means that language is already rooted in pre-linguistic sociality.

The social realism espoused here therefore abandons the theorem that social facts consist in the circumstance that, in a context C, X acts as Y because context C is already social, such that this analytical attempt is thwarted either by a vicious circle or by a regress that cannot be halted in a productive, theoretically controlled way. This does put paid not to the task of social ontology, only to the logical form of Searle's answer.

Anyone who learns to speak is already a member of a community that displays grammatized behaviour – that is, publicly identifiable patterns of behaviour by which different individuals can orient themselves. Human behaviour observed by someone who learns to speak is habitualized in a way that allows others to orient themselves by him. Anyone who follows a rule is initially following a model. Language acquisition is thus grounded in partially pre-linguistic sociality, because those who are inducted into a language already belong to a social structure. *Language is not the phylogenetic, let alone ontological foundation of society.*

What the already existing language community presents to its newborn members through its behaviour is visible normativity. This includes guiding the eyes of infants, giving their daily life a rhythm (which includes the training of sleeping habits that is very familiar to all parents) and thus, on a basic survival level, regulating sensory input, which in turn contributes to the newborn organism. The mere fact that infants are not born as adults means that their nestling in an ecological niche is fundamentally impossible without social conditions.

The human being, as a human animal, is a social product, not some pre-social growth that appears by chance in the presence of a human group. From a different perspective, this means that the central nervous system, and thus also the (as yet unidentified) minimal neuronal correlate of consciousness (assuming there is such a thing), is in fact a social product, since no one has ever been conscious without coming into existence under social conditions. Neuronal tissue does not grow spontaneously, let alone independently of an organism, which never consists solely of neuronal tissue.[9]

The recognition paradigm in social ontology assumes that social facts are generated by discursive practices that construct the existence of a fact by representing this existence. This means that there cannot be social facts if no one believes in their existence. One can hold true and false opinions about a given social fact (social facts are thus 'epistemically objective', as Searle says); but the existence of a social fact is ultimately 'ontologically subjective', since the fact would not exist without a corresponding conviction shared by several people.[10] In the anti-realist paradigm, then, social facts cannot be known without recognition, since they do not even exist without recognition.

Conversely, natural facts exceed our conditions of recognition. For it is inherent in the concept of a natural fact that we cannot rule out a priori the existence of natural facts that, because of the empirical limitations imposed by the architecture of the universe, we fundamentally cannot know and a fortiori cannot recognize. Because of the ontology of their object area (the universe), the natural sciences are constitutively fallible; this follows not from their methods but from the matter itself.[11]

Social constructivism of Searle's type is anti-realistic, since he assumes, for every social fact, that it would not have existed had no one ever referred to it in the logical form of a declaration. The existence and being-already-declared of a social fact coincide ontologically.[12]

Searle's approach to resolving social constructivism based on the validity structure of money seems to rest on an impermissibly simplified 'Marxist' model for distinguishing between use value and exchange value. He argues that the social begins as soon as one assigns to the use value of natural objects an exchange value that is not covered by the use value. It is hardly surprising that Searle's favourite example of exchange value is a banknote. This stands in an incalculably complex representational relationship with those objects of utility for which one can exchange it. The representational relationship does not consist in a visual duplication, let alone a truth function that treats the banknote as a type of statement; in Searle's model, it is a form of validity. The banknote has a borrowed collective intentionality: it refers exclusively through the recognition of its validity to natural objects and artefacts that can be exchanged for it. For Searle, money is objectified validity.

In Searle's construction, the validity of the social breaks ontologically with the anonymity of natural processes, which raises the question of under what conditions the social was even able to emerge. Searle and the projects of philosophical social ontology that followed him view themselves as a metaphysics of the social: they are meant to articulate the trans-empirical foundations of the empirical social sciences. Through the explanation of the difference between social and non-social facts, the empirical social sciences are assigned the task of operating within the framework thus defined.

This is meant to ward off the exaggerated social constructivism that presents itself as 'radical constructivism'.[13] The bogeyman of radical constructivism consists in disputing the existence of non-social facts. By limiting the object area of the social sciences conceptually – that is, a priori – one draws a sharp line between the natural and social sciences that allows us to protect nature from impermissible theoretical assaults.

This manoeuvre is not adequate to stem constructivism, however. Instead of recognizing social constructivism itself as a problem, it is limited to an area specifically designated for it. This results in a sedimentation of massive constructivist residues that leads, for example in the recent work of Maurizio Ferraris, who largely follows Searle, to a formulation of emergentism.[14]

Emergentism assumes that the universe undergoes a local transition at some point from opaque, anonymous states to forms of information-driven self-organization and, later, articulates itself in the form of the mental and the social. For Ferraris, the foundation of the social is the documentation of transactions – that is, the establishment of 'writing-down systems' – to invoke the relevant theoretical construction by Friedrich Kittler.[15]

However, this raises the question of which metaphysics or natural philosophy would actually allow us to localize a number of emergences in the universe. How exactly are the purported levels of the universe that appear diachronically connected synchronically? And how can one guarantee that the relevant categorial caesuras in the universe were adequately drawn? It hardly makes sense a priori that the universe is going through numerous leaps of emergence. If these actually exist, they can only be ascertained with suitable methods. But what methods would these be?

Without natural philosophy and the metaphysics of natural sciences, the vague suspicion that life, mind and sociality must emerge from something that is categorially different from them cannot be confirmed, philosophically or otherwise. Emergentism is a modern mythology that makes sense against the background of a metaphysics that understands the universe as a primarily mind-hostile place of anonymous processes, where one must find a place afterwards for whatever is ontologically unruly.

In addition to the problem that emergentism presupposes a natural philosophy that it does not provide, a graver objection is that social constructivism as such is incoherent, meaning that emergentism offers both an unfounded and an unnecessary procedure to view a fiction of the social wrongly as the essence of the social. If one gives social constructivism an inch, it takes a mile. As soon as one concedes that the social, and thus every form of linguistic normativity, is constructed, one ties the meaning of the word 'nature' (and that of all other terms that are meant to refer to natural things, which *ex hypothesi* includes 'fermion', 'boson', 'molecule', 'Big Bang', 'supernova', 'neocortex', and so forth) to recognition. The term 'nature' only means what Searle or Ferraris claim it means for as long as a language community employs the word mark 'nature' to refer to an X that it considers natural. The knowable status of the natural is thus bestowed via discursive practices, which places the entire edifice of layers at risk of collapsing under the pressure of the social constructivist superstructure.

This framework confirms the claims of Rorty, for whom the sociality of linguistic reference is the argumentative starting point from which he encroaches on truth, and subsequently the factual structure of every purportedly pure natural universe.[16] If the social (and hence language) is constructed, the same applies to linguistic reference, and thus to the ontological obligations of natural-scientific theory-building. If the meaning of 'electron' is socially constructed, it is no longer so simple to maintain the assumption that electrons are not constructed. For one decides on electrons (or, rather, more speculative theoretically postulated entities) by taking on commitments that articulate themselves linguistically, which means that it is not obvious how one sorts the force field of our assumptions into those that do ultimately connect us to language-independent entities and those that do not.[17]

In the framework of FOS, the experimental design of standard social ontology is *a limine* an ontological error that can no longer be satisfactorily corrected after the fact. This ontological error consists in *metaphysically* privileging the universe as an object area of the natural sciences and describing all other fields of sense at best as emergent systems. If one inflates the scientifically explorable into the totality of being, this ultimately leaves no room for entities whose behaviour cannot be predicted through scientific models. This process is a paradigmatic metaphysical error, however – a severe overgeneralization of a given field of sense. It quite simply does not follow from modern physics that everything in existence appears in the field of sense of physics. Anyone who thinks that a general election consists of elementary particles, for example, meaning that the result of the Big Bang was already 'essentially' fixed at the 'moment' of its occurrence, is embroiled in so much nonsense that there is no prospect of imminent rescue.

Searle, of course, bypasses certain outgrowths of this model by viewing the social in normative terms. The social is validity that does not intervene in the causally closed, ultimately only physically describable universe. Let us retrace our steps, then, and begin again elsewhere in order to reconstruct the nature of the social from a different vantage point.

At the first level, there are objects. Secondly, these objects essentially appear in fields of sense, which leads to the formation of a factual structure (that is, ontic truth). In a field of sense, something applies to its objects because there is an ordering function that assigns objects to a field of sense. A proposition to the effect that this or that is the case concerns objects in a field of sense. If the state of affairs is as the proposition describes, the proposition is true. It applies – that is, there is propositional truth.

Whether a proposition is true or not cannot be determined solely by the fact that it is made. Let us call the case of making a proposition, which is characteristic for the question of truth, that of *holding-to-be-true*. Its degree of truth is the relevant fact. The fact is the norm for propositional truth because it locates a given proposition in the realm either of correct or of incorrect judgements. The real, as that which sorts our judgements into successful and failed ones, imposes norms. There is no need for any further normativity consisting in, for example, the fact that those who judge submit to a norm that is immanent in the judgement. Normativity cannot be reconstructed by navel contemplation by the act of judgement of the logical analysis of the propositional form, however technically skilled, if it is not taken into account that there are extra-linguistic facts that enable us to make judgements in the first place.

A proposition claims p, and whoever makes it assumes that this is true. It is impossible to believe something to be true without thus creating a fact, namely the fact of holding-to-be-true. A proposition, from the perspective of a proposition about it, is a fact. After all, it is a fact that someone claims p, regardless of whether p is the case. If one believes the truth to be false or something false to be true, this does not mean one has escaped from the facts; at best it means one has created new facts – that is, doxastic facts.

This brings us to an origin of the mystery of social facts, for social facts seem to be precisely those facts that we *create* through our holding-to-be-true. Based on this reasoning, holding-to-be-true is itself the paradigmatic social fact, since it consists in creating new kinds of facts by asserting them.

What makes these new facts of holding-to-be-true social is that they must be normed through dissent. Based on this model, non-social facts do not prescribe how exactly we should think them, since they themselves are devoid of prescriptive power. One cannot realize that one should judge in a certain way – that is, believe something to be true – if there is no room for corrections. There is only room for corrections of holding-to-be-true if some parts of what one can believe to be true are worse than others. It is in the nature of holding-to-be-true that it is normed by ontic truth; a true statement is (with reference to the norm consisting in the fact) better than a false one.[18]

Assertory propositions are subject to the norm of truth. In so far as propositions are normed in this way, true and false must be distinguishable from each other. They are not distinguishable based solely on whether one believes something to be true, because one cannot simultaneously believe something to be both true and false in the same respect; something *is* true. A false judgement cannot be corrected purely by non-social reality, since correction requires a further, true judgement in whose light the false one is revised. The occasion for the correction cannot come merely from a single subject, since human subjects that judge are already socialized. Someone who reaches the level of practising judgement, who thus lives and survives, is already embedded as a living being in social contexts without which they would not even be an organism.

The attempt to orient oneself by the truth is immanent in holding-to-be-true. Believing something to be true means being convinced that one is orienting oneself by what is true; what is true is indicated purely by a particular holding-to-be-true. One believes p to be true and thus rules out something else. Certain things that are irreconcilable with p, especially not-p, are directly excluded. Here we cannot simply orient ourselves by the truth in order to stay on the winning track of judgement. As soon as inferential conditions become more difficult, we need a further holding-to-be-true regarding existing conditions of inference, though in each case it unsurprisingly applies that one cannot pass through the needle's eye of holding-to-be-true without intending to hit upon the truth.[19]

One cannot correct oneself in a logically private fashion; this is the minimum conclusion from the discussion of Wittgenstein's argument about private language.[20] An individual holding-to-be-true is incorrigible as such. One can replace the belief that p is true with the belief that not-p is true (paradigmatically because q, and from q follows not-p), but the demand to carry out this replacement does not naturally follow from believing p to be true. For believing p to be true entails thinking that one is orienting oneself by the truth. The norm of truth is inherent in holding-to-be-true, which means that orientation by the norm of truth and a successful orientation by what is true cannot be coextensive. If they were, then the fact that we think that something is a particular way would be constitutively impervious to improvement. We are capable of improvement because we do not merely judge serially but make judgements that are connected. The connection between judgements stems from the fact that we learn something, which presupposes that we were corrected or trained – that is, pointed in a particular direction.[21]

This is the origin of the idea of the 'sociality of reason'.[22] We are all beings that make knowledge claims and, hence, take part in the practice of holding-to-be-true; we are constitutively corrigible. Although this corrigibility stems from the idea of holding-to-be-true, it cannot be adequately explained without considering that other people may factually favour a change of direction. For others believe other things to be true, which is what leads to contradiction in the first place. Avoidance of contradictions is therefore not a purely logical – that is, wholly a priori – norm. The pre-social idea of holding-to-be-true does not even yield the *possibility* of error. Rather, the pre-social idea of holding-to-be-true repels the possibility of error. Error and thus contradiction only appear when others make different judgements.

Thus the pre-social idea of holding-to-be-true is not factually instantiated as soon as someone makes a judgement. When people judge, they have long since been conditioned by the fact that they are socially produced as living beings. Even our sensorium stems from processes of social coordination, meaning that we are not born merely with a pre-social central nervous system, for example, in which we have to install a given social order. The idea of a 'pure' holding-to-be-true isolated from factual correction by other beings therefore yields the misleading notion of a logical, maximal private domain that may, of course, strike those who imagine such things as the happiness of immaculate generality.

Contradiction is a problem because someone who contradicts us is pointing out that the real cannot be as we think it is. We think that the real is as we think it is, however, because we believe it to be true that it is so. Whoever contradicts us thus accuses us of violating the norm that we have *nolens volens* imposed on ourselves by making a judgement. Whoever makes a judgement – that is, believes something to be true that others may believe to be false – is thus already in the space of normativity. Reality is a norm one cannot evade, for one already imposes it on oneself before asking which normative order one intends to submit to in future.

Whoever contradicts us strikes at the (paradox-prone) heart of our autonomy: our judgement.[23] Judging is paradox-prone in the sense that we can believe something false to be true without this fact being available to us in the same judgement. We can think wrongly and only notice it when we are corrected. Our judgement cannot correct itself. At some point, someone else joined us and confronted us with the possibility that we might be mistaken. At the same time, this possibility can only be registered if we recognize the other's judgement, which means that we must judge the judgement of another as something that corrects us, such that our own judgement must be able to direct itself against itself. Ultimately, then, we must correct ourselves on the occasion of an outside judgement. No one can relieve us of this course correction; we remain free in our judgements and are therefore open to influence.

This does not mean one cannot correct oneself, only that a given judgement one makes is not corrigible in the respect that one has made it *in that way*, since the judgement consists in believing something to be true and thus factually ruling out believing it to be false. If the possibility that a holding-to-be-true can be false should ever be noticed by someone, it must come from someone else, since one's own doxastic life consists in a number of judgements whose potential or factual incompatibility only becomes apparent to us when someone else points us in a different direction. This is a fact of human life, not a 'transcendental matter of logical form'. One judgement corrects another. One learns to make use of this *in foro interno* for purposes of self-correction, first of all through others.

If we summarize this reflection in the form of individual theses, the following has been said:

1 Judgements – that is, the holding-to-be-true of something – are normative because they are true or false and can therefore be divided into cases of success and failure.
2 A judgement can be true or false but not fallible. A judgement is not mistaken; a person is mistaken. Falsity and error are not the same thing.
3 Fallibility consists in someone being corrigible. Corrigibility is socially acquired as a result of others judging differently and correcting us.
4 The capacity for self-correction is socially acquired and developed. The path to developing the capacity for self-correction varies diachronically and synchronically across an indefinite number of social subsystems.

No transcendental history of judgement's coming-into-itself takes place. Our self-determination, and thus our freedom as minded beings, is set in motion by the fact that others believe other things to be true and thus disclose incompatibilities to us that are not evaluable a priori. The reality shock that demands a course correction stems not from our private holding-to-be-true but from the ever-possible and at some point actual mutual believing-to-be-false that is the formal foundation of human socialization.[24]

Social facts are based on the circumstance that we believe something true which others may consider false, which leads to our being confronted with explicable norms embodied in institutions that are visible as such. The first public sphere of the normative is the existence of natural facts of our survival form, without which there would be no social facts. Natural facts are necessary but fundamentally insufficient conditions for social facts. Furthermore, only a relevant subset of natural facts is a necessary condition for social facts, and we cannot say exactly which subset this is, since we are unimaginably far from having any remotely comprehensive overview of the whole universe. That fermions exist is probably a natural necessary condition for social facts, but less relevant than the existence of the natural necessary conditions for the sexual reproduction of human life. One cannot decide a priori which natural necessary conditions belong to the nature of a given social fact and, hence, cannot decide this on the basis of social ontology either.

Social facts exist because we judge. When we do so, it is fundamentally possible for others to make different judgements. When this occurs, we encounter a form of deviation that is social in a way that can no longer be reduced to natural facts. The judgement of the others is not identical with some processes in my organism, let alone with the fact that there are elementary particles which appear as ensouled foreign bodies on a mesoscopic scale. Judgements thus have a criterion of publicity based on the fact that we, as individuals, perceive things from a particular perspective that gives us occasion to judge that p.[25] *Our judging, then, is the social fact: as* zoon logon echon *[an animal possessing logos], we are social.*

Explicit communitization presupposes an 'agreement in judgements'[26] that, as Wittgenstein rightly points out, is also 'determined by a certain constancy in results of measurement'.[27] 'This seems to abolish logic, but does not do so.'[28] For logic, as the form of theory-building that deals with the structures of the normativity of thought and judgement, cannot have any specific form, and thus any specific content, if one overlooks that it must refer at some point to the practice of judgement among finite, minded beings. A logic is not 'pure' by virtue of there being no possibility to apply it. A logic that is 'pure' in this sense would be an incomprehensible mystery.

We judge differently from others because each of us starts from a different sensory disposition; this is something we cannot and should not pass over. For what makes a judgement objective is not the fact that I abstract from *my* conditions in order to make it but that I, as a judging person, am corrigible in the context of a community. The degree of my doxastic correction is dictated by facts; my correction results from the believing-to-be-false of others. One is originally corrected only because of an existing dissent, which ultimately stems from the circumstances that there are facts which exist on this side of human sociality.[29] Self-correction in the face of the non-human real is thus not only phylo- and ontogenetically but also conceptually secondary to correction through others. We learn to correct ourselves when others have already redirected us – which, admittedly, reaches us only because we are born as minded beings that already judge. Holding-to-be-true must therefore belong to our survival form, otherwise the latter could not be sublimated into a historically variable form of life.

When someone believes p to be true and someone else believes it to be false, this first of all raises the question: p or not-p? Thus the idea that something one believes to be true may be false is a consequence of the reality of dissent.[30] The concept of truth plays the part of resolving the conflict on whose basis Kant, in the third section of the canon of pure reason entitled 'On having opinions, knowing, and believing', already developed his ambitious concept of triangulation. He sees the 'private validity' of a concept in the fact that 'the ground of the judgement, which lies solely in the subject, is held to be objective.'[31] Such a 'taking to be true cannot be communicated',[32] as it consists merely in the fact that someone believes p to be true. The first step in improving the situation is the addition of the 'reason of others',[33] which judges differently. In the second step, however, the 'truth of the judgement' is introduced as the 'touchstone', since, according to Kant, a true judgement 'rests on the common ground, namely the object, with which they all therefore agree.'[34] 'Truth, however, rests upon agreement with the object, with regard to which, consequently, the judgements of every understanding must agree (*consentientia uni tertio, consentiunt inter se*).'[35] Objectivity that thematizes itself (in the medium of the 'thinking of thinking') is thus constitutively social, in that we have access to the thought that we may be mistaken only because we are directed, via the conflict of opinions, to the fact that either p or not-p is true, and that a choice must therefore be possible in principle.

The nature of human sociality is grounded in dissent – that is, in deviation. Deviation consists in judging from a perspective that arises from our factual position in a situation to which we belong as sensorily equipped beings. Dissent need not and cannot be attributed to a mental, linguistic or political social contract that allows a consensus to be established. Consensus cannot be achieved solely through an alignment of opinions, as Kant correctly explains, since the shared focus of agreement necessary for this is the object of which something is true. Objectivity is the epistemological and ontological foundation of society, and thus ineluctably rooted in the real.

Of course, society's participants are always already social animals, since humans are embedded from a very early ontogenetic stage in social contexts without which they could neither live nor survive. Even (phenomenal) consciousness only develops in a human individual when it develops in a symbiosis with another individual (the mother) whose food intake, behaviour, and so on, have a massive impact on the future qualities of the person *in statu nascendi*. Humans (like other animals) are thus constitutively social, since we would have no inner life without sociality. Our inner life is embedded in causal social contexts; without these, there would not even be a development of the minimal neuronal correlate of consciousness (whatever that might be).

The idea of an alignment of opinions presupposes that there is a standard whose existence is not based on gathering further opinions. Given this standard, the only thing that makes sense is to view an existing divergence as dissent. If two opinions exist – that is, two cases of holding-to-be-true – one referring to p and the other to not-p, a stable community only ensues if one concedes that the real decides who is right. If this is ruled out, the result is an irreconcilable contradiction that leads to the collapse of the community of judgement.

Society is grounded in something that does not itself have the character of society. This includes the survival conditions of social animals; there are therefore non-normative (zoological) conditions for normativity.[36] The necessary natural conditions for the existence of social facts are not on the other side of some metaphysical boundary, but rather influence the practice of judgement. Human sociality is not a free-floating mental sphere but a property of beings that depend at every level of their activity on the fulfilment of relevant natural conditions.

We are socialized by the real. This applies not only ontogenetically but also phylogenetically. We consign others to the domain of holding-to-be-true by showing them the real. The demonstration of the real is the basic function on which society rests: as thinkers of thoughts, we demonstrate. The community of thinking, minded beings is essentially a community of dissenters.[37] Yet dissent is not an end in itself, since there is a standard for its success: the real decides who is right. To be sure, the community does not implode merely because wrong opinions circulate and something that is not the case is thus taken to be true. If the idea of truth, and thus the representation of our truth-aptness, goes up in smoke, the community of dissenters crumbles. Legitimate *dissenters* who stake truth claims turn into *dissidents* who are expected to submit to an unfounded, constitutively erratic holding of opinions.[38] Dissidents exist only where the idea of a free, truth-based forming of opinions is structurally undermined, meaning that the role of the dissident is obsolete under ideal discursive conditions. Not every opposition consists of dissidents; opposition is constitutive for opinion-forming, as holding-to-be-true aims for a successful justification in the face of a given believing-to-be-false.

From a socio-ontological perspective, political autonomy consists, in an ideal borderline case, in society becoming itself as an adequate idea of itself. When an ideal political community orients itself fundamentally by the factual structure of human sociality – that is, the idea of a community of stable dissenters – its institutions are judged according to how they balance out dissent and keep neutral spaces open for the adiaphora of the private domain.

It is therefore no coincidence that processes of emancipation go hand in hand with reflection on the philosophical foundations of community. Here the truth about the structure of self-determination constitutes the standard of successful political autonomy. The conflict of political ideas is waged in the name of modern emancipation projects only as long as there is a publicly waged conflict regarding the idea of communitization. It is no coincidence that modernity is essentially connected to theories of the political that enter the self-conception of socialized life; rather, it is a consequence of the form of self-determination that is based on its own specific form of self-determination. That is the idea of social autonomy.

The social autonomy of free, minded beings takes on a reflexive form. We can orient ourselves not only by given, positive norms but also by the fact that we can orient ourselves by norms. Thus our own normativity can become an occasion for orientation. The only reason why this form of recursive self-determination (famously spelled out by Kant) does not collapse is that we determine ourselves in the face of the real. The real passes judgement on the success of our self-determination, which thus never takes place in a vacuum. All self-determination, every judgement about judgement, takes place in the midst of the real.

The real is not identical with the natural. The non-normative conditions for normativity are not exclusively found in nature, as the domain that is paradigmatically examined by the natural sciences. We will refer to the misconception that the nature of the social is identical with the nature of the natural sciences using a phrase that is an obvious choice here: *the naturalist fallacy*.[39]

Social constructivism unsuccessfully attempts to free itself from the naturalist fallacy. That is why it adopts its characteristic opposition to essentialism, because it mistakenly blames the fact that worthwhile projects of emancipation are impeded by the idea that there is anything essential in the social. Yet an insight into the biological, ethological and zoological conditions of human self-determination is not a hindrance to emancipation, but rather enables it by taking over the function of anchoring an otherwise empty discourse in reality. We cannot determine ourselves in a vacuum, which means that this absurd idea cannot act as a foundation for factually successful socialization.

The failure of social constructivism lies in the manifoldly incoherent idea of social construction. One can observe this dialectic paradigmatically in Haslanger's attempt to articulate the idea of social construction in an analytically sharpened form.[40] What is striking first of all is that Haslanger expressly avoids defining the term 'social'. She offers a questionable reason for this:

> I believe that it is not possible to define 'social' in non-circular terms, so an analysis, strictly speaking, is not possible. This does not rule out giving an account of the social, but the contours of this, like those of any account, will depend on the particular project, the purposes for which one needs a notion of the social, and so on. My approach to this, as in other cases, is to employ a focal analysis. For my purposes, coordinated activity is the focal notion.[41]

This would mean that an *analysis, strictly speaking*, of the 'social' is impossible, but a *focal analysis* is possible, though Haslanger here neglects to specify wherein this distinction lies. It is surprising that she attributes the concept of focal analysis specifically to Aristotle's *pros hen* relation, which he shows using the concept of health.[42] Admittedly, she immediately qualifies this analogy because she is aware that an Aristotelian focus is anything but an example of anti-essentialism. For Aristotle, *ousia* is the focus of all judgement, which makes an Aristotelian focal analysis the very epitome of a definition, strictly speaking.[43]

Accordingly, Haslanger hastily adds: 'I differ from many using the concept by emphasizing that the core or focal meaning may differ depending on one's theoretical purposes.'[44] Now, it is *prima facie* unproblematic to make the meaning of the word 'social' contingent on one's theoretical purposes; however, the devil is in the detail here. For, in general, Haslanger feels obliged to semantic externalism, which is not necessarily compatible with the assumption that the meaning of the word 'social' depends on one's theoretical purposes.[45] She even explicitly takes the position that the social sciences are epistemically weighty because they explore 'social kinds'.[46]

According to externalism, however, the meaning of 'water' is not at all dependent on one's interests. According to Haslanger's premises, then, the social cannot itself be a social kind described by the specialist term 'the social'. In this way, she makes her suggestion to view 'the social' as 'coordinated activity' immune to both philosophical critique and social-science expertise. Philosophical critique is kept at bay through an explicit act of stipulation, and social-science expertise by the fact that the social itself is not understood as a social kind. But how does Haslanger know that the social itself has no essence? Why does she think that there are essences, even social essences, but simultaneously dispute that the social has an essence? There may be good reasons, but she does not give them.

Her concept of social construction is equally theoretically problematic. In failing to state what exactly the social is, she undermines the comprehensibility of her own definitions. She distinguishes, only seemingly helpfully, between:

1 generic social construction
2 causal construction
3 constitutive construction
4 discursive construction
5 pragmatic construction.[47]

Let us take a closer look at her definition of generic social construction in particular. Haslanger writes: '*Generic social construction*: Something is a social construction in the generic sense just in case it is an intended or unintended product of a social practice.'[48] This definition leaves much to be desired. As expected, it is first of all hopelessly circular, as it defines the social via social practices. Secondly, and more problematically at this point, we do not learn enough about the meaning of the word 'construction' beyond the fact that it is 'at least initially . . . useful' to conceive construction 'on the model of artefacts'.[49] We do not learn, however, how this model construction proceeds and how Haslanger views artefacts. Instead, we are merely told that there is 'a clear sense' in which institutions are artefacts, and that this is also the sense in which they are social constructions.[50] But that is precisely what is at stake in the question of whether and in what sense institutions are socially constructed! If the desired 'clear sense' existed, it would never have occurred to anyone to be a social constructivist.[51]

Read in a generous light, Haslanger explains the word 'construction' by viewing it as a 'product'. Because she focuses the social on coordinated activity (something on which one can agree with her), her suggestion is therefore that something is socially constructed if it is the product of coordinated activity. However, she considerably weakens this suggestion by adding the word 'unintended' to her definition; the restructuring of elementary particles, for example, is an unintended product of many coordinated activities. When a choir sings 'Ode to Joy', this is certainly a case of coordinated activity. The singers interfere unintentionally with the entire universe, since their singing and their movements modify field structures without which no physically coded information transfer could occur. So the universe is of such a character that it has socially constructed parts, however tiny their quantity. The universe is *ipso facto* (partially) socially constructed, if anything is socially constructed.

Perhaps Haslanger will not shy away from these conclusions; after all, they do away with the socio-ontologically obstructive difference between nature and culture, which may be in her interests.[52] Nonetheless, the entire ecological niche inhabited by humans turns in this model into a social artefact, since humans as such are only capable of survival if they are socialized, which *ex hypothesi* rubs off on the whole human habitat. Yes, Haslanger is consistent in concluding from her definition that fully-grown humans are a 'special kind of artefact'.[53] This is, however, an exaggeration (to put it mildly). While it is at least *prima facie* plausible to view some parts of the whole that we are as 'socially constructed', it is nonsense to view a complete person as an artefact or even socially constructed. For this would impute that the natural forms involved in a human being's survival – our organs and cells, as well as the molecules without which there could be no cells – are socially constructed, unmistakably revealing the absurdity of this position or its transformation into a radical social constructivism.

It is an entirely accurate, but metaphysically harmless observation that much of what is significant in human life is a product of social – that is, coordinated – activity. Because of the division of labour in the relations of production, the sociality of a product they bring about may remain hidden from individual actors. This is a Marxist truism that goes hand in hand with a far more difficult question: what specific relations of production underlie a given product that hides its own sociality?[54] Such an analysis, however, can only be carried out inadequately if one uses the incoherent conceptual tools of 'social construction'.

We should therefore purge social ontology of the jargon of social constructivism once and for all. Baudrillard rightly demanded this in *Forget Foucault*, pointing out that the idea of social construction is thwarted by an inadequately developed conception of power.[55] In Foucault (and subsequently Butler and Searle), the question of constitution arises as well as that of maintaining the social in the face of its (alleged) constructedness. If one reveals something social – sexuality, gender, prisons, the penal system, the classification system for plants and animals, and so forth – as socially constructed, this signifies that it did not come about by natural means. The historicity and thus contingency of discursive practices, examined prominently by Foucault, presupposes that social systems are produced by actors. But how is faith in these systems, without which they could not survive, maintained? How does one maintain something that is essentially historically modifiable?

Foucault's conception of power attempts to perform the theoretical task of explaining the preservation of contingently existing practices, for which he proposed a variety of models in the course of his career. Unlike Foucault, Butler and Searle employ Austin's speech act theory, which they expand in different ways to tie the preservation of social systems to the recognition of actors who do not, at least, offer sufficient resistance to change a social system or abolish it entirely.

Baudrillard, on the other hand, shows that the basic principle of social constructivism – that X is socially constructed if X (a material basis) only exists as Y (a social superstructure) as long as actors jointly ensure that the validity of X continues as Y – follows a specifically modern model of representation that is itself historically contingent. This model claims that the production of facts is what must be taken into account in a social theory: it is based on the explication and knowability of systems, not on what Baudrillard in turn calls an order of 'secrecy and seduction'.[56]

Let us call this *the implicit*. Any linguistically coded explication must follow a sociality that is already implicit, meaning that the model of the declarative or performative situation already draws involuntarily on the social, without being able to explain it or adequately locate it ontologically. One of the existential conditions of the social is that it is always effective in the background, meaning that we can seemingly never grasp it in its efficacy but only in the mode of representation. The binding character of the social and its representation are not the same, however, since the representation of the social rests parasitically on the group stability which is assumed so that the representation can develop its symbolic force.

Because of Searle's virtue of arguing in a theoretically articulated fashion, the problems of prioritizing the explicit become especially clear in his work; he ascribes to social facts a 'world-to-word direction of fit'. This means that, if someone who is authorized baptizes another person 'John', then John is henceforth called John. The sociality of thinking and speaking is thus located in the logical form of declarative speech acts.[57] Our thinking and speaking is social, in that we jointly produce something by representing it as something. We constitute the value of paper money by assigning to a piece of paper a validity that it would not have without the authorizing speech acts. In this way, sociality is tied to representation, which Searle famously locates in the intentionality of consciousness, which in turn emerges – though no one knows how – on the basis of brain areas (which no one can precisely name).

In this sense, Searle does well to naturalize intentionality in order to give representation an anchoring in reality, which is meant to clear it of any suspicion of social construction.[58] Yet this manoeuvre ultimately fails because it remains unclear how naturalized intentionality is meant to provide the foundation for a non-naturalizable – because socially constructed – additional dimension of social facts. Searle's declarative speech acts have a direction of constitution that fits neither into his naturalistic worldview nor his attempt to expand it sufficiently.[59]

Foucault – like Nietzsche before him – sometimes evades this problem by undertaking a quasi-naturalization and making the self come about through discursive practices that have a quasi-natural basis. That is why he ties subjectivity to practices such as sexual abstinence, mutual surveillance, and so on, in order to suggest that subjectivity emerged from rehearsed behavioural patterns. Social systems intervene in the self-constitution of subjects as bodily exercises.

But this theoretical constellation is constitutively blind to its own self-operations; this is why Foucault never wrote a genuine history of the present that was even remotely free of Eurocentric notions, for example (such as the isolation of the Roman territories from Asian influences, which Foucault never mentions). The historical corridor that Foucault describes in order to work his way indirectly towards his own position consists primarily of 'occidental' resources, which, at a minimum, suggests that the modern history of the human sciences is the extension of Athens, Rome and early Christianity. The choice of sources considered relevant clearly shows the signature of the author, who would like to disappear behind his seemingly neutral analyses of power.[60] Far from having killed the author and dethroned the subject, the author of such genealogies proves the master in the house of his own construction, behind which he retreats as an almost anonymous voice.

Given this state of theory, I would suggest following Marx and Baudrillard (albeit from a completely different angle) and replacing references to 'social construction', which fluctuate between vagueness and incoherence, with the concept of *production*.[61] We produce new facts by virtue of being social. These include doxastic and epistemic facts, meaning that an analysis of judgement leads us to the sociality of reason.

The social nature of judgement here consists in the fact that, as thinkers of thoughts, we are constitutively fallible. Thinkers of thoughts are not 'pure' believers-to-be-true, but rather socially produced beings whose mental states are no isolated events of holding-to-be-true in which they remain epistemically trapped. The contents of our holding-to-be-true are shaped, on the one hand, by the non-social real and, on the other hand, by the fact that others present them to us. Here one must take into account that human sensorium is not a non-social anonymous fact but, as an evolutionary product, came about socially through our survival form's conditions of reproduction. As stated above, human neuronal networks are not pre-social growths but sediments of complex selection mechanisms that have been controlled since time immemorial by partly conscious and partly unconscious sociality.

We are in need of correction. Without factual correction, humans cannot even survive. Mind – our capacity for self-images – is therefore social by definition.[62] In being corrected, we acquire the concept of reality as an epistemic modal category. The confrontation with the real, which cannot be achieved in logical privacy, is both the *ratio cognoscendi* and the *ratio essendi* of objectivity.

But the nature of the social is not itself socially produced. The fact that the social consists in beings such as ourselves only being capable of survival through course corrections, which initiate us into the game of giving and demanding reasons, is not in itself something that has been socially produced. We are quite simply beings whose nature is to be capable of survival only under social conditions. As minded beings, we would not exist if we did not constantly reproduce our conditions of survival, which is only possible for social beings such as humans through cooperation. As humans, we learn how to feed ourselves, move, see, hear and interpret; without these elementary exercises, no one reaches adulthood. But there is nothing produced about this architecture itself. We do not make ourselves into social beings in social ways; we are factually social. It is our nature to be social as natural beings. We cannot break out of this structure, whatever fantasies of human self-transcendence might be circulating at a given time.

One cannot reach this facticity naturalistically, since it presupposes the existence and reality of the mind, which cannot be fully naturalized. As minded beings, we are thinkers of thoughts that are social, in the sense that we are and remain fallible. At the latest, this fallibility becomes minded in an articulate way when we control ourselves via the explicit representation of this structure. This self-regulation, a sophisticated form of human action, already breaks at an elemental level from the stimulus–response limits within which our primary, sensory information processing operates, whose parameters are partly explicable in evolutionary terms. Naturally, each of us is born somewhere on a limited spectrum of genetic and neurobiological equipment that is possible for human animals. We interact with this equipment, which can also be epigenetically examined by taking into account behavioural and social environmental factors for genetic expression.[63] However, no zoological autopsy of humans could ever be remotely sufficient to understand our minded form of life and its articulation in the shape of historically grown, corrigible institutions of judgement.

Humans govern themselves via their capacity for self-images. On the basis of a developed sociality, we produce new social facts by forming a picture of how we fit into nature – a picture that affects our actions in one way or another in the age of ecological crises. How we assess our animality, and thus our position in nature, is a factor in determining which social facts we produce. Our articulated capacity for self-images, the reality of the mind, is therefore thoroughly social – which does not mean that specific cases of intentional, truth-apt attitudes are not objective and are instead regulated 'intersubjectively'. The sociality of the articulated mind is not grist for the mill of the ambitious thesis that intentionality is social in every respect. Our thoughts are indeed embedded in causal contexts that would not exist without the social production of living beings; this requires many additional premises, however, if it is to support that conclusion that truth can be replaced by any social norm (such as justified assertibility or consensus under idealized conditions). Not everything is social, not even all the specifically necessary conditions for the existence of social facts.

§13

Our Survival Form: Intransparent Society

The social nature of the mind is grounded in our fallibility. If someone is fallible, they are corrigible and thus the subject of a normalization. Normalization is social if other subjects can undertake it by suggesting a course to a subject. Social groups are not merely aggregates of subjects acting alongside one another, each of them fallible, but the result of an action coordination in the face of the challenges of the real. For the real already normalizes our thoughts and actions implicitly in that intentionality is available to us on the level of perception, and we are thus adapted doxastically to an environment containing objects that are not themselves thoughts, that do not have the form of opinions. Our perception occurs in the midst of the real as something real; it is clearly not a view from nowhere but is situated. The perceptual situation enters our consciousness partially, in so far as we perceive something only if we also exist in other states, such that there is an overall mental state that displays various conscious aspects.

Since perception among social beings is already a partly social product (because our necessary natural preconditions for perception develop in the framework of social reproduction), intentionality is factually social.[1] Yet this is not, as one might assume, primarily because we have to internalize external intentionality. Our self does not come about in the mirror, in the sense that we experience our first models in infancy as an obtrusive non-I without acknowledging ourselves. We could not internalize a self-image without already being attuned intentionally – that is, to facts that are not identical with our eigenstates. One could not demand of a genuine absolute I, which was not originally split into I and non-I, that it recognize an independent reality beyond its control.

The doxastic division of labour in society – the distribution of mutually incompatible holding-to-be-true among a multitude of cooperating actors – thus belongs to the origins of objectivity. The social nature of the mind does not threaten subjective, individual holding-to-be-true, but rather imbues it with epistemic objectivity: because others think differently, we come up against the limits of what convinces us and often find ourselves forced to correct our course or, for good reasons, to look out for better orientation on the path we have taken. If someone is challenged in their knowledge claim p and wishes to stand by it, they cannot avoid consolidating their claim. If one stays with p in the long term out of an unwillingness to countenance non-p, one falls prey to what Hegel aptly referred to in this context as 'self-will' [*Eigensinn*]:

> a freedom which is still enmeshed in servitude. Just as little as the pure form can become essential being for it, just as little is that form, regarded as extended to the particular, a universal formative activity, an absolute Notion; rather it is a skill which is master over some things, but not over the universal power and the whole of objective being.[2]

The thought expressed here can be reconstructed as follows: if we believe p to be true, there is either an *occasion* or a *reason* for this. An occasion is something that puts us in a mental state that is directly registered as a change in the state of information.[3] Our mental life essentially takes place in such a way that in every nameable situation we are exposed to a different state of information. We experience the 'stream of thoughts and life'[4] as a sequence of states. The overall mental states in which we respectively live as minded beings are finely individuated as events in the universe: they are exactly what they are, and nothing else.[5]

Overall mental states are radically singular and thus unrepeatable. They are respective, otherwise I could not ascribe them to myself.[6] The transition from one mental state to another generates a new state of information that has never existed before; in this way, the mind takes place as an event that can acknowledge itself. As self-conscious speech-capable beings, we have a vocabulary to reidentify elements of the state of information across different states, which enables us to name occasions. What we successfully name in this way (an object) is an occasion for believing something to be true; for objects are always part of an environment (a field of sense) without which they could not exist.

One should note that an *occasion* is not to be confused with a *stimulus*. 'Stimulus' is already a concept with a nuanced theoretical role, and certainly nothing that can be 'directly' observed. Stimuli are postulated, occasions are obvious. Whether occasions can be reduced to stimuli is at stake in the debate between illusionism and realism. As we have seen, it is a futile endeavour to identify all occasions with clusters of stimuli that are effective below our attention threshold, since this would deny us access to the attention threshold itself, which would obviously not be effective only below itself. Applied thoroughly to its own experimental design, illusionism exposes itself as bad magic.

In contrast to an occasion, a *reason* is a move in the game of giving and demanding reasons.[7] A reason is something we can adduce in order to secure p against a legitimate objection. A legitimate objection to p increases the plausibility of non-p in a context in which something is at stake. The contexts in which we judge lend their ontological weight. There is no point in proving to oneself that there is some p (such as 'I am conscious', 'I judge that p', 'I am alive' or 'I = I') that one *must* believe to be true when one considers it. For this project overlooks that there is a context – for example, a philosophical inquiry into propositional contents – in which it makes sense to point out something obvious. Simply put, every cogito and every consciousness finds itself in a situation it has not produced itself, for example in a 'backwater near Ulm'.[8] The ability to assure oneself of oneself, which goes hand in hand with self-consciousness, only comes about in the context of a doxastic division of labour that enables us to accomplish our survival as minded beings. A causally isolated cogito freezes; even Descartes needs an oven.

Reasons generate epistemic asymmetries and thus create the idea of an opposition.[9] This means that the logical space in which we judge is always already curved; the measure of its curvature is the trace of the other. Because there can be no flat logical space, whatever supports p always *factually* contradicts non-p. So there are incompatibilities that are not defined via an all-encompassing logical space. Negation is therefore not some logical carte blanche that surrounds 'p', as it were, and isolates it from everything else. Anyone who disputes p can only do so successfully in the name of q. Negation refers to the irreconcilability of the holding-to-be-true of p with that of q. *Someone who negates productively (that is, gives a substantive alternative) is countering; whoever negates haphazardly and universally (that is, says 'no' without giving alternatives) is being defensive at best.*

This social structure of holding-to-be-true can be mapped onto social theory. For society has blind spots, which is a constitutive motor for its differentiation into subsystems that are not subject to any centrally identifiable rule. Society has no power centre, otherwise it would be incapable of functioning. This is one of the basic insights of systems theory and must be taken into account socio-ontologically.

Let us be more specific. We are fallible; here we find the other who leads us to correct our course. Other people judge differently. We cannot have a complete idea of how others 'as a whole' judge, since such an overview would amount to having a body of thought that could no longer be disputed. An overview of society *as such* would not offer a view of anything. What exactly others think ultimately remains unavailable; the others always surprise us.

No surveillance apparatus, however perfect, can control society. Thus the power of a surveillance apparatus does not lie in monitoring the opinions of the masses and potentially intervening if the judgements are not as the power centre intends. Rather, a surveillance apparatus at best controls a large majority because its subjects orient themselves by the fiction of its omnipotence. Successful censorship relies on self-censorship, transforming the notion that everything is being monitored into effective behavioural models for the actors, who ultimately impose these on themselves.

Because we do not know how the others as a whole judge, we stay on course for corrections. This allows a community of minded beings to survive through cooperation and work towards the systematic improvement of its living conditions. The reasons we can give to reach a particular goal in the smallest possible number of suitable steps is always contestable; where exactly the contestation comes from is always a posteriori – for everyone.

This is where one paradox of the perfect dictator lies: in case of success, the perfect dictator becomes paranoid because they can no longer admit to any external source of holding-to-be-true whose course they cannot anticipate through the production of a surveillance apparatus. Committing senseless murders in order to spread fear among subjects – that is, totalitarian state terror – does not solve the problem; it consolidates it by spreading a constant fear of turmoil. The widely perceived threat to the idea of the democratic constitutional state as a theoretically justifiable form of rule comes from the fact that its opponents are not totalitarian dictators on the model of the twentieth century. Today, the conceptual challenge to the idea of the democratic constitutional state feeds on the fact that soft forms of total socialization have become possible.

I mention this latitude, which extends from the idea of systematically distributed power to the idea of an all-encompassing power centre, only as an example of how social systems, via the fiction of a power centre, themselves control something we refer to as 'the state'. A totalitarian state is one that identifies the state *with* society and attributes the latter to the foundation of an identifiable 'we' that stands for society as a whole. A totalitarian state is constitutively opposed to the others outside its borders, and is thus political in Carl Schmitt's sense.[10] What we are experiencing today as a resurgence of nationalism is the return of the political as conceived by Schmitt on a global stage – a movement that takes on mythological qualities, as we will see (see below, §15).

Society is possible and actual because social facts fundamentally do not consist of declarations. There is no primordial act of recognition that brings the social into being. As we have seen, this model already fails because the alleged act itself must be social in order to achieve the necessary recognition for the theorist to enter either a vicious circle or a regress. In this way, a consensus-based social ontology generates a mythology of distant origin – that is, an archaeology of knowledge. We do not cooperate because we realize at some point that it is a good idea, since such a realization would already be a cooperation; we thus cooperate for no reason. There is sufficient occasion for cooperation, which is why social biology is on the right track in tying the fact of the social to the fact that we are living beings. The human form of life participates in mind but is biologically impregnated.

Our survival form is thoroughly cooperative. We are connected not only by our sapience – that is, by explicable self-models – but already by being hominids. Before any imagined or actual cultural embedding, we belong, as hominids, to the human group that does not need to be put together before proceeding. On a fundamental level, then, human sociality is not socially constructed in any case, assuming this attribute contrasts with 'natural'.

We are social by nature; this is an expression of our survival form, which generates a statistically averaged universal.[11] Human scopes of action are embedded at a fundamental biological level in an ecological niche on which our daily lives feed. Survival, death, sexual reproduction, our elemental emotional repertoire, and so on, form universal patterns in which humans have been able to recognize themselves for over a hundred thousand years. Cultural, local impregnation does not modify this core but embeds it in historically contingent practices without consequently annulling it.

Because of this, our *survival form* is not separated from our *mental life form* by a conceptual, let alone metaphysical chasm. They are not identical, however, which is why the social remains fundamentally intransparent. For our nature is not wholly known to us in the medium of mind, meaning that we, as human animals, will always generate circumstances whose context indefinitely exceeds any state of empirical knowledge. Humans will never fully decipher themselves, as we are essentially embedded in an environment whose systemic complexity prevents us from ever gaining full control of them. Armin Nassehi puts it in a nutshell: 'We are intransparent to ourselves.'[12] I also agree with him completely when he states:

> There are few universal rules in the social realm. Everything is historically relative and depends on countless empirical constraints. I would, however, go so far as to say that if something can genuinely be ruled out, it is open and free communication and the possibility of communitization. Communitization is more like an effect that one can dispense with communication. . . . Communities are established primarily by ensuring that certain communicative [sic!] contents, demands, forms and deviations precisely *do not* occur.[13]

Our fallibility as thinkers of thoughts does not stem entirely from our survival form, which is a barb of the related primal scene of the Thracian maid; she pokes fun at Thales, who is unfit for survival because his view into the distance prevents him from seeing the obvious.[14] Human thought goes far beyond the circumstance that we need to survive. Consequently, our conceptual faculty cannot remotely be reduced to one evolutionarily privileged basic pattern. The fictions do not disappear; they cannot be replaced by a collectively explicit set of rules that is immune to ideological infringements.

Our thought is thus not merely the extension of evolution. Thought is not some evolutionary feeler with which the mysterious urge to live gains an idea of its surroundings. To be sure, one can ascribe an arbitrary adaptive advantage to any behaviour, as illustrated *ad nauseam* by the many nonsensical treatises in the genre of evolutionary psychology.[15] Yet this same arbitrariness shows that evolutionary explanations of the mind 'from bacteria to Bach' are unscientific (or, less polemically coded, trans-empirical). Since one can invent any number of stories that treat a given human (or non-human) behaviour as adaptive, recourse to the metaphors of evolutionary theory explains nothing whatsoever. One can recognize the explanatory lunacy of overstretched, ultimately pseudo-biological models in the fact that they take the mere existence of a behaviour – falling in love, walking upright, scientific theory-building, ludic drive, nutritional preferences, and so forth – as proof that it serves the purpose of survival and is therefore adaptive. However, it does not follow from the fact that a particular behaviour does not kill us that it is adaptive. Otherwise, all behaviour (except suicide) would be adaptive, since it ensures that the organism is doing something (namely performing this behaviour).[16]

The social rests phylogenetically on intransparency because we, as minded *living beings*, must rely on cooperation in our survival form. Because one can never know exactly what everyone else knows, any explicit action coordination depends on the involvement of fictions that allow the participant perspective to be upheld. Society thus does not emerge from a knowledge claim or any other effective claim to shape the community, but already exists if such claims can be made. The zone of intransparency is not clearly delineated; since the participants do not know what everyone else knows, they are equally unaware of what everyone else does not know. The exact level of knowledge remains beyond explicability, a circumstance that Max Weber examined in the context of rationalization. This consists not in the fact that modern societies are more rational than supposedly pre- or non-modern ones, but rather in the circulation of the fiction of an omniscient observer (an expert committee), which relieves individuals of the task of constantly testing the functioning of institutions.[17]

The sociality of *minded* beings consists in raising themselves from the swamp of their survival. Human beings are sublime.[18] Viewed in a different way, we exist in the emphatic sense of existentialism. This means that we are at a distance from the necessary natural conditions for our survival. We are clearly capable of leading our mental lives in light of a self-portrait (a concept of humans).

Different conceptions of humans rule one another out. In practice, what happens is that we form an idea of what constitutes our survival that does not take its natural conditions sufficiently into account. This, in turn, is obvious to the extent that we are far from having complete knowledge of the self-organization of our survival form (the human body). We are and will remain at the mercy of sickness and health and life and death as processes that we cannot completely control. In some sense, life emerges; it is tied to the coordination of subsystems, which is incomprehensible without vertical causation from the whole upon its parts. Beyond this, our very survival is tied to social conditions, meaning that, in addition to the ecological niche of our individual organism, a social environment contributes causally to how exactly we develop, and that we do so at all.

Since we are far from explaining the biological complexity of our environmental adaptation mechanistically with recourse to the isolated causality of individual, even molecular components, we are also at a distance from our own animality in theoretical terms. We depend on a conception of humans in order to be able to thematize our mere survival. These conceptions of humans guide our behaviour: *we act in light of a view of our own animality*.

Anyone who follows a self-model as a more or less altruistic killer ape or some other zoological model, like the common-or-garden naturalists of our time, has a fundamentally different attitude to their survival from someone who believes themselves capable of having an immortal soul. Naturalism and religion are, among other things, two poles of the answer to the question of why we survive. Contrary to what naturalists insist, the question of what life is has not been reductionistically or mechanistically settled. Vitalism is wrongly thought to be clearly out of date; this usually stems from a failure to gain any insight into the discourse in which Driesch and Bergson once intervened, to name only two protagonists.[19] I mention this not to take sides for the (immortal) soul – which vitalists reject, incidentally – but merely to articulate the thought that our minded form of life already comes to light at the level of our own relationship with our animality. Humans are unsettled as beings; we are not at home in our animality in the same way as other animals, whose self-control does not take the detour of self-description. 'Human beings are the reluctant animals.'[20]

There is some conception of humans that captures the essence of our animality, which is interwoven in manifold ways with the causal architecture of the non-human universe (our behaviour takes place in the space of forces and natural laws). We simply do not know which object-level anthropology – that is, which conception of humans – adequately grasps our animality. Humans are still downwardly open in zoological terms, as it were. The response to this problem is the conflict between different conceptions of humans.

In this respect, Yuval Noah Harari hit the mark in *Sapiens: A Brief History of Humankind*.[21] Humans form groups that one can call 'societies' based on stories they tell to domesticate the mystery of their survival. Medicine thus takes on a philosophically neglected centrality in the construction of society, which is no less constitutive for 'modern' societies than for those one may be accustomed to classifying as 'pre-modern'.[22] Medical progress is closely connected to the history of our self-images, since natural science has not yet settled the question of how exactly the still unfathomably complex control circuits in a human organism are connected and how exactly one can classify health as the normal state of coordination between the individually complex systems that converge in an organism.

Human socialization is fundamentally fictional. The connection of human groups we are accustomed to calling 'society' or 'culture' is historically a result of myth-making. Humans cannot be understood without the mythological consciousness of their position in the non-human cosmos.[23] Admittedly, Harari immediately squanders this insight by telling a one-sidedly naturalistic *story* of humankind that repeats all the commonplace teleological patterns, leading from primitive survival to modern European civilization and reaching their culmination – not by chance – in California.[24] Like his true model, Nietzsche, he draws on the inevitable narrativity of our self-being to prepare the *Übermensch*. Harari uses stories to work cunningly and covertly on the self-destruction of humanity; it is very much in keeping with this that he propagates the philosophically nonsensical claim that the new digital surveillance apparatuses are the ultimate disproof of free will, and thus the beginning of the end of *liberal democracy*.[25]

Instead of this arbitrary manoeuvre, which pits an object-level anthropology – that of transhumanism – against others (especially theistic conceptions of humans), the neo-existentialism espoused here recommends the idea of a *higher-order anthropology*. This rests on the anthropological invariant of the indispensability of conceptions of humans, which is the source of universal validities. Wherever we encounter humans, they control their socialization through object-level views of life and death, and so on. Cures and funerals happen everywhere.

This is the origin of localization problems in philosophy: the question of how values, mind, consciousness, life, beauty, numbers, colour impressions, and so forth, fit into the universe raises ontological and epistemological problems of the highest order. For our conception of humans is always a result of the fact that we stand out from the non-human environment, something that has not been changed by modern astrophysics, which has become the paradigm of our 'excentric positionality'.[26] We constantly remove ourselves from every alleged centre into which we have previously imagined ourselves. In so-called modernity, this self-dispute takes on the form of a suspicion of meaninglessness, culminating in the idea that our life cannot have any purpose significantly exceeding survival, since we see nothing in ourselves except stardust, which, from a cosmic perspective – in Schopenhauer's oft-cited words – becomes a 'film of mildew' that 'has generated living beings with cognition'.[27]

For all this, however, Schopenhauer senses that this excentric perspective is assumed by us and thus in turn assumes a function in our self-description that, in spite of itself, is not restricted to being 'the empirical truth, the real, the world'.[28] The description of life from a cosmic perspective only threatens the meaning of life because we ourselves assume that perspective. Thus it turns out to be a contribution to human self-determination. It is by no means 'the empirical truth, the real, the world', but rather an atmospheric impression that results from a particular metaphysics or speaks out as metaphysics.[29]

Such a metaphysical atmosphere in the face of an unsettled conception of humans is, according to the diagnosis proposed here, an expression of social conditions. For society is part of the answer to the question of what or who we want to be. Social systems are controlled from the participant perspective through their members forming an idea of their situation. Social systems are interactive in Ian Hacking's sense: our understanding of what they are and how they work is a substantial factor in determining what they are and how they work.[30]

This phenomenal situation can easily tempt us into social constructivism, since the social is not independent from how actors behave towards it. The social is produced by dissent management, and this production is changeable – that is, contingent. In this minimal sense, one could say that some things (especially the social) are constructed without this meaning that everything is constructed, though the concept of construction would then require further clarification.[31] This clarification will follow here in Part III by replacing 'construction' with its realist counterpart, production.

That social systems are produced and reproduced does not rule out the possibility that all participants may be mistaken about them. For social systems are fabricated not through a conscious or transparent act of construction but always under intransparent conditions that go far beyond what is directly accessible to the founders of a social system.[32] That is why, in complex societies with an incalculable number of subsystems, higher-order social systems are established that set up risk assessments and other evaluative parameters in order to make explicit the basic conditions for given lower-level social systems. This is only partly successful, for there is immediately a potentially vicious regress that is familiar from the founding documents of political and legal philosophy: as soon as a higher-order monitoring system for a given social system (such as a police department responsible for a particular district) is suspected of intervening in the monitored social system in an impermissible (for example discriminatory) fashion, there will be demands to involve a further social system (such as the public prosecutor's office or the interior ministry) that observes the functioning of the higher-order monitoring system on a further level, and so on *ad infinitum*. Under these conditions of labour division, it is fundamentally impossible to create complete transparency, since every system of observation has a 'blind spot', to invoke one of the accurate central insights of systems theory.[33]

This is all public property from the social sciences that should not be neglected in the context of socio-ontological realism. One must not overlook that our socialization does not proceed under optimal, idealized epistemic conditions, and this has feedback effects on philosophy theory-building. For the latter takes place not in a social vacuum but in the medium of printing, the university, public debate, at conferences, in specialist societies, and so forth.

The social conditions for philosophical theory-building concerning the social should not be permanently ignored, since this could lead to a crude confusion between model and reality in the following sense: every specific socio-ontological approach chooses a basic concept on which its theory-building is focused – normativity, recognition, power, sovereignty, communication, systems, and so on. The construction of theories that follows on from this establishes inferential networks that allow us to formulate a model representing the behaviour in theoretical statements. Models are never identical with the things they aim at. With some elements in models, one must ascribe to them a reference to something real without which the model would run dry. Quine famously termed this ascription 'ontological commitment'. The ontological commitments of a model presuppose that there is something real which can be modelled. One cannot say wherein they consist without analysing an already given and established model.

The ontological commitments of a social theory are partially intransparent in the act of their construction; this reflects that there are social conditions for the theoretical construction of the social which the activity of mutual critique among available theories attempts to capture. A social theory that seeks to free itself from critique, and thus from the legitimacy of alternatives, will be doomed by its successful autopoiesis because it makes its fallibility invisible. The epistemic modal category of reality, and hence fallibility, is replaced by the false consciousness of a definitively successful paradigm of social research – something that Lewis Gordon has examined as 'disciplinary decadence'.[34]

Consider the *disciplinary fallacy*. This concludes whether the commitments of a group that is in an exchange about the details of a shared model's properties are ontologically true based on the group's closure.[35] Such a fallacy becomes canonic through the pragmatist theory of truth, which identifies truth with consensus or some other norm of rational acceptability, and thus keeps the concept of reality away from modelling.

Scientific paradigms are conceptually closer to the mythological then one might think. Quine pointed this out with his drastic remark that the ontological commitments of modern physics are not categorially superior to Homer's pantheon, which is by no means a reason to give up the former in favour of the latter.[36] 'To call a posit a posit is not to patronize it.'[37]

The general problem with this model of a model is that it conceptually places the real at an unbridgeable distance.[38] That is why – as in all pragmatist and neo-pragmatist theoretical constructions – truth is replaced by a non-alethic criterion for success, such as the decision to adopt a worldview based on its technological or social effectiveness. This weakness is manifest specifically in the socio-ontological context in the fact that its own positioning cannot be grasped as social, otherwise the supposedly categorial distinction between an observable system of aims and an explanatory model could be bypassed. If model construction is already social, then the property one aims for via a model – in this case sociality – is *ipso facto* already a model property.

This is manifested indirectly in Quine's concession that radical translation begins 'at home' – that is, where the theorist attempts to explain his own vocabulary and assure themselves reflexively of the semantics of their language.[39] He argues that linguistic terms do not refer to things 'just like that', but only in the respect that a model-like context is in place that assigns meanings. Therefore he does not consider meanings non-naturalistic, which makes them ineligible for ontological commitment from a naturalist perspective. This causes the social stabilizer of meaning to disappear from view that I will examine in the following paragraphs based on neo-realist premises, namely the fact that linguistic meaning is only possible in contexts of joint rule-following. To the extent that thought has a social nature, the fact that we are recognizably fallible, every discourse is already the 'discourse of the other'.[40] The character of our fallibility results from natural and social conditions that, *in ipso actu operandi*, are always partially intransparent. No one deludes themselves alone.

This can be illustrated with recourse to the condition of justification for knowledge claims that ignite the dispute over fallibility. If S knows that p, there is some reason why S believes p to be true. This reason, in the successful case of knowledge, is sufficient for that which S believes to be true to be believed true (because it is true). In the successful case of knowledge, the reason for holding-to-be-true coincides with that which is believed to be true, which has led Williamson and other epistemological externalists not to consider the condition of justification genuine and to treat knowledge as an unanalysable mental state *sui generis*.[41] After all, the best reason for a knowledge claim to the effect that I have two hands is some fact – for example, that I have two hands – to which I have an epistemic attitude, especially that of holding-to-be-true. As Plato already saw clearly, the classical definition of knowledge is harmlessly circular: the condition of justification is implicit in the knowledge claim, since, in the case of success, one believes that which is true to be true, and ultimately does so because it is true. In the case of success, truth and holding-to-be-true are bound to each other. Plato's name for this bond is *logos*.[42]

Whether the reason for knowledge is the fact that I have to reason or the fact that I perceive that I have two hands is secondary in this context, since the analysis of knowledge boils down to the circumstance that some fact – something that is true – is the reason for my knowledge, which is why it is possible (but not necessary) to know that one knows that p. Knowledge claims are fundamentally *iterable*, but not *iterative*.

Yet how can one adequately think fallibility under such conditions? If knowledge is our name for the case of success, then it goes without saying that knowledge is not fallible. Since one cannot successfully remove the idea of the case of success from the analysis of our epistemological position, something else must be fallible.

Unfortunately, the bearer of fallibility cannot simply be located in the knowledge *claim*. The problem with this suggestion is that it cannot know any successful knowledge claim, since the successful case of a knowledge claim is knowledge, which is *ex hypothesi* neither fallible nor infallible, but rather a non-coincidentally justified holding-to-be-true.[43] If knowledge claims were constitutively fallible, they could not succeed. Here one cannot retreat to a purportedly 'healthy' fallibilism, for the thesis that all knowledge claims are fallible (because knowledge claims are constitutively fallible) amounts to a denial of knowledge.

One cannot improve this epistemological situation by falling back on a justificatory holism, or some other variety of coherentism, in order to make knowledge claims so complicated as to underpin the impression that they can never unreservedly succeed by drawing on the theory or history of science. It is especially unproductive to plunge into the depths of a genealogy of objectivity or the archaeology of knowledge.[44] The attempt to historicize epistemology at best describes the modification of experimental designs and social mechanisms of recognition, without achieving any conceptual progress beyond the nonsensical claim that we can never really know anything.[45] The historicization of 'knowledge' is at best only deferred scepticism.

If knowledge claims can be successful, then factually made first-order knowledge claims cannot be fallible, only successful or unsuccessful in individual cases. Each respective knowledge claims succeeds or it does not. Thus the knowledge claim does not fluctuate between success and failure; it is we who fluctuate – that is, minded beings whose sequences of states and mental organization lead to the possibility of being mistaken. What are mistaken are not any verbally articulated knowledge claims, but rather the beings that make them.

A given knowledge claim, to the effect that p, is successful; another, to the effect that non-p, fails – a genuine case of *tertium non datur*. Here this is no third or neutral case that oscillates between success and failure and needs to be pinned down through some justificatory manoeuvre.[46] So why is it that we are fallible, if not because we make *knowledge claims*?

The answer is that *we* are fallible, not our factual knowledge claims.[47] If someone makes a knowledge claim, they may fail because, as a minded being, they experience an empirically and fundamentally incalculable complexity and sequence of states; this allows them to favour p over a given selection of alternatives. The favouring of p leads to a holding-to-be-true, which is supported in its specifics by incalculably many states of holding-to-be-true. The reason for the error is not the knowledge claim – that is, in a particular judgement – but in the fact that other factors of judgement cloud the judgement. If it were transparent in the judgement whether it is true or false, there would not be any conflict with other states of the error-prone subject. These states do not only include other judgements, since we as living beings do not only judge but have attitudes of different kinds that influence and enable the formation of our judgements.

Without the sensorium with which I happen to be equipped, I could not put these judgements about my judgements on paper. My sensorium, in a never fully transparent interaction with all other real facts of my judgement formation, generates an area of plausibility (the evidence available to me at a given time) that causes (but does not force) me to make a judgement.[48] This entire process, which is always fundamentally intransparent, is the reason for my fallibility, not my generally communicable knowledge claim.

If we judge that p, and thus make a knowledge claim, this fulfils conditions B_1, B_2, ..., B_n, which ensure that the event of judgement takes place. One judges at a point in time that p, and the judgement takes place in a context. Judgements manifest themselves as objects of examination in fields of sense. Judgements exist. When we do something as minded beings, such as judging, then the natural and social conditions for the knowability of our activity are fulfilled. The knowledge claim made by us is not completely invisible, otherwise its assessment could not be theorized.

Not all conditions of the asserted knowledge claim are completely visible, however, since that would rule us out as its carriers. So there is no objectivity without subjectivity. This does not mean abandoning the idea that knowledge is the successful case of knowledge claims, which thus fall into two categories: successful and failed ones. Classically formulated: judgement splits our epistemic life into two types of cases. To judge is to see oneself on a side to which there is an alternative. Of course, we thus ultimately refer to ourselves as minded beings that make factual knowledge claims. This facticity is too complex to be comprehended fully. Part of our life is always slipping away from us, without a fixed boundary that would allow us to divide our life into what is transparent and what remains opaque. Factually, this boundary shifts according to criteria that are not fixed a priori.

I have referred to this circumstance elsewhere as *Ge-schichtlichkeit*.[49] The overall sufficient conditions for an epistemological event can in part be analytically assessed after the fact and assigned to different fields of sense that can be archaeologically isolated as layers. We are fallible because the interplay of these elements cannot be subject to higher-order inspection. *Any reflexive control of the modules that we employ in order to know something modifies the overall state in which we find ourselves, potentially to the extent that we would always require a further assessment for the same reasons that led us to call for an inspection.*

This creates the danger of a textbook example of vicious infinite regress. An infinite regress is generally the interminable reapplication of a rule whose activation is forced in the framework of a registration process, meaning that there is an algorithm for every infinite regress – for example, that every factual thought must be accompaniable by an 'I think'.[50] In the justificatory context of epistemology – which makes knowledge claims about knowledge (claims) – an infinite regress becomes *vicious* if the entitlement we acquire to represent p in contrast to a recognizable case of non-p (one position in contrast to another) can only be gained if q must be adduced in order to rule out non-p – a procedure that is repeated for q.[51] If I can only judge p if I rule out non-p by judging p, then I cannot say a priori why I can judge q without ruling out non-q, which brings r into play, and so on.

If there are non-a priori and thus empirical regress blockers that serve as a legitimation, however, then we evade this problem. We are therefore justified quasi-a priori – that is, by comparing theories – to presume empirical regress blockers. I say 'quasi-a priori' because the point of introducing facticity into the supposedly pure thought of epistemology is that philosophical knowledge claims are made in factual and thus reality-saturated contexts that cannot rid themselves of the historical finitude that allows us to judge successfully at all. For, without these contexts, *our kind* would not exist, and thus *our* judgements would not be at issue.[52]

In this context, society is one of the partially intransparent conditions of realization for facticity. That facts differ recognizably from holding-to-be-true is not exclusively because there are natural species. Nature – understood as the field of sense of natural species – is not mistaken about itself in our mistaken opinions about it. In humans, nature neither opens its eyes nor deludes itself with false opinions by producing humans and leaving them partly in the dark. For there are not only natural conditions for holding-to-be-true but also social ones. These are partially non-natural in so far as they consist essentially in our living life in light of self-portraits.

We can illustrate that social species can be distinguished from natural ones with recourse to three types of error.[53]

A) *Error about natural species*: If I am mistaken about a natural species, this does not change any of its intrinsic characteristics. This is one reason why it seems useful to ascribe intrinsic characteristics to natural species, because our knowledge or mistaken opinions about them do not automatically lead to a modification of their characteristics. The number of types of elementary particles in a distant region of the universe (where there are no particle accelerators generating new elementary particles through collisions and so forth) is determinate. Let us say that there are exactly six types of quarks there. Perhaps someone heard something about quarks but confused them with bosons, leading them to believe that there are five types of quarks in said region.[54] A person's true or false opinions about quarks and bosons do not change their properties.

B) *Self-delusion*: Someone who is deluded about themselves modifies their status. If I am mistaken about myself – for example, if I think that I have no immortal soul when I actually do; if I think I am adopting an excellent posture while dancing tango, yet others do not even consider my dance steps recognizable tango moves; if I think I know something but am in error; and so on – then I change as a result. This status modification is measured in the category of normality with the measuring units of social classification systems, which enables us to label certain behaviours in given social systems 'normal' – that is, unremarkable – and others as 'abnormal' – that is, an offence; herein lies the origin of normativity.[55]

C) *Naturalization of the social*: A third type of error consists in over-extending the naturalization of the social – that is, drawing the boundary between the natural and the mental in the wrong place, in the main area of the mind. This corresponds to the pathogenic potential of second nature, which invites us to understand our rooting in anonymous nature not only as a causal foundation but also as an occasion for a revision of the order of justification. That habituation and rehearsal of a discursive practice does not presuppose guided, semantically blind repetitions does not mean that intentionality can be adapted to basal, naturalizable forms of representation. Whoever sees no more in social systems than an expression of pre-social, anonymous natural processes hidden by their complexity fails to recognize the structure of institutions, and thus increases the likelihood of a factual reduction of objective mind to the pre-social. Such a factual reduction is manifested in social systems as a dismantling of institutions.

Social species differ based on their constitutive embeddedness in specifically human formats of self-delusion. The humanities and social sciences examine facts, events, texts, art works, and so on, from the perspective of the human capacity for self-determination, which can fail in the form of self-delusion and naturalization of the social. A society is a space for self-making: which forms of self-determination are considered successful, failed or neutral contributes to determining the requirements for a successful life.

Without this dimension, actors cannot experience sanctions for violating norms as punishment. The success of our life is determined, among other things, by the social perception of the background of largely implicitly shared norms, which measure our self-determination by external standards. Whether a dancing style is really accomplished, a behavioural pattern is a form of sexual harassment, a series of mental states is an indication of an adaptive disorder, a style of beard is hip, a socioeconomic transaction is a case of corruption, a loud laugh is exuberant or threatening, and so forth, is not only in the hands of an actor whose actions are assessed. Continuously failing self-determination leads to social sanction extending from mild forms of exclusion to imprisonment or, depending on the legal system, even death.

Natural species contribute to successful and failed self-determination. Social species do not float above other facts at an unreachable distance.

How one dances depends on how far one's own neuronal history, as well as one's general bodily attributes and exercises, enable one to perform sequences of movements; adaptive disorders, which we classify as 'sick' in social and other terms, can be effects of dysfunctional biochemical processes. The life of the mind is subject to natural conditions, though these are fundamentally insufficient to provide self-determination.

The mereology of the mind turns the prevailing order, which is metaphysical and therefore purportedly stable a priori, on its head. The naturalist considers this order either self-evident or an inductive result of the explanatory success of the natural sciences: the mind is not part of nature, but nature is part of the mind.

This ontologically significant transformation is codified in social units of measurement – that is, in explicable norms that act as signposts – to invoke one of Wittgenstein's famous analogies.[56] Norms are originally implicit; they stem from unwritten laws. One can see this in the fact that behaviours are modified through factual correction – even if we only notice them as such through a confrontation with alternatives that we consider exemplary. The implicit is the starting point of every socio-ontological analysis because its concept aligns with the fact of our intransparent entanglements. As Bourdieu aptly remarks: 'It is because we are implicated in the world that there is implicit content in what we think and say about it.'[57]

Here one can introduce the much discussed example of manners, of which one only becomes aware as social norms when one encounters alternatives that one finds difficult to comprehend and for which one desperately seeks some articulation and justification – an experience any traveller can easily have in a very unfamiliar country. Table manners that are widespread in China or Japan differ significantly from those that apply at the Munich Oktoberfest or a Michelin-starred restaurant in Paris. The same applies to greeting rituals, such as the handshake, which was probably introduced by the Quakers as a gesture of universal equality. We take the use of such manners for granted and only notice them *as* norms when we encounter alternatives.

This contrasts with a point made by Christoph Möllers, who concludes from his concept of norms that 'Peaking of implicit norms is thus pointless as norms only arise on the basis of an experience which combines a nega- tive evaluation with a generalization pointing *toward the future*.'[58] Möllers recommends a 'reduced concept of normativity, which consists in just two elements.'[59] 'Norms, so runs the claim, consist of the representation of a *possibility* and a positive evaluation of its realization, one that I will characterize as a *realizing marker*.'[60] The argument advanced here against implicit norms does not convince on the general scale claimed by Möllers, because he mistakenly believes that it remains unclear

what the difference would consist in between the situation being described as one in which a norm referring back to the past situation only arises in the moment of its breach, and a situation in which the event is described without any recourse to a social norm. To speak of an implicit norm then gives the impression that one could speak of a sanction without being able to identify what said sanction is referring to. If I have no means of identifying a norm other than a reaction to it, then I shouldn't classify the event as a 'reaction.'[61]

The last sentence is not formulated very well, since a reaction to a norm obviously points to its existence. In any case: why should one not 'classify the event as a "reaction"'? The argument that this wording is intended as a justification leads nowhere, but rather, *pace* Möllers, takes us into the depths of the Kripkenstein[62] rule problem, which will be examined in the following section.[63] The idea of an implicit norm states that a situation can be normatively charged even if the norm is communally constitutive and has thus gone unnoticed by those who belong to a community. If, for example, a particular group has eaten with chopsticks since time immemorial and one day encounters a group that requests a knife and fork, the use of chopsticks becomes visible as a norm because others deviate from it. The norm was implicit and now becomes explicit for those involved. Before that, their bond was either invisible to them or was perhaps treated in a mythological way, for example, through circulation as destiny, nature or a divine command.

If something social is considered something natural, its normativity is concealed. In my classification, mythology and ideology (see below, §15) latch onto cases of implicit norms because the registration of norms proceeds in such a way that their normativity is overlooked. Any normatively describable event can also be described without norms. The question is: who is right? Whether a social theorist characterizes a situation as normative or non-normative is not usually decisive for the question of what type of situation it actually is. Social theory does not produce all of its objects, only those that come about because the social theorist intervenes in social systems without which their foray into matters of scientific claims could not be effective.

Möllers infers the ontology of factually existing norms from their conditions of social-scientific knowability.[64] Taking a formulation by Blumenberg, he imputes a 'consciousness of possibility' to normatively bound actors.[65] Perhaps such a thing exists, but this does not mean that implicit norms collide with the general consciousness of possibility which distinguishes us as actors from the *differentia specifica* of other life forms or that we cultivate social attitudes to *possibilia*.

Our consciousness of freedom is a prerequisite for normativity. Because others are in a state of dissent with us, we have the concept of the epistemic possibility of being wrong. Where there is no dissent, no society comes about, and a society developed in a completely consensual way would collapse. If we always agreed on everything – if there were universal agreement in all cases – there would be no society.

But this does not happen, if only because the participants of social practices (as subjects) are defined via an egocentric index that always causes them to perceive a thing differently from others. Our mere perceptual judgements already set up relationships of dissent, because we imagine the same real constitutively differently.[66] The continued existence of factual dissent is guaranteed as long as humans judge, which reproduces complexity that already exists on a registration level that is pre-social in terms of its substance and object.[67]

This socio-ontologically fundamental finding does not conflict with the existence of implicit norms. Although they only become conspicuous through dissent, this dissent can come to light in the interaction of the social scientist (or any outside observer who finds themselves in a social system that is partially transparent to them) with the observed system. It is part of the objectivity of the social sciences that implicit norms contribute to the constitution of a society – that is, norms that can emerge for the first time through social-scientific observation.[68]

This is exactly what applies to grammatical norms, for example, which one can attempt to capture through a scientific grammar. Language is very much normative (*pace* Möllers), because linguistic behaviour is subject to mutual correction procedures, whose unit of measurement is explicated by a scientific grammar with its own specially developed vocabulary.[69] Möllers, on the other hand, does not regard linguistic rules as norms. To show this, he advances the unconvincing argument that Brandom's variant of a normativity of the linguistic leads to a problematic 'pan-normativism'. Even if this were true, this would obviously not prove that linguistic rules are not norms, only that Brandom's theory of this normativity is overgeneralized. On the other hand, he formulates an independent argument that is presented expressly as a reason for rejecting the idea of implicit norms. He encapsulates it as follows: 'It is impossible for us to have assented to the conventions that shape our language beforehand. We assent in the execution of language, not in advance.'[70] This argument, of course, presupposes what is meant to be proved, namely that language cannot be normative since all norms are explicit. We do not have to agree to norms beforehand – in fact, we do not have to agree to them at all for them to apply and take effect. No one agreed to the norm of truth before working closely with facts at the level of perception, which is already a form of normativity.

Möllers underestimates rule scepticism and becomes entangled in it when he invokes Quine to prove that there are no linguistic norms prescribing behaviour, such that linguistics or philologically schooled scientific grammar 'quickly turns into the construction of ad hoc conventions that need to adapt to every practice; that is, they don't prescribe anything in the end but only reconstruct something.'[71] This overlooks that scientific grammar leads to spelling reforms and dictionaries, among other things, and is used to teach and learn grammatically well-researched languages. Precisely because there are manifold irregularities resulting from the diachronic and synchronic social differentiation of language use (such as irregular verbs in inflected languages), there are sanctions in language acquisition without which no *infans* will become a linguistically mature minded being.[72]

Unlike Möllers, Searle and others, I consider the implicit and intransparent the socio-ontologically decisive factor – that is, a relevant and necessary condition for the existence of normativity. The 'uncertainty' that Möllers ascribes to the concept of norms is not only *epistemic* but also *social*. Norms react to uncertainty because our survival form is social and none of us have a full view of how our survival succeeds.

The scale of labour division is already complex in small groups, which stems from the fact that, because of their respective egocentric indices, the individuals involved have had different experiences that communicatively collide. Our reciprocal observation should be understood not on the model of social-scientific theoretical construction, but rather as a largely unconscious process whereby norms circulate in the mode of rituals.

Belonging to a group, a society, does not primarily require that one knows or claims to know which norms constitute this group and distinguish it from other 'norm circles'.[73] Following a rule, after all, is not as such an interpretation of the rule. The inevitable blindness of rule-following is the signature of the social at the fundamental level of socialization. Normativity is not generally a result of some explication process, but rather begins where the cohesion of a group is required.

In this context, I understand Wittgenstein's famous recourse to 'agreement in judgements' in §242 of *Philosophical Investigations* as an argument against the prerequisite for knowability adduced by Möllers.

> It is not only agreement in definitions, but also (odd as it may sound) agreement in judgements that is required for communication by means of language. This seems to abolish logic, but does not do so. – It is one thing to describe methods of measurement, and another to obtain and state results of measurement. But what we call 'measuring' is in part determined by a certain constancy in results of measurement.[74]

A norm does not have to be noticed by a social scientist in order to be effective. Part of the description of the measuring method is that a norm must be noticed as such before one can devote a study to it. It is correct that one cannot ascertain norms simply by describing the regularities in the behaviour of a group; that someone does something regularly does not mean that this behaviour is normative. Not every action is guided by a definition of goals, otherwise it would be difficult to subsume the action of walking cheerily through a park or looking calmly out of the window under the thus overextended concept of an intentional action.[75]

Measurement itself is subject to three rules – a measuring method – that cannot be measured on the same theoretical level. Social scientists must first of all agree in the judgements whereby they examine the normativity of an unfamiliar rule-following. No matter how one looks at it, it leads nowhere to think that one can fully explicate the rule apparatus of such a measuring method. Nonetheless, it claims normative force for itself, which becomes apparent when someone bizarrely – for example in the mode of a conspiracy theory, or in the less empirically vulnerable form of sceptical hypotheses – disables the apparatus of assumptions without which a given measuring method cannot produce any identifiable results.[76] Hence Wittgenstein's constant recourse to ethnological speculations, whose aim is to defamiliarize our own judgements and show us that there could always be some normatively charged level that we have hitherto overlooked.

The social sciences can examine themselves, and will then, like any recursive examination, encounter at some point the finitude of possible surveys of the state of information. Sceptical hypotheses, confrontation with far-reaching cultural difference, conspiracy theories and extreme political conflicts are stumbling-blocks for theory-building which show us that we share with some people (as opposed to others) a set of normatively charged background convictions that enable an ostensible negotiation of norms. An explicit legal system that pushes for the explication and publication of its own norms in the mode of democratic constitutional states should not make us forget that this system, for its part, rests on an agreement in judgements that it cannot make fully public. Ultimately, the framework of validity in which we move like a fish in water more or less functions only as long as there are implicit norms that affect our actions.

Viewed in this light, Möllers's vacillation between affirmation and negation is understandable. 'We take norms to be the affirmation of the realization of a possibility.'[77] What he means is that this affirmation must be explicit, since, as we have seen, he disputes the possibility of implicit norms (through the introduction of a revisionary or, as he concedes, 'reduced' concept of norms). A norm evaluates a possibility as something that is meant to be realized and thus indeed makes room for deviation.

Norms that cannot be breached are not norms; so far, so good. But this does not show that norms presuppose a factual breach, that areas of action are hence only normed if an explicit breach is noticed or previously non-normed actions are re-evaluated in light of a publicly accessible norm. In this context, Möllers identifies negation and negatability, as shown in the following passage, in which he makes affirmation switch to negation.

> The possibility of denying reality thus marks the departing point of every normative practice. Affirmation as a normative form always builds on negation. The recognition that something has been realized is only conceivable under the condition of its possible negation. Affirmation is reflection upon a negation having been omitted, not vice versa. The base operation of the normative is negative. It rejects the world in its current state. Without this operation, norms are inconceivable.[78]

It is true that norms as such are only conceivable because of a deviation that is registered as such. An omitted negation is possible *ex hypothesi*, however, and factually always real, since there is some norm that is used by the norm theorist to support their statements about normativity. One cannot successfully reject 'the world in its current state', however, as this would at best produce a different state of the world – that of rejecting a particular fact – that could then be examined through social science, for example. Because there is social-scientific knowledge, norms must *nolens volens* belong to the real. Möllers concedes this too, albeit again in the form of a vacillation that leads to a paradoxical formulation: 'Beyond the question of how the two relate to each other, and whether inferences from "is" statements are permissible for "ought" statements, normativity is still part of the entirety of facts. It is a counter-world that is part of the world.'[79] This is where ontological reflection throws a spanner in the works; Möller certainly discusses it but does not attempt to pin it down despite offering a theoretically rich modal package to bring the possibility of norms within reach. But how can a counter-world be part of the world if this latter, as Möllers assumes, is the totality of facts? A subset of facts cannot be a counter-world. Möllers's recourse to the theological language game – in our case the metaphor of the kingdom of God, which is not of this world – does not significantly increase the coherence of the idea of 'a counter-world that is part of the world'.[80]

On closer inspection, the theoretical position taken by Möllers soon proves to be normative itself. His theory of normativity is, like many other current suggestions, indebted to the model of reflexive autonomy to which I refer, using a Kantian neologism (*mutatis mutandis*!), as *heautonomy*.[81] Here I am thinking of Pippin's and Brandom's contributions to the theory of modernity, which follow on from Hegel's diagnosis that orientation towards norms in modernity itself becomes a norm by which we can orient ourselves.[82] But not all norms exhibit the logical form of right (understood as an explicable regulation of conflicts of interest). And even right, from a strict Hegelian perspective, rests on morality, which cannot exist without implicit forms of socialization.

Society is therefore fundamentally intransparent; this imposes limits on the public sphere, which it keeps forcing to recalibrate its apparatuses of observation, and these comprise not only the familiar media of modernity – including the publication conditions in the academic world, which are modified by the press – but more recently also the aptly named *social media* (see below, §16). The observation industry, taken to its social-scientific extreme by systems theory, is fundamentally endless, since there is always an as yet unexplicated but normative remainder on which the game of giving and demanding reasons feeds, as do normative practices that rely on exerting power through the symbolic designation of norms. The social dynamics of transparency and intransparency cannot reach a final resolution, because it is in the nature of the normative – the nature of the social – that the negotiation of dissent presupposes the involvement of norms not explicitly envisaged by the discourse's participants.

Our survival form as such is intransparent. We explicate it in the framework of human-biological self-examinations whereby we simultaneously insert ourselves into a conception of nature. Our natural-scientific knowledge is not complete – and cannot be completed, strictly speaking – which means that we cannot transcend the intransparency of our survival form in a productive act of transparency in favour of a transparent form of life in the space of reasons. However much the mind comes to itself in the form of its self-consciousness, it does not come to terms with its normativity in this way, since there is always some norm that is effective on an implicit level and demands behavioural adjustments that had hitherto gone unnoticed.

§14

Rule-Following, Realistically Conceived

Since Kripke's influential reading of Wittgenstein, the problem area of rule-following has been a staple among the tasks of social philosophy.[1] For Kripke thinks that Wittgenstein's *Philosophical Investigations* can be taken as the basis for developing a new, sharpened sceptical paradox whose conclusion is that no one has ever truly followed a rule.[2] This conclusion follows – as is usually the case with paradoxes – from individually questionable points whose semblance of plausibility requires an explanation.

What is special about the paradox of rule-following is that both its motivation and its conclusion can be understood as expressions of social alienation. For the paradox corresponds to the impression that we often think we cannot recognize the norms constituting a group or specific social situation because there are none. Consider the supposition that (social) identity, which is discussed so widely and articulates itself in stereotypical explanations of actions, is an illusion because social identities do not (really) exist.[3] *If there are no social facts determining what someone should do in a given situation, then what we do cannot meaningfully be reconstructed as an application of rules that subsist independently of a completely unfounded behaviour.*

In the following, I would like to argue with reference to the problem area of rule-following that there are irreducibly social facts which act as norms for action. The conclusion of the 'Kripkenstein' paradox is thus false. The *proton pseudos* of the defining premises is the assumption that the mental apprehension of a universal rule by actors who are evaluating one another's social performance is a necessary precondition for a given behaviour being classified as correct or incorrect. Since the socio-ontologically fundamental case of rule-following is constitutively implicit and epistemically opaque, the specification of a norm cannot be based on someone choosing from a collection of possible rules the one by which they can subsequently be judged.

Normative, social facts are irreducibly effective. The circumstance that actors assess each other's performance, leading to a system of sanctions that eventually become explicable and thus (symbolically, linguistically, textually and institutionally) encodable, is grounded in non-conscious social facts of action coordination. We therefore never fully know what rules some group is following, which is why those involved can always ask for further explications of their implicitly shared belonging. However, the circumstance that we cannot fully recognize the respective rules bestowing validity clearly does not mean that there are no social facts determining which rule someone is meant to follow.[4]

A rule divides given behaviour into correct (rule-compliant) and incorrect (deviant) actions. Given behaviour appears against its background as application. Not every application is reconcilable with the rule itself; a rule that is fulfilled by all behaviour does not regulate anything.

From a perspective of empirical observation, any given behaviour conforms to a potentially infinite number of rules. That is why one needs some explanation for why a given behaviour B should be judged by the rule R_1, not by the rule R_2, R_3, . . . or R_n. A successful explanation refers to a social fact, in so far as rules can only exist because the egocentric indices of a majority of actors are entangled in dissent. Rules are as fundamental as the sociality of our minded form of life. Mind emerges not from pre-social mental states but through the social reproduction of our survival form. Which rule someone should follow can therefore be determined with reference to numerous factors.

But what about the seemingly harder question of which rule someone is following in a given situation? Here, too, the idea that someone holds an opinion and accordingly chooses *in foro interno* which rule to follow, and thus to be measured against it, is far-fetched from the start. Which rule someone follows is not based on their anticipating an indefinitely large number of application cases by deciding to follow R_1 rather than R_2. Our inner mental life is already socialized by the time we develop the faculty of explicit self-regulation.

One could certainly say, then, that there are facts of opinion-holding and perhaps also phenomenological experiences of meaning, but these are effective qua social products – not because of a commitment to R_1 as opposed to R_2 and so forth, based only on the controlling power of the subject. Which rule someone decides to follow is explicable through the same methods from the humanities, the social and natural sciences as well as the historically enriched everyday knowledge of actors that one uses to establish what rule applies to them.

The socio-ontological motif of social and constitutively implicit normativity becomes visible at the hinges that connect Wittgenstein's *Philosophical Investigations* with *On Certainty*.[5] According to my suggested interpretation, Wittgenstein infers from the ineluctable imprecision of all meaningful use of rules (demonstrated paradigmatically with reference to language) that our multiple group affiliations are constitutively intransparent. For epistemologically justified reasons, the subject of 'constitutive rules' thus turns out to be a key to the understanding of the social.

In order to make this transition fruitful for a neo-realist social ontology, I will show that a treatment of the problem of rule-following, including its social dissolution, need not drift into anti-realist territory. To be sure, anti-realist or neo-pragmatist models for resolution suggest themselves because of Kripke's influential experimental design, which draws on the intuition that there is a conceptual tension between norms and facts that can be used to make normativity comprehensible.[6] It is no coincidence that Kripke follows on explicitly from Hume in his reading of Wittgenstein, imputing to Wittgenstein a sceptical paradox along with a sceptical solution analogous to Hume's anti-realism with reference to causal relationships.[7]

This section will undertake a realist solution of the (alleged) problem of rule-following. This solution provides a contribution to neo-realist social ontology that no longer obstructs the sceptical ghost of rule-following, because the variant of a norm-nature or norm-fact distinction that encourages it has been overcome.

To define this option more precisely in conceptual terms, it is indispensable to call to mind the opening moves of Kripke's problem set-up. To reconstruct it, let us begin with an especially striking interim result. According to Kripke, this interim result consists in a sceptical paradox whose conclusion is that 'no fact about me constitutes my meaning plus.'[8]

> This, then, is the sceptical paradox. When I respond in one way rather than another to such a problem as '68+57', I can have no justification for one response rather than another. Since the sceptic who supposes that I meant quus cannot be answered, there is no fact about me that distinguishes between my meaning plus and my meaning quus. Indeed, there is no fact about me that distinguishes between my meaning a definite function by 'plus' (which determines my responses in new cases) and my meaning nothing at all.[9]

In my view, the crucial point in the construction of the paradox is the assumption that the result of a calculation that I must carry out in order to obtain a result definable as such fundamentally cannot be determined by a mental state. For the meaning of a term that is used to commit to *one* of an essentially infinite number of rules followed by a given behaviour from an observer's perspective does not consist in a reality of infinitely many applications. To understand the meaning of the expression of a rule, one does not need to have run through all its applications, which is impossible in many cases.

This line of thought underlies Kant's thesis that mathematical judgements are synthetic: however long one looks at '68', '+' and '57', the conclusion that follows from the assignment to add 68 to 57 cannot productively be reached by already having 125 in mind. There must be a point at which it is open what result one will reach if the function termed '+' is subject to corrigible conditions of application. No one can factually apply such a rule and simultaneously have an overview of all its possible applications.

This makes room for a 'sceptical hypothesis about a change in my usage'.[10] One fundamentally cannot apply the plus rule in such a way that one rules out all possible alternative rules that come into force as soon as when a certain threshold of use cases is passed. If someone does not follow one or more rules (or even an infinite number of them) that classify a given behaviour as correct, they are clearly not following any rule. Anyone who follows a rule is following a (more or less) determinate rule. This already shows that no theoretical construction, and hence no framework of premises, is stable if it violates this simple principle. Some rule has to be followed.

One cannot explicitly dictate to oneself to follow the plus rule in contrast to all other possible rules, since one cannot gain the necessary overview. Out of the infinite number of rules one could follow, one only sees a vanishingly small subset. My mental history, then, does not contain any overview of my future applicatory behaviour that could act as a pre-scription ensuring that my current behaviour still follows this direction.

The misleading impression of an imminent paradox depends (here and elsewhere) on the involvement of advance assumptions that generate the incoherence-infected framework of premises. These assumptions always seem natural (though they are not), because otherwise there could not be any paradox.

In Kripke's set-up, the gateway to the paradoxical is the mentalist vocabulary used from the start, which especially includes the reference of the possessive pronoun 'my' in 'my mental state'. In what sense is it not a fact about *me* that I was expected to add at an early age when instructed to calculate 1+2 by counting on my fingers? When I was expected to carry out addition, it was possible to correct me because there was always a fact determining which rule I followed. If someone does not follow any rule, they cannot be corrected. Therefore, assuming I can ever be corrected, there must be a fact relating to me that determines which rule I follow, though it is not clear here what kind of fact it is.

When rehearsing the practice of addition, of course, it was almost impossible to learn the rule and simultaneously gain an insight into this learning behaviour. Moreover, it would be fundamentally impossible to learn the rule of addition based on an insight into learning behaviour if it were another requirement to learn the rules for insight into learning behaviour.

Since Plato's theory of knowledge acquisition, there have been many arguments supporting the view that gaining an understanding of rules need not (and cannot universally) depend on the universality of a rule.[11] One should note the conclusion that *the exercise of a faculty – which includes learning the rules of addition – cannot ground in rehearsing every faculty with recourse to the exercise of a further faculty*. Someone who learns something does not first have to be informed about the rules of learning and teaching.

One does not start by learning with recourse to explicit systems of self-regulation; self-regulation develops out of prior regulation by others.

Faculties can be intertwined; the complexity of cooperating epistemic faculties increases in the course of a human life through differentiated knowledge acquisition (education).[12] Yet this does not manoeuvre anyone into the fatal situation imagined by Kripke. For the facts about me that have allowed me to perform addition (as opposed to quaddition) obviously do not consist in my being subject to a rule regress against which I cannot mentally – logically privately – equip myself. Otherwise, no one would do sums, and this is not really what Kripke wants to assume at the beginning of the argument, since, in the construction of his sceptical paradox, he employs facts of addition for which one cannot identify any mental evidence in the past; this leads to self-undermining, sceptical conclusions.[13]

It is no coincidence that it is not easy to shake the holding-to-be-true of young children by adducing sceptical hypotheses, since their convictions are naturally primarily object-based and they cannot be ruffled by a higher-order distrust of their conceptual abilities. Young children are not born sceptics; rather, they rehearse rule-following by operating in a context that determines which rules they follow. When children quadd rather than add, one corrects them. Their deviant behaviour may be more or less well concealed by skilled or coincidental adaptation, but this does not mean that it does not exist. That is to say, normative facts of rule-following are constitutively social because there can be dissent in the form of observable deviation that leads to someone being corrected for following a different rule from the one that is appropriate to the given context. There are no further facts (such as mental or biological ones) behind these normative social facts that form the *ontological* or even *metaphysical* basis for social facts. Social facts are *sui generis* and are made scientifically identifiable using methods developed especially for this purpose.

Kripke does not dispute that '+' means that there is hence some rule of meaning for '+'. His problem is equally explicitly *not* epistemological; his concern is not 'that we cannot know whether a rule was followed'.[14]

Admittedly, he presents this as the conclusion from the sceptical paradox that there is no fact above me which distinguishes between my opinion that I have followed '+1!', say, rather than '#1!'. Therefore the trigger for his paradox must be located elsewhere, neither in an independent suspicion towards the existence of rules of meaning nor in epistemological reflections that are directly susceptible to scepticism.

However, closer inspection does not reveal what exactly Kripke's problem is; its formulation is nebulous. To motivate a problem or paradox, one can at best adduce his suggestion that past applications of the plus rule do not offer any instructions for answering the question 'What is x in 68+57 = x?' with '125'.[15] Instead of 'instructions', Kripke speaks of 'justification'. According to him, no past application of the rule of addition justifies a present continuation of the rule used back then. However, this is precisely not the case: because I once learned addition, I would be making a mistake today if I gave any other answer than '4' to the question of which whole natural number is the only possible value of x in '2 + 2 = x', and this would apply *mutatis mutandis* to any other number. This obviously does not mean that I need an overview of *all* applications of some past, present or future expression of such-and-such a rule in order to apply it. The facts on whose account I have followed a rule of addition in the past, something that is still binding in the present, are social and hence cannot be found 'in my mental history', assuming one takes this to be a private interior completely isolated from social facts. Yet this private interior does not exist, so there is likewise nothing resembling 'my mental history' in the sense claimed by Kripke. The 'argument' collapses because it draws on an absurd metaphysics of intentionality from which it actually follows that, if we had a private 'mental history', no one would ever follow any rules. But the idea of such a mental history cannot be meaningfully explained; it is an incoherent fiction, because it represents our factual inner life in distorted fashion – in short, a self-delusion.

At best, Kripke reminds us of the banal fact that normativity cannot mean having an a priori overview of all cases of a completely clear norm, such as summative addition of the rules of a deterministic game (in which there is a deterministic algorithm for the ideal course of a game, as in 'Connect Four'). That is why finite thinkers can be expected to commit calculation errors when confronted with rules that conflict with different expectations or mental operations (short-term memory span, attention disorder, and so forth). Wherever *we* can calculate, we can *miscalculate*.

That we can miscalculate means that we are subject to norms which we have not set in such a way as to be entitled to ad hoc modifications. The final balance of our rule applications is therefore documented by recording systems that allow us to transport a past rule expression successfully into the present. This does not mean that we either rely or have relied on explicitly calling to mind, in a single given code (for example, in the form of psychic states), the rules we intend to follow. Which rule one follows and which rule one should follow because of social circumstances cannot be reduced to someone's explicit attitude to the rules; this does not, of course, rule out occasional explicit attitudes that allow us to adduce a rule expression to justify our own actions.

Now, one may wish to counter that we must always subject the past rule expression, along with its institutional commentary – as in the case of the law and its practice of commentaries or the effective history of a canonic literary text – to a present *interpretation*, meaning that no recourse to the past alone justifies a present continuation of the practice. Yet this overlooks the fact that the hermeneutical situation of the law or the interpretation of canonic texts differs fundamentally from the continuation of a deterministic rule that can be captured in the form of an algorithm. Even a pocket calculator cannot take into account all cases of the rule of addition if we use it to collect several large numbers, thanks to addition, to form a single whole number, and yet it is not fallible and has no mental history that might cast sceptical doubts. Anyone who wanted to add in the past can be reminded of this by a calculator if, in the present, they answer not '125' but '5' when posed the task of 'Find the natural number that is the only permissible value for "x" in "68 + 57 = x"!'; for the calculator answers the question '68 + 57 = ?' in the desired sense with the correct sum, 125.

The application of a rule in a given case is not always a form of interpretation, since some rules are deterministic. Those rule systems that cannot exist without interpretation (such as art works) are constitutively open, meaning that there are possible interpretations whose possibility could not be contained in the past.

It is not difficult to name independent criteria for normativity that are not merely aggregates of mental states among actors. Following on from Elder-Vass, I will term these criteria 'norm circles'.[16] Here a norm circle cannot be understood merely as a set or formal mereological sum of otherwise logically private subjects; many intentionally equipped brains do not produce normativity. This is where Searle is wrong: like other social ontologists, he ultimately considers mental states insurmountable, and therefore cannot see that collective intentionality is not the logical form of a heap of individuals flocking together.[17]

Normativity emerges in the context of human action coordination through the fact that we use, in the mode of tradition, a rule set in the past to normalize our mental life. Therefore my mental life never has the form surmised by Kripke, where I imagine a rule *in foro interno*, as it were, without ever having an overview of all its applications in advance, since I am finite. Rather, our mind easily makes contact with the infinite, since we have established this connection in finite steps via the necessary procedures for rehearsing and passing it on.[18]

It is important to note that we create the connection to the infinite in finite steps, yet do not create the infinite. Thus the polarization of moves in the philosophy of arithmetic is mistaken, as it marks an extreme, robust realism and an extreme anti-realism as its limiting points. The fact that there may (depending on the chosen formal system) be an infinite number of permissible values for x in '68 + 57 = x' which are compatible with the rule of addition, or that a rule of addition defines a successor for every natural number, such that the series of natural numbers instantiates the concept of enumerable infinity, does not mean that finite beings are prevented from understanding this. Mathematical objects cannot mostly lie beyond our cognitive reach because of the infinity (or infinities) observable in them, as an extreme, robust realism would assume. This realism, however, is merely the other side of an equally extreme anti-realism that regards arithmetic as no more than a description of a human proof practice.

Yet, in contrast to Kripkenstein, none other than Plato and – closer to our time – Wittgenstein point out that our normative situation should not be understood as a hopeless shot in the dark. Following the rule blindly does not mean that we are shackled to our finitude, as Kripke suggests.[19] Against this background, let us turn to the game-changing §§217–19 in *Philosophical Investigations*, which can be read in light of New Realism. Here is the relevant passage from §217:

> 'How am I able to follow a rule?' – If this is not a question about causes, then it is about the justification for my acting in *this* way in complying with the rule.
>
> Once I have exhausted the justifications, I have reached bedrock, and my spade is turned. Then I am inclined to say: 'This is simply what I do.'[20]

When someone follows a rule, they do not do so in every conceivable way. One follows a rule in some way that is compatible with the rule. More specifically, one does something that exhibits a regularity that can be measured against a standard. One goes for a walk, cooks, thinks, checks the heartbeat of a newborn, calls a taxi, adds up, and so forth. To carry out any of these actions, one must follow various rules; this allows us to evaluate the success of the action. One can trip when going for a walk, one can descend into dangerous rumination when reflecting, one can miscalculate during addition, and so on. There are different ways to go for a walk, check the heartbeat of a newborn, add up (in one's head, with a calculator, on paper), and so forth. From the outset, the issue Wittgenstein has in mind here is not some variant of a Cartesian or Kantian question as to how rule-following or acting are possible at all. The sum of 'methods' in *Philosophical Investigations* develops from Wittgenstein's attempt to characterize our situation with realistic sense. The idea that we need to find a justification for the fact that we can add up *at all* or follow any rule *at all* is based on a manoeuvre that problematizes an obviously well-functioning practice in such an impermissible way that one must pose the diagnostic question of what conceptual tentacles have entangled the theorist.

In this light, Wittgenstein is justified, in the middle of *Philosophical Investigations* (where we have long been operating with the sections that are central to our subject matter), in identifying a solution process grounded in the reality of our actions. The reality of our actions, the fact that we do such-and-such, is the 'hard rock' we encounter when we probe the concept of action. We can then consider an action a legitimate example of how we follow a rule: *thus*. The fact that someone is adding up, for example (in one's head, with a calculator, on paper), is the best conceivable example of how one follows a rule. Since one can not only add up in one's head but also on paper or using a calculator (for purposes of everyday sum calculation), the question is which facts in my mental history can be adduced to justify following the rule of addition, since there may be different facts supporting the statement that one is adding up. A general answer explaining how one can follow a rule at all is fundamentally not to be expected, which is a point of the regress arguments familiar since Plato's discussion of the situation, on which Wittgenstein sometimes relies.[21]

What is true is that we could not follow any rule if the justification for continuing to follow a particular rule we had followed in the past could only be that we had recited all rules to ourselves in the past. It is equally true that a past experience of meaning alone cannot be a justification for continuing to follow the rule I wanted to follow at that time. Wittgenstein undermines these notions in §218: 'Whence the idea that the beginning of a series is a visible section of rails invisibly laid to infinity? Well, we might imagine rails instead of a rule. And infinitely long rails correspond to the unlimited application of a rule.'[22] We should note that Wittgenstein is not disputing that there are rails laid to infinity but pointing out that there are rules whose area of application is unlimited, which does not refer only to mathematical cases. Going for a walk is not restricted to a particular length; one can walk for as long as one wants and is able to walk. The application of the rule is open, which does not mean that the rule itself is indeterminate in the sense that one cannot follow it sufficiently clearly. One can go for a walk, clearly. How the rule is factually applied is not determined by the rule. That is why we can break it by treating something as a case of application that is not.

The following §219, admittedly, seems to be grist for Kripkenstein's mill:

> 'All the steps are really already taken' means: I no longer have any choice. The rule, once stamped with a particular meaning, traces the lines along which it is to be followed through the whole of space. – But if something of this sort really were the case, how would it help me?
>
> No; my description made sense only if it was to be understood symbolically. – I should say: *This is how it strikes me.*
>
> When I follow the rule, I do not choose.
>
> I follow the rule *blindly*.[23]

Following a rule in a particular way – that is, following a particular rule – does not consist in choosing between different rules in every case of application. This is precisely the false assumption that entangles the theorist in a vicious regress, since the choice to follow one rule and not another in turn either follows a rule or is completely arbitrary. The arbitrary choice sometimes to follow one rule and sometimes another can *trivialiter* not form the basis for following a particular rule. If one follows a rule – that is, if one repeatedly applies it – then one is not *ipso facto* following the differently constituted higher-order rule that one should follow *this* rule. Rule-following is not interpreting (which does not rule out the possibility of interpreting practices or sets of rules).[24]

Whoever knowingly follows the rule of addition is not knowingly following the rule of following the rule of addition rather than the rule of quaddition. Since there are an unlimited number of alternatives when one performs a particular action, there is always something that sufficiently resembles what one is doing that one can more or less easily get off course when confronted with an alternative. This is especially striking in the case of social norms such as fashion or table manners on travels. But going for walks and adding up also belong to this in a certain sense, because they likewise involve patterns of action that can be carried out in different ways.

Yet all this, as Kripke himself admits, does not mean that no one ever does anything determinate, only that what we do cannot be limited to the way we as individuals imagine it. Feeling fashionably dressed is not the same as being fashionably dressed; having the impression of acting appropriately at the table is not the same as acting appropriately; and so on.

A norm circle determines in extremely detailed fashion which action types are counted as this or that. How one follows a rule is not determined by individuals, who are only the individuals who can inspect their mental states because these states have long belonged to norm circles. Calling up one's mental history in order not to find any traces of rules that justify current behaviour is itself a rule one must be trained to follow – for example, by enacting Kripke's 'elementary exposition' of the (alleged) problem of rule-following. The community does not simply present itself as a stabilizing result of a critical meditation on rules; rather, it already structures the elements that motivate the 'paradox'. That is why the recourse to the community is not an element of a sceptical solution, but rather a reference to the relevant architecture of facts that allows us as minded beings to follow certain rules.

This does not mean that we have somehow successfully avoided the infinite, however. Here one must take care not to fall prey to what might be termed *sociologism*.[25] Sociologism states that we can only explain actions with reference to structural conditions, which deviate from the reasons given by an individual actor when asked what they are doing. A single action is presented as an example of a structure whose existence can be historically researched and sociologically explained. It corresponds conceptually to a number of conclusions that some people feel compelled to draw if they take Kripke's problem and its sceptical solution for an adequate description of rule-following. What is impossible for the individual in Kripke's model is, according to sociologism, achieved by the community (a social system, communication, classes, mutual recognition, or whatever other socio-theoretical features one ascribes to this). As soon as one steps onto the slippery slope of Kripke's 'paradox', it is too late for any social rescue attempt. If an individual cannot follow a rule indefinitely often, then it makes no difference if others ascribe this impossible faculty to them from the outside. The fictive community of the so-called community view is an impermissible multiplication of semblance; one might even call it a *context of delusion*.

There are facts of different kinds that determine which rule a person follows. These facts include other norms – that is, patterns that divide actions into those that correspond to them, and are therefore allowed or recommended, and those that go against them, which are therefore at best tolerated and at worst punished. The normalization of actions is already a social practice; it results from our assessment of our own actions by forming an idea of how others perceive, think, and so on. Sociality as management of dissent is explicated in normative codices without automatically being correctly grasped in its socio-ontological nature. The visible existence of institutions, and hence social facts, does not guarantee that one will grasp this circumstance in a socio-ontologically appropriate way. Even if we successfully explicate norms, we can still be in error about the foundations of human sociality, which are always effective in the background during explicit rule-following in the sense that the explicit characterization of a rule as a norm can deviate from the norm that is factually followed. Rule-following and the description thereof are not the same, although the description of rule-following naturally follows rules of its own.

A basis of fundamental dissent results in the crystallization of norms that lead to the creation of norm circles. Once these exist, it is essentially possible to formulate explicitly what unites them and give a norm an articulated symbolic form. The social sciences provide the theoretical vocabulary corresponding to the differentiation of norm circles in institutions, organizations, states, milieus, and so forth; their vocabulary is synchronically and diachronically variable, since norm circles emerge and expire without there being any a priori canon that delineates the human radius of action as such. Which form of action humans carry out, which norm circle they form, and which practices of sanction and recommendation guarantee their continuation over generations cannot be ascertained with recourse to a general problem of rule-following.

That is why the social sciences possess an objectivity *sui generis* that is synchronically and diachronically variable, since the social sciences have to include themselves in their examination. Universities, with their differentiated subsystems (departments, students, teaching positions, seminars, lecture halls, and so on), are themselves an object of social-scientific studies, which means they are subject to conditions of preservation that cannot be reduced to individuals deciding to do one thing or another in their mental histories.

The natural sciences cannot make any meaningful statements within their methodological framework about how a university is or should be organized. Certainly natural scientists can have roles that allow them to shape institutions, but this does not mean that they are successfully applying natural-scientific methods in the strict sense. If they think otherwise, they are being misled by social systems that justify their administrative actions on the basis of a naturalist ideology. When a naturalist view of historically grown institutions is fostered, there are specifically socio-economic reasons for the actors imagining their actions in a particular – distorted – fashion. The old organicist confusion of an organization with an organism familiar from political philosophy may have a certain heuristic value, but it should not be taken literally – unless contemporary sociobiology could boast of the truly spectacular discovery that human groups form genuine macroorganisms.

The objectivity of social-scientific knowledge imposes conditions for knowability on its objects which simultaneously ensure that one can be wrong about them. Here as elsewhere, the real potentially resists being grasped, which is exacerbated in the case of norm circles by their active resistance to being known. The social is intransparent in a specific way, since the type of complex differentiation enabled by asymmetries and chains of command would never come about without an ill-defined degree of intransparency. Social cooperation among minded beings only works because a decision is made somewhere that can at best be justified *post factum*. Norm circles do not constitutively ensue in the mode of their justification.

Let us call the circumstance that there is a rule which has normative power over actors the *binding force* of that rule. The binding force of the normative (normativity) develops under conditions that entail an ill-defined degree of indeterminacy; this allows a decision to be made that is only subject to deliberation after the event. Consequently, the binding force always generates a zone of intransparency. Where norms exist, they make room for a hermeneutics of suspicion that no one and nothing (not even the theoretically postulated sovereign) can escape. The social and the resistance to its being known coincide at this fundamental socio-ontological level.

The basic ontological form of the social is the alignment of holding-to-be-true. One believes something to be true that someone else considers false, so the real comes into play as the third element in a constitutive tri-angulation. Möllers illustrates this using the case of 'a norm arising from error'.[26] He uses the example of a situation in which someone decides to wear a tie to an event because, out of insecurity, he thinks that men are expected to wear one. He is mistaken about the customs and expectations of the hosts but shares his mistaken assessment with others. Another group of men likewise appears wearing ties, since it comprises those who like to wear a tie in the evening. This may go so far that someone who appears without a tie faces criticism that does not come from the hosts but from a norm 'created by custom' by the guests.[27] Norms can thus ensue through errors about existing norms, which means that social systems are themselves something real about which there is objectivity (and hence error-proneness among actors). From this, Möllers infers a 'commonality' between norms and fictions:

> Just as with fictions, norms do not operate independently of the factual world, one could even say that imagined norms are more dependent on facts and existing normative contexts than other norms since the error rests on a misinterpretation of given conditions, and cannot, unlike with other norms, be posited in wilful ignorance or conscious opposition to the status quo.[28]

With this, he opposes the misguided heautonomy model of normativity, which states that there must be a specific, non-cognitive normative attitude to norms if they are to develop binding force in actors.[29] Möllers's suggestion can therefore be classified as realistic; this is already true because he recognizes cognitive attitudes to norms that place actors and theorists in an objective attitude of assessing facts, which can have normative consequences because the facts in question are social norms.

Social systems permit indefinite nesting – recursive complexity – because a social system can itself be something real that takes up the position of the real in the triad of subject[1]–real–subject[2].[30] Subjects can be in conflict over what social system unites them – a complexity that can be modelled using the thoroughly studied rules of prisoner's dilemmas and other basic concepts from game theory.

Concrete social systems such as a given institution serve the purpose of eliminating paradoxes by passing a literal (juridical) judgement, and thus determining what is the real that should be taken into account for the social system of a judge's decision. The gathering of evidence, of witness statements, documents, and so on, in the context of a lawsuit serves to establish a framework of the real with which the subjects in conflict are made to align. The equalizing justice of the verdict consists in changing the social situation in which the actors are operating. The juridical verdict is not a truth-apt statement to the effect that p ('The act of the defendant is a case of manslaughter'), but rather the establishment of a new social system, such as sentencing. Someone who is sentenced or condemned is subjected to a social transformation, not a scientific study.

On a socio-ontological level, the methodological problem of the social sciences lies in their tendency to have a normative effect because they ultimately contribute, in a self-conscious (reflexively accessible) manner, to changing a social situation. When a text about a social system is accepted for publication by a specialist journal, this means (among other things) that a judgement has been made that a group of subjects is focusing discursively on the real in a relevant fashion that is suitable for that norm circle. The social sciences are constitutively reflexively jaded, because they must (be able to) examine their own inception according to the cognitive criteria available to them. There is evidently no objectively grounded way to evade this, only an escape to the naturalization of methods.

This creates the impression that social facts must arise and be maintained through a special causality, the social construction, since there are good methodological reasons to avoid impermissible naturalization. Yet this move overlooks the fact that the social sciences, as social systems, share the intransparency of their subject matter; a social theorist is justified in applying their insight into the 'unreflective nature of rule-following'[31] to themselves without seeing it as a work of nature.[32]

Any examination of a social system leads to a social modification, since one can only causally explain something if one can interact with the target system – that is, intervene in it. This applies in general, which is why interventionist causal theory continues to be in great demand.[33] When one interacts with a social system, one must find methodological ways of taking one's own contribution to the change of course in the observed system out of the equation, which has led to the development of social-scientific methods.

§15

Mythology, Ideology, Fiction

The objects of social-scientific examination, or of an understanding of social systems not supported by the appropriate methods, are not fictions in the usual sense criticized in depth in Part I. Moreover, social facts are precisely not interpretation-dependent on the socio-ontologically constitutive level and should therefore not be constructed on the hermeneutical model of aesthetic experience. Social production and reproduction take place at the level of implicit rule-following that allows us to interfere via interpretations, though these are in turn subject to implicit conditions, meaning that any attempt to clarify the social as a whole is doomed to failure.

This part of the book has concerned itself mostly with pointing out, in opposition to the climate of social constructivism, that there are genuine forms of social alienation that are not in the eye of the beholder in any relevant metaphysical or logico-semantic sense. Rather, the eye of the beholder is socially produced, as shown by Bourdieu in the case of factually occurring taste judgements.[1] Normative social facts acquire their effectiveness not as a consequence of performative speech acts or logically equivalent representation relationships but in the framework of largely unconscious processes of adaptation to and deviation from existing, passed-on, symbolically documented norms. As soon as we possess the reflexive faculty of self-regulation with recourse to the thought thereof, we also find ourselves in circumstances that are sediments of intransparent social transactions. There is no way out of this situation.

This does not, however, mean that the dimension of fictions and illusions examined in Part I and Part II in the *pars construens* is socially inert. Social ontology, as a discipline that keeps an eye out for constitutive sociality, is susceptible to interactive forms of error: by imagining the social in a particular way, one modifies it. Consider the case of the media dissemination of social statistics, whose very nature has socio-ontological premises inscribed in it; this leads humans to behave in a certain way because of their notion of scientific objectivity. Election forecasts are part of the social conditions of production for electoral successes as much as the media reporting, which reflects how its authors imagine the inner thoughts of voters who are unknown to them as individuals. Stereotypical ideas about Britons, Saxons, Bavarians, Indians, the US middle class, and so forth, thus become causally effective, and hence social-scientifically measurable, by filtering through into the background of implicitly shared rule-following, which in turn provides the social conditions of production and reproduction. This cycle undermines every layered model in social ontology consisting of base and superstructure: how we imagine the social as such, or a specific social system, has effects at the socioeconomic level, and vice versa.

This universally known fact has a special significance in the socio-ontological context, because it can be identified as a theoretical foundation of the ever-present suspicion of ideology that the social sciences (should) direct at themselves. How one imagines a social system depends on what prior assumptions enter the framework of premises whereby one seeks to approach the system. This framework of premises necessarily encompasses social systems, something that the social sciences cannot take out of the equation in their area of examination without potentially falling prey to specific fictions that are not recognized as such.

In the following, I would like to distinguish between two forms of socio-ontologically relevant fictions.

I will call the first form *mythology*. As stated above, this consists in the influence of implicit models on the behaviour of actors belonging to a social system. At the representational level, this manifests historically in the form of a theogonic consciousness and is perpetuated in our time especially in tales of super heroes and other everyday myths, to say nothing of the continued existence of world religions.

In contrast to mythology, an *ideology* is an edifice of ideas whose function is to legitimize a given asymmetrical distribution of socioeconomically valuable resources by diverting the attention of the actors involved in the production and reproduction of the edifice from said situation. Ideologies do not need to be explicitly asserted; they are usually implicitly effective and are not passed down by a central authority (which distinguishes ideology from propaganda).[2] Moreover, ideologies do not necessarily consist of false or illusory convictions or representations. One can dominate with true statements too, depending on how they are employed.[3]

The social function of the fictions of mythology and their scientific-sounding supplementary ideological modules amounts to this: legitimizing something that would be untenable under idealized conditions of justification by cloaking it in an aura of semblance.[4] Art and design contribute substantially to the production of this aura, as does reporting on alleged futuristic scientific breakthroughs (such as superintelligence, settling on Mars or final cancer therapy).[5] That is why one purpose served by the ontological calibration of the relationship between reality and fiction – that is, the philosophical work on the concept – is the social cause of making society more informed about itself. That a particular social practice is justified in the eyes of its participants certainly does not mean that it can be justified. Justification is a normatively undemanding but socially extremely effective status that one should not lose sight of. Transferring idealized notions of the game of giving and taking reasons to areas based on different sources of legitimacy is a socio-ontological error whose implementation has a pathogenic effect.

Ideological thinking often relies on a mythological substructure, since the heteronomy of archaic thinking makes it especially well-suited to ignoring the otherwise obvious problems of the present. At the representational level, the mythological manifests paradigmatically in the form of a theogonic, genealogical consciousness.[6] Mythologies make available the framework in which it seems productive to answer the question as to why a given behavioural pattern of which actors have become aware is considered valid, even though it cannot be explicitly justified in the mode of the game of giving and demanding reasons. In this way, mythology *entitles* us to continue practices that cannot be *justified*. An explicit justification is replaced by recourse to an imagined deep past that is meant to explain why the practice exists and continues.

This conceptual suggestion for defining the role of the mythological makes it possible to recognize mythology in modern forms of human self-assurance – even and especially where it is officially disavowed in the name of science and logos.[7] A central example of this structure is the notion that the human being is a complex cognitive system that cobbles together a worldview through more or less skilled, usually implicit extrapolations, while never being in contact with reality without the aid of models. We shall call this self-image *modellism*.[8]

Modellism is based on a model of the system of the 'human', which is essentially oriented towards a positivist theory of science. Nowadays, people often locate the construction of models in the brain or a subsystem thereof, which is understood as a calculating machine whose function is to make predictions on timescales that are not consciously available to us ('predictive coding'). The mythology of modellism consists in tailoring humans to a paleo-anthropological corridor and attempting to explain current, observable behaviour with recourse to (purported) strategies of evolutionary adaptation in a past that can no longer be empirically observed.[9]

In particular, the experimental design of illusionism and related efforts rests on a mythology that projects an as such largely implicit conception of humans into the deep past of our species in order to justify current research behaviour. If humans were ultimately identical with their consciousness, and that consciousness with some mechanics of the brain that could be explained with reference to its evolutionary usefulness, one would have to adapt the scientific self-examination of humans to this paradigm. A philosophically rigorous theory of mind would be replaced by a positivistically reduced understanding of consciousness that would rule out any historical self-conception.

An exemplary case is an article by Stanislas Dehaene, Hakwan Lau and Sid Koudier that examines the question of what consciousness is and whether machines can have it.[10] Amazingly enough, the authors take less than a page to answer the question of what consciousness is. Without offering any credible method, they distinguish between three meanings of 'consciousness' and claim to be bracketing the first of these, 'subjective experience', yet simultaneously paint a veritably absurd picture of this meaning.

> The word 'consciousness', like many prescientific terms, is used in widely different senses. In a medical context, it is often used in an intransitive sense (as in, 'the patient was no longer conscious'), in the context of assessing vigilance and wakefulness. ... For lack of space, we do not deal with this aspect here, however, because its computational impact seems minimal: Obviously, a machine must be properly turned on for its computations to unfold normally.[11]

Where to begin listing the manifold errors contained in this passage? How do the authors know that 'consciousness' is a 'prescientific term'? When is a term 'scientific'? If 'consciousness' is a pre-scientific term that is used in a medical context, then how can medicine be a science in this respect? If consciousness in the sense of wakefulness consists in our machine being switched on, then in what sense, pray tell, are we switched off when in a coma or unconscious deep sleep? Not being conscious is not the same as being dead! And how do the authors know that 'consciousness' is used with different meanings? What are these and how are they established? What natural language do they examine, since 'conscious' in English is not identical to the German equivalent *Bewusstsein* or the French *conscience*? Have they consulted linguistics, philosophy, the history of ideas or any discipline which would prove scientifically that consciousness is a pre-scientific concept?[12]

The authors' self-model asserts something it does not remotely prove, namely that we are machines in the same sense as human-made artefacts that can be switched on and off. Yet an organism cannot be switched off without the consequence that it can no longer be switched on; dead is dead. And this is only one of countless highly relevant ontological differences between human-made mechanical artefacts and us as conscious, minded beings.

The two other aspects of the meaning of 'consciousness' are, according to the authors, the 'global availability' of information in an organism and 'self-monitoring'. Global availability supposedly consists in the 'transitive meaning of consciousness'[13] – that is, in the 'relationship between a cognitive system and a specific object of thought'.[14] Here the authors should present a theory of intentionality, which they do not. Significantly, they do not tell us anything about the meanings of their terms 'thought', 'mental representation', and so forth, which they use to explain the concept of consciousness. We learn even less about why the meaning of 'conscious-ness' as 'global availability' is supposedly 'synonymous' with 'having the information in mind'.[15]

Global availability is not meant to be connected to the second sense of 'consciousness', postulated once again by the authors without any reasons: self-surveillance. In this context we learn: 'Human beings know a lot about themselves, including such diverse information as the layout and position of their body, whether they know or perceive something, or whether they just made an error.'[16] This form of self-consciousness (or, in neurospeak, 'metacognition') is separated from consciousness in the first sense, the authors argue, as it supposedly exists even without a person being conscious thereof. They aggressively avoid any engagement with the philosophical tradition from which the meanings of 'consciousness' have emerged, however, invoking them uncritically in an unacceptably simplified form.

'Consciousness', like many other central elements of our mental-ist vocabulary, is anything but a pre-scientific term, as claimed by the authors. This term is a fixed part of the purported everyday language on which the authors rely, without giving any sources, as a result of its philosophical and scientific history. Instead of a historically informed survey of human self-exploration, they present a modellistic self-model that describes the human being as a cognitive system of self-surveillance.

But this self-model has a history of its own that is not fully reconstructed, as it would have to take into account, in addition to the Greco-Roman tradition of subjectivity theory, other self-models that operate outside this more or less intra-European history of self-determination. The authors consequently examine at best the neuronal signatures of a very limited area of a given conception of humans, with no consideration whatsoever for its origins or meanings. Instead, they employ evolutionary parameters that present the human organism as a consequence of unconscious calcu-lations that have enabled us to reach the point we have in the struggle for survival, namely conscious life.

This especially crude variant of a computational model of mind is a paradigmatic case of an ideological use of mythology, for it adopts the function of an explicit justification of an unjustifiable distribution of resources (for example, among academic disciplines in the context of the competition for funding). The underlying mythology is the conception of humans as complex calculation machines with a surprising number of layers whose simultaneous processes generate consciousness. This mythology arises from dividing humans quasi-geologically into layers, of which the oldest are classified as elemental, so that the interplay of many such elemental processes gives rise – it is never explained how – to a 'consciousness' if one waves the magic wand of emergence. The explicit justification promises a technological production of 'artificial con-sciousness', which cannot remotely succeed without a sufficiently precise, properly theoretically elaborated understanding of the meaning of 'consciousness'.[17] No one, including the authors, knows *what* they intend to produce. Nor does anyone, including the authors, know *how* one might go about producing it.

Because humans, as minded beings, develop their conceptual faculty under social conditions and can therefore modify them, we are always susceptible to ideology. For we do not have any external criterion extending beyond the human form of life whereby we can determine who or what humans are.[18] According to neo-existentialism, of course, this circumstance is the relevant anthropological constant, and thus the starting point of a systematic philosophy of mind that takes into account the historicity of mind as well as its synchronically and diachronically plural manifestations.

One currently rampant ideology latches onto progress in the neurosciences and computer science and is connected to murmurings about 'Artificial Intelligence' – a term that, like 'digitalization', is normally used without the slightest specification, which immediately spawns futuristic narratives (see transhumanism) intended to deliver humans from themselves once and for all.[19] The ideological dimension of this discourse consists in the fact that humans do not enlighten themselves about themselves, instead using a product of their social activity (the technosphere) to adapt these products' historical conditions of production to an automatized fate. In this way, the progressive automatization of certain work processes in different sectors of a society based on division of labour is presented as a quasi-theological process of manifesting mind in non-organic material. This repeats the mythological format of the origin of mind in the non-mental – that is, a kind of primordial ignition of mental life – of which we have no adequate natural-scientific knowledge.[20]

It is fundamentally impossible to discover the origin of the historically variable mind through natural science, since it is in the nature of a natural-scientific explanation that its objects do not have a history in the sense studied in the field of history. Evolution in the strict sense and history as a social process of human self-determination cannot be reduced to each other. History is not a continuation of evolution by other (mental) means, nor is evolution natural history – that is, a form of anonymous, blind *historical* process.[21] Any attempt to merge evolutionary theory and historical science by brute metaphysical force completely overlooks the fact that history only takes place where actors appear as minded beings living a life in light of self-images, which can never be identical with organic processes. The wish to live in a just, solidary community, with the accompanying willingness to recognize certain institutions and their decisions, cannot be explained remotely comprehensively by the fact that apes, like other animals, also have an evolutionarily useful 'fairness' detector. No specific socioeconomic, politically considered order can be understood in its genesis or validity in this way.

In addition, I am quite convinced that we will never find out what factually served as the starting shot for mind, the origin of our historical existence. There is no available information from which we will infer any self-models that are reliable, not ultimately mythological. Digging in desert sand, speculations based on chance archaeological finds, genetic data collection or whatever else one resorts to in order to approach the origin of mind – all this is hopelessly mythological from the perspective adopted here. *Ignoramus et ignorabimus*. This inability to know is part of a truly enlightened humanism that does not rely *sotto voce* on scientistic mythology – that is, ideology. Whoever claims knowledge where there is nothing for us to know, and calls for an ideologically dressed-up ignorance of social consequences on this basis, damages the architecture of our minded form of life by using a bad archaeology of knowledge.

Humans are historical beings. This historicity cannot be brought to a halt by any process of naturalization seeking to convince us that everything proceeds completely naturally in a human society. For wherever humans act, they exceed the necessary, natural conditions of their occurrence by the dimension of the fictional. We have long moved so far beyond any given stimulus scene that the notion that we are ultimately complex 'feeding and fleeing machines' can be exposed as mythology and ideology.

A human being can, of course, be largely transformed into a machine. In addition to forcing humans to submit to a notion of the machine by threatening and carrying out violence, this can be achieved especially by spreading the ideology that we know everything there is to know about humans through natural-scientific research and can therefore be sure that we are complex machines, such as cellular automata, that realize certain functions which can also be implemented in non-biological 'hardware'. From the perspective adopted here, the grandiose visions of the future circulating in the current AI discourse (mostly of Californian provenance) serve to relieve humans of their self-determination.[22] This relief, if successful, leads to the illusion of an ahistorical existence whose political administration consists merely in creating the basic conditions for applied scientific research, which is meant to yield the technological prostheses of being-human.

This self-model is a severe case of (literally) false consciousness, since it relies on a false image of consciousness in order to keep humans away from any higher spirituality. The foundation of any higher spirituality is a concept of mind that avoids the mistake of confusing our indispensable starting position with a subset of its necessary, natural conditions. Let us not forget that we must overcome the naturalism which countless metaphysical manoeuvres hide behind, drawing on (alleged) empirical knowledge to develop a conception of humans that takes normative effect.

Human is and ought coincide on the standpoint of neo-existentialism. Because of our inevitable ability of self-determination, we commit an existential error if we attempt to deviate from the norm of being-human. To be sure, humans are incapable of not being humans; they are, however, capable of basing their being-human on a misconception of what it consists in. This gives rise to a space of pathologies that is the occasion for a hitherto unknown philosophical taxonomy of error. For, in addition to conventional false convictions, whose form consists merely in a person believing something to be true that is false (and vice versa), there are an infinite number of errors, including the modes of self-delusion in particular.

A *self-delusion* is generally an error about who or what a human self is that affects someone's actions. Because we are capable of this form of self-delusion, our mental life is differentiated into an indefinite number of forms that we measure via historically variable medical categories of the normal and the pathological.

Here one can apply a scale extending from maximum objectivity to maximum subjectivity of convictions. A conviction is *maximally objective* if it concerns a fact that would exist in every way even if there were no one who had a conviction about it.[23] Conversely, a conviction is *maximally subjective* if it relates to a fleeting state in a subject that acknowledges that state's existence yet cannot name an object of comparison that would allow the subject to identify the state as a case of any particular kind. If there were qualia whose existence and appearance were so 'welded together' that the subject had no space to classify their existence, these would be maximally subjective.

We can leave open whether maximally objective and maximally subjective facts exist in a pure form, since the normal case of our convictions relates to hybrid cases. As a rule, we are convinced that something is the case because we judge from the standpoint of our information assessment. We do not judge 'from nowhere', even if we abstract from the circumstance that we judge and make facts communicatively available whose confirmation can be taken up by others.

If I judge that p, then there is room for someone else to judge the same – that is, that p. My judgement does not always or essentially relate to this as it relates to the fact that p, otherwise it could not be taken up. A consequence of this is that, in a case of the judgement, one has the situation that a fact exists – namely, the fact that I judge that p. The affirmation of this fact can in turn be taken up, whether by me or by others. Judgements are then 'subjective' in that they can be made from a standpoint which, as my own standpoint, can exhibit defects that are unknown to me in my judgement. Otherwise, I would be unable to judge falsely and would thus not be fallible. At the same time, they are 'objective' because they are based in the realm of facts. One does not judge from 'cosmic exile'[24], but rather from where one is standing. That judgements are objective, then, does not mean that they are not subjective, that their substance is in every way independent of the judgement of someone who is an individual and therefore exhibits mental states that are inseparable from other mental states affecting the judgement. That judgements are objective means that they can in turn become the substance of other judgements – that is, that they are affirmable and thus publicly accessible.

The fact that I judge has an unquestionable effect at the content level only in cases where I make judgements about myself. Self-referential judgements exist; they are a paradigmatic object of philosophy. Self-referential judgements, however, are not transparent as such. Because of their opacity, it is impossible to rule out any possible errors from our self-relations. If an error occurs, this produces specific forms of error that – as far as we know – are restricted to the human form of life. Humans can believe themselves to be something they are not (such as computing programmes running on wetware, culturally upgraded killer apes, brains, and so on) and thus develop patterns of behaviour that can be classified as pathological.

Mythology and ideology are modes of self-delusion. They cannot be eliminated entirely, since we can only cognize the norm of being-human from the historically situated standpoint of a human. To assure us of ourselves historically, we will always use forms of autobiographical narrative that we apply in the medium of our individual lifestyles to understand ourselves as being on a path through life with the most profound meaning for those involved. *Ethos anthropo daimon.*[25]

The narratives available to us come from different traditions whose contexts and elements of incoherence can probably be clarified only in the framework of what Axel Hutter calls 'narrative ontology'.[26] What it means to be someone and what social identity one has depends essentially on the desired continuation of the autobiography one is working on.

There is no alternative to this narrative statement as long as we live a minded life. Accordingly, all finite, minded life is characterized by mythology, ideology and fictions, which only becomes a problem through the growth of an ideological apparatus that intervenes in the design of the chaotic fabric of mythologies to control the narrative fields of sense of subjects, be it consciously or unconsciously.

The current ideological constellation of a cooperation between neuroscience and computer science threatens humans by cutting off the self-examination of the narrative structure of being-human in the humanities and social sciences through at times aggressive socioeconomic steps. Humans are trained to become suppliers and producers of data, without being given the slightest explanation of what 'data' actually is, and that it only comes about because we direct human behaviour in channels constructed *a limine* in such a way that they restrict our scope of action by intervening in our imagination. The mistaken notion that our mental life is a neuronal storm that generates computational powers of some kind factually effects a depletion of our imaginative capabilities, which is in turn used for media technology purposes – such as marketing narratively simplified patterns of cultural mass production, which streaming services can produce continuously.

Many processes that lie behind the word 'digitalization' amount to interventions in the imaginative faculty of actors whose attention economy, with a little psychological expertise, can be manipulated by applying psychometric methods to data sets willingly provided by the actors because they are unaware of what is happening to them. This process continues undisturbed, or even accelerates further, only as long as access to our being-human slips out of reach. That is why the spread of the ideology of future immortality, ultimate medical progress, basic income generated by robots, and so forth, is closely connected to an intervention in the architecture of the humanities and social sciences.[27] These latter are led away from their well-founded humanist self-conception through the replacement of informed mental self-mediation by neurocentric nonsense. For if one stops humans from agreeing on who they are, it is easy to fool them into wanting to be something in which they actually have no interest.

It is therefore correct that we need a new enlightenment; strictly speaking, of course, we only need to adhere to the existing idea of enlightenment, in so far as this means that humans have the courage to demand knowledge instead of mere probability.[28] We should not dissolve humans into a probabilistic function to which we can ascribe a degree of predictability by controlling human behaviour through ideologically wrapped propaganda.

The Ontology of Social Networks

This brings us to the eye of the hurricane that is 'digitalization'. Fundamentally, the processes of *digitalization* collectively refer to the project of transforming something analogue as completely as possible into a different resolution format, namely the digital. Digitalization is a modelling process that inevitably falls short of what it seeks to capture. What can be digitalized is base reality, which is fundamentally analogue. The universe is not a computer, but rather a dimension of the real that is ultimately irreducible to terminology; this insight is the quintessence of natural philosophy.[1]

In my concluding remarks, however, the concern is not to present further arguments showing that it is inherently impossible to make the real entirely conceptually transparent, and thus to digitalize it fully.[2] Rather, I am specifically attempting to diagnose the pathologies of what are aptly described as 'social networks'.

In the following, what I refer to as a *social network* is a globally – that is, location-independently – accessible media platform that enables communication under specific basic conditions of information processing. In particular, communication in social networks is tied to the introduction of additional modules that go beyond a simulation of analogue communication in the form of video calls and text messages. The additional modules (such as newsfeeds, advertisements, timelines, behavioural recommendations and, most importantly of all, the 'posts' of the others) generate the attractiveness of social networks, which one joins precisely because of such an array. One does not need social networks to make telephone calls.

The attractiveness of media formats always remains intransparent to their users, otherwise it would not be effective. This intransparency is used *socially* by social media, as their name already indicates – more precisely, to generate courses of action by circulating ideas of norms.[3] Someone who posts pictures of their leisure behaviour in an appropriate medium, for example, is thus making available an image of a succeeding life. One posts an idealized self-image, thus making oneself vulnerable at the core of one's selfhood. On the whole, people do not like to post their weakest sides.

Here, a datum is the measurable difference between base reality and the small area we select and digitalize. The barbecue party, with its immensely complex embedding in a transfinite number of fields of sense, is reduced to snapshots that express one standpoint. The more such data and data points exist, the more one can learn about the barbecue. Since barbecue parties are essentially connected to what we expect of them, how we imagine ourselves and others (assuming they take part in barbecue parties), our data reveals something about how we think. A datum is a little piece in the mosaic of a self-image. Because we control ourselves via self-images, we can be controlled from the outside through interventions in our production of self-images (which has happened to each one of us through our early upbringing, and so on). Big Data, metadata and all the rest are the new oil because data is not neutral, but rather an expression of value judgements. There is no neutral data, since data is selected by presetting search engines; in the case of living beings, these pre-settings are evolutionary parameters, and for minded beings they are also imaginary, fictional and other historico-cultural object formats whose ontological texture is intransparent to us in the course of its use.

There are no unbiased algorithms or neutral online platforms, then, because the data on which they feed for their functions is an expression of biases that have not been interrogated in advance as to their morality but all uncritically uploaded. This is the irreparable malposition of the digital infrastructure, which renders explicit what is already implicitly effective, with the result that we look in the mirror of our own biases in digital formats.[4]

Social networks are personalization machines.[5] They transfer the not-yet-social mental states of an individual into formats of a mask of self-presentation, a *persona*. It is no coincidence, then, that especially successful online platforms base their business models precisely on giving their users the chance to socialize their 'private lives' as completely as possible, and thus share them. A genuinely finite, fleeting mode of experience restricted to the moment is replaced by the possibility of digitalizing and hence externalizing the experience. This externalization creates a semblance of memory, but people overlook the fact that a scene filmed with a smartphone already differs from the experienced scene because, in most cases, one is incompetent as the director of one's own experiences. Someone who films themselves experiencing something they wish to convey to others does not, in so doing, experience what they wish to convey – unless one wishes to convey that one is filming rather than experiencing (which is also a form of experience, only not the form one is attempting to capture in this way).

Social networks are worthy of their name. They follow on from social ontology in that they paradigmatically rely on the dissemination of dissent. The irregular articulation of opinions, the out-of-control freedom of speech, which does not have to follow nationally applicable laws thanks to the supranational organization of large firms, is not some incidental lapse, but rather an expression of the socio-ontological intensity of social media.[6] They are social precisely because they allow users to voice dissent directly and publicly, without any genuine examination of the content of their statements. Since there does not need to be any delay between articulatory intention and publication in social media, the rehearsed procedures of impulse control whereby, in the usual analogue media situations, we ensure that the existence of dissent remains tied to the possibility of its institutional administration, fall away. *Social networks are flow heaters of unfiltered dissent; their essence is the shitstorm. In this way, they induce us to produce data, since we defend ourselves and keep returning to produce new data. Thus we gradually turn into a digital proletariat, producing huge added value without a minimum wage and no longer noticing this process as such.*

Social networks do not have any juridically and hence adequately nationally secured, effective control system for opinion-forming. No one mediates between the quarrelling parties, who are instead let loose upon one another in unfiltered sociality like virtual gladiators. Someone without independent practice in dissent culture will not be prevented from freely venting their opinion, independently of the fact that this is subject to a norm of truth without which dissent would not be measurable. After all, dissenting parties must be in a dispute over a set of facts, otherwise there would be no dissent – only different emotional temperatures, which constitutes the extreme case of the collapse of a social system.

If the participants in a social system are reduced to their subjective individuality, and there is no more institution to intervene and allow the emerging conflicts of interest to be processed, the social system collapses. When the norm of truth is marked as unwanted in the pure opinion-holding of social networks, the social system breaks up into its constituent parts. This decline is only virtual, however, since in reality there certainly is an institution that administers the plurality of opinions by employing them for advertising and propaganda. This institution is the operator of a system offered as a social network. To quote Nassehi again, who describes the context in question with sociological precision:

> Let me offer a somewhat bold example: if data is the new oil, then the virtually unsuspicious daily activities of the users are like the plants, forests, animals and oils that once supplied the basis of this viscous fuel and lubricant through the constant decay of their existence. Today, the constant decay of communication events on the Internet and at the sensors registering events everywhere supplies the basis for the maturation of the raw material.[7]

The social networks are media of decay to the extent that they are geared towards dismantling the norm of truth as a discursive guideline. Here truth is a norm in so far as ontic truths – that is, facts – form the decisive criterion for whether a holding-to-be-true succeeds or not. What is the case determines what sort of conviction a person has. No formatting of our convictions alone is capable of overwriting the criterion of truth.

It is decisive for the business model of social networks that their algorithms – and thus, in reality, the staff producing them – remove the two factors of truth and freedom from the conditions of production for self-models in order to simulate a 'world without mind'.[8] But the appearance of mindlessness is deceptive; rather, social networks stage the pure intensity of mind without its extension – that is, without embodiment. Sociality is essentially embodied, for our body is the starting point of our indexical positioning in the real. Because of our finite hereness, we are ontologically isolated from the fields of sense of the fictive.

Therefore one could almost distinguish between the *deictic* and the *digital*. The digital is ontologically defective, as it is a second-order reality that attempts to break free of its analogue location. Digitalization as the overall project of overcoming analogue humans is doomed to fail because of the reality of humans, who, in an act of existential desperation, attempt to evade their responsibility in the factual here and now – that is, in their hereness. The meanwhile obvious addictive potential of social networks stems from the fact that they deliver social intensity without responsibility.[9] Anyone who applauds a fleeting self-presentation on a relevant channel with a click grants the self-presenter the impression of interconnection.

However, one must take into account that the sociality of social networks is not fictive. Our avatar is not ontologically isolated from us to the extent of a fictional *dramatis persona*, which may resemble us but cannot be strictly identical with us or any part of us.

In light of this, one can separate the fictive from the virtual. The *virtual* is the objectification of a fiction, but this by no means makes it fictive. We are not shielded from the virtual; rather, it enters our self-model because aspects of our personality are reinforced through the media format of platforms that, through applause and attention, control what we will mean to ourselves in the future.

In every analogue social situation in which our expressive demeanour is visible, the actors belonging to a social system adapt to one another perceptibly and imperceptibly. Analogue communication is physical, which obviously involves more than merely the visual sensory modality. Our hereness is multi-modally sensory, even – and especially – if others are involved in the construction of a scene. If one sheds this dimension and distils the pure intensity of the social (that is, dissent as a source of objectivity), one replaces the social with statistics, for mutual adaptation then takes place via expressive media whose conditions of articulation are completely transparent to their producers.[10]

What is not transparent to the producers are the conditions of production of the social system that allows them to produce social networks and maintain them through skilful updates. Social networks are produced under analogue socioeconomic conditions, and thus necessarily inherit the constitutive intransparency of the social. This manifests in the digital through the bias of the producers, who sooner or later become visible in an analogue form, with the creation of massive, digitally induced, analogue socioeconomic inequality.

A simple example of this meanwhile familiar process is the fact that users of social networks perform work by publicizing their self-models (their data). Whoever produces photos, videos, text messages or political commentaries and disseminates links and makes these available on a platform is working without any claim to payment (let alone minimum wage) for a platform that exploits this work in the form of added value.

The billions of users of social networks thus form a digital proletariat that is still almost entirely unconscious of its status.[11] The digital proletariat is not exploited through the sprinkling of advertising and buying recommendations in its virtual transactions, but rather through its enablement of the further development of software, for which the programmers require access to huge amounts of data; these can be used to test one's skill in using statistical procedures to highlight patterns that allow one to make predictions. If there are sufficiently large data sets that document what people do by containing the self-presentation of their thinking, it is possible to foresee their behaviour with statistically calibrated accuracy.

This can only succeed, however, as long as the actors are not aware of it. For social facts are interactive: someone who knows the rules of a social system has an advantage over someone who is blindly at their mercy. As soon as the rules have been made largely public, it is possible to change them. Someone who knows how they are being observed can at least make an attempt to change their behaviour in the hope of evading surveillance.

A surveillance so complete that it would eradicate the freedom of minded beings is impossible; for such a surveillance apparatus would have to be maintained by minded beings, who could in turn not be subjected to it, otherwise the necessary updates could not be brought about. The collapse of large-scale dictatorships, in particular those familiar from the last century, as well as their transition to softer formats, is also due to the fact that the leadership of a dictatorial state apparatus knows this. Thus the social competition to control the narrative is shifted to the small group that plans to systematically determine their subjects' scope of action. For the social as a whole is not merely a simulation game.

All social systems are unstable in one way or another on account of their ineradicable zones of intransparency. There are two decisive reasons for this.

On the one hand, sociality is tied to truth, since our opinions only diverge in dissent if there are facts that pass judgement on them. Whatever is the case generally or individually when one judges is not transparent in the overall judgement. Whichever way one turns, one cannot know the whole truth – which does not, of course, mean that one cannot know that some thing or another is true. The perfect large-scale dictatorship would presuppose a form of omniscience that cannot be achieved, not even through some progress in the AI industry. *Whoever judges is judgeable, in so far as there are facts that determine what kind of judgement someone has made.*

On the other hand, sociality is a manifestation of freedom, since freedom among minded beings consists in the exercise of their self-determination. By imagining what we are like, we turn ourselves into something we want to be. Conceptions of humans affect our actions. The production and transformation of conceptions of humans is unpredictable; we cannot fully control as who or as what humans manifest themselves.

The innovation of social networks lies in making this circumstance invisible and, through merely statistical procedures, pretending merely to state what we are like without intervening in our self-determination through the basic conditions of this description. This illusion should really have been dispelled at least since the exposure of the manifold scandals relating to social networks and their critical influence on the continued existence of the democratic constitutional state.[12]

Because of their formatting, social networks modify the analogue transactions of their members. The effects of digital on analogue reality appear on different levels, including the far from banal fact that the users of social networks spend their very much analogue time of finite survival working on their self-presentation. Slipping into the role of my avatar does not allow me to escape from my analogue status as a mortal being for even one second.

Yet the feedback effect of the social networks on analogue communication extends much further, as conceptions of humans are generated that affect actions under analogue conditions. This especially includes the widespread statistical conception of humans and the world, in which reality as a whole is a large-scale calculation that can only be appropriated through statistical approximation procedures. Knowledge claims – and thus contact with the truth – are replaced by suppositions from which one thinks one is harvesting large data sets, without realizing that the data sets already contain implicit and explicit knowledge claims as well as manifold errors.

This problem can be illustrated using the fundamentally misguided 'method' of so-called experimental philosophy, which has a particularly drastic effect on epistemology. One might hold the opinion that one can resolve the concept of knowledge by undertaking surveys to determine under what conditions a true opinion is considered justified. In this way, one could only privilege a given theory of science over others by using the linguistic 'intuitions' of German-speakers, say, as data sets from which to derive a concept of knowledge in a statistically averaged fashion.

This project is immediately thwarted, however, by the fact that the knowledge claims made about the knowledge gathered themselves surely (or should I say hopefully?) do not come about through surveys, since the purported group of pre-theoretical, unphilosophical 'normal speakers' along with their intuitions, *ex hypothesi*, do not belong to the expert committee of professional philosophers working on presenting a theory of knowledge. Epistemology makes classic knowledge claims as to what knowledge is – a situation one cannot escape by documenting what 'people in general' mean when they use the word 'knowledge'. The concept of knowledge is as difficult to identify statistically as any other philosophical concept.

Knowledge – including scientific knowledge – cannot be reduced to a supposition that relies on statistical procedures for pattern detection in large data sets, because any experimental design that generates statistical procedures itself presupposes, somewhere or other, knowledge claims that were not generated via statistical procedures. If a physicist logs into the data sets of the CERN, they draw on their sensory modalities and practical knowledge about the evaluation of pictures to apply statistical methods. From a different perspective, knowledge claims are not statistics all the way down; the foundation we stand on when we judge is never completely digitalized. Someone who judges is and remains a human being, and humans are not statistically ascertained data sets.

One cannot successfully reduce humans to the digital. To hide this, some people spread the ideology of complete transparency and a surveillance apparatus we supposedly cannot resist. Digitalization thus becomes the new name for a fate that, like the purported singularity, is more or less imminent. This grand metaphysical narrative of our time is disseminated in the medium of social networks and then spreads to the conditions of analogue publication, whose task in the age of enlightenment should still be the critical assessment of knowledge claims.

In this context, the role of social ontology is to point out that social networks are in fact fundamentally social, but that their ontology is virtual. I see the virtuality of social networks in the fact that they promise pure sociality without embodiment. The body one displays in social networks is already formatted via the publication conditions of the platforms (including censorship of nudity). One makes available a self-image, a bodily schema, that does not coincide with the body without which one would not be anyone. Hence the increasing prominence of video platforms on which users can act out their fantasy of being a starlet just once. The immeasurable amounts of data that heat up servers and computers have unsuspected ecological and hence economic consequences, as shown by the discussion about cryptocurrencies. The internet as a whole contributes to the ecological crisis because human self-modelling in social networks costs a great deal of energy. One is easily distracted from this, because the internet gives the false impression of a modernized noosphere – that is, an 'infosphere', as Floridi aptly terms it (albeit without critical intentions).[13]

The essence of these reflections is that we urgently need a true digital revolution, which presupposes an enlightenment about the ontological architecture of the digital age, and thus of social networks. What is fateful is not disembodied virtual sociality, but rather the fact that users of social media channels are not only exploited by the producers but also controlled in their thought models and, among other things, systematically manipulated through the dissemination of mythology and ideology.

As one would expect in fully ideologized circumstances, this does not mean that the producers of ideology are necessarily informed about their own activities.[14] Because the context of delusion is social, it is by definition insufficiently transparent to create an ordered hierarchy headed by a self-consciously ruling class that is aware of the conditions of its rule.

§17

The Public Sphere of Mind

The 'crisis of the public sphere' has been on everyone's lips at least since Habermas formulated his influential assertion of a structural trans-formation of the public sphere.[1] In 1990, in the preface to the second edition, he articulated a difficulty that was not only sociological but also philosophical-conceptual, based on the 'growing selective constraints imposed by electronic mass communication'.[2] He argues that mass media have 'contradictory effects', including 'deracination' on the one hand and 'levelling of differences' on the other, yet does not assign the 'pluraliza-tion of forms of life' and the 'individualization of life plans' clearly to each of these tendencies.[3] He explains this diagnosis with the following obser-vation: 'The dedifferentiation and destructuring affecting our lifeworld as a result of the electronically produced omnipresence of events and of the synchronization of non-simultaneities certainly have a considerable impact on social self-perception.'[4] According to Habermas, the 'demo-cratic potential of a public sphere'[5] shaped by an electronic infrastructure is 'ambivalent',[6] which ultimately means that one cannot easily ascertain whether global mass communication supports or obstructs the spread of the democratic constitutional state.

This is a problem that Habermas tackles against the background of his ambivalent thesis that communication can be conceptually (if not factu-ally) separated from a strategic display of power, meaning that one could postulate a form of communicative reason as the underlying principle of a public sphere developing in a direction that can be encouraged based on the later criteria of discourse ethics.[7]

In this context he formulates what he calls the 'principle of publicity', which he defines as the 'universal accessibility of that domain in which is to be rationally decided what is practically necessary in the general inter-est',[8] though there is an ambivalent stance that runs through the whole of *The Structural Transformation of the Public Sphere* and is connected to the fact that, on the one hand, Habermas envisages the variant of universal communicative reason developed later on but, on the other hand, he does not want to infer from this that humans are the universal that justifies 'universal accessibility'.[9] For he considers an argumentation that conceives the public sphere as the development of humans as such, and thus of human rights, a historically locatable and paradox-prone constellation that he describes as the 'public sphere of civil society'.[10]

Therefore the public sphere is essentially a crisis phenomenon for Habermas, because he describes it as a historically contingent, unstable formation with a questionable genealogy. If the idea of a universal form of humanity (and thus the concept of communicative reason) is an expression of a civil infrastructure that, contrary to its publicized commitment to universal accessibility, generates exclusion mechanisms via property relations, then the invocation of the emancipatory potential of the public sphere is *always* ideology.[11]

Habermas wriggles out of this dialectic by not only defining ideologies as the 'socially necessary consciousness in its falsity' but also ascribing to them an aspect 'that can lay a claim to truth inasmuch as it transcends the status quo in utopian fashion, even if only for purposes of justification.'[12] Thus the bourgeois public sphere becomes, in spite of itself, the origin of a utopia of equality that it is neither willing nor able to fulfil.

However, this influential theory of the public sphere overlooks the fact that the structural transformation it posits is based on a uniform pattern: the concept of the public sphere. The point of the first philosophical theories of the public sphere, however, to which Habermas himself refers, is that universal accessibility is the 'eternal logos' hidden from those who know not what they do.[13] Like the Eleatics, Heraclitus – the pioneer of the public sphere overlooked by Habermas – infers from his insight into the structure of the existent that there is something which is common to everything, but which 'the many' attempt to dispute because of their self-will, their privacy.[14] The idea of a radical particular holding-to-be-true that is not translated communicatively into a universal is rejected by the founding acts of philosophy, which is why the Platonic opposition between philosophy and Sophism is not a late artefact of a specific constellation but an element of the concept of philosophy. A philosophy whose function is to remove the universal from the form of holding-to-be-true in favour of supposedly radical alterity will always be a betrayal of its own concept. The rejection of the universal in favour of a particular is always exposed at best as the staking of a conceptually irrelevant claim to power – that is, as discursive violence.[15]

The foundation of the public sphere, then, is indeed the universal accessibility of the sphere of practical necessity. As this sphere has always concerned humans as such, however, one falls short of the concept of a genuinely universal accessibility if, like Habermas, one ties it to a historically contingent formation. If publicity were a contingent byproduct of modern socioeconomic processes, there would be no difficult-to-revise reason to recognize it as a norm. If the reason for the fact that the democratic constitutional state is aimed at all people as such, not only a group of stakeholders, were no more than the unstable result of a dialectic of enlightenment, it would lose its justification. The thesis of *The Structural Transformation of the Public Sphere* thus particularizes the universal and invalidates the public sphere's claim to be the ground of universality.

Based on this, one cannot formulate an adequately temporally neutral, transhistorical claim with which to critically examine the challenges of the digitalized public spheres. If there were many public spheres resulting from local socioeconomic constellations (let us say, far too crudely: an American one, a Chinese one, a European one, and so on), their digital collision in the medium of the internet would be inherently incapable of reason. The collision would automatically result in a provisionally uncontainable cyberwar of all against all. Any invocation of a universal transcending this cacophony would fail if the idea of humanity, of the human being as such, remained confined to a specific constellation (the 'West', the 'occident', 'Europe' or whatever questionable entity one might name here).

For this reason, I consider it theoretically and practically imperative to tie the theory of the public sphere to the historically unmediated concept of humanity. It may be the case that humans only became aware at a particular point in their historical self-examination (such as the Axial Age) that they have a general capacity for self-images that connects them to all other humans.[16] Without further assumptions, however, it does not follow from this that the status of being a human is historically contingent. Here, as elsewhere, it applies that genesis and validity do not come into conflict without further premises; this is the decisive argumentation gap in all purportedly undermining genealogical projects, from Nietzsche to Foucault.

The concept of mind as the indispensable human capacity for self-images developed in this study is an element of a groundwork for a theory of genuine publicity. *Genuine publicity* consists in social reality being fundamentally universally accessible. Universal accessibility does not mean that it is possible to remove all zones of intransparency, which would amount to an abolition of the social. Rather, it means that we have no reason to assume that there is any insoluble, eternal secret of the social that cannot be explored through scientific efforts. The zones of intransparency change, because society is not a pyramid with a foundation (be it implicit or explicit). It is therefore a principle of genuine publicity to be allowed, under regulated conditions, to demand the release of documents that may bring facts to light in public that will contribute to an institutional course correction. The model for this process presupposes that such a process of exploration and publication of facts, always limited by moral and juridical norms, serves to improve the human form of life as a whole.

Since the public sphere sets itself apart from the private sphere, what follows from the concept of genuine publicity is not socio-ontological transparentism: the public sphere presupposes the private, which no system of observation that completely socializes private processes may infiltrate. Because of their digital infrastructure, which extends to all households and situations, the social networks automatically contribute to undermining the public sphere, and thus the democratic constitutional state, since it has become almost impossible to shut them down entirely. Defending the democratic constitutional state in the face of digitalization, then, includes demanding packages to secure privacy, which must go much further than is currently intended. Not every digitalization is desirable.

Publication is not an end in itself; this is secured by the concept of a legitimate private sphere. The publicized and the private must be coordinated in such a way as to open up a space for actions that are neither morally, nor juridically, nor or even politically suspicious. Actions that should not come under suspicion can be described as *neutral*. They belong to the category of adiaphora – that is, the realm which should not be regulated by universalizable norms. Going for a walk, drinking orange juice and – a less obvious case for many people – practising certain forms of sexual interaction that some would consider offensive, along with an indefinite number of human actions, all belong to the adiaphoric realm that must be secured by the public sphere. *The* private sphere *is the area of the individualizing adiaphora – that is, that which one is free to do and harms no one else. The value of the private lies in protecting us as private persons from the politicization of the adiaphora, which is why a state that flirts with totalitarianism targets precisely this area and declares adiaphora a state matter.*

Genuine publicity, then, does not consist of what is publicized. Rather, it serves to regulate publications, since it is guided by the idea that the universal human form of life leaves indefinite room for adiaphora. Since one cannot infer a priori from an inspection of the concept of the human being what factual action patterns are included in adiaphora, the space of genuine publicity constantly moves the boundary between the publicized and the private.

Therein lies the ever-advancing structural transformation of the public sphere, which does not mean that publicity or the social as such can be historicized.[17] That humans produce historicizable constellations of the social is not itself a historicizable circumstance, but rather an essential feature of humans as such. There is therefore *prima facie* no cause to overextend the concept of the historicizable and thus to abandon the logos that unites us.

From this perspective, the crisis of the public sphere lies in the fact that the new platforms of immediate publicity weaken the institutional regulation of the publicized to such an extent that the private sphere is rapidly dissolving. An essential process that is conventionally assigned to the nebulous category of 'digitalization' consists precisely in turning the idea of genuine publicity against itself. Users of social networks who protest, sometimes quite rightly, overlook that the articulation of their critical contributions to the course correction of the democratic constitutional state occurs under conditions that are imposed on them by the platforms. These conditions especially include the undermining of their privacy, whose continued survival they are therefore quarrelling about in the wrong medium. Anyone arguing the case for their privacy online has already forfeited it.

Here Habermas was already spot on in the 1960s when he and others observed a '"disappearance of the private" in the sphere of social labour',[18] which he connects to the concept of the 'large enterprise' (what we now call a 'corporation'). He uses the term 'industrial feudalism' to describe the phenomenon, known especially from the USA, that corporations completely deprive their employees of privacy by creating a social infrastructure (housing, childcare, schools, cultural events, gyms, and so forth) which guarantees that their staff are essentially working whenever they are awake. The seemingly highly privileged form of life among the employees of dominant internet corporations rests on the absorption of their private sphere into the corporation's surveillance apparatus, as strikingly depicted by Dave Eggers in *The Circle*.[19]

This reveals the problem that endangers the survival of an institutionally implemented genuine publicity: the private sphere is disappearing in favour of the activity of publicizing the private to the quantifiable extent to which users of the internet, through their searching and publication behaviour, produce data whereby they make their mind – that is, their self-image – available in objectified form. Whoever publishes images online of who they want to be makes themselves vulnerable, since they allow their privacy to be subjected to a public norm. This vulnerability is not a contribution to genuine publicity, but rather an uncontrolled shifting of boundaries whose contribution to democracy is not only ambivalent but even clearly damaging. Our self-presentation in social media as well as our addictive online behaviour, which is controlled by the formation of appropriate monopolies by search engines, means that our private sphere turns into work for corporations in a way that is not transparent to us.

Therefore this is not an emancipatory recourse to the principle of publicity, but rather an indirect undermining thereof. Habermas once again describes this accurately, drawing on an analysis of programmes in 'radio, film and television':[20] 'The world fashioned by the mass media is a public sphere in appearance only. By the same token the integrity of the private sphere which they promise to their consumers is also an illusion.'[21] Like mind, publicity is a normative concept: it refers to the dimension in which we can mistake ourselves. Self-mistaking, however, is not an error like any other, but rather an intervention in the concrete –that is, the historically situated structure of subjectivity. The pathology of publicity that is currently observable under the catchword 'digitalization' is a process of labour automation that hides behind an ideology of progress. The specific ideology of progress found in digitalization consists in presenting the accelerated establishment of surveillance systems fostered by information technology as a destiny to which there is no alternative, and which is carried out by an ultimately unpredictable superintelligence.[22] Instead of an analysis of the socioeconomic operating conditions of the age of information, we are presented with the farce of a grand narrative that passes off a contingent phase of industrialization as inescapable destiny. In this way, the mind sets itself a trap that allows it to remove mental freedom in favour of a false self-conception.[23]

This is the appropriate context for some concluding remarks that take a stance on the supposed post-truth era, based on the developed ontological foundation of New Realism. There is no such thing as a post-truth era; rather, digitalization enables a faster dissemination of addictive ideological material. The public sphere is undermined by the fact that it infiltrates what was the private sphere, such that publicity occurs everywhere and thus essentially nowhere. The data quantities we generate by using the internet accompany us around the clock, wherever we might be. This is made possible by so-called Artificial Intelligence, which essentially consists in automatized pattern detection infiltrating our digital work routine. This pattern detection, which is performed using appropriate algorithms based on large data quantities, produces spaces of subjugation by one's own self-images, which are reflected in the machines.[24]

The omnipresent screens of our day are projection surfaces for our view of ourselves, which we can no longer see through as such. To make the ideology of digitalization lead to the self-subjugation of subjects, there is an ideological superstructure which would have us believe that today's information technology is intelligent ('smart', 'learning', and so on) – which, on closer inspection, is a rather absurd notion that was already disproved in the first wave of a critical philosophy of AI.[25]

The success of many large digitalization companies consists in providing platforms rather than content. These platforms serve to let us express how we see ourselves by generating an illusory publicity in which we display ourselves. This display is then used for profit: the platform is adapted to the users' patterns until the competition is left behind. This is followed by an unfettered manipulation that keeps the users addicted.[26]

The manifold platforms of our time play into each other's hands: the series one watches, the flats one sublets, the videos and pictures one posts, the news one spreads, the food one orders, the sexual partners one chooses – they are all connected, meaning that we all more or less unconsciously produce an avatar of ourselves whose digital cells are our data points.

We should note, however, that this virtual avatar is not a fictive object, but rather an aspect of ourselves: a hybrid of facts and wishful thoughts with which we design ourselves. Unlike Faust, my virtual avatar is neither ontologically nor causally isolated from me. It is a genuine part of me as a minded being. To be sure, the ontology of virtual reality is intertwined with art history and therefore contains genuine fictional references (in computer games, for example). However, it differs from the reality of the fictive in being fundamentally social. In virtual reality we present facets of ourselves; it is a (more or less badly controlled) form of psychological experiment in which we participate willingly (and largely without socioeconomic compensation). Our virtual avatar is an expression of our self-referential thoughts, which encounter the expression of others at a distance from the facts that accompany our corporealization in the base reality in which we are indexically anchored.

Our virtual avatar is not produced under conditions that we can control, as it clings to the innate structure of platforms whose business model is to keep us interested so that we will produce new data that can be fed into statistical analyses, which in turn improve the user experience. This sets up a cycle of reproduction that creates monopolies if it succeeds, and this monopolization cannot be prevented because the legal apparatus has no means against these newly emerged social systems; herein lies the much discussed powerlessness of nation states to oppose the transnational order of virtual reality. This tension accordingly leads to direct attacks by virtual reality on analogue reality; election manipulation is only one especially visible form of cyberattack by digital monopolies on the primacy of the rule of law, which might get in their way. Election manipulation on social platforms is thus not a contingent byproduct of an otherwise neutral information supply, but rather a palpable intrusion on analogue social systems by the digital click farms.

This intrusion contributes to undermining the truth claims of the modern public sphere and the legal systems tailored to it, which traditionally countered newspaper hoaxes – or 'fake news', as one now calls them – with boards of inquiry and libel suits in order to support the idea of a discourse that promotes rationality.[27]

On a Final Note:
We Must Chase away the Spectre
of the Post-Truth Era

The need to trawl through the dimensions of semblance ontologically is motivated, among other things, by the fact that the digital age is seeing an intensified, socioeconomically and politically extremely effective confusion of fiction and reality. I here offer a theory in opposition to this, one that ontologically enables us to distinguish fiction from reality without disputing the reality of fiction.

Here it is germane to recall critically the epitome of all postmodern diagnoses, Jean Baudrillard's *Simulacra and Simulation*.[1] Baudrillard introduces the concept of hyperreality to describe social relations of production built on the fact that the real is understood through its cartography, not vice versa. He goes so far as to claim that the American form of society in particular as a whole is turning into a hyperreality – in his example, on the model of Disneyland. According to Baudrillard, what he calls 'America' is merely a kind of emanation from an imaginary Los Angeles that supplies the rest of the globe with self-models that can no longer be distinguished from an original. Everything becomes a 'fake', one might say, which is thus the model for the real that must be produced.[2]

It is not hard to extrapolate from this and, with some postmodern imagination, Donald Trump becomes Donald Duck. That Donald Trump is elected president in an episode of *The Simpsons* titled 'Bart to the Future' (series 11, episode 17) from 2000, and some scenes almost seem like predictions, led – predictably enough – to the spread of conspiracy theories. One of these was that *The Simpsons* had predicted the future with conspicuous regularity, and so on.

Today, Baudrillard's work in general reads like an applicable and indirectly self-applicable commentary on the ontological confusions of the digital age, which could thus almost be viewed as the culmination of postmodernity.[3] Indeed, one can observe a spread of what Baudrillard calls simulation in the form of the so-called post-truth era: first-order facts (base reality) of human life evidently no longer play a part in the reproduction of socioeconomic structures because they have been placed by the purely symbolic order, in which there is no longer any reference to the real. Reality seems lost, or at least in crisis.

For all its undeniable semblance of plausibility, however, this diagnosis is ultimately deeply flawed. Baudrillard seems to hit the mark because he encapsulates the ideology of the post-truth era in a heightened form; yet, in so doing, he reproduces it in theoretical form rather than seeing through it. This makes him a postmodern theorist *par excellence*.[4] Baudrillard slips (convincingly) into the role of the simulation; it is therefore no coincidence that his work falls into the hands of Neo (played by Keanu Reeves) in *The Matrix*.

Resisting the temptation to view our digital age as post-truth, we must conclude by hammering home three points.

Firstly, we live in advanced industrialized states in a society of knowledge and information whose data traffic now reaches anyone with internet access. To be sure, the internet is essentially an illusion generator, since it does not allow any distinction between real and false information within its medium. Nonetheless, it simultaneously brings about the dissemination of truths and the production of new facts. For digital infrastructure is by no means located in our heads, but rather is a social system that is effective in material and energetic dimensions.

We know more in real time today than ever before, which creates new challenges for the analogue social systems reacting to this. Digitalization brings facts to light that would remain hidden under analogue conditions. At the same time, it creates new industrial facts and thus also contributes to the climate catastrophe.

In so doing, it generates new zones of intransparency. It is not an unconditional process of emancipation, since it is accompanied by an ideology of automatizing the reduction of freedom that is historically evident in the form of new possibilities for exploitation, something that we do not adequately acknowledge because of the manifold postmodern smokescreens produced as an accompanying text to digitalization.

Secondly, the base-reality industrial conditions of production and reproduction in digitally accelerated consumer and affluent societies are in no way digitalizable. The material conditions for the continued existence of the internet and the global transportation of goods are highly analogue: without good old oil, the new oil of digitalization, namely data, would have no *raison d'être*. Someone who films themselves during a barbecue for social networks is burning fossil fuels – not only for the barbecue but also for the dissemination of their video clip on the internet. It is a dangerous illusion to take the mind-shaped user interface of digital realities at face value. Their foundation is a not inconsiderable contribution to the climate crisis, since the factual conditions of production in a global society do not cease to be real in every relevant sense.

Thirdly, Baudrillard, like some other theorists of illusion cited in this book, uses a theoretically ill-considered vocabulary to describe the flipside of the truth, namely the untrue and illusory. This creates the misleading impression that, because we basically do not separate fiction from reality, we can no longer distinguish between them. This postmodern ideology involuntarily sustains the mechanisms of the alleged post-truth era, whose main feature is supposedly that feelings count rather than facts.

The ontological, meontological and fictionality-theoretical manoeuvres undertaken in this book are directed against this sophisticated and multi-faceted constellation of post-truth semblance. The function of the theory formation here consists in making available instruments for the destruction (not only deconstruction) of this semblance. The destruction of semblance can only succeed if we recognize that it leads an ontological life of its own, that it is real and leads to the extermination of our own form of life through implementation in human self-images. This extermination takes many forms and is fuelled by the bad fiction of an all-encompassing automatization and digitalization that, on closer inspection, is an ostensibly progressive drive to self-destruction. This drive articulates itself by disputing the existence of a self, based on the postmodern semblance of the death of the subject, which has now formed an alliance with naturalism. Baudrillard's hypothesis of simulation has unexpectedly been resurrected in the form of an ontologically misguided neuroinformatics which would have us believe that we are on the way to eradicating the supposed illusion of mind.

But this is anti-mind: mind turns against mind. This self-rupture can succeed, but only at the price of exterminating the human form of life, and thus the human survival form. We must bear in mind that nothing remains after this extermination: no mind will ever be rushing through the cables, enjoying its superintelligence and disembodiment. Cable spaghetti and microchips do not enjoy anything; they are not even dead.

The dream of the post-truth era, in which facts will finally stop mattering, fulfils the human, all-too-human wish to break free of finitude. Metaphysical naturalism, which allies itself with this wish, represents an enormous danger today. We should note that the error does not, of course, lie in scientific insights. What we find out about the universe with the appropriate methods of the natural science are precisely facts. The error lies in the scientific worldview, which presumes to supplant philosophy and pass off a metaphysics gone wild as a successful interpretation of genuine scientific research.

That is why, with this book, I have attempted to breathe new life into the dialogic format of philosophy and the humanities. This requires overcoming the unfortunate postmodern constellation and reminding ourselves of the ontological weight of the fictional, as the dimension of the reality of mind that generates the respective *zeitgeist*-specific semblance that we must examine, see through and potentially destroy using the methods of philosophy and the humanities developed for this purpose.

The purpose of this undertaking is a recalibration of the meaning of life: we must recognize that human life, in its embeddedness in a complex ecological niche (which naturally includes countless other life forms with which we, as organisms, live in constant symbiosis), is an indispensable source of existential meaning that is necessary for our existence. Our minded form of life does not continue to exist without our animal survival form. Our animality is a condition that is necessary (albeit insufficient), and thus must never be cast aside, for the existence of spirit, consciousness and the experience of sense. To ensure that the series of *Terminator* films finally comes to an end, we must find a way to lessen the attraction of the idea that there could be intelligent machines which are non-biologically adapted to a niche and will come for us. This sort of thing exists only in fictions: the Terminator is a fictive object and thus at best a distraction from the real danger of human self-extermination through the destruction of our ecological niche (which Arnold Schwarzenegger managed to increase in his role as governor of California).

Let us abandon our trust in Hölderlin's lyrical subject! It is simply untrue that where there is danger, salvation also grows. Whether humans can be saved from self-extinction also depends on whether we overcome the semblance whose deep logical structure the book I now conclude has attempted to explicate.

The spectre of the post-truth era is a *danse macabre* brought forward, the intimation that our current global order is not sustainable.[5] The game is not lost yet: since knowing through the progress of scientific society that the human species has prepared a self-imposed end, everything depends on placing sustainability at the top of our structure of priorities in the right way. This structure can only be implemented successfully if we face the facts, which includes taking into account their breadth. This is impossible without research in the humanities and, thus, insight into the reality of mind.

Notes

Preface

1 See, with more specific indications of the respective context, Markus Gabriel, *Propos réalistes* (Paris: Librairie Philosophique J. Vrin, 2019). Regarding the state of discussion within New Realism between the ontology of fields of sense and Benoist's contextualism, see Jocelyn Benoist, *L'adresse du réel* (Paris: Librairie philosophique J. Vrin, 2017) and Markus Gabriel, 'Être vrai', *Philosophiques*, 45/1 (2018): 239–47, as well as the special issue of *Critique: Revue générale des publications françaises et étrangères*, 72/862 (2019) devoted to Jocelyn Benoist containing my statement 'Concepts et objects dans les "nouveaux réalismes"', pp. 202–14.

2 A first step will be taken in Markus Gabriel, *The Reality of the Universe* (forthcoming).

3 A historical building in Tübingen used as a centre for philosophical studies since it was built in 1482 (Trans.).

Introduction

1 One might wonder whether it is even desirable that everything and anything be 'digitalized' and made the object of a futuristic artificial intelligence. Yet this question tends to be left aside with the dubious argument that 'digitalization' is a process not only of automating the socioeconomic means of producing surplus value, but one that automatically results from the inherent logic of global capitalist competition. According to this widespread techno-philosophical fatalism, whoever fails to participate energetically in digitalization (even though no one knows exactly what this means . . .) will simply be swept aside by the supposedly unstoppable onward march of 'progress'.

2 See Bruno Latour's pioneering reconstruction 'Why has critique run out of steam? From matters of fact to matters of concern', *Critical Inquiry*, 30/2 (2004): 225–48. Latour's proclaimed return to realism in this text (pp. 231f.) is stymied, however, by his continued adherence to the idea that 'matters of fact' are

constructed, while he supports an unconditional commitment to 'matters of concern'. His position thus boils down to a variant of the Rortyan conception that knowledge claims are ultimately claims on a community, not claims to truth. I therefore thoroughly disagree with the details of Latour's position, which still attempts to step beyond modernity and replace it with some kind of non-modernity, for he (very much in the style of the 'deconstruction' he attacks) doubts, on the one hand, that modernity ever really existed and, on the other hand, criticizes the recourse to said modernity after the failure of postmodernity. See Latour's ambivalent stance in *We Have Never Been Modern*, trans. Catherine Porter (Cambridge, MA: Harvard University Press, 2012).

3 As was influentially undertaken in Lorraine Daston and Peter Galison, *Objectivity* (New York: Zone Books, 2007).

4 This criticism also applies to Quentin Meillassoux's critique of correlationism in *After Finitude: An Essay on the Necessity of Contingency*, trans. Ray Brassier (London: Continuum, 2008). *Mutatis mutandis*, the projects of so-called speculative realism also fail due to their attempts to overcome the human standpoint with an epistemological and ontological *coup de force*. This move is supposed to spare them from having to prove the credentials of their mode of theorizing, so that they can go on a metaphysical poaching trip in the 'great outdoors' of a nature supposedly untouched by human hands. See Markus Gabriel, 'Tatsachen statt Fossilien – Neuer vs. Spekulativer Realismus', *Zeitschrift für Medien und Kulturforschung*, 7/2 (2016): 187–204, and Stephen Mulhall's critique of Harman in 'How complex is a lemon?', *London Review of Books*, 40/18 (2018): 27–30.

5 On this, see most recently Jacques Derrida, 'The university without condition', in *Without Alibi*, ed. and trans. Peggy Kamuf (Stanford, CA: Stanford University Press, 2002), pp. 202–37.

6 For this space, Wolfram Hogrebe has elaborated an anthropology and metaphysics of the surreal in a series of books. See Wolfram Hogrebe, *Der implizite Mensch* (Berlin: Akademie, 2013); *Philosophischer Surrealismus* (Berlin: Akademie, 2014); *Metaphysische Einflüsterungen* (Frankfurt: Klostermann, 2017); *Duplex: Strukturen der Intelligibilität* (Frankfurt: Klostermann, 2018); *Szenische Metaphysik* (Frankfurt: Klostermann, 2019).

7 On this, see Wolfram Hogrebe, 'Risky proximity to life', trans. Adam Knowles, *Graduate Faculty Philosophy Journal*, 31/2 (2010): 219–312.

8 For the derivation of this concept of fictions from an epistemological exercise, see Markus Gabriel, 'The art of skepticism and the skepticism of art', *Philosophy Today*, 53/1 (2009): 58f.

9 Stanley Cavell, *The World Viewed: Reflections on the Ontology of Film* (Cambridge, MA: Harvard University Press, 1979), p. 85.

10 See of course Jürgen Habermas, *The Structural Transformation of the Public Sphere: An Inquiry into a Category of Bourgeois Society*, trans. Thomas Burger (Cambridge: Polity, 1989). For a sociological perspective on the recent state of the debate, see Dirk Baecker, *4.0 oder Die Lücke die der Rechner lässt* (Leipzig: Merve, 2018), and Armin Nassehi, *Muster: Theorie der digitalen Gesellschaft* (Munich: C. H. Beck, 2019).

11 For an especially trenchant presentation, see Graham Priest, *Towards Non-Being: The Logic and Metaphysics of Intentionality* (Oxford: Oxford University Press, 2016). See also Francesco Berto, *Existence as a Real Property* (Dordrecht: Springer, 2013), and Priest's model Richard Routley, *Exploring Meinong's Jungle and Beyond* (Canberra: Australian National University, 1980).

12 Markus Gabriel, *Sinn und Existenz: Eine realistische Ontologie* (Berlin: Suhrkamp, 2016). On the problem area of Meinongianism, see especially pp. 212–20.

13 For a paradigmatic example of how to bring analytical clarity into this convoluted discussion, see Kwame Anthony Appiah, *The Lies That Bind: Rethinking Identity* (London: Profile Books, 2018).

14 See Markus Gabriel, *I Am Not a Brain: Philosophy of Mind for the Twenty-First Century*, trans. Christopher Turner (Cambridge: Polity 2017), as well as my elaboration and defence of the neo-existentialist paradigm in *Neo-Existentialism: How to Conceive of the Mind after Naturalism's Failure* (Cambridge: Polity, 2018). See also Georg W. Bertram, *Was ist der Mensch? Warum wir nach uns fragen* (Stuttgart: Reclam, 2018). In my view Bertram goes too far when, in an earlier work, he writes:

> Humans are not what they are simply by nature. We are not determined by our cultural traditions to come out a certain way. Rather, as humans, we always have to define what we are anew. What we become as humans is always the result of taking a stance, indeed, a stance on ourselves, and this 'taking a stance' has to be grasped as a practical occurrence. This means that the continual process of redefining what it means to be human involves a component of reflection that is essential to all of our practices. (*Art as Human Practice: An Aesthetics*, trans. Nathan Ross [London: Bloomsbury, 2019], p. 3)

Rather, I think that the human being is thoroughly determined in its self-determination: our capacity to generate self-images is our historically invariant essence, which we grasp in the reflexive practice of philosophy. In a certain sense, then, we are what we are (that is, human beings) by nature. Humans do not need to become humans first, but already are (because they are essentially) humans from the start. One does not become human; one is human.

15 Martin Heidegger, *Contributions to Philosophy (of the Event)*, trans. Richard Rojcewicz and Daniela Vallega-Neu (Bloomington: Indiana University Press, 2012), p. 315. See Wolfram Hogrebe, 'Riskante Lebensnähe', in Carl Friedrich Gethmann (ed.), *Lebenswelt und Wissenschaft: XXI. Deutscher Kongress für Philosophie 15.–19. September 2008 an der Universität Duisberg-Essen* (Hamburg: Felix Meiner, 2011), pp. 40–62, esp. pp. 52–5, and the detailed discussion in Jaroslaw Bledowski, *Zugang und Fraktur: Heideggers Subjektivitätstheorie in Sein und Zeit* (Tübingen: Mohr Siebeck, 2021).

16 See my earlier discussion in Markus Gabriel, 'The mythological being of reflection – an essay on Hegel, Schelling and the contingency of necessity', in Markus Gabriel and Slavoj Žižek, *Mythology, Madness and Laughter: Subjectivity in German Idealism* (London: Continuum, 2009), pp. 15–94.

17 Willard Van Orman Quine, *Word and Object* (new edn, Cambridge, MA: MIT Press, 2013), p. 275.

18 Markus Gabriel, 'Cosmological idealism', in Joshua R. Farris and Benedikt P. Göcke (eds), *The Routledge Handbook of Idealism and Immaterialism* (London: Routledge, 2022), and *The Reality of the Universe* (forthcoming). See also Thomas Nagel's fairly recent attempt to appropriate objective idealism in *Mind and Cosmos: Why the Materialist Neo-Darwinian Conception of Nature is Almost Certainly False* (Oxford: Oxford University Press, 2012). Unfortunately, Nagel remains captive to the fantasy of a view from nowhere that we must strive for but can never reach – a fantasy whose various paradoxes he elaborated in *The View from Nowhere* (Oxford: Oxford University Press, 1986). Compare the rejection of Nagel's conception of objectivity in Sebastian Rödl, *Self-Consciousness and Objectivity: An Introduction to Absolute Idealism* (Cambridge, MA: Harvard University Press, 2018).

19 One way out of this cul-de-sac is to recognize the irreducible existence of a human context. Doing so results, by means of the concept of top-down causation, in solutions to such puzzles as the measurement problem and the relation of mind and nature in the universe. See George Ellis, *How Can Physics Underlie the Mind: Top-Down Causation in the Human Context* (Berlin: Springer, 2016); Barbara Drossel and George Ellis, 'Contextual wavefunction collapse: an integrated theory of quantum measurement', *New Journal of Physics*, 20 (2018): 1–35; George Ellis and Markus Gabriel: 'Physical, logical, and mental top-down effects', in Markus Gabriel and Jan Voosholz (eds), *Top-Down Causation and Emergence* (Dordrecht: Springer, 2021).

20 In Sainsbury's cartography, the position adopted here apparently does not count as fictional realism, since he understands this as the 'controversial claim that reality (our reality) contains such things as Kilgore Trout and Sherlock Holmes. It argues for what I call robust fictional characters, by which I mean that it claims that fictional characters belong to our reality, and not just to some fictional world' (Richard Mark Sainsbury, *Fiction and Fictionalism* [Oxford: Oxford University Press, 2010], p. 32) As we shall see, this is not the case, especially as Sainsbury deploys a criterion of realism that understands 'reality' as participation in 'our world, the one and only real and actual world' (ibid.). This contradicts the no-world-view I shall be applying here. The alternative between (robust) fictional realism and fictional irrealism is thus incomplete.

21 As I argue at length in Gabriel, *Sinn und Existenz*. For further discussion and defence of the thesis, see Markus Gabriel, 'Neutraler Realismus', in Thomas Buchheim (ed.), *Jahrbuch-Kontroversen 2* (Freiburg: Karl Alber, 2016); Peter Gaitsch et al. (eds), *Eine Diskussion mit Markus Gabriel: Phänomenologische Positionen zum Neuen Realismus* (Vienna: Turia + Kant, 2017); Otávio Bueno and Jan Voosholz (eds), *Gabriel's New Realism* (Dordrecht: Springer, forthcoming).

22 In short, the relation of appearing-in-a-field-of-sense is not transitive in every case, for something can appear in sense field S^2 of a sense field S^1 without thereby appearing in S^1. See Markus Gabriel, *Why the World Does Not Exist*, trans. Gregory S. Moss (Cambridge: Polity, 2015), and Romain Leick, '"Eine Reise durch das Unendliche": SPIEGEL-Gespräch mit Markus Gabriel über

die Grenzen der naturwissenschaftlichen Erkenntnis und die Frage nach dem Sinn', *Der Spiegel*, 27 (2013): 122–4. To be sure, there are both transitive and intransitive cases. The field of sense of a neighbourhood in a city appears in a city, which is itself a field of sense. The objects of the neighbourhood are also objects of the city. One could list any number of transitive and intransitive cases. Incidentally, it follows from the no-world-view that there can be no complete axiomatization of FOS. Besides general, (meta-)mathematical and (meta-)logical incompleteness theorems, this follows from the fact that the domain of empirical truths cannot be restricted a priori such that there would be an evident reason to expect no further, as yet unregistered, empirical truths. An ontology that does not take this fact into account – that is, a 'purely formal' ontology – is nonsense. On this matter, following on from a reflection by Husserl, see Gabriel, *Sinn und Existenz*, pp. 172–4; 268–70; 297f.

23 For more details, see, besides *Sinn und Existenz*, in particular 'Der Neue Realismus zwischen Konstruktion und Wirklichkeit', in Ekkehard Felder and Andreas Gardt (eds), *Wirklichkeit oder Konstruktion? Sprachtheoretische und interdisziplinäre Aspekte einer brisanten Alternative* (Berlin: de Gruyter, 2018), pp. 45–65.

24 On this particular issue, see Markus Gabriel and Graham Priest, *Everything and Nothing* (Cambridge: Polity, 2022).

25 Mereological structures are not restricted to material-energetic systems ('bodies'). Thoughts can have parts just as much as sets, cities, mental states, and so on. Precisely which mereological axioms need to be taken into account for which system of elements is not something that can be decided a priori, which is why I do not see mereology as a form of metaphysics – here understood as a form of knowledge that is formal-logical on the one hand but on the other hand grants substantial insights into empirical reality. See Gabriel, *Why the World Does Not Exist*.

26 On this point, see the impressive, though unjustly neglected study by Josef Simon, *Wahrheit als Freiheit: Zur Entwicklung der Wahrheitsfrage in der neueren Philosophie* (Berlin: de Gruyter, 1978), and more recently Jens Rometsch, *Freiheit zur Wahrheit: Grundlagen der Erkenntnis am Beispiel von Descartes und Locke* (Frankfurt: Klostermann, 2018). See also my 'Dissens und Gegenstand: Vom Außenwelt- zum Weltproblem', in Markus Gabriel (ed.), *Skeptizismus und Metaphysik* (Berlin: Akademie, 2011), pp. 73–92. For a critique of mainstream versions of the recognition model, see Jens Rometsch, 'Why there is no "recognition theory" in Hegel's "struggle of recognition": towards an epistemological reading of the Lord-Servant-relationship', in Markus Gabriel and Anders Moe Rasmussen (eds), *German Idealism Today* (Berlin: de Gruyter, 2017), pp. 159–85, and Markus Gabriel, 'A very heterodox reading of the lord-servant-allegory in Hegel's Phenomenology of Spirit', in Gabriel and Rasmussen, *German Idealism Today*, pp. 95–120.

27 For a defence of the concept of knowledge in the context of debates on the architecture of perceptual knowledge, see Andrea Kern, *Sources of Knowledge: On the Concept of a Rational Capacity for Knowledge*, trans. Daniel Smyth (Cambridge, MA: Harvard University Press, 2017), and my review 'Die Wiederkehr des Nichtwissens: Perspektiven der zeitgenössischen Skeptizismus-Debatte',

Philosophische Rundschau, 54/1 (2007): 149–78, as well as my more extensive engagement with Kern in *The Limits of Epistemology,* trans. Alex Englander (Cambridge: Polity, 2020).

28 On this, see Josef Simon's late work *Kant: Die fremde Vernunft und die Sprache der Philosophie* (Berlin: de Gruyter, 2003).

29 A similar approach can be found in so-called critical realism, which receives an especially clear articulation in Dave Elder-Vass, *The Reality of Social Construction* (Cambridge: Cambridge University Press, 2012), and *The Causal Powers of Social Structures: Emergence, Structure and Agency* (Cambridge: Cambridge University Press, 2010). See also the recent attempt to argue for an equally realist 'general ontological turn' (p. xii) in the social sciences in Tony Lawson, *The Nature of Social Reality: Issues in Social Ontology* (Abingdon: Routledge, 2019).

30 Pierre Bourdieu, *Pascalian Meditations,* trans. Richard Nice (Cambridge: Polity, 2000), p. 108.

31 As famously asserted by Jacques Rancière in *Disagreement: Politics and Philosophy* (Minneapolis: University of Minnesota Press, 1999). I follow Rancière to the extent that he makes disagreement integral to politics, but I do not share the notion of an opposition between the idea of justice and the presence of police. The idea that the existence of institutions as such is already an unjust solution of a paradox betrays, in my view, a badly constructed social ontology.

32 Displaying the irony seemingly inherent in the genre, Gregor Dotzauer, in his review of *Why the World Does Not Exist,* labels new realism a position of the 'radical centre' (Gregor Dotzauer, 'Radikale Mitte. Der Philosoph Markus Gabriel erklärt, warum es die Welt nicht gibt', *Die Zeit,* 34 (2013): 48). This is, however, an accurate characterization of the critical social ontology developed here. It is necessary to shift the mode of critique to the centre of society and thus avoid the invariably false solidarity with the disadvantaged that creates an impression of still somehow being on the side of Marx while belonging to the class of academically trained theorists. We ought not to forget that Marx had good reasons to style himself as an anti-philosopher who (being solidly middle-class) banked on others changing the world. Social-ontological realism is not any kind of justification of an unjust status quo but a critical position that is under no illusion about itself and does not deny its real implication in social systems. That the theorizing of social ontology emerges under historically specific conditions of production does not entail that there are no social facts, of which some are objectively unjust and thus ought to be changed.

33 See my interview from May 2019 with Ana Carbajosa, 'Silicon Valley y las redes sociales son unos grandes criminales', *El País,* 15266 (2019), pp. 35f.

34 Martin Heidegger, *Bremen and Freiburg Lectures: Insight into That Which is and Basic Principles of Thinking,* trans. Andrew J. Mitchell (Bloomington: Indiana University Press, 2012), p. 36 (translation modified).

35 Despite an unmistakably nostalgic tone, Rüdiger Bubner captures the present situation in *Ästhetische Erfahrung* (Frankfurt: Suhrkamp, 1989), p. 150: 'In the media age, the tendency to transform all content into images before a large audience and to recruit the audience itself as a co-actor is triumphant. Social action becomes staged action, subjects stylize their wishes and interests

into poses. Reality renounces its ontological dignity in favour of universally applauded semblance.'

36 This ideological architecture can be altered. Its modification should follow the objective of realizing a humanistically enlightened digital infrastructure for constitutional democracies. A genuine ethics of digitalization insists upon this point. See Markus Gabriel, *The Meaning of Thought*, trans. Alex Englander (Cambridge: Polity, 2020), as well as Julian Nida-Rümelin and Nathalie Weidenfeld, *Digitaler Humanismus: Eine Ethik für das Zeitalter der Künstlichen Intelligenz* (Munich: Piper, 2018), which has similar premises and results.

37 This is the subject of Cornelius Castoriadis's magnum opus *The Imaginary Institution of Society*, trans. Kathleen Blamey (Cambridge, MA: MIT Press, 1997). See also Jens Beckert, *Imagined Futures: Fictional Expectations and Capitalist Dynamics* (Cambridge, MA: Harvard University Press, 2016).

Part I Fictional Realism

1 See, for example, the suggestion in Tilmann Köppe and Tom Kindt, *Erzähltheorie: Eine Einführung* (Stuttgart: Reclam, 2014), p. 81. In a certain sense, I agree with the thesis that 'fictive entities have no existence independent of texts and the rule-governed representational activities of persons.' This thesis needs to be substantially modified, however: for one thing, it is clearly false in *Faust* that Gretchen, for example, is dependent on texts or representational activities. Sainsbury's definition in *Fiction and Fictionalism*, by contrast, is hopelessly circular: 'a work is fictional if and only if it results from some interconnected utterances, a reasonable number of which count as "fictive", that is, produced with distinctively fictive intentions' (p. 7). This sequence of words does not even serve as a meaningful clarification and entangles Sainsbury in absurd assumptions, since he thus cannot even treat myths, for example, as fictions.

2 Michel Houellebecq, *The Map and the Territory*, trans. Gavin Bowd (London: Vintage, 2012).

3 A fictional depiction that portrayed only facts obtaining independently of the fiction would thus no longer be a case of fiction, but rather – what else? – a very well-made factual report. Fictions, therefore, cannot be composed of true statements that refer purely to non-fictive objects.

4 Regarding this point, Daniel Kehlmann has asked how we should think of the genre of travel guides, which seem to make partially literary claims and so touch on the ontology of art. I would classify texts of this kind as ontological hybrids. In such cases, some objects are in fact fictive while others are non-fictive. The totality of such texts is thus not fictional, even if they contain intentionally fictional sections.

5 It should be noted that there can be no access to meta-hermeneutical objects unless the person researching them has an eye on the hermeneutical objects that exist owing to a prior history of aesthetic experiences – experiences in which the scholarly interpreter must have a share. Access to meta-hermeneutical objects occurs via hermeneutical ones.

6 Bubner, *Ästhetische Erfahrung*, p. 151 (my translation, WH). See the similar line of thought in Martin Seel, *Ästhetik des Erscheinens* (Berlin: Suhrkamp, 2016), pp. 44f.

7 See Bubner's succinct formulation of this state of affairs in *Ästhetische Erfahrung*, p. 35: 'What aesthetic experience experiences is constituted in and through the experience, such that the content of each experience cannot be objectified independently of the experience itself.'

8 This space is historically open and can be brought to completion only when a work ceases to be interpreted. That is why works of art can never be interpreted completely; there is always a further possible interpretation. Yet this openness does not lead to any meta-hermeneutical arbitrariness. The plurality and historicity of interpretations are compatible with the objectivity of scholarly research into art works and the dimensions of aesthetic experience. For what is by now a classic discussion, see Umberto Eco, *The Open Work*, trans. Anna Cancogni (Cambridge, MA: Harvard University Press, 1989).

9 For an overview of the assumptions common to recent approaches, see Tilmann Köppe and Tobias Klauk (eds), *Fiktionalität: Ein interdisziplinäres Handbuch* (Berlin: de Gruyter, 2014). Some more nuanced discussions can be found in Dieter Henrich and Wolfgang Iser (eds), *Funktionen des Fiktiven* (Munich: Fink, 1986).

10 The fictional representations of art involve fictive objects. This does not mean, however, that there are unequivocal signs of fictionality, signals that one could take as necessary and collectively sufficient criteria and transpose into a definition we can apply to distinguish between reports expressing truth claims and mere tales without any possibility of referentiality.

11 In this sense, one might try partially to reconcile the approach developed here and the much discussed distinction between *encoding* and *exemplifying* attributed to Ernst Mally. For the technical details, see Edward N. Zalta, *Abstract Objects: An Introduction to Axiomatic Metaphysics* (Dordrecht: Reidel, 1983). The shortcoming of this approach is that it leaves the property-property untouched and merely modifies what it means to fall under a concept. Yet fictive objects do not have any of the properties familiar to us, nor do they encode them. The meontological isolationism to be developed in the following goes much further, by thinking of the fictive strictly and entirely as semblance, without committing the error of keeping semblance at a distance from being. Semblance has, one might say, a being in being.

12 Hans Blumenberg, *Theorie der Unbegrifflichkeit* (Frankfurt: Suhrkamp, 2007), p. 76 (my translation, WH).

13 See also the major attempt to connect the fictive with the imaginary via the idea that the former consists in 'opening up a space of play', in Wolfgang Iser, *The Fictive and the Imaginary: Charting Literary Anthropology*, trans. David Henry Wilson (Baltimore: Johns Hopkins University Press, 1993), p. xvii:

> By opening up spaces of play, the fictive compels the imaginary to take on a form at the same time that it acts as a medium for its manifestation. What the fictive targets is as yet empty and thus requires filling; and

what is characteristic of the imaginary is its featurelessness, which thus requires form for its unfolding. Consequently, play arises out of the coexistence of the fictive and the imaginary.

14 Paul Boghossian has pointed out to me that what is frequently referred to as 'interpretation' could actually be a third category of objectivity in the humanities. This third category consists in developing interpretations (that is, performances) that exhibit the technical expertise of analytical readings in outstanding fashion – that is, especially skilful ones. A new paradigmatic interpretation of a classic published by an expert, one that casts new light on said classic, would be such a case, since it showcases particularly sophisticated exercises of the imagination in objectified form. One especially accomplished work that embodies this third category fashion is Pierre Bourdieu, *Manet: A Symbolic Revolution*, trans. Margaret Rigaud-Drayton and Peter Collier (Cambridge: Polity, 2017).

15 On the concept of gaps, see the *locus classicus* Wolfgang Iser, *The Implied Reader: Patterns of Communication in Prose Fiction from Bunyan to Beckett*, trans. David Henry Wilson (Baltimore: John Hopkins University Press, 1974), and Wolfgang Iser, *The Act of Reading: A Theory of Aesthetic Response*, trans. David Henry Wilson (Baltimore: Johns Hopkins University Press, 1980).

16 Therein lies, as a side note, the specific objectivity of philology, whose virtue Nietzsche quite correctly saw in the practice of reading slowly. See Friedrich Nietzsche, *Daybreak: Thoughts on the Prejudices of Morality*, trans. R. J. Hollingdale (Cambridge: Cambridge University Press, 1997), p. 5:

> It is not for nothing that I have been a philologist, perhaps I am a philologist still, that is to say, a teacher of slow reading. . . . For philology is that venerable art which demands of its votaries one thing above all: to go aside, to take time, to become still, to become slow – it is a goldsmith's art and connoisseurship of the *word* which has nothing but delicate, cautious work to do and achieves nothing if it does not achieve it *lento*. But for precisely this very reason it is more necessary than ever today, by precisely this means does it entice and enchant us the most, in the midst of an age of 'work', that is to say, of hurry, of indecent and perspiring haste, which wants to 'get everything done' at once, including every old and new book. . . .

17 See the related concept of presentation [*Darstellung*] as the 'mode of being of the work of art' in Hans-Georg Gadamer, *Truth and Method*, trans. Joel Weinsheimer and Donald G. Marshall (London: Bloomsbury, 2013), p. 120. Here, Gadamer argues for the necessity of performance. I share the thesis he derives from this point, namely that 'the being of art cannot be defined as an object of an aesthetic consciousness because, on the contrary, the aesthetic attitude is more than it knows of itself. It is a part of the *event of being that occurs in presentation*, and belongs essentially to play as play' (ibid.).

18 On this, see Markus Gabriel, *The Power of Art* (Cambridge: Polity, 2020),

and the much discussed reflections on suddenness in Karl Heinz Bohrer, *Suddenness: On the Moment of Aesthetic Appearance*, trans. Ruth Crowley (New York: Columbia University Press, 1994).

19 The same can be said for Derrida's contributions to the topic of the 'urtext', which has recently been the object of a masterful reconstruction by Philip Freytag, *Die Rahmung des Hintergrunds: Untersuchungen über die Voraussetzungen von Sprachtheorien am Leitfaden der Debatten Derrida–Searle und Derrida–Habermas* (Frankfurt: Klostermann, 2019). Freytag shows that Derrida puts forward an extreme realist position, including in semantics and hermeneutics, which hardly resembles the caricature drawn by Habermas and Searle (whose critiques were in any case developed with only scant knowledge of Derrida's texts). Searle and Habermas mistake their miscomprehension of Derrida's texts for the incomprehensibility of the texts themselves, a procedure that may frequently serve polemical ends but hardly furthers understanding. If one does not understand a text, how can one criticize its author for their supposed errors?

20 I have given an extensive presentation of FOS in *Sinn und Existenz* and *Fields of Sense*. For a defence of the position against a series of objections, see the discussion in Buchheim (ed.), *Jahrbuchkontroversen 2*, in Gaitsch et al. (eds), *Eine Diskussion mit Markus Gabriel*, and in Bueno and Voosholz (eds), *Gabriel's New Realism*. My arguments in the present work presuppose the concepts of FOS, although I will, where necessary, provide brief elaborations of the key ideas which do not require any familiarity with my previous accounts of the theory.

21 Narrative formats that are classified as 'realism' do not, therefore, overcome the illusory character of art. Rather, they strengthen it by introducing ghosts – that is, uncanny revenants of our own reality. In this context, see Elisabeth Strowick, *Gespenster des Realismus: Zur literarischen Wahrnehmung von Wirklichkeit* (Paderborn: Fink, 2019).

22 Saul A. Kripke, *Naming and Necessity* (Cambridge, MA: Harvard University Press, 1980), pp. 44–53.

23 A paradigmatic discussion can be found in Kit Fine, 'The question of ontology', in David Chalmers et al. (eds), *Metametaphysics: New Essays on the Foundations of Ontology* (Oxford: Oxford University Press, 2009), pp. 157–78; see also Tuomas E. Tahko (ed.), *Contemporary Aristotelian Metaphysics* (Cambridge: Cambridge University Press, 2012).

24 See the astute and intense reckoning with metaphysical realism in Shamik Dasgupta, 'Realism and the absence of value', *Philosophical Review*, 127/3 (2018): 279–322. Since Dasgupta ends up advocating the opposite extreme of the debate, however, namely an irrealism à la Goodman, he overshoots his critical target with dogmatism, for the choice between a metaphysical realism on the one hand, which produces a reductionist catalogue of the inventory of the world, and an arbitrary concoction of predicates for propositional data processing on the other, is far from reflecting a complete meta-metaphysical disjunction. Compare the subtler approach, in the tradition of Wittgenstein and Putnam, in Jocelyn Benoist, 'Realismus ohne Metaphysik', in Markus Gabriel (ed.), *Der Neue Realismus* (Berlin: Suhrkamp, 2016), pp. 133–53. For an equally

insightful description of the logical form of a middle position – neither meta-physically realist nor irrealist – see, as more recent *loci classici*, Hilary Putnam's works *Realism with a Human Face* (Cambridge, MA: Harvard University Press, 1992), *Renewing Philosophy* (Cambridge, MA: Harvard University Press, 1995), *The Threefold Cord: Mind, Body and World* (New York: Columbia University Press, 1999) and *Ethics without Ontology* (Cambridge, MA: Harvard University Press, 2009). Concerning my own position in relation to Benoist and his use of a Wittgensteinian point of departure, see Gabriel, *Propos réalistes*. For a recent reconstruction of Putnam's model-theoretic argument against metaphysical realism, see Tim Button, *The Limits of Realism* (Oxford: Oxford University Press, 2013).

25 Dennis Lehmkul has alerted me to cases in the history of science in which the reverse took place: an object assumed to be fictive (such as quarks) actually turned out to exist.

26 This is paradigmatically explained in the form of a much discussed error theory in John L. Mackie, *Ethics: Inventing Right and Wrong* (London: Penguin, 1990).

27 For an extensive presentation of the argument, see Gabriel, *Sinn und Existenz*, §6. An introductory account can be found in *Why the World Does Not Exist*. For a concise presentation of the thrust of the argument, which reduces it to a variant of Russell's antinomy, see Hans Jürgen Pirner, *Virtuelle und mögliche Welten in Physik und Philosophie* (Berlin: Springer, 2018), pp. 305–9. Pirner sees the resultant ontological pluralism as grist to the mill of the many-worlds interpretation of quantum mechanics, though this does not follow without to my mind debatable supplementary assumptions.

28 See, for example, Luther's infamous sermon on Exodus 22:17 ('You shall not permit a female sorcerer to live'), which he gave between 11 March and 6 May 1526. Quoted in *Luther on Women: A Sourcebook*, ed. Susan C. Karant-Nunn and Merry E. Wiesner-Hanks (Cambridge: Cambridge University Press, 2003), p. 231.

29 It follows from meontological isolationism that Jesus only performed miracles *in the Bible* that he did not perform *in Bethany* if Jesus is not identical to Jesus; more precisely, if Jesus *in the Bible* differs from the historical Jesus who resided in the Near East.

30 See the famous passage in Gilbert Ryle, *The Concept of Mind* (London: Routledge, 2000), p. 24:

> It is perfectly proper to say, in one logical tone of voice, that there exist minds and to say, in another logical tone of voice, that there exist bodies. But these expressions do not indicate two different species of existence, for 'existence' is not a generic word like 'coloured' or 'sexed'. They indi-cate two different senses of 'exist', somewhat as 'rising' has different senses in 'the tide is rising', 'hopes are rising', and 'the average age of death is rising'. A man would be thought to be making a poor joke who said that three things are now rising, namely the tide, hopes and the average age of death. It would be just as good or bad a joke to say that

there exist prime numbers and Wednesdays and public opinions and navies; or that there exist both minds and bodies.

31 This might seem to be grist to the mill of Quentin Meillassoux's speculative realism. However, his argumentation rests on an assumption that is actually refuted by his own theory, namely that the concept of possible worlds is ultimately coherent.

32 Berlin Brandenburg Airport opened on 31 October 2020 (Trans.).

33 Ultimately, the metaphysical vocabulary of possible worlds is impermissible, since there is not even a single possible world if *the* (actual) world does not exist. The modal apparatus of FOS therefore consistently avoids the assumption that *possibilia* are variations on the actual and, instead, understands the possible in terms of the concept of sense – that is, as compatibility with the framework conditions of a given field of sense. The given structures of the reality of a field of sense demarcate a space that dictates the measure of possibility. See Gabriel, *Sinn und Existenz*, §§9f., and 'Was ist (die) Wirklichkeit?', in Markus Gabriel and Malte Dominik Krüger (eds), *Was ist Wirklichkeit? Neuer Realismus und Hermeneutische Theologie* (Tübingen: Mohr Siebeck, 2018), pp. 63–118.

34 Julia Mehlich, 'Kopernikanischer Salto: Über den neuen neutralen Realismus (Gedanken zum Vortrag von Markus Gabriel)', in Markus Gabriel, Метафизика или онтология? Нейтральный реализм [Metaphysics or ontology? Neutral realism] (Moscow: Lomonosov Moscow State University, 2017), pp. 116–17. See Anton Friedrich Koch, *Hermeneutischer Realismus* (Tübingen: Mohr Siebeck, 2016).

35 This fictionalism is certainly distinct from the semantic positions that currently go by this name, even if there are some conceptual commonalities. In recent debates, which many authors see as having begun in the 1980s with the publication of Hartry Field's *Science without Numbers: A Defence of Nominalism* (Oxford: Oxford University Press, 2016), fictionalism is commonly seen as a discourse theory that assumes of a given object domain (numbers, possible worlds, moral values, natural scientific facts, etc.) that statements about the domain (1) are to be taken literally, while it is (2) generally recognized that they are, taken literally, false, which (3) nevertheless has a pragmatic function, meaning there is no reason to abandon the discourse. There is then an additional assumption (4) that the construction of the discourse takes narrative patterns into account. For an overview of the theoretical landscape, see Frederick Kroon et al. (eds), *A Critical Introduction to Fictionalism* (London: Bloomsbury, 2019). See also Mark Eli Kalderon (ed.), *Fictionalism in Metaphysics* (Oxford: Oxford University Press, 2005). Regarding the topic of fictional objects and possible worlds, see also Sainsbury, *Fiction and Fictionalism*. An introductory work that explicitly engages with Vaihinger is Kwame Anthony Appiah, *As If: Idealization and Ideals* (Cambridge, MA: Harvard University Press, 2017).

36 On the prospects of handling antinomies of totality dialetheistically, see Graham Priest, *Beyond the Limits of Thought* (Oxford: Oxford University Press, 2002).

37 Gabriel and Priest, *Everything and Nothing*. I am grateful to Graham Priest for

extensive discussions during his visiting professorship at the International Centre for Philosophy NRW in June 2019, which referred to his lecture for the Ernst Robert Curtius Lecture series on 9 November 2017.

38 An overview and defence of mereological orthodoxy can be found in Giorgio Lando, *Mereology: A Philosophical Introduction* (London: Bloomsbury, 2018).

39 For Priest and other neo-Meinongians, the situation is actually more complicated, because they banish existing fictive objects to possible worlds in which they possess the existence property (of being causally embedded). This raises the difficulty of how we individuate the supposedly actual world in which we find ourselves – hence we will never bump into Sherlock Holmes in London. On this problem, see Gabriel, 'Was ist (die) Wirklichkeit?'.

40 For a discussion of whether neo-Meinongianism does entail logical explosion after all, see Otávio Bueno and Edward N. Zalta, 'Object theory and modal Meinongianism', *Australasian Journal of Philosophy*, 95/4 (2017): 761–78. See also the pioneering essays in Graham Priest et al. (eds), *The Law of Non-Contradiction: New Philosophical Essays* (Oxford: Oxford University Press, 2004).

§1 Interpretation and Reading

1 A paradigmatic elaboration of this position can be found in Anthony Everett, *The Nonexistent* (Oxford: Oxford University Press, 2013). Everett takes his bearings from Kendall Walton's influential make-believe theory, which is defended at length in Kendall Walton, *Mimesis as Make-Believe: On the Foundation of the Representational Arts* (Cambridge, MA: Harvard University Press, 1990).

2 See especially Peter van Inwagen, 'Fiction and metaphysics', *Philosophy and Literature*, 7/1 (1983): 67–77, 'Creatures of fiction', *American Philosophical Quarterly*, 14/4 (1977): 331–7, and 'Existence, ontological commitment, and fictional entities', in *Existence: Essays in Ontology* (Cambridge: Cambridge University Press, 2014), pp. 87–115; Amie L. Thomasson, *Fiction and Metaphysics* (Cambridge: Cambridge University Press, 1999), and *Ontology Made Easy* (Oxford: Oxford University Press, 2015).

3 John R. Searle, 'The logical status of fictional discourse', *New Literary History*, 6/2 (1975): 319–32.

4 For interesting suggestions on how to combine Walton's position with narratological and psychological theory so as to merge pretence theory with a theory of imagination, see Everett, *The Nonexistent*, pp. 6–37, and Derek Matravers, *Fiction and Narrative* (Oxford: Oxford University Press, 2014), pp. 7–21.

5 Jody Azzouni, *Talking about Nothing: Numbers, Hallucinations and Fiction* (Oxford: Oxford University Press, 2010), pp. 110–50.

6 See Jody Azzouni, *Tracking Reason: Proof, Consequence and Truth* (Oxford: Oxford University Press, 2006), pp. 9–116.

7 On this problem, see Antony Everett, 'Against fictional realism', *Journal of Philosophy*, 102/12 (2005): 624–49; for an opposing position, see Benjamin Schnieder and Tatjana von Solodkoff, 'In defense of fictional realism', *Philosophical Quarterly*, 59 (2009): 138–49. For a defence of Everett's arguments

against Schnieder and von Solodkoff, see Ben Caplan and Cathleen Muller, 'Against a defense of fictional realism', *Philosophical Quarterly*, 64 (2014): 211–24.

8 Generally, one can speak of an *embedding* of sense field when the objects of a sense field S^1 appear in another field S^2 only if they appear within their field in the other field.

9 Gabriel, *Why the World Does Not Exist*, p. 88.

10 On the concept of sense as an ordering function, see Gabriel 'Der Neue Realismus zwischen Konstruktion und Wirklichkeit'.

11 FOS's relation to the landscape of theories of causality – and especially to the question of whether the universe as the object domain of natural science is causally privileged – remains unresolved. I therefore withhold judgement here on the problem of how exactly the universe is embedded in its field environment and which kinds of non-physical objects causally interfere with it, directly or indirectly. On the discussion relating to this, see Gabriel and Voosholz (eds), *Top-Down Causation and Emergence*, especially the essay Ellis and Gabriel, 'Physical, logical, and mental top-down effects'. However, I proceed from the assumption that, under event conditions – that is, where temporal processes are at issue – causality can be reduced to the principle of sufficient reason; that is, it can be determined in terms of the necessary conditions of the occurrence of a given event being collectively sufficient. This is compatible with the existence of indeterministic systems whose probabilistic nature is ontic and not merely epistemic (which is, among other things, a consequence of quantum mechanics). The principle of sufficient reason does not assert that all objects are predictable for an ideal observer, but only that, for any given event, necessary conditions of its occurrence can be given (retrospectively) that are jointly sufficient. Concerning the principle in the context of the discussion on free will, see Gabriel, *I Am Not a Brain*, pp. 178–220.

12 See Andreas Kablitz, *Kunst des Möglichen: Theorie der Literatur* (Freiburg: Rombach, 2013), pp. 149–219. Moreover, it is a universally recognized finding of narratology that literary texts presuppose 'that the reader applies their knowledge of the world in the act of reading. The encyclopaedia of the actual world is thus imported into the fictional world' (Fotis Jannidis, *Figur und Person: Beitrag zu einer historischen Narratologie* [Berlin: de Gruyter, 2004], p. 176). To be sure, FOS would formulate this point rather differently, namely in terms of the assumption that we exploit background knowledge of what is the case in our field of sense in order to have an aesthetic experience occasioned by a work and to perform the figures presented in it.

13 To borrow Heidegger's vocabulary, the aesthetic world would become incomprehensible earth. Heidegger saw the work of art in terms of a 'fight between world and earth'. See Martin Heidegger, 'The origin of the work of Art', in *Off the Beaten Track*, ed. and trans. Julian Young and Kenneth Haynes (Cambridge: Cambridge University Press, 2002), p. 27. On the concept of earth and its prehistory in Hegel and Husserl, see the reconstruction in Tobias Keiling, 'Of the Earth: Heidegger's philosophy and the art of Andy Goldsworthy', *Journal of Aesthetics and Phenomenology*, 4/2 (2017): 125–38.

14 An aesthetic judgement in its standard categorical form consists in ascribing properties to a fictive object. This process takes place not in an explicitly propositional, linguistically articulated code but in the medium of imagination in which fictive objects are performed. A paradigmatic manifestation of this process is the imaginative reading experience, which readers can describe by stating, for example, how they imagine a particular *dramatis persona*.

15 This means that not every narration or coherence formation deals with fictive objects. Factual reports can take the form of narrations and employ types of coherence formation that follow on stylistically from fictions containing fictive objects.

16 See Michael N. Forster, *Herder's Philosophy* (Oxford: Oxford University Press, 2018), as well as, proceeding from Schleiermacher, Manfred Frank's classic study *Das individuelle Allgemeine: Textstrukturierung und -interpretation nach Schleiermacher* (Frankfurt: Suhrkamp, 1985). All individuality exists within a universal framework shared by all recipients of a given art work. This framework is stamped by practices of presentation and aesthetic experience. This means, incidentally, that it cannot be reduced to how human animals exhibit a certain image-processing system that can be neuroaesthetically decoded. Neuroaesthetics at best describes one part of the general reception framework of an art work, but never the art work itself.

17 On the concept of reception as the irradiation of the work into the recipient, see Gabriel, *The Power of Art*.

18 I here largely follow Kablitz, *Kunst des Möglichen*. In particular, I agree with his reading of the contract of fiction, which stipulates that what 'constitutes the peculiarity of fictional discourse is that it is relieved from the duty of making statements about factual states of affairs' (p. 154). 'Fictionality, the famous contract of fiction, releases the text from the otherwise obtaining rule that the content of its predications must depict true states of affairs' (ibid., p. 166). At the same time, I do not see how Kablitz means to reconcile this assumption with his 'one-world-semantics' (which I by no means share), according to which 'all fictional discourse always refers to the given world as we know it, as long as it does not subject it to any explicit alterations' (ibid., p. 175). It is precisely this assumption that I am challenging here.

19 On this, see Andreas Kablitz, *Der Zauberberg: Die Zergliederung der Welt* (Heidelberg: Winter, 2017).

20 This is the downfall of the type of pure reception aesthetics that decouples aesthetic experience from the work. In Bubner's case, such an aesthetics takes its orientation from the Kantian model, its πρῶτον ψεῦδος. Thus Bubner states: 'What aesthetic experience experiences constitutes itself in experience and through experience, such that the content of this experience cannot be independently objectified, in a work, for example' (*Ästhetische Erfahrung*, p. 35). This is the basic tenor of the Constance School of reception aesthetics, which Bubner regards as paradigmatic, especially Hans Robert Jauss, *Ästhetische Erfahrung und literarische Hermeneutik* (Frankfurt: Suhrkamp, 1982). Here, Bubner falls victim to the very 'aestheticization of the lifeworld' that he himself diagnoses.

He develops his theory as if any given object could be the trigger of an aesthetic experience.

21 The year stated changes with each individual series; all are variations on the theme of the original film. This naturally has consequences at the intertextual level, which also brings various genres – film and television series – into conversation. It would lead us too far afield from our ontological concerns to analyse these details here.

22 The German word for 'true', *wahr*, is related (like *verum*) to ὁρᾶν, 'with direct sight'. The true is the public, the obvious.

23 On the connection between manticism and hermeneutics, see Wolfram Hogrebe, *Metaphysik und Mantik: Die Deutungsnatur des Menschen (Système orphique de Ièna)* (Frankfurt: Suhrkamp, 1992). I have elsewhere interpreted the materiality of Hitchcock's birds from this perspective. As is well known, only some of the birds in the film of the same name are genuine birds that Hitchcock filmed. At the material level of the film, he merges multiple layers of meaning that have to be combined and reworked into a unified depiction in the imagination. See 'The bird's eye view: ornithology and ontology in Hitchcock's *The Birds*', in Christine Reeh-Peters et al. (eds), *The Real of Reality: The Realist Turn in Contemporary Film Theory* (Leiden: Brill, 2021), pp. 181–94.

24 I do not share Bassler's assessment that Kehlmann belongs in the category of popular realism, which Bassler presents and ultimately denigrates in 'Populärer Realismus', in Roger Lüdeke (ed.), *Kommunikation im Populären: Interdisziplinäre Perspektiven auf ein ganzheitliches Phänomen* (Bielefeld: transcript, 2011), pp. 91–103.

25 Daniel Kehlmann, *F: A Novel*, trans. Carol Brown Janeway (New York: Vintage, 2014), p. 3.

26 Ibid. Bernard Géniès rightly emphasizes that New Realism's conception of autonomy draws paradigmatically on *mise en abyme* as the logical form of fictional reference. Bernard Géniès, 'Préface', in Gabriel, *Le pouvoir de l'art*, pp. 7–11 (there is no preface in the English edition).

27 Kehlmann, *F*, p. 56.

28 Ibid.

29 Ibid., p. 57.

30 Ibid.

31 Ibid., p. 58.

32 Fernando Pessoa, *The Book of Disquiet: The Complete Edition*, ed. Jerónimo Pizarro, trans. Margaret Jull Costa (New York: New Directions, 2017). This passage does not appear in the English edition (Trans.).

33 That linguistic meaning always ultimately rests upon an inextinguishable vagueness and thus cannot be overcome by a misplaced ideal of thoroughgoing determinacy is perceptively shown by Stephen Schiffer, *The Things We Mean* (Oxford: Oxford University Pres, 2003).

34 See van Inwagen, 'Creatures of fiction'.

35 On this concept of reception aesthetics, see Thomas Szlezák, *Platon und die Schriftlichkeit der Philosophie* (Berlin: de Gruyter, 1985). Szlezák overlooks how the Platonic dialogues contain fictional elements, meaning they cannot simply

be reconstructed on the model of an incomplete and fragmentary presentation of a non-fictional unwritten doctrine – if only because many of the featured characters did not exist outside the text or, even when they did, they did not advocate the positions ascribed to them within the text, where they instead play specific allegorical roles. Szlezák thus ignores the fictionality of the Platonic dialogues and overlooks how ontological problems of self-reference arise when Plato has his characters give voice to a critique of art, thus indicating that the texts should be understood as neither direct nor indirect references to an independently pre-existent truth.

36 See the *locus classicus* Gadamer, *Truth and Method*, pp. 311–17. Here Gadamer expressly rejects a conception of a culture as a closed horizon from which one might disclose a past. Such a conception of a cultural environment [*Kulturkreis*] is incompatible with the concept of the hermeneutical situation.

> Just as the individual is never simply an individual because he is always in understanding with others, so too the closed horizon that is supposed to enclose a culture is an abstraction. The historical movement of human life consists in the fact that it is never absolutely bound to any one standpoint, and hence can never have a truly closed horizon. The horizon is, rather, something into which we move and that moves with us. Horizons change for a person who is moving. (Ibid., p. 315)

Incidentally, Thomas Szlezák also misses this point in his *Was Europa den Griechen verdankt: Von den Grundlagen unserer Kultur in der griechischen Antike* (Tübingen: Mohr Siebeck, 2010). Szlezák uncritically trades in such stereotypes as 'the Greeks' and 'Europe'.

37 Faust and Gretchen are thus historical objects – that is, objects that essentially appear in histories whose coherence emerges at the level of the imagination. As a side note, the error of the narrative theory of personal identity consists in transferring this property of hermeneutical objects onto our subjectivity. For while we do tell stories about ourselves, we are not identical with these, as I will explain in Part II.

38 See the misguided anti-realist reading of Gadamer in Hans Joachim Krämer, *Kritik der Hermeneutik: Interpretationsphilosophie und Realismus* (Munich: Beck, 2007). I share Krämer's critique of anti-realism, but not his interpretation of Gadamer. Gadamer's theory of truth is not, in my view, anti-realist, but contextualist, because he rightly points out how the meaning of an expression (and thus its truth value) is explicable only within the historically variable and ultimately incalculable contexts of use in which it features. See Hans-Georg Gadamer, 'What is truth?', trans. Brice R. Wachterhauser, in Wachterhauser (ed.), *Hermeneutics and Truth* (Evanston, IL: Northwestern University Press, 1994), pp. 33–46. Moreover, it should be beyond doubt that Gadamer is a hermeneutical realist, in the sense that a central thesis of *Truth and Method* is that art is 'knowledge' – that is, 'conveying truth' (*Truth and Method*, p. 88). See the discussion and refutation of hermeneutical nihilism and subjectivism, ibid., pp. 86–8).

39 See, once again, Eco, *The Open Work,* and also *The Limits of Interpretation* (Bloomington: Indiana University Press, 1994).

40 Contrary to the widespread myth that Gadamer denied authorial intention, one need only consider *Truth and Method,* pp. 425f., where he defends Kant's intentions against misinterpretations, pp. 14 and 59f. or a passage such as the following: 'Even if we exclude the initially great influence of English empiricism and the epistemology of the natural sciences as being a distortion of his real intentions, it is still not so easy to understand what these intentions were. Georg Misch has taken an important step in this direction' (p. 222, translation modified). The expression *intentio auctoris* appears only once in *Truth and Method,* within a citation from Chladenius. Thus the claim that Gadamer denied authorial intention is untrue; rather, he continually makes use of it in order to distinguish one reading of a text from another.

41 See the defence of Gadamer's position against widespread accusations of relativism, in David Weberman, 'A new defense of Gadamer's hermeneutics', *Philosophy and Phenomenological Research,* 60/1 (2000): 45–56.

42 This happens frequently during the production phase, since artists do not immediately publish the first version of an intended work. Rather, on the basis of aesthetic experience occasioned by a material of their own making, they decide which work they wish to make available as an occasion for others to undergo an aesthetic experience. Prior to making a work public, the artist evaluates fragments of a material architecture *in statu nascendi* with recourse to the aesthetic experiences triggered within themselves. To be sure, this does not make them any kind of theoretical expert about the work (an epistemic *authority*), only its *author*.

43 See Immanuel Kant, *Critique of Pure Reason,* ed. and trans. Paul Guyer and Allen W. Wood (Cambridge: Cambridge University Press, 1998), pp. 328f. (B278f.). For the thought that we might thereby draw on this general concept of a limit to the imagination in order to found an aesthetic realism, I am indebted to conversations with Wolfram Hogrebe. See also Kant, *Critique of Pure Reason,* p. 659 (A770/B798): 'If the imagination is not simply to enthuse but is, under the strict oversight of reason, to invent, something must always first be fully certain and not invented, or a mere opinion, and that is the possibility of the object itself.'

44 See Gabriel, 'Was ist (die) Wirklichkeit?'. This is a partial course correction from Gabriel, *Sinn und Existenz,* §§ 9–10.

45 Things are different in the context of discussions of 'hallucination', although we should reject the philosophical concept of a hallucination as a representation (content) without an existing object. Actually occurring hallucinations do have an object that causally triggers them.

§2 There Are No Fictional Objects

1 See the excellent overview provided by Frank Zipfel, *Fiktion, Fiktivität, Fiktionalität: Analysen zur Fiktion in der Literatur und zum Fiktionsbegriff in der Literaturwissenschaft* (Berlin: Erich Schmidt, 2001).

2 For an alternative view, see the Frege-inspired strategy of 'deontologization' pursued in Gottfried Gabriel, *Fiktion und Wahrheit: Eine semantische Theorie der Literatur* (Stuttgart-Bad Cannstatt: frommann-holzboog, 1975), p. 10. Gabriel's semantic thesis that fictional discourse lacks the necessary properties to render it referential aims at 'the elimination of discourse about fictional objects' (p. 38). His approach, however, falls at the first hurdle because of its own conditions of expression, as it treats the non-fictional expression 'Pegasus exists' as a statement about the use of 'Pegasus', not as one about Pegasus. Gabriel, therefore, has to analyse away the expression 'Pegasus does not exist' in order to replace it with a statement taking the form '"Pegasus" cannot be rendered referential'. This leads not only to insurmountable semantic-ontological difficulties (since, for one thing, this whole approach leaves the general problem of non-existence untouched) but also to the absurd consequence that the 'reader's experience' of a literary text – what I am here calling a 'performance' or 'interpretation' – is a 'phenomenon of illusion' that Gabriel does not even regard as 'a necessary condition for the successful reading of a novel' (p. 81). How one might understand a literary text, a theatrical performance or a film (to name but a few examples) without imagining anything (for example, that one is witnessing the adventures of Indiana Jones) remains a mystery to me. One cannot do away with hermeneutics, and thus the ontology of art works, through semantic decrees that may well lead to deontologization, but at the price of denying the very phenomena in question. Far from being a successful theory, it is a case of exaggerated ontological elimination. See the contrasting view in Iser, *The Act of Reading*, ch. 3, in which Iser develops a 'phenomenology of reading'.

3 See Kripke, *Naming and Necessity*, pp. 44ff.

4 See Walton, *Mimesis as Make-Believe*. Walton states that participants in the game of fiction can appear in the object domain of fiction together with their actions, which he describes as 'reflexive props' (pp. 210–13). In particular, he recognizes that the position of the interpreter is due to an activity of the imagination whereby the reader imagines themselves witnessing a documentation of events that do not exist in the reader's own non-fictive sense field. In this way, the reader as a reflexive prop is a participant (see pp. 213–20). However, Walton overlooks the fact that this position was already developed in much greater depth in Gadamer's ontology of the art work as play. See Gadamer, *Truth and Method*, pp. 106–67, esp. pp. 119–22.

5 A significant exception is a once-only enactment of an art work by the artist themselves that they never report. These occur fairly frequently, as artists often reject sketches, melodies, and so forth. The production of a score succeeds only because artists have aesthetic experiences in the process that serve as experiments for possible publication. Publication generates the hermeneutical plurality that the artist can suppress *in statu nascendi*. Such is the peculiar status of the producer of a score, which makes them not simply the spectator of an anonymous production, a mere medium, but, in the best case, an artistic genius, the producer of endlessly reinterpretable works. Once produced, works bearing the character of genius are there to stay. For an ontological interpretation of the concept of genius, see Philipp Hesseler, *Grundlose Gestaltung:*

Kunstphilosophische Überlegungen zu Schelling und Mondrian (Paderborn: Brill, 2017).

6 Once again, see Kablitz's concept of coherence formation in *Kunst des Möglichen*.

7 At this point we encounter ontological and causal feedback effects. How one imagines Paris in the course of reading a novel has a bearing on how Paris is (among other things). Highly aestheticized environments such as Paris or Venice are continually reshaped by people who, having had aesthetic experiences in these environments (such as Paris in Proust's *In Search of Lost Time* or Venice in Mann's *Death in Venice*), intervene in the fields of sense from which Paris is constituted. This circumstance does not overturn the ontological isolation of art, as it can be modelled as a causality between fields of sense without any need for the isolated objects to interact causally.

8 This is demonstrated paradigmatically by Pierre Bourdieu in *Distinction: A Social Critique of the Judgement of Taste*, trans. Richard Nice (Cambridge, MA: Harvard University Press, 1984), and *The Rules of Art: Genesis and Structure of the Literary Field*, trans. Susan Emanuel (Stanford, CA: Stanford University Press, 1996).

9 See Hogrebe, *Der implizite Mensch* and *Philosophischer Surrealismus*.

10 See Gabriel, 'Was ist (die) Wirklichkeit?'.

11 This does not settle the matter of whether Faust and Gretchen are a couple in a different sense (for example, in another universe); this would take us into the semantic debate on descriptivism. If, in a different universe beyond the event horizon of our own, there were a constellation of facts that we found indistinguishable from those of an interpretation of Faust, the objects appearing there would nonetheless not be identical with Faust and Gretchen, since they would precisely not be similarly interpretation-dependent but, rather, interpretation-independently complete. I would therefore argue that Faust and Gretchen are essentially fictive, which implies, among other things, that they cannot exist in other universes without in turn being embedded in fictional fields of sense as isolated elements.

12 I thus concede to Jens Rometsch (based on a conversation) that a punctuation mark appearing in a copy of a novel can be used as a statement and, accordingly, be true in our field of sense. But this use of the punctuation mark is not an interpretation, so it makes the mistake of revoking the fictionality contract (which can make sense for other reasons). Thus, on the one hand, someone who finds ruins based on Homer's epics or chooses a restaurant in Paris based on Proust's *In Search of Lost Time* is making a mistake; on the other hand, it is justified by the fact that authors and recipients use non-fictional background knowledge to build up a fictional sense field, meaning that one clearly can distil non-fictional factual knowledge from an analytical reading of fictional material. Ontologically speaking, this is the same situation as determining the weight of a bronze statue in order to calculate its material value. So I still disagree with Rometsch in the respect that this does not mean literary texts contain true statements. Qua literature, this is precisely not the case for texts as works of art.

13 For a recent rebuttal of pan-fictionalism, see Françoise Lavocat, *Fait et fiction: pour une frontière* (Paris: Seuil, 2016).

14 See Zipfel, *Fiktion, Fiktivität, Fiktionalität*, pp. 229–47. Zipfel is right that it is 'doubtful whether, considering the wealth of possibility for literary-fictional narration, it is possible to draw up a complete list of fiction signals' (p. 233). Contrary to Gabriel's approach in *Fiktion und Wahrheit*, Zipfel rightly maintains that fiction is 'not only a way of dealing with texts', meaning that it cannot be described exhaustively 'as a processing mode for literary texts' (ibid., p. 231). Hence there are fictionality signals, but there is no exhaustive list of all possible signals of this kind.

15 In aesthetic experiences of the musical, the fictional objects are rules of arrangement (sequences) that may play with our expectations – that is, with the pure temporality of aesthetic experience – in so far as the music does not represent anything outside of tonality.

16 See the classic argumentation in the ninth chapter of Aristotle's *Poetics*, 1451b36–1452a11.

17 It would be a different matter if I appeared essentially in some fiction. One can construct metaphysical hypotheses in which this would be the case. If I were a figure in a novel or a video game in someone's mind, for example, without being able to notice this (according to the model of the simulation hypothesis, perhaps), the situation would be different. But I cannot offer any good reason for why this is the case, and therefore consider myself entitled to be a non-fictional realist with reference to my conditions of survival, which does not rule out the possibility that I might be mistaken about this.

18 Regarding the concept of gaps, see again the *locus classicus* Iser, *The Implied Reader* and *The Act of Reading*.

19 See to that effect also Johannes Anderegg, *Sprache und Verwandlung: Zur literarischen Ästhetik* (Göttingen: Vandenhoeck & Ruprecht, 1985), p. 113: 'Fiction comes about when we understand a text as a score for the staging of mental representations.'

20 This is what distinguishes 'Gretchen' from 'Merkel'. Angela Merkel is not a fictional object, even if her political role means that there are many myths and conceits about her from which, with the aid of her advisory team, she can draw socioeconomic profit, as befits a complex modern media democracy. Fact-based and symbol politics cannot be completely separated, though this does not mean that Merkel is a fictional, let alone fictive object.

21 See Köppe and Klauk (eds), *Fiktionalität*, p. 6. Maria E. Reicher argues more subtly in her essay 'Ontologie fiktiver Gegenstände' in the same volume, pp. 159–89.

22 In literary scholarship, the term 'metafiction' refers to a fiction that deals within its own medium with the fact that it is fictional. See Ansgar Nünning, *Von historischer Fiktion zu historiographischer Metafiktion: Theorie, Typologie und Poetik des historischen Romans* (Trier: WVT Wissenschaftlicher Verlag, 1995), and, more recently, Ilona Mader, *Metafiktionalität als Selbst-Dekonstruktion* (Würzburg: Königshausen & Neumann, 2017). On this discussion, see also the essays in Marc Currie (ed.), *Metafiction* (London: Routledge, 1995). In the philosophical discourse, however, 'metafictional' usually refers to assertions about fictional objects.

23 Stuart Brock and Anthony Everett (eds), *Fictional Objects* (Oxford: Oxford University Press, 2015).

24 Ibid., p. 3.

25 In addition, it is indeed the case that, since the pre-Socratic philosophers, many discoveries in nature have been canonically represented in literary form – from Lucretius via Galileo to modernity.

26 Like Oliver Scholz, who openly declares it a criterion of fiction that, 'as a rule, someone is pretending that the world is in certain ways different from how it actually is, or that things exist in it which in reality do not exist' (Oliver R. Scholz, 'Fiktionen, Wissen und andere kognitive Güter', in Köppe and Klauk (eds), *Fiktionalität*, p. 210).

27 For a recent historical overview, see Ursula Peters and Rainer Warning (eds), *Fiktion und Fiktionalität in den Literaturen des Mittelalters* (Munich: Fink, 2009). On the classical origins, see the essay in the same volume by Oliver Primavesi, 'Zum Problem der epischen Fiktion in der vorplatonischen Poetik', pp. 105–20.

28 To the best of my knowledge, the very first articulation of the concept of fiction comes from Xenophanes (DK 21 B 1, 22), where the battle between titans and giants is described as *plasmata ton proteron* – that is, as inventions of earlier singers. However, Xenophanes does not treat the gods per se as inventions here. Rather, what he criticizes in the name of his emphatic monotheism (DK 21 B 23) are the anthropomorphic gods generated (*gennasthai*) by humans.

29 Azzouni, *Talking about Nothing*, p. 14. See also ibid., p. 139. Similarly, see the explanation of the 'notion of independent reality' in Sally Haslanger, *Resisting Reality: Social Construction and Social Critique* (Oxford: Oxford University Press, 2012), pp. 84f. Haslanger notes, 'To bring about a change in the world, you have to do more than just think about it' (ibid., p. 85). This is not entirely true, however; by thinking about reality, I obviously change it – at least, in so far as, at the moment of my thinking, it is a new fact that I am now thinking this particular thought. Admittedly, Haslinger does explicitly concede that not only what is independent in her sense is real (see ibid., p. 98, note 27 and *passim*).

30 See Gabriel, *The Limits of Epistemology*, p. 34, and Anton Friedrich Koch, *Versuch über Wahrheit und Zeit* (Paderborn: Brill, 2006). At an object level, one can also determine the contrast of objectivity by differentiating between registry-dependence and registry-independence. Something is dependent on a registry if it would not have existed without the respective registry. Conversely, something is independent of a registry if it would still have existed without the respective registry. Certainly, a further analysis of such a counterfactual criterion for realism would require a more detailed explanation of how these conditions are to be understood. See Markus Gabriel, 'Existenz, realistisch gedacht', in *Der Neue Realismus*, pp. 171–99.

31 During the discussion of my plenary speech at the congress of the German Society for Phenomenological Research in Vienna on 19 September 2019, Lambert Wiesing posed the question of whether the paradigmatically real is not rather that about which we cannot be mistaken – that is, the first-person perspective that is epistemically available in the mode of self-consciousness. This was discussed with reference to sensations of pain. However, one can be

mistaken about both whether someone else with a first-person experience has sensations of pain and what kind of sensations they are; then such sensations would be an exception at best, as they involve first-person familiarity. In addition, I can be mistaken about my pain and other mental states in a first-person situation, since the experience of a sensation (consciousness) does not coincide with the epistemic attitude whereby I register this experience (even if it is supposedly immune to error). Sensations and epistemic states are subject to a different code. Thirdly, I can be mistaken about my own pain by localizing it wrongly, for example. From a human-science and medical perspective, it is also far from obvious to what extent toothache takes place within the tooth, or whether all pain is actually consciously registered in a different part of the central nervous system. As we do not know what exactly constitutes the minimum neuronal correlate of consciousness, it is an open question whether they are registered in another processing location as taking place in the tooth – which would mean that one could cause toothache without there being any toothache. In short, Wiesing's assumption that he is more certain of some of his mental states than is necessary for his theory of reality is not adequately supported.

32 Paradigmatically, because we acknowledge existence and, based on this, learn that many things exist with which we will never have epistemic contact. Admittedly, we do encounter this bloc of unknowable objects in the mode of the *de dicto* idea that there is much we will never know – which does not mean that we consequently know it.

33 According to the theory proposed here, the imaginings of the episodic memory are fictive objects whose score is our motoric, material memory. Accordingly, I would distinguish between propositional memory, which is epistemic, and episodic memory, which seeks to fool us about past episodes that never took place. Nonetheless, we can make epistemic use of the episodic memory.

34 See the *locus classicus* Herbert Grabes, 'Wie aus Sätzen Personen werden', *Poetica*, 10/4 (1978): 405–28. For a comprehensive treatment of the relationship between the development of figures and personal knowledge rehearsed in one's lifeworld, see Fotidis, *Figur und Person*, following on from Grabes, on pp. 178ff.

35 One can find an interesting portfolio showing the range of actually existing hallucinations in Oliver Sacks, *Hallucinations* (London: Picador, 2012).

36 Everett, *The Nonexistent*, p. 63.

37 Ibid.

38 As mentioned above, I understand fictional irrealism as a reaction to the problem of emptiness. It avoids emptiness by completely abolishing fictional objects, such that it is no longer analytically true that they do not exist, as they are not even objects of a well-formulated negative statement of existence; rather, they are nothing at all. Everett fluctuates somewhat in this regard when he writes:

> We would certainly find it bizarre if someone, upon being told that Holmes is a fictional character, asserted that Holmes exists. Now I don't

think that these sorts of facts establish that it is a *conceptual truth* or a *linguistic truth* that fictional characters don't exist. For I don't think there are conceptual or linguistic truths about fictional characters. But if *you* think there are conceptual or linguistic truths about fictional characters then I think you should take the fact that fictional characters don't exist to be one of them. (*The Nonexistent*, p. 132)

§3 Meontology in Ontology of Fields of Sense

1 The paradigmatic work in this context is naturally Plato's *Sophist*, which presents the first theory of non-existence or non-being in order to decompress the Eleatic *One*. Here I am very much following Plato's basic idea that non-being should be modelled as otherness (*thateron*), though, in sense field ontology, the entities whose relation is non-existence are not Platonic forms in the strict sense but, rather, fields of sense.

2 Regarding this term, see Gabriel, 'Der Neue Realismus zwischen Konstruktion und Wirklichkeit'.

3 To quote a well-coined phrase from Durs Grünbein, 'The thinker's voice', in *The Bars of Atlantis: Selected Essays*, ed. Michael Eskin, trans. John Crutchfield, Andrew Shields and Michael Hofmann (New York: Farrar, Straus & Giroux, 2010), pp. 228–45.

4 Against the concept of consciousness-independence as a criterion for realism, see Gabriel, 'Neutraler Realismus'.

5 The qualification 'in part pre-theoretically' takes account of the fact that we also model objects that exist only as theoretical terms, such as the object 'theoretical term'.

6 See on this Gabriel, *The Meaning of Thought*.

7 Some natural scientists, drawing on quantum mechanics or neuroscientific examinations of consciousness, claim that the 'phenomenal character of the world' is fundamental (Hartmann Römer, 'Emergenz und Evolution', *Zeitschrift für Parapsychologie und Grenzgebiete der Psychologie*, 50 [2017]: 68–98, here p. 74). For a few examples among many others, see Erwin Schrödinger, *Mind and Matter: The Tarner Lectures* (Cambridge: Cambridge University Press, 1958); Giulio Tononi and Christof Koch, 'Consciousness: here, there and everywhere?', *Philosophical Transactions of the Royal Society*, 370/1668 (2015); Brigitte Görnitz and Thomas Görnitz, *Von der Quantenphysik zum Bewusstsein: Kosmos, Geist und Materie* (Berlin: Springer, 2016). I will address the position of OFS regarding such nature-philosophical questions elsewhere. See also the recent ontologically fruitful analysis of the threshold discussions in contemporary quantum mechanics in Slavoj Žižek, *Sex and the Failed Absolute* (London: Bloomsbury, 2020), pp. 273–308, and pp. 333–42.

8 See Gabriel, 'Neutraler Realismus'.

9 Ibid. See also Gabriel, 'Existenz, realistisch gedacht'.

10 Peter van Inwagen argues along similar lines in *Metaphysics* (New York: Routledge, 2018), pp. 3f.; unfortunately, however, he proceeds from his con-

vincing argument that reality as a whole cannot be reduced to appearances for subjects to the inference that an all-encompassing object area (called 'the world') exists.

11 See the extensive argumentation in Koch, *Versuch über Wahrheit und Zeit*, ch. 1, esp. §13, where Koch shows that there is no primal fact, no 'pre-propositional (pre-discursive), immediately given original' (p. 105) fact whose structure dictates that it can only be acknowledged in an error-immune fashion.

12 This position is rigorously articulated in Rödl, *Self-Consciousness and Objectivity*. For a similar approach, but without the optimistic belief that philosophy articulates an eminent concept of science as such, see Michael Hampe, *Die Lehren der Philosophie: Eine Kritik* (Berlin: Suhrkamp, 2014). One need hardly point out that these positions are inspired by Wittgenstein's deliberate anti-philosophy. For a truly resolute reading of Wittgenstein that theoretically reconstructs the anti-theoretical impetus, see Paul Horwich, *Wittgenstein's Metaphilosophy* (Oxford: Oxford University Press, 2012).

13 It should be noted that, like existence, non-existence is a higher-order property that distinguishes fields of sense from one another, not an object-level property that distinguishes given objects in a field from one another. In a given field, all objects that appear exist, and all objects that do not appear do not exist. Here non-existence already serves the demarcation of fields of sense, and thus the self-determination of the field as such. What it means for a given meaning to have a structuring effect within a given field of sense becomes apparent in that field through the fact that other objects are excluded.

14 Hegel famously presented an attempt at such a self-guaranteeing theory in *The Science of Logic*. I cannot show here that this project fails. Gregory Moss undertakes an extensive discussion, including a state of the art defence of Hegel against FOS in *Hegel's Foundation Free Metaphysics: The Logic of Singularity* (London: Routledge, 2020), which specifically discusses my critique of Hegel from *Sinn und Existenz* in detail. Unfortunately, I obtained that manuscript only shortly before completing the present one, so there was no time to address Moss's argumentation with the necessary care; this will happen elsewhere. For an outline of the case against the possibility of a completely self-authenticating philosophical argument, see Markus Gabriel, 'Die Endlichkeit der Gründe und die notwendige Unvollständigkeit der Tatsachen', in Julian Nida-Rümelin and Elif Özmen (eds), *Die Welt der Gründe: Deutsches Jahrbuch Philosophie* 4 (2012), pp. 696–710.

15 The 'method' that is currently very popular in the German-speaking world for establishing what people are thinking in the English-speaking world, followed by classifying and weighing up the arguments for and against in charts, contributes too little to finding the truth for it to pave the way for genuine philosophical progress. Strictly speaking, this procedure is a largely irrelevant sideshow for the production of PowerPoint presentations, and one should not participate in it.

16 This is also supported by the fact that it is still unclear what ontological categories actually exist. See Jan Westerhoff, *Ontological Categories: Their Nature and Significance* (Oxford: Oxford University Press, 2005), which shows that there is

a still unsolved 'cut-off problem' (p. 56) that does not allow us to distinguish between categorical and empirical concepts.

17 On realism as a theory of contact, see Hubert Dreyfus and Charles Taylor, *Retrieving Realism* (Cambridge, MA: Harvard University Press, 2015).

18 Kant, *Critique of Pure Reason*, A19/B33: 'In whatever way and through whatever means a cognition may relate to objects, that through which it relates immediately to them, and at which all thought as a means is directed as an end, is intuition' (p. 155). On the concept of intuition, see Pirmin Stekeler-Weithofer, *Formen der Anschauung: Eine Philosophie der Mathematik* (Berlin: de Gruyter, 2008).

19 For a critical view of this, see Markus Gabriel, 'Hegel's account of perceptual experience in his philosophy of subjective spirit', in Marina F. Bykova (ed.), *Hegel's Philosophy of Spirit: A Critical Guide* (Cambridge: Cambridge University Press, 2019), pp. 104–24, and 'Intuition, representation and thinking: Hegel's psychology and the placement problem', in Marina F. Bykova and Kenneth R. Westphal (eds), *The Palgrave Hegel Handbook* (Basingstoke: Palgrave Macmillan, 2020).

20 Tyler Burge has presented a theory of objectivity that places conditions of accuracy far below the threshold of conscious perception in living beings. See Tyler Burge, *Origins of Objectivity* (Oxford: Oxford University Press, 2010). I do not dispute that the phenomena Burge investigates exist; rather, my presentation of the main text is deliberately restricted to the concept of conscious perception as an epistemologically privileged interface. If we had no faculty of conscious perception, which is the foundation for the exercise of self-consciousness, we would not have any theoretical access to perceptions. Someone only capable of seeing blindly would presumably not be aware of it.

21 For a paradigmatic example, see Stanislas Dehaene, *Consciousness and the Brain: Deciphering How the Brain Codes Our Thoughts* (New York: Penguin, 2014). For an opposing approach to this variety of neurocentrism, see Gabriel, *I Am Not a Brain, Neo-Existentialism* and *The Meaning of Thought* (Cambridge: Polity, 2020).

22 Derek Parfit, *On What Matters*, vol. 2 (Oxford: Oxford University Press, 2013), p. 473.

23 On the concept of existence as formal being, see Anton Friedrich Koch, 'Die Offenheit der Welt und der euklidische Raum der Imagination', in Markus Gabriel et al. (eds), *Welt und Unendlichkeit: Ein deutsch–ungarischer Dialog in memoriam László Tengelyi* (Freiburg: Alber, 2017), pp. 68–78. Admittedly, I do not share Koch's assumption that existence is a non-discriminating property of all objects because universal metaphysical quantification, which applies to all objects without restrictions, is thwarted by the no-world intuition (Gabriel, *Sinn und Existenz*, §6). There is no allness of objects that could bestow properties – such as the property of non-discriminating existence – on those objects by virtue of their belonging to such an allness.

24 As in Tobias Rosefeldt and Catharine Diehl, 'Antwort auf Gabriel', in Buchheim (ed.), *Jahrbuch-Kontroversen 2*, pp. 230–9.

25 See also below, pp. 69f.

26 For an opposing view, see Gabriel, 'Neutraler Realismus', pp. 28f., and *Sinn und Existenz*, §2b.
27 See for example Jody Azzouni, Deflating Existential Consequence: A Case for Nominalism (Oxford: Oxford University Press, 2004), as well as Graham Priest, One: Being an Investigation into the Unity of Reality and its Parts, including the Singular Object which is Nothingness (Oxford: Oxford University Press, 2014), pp. xiif.
28 Gabriel, *Sinn und Existenz*, p. 214.
29 Thus Priest's argument in Gabriel and Priest, *Everything and Nothing*.
30 Conversational remark to the author. See my response in Gabriel, *Propos réalistes* and 'Être vrai'.
31 See the remarks on this in the introduction to Gabriel, *Propos réalistes*, pp. 7–52.
32 See the famous passage in Bertrand Russell, *Introduction to Mathematical Philosophy* (New York: Cosimo, 2007), p. 169:

> Logic, I should maintain, must no more admit a unicorn than zoology can; for logic is concerned with the real world just as truly as zoology, though with its more abstract and general features. To say that unicorns have an existence in heraldry, or in literature, or in imagination, is a most pitiful and paltry evasion. What exists in heraldry is not an animal, made of flesh and blood, moving and breathing of its own initiative. What exists is a picture, or a description in words.

33 In the field of narratology, Peter Rabinowitz has defined three different types of audience: the real, the authorial and the narrative. See Peter J. Rabinowitz, 'Truth in fiction: a reexamination of audiences', *Critical Inquiry*, 4/1 (1977): 121–41. This classification goes beyond the simple distinction between intra-fictional and metafictional speech, since it does justice to a genuinely literary phenomenon: the function of the 'implicit reader', formulated by the Constance School of reception aesthetics. See the *locus classicus* Iser, *The Implicit Reader*. It is a mystery why narratology is almost entirely ignored in the analytical debate on fictional entities. It has recently made an indirect appearance in Derek Matravers, *Fiction and Narrative*. By contrast, a paradigmatic example of work that keeps abreast of narratological research can be found in Albrecht Koschorke, *Fact and Fiction: Elements of a General Theory of Narrative*, trans. Joel Golb (Berlin: de Gruyter, 2018).
34 One might say that FOS implies a generalized ontological deflationism, as it disputes that there is such a thing as 'heavy-duty' existence. Superficially, then, FOS resembles the 'easy ontology' of Annie Thomasson, as described in her *Ontology Made Easy*. This analogy is deceptive, however, since Thomasson is not an exponent of meta-ontological realism. She defines her concept of existence as follows: 'Ks exist iff [if and only if] the application conditions actually associated with "K" are fulfilled' (p. 86). From this she infers an ontological pluralism based on Huw Price's 'functional pluralism'. See Price, *Naturalism without Mirrors* (Oxford: Oxford University Press, 2011), esp. p. 300. As with FOS, Thomasson argues that 'we should expect no uniform, across-the-board

answer to the question of what it takes to exist. Thus, again we have a purely formal answer, not one with across-the-board material content' (*Ontology Made Easy*, p. 89). However, the reason she gives for this pluralism is a variation on the application conditions of term, such that she disputes that there are any 'across-the-board, shared criteria of existence' (ibid.) – which does not necessarily mean that any uniform total sense field exists independently of our language experience. She consistently treats existence as a 'notion' (p. 116) rather than a property of objects, something with which I disagree. According to OFS, the reason why there is no material '*substantive* criterion for existence' (ibid.) is that existence is plural; this is not primarily, let alone exclusively, made true by the fact that our concept of existence exhibits plural application conditions.

35 Henri Bergson, *Creative Evolution*, trans. Arthur Mitchell (Lanham, MD: University Press of America, 1984), pp. 272–98.

36 Ibid., p. 283.

37 Ibid., p. 286:

> In other words, and however strange our assertion may seem, there is more, and not less, in the idea of an object conceived as 'not existing' than in the idea of this same object conceived as 'existing'; for the idea of the object 'not existing' is necessarily the idea of the object 'existing' with, in addition, the representation of an exclusion of this object by the actual reality taken in block.

Bergson sees nothing problematic about the 'idée de Tout', whose meaning he considers indirectly affirmed through the illusion of absolute Nothing (see ibid., p. 296).

38 In this statement, 'absolute totality' and the 'complete absence' thereof are likewise words that refer to nothing. One cannot conclude from this that FOS has a terminological problem, however, as it is rather the metaphysician's task to show that such words should refer to something. See below, §10.

39 See, of course, Lewis's *magnum opus*, *On the Plurality of Worlds* (Oxford: Oxford University Press, 1986).

40 Quentin Meillassoux, *Trassierungen: Zur Wegbereitung spekulativen Denkens*, trans. Roland Frommel (Leipzig: Merve, 2017).

41 See Gabriel, *Sinn und Existenz*, §3.

42 For an overview, see Graham Priest, *An Introduction to Non-Classical Logic: From If to Is* (Cambridge: Cambridge University Press, 2008). Badiou operates uncritically with classical logics without philosophically justifying this weighty preselection. See Alain Badiou, *Being and Event*, trans. Oliver Feltham (London: Continuum, 2006), and *Logics of Worlds*, trans. Alberto Toscano (London: Bloomsbury, 2019).

43 It is different in the case of classical metaphysical projects developed in neo-Platonism, medieval philosophy and German Idealism, for example, as these do not treat the absolute as an *object* of theorizing based on the model of modern natural science or propositional logic. See, for example,

Jens Halfwassen, *Auf den Spuren des Einen: Studien zur Metaphysik und ihrer Geschichte* (Tübingen: Mohr Siebeck, 2015), as well as the paradigmatic works by Werner Beierwaltes: *Identität und Differenz* (Frankfurt: Klostermann, 1980), and, more recently, *Catena Aurea* (Frankfurt: Klostermann, 2017). It is an open question how exactly a non-objective metaphysics of the absolute would be reformulated in the light of current theoretical requirements, though it may have particular advantages at the limits of current theoretical physics, where one finds conceptual situations that have reminded Carlo Rovelli and others more or less coincidentally of Dante, whose *Divine Comedy* is dominated by neo-Platonic metaphysics. See Carlo Rovelli, *Reality Is Not What it Seems: The Journey to Quantum Gravity*, trans. Simon Carnell and Erica Segre (London: Penguin, 2016), pp. 97–106. Admittedly, Rovelli not only twists the meaning of the Dante passage he cites but also invents the text he seems to be quoting. Canto XXVII of *The Divine Comedy* does not actually contain the lines presented by Rovelli: 'This other part of the universe surrounds the first like the first surrounds the others' (Questa altra parte dell'Universo d'un cerchio lui comprende, / si come questo li altri) (p. 98). The actual text reads 'Luce ed amor d'un cerchio lui comprende, / sì come questo li altrí; e quell precinto / colui che l'cinge solamente intende' (Canto XXVII, 112–14); in English: 'By circling light and love it [heaven] is contained / as it contains the rest: and only He / Who bound them comprehends how they [spheres] were bound' (Dante Alighieri, *The Divine Comedy*, vol. III: *Paradise*, trans. Mark Musa [London: Penguin, 1986], p. 321). Here heaven is contained (as it was for Aristotle, who is Dante's source) in the 'divine mind' [*mente divina*] (Canto XXVII, 110), meaning that no paradox-ridden structure appears in the self-contained universe.

44 In this sense, as shown in Gabriel, *Sinn und Existenz*, FOS respects the idealistic requirements of a transcendental ontology, which I outlined especially using studies on Schelling and Hegel in Markus Gabriel, *Transcendental Ontology: Essays in German Idealism* (London: Continuum, 2011). This does not make it an idealistic ontology, however, though I also have my doubts that one can prove the existence of an idealistic ontology in Schelling or Hegel. See especially Markus Gabriel, 'What kind of an idealist (if any) is Hegel?', *Hegel Bulletin*, 27/2 (2016): 181–208, which argues especially against readings such as Rolf-Peter Horstmann, 'Hegel's *Phenomenology of Spirit* as an argument for a monistic ontology', *Inquiry*, 49/1 (2006): 103–18.

45 This effort is not made by Williamson, for example, who therefore fails to offer any proof that his approach is epistemologically tenable. See his inadequate methodological self-appraisal in Timothy Williamson, *Modal Logics as Metaphysics* (Oxford: Oxford University Press, 2013), pp. 423–9. It is not enough to point out that one can generally differentiate between metaphysical and epistemological matters if one does not take into account that the real and our cognition are connected. This already results from the fact that our cognition of the real is itself something real that can be cognized, meaning that one cannot draw any categorial distinction between metaphysical and epistemological matters.

46 See Charles Kahn, *Essays on Being* (Oxford: Oxford University Press, 2009); Ernst Tugendhat, *Aufsätze 1992–2000* (Frankfurt: Suhrkamp, 2001); and Graham Priest, 'Sein language', *The Monist*, 97/4 (2014): 430–42.

47 Regarding the ontology of 'real objects' in 'fictive stories', see Zipfel, *Fiktion, Fiktivität, Fiktionalität*, pp. 92–7. Rudolf Haller also defends the claim that no fictional objects are identical with real objects in 'Wirkliche und fiktive Gegenstände', in *Facta und Ficta: Studien zu ästhetischen Grundlagenfragen* (Stuttgart: Reclam, 1986), pp. 57–93. Haller considers fictive objects incomplete, however, which is irreconcilable with the position espoused here, which states that fictive (in my vocabulary: hermeneutical) objects are not incomplete in the framework of an interpretation, and their meta-hermeneutical basis (the figure expressly named as a *dramatis figura*, for example) is not incomplete anyway. The semblance of incompleteness stems from a confusion of these two objects, which seemingly coalesce in aesthetic experience.

48 See Tim Crane, *The Objects of Thought* (Oxford: Oxford University Press, 2013), p. 17.

49 Žižek rightly points out that the real as such often appears in the form of a fiction within a fiction; we recognize the real in the contrast to a variation upon it. The contrast area in which it is thus embedded determines its position in the mental life of humans, which is fundamentally built up around fictions; I agree with Žižek, who deals with this using the concept of 'phantasy'. See his ingenious reading of *The Man in the High Castle* in *Sex and the Failed Absolute*, p. 338. We discover the real in the contrast area of fictions, though this does not mean that everything real is fictional or even fictive. Realism is not restricted by the central role of fictions in the human mind; it is merely located in the right position.

50 See the *locus classicus* Aristotle, *Poetics*, 1451b36–1452a11.

51 For a similarly broad concept of the score, and accordingly its performance, see Christoph Möllers, *The Possibility of Norms: Social Practice beyond Morals and Causes*, trans. Alex Holznienkemper (Oxford: Oxford University Press, 2020). Möllers establishes a connection between aesthetics and the application of juridical norms by treating a legal text as a score, and thus tying the court's verdict to conditions of performance.

52 Matravers largely subscribes to Walton's view, which closely aligns representation and fiction. For an overview of the potential difficulties in the accompanying 'unusual terminological posits', see Zipfel, *Fiktion, Fiktivität, Fiktionalität*, pp. 23f.

53 Hans Blumenberg, *Theorie der Unbegrifflichkeit*, p. 10. As the reference to cave paintings suggests, what unites concept and fiction is the idea of a representation of the absent.

54 See Gabriel, *The Meaning of Thought*.

55 Hans-Georg Gadamer, 'The relevance of the beautiful', in *The Relevance of the Beautiful and Other Essays*, trans. Nicholas Walker (Cambridge: Cambridge University Press, 1986). Nicolas Bourriaud has prominently expanded this basic structure of the work into the concept of a relational art. See, with examples, Wolfgang Kemp, *Der explizite Betrachter: Zur Rezeption zeitgenössischer*

Kunst (Konstanz: Konstanz University Press, 2015), pp. 145–64. Bourriaud and Kemp overlook Gadamer's point that this relationality belongs to the ontology of art and does not constitute a historically striking figure of modernity. See Gadamer, 'The relevance of the beautiful', in which he refutes the prejudice that he treats tradition as 'conservation' (p. 49). On the contrary, Gadamer develops an insight into the historicity of understanding, which is reconcilable with an ontology of historical events. Historicity is not in turn historical but, rather, belongs to the totality of things that we are as minded beings.

56 They are part of our 'symbolic life', as Catherine Malabou recently called it, in *Morphing Intelligence: From IQ Measurement to Artificial Brains*, trans. Carolyn Shread (New York: Columbia University Press, 2019), pp. xv–xvi. However, I in no way share Malabou's diagnosis that a theoretical alternative to the 'reduction of the intellect to the two forms – neuronal and cybernetic' – has no future (p. 9) or her opinion that a brain simulation is indistinguishable from a brain. It is notable that Malabou expressly speaks of being convinced by Kurzweil, and by Spike Jonze's film *Her*, that 'plasticity is progammable' (p. 91 and pp. 91–2). This amounts to a fundamental confusion of fiction and reality, as no science fiction film should convince anyone of a real future possibility, let alone reality!

57 See the outstanding cinematic representation in Ruben Östlund's *The Square* (2017).

58 Gadamer, 'The relevance of the beautiful', p. 23.

59 See again Kemp, Der explizite Betrachter, as well as Gabriel, *The Power of Art*.

60 See Markus Gabriel, 'Für einen nicht-naturalistischen Realismus', in Magdalena Marszałek and Dieter Mersch (eds), *Seien wir realistisch: Neue Realismen und Dokumentarismen in Philosophie und Kunst* (Zurich: Diaphanes, 2016), pp. 59–88.

61 As correctly described by Kripke in *Naming und Necessity*. See also Gabriel, 'Was ist (die) Wirklichkeit?'.

62 Similarly, see Zipfel, *Fiktion, Fiktivität, Fiktionalität*, pp. 74f., who follows on from Goodman: 'Our everyday reality is a version of the world that – like all versions, but in a particularly clear fashion – is composed of different available versions. We refer to this reality when we say that figures in novels do not really exist, that events described in fictional literature did not really take place, that stories are entirely invented.' On the concept of everyday reality as lifeworld, see §8 below.

63 This ontological structure is not a particularity of fictive objects. I myself currently exist in Paris but not in *The Count of Monte Christo*, which means that I exist in one respect but not in another. Note, however, that the Count of Monte Christo cannot detect my non-existence in his sense field. Even if, in a field of sense, there existed a novel with the title *The Author of the Philosophical Book Fictions*, this novel could not be about me, only about a fictive object that resembles me. The Count of Monte Christo cannot cognize me, but I can cognize him. That is an epistemic privilege of the real over the fictive, albeit one from which only we profit.

64 See the discussion in Gabriel and Priest, *Everything and Nothing*.

§4 The World Is Not a Fiction

1 Jorge Luis Borges, *The Aleph*, in *Borges, a Reader: A Selection from the Writings of Jorge Luis Borges*, ed. Emir Rodríguez Monegal and Alastair Reid (New York: Dutton, 1981), p. 160: '"Beatriz, Beatriz Elena, Beatriz Elena Viterbo darling Beatriz, Beatriz now gone forever, it's me, it's me, Borges."'

2 On Borges's use of proper names in general, see Daniel Balderstrom, *Out of Context: Historical Reference and the Representation of Reality in Borges* (Durham, NC: Duke University Press, 1993). 'Daneri' probably also alludes to Ner[u]da and R[ub]én Darí[o]. See Humberto Núñez-Faraco, 'In search of the Aleph: memory, truth and falsehood in Borges's Poetics', *Modern Language Review*, 92/3 (1997): 613–29. Daneri is formed from Dan- and -eri, meaning that 'te alighi' is omitted, which alludes to the title 'El Aleph'; 'te alighi' sounds like a pseudo-Italian corruption of 'El Aleph'. However far such word games might extend at the level of signifiers, we must definitely take into account that a story creates complex conditions of reference for its use of proper names that cannot be described using the naïve schema of 'empty proper names'.

3 On the role of names in literary contexts, see Dieter Lamping, *Der Name in der Erzählung: Zur Poetik des Personennamens* (Bonn: Bouvier, 1983).

4 'In one and the same act' (Trans.).

5 Borges, *The Aleph*, p. 159.

6 Ibid.

7 Ibid.

8 Ibid.

9 In addition to the obvious and explicit reference to transfinite set theory already made with the word 'Aleph', there is also a possible connection to the 'Alpha body' mentioned by Vaihinger in *The Philosophy of 'As If'*, quoted by Borges in the story 'Tlön, Uqbar, Orbis Tertius'. This body is a fictive concept, 'the immovable central point of absolute space' (Hans Vaihinger, *The Philosophy of 'As If'* [London: Routledge, 2021], p. 66). Vaihinger advocates a 'metaphysics of sensations' whose fictionality Borges reveals in 'Tlön, Uqbar, Orbis Tertius'.

10 On this distinction, established in literary criticism, see Monika Fludernik et al. (eds), *Faktuales und fiktionales Erzählen: Interdisziplinäre Perspektive* (Baden-Baden: Ergon, 2015).

11 See the much-discussed studies in Paul de Man, *Allegories of Reading: Figural Language in Rousseau, Nietzsche, Rilke, and Proust* (New Haven, CT: Yale University Press, 1979).

12 See the famous phrase *hos eide ta t'eonta ta t'essomena pro t'eonta*, which describes the temporal omniscience of Calchas the seer in *Iliad* 1, 70. This omniscience is also attributed to the muses, for example in Hesiod, *Theogony*, 38, where this phrase is repeated. In the *Iliad* (2, 484–6) the omniscience of the muses is compared to the ignorance of the recipients, who acquire the knowledge that is passed on to the singer only through hearsay.

13 Borges, *The Aleph*, p. 160. On the role of the authorial fiction in Borges, see Jean-Pierre Mourrey, '"Borges" chez Borges', *Poétique*, 16 (1985): 313–24.

14 See Núñez-Faraco, 'In search of the Aleph'.

15 The technical details of a mereology without anti-symmetry (especially with non-well-founded, recurring loops) were discussed at length in June 2020 during Graham Priest's time as visiting professor in Bonn, at the invitation of the International Centre for Philosophy of North Rhine-Westphalia, which is expanded upon in Gabriel and Priest, *Everything and Nothing*.

16 This, it should be noted, does not generate any variant of Russell's paradox in FOS, as the field of all fields of sense, whose sense does not itself appear in them, does not exist. And, even if such a field could be constructed, this would not prove without additional assumptions that this generates a paradox. See Gabriel, *Sinn und Existenz*, pp. 340–7.

17 I have made this clear beyond any doubt in the texts familiar to Priest, for example in Gabriel, *Sinn und Existenz*, pp. 235–9, and already in Gabriel, *Why the World Does Not Exist*.

18 See Graham Priest, 'Everything and nothing', in Gabriel and Priest, *Everything and Nothing*, p. 10.

19 See, for example, Jorge Luis Borges, *Labyrinths: Selected Stories & Other Writings*, ed. Donald A. Yates and James E. Irby (New York: New Directions, 2007), p. 10: 'They [the metaphysicians of Tlön] judge that metaphysics is a branch of fantastic literature.' Here, of course, Borges is not speaking *in propria persona*.

20 Borges, *The Aleph*, p. 163. See Jon Thiem, 'Borges, Dante, and the poetics of total vision', *Comparative Literature*, 40/2 (1988): 97–120, here p. 112:

> Daneri trivializes the Aleph. He reduces it to the order of such modern inventions as the telephone, the moving picture, and the astronomical observatory. . . . Using the Aleph as a kind of panoptic videotape machine, he fails to view it as anything more than a total repository of real life images. He ignores its truly marvellous feature: the capacity to annihilate the limits of human spatial perception, to convey visually a transcendental order of space. Narrator and reader alike recognize that this Aleph, the Aleph that 'The Aleph' makes us see, is far more fascinating than Daneri's universal peephole.

21 Borges, *The Aleph*, p. 161.

22 Jorges Luis Borges, 'The yellow rose', in *A Personal Anthology*, ed. Anthony Kerrigan (New York: Grove, 1967), p. 83. Like the encyclopedic tomes in the miniature, the Aleph is also located in a corner (*ángulo*).

23 Borges, *The Aleph*, p. 156: 'So foolish did his ideas seem to me, so pompous and drawn out his exposition, that I linked them at once to literature. . . .'

24 In this context, see the structural analysis of a fictional scene from *Escape from the Planet of the Apes* in Gabriel, *Why the World Does Not Exist*.

25 See Priest, *Beyond the Limits of Thought*.

26 Strictly speaking, Borges's metaphysical-sounding stories argue neither for nor against thinking the absolute, since their character as works of art makes them self-enclosed, meaning that they do not espouse any metaphysical or meta-metaphysical theses. This follows from meontological isolationism.

27 Meinong's theory of objects is expressly conceived as a 'theory of objects of knowledge'. See Meinong, *Über Gegenstandstheorie: Selbstdarstellung* (Hamburg: Meiner, 1988), §6. Here he touches on metaphysical fictionalism by tying the knowability of the total realm of objects (and hence metaphysics in his sense) to a 'very instructive . . . fiction':

> Assuming an intelligence of unlimited capacity, then, there is nothing unknowable, and whatever is knowable exists; or, because one tends to say 'there is' of that which is, that which specifically exists, it would perhaps be clearer to say that everything knowable is given – given to knowing. And, to the extent that all objects are knowable, one can without exception, whether they *are* or not, ascribe givenness to them as a most universal type of property. (Ibid., p. 19)

28 Literally 'much in little', in the sense of something great in a small place (Trans.).
29 Zipfel rightly assigns *The Aleph* to the realm of fantastic rather than realistic stories. See Zipfel, *Fiktion, Fiktivität, Fiktionalität*, pp. 109–12. The Aleph crosses the threshold of fantasy set by the context of an everyday reality imposed by a basement in Buenos Aires.
30 For an extensive analysis, see Gabriel, *An den Grenzen der Erkenntnistheorie*.
31 Priest cites Gabriel, *Fields of Sense*, pp. 188f., to point out that I would even accept a non-well-founded mereology, since I actually acknowledge 'that some field can appear within itself.' By contrast, see the reconstruction of the argument in James Hill, 'Markus Gabriel against the world', *Sophia*, 56/3 (2017): 471–81, which follows the individual steps of the argument more closely, because Hill takes into account the additional argument introduced in *Fields of Sense*, p. 140, and taken as given on pp. 188f.
32 See Markus Gabriel, *Fictions*, trans. Wieland Hoban (Cambridge: Polity, 2024), p. 89.
33 For a discussion of the role of Kant's concept of heuristic fiction in Vaihinger's reading (which was treated by Borges) for Borges's *Fictions*, see Floyd Merrell, *Unthinking Thinking: Jorge Luis Borges, Mathematics and the New Physics* (West Lafayette, IN: Purdue University Press, 1991); Silvia G. Dapía, *Jorge Luis Borges, Post-Analytic Philosophy, and Representation* (London: Routledge, 2016).
34 See the role of contexts in Graham Priest, *Towards Non-Being: The Logic and Metaphysics of Intentionality* (Oxford: Oxford University Press, 2016), pp. 112f.
35 A mereological atom or basic object is a part of a system that would not have actual parts in any system. There is room in FOS for the idea that there certainly can be genuine atoms in some systems, such as the universe, on some not yet clearly identified scale. We do not know if space–time is atomistic ('grainy') or continuous at the level of the Planck length, or what exactly this means for the question of genuine mereological atoms in the universe. There can be basic objects in some fields of sense without this meaning that there are basic objects which are built into all fields of sense, since, independently of this question, we know that there is nothing which appears in all fields of sense,

because the relevant totality distributing something across *all* fields of sense does not exist.

36 Jorge Luis Borges, *Dreamtigers*, trans. Mildred Boyer and Harold Morland (Austin: University of Texas Press, 1964), p. 90.

37 The conference was held by the Institut des Sciences Juridiques & Philosophiques de la Sorbonne on 29 March 2017 at the CNRS in Paris. Meillassoux's lecture was entitled 'Corrélation et nécessité'.

38 See Cantor's much discussed concept of the Absolute Infinite, which he calls the 'simply *absolute*', in Georg Cantor, *Gesammelte Abhandlungen mathematischen und philosophischen Inhalts*, including commentary and additions from the Cantor–Dedekind correspondence, ed. Ernst Zermelo (Berlin: Springer, 1932), pp. 378–439. See also the discussion in Guido Kreis, *Negative Dialektik des Unendlichen: Kant, Hegel, Cantor* (Berlin: Suhrkamp, 2015), pp. 393–406. Admittedly, Kreis's discussion is flawed because it passes over Cantor's main argument against Kant, which one finds in Cantor, *Gesammelte Abhandlungen*, p. 375. Simply put, Cantor rightly points out that Kant does not have an acceptable concept of the mathematical infinite (such as that offered by Cantor himself), which means that the limitative dialectics proposed by Kreis cannot get off the ground to begin with. Like Kreis, Zermelo assesses this manoeuvre incorrectly (ibid., p. 377). It is likewise not the case that Cantor, as Kreis claims, advocates a negative theology of the absolute, which would mean that one cannot know anything about it. Rather, Cantor develops an argumentation that 'infers the necessity of the actual creation of a transfinite from the highest perfection of God's nature, from his infinite goodness and glory' (ibid., p. 400). Instead of a strict negative theology, Cantor assigns his metaphysical reflections to '*speculative theology*' (ibid., p. 378). Kreis's localization of Cantor somewhere in the incoherent no man's land of limitative dialectics is therefore wholly lacking in any factual or textual basis.

39 For more detail, see Gabriel, *Der Sinn des Denkens*.

§5 FOS Is Not a Meinongian Theory of Objects

1 Following on from Pierre Aubenque's concept of a tinology and its elaboration in Jean-François Courtine's Suárez interpretation, László Tengelyi, *Welt und Unendlichkeit: Zum Problem phänomenologischer Metaphysik* (Freiburg: Karl Alber, 2016), pp. 84–113.

2 *Critique of Pure Reason*, A292/B349.

3 Ibid., A771/B799.

4 See Meinong, *Über Gegenstandstheorie*, pp. 8–10. It was only with the polemics of Russell and Quine that Meinong's own position was reconstructed in such a way that it walks blindly into the traps that it made famous. Meinong's notion of a solution consists in the introduction of the 'pure object' (ibid., p. 12), which is 'by nature outside of being [*ausserseiend*]' (ibid.) – an assumption that does away 'once and for all with the semblance of the paradoxical' (ibid.). Through the 'principle of the outside-being of the pure object' (ibid.), Meinong shifts the

totality of objects into cognition. Yet this means it is no longer certain that the object area of pure objects can be totalized without paradoxes. Perhaps this is where psychoanalysis is right, which has assumed since Freud and Jung that there is a form of reference (the unconscious) that operates below the threshold of classical logic. See, for example, C. G. Jung, *The Archetypes and the Collective Unconscious*, trans. R. F. C. Hull (Princeton, NJ: Princeton University Press, 1969), p. 230: 'Logic says *tertium no datur*, meaning that we cannot envisage the opposites in their oneness. In other words, while the abolition of an obstinate antinomy can be no more than a postulate for us, this is by no means so for the unconscious, whose contents are without exception paradoxical or antinomial by nature, not excluding the category of being.' For a precise overview of the contradictions that result when one introduces a Meinongian realm of being, see Sainsbury, *Fiction and Fictionalism*, pp. 44–67.

5 See especially Priest, *Towards Non-Being*, pp. vii–viii, as well as ch. 4, in which Priest presents his own solution. Other much discussed Meinongian positions are espoused in Routley, *Exploring Meinong's Jungle and Beyond*; Edward N. Zalta, *Abstract Objects: An Introduction to Axiomatic Metaphysics* (Dordrecht: D. Reidel, 1983), and *Intensional Logic and the Metaphysics of Intentionality* (Cambridge, MA: MIT Press, 1988); Terence Parsons, *Nonexistent Objects* (New Haven, CT: Yale University Press, 1980); Berto, *Existence as a Real Property*.

6 Priest, *Towards Non-Being*, p. viii.

7 Ibid.

8 Ibid., p. 13.

9 Priest, *One*, p. xxii: 'For the record, I take it to be to have the potential to enter into causal relations.' For a contrasting view, see Gabriel, 'Was ist (die) Wirklichkeit?', pp. 67f.

10 Priest, *Towards Non-Being*, p. 13.

11 Priest, 'Everything and nothing', p. 19. He continues: 'Thus, Australia is an object, since one can say "Australia has six states", so predicating "has six states" of it. It is an object, since one can quantify over *it*, as in saying that some continents (such as Australia) are entirely in the southern hemisphere. And Australia is an object, since one can think about it, wish one were *there*, and so on.'

12 Ibid. Priest uses 'S' for the particular quantifier (= some), which he distinguishes from the existential quantifier (= there exists something, such that).

13 On the identity riddle and its ontological background, see Markus Gabriel, 'Die Ontologie der Prädikation in Schellings *Die Weltalter*', *Schelling-Studien: Internationale Zeitschrift zur klassischen deutschen Philosophie*, 2 (2014): 3–20. For more recent work, see Manfred Frank, '*Reduplikative Identität*': *Der Schlüssel zu Schellings reifer Philosophie* (Stuttgart-Bad Cannstatt: frommann-holzboog, 2018).

14 See Priest, *Towards Non-Being*, p. 20: 'It is clear, however, that some non-intentional predicates are not existence-entailing. Thus, logical predicates, such as identity, are not: even if *a* does not exist, it is still true that *a* is self-identical, *a* = *a*.'

15 See the details of a promising local anti-realism in Crispin Wright, *Truth and Objectivity* (Cambridge, MA: Harvard University Press, 1992).

16 Admittedly, considering the metamathematical incompleteness theorems of the century since Gödel, it seems to me that we should espouse a form of realism in mathematics, which is why Gödel himself adheres to a Platonist ontology. That is a different matter, however. See Gabriel, *Sinn und Existenz*, pp. 148–57.

17 For a paradigmatic example, see Rödl, *Self-Consciousness and Objectivity*. Regarding the concept of idealism in this context, see Markus Gabriel, *Skeptizismus und Idealismus in der Antike* (Frankfurt: Suhrkamp, 2009), §3.

18 See Rödl, Self-Consciousness and Objectivity.

19 Koch, *Hermeneutischer Realismus*, ch. 5.

20 See Markus Gabriel, 'Gegenständliches Denken', in Antonia Egel et al. (eds), *Die Gegenständlichkeit der Welt: Festschrift für Günter Figal* (Tübingen: Mohr Siebeck, 2019), pp. 37–55.

21 See Gabriel, 'Cosmological idealism'.

22 See Markus Gabriel, 'Transcendental ontology in Fichte's Wissenschaftslehre 1804', in Steven Hoeltzel (ed.), *The Palgrave Fichte Handbook* (Basingstoke: Palgrave Macmillan, 2019), pp. 443–60.

23 See in particular the subtle reconstruction of the argumentative area in Sebastian Gardner, 'The limits of naturalism and the metaphysics of German Idealism', in Espen Hammer (ed.), *German Idealism: Contemporary Perspectives* (London: Routledge, 2007), pp. 19–49. See also Markus Gabriel, 'Endlichkeit und absolutes Ich: Heideggers Fichtekritik', *Fichte-Studien*, 37 (2013): 241–61, as well as Gabriel, *I Am Not a Brain*.

24 Gabriel, 'Für einen nicht-naturalistischen Realismus'.

25 For greater detail, see Gabriel, 'Existenz, realistisch gedacht'.

26 Of course, our statements themselves belong to this ground; we do not escape it by making statements about it. It does not follow from our position as assertory beings that we are subjects standing opposite an object. See Gabriel, *Der Sinn des Denkens*, pp. 222–7.

27 Burge convincingly puts naturalism in his place in *Origins of Objectivity*, p. 308, where he defines naturalism as 'the idea that properties recognized by natural sciences are all the properties science should recognize' and concludes: 'Naturalism does not connect well with actual scientific explanation. It has yielded little of scientific or philosophical value.' Voilà!

28 Meinong, *Über Gegenstandstheorie*, p. 17.

29 Ibid., p. 4.

30 Ibid.

31 Ibid., p. 19.

32 Edmund Husserl, *Formal and Transcendental Logic*, trans. Dorion Cairns (Dordrecht: Springer, 2013), p. 148.

33 See the corresponding argumentation in Gabriel, *An den Grenzen der Erkenntnistheorie*.

34 Kant, *Critique of Pure Reason*, A290/B346.

35 Ibid., A 292/B 348.

36 Priest, *Towards Non-Being*, pp. 118–21.

37 Ibid., p. 120.

38 According to the classification employed here, what I call 'blind fictional realism' is theoretically superior to the average fictional realism because it includes an articulated ontology that allows us to conduct the discussion about realism and irrealism based on an elaborated, and hence well-founded, theory of objects.

39 Trivially speaking, detectives are characterized by their being-a-detective. If one viewed Holmes's career as contingent, one could introduce a detective called 'Shmolmes' who would be essentially a detective; he would not be Shmolmes if he were not a detective. Unlike Holmes, Shmolmes is ontologically predestined for being-a-detective. Since Shmolmes is a proper object for Priest, his introduction is entirely unproblematic.

40 Not all social attributes are recognition-dependent. See Markus Gabriel, 'Facts, social facts, and sociology', in Werner Gephart and Jan Christoph Suntrup (eds), *The Normative Structure of Human Civilization: Readings in John Searle's Social Ontology* (Frankfurt: Klostermann, 2017), pp. 49–68, as well as Part III of this book.

41 Priest, *Towards Non-Being*, p. 119.

42 On this distinction, see Markus Gabriel, 'Repliken auf Beisbart, García, Gerhardt und Koch', in Buchheim (ed.), *Jahrbuch-Kontroversen* 2, p. 113.

43 This does not mean that such objects are not real, however, since we can be mistaken about them. Having pains does not mean knowing what exactly these pains are. One can view pains as states of an immaterial soul and therefore be wrong.

44 According to Priest, furthermore, A belongs to itself as a part.

45 João Branquinho and Mattia Riccardi pointed out to me that whether pains are ideal objects depends on the concept of pain. In his keynote presentation at the third congress of the Portuguese Society of Philosophy on 6 September 2018, Branquinho concluded from Williamson's arguments against epistemic luminosity that pains are not ideal, though this is questionable as a metaphysical argument. For a discussion of the concepts of pain employed there, see Murat Aydede (ed.), *Pain: New Essays on its Nature and the Methodology of its Study* (Cambridge, MA: MIT Press, 2005).

46 See Mehlich, 'Kopernikanischer Salto', pp. 107–17.

47 Anton Friedrich Koch, 'Sein und Existenz', in Sebastian Ostritsch and Andreas Luckner (eds), *Philosophie der Existenz: Aktuelle Beiträge von der Ontologie bis zur Ethik* (Stuttgart: J. B. Metzler, 2019), pp. 46–66.

48 See Markus Gabriel, 'Sinnfeldontologie oder reformierte Metaphysik? Replik auf Le Moli', *Perspektiven der Philosophie: Neues Jahrbuch*, 42 (2016): 110–25.

49 See the arguments in Gabriel, *Sinn und Existenz*, §3.

50 The neo-Meinongian theory of objects is a textbook case of what Heidegger rejects as stock metaphysics. Its objectification knows no boundaries, not even nothingness. This is not the place to address Priest's own reading of Heidegger, which possibly finds a way to defend itself against this reservation. See Priest, *Beyond the Limits of Thought*, ch. 15.

51 Admittedly, this leaves open whether one can introduce a different interpretation of the unrestricted universal FOS, for example on the model of

substitutionally understood quantification, that might be conducive to FOS. I will leave aside the accompanying discussion, which is both interesting and relevant, since one clearly cannot base counterarguments to the no-world intuition on models of the workings of unrestricted universal quantification that do not draw on any metaphysically useful, unrestricted domain of discourse without doing additional philosophical work. For more detail, see Gabriel and Priest, *Everything and Nothing*.

Part II Mental Realism

1 For a literary-criticism perspective, following on from Goethe's *Theory of Colours* and drawing on Derrida's *Spectres of Marx*, see Elisabeth Strowick, *Gespenster des Realismus: Zur literarischen Wahrnehmung von Wirklichkeit* (Paderborn: Fink, 2019). Translator's note: the author's comment is based on the fact that the word *Geist* refers to both 'mind' (as in the philosophy of mind) and 'spirit', also in the sense of 'ghost'.

2 I only realized quite recently that Scheler actually developed a robust philosophy of mind – one that also kept pace with the natural science of his time (which included, no less than quantum mechanics, Darwinism and empirical psychology, which was very advanced by then) – that coincides at many decisive points with the position of neo-existentialism developed here. See Max Scheler, *The Human Place in the Cosmos*, trans. Manfred S. Frings (Evanston, IL: Northwestern University Press, 2009).

3 Gabriel, *Neo-Existentialism* (Cambridge: Polity, 2018), and, by way of introduction, *I Am Not a Brain* (Cambridge: Polity, 2017).

4 Martin Heidegger, *Being and Time*, trans. John Macquarrie and Edward Robinson (New York: HarperCollins, 2008), p. 67.

5 See Charles Taylor, *A Secular Age* (Cambridge, MA: Harvard University Press, 2009).

6 I am here following suggestions by Werner Gephart and Rudolf Stichweh made in conversation at the first research conference of the philosophy department at the University of Bonn on 1 February 2019.

7 Here I distinguish between the philosophy of biology and that of the living. While the former examines the structure of existing, already established biological theories about a particular object area with the general methods of the theory of science, the latter deals directly with the objects examined by biology. The philosophy of biology examines theories, while the philosophy of the living examines living systems. In my view, one should also consider a similar distinction with reference to other areas of research in natural science, such as by distinguishing the philosophy of physics from the philosophy of nature.

8 Denis Noble, *Dance to the Tune of Life: Biological Relativity* (Cambridge: Cambridge University Press, 2017), p. 6. Similarly, see Laurent Nottale, *La relativité dans tous ses états: au-delà de l'espace-temps* (Paris: Hachette, 1998).

9 Noble, *Dance to the Tune of Life*, p. 262.

10 The human sciences encompass every form of human self-exploration, which

obviously crosses disciplinary boundaries. The human being is not the object of some individual science but, rather, the creature that studies itself, the implicit or explicit topic of every research project. Disputing this state of affairs through a reduction or even elimination of the human standpoint is a source of pathologies that, without any claim to completeness, will be diagnosed in the following.

11 I am grateful to Werner Gephart for pointing out in conversation and writing that one must take the theoretical level of what he calls 'homunculi' into consideration to define the standpoint of sociology in science-theoretical terms. The homunculi populate the intermediate metaphysical realm between observable behaviour and meaningfully understandable actions. They therefore belong in the portfolio of self-exploration in the categorial apparatus of sociology and, because of the empirical openness of theorizing, float between 'truth' and 'posit' in the sense of Quine, *Word and Object* (Cambridge, MA: MIT Press, 2013), §6.

12 It has not even been established that said minimum correlate must be neuronal. Noble, for example, is not alone in the assumption that 'conscious experience is a property of the body as a whole' (Noble, *Dance to the Tune of Life*, p. 68). See Denis Noble et al., 'What is it to be conscious?', in John R. Smythies et al. (eds), *The Claustrum: Structural, Functional, and Clinical Neuroscience* (San Diego: Elsevier, 2014), pp. 353–63.

13 This is the state of theory in Daniel C. Dennett, *The Intentional Stance* (Cambridge, MA: MIT Press, 1987). See the current state of Dennett's contributions to illusionism in *From Bacteria to Bach and Back: The Evolution of Minds* (New York: W. W. Norton, 2017).

14 See the classic study: Bruno Snell, *The Discovery of the Mind in Greek Philosophy and Literature* (New York: Dover, 2012).

15 Laplace was even Napoleon's minister of the interior and played an important part in turning the school of ideology towards the ends of the new regime.

16 Ludwig Wittgenstein, *Philosophical Investigations*, trans. G. E. M. Anscombe, P. M. S. Hacker and Joachim Schulte (Oxford: Wiley-Blackwell, 2010), p. 110 (§309): 'What is your aim in philosophy? – To show the fly the way out of the fly-bottle.'

17 Kant, *Critique of Pure Reason*, A26/B42.

18 For an articulation of this programme, see Edmund Husserl, 'Philosophy as rigorous science', trans. Quentin Lauer, in *Phenomenology and the Crisis of Philosophy* (New York: Harper & Row, 1965), pp. 71–148.

19 Ibid., p. 106.

20 Blumenberg, *Theorie der Unbegrifflichkeit* (Frankfurt: Suhrkamp, 2007), p. 38. Regarding the concept of the absolute metaphor, see of course Hans Blumenberg, *Paradigms for a Metaphorology*, trans. Robert Savage (Ithaca: Cornell University Press, 2010).

§6 From Naïve Realism to Illusionism

1 See Gabriel, 'Neutraler Realismus', in Thomas Buchheim (ed.), *Jahrbuch-Kontroversen 2* (Freiburg: Karl Alber, 2016) and 'Existenz, realistisch gedacht', in *Der Neue Realismus* (Berlin: Suhrkamp, 2016), pp. 171–99.

2 See, for example, Stephen L. Macknik et al., *Sleights of Mind: What the Neuroscience of Magic Reveals about Our Everyday Deceptions* (New York: Henry Holt, 2010), as well as Susana Martinez-Conde and Stephen L. Macknik, *Champions of Illusion: The Science Behind Mind-Boggling Images and Mystifying Brain Puzzles* (New York: Farrar, Straus & Giroux, 2017).

3 John R. Searle, *Intentionality: An Essay in the Philosophy of Mind* (Cambridge: Cambridge University Press, 1983).

4 For a defence of a minimal cogito at the same time as overcoming ontological dualism in readings of Descartes, see Jens Rometsch, *Freiheit zur Wahrheit* (Frankfurt: Klostermann, 2018).

5 Daniel C. Dennett, *Consciousness Explained* (London: Penguin, 1993).

6 See Dennett, *From Bacteria to Bach and Back* (New York: W. W. Norton, 2017), p. 9: '"Everything is the way it is because it got that way."' Dennett is quoting from D'Arcy Wentworth Thompson, *On Growth and Form* (Cambridge: Cambridge University Press, 1992). Admittedly, this principle applies at most to processes, more specifically processes that can be examined with the methods of evolutionary biology, which raises science-theoretical problems about the interpretation of evolutionary biology that Dennett does not even attempt to address. Instead, he relies essentially on vulgar mechanist-metaphysical readings à la Dawkins.

7 On this gesture, see Claus Beisbart, 'Wie viele Äpfel sind wirklich im Kühlschrank', in Buchheim (ed.), *Jahrbuch-Kontroversen 2*, pp. 223–9, in particular p. 224.

8 George Berkeley, *Philosophical Commentaries* (London: Routledge, 2019), p. 429.

9 John Campbell and Quassim Cassam, *Berkeley's Puzzle: What Does Experience Teach Us?* (Oxford: Oxford University Press, 2014).

10 Huw Price, *Naturalism without Mirrors* (Oxford: Oxford University Press, 2011), pp. 253–79.

11 See, for example, the representative study by Jay L. Garfield, *Engaging Buddhism: Why it Matters to Philosophy* (Oxford: Oxford University Press, 2015). For a metaphysical interpretation, see the typically incisive description in Graham Priest, *The Fifth Corner of Four: An Essay on Buddhist Metaphysics and the Catuṣkoṭi* (Oxford: Oxford University Press, 2018).

12 Daniel C. Dennett, 'Illusionism as the obvious default theory of consciousness', *Journal of Consciousness Studies*, 23/11–12 (2016): 65–72.

13 Keith Frankish, 'Illusionism as a theory of consciousness', *Journal of Consciousness Studies*, 23/11–12 (2016): 11–39, at p. 11.

14 Ibid., p. 15.

15 Ibid.

16 Ibid., p. 18.

17 Regarding this ultimately arbitrary strategy of a pathology that Raymond Tallis has termed 'neuro-Darwinitis', see his book *Aping Mankind: Neuromania, Darwinitis and the Misrepresentation of Humanity* (London: Routledge, 2011), as well as Gabriel, *I Am Not a Brain*.

18 Nicholas Humphrey, *Soul Dust: The Magic of Consciousness* (Princeton, NJ: Princeton University Press, 2011), p. 204, quoted in Frankish, 'Illusionism as a theory of consciousness', p. 17.

19 Frankish, 'Illusionism as a theory of consciousness', p. 17.

20 Nicholas Humphrey, 'The invention of consciousness', *Topoi*, 39 (2017): 13–21, here p. 13.

21 Searle, *Intentionality*, ch. 10.

22 Derk Pereboom, *Consciousness and the Prospects of Physicalism* (Oxford: Oxford University Press, 2011), pp. 15–40, quoted in Frankish, 'Illusionism as a theory of consciousness', pp. 17f.

23 An indirect reference to George Ray in Frankish, 'Illusionism as a theory of consciousness', p. 18.

24 At this point, one could also consider the discourse-theoretical variant of mental fictionalism, which holds that discourse about the mental is (1) truth-apt/cognitive, (2) to be understood literally, without paraphrase, but nonetheless (3) false, although the statements about the mental (4) play a useful part, meaning that we should not break off the discourse for rationality-theoretical reasons. For a discussion of this position, see the contributions in *The Monist*, 96/4 (2013), an issue devoted to 'mental fictionalism'. The decisive objection to mental fictionalism can be found in that issue, in Miklós Márton and János Töszér, 'Mental fictionalism as an undermotivated theory', pp. 622–38. Márton and Töszér show that there is no reason to view consciousness as a point of reference for motivating a factionalist discourse theory, which means that there is *a fortiori* no reason to accept a general mental fictionalism.

25 See Gabriel, *Propos réalistes* (Paris: Librairie Philosophique J. Vrin, 2019), pp. 189–207.

26 See Aristotle, *De anima* III 6, 430a26–28.

27 See my reconstruction of this much discussed state of affairs in Gabriel, *The Limits of Epistemology* (Cambridge: Polity, 2020), §§8f.

28 Frankish, 'Illusionism as a theory of consciousness', p. 27: 'If people's claims and beliefs about something (God, say, or UFOs) can be fully explained as arising from causes having no connection with the thing itself, then this is a reason for discounting them and regarding the thing as illusory.'

29 *Critique of Pure Reason*, B123f.

30 I thank Ned Block and Tyler Burge for an extensive discussion of this problem during the Ernst Robert Curtius Lectures in Bonn on 12 December 2016.

31 Immanuel Kant, *Dreams of a Spirit-Seer*, in *Kant on Swedenborg: Dreams of a Spirit-Seer and Other Writings*, ed. Gregory R. Johnson, trans. Gregory R. Johnson and Glenn Alexander Magee (New York: Swedenborg Foundation, 2002), p. 10.

32 Ibid.

33 Ibid., p. 12.

34 Ibid.

35 Frankish, 'Illusionism as a theory of consciousness', p. 22. This passage is directly preceded by an instructive one in which Frankish imagines someone who 'is referring to a fictional agony, entering into the world of the play and responding to the emotions of the characters as if they were real. . . . Of course, most people do not regard their phenomenology as illusory; they are like naive theatregoers who take the action on stage for real.'

36 Ibid., p. 34.

37 Tyler Burge, 'Self and self-conception', *Journal of Philosophy*, 108/6–7 (2007): 287–383.

38 From the human standpoint, the relevant whole whose parts include phenomenal consciousness is the mind, and thus neither the organism at any given moment nor a subsystem of the organism (such as a subsystem of the central nervous system). Mind is the whole from which we can grasp ourselves as beings that essentially have mental states, some of which cannot be successfully identified by correlating them with natural species, and ultimately tracing them back to these. That is why mind is not a natural species, and consequently not as such an object of any natural-scientific examination.

39 G. W. F. Hegel, *The Science of Logic*, trans. George di Giovanni (Cambridge: Cambridge University Press, 2010), p. 69.

40 Christoph Chabris and Daniel Simons, *The Invisible Gorilla, and Other Ways Our Intuition Deceives Us* (New York: Crown, 2010).

§7 The Indispensability of Mind

1 See also Wolfram Hogrebe, *Szenische Metaphysik* (Frankfurt: Klostermann, 2019).

2 For a recent perspective on these issues, see Dieter Henrich, *Dies Ich, das viel besagt: Fichtes Einsicht nachdenken* (Frankfurt: Klostermann, 2019).

3 Aristotle, *Metaphysics* XII 9, 1074b36. For an interpretation, see Markus Gabriel, 'God's transcendent activity: ontotheology in *Metaphysics* 12', *Review of Metaphysics*, 250 (2009): 385–414.

4 See the concept of sensations in Bertrand Russell, *The Analysis of Mind* (London: Allen & Unwin, 1921). Russell understands sensory data not as subjective mental states but as the 'intersection of mind and matter' (p. 144). According to this model, objects are not located behind their aspects but are bundles of particularity. In response to the natural objection that this causes the substance of reality to crumble, Russell trenchantly states: 'It may be said: If there is no single existent which is the source of all these "aspects," how are they collected together? The answer is simple: Just as they would be if there were such a single existent' (p. 98). On the history of the concept of intensity in psychophysics and related areas, see Andrea Schütte, *Intensität: Ästhetik und Poetik eines literarischen Phänomens* (habilitation thesis, University of Bonn, 2018).

5 Thus also Hubert Dreyfus and Charles Taylor, *Retrieving Realism* (Cambridge, MA: Harvard University Press, 2015).

6 See the discussion of this in Michael S. Gazzaniga, 'On determinism and

human responsibility', in Gregg D. Caruso and Owen Flanagan (eds), *Neuroexistentialism: Meaning, Morals, and Purpose in the Age of Neuroscience* (Oxford: Oxford University Press, 2018), pp. 223–34.

7 It does not aid the cause of epiphenomenalism to postulate that refrigerators, cold drinks, and so on, become effective as represented objects in the form of neuronal patterns, since the representations represented by the refrigerators, cold drinks, and so forth, must somehow deal with them in order for correlating mental states to exist at all. They do not deal with them, however, merely by virtue of being caused by them, unless one smuggles the relation of intentionality into the concept of causation. Representing something and having been caused by something are not generally the same thing, of course, so the epiphenomenalist would have to explain why this should apply to neuronal patterns, assuming they are caused by environmental things or objects.

8 Timothy Williamson, *Knowledge and its Limits* (Oxford: Oxford University Press, 2000), pp. 93f.

9 Ibid., p. 93.

10 Ibid., p. 95.

11 Here I am largely following Anthony Brueckner and M. Oreste Fiocco, 'Williamson's anti-luminosity argument', *Philosophical Studies*, 110/3 (2002): 285–93.

12 Williamson, *Knowledge and its Limits*, pp. 106–9.

13 Ibid., p. 107.

14 Rometsch, *Freiheit zur Wahrheit*, ch. 4.

15 See the arguments for a biological externalism in Gabriel, *Der Sinn des Denkens*, pp. 197–204.

16 In the German text, Gabriel translates 'entertain the proposition' as *urteilen*, which is more like 'to judge'. Outside of Williamson's specific argumentation, the word has therefore been translated accordingly, rather than adapting it to the original English terminology (Trans.).

17 Williamson, *Knowledge and its Limits*, pp. 108f.

18 This is shown especially well in Sebastian Rödl, *Self-Consciousness and Objectivity* (Cambridge, MA: Harvard University Press, 2018). See also Irad Kimhi, *Thinking and Being* (Cambridge, MA: Harvard University Press, 2018).

19 Based on this, Anton Friedrich Koch has shown that we cannot be in a sceptical dream scenario. See his anti-sceptical strategy in 'Wir sind kein Zufall: Die Subjektivitätsthese als Grundlage eines hermeneutischen Realismus', in Gabriel, *Der Neue Realismus*, pp. 230–423, as well as 'Der metaphysische Realismus und seine skeptizistische Rückseite', in Gabriel (ed.), *Skeptizisimus und Metaphysik: Deutsche Zeitschrift für Philosophie*, 28 (2011): 93–104 [special issue].

20 Here one might fear that this would endanger the comprehensibility of outside judgements, since it seems as if the fact that something thinks *p* colours what they think. Yet this overlooks the fact that the situation in which the person who judges is operating is in fact incorporated into the judgement's content, not least if another person judges the judgement someone makes. Subjectivity is not a private standpoint that inscribes itself on the objective judgement and

thus cloaks it in ineffability; rather, it is a public event of embedding a judging being in real surroundings.

21 For a critique of the formally misleading notion that knowledge ultimately has the same form in all cases, namely 'S knows that p', see Rödl, *Selbstbewusstsein und Objektivität* (Berlin: Suhrkamp, 2019). For a different view, see Saul A. Kripke, 'Nozick on knowledge', in *Philosophical Troubles* (Oxford: Oxford University Press, 2011), pp. 162–224, here pp. 210f.: 'It is very plausible that a unified account [of knowledge] is indeed desirable; prima facie it would seem that "*S* knows that *p*" expresses one and the same relation between *S* and *p*, regardless of what proposition *p* is, or for that matter, who *S* is.' By contrast, see Gabriel, *Sinn und Existenz* (Berlin: Suhrkamp, 2016), §11.

22 Carlo Rovelli, *The Order of Time*, trans. Erica Segre and Simon Carnell (New York: Riverhead, 2018), p. 134.

23 By contrast, see Gabriel, 'Für einen nicht-naturalistischen Realismus', in Magdalena Marszałek and Dieter Mersch (eds), *Seien wir realistisch* (Zurich: Diaphanes, 2016), pp. 58–9.

24 Rovelli, *The Order of Time*, p. 31.

25 For a subtle reconstruction of this problem area, which has famously been known since Sellars as the 'myth of the given', see John McDowell, *Having the World in View: Essays on Kant, Hegel, and Sellars* (Cambridge, MA: Harvard University Press, 2013).

26 Here Rovelli largely follows Huw Price, *Time's Arrow and Archimedes' Point: New Directions for the Physics of Time* (Oxford: Oxford University press, 1997).

27 Rovelli, *The Order of Time*, p. 210.

28 Ibid., p. 211.

29 Ibid.

30 Ibid.

31 Ibid., pp. 211f.

32 Ibid., p. 210.

33 Wolfgang Detel, *Warum wir nichts über Gott wissen können* (Hamburg: Meiner, 2018), pp. 31–3.

34 Ibid., p. 32.

35 Regarding this model, see the deliberations in Wolfgang Prinz, *Selbst im Spiegel: Die soziale Konstruktion von Subjektivität* (Berlin: Suhrkamp, 2013).

36 This is precisely what has been opposed by the recourse to the mythological consciousness since Schelling's positive philosophy. For a comprehensive account, see my reconstruction in Markus Gabriel, *Der Mensch im Mythos: Untersuchungen über Ontotheologie, Anthropologie und Selbstbewusstseinsgeschichte in Schellings 'Philosophie der Mythologie'* (Berlin: de Gruyter, 2006). On the mythological consciousness and its omnipresence in the naturalist self-conception of modernity, see Hans Blumenberg, *Work on Myth*, trans. Robert M. Wallace (Cambridge, MA: MIT Press, 1988), and Kurt Hübner, *Die Wahrheit des Mythos* (Munich: C. H. Beck, 1985).

37 See George Ellis and Markus Gabriel: 'Physical, logical, and mental top-down effects', in Markus Gabriel and Jan Voosholz (eds), *Top-Down Causation and Emergence* (Dordrecht: Springer, 2021).

§8 The Lifeworld of Ontology of Fields of Sense

1 Edmund Husserl, *The Crisis of European Sciences and Transcendental Phenomenology: An Introduction to Phenomenological Philosophy*, trans. David Carr (Evanston, IL: Northwestern University Press, 1970), pp. 48f. A particularly glaring example of this tendency in contemporary physics can be found in Max Tegmark, *Our Mathematical Universe: My Quest for the Ultimate Nature of Reality* (New York: Knopf, 2014), as well as the same author's recent attempt to characterize life as a technical function, in *Life 3.0: Being Human in the Age of Artificial Intelligence* (New York: Knopf, 2017).

2 Husserl, *The Crisis of European Sciences and Transcendental Phenomenology*, p. 49.

3 Ibid., p. 50.

4 Ibid., p. 51.

5 Ibid.

6 See Edmund Husserl, *Logical Investigations*, vol. 2, trans. J. N. Findlay (London: Routledge, 2013), pp. 220–5.

7 Ibid., p. 220.

8 Husserl, *The Crisis of European Sciences and Transcendental Phenomenology*, p. 51.

9 Ibid.

10 The methodological individualism also employed by Husserl generally has a deleterious effect at this level, something already pointed out by Karl Mannheim. If knowledge were an accumulation of individual perspectives or knowledge claims, the result would be the absurd image of a community, and 'in a certain discussion the true worldview is brought to light' (Karl Mannheim, *Ideology and Utopia*, trans. Louis Wirth and Edward Shils [London: Routledge, 2013], p. 26).

11 Edmund Husserl, *Die Lebenswelt: Auslegungen der vorgegebenen Welt und ihrer Konstitution* (Dordrecht: Springer, 2008), p. 158: 'Our whole interpretation of the pre-scientific lifeworld, and from there of science and all products of the radical enlightenment of science on this path, is my interpretation, the European's. The primitive has an entirely different lifeworld; for him there is no path to European science. Our logic – the logic of the primitives. But I am the one who makes these distinctions etc.' For a discussion of 'primitive Dasein', see Heidegger, *Being and Time*, §11.

12 Husserl, *Die Lebenswelt*, p. 168.

13 Admittedly, Husserl himself is not an outright advocate of the phenomenological argument, as one can find such statements in his writings as 'I do not see colour-sensations but coloured things, I do not hear tone-sensations but the singer's song, etc. etc.' (*Logical Investigations*, vol. 2, p. 99). However, there are passages in Husserl that implicate him in a problematic representationalism, as well as passages that portray adumbrations as concepts gained through an analysis of a complete perceptual situation, meaning that perceptions do not *in reality* contain adumbrations but can only be viewed as such in order to divide

actually successful perception into partial conceptual aspects in an explanatory mode. However, the at times extreme divergence of interpretations in Husserl scholarship ultimately shows that Husserl did not articulate a sufficiently clear position on the realism/idealism complex. One can find a cursory doxographic overview in Dan Zahavi, *Husserl's Legacy: Phenomenology, Metaphysics, and Transcendental Philosophy* (Oxford: Oxford University Press, 2017), esp. ch. 4. I am grateful to Tobias Keiling for an extensive discussion of the ontology of the noema and the research landscape. On the relation between phenomenology and the landscape of New Realism, see Tobias Streubel, 'Inwiefern ist die Phänomenologie eine "realistische" Philosophie', *Deutsche Zeitschrift für Philosophie*, 67/2 (2019): 192–210.

14 On these 'generic objects' and their role in epistemology, see Stanley Cavell, *The Claim of Reason: Wittgenstein, Skepticism, Morality, and Tragedy* (Oxford: Oxford University Press, 1999), ch. 6. Husserl expressly terms the object of a perception a 'thing', for example in *Logical Investigations*, vol. 2, p. 211:

> All perceiving and imagining is, on our view, a web of partial intentions, fused together in the unity of a single, total intention. The correlate of this last intention is the thing, while the correlates of its partial intentions are *the thing's parts and moments*. Only in this way can we understand how consciousness reaches out beyond what it actually experiences. It can so to say mean beyond itself, and its meaning can be fulfilled.

Husserl, then, would officially dispute that one perceives sides of things. Nonetheless, an act of 'meaning beyond itself' is necessary, which means that one initially apprehends something (in the mode of partial intentions) that must then be connected to a total intention. Yet this triggers a variation on the phenomenological argument, since one cannot perceive a thing directly but only through an indefinite number of partial operations. The thingly parts are potentially in the way. While this explains the fallibility of perception, its result is that one must view a case of success not as direct perception but as a successful detour, which takes us back to the problems discussed in the main text.

15 Husserl cannot be entirely absolved of the suspicion of employing a variant of this argument, as shown by *Logical Investigations*, vol. 2, pp. 220ff., where the adumbration theorem is tested in the context of the theory of perception. At the very start of this passage we read: 'The object is not actually given, it is not given wholly and entirely as that which it itself is. It is only given "from the front", only "perspectivally foreshortened and projected" etc.' Husserl presumably realizes that this can lead in the wrong direction, and adds a few lines later: 'We must note, however, that the object, as it is *in itself* – in the only sense relevant and understandable in our context, the sense which the fulfilment of the perceptual intention would carry out – is *not wholly different* from the object realized, however imperfectly, in the percept.' But even this is further qualified, culminating in the statement that 'it yet, as a *total act*, grasps the object itself, even if only by way of an adumbration'. This raises the question of how

one can actually grasp the object itself, which is not really given, 'even if only by way of an adumbration', which brings up the problem area pointed out in the main text.

16 Thus Tobias Keiling in a written message on a previous version of the main text.

17 Husserl, *Logical Investigations*, vol. 2, pp. 220.

18 Ibid.

19 Ibid., p. 211.

20 See the much discussed essay by Dagfinn Føllesdal, 'Husserl's theory of perception', *Ajatus: Yearbook of the Philosophical Society of Finland*, 36 (1976): 95–105.

21 For a systematically ambitious variant, see the argumentation in Steven Crowell, *Normativity and Phenomenology in Husserl and Heidegger* (Cambridge: Cambridge University Press, 2013).

22 See the sketch of a deduction of the existence of veridic normativity in Detel, *Warum wir nichts über Gott wissen können*, pp. 61–3. Detel works with a dualism between semantic substance and 'physical states in the world', which confronts him with the problem of explaining the 'strange, even mysterious' property of representations of being 'correct-or-incorrect, fulfilled-or-not-fulfilled, true-or-false' (ibid., p. 61). Here Detel overlooks that a given mental state whereby a subject can refer to something that is not in all cases a mental state is never true-or-false, but rather true or false. Mental states do not oscillate between truth values, which means that there is no need to impute these from without in order to tie them to physical states of the world. Our thoughts are already where they want to go or where they belong – that is, factually true or factually false. To the extent that they meet the minimum requirements of truth-aptness, normativity does not apply. For the phenomenological context in the strict sense, see Crowell, *Normativity and Phenomenology in Husserl and Heidegger*.

23 Direct realism does not deny that there are substances which can be understood as media. These media are something thoroughly real, however – in this case even causally active. They can be examined with the suitable methods of physics and sensory physiology, though they do not exhaust themselves in this, as perceptual substances are essentially conscious, and thus processed in modules of the mind.

24 Tobias Keiling has remarked that Husserl's theory of perception should be understood to the effect that, based on (T+S^i), (T+S$^#$) should be rejected, though this does not rule out the possibility of a substance S^{ii} that is more adequate than S^i. However, this presupposes that there may not be a maximally adequate substance S*. In keeping with the object theory of FOS, I would counter that we can introduce a conjunction of all perceptual substances that adequately represent their perceptual thing. Taken together, they form the maximally adequate substance S* – which, one should note, can probably no longer be a perceptual substance according to Husserl. For a comprehensive opposing perspective, see Gabriel, *The Meaning of Thought*, where I hold that maximally adequate substances qua objects of thinking –that is, qua thoughts – certainly can be perceived; for thinking as the grasping of thoughts is perception of concepts. This option is located outside the phenomenological framework, though this is

not a flaw within the perspective taken here but in fact the decisive advantage for avoiding the phenomenological arguments in all its variations.

25 Detel, *Warum wir nichts über Gott wissen können*, p. 61.

26 Ibid., p. 89.

27 Ibid., p. 87.

28 Ibid., p. 89.

29 See, paradigmatically, Jean-Luc Marion, *Givenness and Revelation* (Oxford: Oxford University Press, 2018).

30 I am grateful to Eduardo Viveiros de Castro for discussions about the status of symmetrical anthology in light of the challenges of ethnological research during our meetings in Porto Alegre and Rio de Janeiro. For an overview of his position, see Eduardo Viveiros de Castro, *The Inconstancy of the Indian Soul: The Encounter of Catholics and Cannibals in 16th-Century Brazil*, trans. Gregory Duff Morton (Chicago: Prickly Paradigm Press, 2011). For a discussion of circumstances amenable to New Realism in contemporary cultural anthropology, see the collection by Martin Holbraad and Morten Axel Pedersen, *The Ontological Turn: An Anthropological Exposition* (Cambridge: Cambridge University Press, 2017). I am also grateful for an extensive analysis of the scope of New Realism and neo-existentialism for ethnology by Susan Gal and Celia Lowe, with whom I was able to discuss the associated methodological questions during my time as Walker Ames Lecturer at the University of Washington in Seattle in March 2019.

31 Gabriel, *Sinn und Existenz*, pp. 88f, 193–6, 304–6. See also ibid., pp. 356–68. In Gabriel, *The Limits of Epistemology*, I developed a number of meta-epistemological arguments that the contextuality of knowledge claims implies that there is no redeemable knowledge claim which turns all contexts into some kind of object (even if it is a mereologically generated one).

32 With this distinction I am following the basic idea of Peter Strawson's reconstruction of the thrust of a transcendental deduction in Strawson, *The Bounds of Sense: An Essay on Kant's Critique of Pure Reason* (Abingdon: Routledge, 2019). On this reconstruction, see Markus Gabriel, *Die Erkenntnis der Welt* (Freiburg: Alber, 2012), ch. III.2.2.

33 Campbell and Cassam, *Berkeley's Puzzle*, pp. 2–4.

34 This was already critically rejected in John McDowell, *Mind and World* (Cambridge, MA: Harvard University Press, 1996), p. 75, n. 6.

35 Immanuel Kant, *Groundwork of the Metaphysics of Morals*, trans. Mary Gregor (Cambridge: Cambridge University Press, 1996), pp. 24f.

36 See Thomas Nagel's brief deliberations at the end of 'What is it like to be a bat?', *Philosophical Review*, 83/4 (1974): 435–50, esp. pp. 449f. See, more recently, Tilman Staemmler, *Thomas Nagel: Eine phänomenologische Intuition in der Philosophie des Geistes* (Würzburg: Königshausen & Neumann, 2018). Naturally 'appearances' [*Erscheinungen*] in the Kantian sense are paradigmatic elements of the causal order. Yet appearances, in a way that is not simply epistemically graspable (knowable), are in turn 'caused' by things in themselves, which takes us to the much discussed and never adequately resolved debate on the relation between things in themselves and appearances. An objective phenomenology

in the sense aimed for in the main text grasps appearances both causally and as things in themselves, which means that the Kantian division of labour is overcome (or its motivation circumvented).

37 As noted above, there are many reflections in Husserl's own work in which he expressly distances himself from such theoretical figures. For a representative example, see *Logical Investigations*, vol. 1, p. 299: 'That the so-called immanent object is not in a serious sense an object in our presentation [*Vorstellung*] . . . is naturally my definite opinion too; on the side of the presentation nothing exists but the reference-to-this-object, the significant scope [*Bedeutungsinhalt*], as it were, of the presentation.'

38 For a critique of such a model, see (of course) Richard Rorty, *Philosophy and the Mirror of Nature* (Princeton, NJ: Princeton University Press, 2009), as well as Hilary Putnam, *The Threefold Cord* (New York: Columbia University Press, 1999). The relevant rejection of mental representationalism, which was a central philosophical issue in the 1920s, is simply ignored in many areas of contemporary cognitive research, without any attempt to show first how one opposes all these objections argumentatively. This is an unfortunate regression to an untenable methodology that will have consequences sooner or later in the form of incorrect data and failed experiments.

39 Thus an apt formulation by Kurt Flasch in *Die Metaphysik de Einen bei Nikolaus von Kues: Problemgeschichtliche Stellung und systematische Bedeutung* (Leiden: Brill, 1973), p. xii. For a critique of the idea of nature as the 'bedrock of being' that is presumably alluded to by Flasch, see Theodor W. Adorno, *Negative Dialectics*, trans. E. B. Ashton (New York: Continuum, 2007), p. 368.

40 See the presentation of a direct perceptual realism in John R. Searle, *Seeing Things as They Are: A Theory of Perception* (Oxford: Oxford University Press, 2015).

41 In keeping with this, see the comprehensive phenomenological sketch in Evan Thompson, *Mind in Life: Biology, Phenomenology, and the Science of Mind* (Cambridge, MA: Harvard University Press, 2007).

42 Husserl, The Crisis of European Sciences and Transcendental Phenomenology, p. 2.

43 Rometsch, *Freiheit zur Wahrheit*, chs 15–17, shows that the transition to such a conception of mental representations in the modern age was circumvented by Descartes and became a paradigm only with Locke. Rometsch identifies the reasons for this shift in Locke's theory of signs.

§9 Objective Phenomenology

1 The perceived suchness has a factual format; that is, there is a categorial difference between our perceptual form and the form in which we encounter things. These two formats are intertwined in perception but are differently coded, which is why it is legitimate to argue that the facts we perceive would often still be much the same as our perceptions, even if we did not perceive them. Since perceptions constitute a causal contribution to events in the universe, it is

not strictly the case that the things we perceive are independent of perception. However, not all of the perceived facts exist because we perceive them, which is where I bring the idea of different codings into play.

2 It is no coincidence that Russell, as an exponent of a purely causal theory of perception, considers our perception so fragmentary that we can remove one individual thing in the series *x*, *y*, *z* at any time. See Bertrand Russell, *The Analysis of Matter* (London: Routledge, 1992), p. 200. What Russell overlooks here, however, is that perceptual processes are essentially causally connected to processes that are only explicable via quantum mechanics, so one precisely cannot undo the relations between the individual things that we observe in the act of perception and our observation itself without thus changing other individual things. The causal texture of perceptual fields of sense cannot be grasped without quantum-theoretical interconnections. Causal transmission of information does not work in the manner of a classical Newtonian perspective – that is, by a source transmitting something that is causally independent of the process of its apprehension. Perception is a case of what is known in quantum mechanics as observation – that is, a causal intervention into the surroundings, not a mere apprehension.

3 See, famously, Wilfrid Sellars, *Empiricism and the Philosophy of Mind* (Cambridge, MA: Harvard University Press, 1997), which gave rise to a tradition of rejecting the idea that concepts are interventions in a non-conceptual material. However, one should not conclude too hastily from this that there is no non-conceptual sensory material, something rightly pointed out by Charles Travis and Jocelyn Benoist. See Travis, 'The silence of the senses', *Mind*, 113/449 (2004): 57–94, and Benoist, *Le bruit du sensible* (Paris: Cerf, 2013).

4 See Kripke, *Reference and Existence: The John Locke Lectures* (Oxford: Oxford University Press, 2013), Lecture IV.

5 Heine reports that Hegel once referred to the stars in conversation as 'a shiny leprosy in the sky' (Heinrich Heine, *Confessions*, trans. Peter Heinegg [Malibu: J. Simon, 1981], p. 46). This statement is presumably directed against Kant's famous reference to the 'starry heavens' and human, moral significance, which is a different matter.

6 What I mean by the 'subjective visual field' is the object area consisting of what I consciously perceive from my literal standpoint, as opposed to what another living being located somewhere else perceives. Certainly the objects within two different subjective visual fields can overlap; we can in part perceive the same things, albeit differently. Two subjective visual fields can never be extensionally identical. It is not part of this concept that subjective visual fields employ mental representations, notions or any other structure found in 'someone's head' or 'consciousness'.

7 See Kripke, *Reference and Existence*, p. 93.

8 See, despite its rejection in the majority of recent Husserl scholarship, the interpretation in Dagfinn Føllesdal, *Husserl und Frege: Ein Beitrag zur Beleuchtung der Entstehung der phänomenologischen Philsophie* (Oslo: Norwegian Academy of Sciences, 1958).

9 Gabriel, 'Neutraler Realismus'.

10 The type of 'naïve realism' criticized here can be traced to G. E. Moore. For more detail with sources, see Gabriel, *The Limits of Epistemology*, §3. A different form of 'naïve realism' is connected to disjunctivism, though this is not specifically addressed at this point. For a paradigmatic description, see the reflections on the relation between naïve realism and disjunctivism in Michael G. F. Martin, 'The reality of appearances', in Richard Mark Sainsbury (ed.), *Thought and Ontology* (Milan: FrancoAngeli, 1997), pp. 77–96.

11 I do not see how disjunctivist theories deal with the relation between different fields of sense – that is, how they determine the relation between electromagnetic radiation and perceptible, colourful objects, and so forth. Here it is not sufficient to rely on the fact that appearances manifest things in themselves, since these things seem to have a plurality of descriptions, some of which entail the fact that the things in themselves cannot appear visually at all in those descriptions (such as quantum physics).

12 Geert Keil, *Willensfreiheit: Grundthemen Philosophie* (Berlin: de Gruyter, 2012), p. 41. See also Brigitte Falkenburg, *Mythos Determinismus: Wieviel erklärt uns die Hirnforschung* (Berlin: Springer, 2012), as well as Jenann T. Ismael, *The Situated Self* (Oxford: Oxford University Press, 2009), and *How Physics Makes Us Free* (Oxford: Oxford University Press, 2016).

13 At a panel discussion in Marseilles on 31 October 2015.

14 Rovelli, *The Order of Time*, p. 75.

15 Naturally there are also perceptual systems that are directed not at the organism's environment but, rather, at its states, such as sensations of pain, the sense of balance, and so on.

16 A paradigmatic example of this incurable imbalance can be found in Michael Esfeld, *Naturphilosophie als Metaphysik der Natur* (Frankfurt: Suhrkamp, 2008). Where physics does not support his outlandish metaphysical construction, Esfeld corrects physics itself in order to create the desired balance between empirical input and free-floating metaphysical construction; however, this cannot succeed as long as one understands the philosophy of nature as metaphysics. Esfeld jumps back and forth at will between a priori and a posteriori to justify a naturalist worldview for which he does not adduce any reasons that are independent of this ideology.

17 See here the reflections on the concept of mind in Scheler, *The Human Place in the Cosmos*.

18 Hans Vaihinger, *The Philosophy of 'As If'* (London: Routledge, 2021), pp. 18ff. and *passim*. Vaihinger is largely drawing on *Critique of Pure Reason*, A771f./B799f.

19 Vaihinger builds his own theory of fictions on this fiction. See for example Vaihinger, *The Philosophy of 'As If'*, p. 60:

> The entire conceptual world [*Vorstellungswelt*] lies between these two poles of sensation and motion. The psyche continually adds new members between these two points, and the delicacy and elaboration of its interpolations, pictures and auxiliary concepts develop with the growth of the nerve-mass and the increasing isolation of the brain from

the spine. Our conceptual world lies between the sensory and motor nerves, an infinite intermediate world, and serves merely to make the interconnection between them richer and easier, more delicate and more serviceable. Science is concerned with the elaboration of this conceptual world, and with the adjustment of this instrument to the objective relations of sequence and coexistence which make themselves perceptible.

Vaihinger recognizes that he himself uses a 'fictional language' (ibid.). But he does not seem to go far enough, because he then introduces sensations as factual (which here presumably means non-fictive) 'given' sensations (ibid.), which is why he defines his philosophy as idealistic positivism (sic!). The position from which Vaihinger defines fictions as such is ultimately wilful, since it exempts itself from fictionality for no reason. See p. 70: 'The only fictionless doctrine in the world is that of Critical Positivism.' It becomes evident at several points in Vaihinger's deliberations that this position is contradictory (which, according to his own premises, is a signal of fictionality). For example, he refers on one occasion to the 'conceptual world' or the 'world of sensory appearance' as 'mere illusion' (p. 126), albeit based somehow on experience as pure Being, though we read only a little later that 'the phenomenal world' is 'not a mere illusion' but, rather, a 'conceptual construct which has become more appropriate and suitable through a progressively richer experience' (p. 127).

20 One can find what is hopefully a deterrent example of the epistemological incoherence that results from viewing the elements of a reconstructive analysis as autonomously acting systems from which the unity of thinking can never be regained in the following passage from Neil Levy, 'Choices without choosers: toward a neuropsychologically plausible existentialism', in Gregg D. Caruso and Owen Flanagan (eds), *Neuroexistentialism: Meaning, Morals, and Purpose in the Age of Neuroscience* (Oxford: Oxford University Press, 2018), p. 115:

It is now a commonplace in cognitive science that the mind is *modular*. Minds do not consist of a central executive in addition to a multiplicity of inflexible and rather unintelligent mechanisms. Rather, the mind consists of *nothing but* such unintelligent mechanisms. There is no such central executive: nothing which occupies a seat of power, and nothing which has sufficient intelligence to even understand what that power consists in, let alone use it wisely.

Is this an expression of self-knowledge?

21 For a discussion of the question of whether generalized quantum theory boils down to a process ontology, or whether one can rather make an epistemic cut that introduces stable objects with substance form into the universe, see Hartmann Römer, 'Substanz, Veränderung und Komplementarität', *Philosophisches Jahrbuch*, 113/1 (2006): 118–36. See also the reflections in Karen Barad, *Meeting the Universe Halfway: Quantum Physics and the Entanglement of Matter and Meaning* (Durham, NC: Duke University Press, 2007).

22 See Anton Friedrich Koch, 'Die Bildtheorie des Elementarsatzes und die Lesbarkeit der Dinge (Wittgenstein, Sellars, Kant)', in Siri Granum Carson et al. (eds), *Kant: Here, Now, and How: Essays in Honour of Truly Wyller* (Paderborn: Mentis, 2011), pp. 179–92.

23 See the incisive description of his position in Benoist, 'Realismus ohne Metaphysik', in Markus Gabriel (ed.), *Der Neue Realismus* (Berlin: Suhrkamp, 2016), pp. 133–53, and in greater detail in *Éléments de philosophie réaliste* (Paris: Vrin, 2011).

24 See Markus Gabriel, 'Dissens und Gegenstand: Vom Außenwelt- zum Weltproblem', in Gabriel (ed.), *Skeptizismus und Metaphysik* (Berlin: Akademie, 2011), pp. 73–92.

25 Let me repeat here that the lines in a Müller–Lyer illusion are, of course, never really equally long. Perceptible lines are not geometric lines. This is more significant than one might suppose, for it shows that the concept of perceptual delusion contains an element of Vaihinger's fictions, as it presents the perception with geometrical dimensions that do not literally apply.

26 This corresponds to Russell's concept of the sensory datum in *The Analysis of Mind*, with which, in spite of himself, he takes up the basic idea developed by Henri Bergson (far more elegantly) in *Matter and Memory*, trans. N. M. Paul and W. S. Palmer (New York: Cosimo, 2007).

27 Gabriel, *Sinn und Existenz*, pp. 193–7.

28 See especially Jocelyn Benoist, *Sens et sensibilité: l'intentionnalité en contexte* (Paris: Cerf, 2009).

29 See the science-historical sketch in the context of a theory of the imagination that pursues similar goals to FOS in John Stallis, *Logic of Imagination: The Expanse of the Elemental* (Bloomington: Indiana University Press, 2012), ch. 7. I am grateful to Tobias Keiling for pointing me to this study and its parallels with the objective phenomenology developed in the main text (which also become clear in chapter 4 of Sallis's book).

30 See Alexander Kanev, 'New realism, pluralism and science', in Luca Taddio (ed.), *New Perspectives on Realism* (Milan: Mimesis International, 2017), pp. 191–214.

31 Regarding the failure of the requirement of iterativity, demands that there is knowledge of knowledge, or at least that it must general be possible, see Gabriel, *The Limits of Epistemology*, pp. 93–5 and 97–100.

32 Russell, *The Analysis of Matter*, p. 197.

33 Admittedly, Russell sees another grave problem in the fact that he wishes to remove the concept of cause from science, which means that, in spite of himself, he cannot advocate a scientifically based causal theory of perception anyway, since science lacks the concept of cause. See Bertrand Russell, 'On the notion of cause', in John G. Slater (ed.), *The Collected Papers of Bertrand Russell*, vol. 6: *Logical and Philosophical Papers 1909–1913* (London: Routledge, 1992), pp. 193–210.

34 For a clarification of the concept of information, see Luciano Floridi, *The Philosophy of Information* (Oxford: Oxford University Press, 2013).

35 Aristotle, *De anima* 426b3–24, where Aristotle establishes a connection between

the objective structure (*logos*) and the fact that it judges (*krinei*). See Gabriel, *Der Sinn des Denkens*, pp. 50–5.

§10 Ontology of the Imagination

1 David Hume, *An Enquiry Concerning Human Understanding and Other Writings*, ed. Stephen Buckle (Cambridge: Cambridge University Press, 2007), p. 47.
2 See the historically and systematically skilful defence of a Cartesian position in Rometsch, *Freiheit zur Wahrheit*, ch. 4.
3 Horst Bredekamp, *Thomas Hobbes visuelle Strategien: Der Leviathan, Urbild des modernen Staates, Werkillustrationen und Portraits* (Berlin: de Gruyter, 1999); *Die Fenster der Monade: Gottfried Wilhelm Leibniz' Theater der Natur und Kunst* (Berlin: de Gruyter, 2004); *Darwins Korallen: Die grünen Evolutionsdiagramme und die Tradition der Naturgeschichte* (Berlin: de Gruyter, 2005).
4 See Gabriel, *Der Mensch im Mythos*, which forms the basis for my subsequent studies on the relation between scepticism and metaphysics. See Gabriel, *Skeptizismus und Idealismus in der Antike* (Frankfurt: Suhrkamp, 2009), and Gabriel (ed.), *Skeptizismus und Metaphysik*.
5 Rovelli, *Reality Is Not What It Seems*.
6 For arguments in this direction, see James Ladyman et al., *Every Thing Must Go: Metaphysics Naturalized* (Oxford: Oxford University Press, 2007). See also Harold Kincaid, James Ladyman and Don Ross (eds), *Scientific Metaphysics* (Oxford: Oxford University Press, 2015).
7 Caruso and Flanagan (eds), *Neuroexistentialism*. See my review in *Notre Dame Philosophical Reviews* of 25 November 2018 (https://ndpr.nd.edu/reviews/neuro existentialism-meaning-morals-and-purpose-in-the-age-of-neuroscience/).
8 Owen Flanagan and Gregg D. Caruso, 'Neuroexistentialism: third-wave existentialism', in Caruso and Flanagan (eds), *Neuroexistentialism*, p. 2. The authors obviously do not understand German, as they do not recognize *Geisteswissenschaften* as the plural and suppose that *Geist* means 'ghost', whereas *Geisteswissenschaft(en)* is the term for the humanities. What is even worse is that Friedrich Adolf Kittler makes the same mistake in his (unfortunately) highly influential essay collection *Die Austreibung des Geistes aus den Geisteswissenschaften: Programme des Poststrukturalismus* (Paderborn: Schöningh, 1980).
9 Flanagan and Caruso, 'Neuroexistentialism', p. 2.
10 Ibid., p. 8. Both claims are scientifically false, or at best highly unsubstantiated. See Ellis and Gabriel, 'Physical, logical, and mental top-down effects' and, more comprehensively, Noble, *Dance to the Tune of Life*.
11 A recent example is Maurizio Ferraris, *Intorno agli unicorni: supercazzole, ornitorinchi e ircocervi* (Bologna: il Mulino, 2018).
12 Kant, *Critique of Pure Reason*, A771/B799.
13 Thus the famous formulation from Anaxagoras, DK 59 B 1, which was notably taken up by Plotin. See the difficulties of a meta-metaphysical fictionalism, which I have shown in Gabriel, *Sinn und Existenz*, pp. 367f.

14 Hill, 'Markus Gabriel against the world', *Sophia*, 56/3 (2017): 471–81, at p. 471.

15 Ibid.

16 For a discussion, see Jocelyn Benoist, '*Plus ultra*: méditation sur le carré rond', *Archivio di filosofia*, 78/1 (2010): 209–16.

17 Hill, 'Markus Gabriel against the world', p. 474. Note that the word 'any' does not refer to any case, since quantifiers do not refer.

18 That is why Timothy Williamson's argumentation is methodologically and meta-logically misguided in 'Everything', *Philosophical Perspectives*, 17/1 (2003): 415–65.

19 See Markus Gabriel, 'Die Metaphysik als Denken des Ungegenständlichen', in Tobias Dangel and Markus Gabriel (eds), *Metaphysik und Religion: Festschrift für Jens Halfwassen zum 60. Geburtstag* (Tübingen: Mohr Siebeck, 2020).

20 It is irksome that there are nonetheless attempts to trump the mathematical metalogic of the twentieth century a priori with recourse to the myth of metaphysical universal quantification. See the discussion in Augustín Rayo and Gabriel Uzquiano (eds), *Absolute Generality* (Oxford: Oxford University Press, 2006).

21 Priest, *Towards Non-Being* (Oxford: Oxford University Press, 2016), pp. 13f.

22 I therefore agree entirely with Nick Stang (based on many conversational exchanges) that metaphysics is only possible if it makes statements about the world that are synthetic and a priori; that is precisely its aim. I do not, however, agree with his feeling that Kant may have achieved this. See Nicholas F. Stang, 'Transcendental idealism without tears', in Tyron Goldschmidt and Kenneth L. Pears (eds), *Idealism: New Essays in Metaphysics* (Oxford: Oxford University Press, 2017), pp. 82–103.

23 Hill, 'Markus Gabriel against the world', p. 475. Specifically on this problem, see Gabriel, *Sinn und Existenz*, §2a.

24 Guido Kreis remains stuck in this neo-Romantic framework of an unhappy infinite approximation; see *Negative Dialektik des Unendlichen* (Berlin: Suhrkamp, 2015).

25 I am grateful to Ulf-G. Meissner, Hans-Peter Nilles, Yasunori Nomura and Hitoshi Murayama for explaining the theoretical foundations of this physical incompleteness at the Bethe Centre for Theoretical Physics in Bonn and during my residencies at the Institute for the Physics and Mathematics of the Universe at Tokyo University.

26 Hill, 'Markus Gabriel against the world', p. 476.

27 Aristotle already pointed out accurately that being cannot be the highest form of genus, meaning that he precisely cannot view ontology as a metaphysical theory of totality, as this is intended by today's advocates of absolute universal quantification. See the illuminating reconstruction in Anton Friedrich Koch, 'Warum ist das Seiende keine Gattung', *prima philosophia*, 6 (1993): 133–42.

28 See also Wittgenstein's comment in *Philosophical Investigations*, §216: '"A thing is identical with itself." There is no finer example of a useless sentence, which

nevertheless is connected with a certain play of the imagination. It is as if in our imagination we put a thing into its own shape and saw that it fitted.'

29 William James, *A Pluralistic Universe: Hibbert Lectures at Manchester College on the Present Situation in Philosophy* (London: Longmans, Green, 1920).

30 Ibid., p. 34.

31 Ibid.

32 Ibid., p. 212.

33 Ibid.

34 Ibid., p. 319.

35 According to Hilary Putnam, 'metaphysical realism' is a perspective from which 'the world consists of some fixed totality of mind-independent objects. There is exactly one true and complete description of "the way the world is". Truth involves some sort of correspondence relation between words or thought-signs and external things and sets of things' (Putnam, *Reason, Truth and History* [Cambridge: Cambridge University Press, 1981], p. 49). See, also by Putnam, *Realism with a Human Face* (Cambridge, MA: Harvard University Press, 1992); *Renewing Philosophy* (Cambridge, MA: Harvard University Press, 1995); and *The Threefold Cord*; as well 'Why there is no ready-made world', in *Realism and Reason* (Cambridge: Cambridge University Press, 1983), pp. 205–28. The recent reconstruction and defence of the model-theoretical arguments against metaphysical realism thus understood can be found in Tim Button, *The Limits of Realism* (Oxford: Oxford University Press, 2013).

36 James, *A Pluralistic Universe*, p. 325.

37 Ibid., p. 325:

> for every part, though it may not be in actual or immediate connexion, is nevertheless in some possible or mediated connexion, with every other part however remote, through the fact that each part hangs together with its very next neighbours in inextricable interfusion. The type of union, it is true, is different here from the monistic type of *alleinheit*. It is not a universal co-implication, or integration of all things *durcheinander*. It is what I call the strung-along type, the type of continuity, contiguity, or concatenation. If you prefer Greek words, you may call it the synechistic type.

38 See Anton Friedrich Koch, *Hermeneutischer Realismus* (Tübingen: Mohr Siebeck, 2016).

39 Ibid., pp. 88–96.

40 Ibid., p. 88.

41 Ibid.

42 The objectification already takes place below the conceptual threshold of conscious perception. See Tyler Burge, *Origins of Objectivity* (Oxford: Oxford University Press, 2010).

43 Koch, *Hermeneutischer Realismus*, p. 88.

44 Ibid., p. 89: 'It is probable that what we call the imagination is a somewhat

ill-defined bundle of many cognitive faculties into which we can expect insights through sensory physiology, neurology and cognitive science.'

45 Ibid.

46 Ibid.

47 Ibid., p. 151.

48 Ibid.

49 As a discursive formation, Euclidean geometry has properties of a deductive system whose theorems express truth-apt, and hence fallible, statements about spatial forms. See Michael N. Forster, 'Kants transzendentaler Idealismus: Das Argument hinsichtlich des Raumes und der Geometrie', in David Espinet et al. (eds), *Raum erfahren: Epistemologische, ethische und ästhetische Zugänge* (Tübingen: Mohr Siebeck, 2017), pp. 63–82.

50 Koch, *Hermeneutischer Realismus*, p. 44.

51 Ibid., p. 66.

52 Ibid. The formulation is admittedly problematic, as Koch adduces a reason for the world's non-existence in order to conclude that it does exist. My thesis, however, is that it does not exist at all, not even as an open horizon, which does not mean that there is no open horizon; that is a different issue.

53 This is shown paradigmatically in Koch, *Versuch über Wahrheit und Zeit* (Paderborn: Brill, 2006). For a discussion of this thesis, see the reconstruction in Thomas Hofweber, 'The place of subjects in the metaphysics of material objects', *Dialectica*, 69/4 (2015): 473–90.

54 Koch, *Hermeneutischer Realismus*, p. 67.

55 Ibid.

56 Ibid., p. 68.

57 See Gabriel, *Sinn und Existenz*, pp. 353–5.

§11 Fictive, Imaginary and Intentional Objects

1 Travis, 'The silence of the senses', and Benoist, *Le bruit du sensible*.

2 Regarding this understanding of intuition, see Gabriel, 'Intuition, representation and thinking: Hegel's psychology and the placement problem', in Marina F. Bykova and Kenneth R. Westphal (eds), *The Palgrave Hegel Handbook* (Basingstoke: Palgrave Macmillan, 2020).

3 To know truths about an object, it is not sufficient to think the *de dicto* thought that there are objects about which we cannot know anything except the fact that we know nothing about them. For it is not through such ideas that we direct ourselves at objects, which is the entire point of the insight that there are unknowable objects. Unknowable objects are not knowable through the back door of their non-object character.

4 See *Critique of Pure Reason*, A19/B33: 'In whatever way and through whatever means a cognition may relate to objects, that through which it relates immediately to them, and at which all thought as a means is directed as an end, is *intuition*.' See also ibid., A68/B93: 'Since no representation pertains to the object immediately except intuition alone, a concept is thus never immediately

related to an object, but is always related to some other representation of it (whether that be an intuition or itself already a concept). Judgment is therefore the mediate cognition of an object, hence the representation of a representation of it.' In the A deduction, we also read this: 'Appearances are the only objects that can be given to us immediately, and that in them which is immediately related to the object is called intuition' (ibid., A108f.). On this level, Kant thus espouses a direct (empirical) realism. For an interpretation, see Lucy Allais, *Manifest Reality: Kant's Idealism and His Realism* (Oxford: Oxford University Press, 2015).

5 For an extensive discussion, see Gabriel, *The Limits of Epistemology*.

6 On the quantum theory of cognition, see Römer, 'Substanz, Veränderung und Komplementarität'.

7 Johann Gottlieb Fichte, *Science of Knowledge*, trans. A. E. Kroeger (London: Trübner, 1889), p. 94.

8 Ibid.

9 See the impressively clear, naturalistic self-description in Theodor Lessing, 'Haarmann: the story of a werewolf', in *Monsters of Weimar: Comprising the Classic Case Histories Haarmann, the Story of a Werewolf, Kürten, the Vampire of Düsseldorf* (Nashville, TN: Nemesis, 1993). 'A tailless ape that walks on its hind legs, is gregarious, omnivorous, unquiet of heart, lying-minded, thieving, lecherous, pugnacious, but a creature of many accomplishments. The enemy of all other earthly beings, and its own most redoubtable foe.'

10 See also Jocelyn Benoist, *Logique du phénomène* (Paris: Hermann, 2016), p. 74: 'It is only by passing through the imaginary that that which, in our ordinary transactions with what we refer to, we always already call "real" can become "appearing".'

11 See the project of a fundamental heuristics, also known as manticism, in Wolfram Hogrebe, *Prädikation und Genesis: Metaphysik als Fundamentalheuristik im Ausgang von Schellings 'Die Weltalter'* (Frankfurt: Suhrkamp, 1989); also Hogrebe, *Metaphysik und Mantik* (Frankfurt: Suhrkamp, 1992).

12 Gabriel, *Sinn und Existenz*, pp. 353–5. For a rejection of the possibility of metaphysical categories, see, by the same author, *Propos réalistes*, pp. 7–51, as well as 'Hegel's Kategorienkritik', in Rainer Schäfer et al. (eds), *Kategoriendeduktion im deutschen Idealismus* (Berlin: Duncker & Humblot, forthcoming).

13 A similar conclusion is reached in Jan Westerhoff, *Ontological Categories* (Oxford: Oxford University Press, 2005), and Otávio Bueno et al., 'The no-category-ontology', *The Monist*, 98/3 (2015): 233–45.

14 See also the argumentation in Anjan Chakravartty, *Scientific Ontology: Integrating Naturalized Metaphysics and Voluntarist Epistemology* (Oxford: Oxford University Press, 2017).

15 Friedrich Nietzsche, *Late Notebooks*, ed. Rüdiger Bittner (Cambridge: Cambridge University Press, 2003), p. 139.

16 Benoist, *Logique du phénomène*, pp. 114–22.

17 Ibid., p. 117.

18 As an aside, the recent naturalistic interpretations fall short of Vaihinger's positivism, because they use a deflationary vocabulary in order to ascribe to

Nietzsche, despite his explicit rejection thereof, causal explanatory models and an atomism that he famously opposes in many parts of his published and posthumous writings. On the level of philosophy, Nietzsche is a methodological factionalist, not a naturalist who relies purely on given knowledge about nature, let alone natural science. A paradigmatic example is Brian Leiter, *Nietzsche on Morality* (London: Routledge, 2015). When I made this point after his keynote presentation at the eighth International Summer School in German Philosophy in July 2018, he countered that Nietzsche rejected a certain notion of causality but not causal explanations in a broader sense, and could therefore be considered a 'speculative naturalist' in a contemporary sense. I concede that this is true of Nietzsche's forays into natural philosophy as well as his recourse to drives, which he assigns to the realm of perspectives, but would argue that the overall position he adopts is more on the side of aestheticism than that of an anticipation of natural-scientific overall explanations of human behaviour. To be sure, this is not central to the argumentation in the main text, since it is unquestionably the case that there are many metaphysical fictionalists, especially Vaihinger, who adopt an unambiguous stance and can be considered representatives of the state of theory at issue here. Regarding a similar problem in Foucault, see Dave Elder-Vass, *The Reality of Social Construction* (Cambridge: Cambridge University Press, 2012), pp. 143–58, esp. p. 151.

19 Jacques Derrida, *Of Grammatology*, trans. Gayatri Chakravorty Spivak (Baltimore: Johns Hopkins University Press, 1997), p. 158.

20 For example, ibid., p. 193.

21 Ibid., p. 56.

22 Ibid., p. 57.

23 One could certainly also take Derrida as a realist, since he does indeed represent a radical empiricism that acknowledges no recognizable, transcendental frame – a manoeuvre that is reconcilable with his fictionalism. For a convincing reconstruction of such a position, see Philip Freytag, *Die Rahmung des Hintergrunds* (Frankfurt: Klostermann, 2019). For a newer transcendental perspective, on the other hand, see Martin Hägglund, *Radical Atheism: Derrida and the Time of Life* (Stanford, CA: Stanford University Press, 2008).

24 Römer, 'Emergenz und Evolution', *Zeitschrift für Parapsychologie und Grenzgebiete der Psychologie*, 50 (2017): 68–98, here p. 74.

25 Ibid., p. 84.

26 I am grateful to Hartmann Römer and George Ellis for intense conversations about the relation between physics and FOS in Paris from 14 to 16 November and 3 to 4 December 2018. To be sure, Ellis's position is a classical epistemological one, whereas Römer believes that the cognitive process in a living being has a non-classical form, which justifies the application of terminology from quantum theory. I am also grateful for a corresponding discussion at the Institute for the Physics and Mathematics and the Universe at the University of Tokyo in June 2018 with Hitoshi Murayama and Yasunori Nomura, who likewise argued plausibly that quantum theory is fundamental – at least in the sense that it affects our fallibility, which also implies that it is probable (though

never deterministically predictable) that a relevant subset of our truth-apt mental episodes is factually true.

27 This means neither that perception is fundamental nor that it is the overall sense field of a mental life. The fact that we always also perceive merely commits us to an obviously correct minimal empiricism, according to which we must take into account that we can attain perceptual knowledge.

28 Heinrich von Kleist, 'Über das Marionettentheater', in *Sämtliche Werke und Briefe*, vol. 2 (Munich: Hanser, 1965), pp. 338–45, and 'Über die allmähliche Verfertigung der Gedanken beim Reden', ibid., pp. 319–23.

29 See Eugene Paul Wigner, *Philosophical Reflections and Syntheses* (Berlin: Springer, 1995). Of course, Römer does not at all mean that *consciousness* triggers the collapse of the wave function, since his generalized quantum theory does not postulate a causal role of consciousness in the measuring process but, rather, discusses general ontological parameters on the theoretical level of FOS. However, this raises the question of whether the cognitive process is not causally embedded after all, to which Römer replies with a theory of time that views the quantum universe as atemporal; this would require a lengthy discussion that would be out of place here. There is an intermediate position in Michel Bitbol, *Mécanique quantique: une introduction philosophique* (Paris: Flammarion, 2008). Based on this, see his recent positioning against Meillassoux, in Michel Bitbol, *Maintenant la finitude: peut-on penser l'absolu?* (Paris: Flammarion, 2019).

30 This is not my last word on the matter of how we can understand the cognitive process as something that is real without treating a reality as a total object. This aspect of FOS can only be clarified as part of a natural philosophy, whose main features I am currently working on at the Bonn Centre for Science and Thought and the Institute for the Physics and Mathematics of the Universe at the University of Tokyo. I am especially grateful to Alexander Kanev, who drew my attention early on during his time in Bonn in the alumnus programme of the Alexander von Humboldt Stiftung (2014) to the fact that FOS has natural-philosophical implications that allow us to give more conceptual precision to the fallibility condition of our knowledge acquisition. I am also grateful to Jan Voosholz, who convinced me at the Humboldt Kolleg on New Realism in Sofia (25–7 October 2017), if not earlier, that New Realism has crucial science-theoretical implications.

31 Meillassoux, *After Finitude* (London: Continuum, 2008).

32 Quine, *Word and Object*, p. 20. On Quine's connection to post-Kantian idealism, see Paul W. Franks, 'From Quine to Hegel: naturalism, anti-realism, and Maimon's question *quid facti*', in Espen Hammer (ed.), *German Idealism: Contemporary Perspectives* (London: Routledge, 2007), pp. 50–69.

33 The familiar, picturesque variant of this is that the universe will at some point open its eyes, as it were, and retroactively prove to be legible, and so on. My concern here, however, is the ontological deep structure of such theoretical frameworks.

34 Adorno, *Negative Dialectics*, p. 368.

35 This ontological architecture has its correlate in manifold elaborations, from

the classical global distinction between being and semblance to the modern variations on the veil of representation that cannot be lifted, and so on. In some variants, the non-intentional becomes a fetish that can only be apophatically encircled. This was opposed by Levinas, who therefore developed an understanding of intentionality that treats intentionality not as a closed sense field but as a respectively specific contact with something that is not necessarily intentional. For a paradigmatic example, see Emmanuel Levinas, *Totality and Infinity: An Essay on Exteriority*, trans. Alphonso Lingis (Pittsburgh: Duquesne University Press, 1969). In this way, Levinas breaks open Meillassoux's 'correlationist circle' from the inside and circumvents metaphysics, which caused Derrida to accuse him of trying to skip over intentionality by force. See, famously, Jacques Derrida, 'Violence and metaphysics: an essay on the thought of Emmanuel Levinas', in *Writing and Difference*, trans. Alan Bass (Chicago: University of Chicago Press, 1978), pp. 79–153. Here one sees that Derrida's early coinage remains within Husserl's framework, of which he originally sought only to correct a few details before this project turned into a proliferation machine for paradoxes.

36 See Goldschmidt and Pearce (eds), *Idealism: New Essays in Metaphysics*.

37 On the general concept of 'correlationism', see Quentin Meillassoux, 'Iteration, reiteration, repetition: a speculative analysis of the sign devoid of meaning', in Armen Avanessian and Suhail Malik (eds), *Genealogies of Speculation: Materialism and Subjectivity since Structuralism* (London: Bloomsbury Academic, 2016), p. 118:

> By correlationism I mean, in a first approximation, any philosophy that maintains the impossibility of acceding, through thought, to a being *independent* of thought. According to this type of philosophy, we never have access to any intended thing (understood in the most general sense, not necessarily in the phenomenological sense) that is not always-already correlated to an 'act of thinking' (understood, again, in the most general sense).

On the distinction between *weak* and *strong correlationism*, see Meillassoux, *After Finitude*, ch. 2. On the incoherence of this concept, on the other hand, see Gabriel, *Sinn und Existenz*, pp. 396–9.

38 See, for example, *Critique of Pure Reason*, A601/B629:

> Thus whatever and however much our concept of an object may contain, we have to go out beyond it in order to provide it with existence. With objects of sense this happens through the connection with some perception of mine in accordance with empirical laws; but for objects of pure thinking there is no means whatever for cognizing their existence, because it would have to be cognized entirely a priori, but our consciousness of all existence (whether immediately through perception or through inferences connecting something with perception) belongs entirely and without exception to the unity of experience, and though an

existence outside this field cannot be declared absolutely impossible, it is a presupposition that we cannot justify through anything.

See Gabriel, *Sinn und Existenz*, §2a.

39 See the introduction of this term into the language of philosophy, in J. G. Fichte, *The Science of Knowing: J. G. Fichte's 1804 Lectures on the Wissenschaftslehre*, trans. Walter E. Wright (Albany: SUNY Press, 2012), p. 38 and *passim*. Facticity consists in the 'insight into knowing's absolute self-sufficiency, without any determination by anything outside itself, anything changeable' (p. 38).

40 While introducing the idea of 'basic concepts' (without which one cannot have any other concepts), Fichte introduces the concept of reflection [*Besinnung*] as 'reflexibility', on which he comments as follows: 'looking at the factum in relation to justifiability' (J. G. Fichte, *Die späten wissenschaftlichen Vorlesungen I: 1809–1811* [Stuttgart-Bad Canstatt: frommann-holzboog, 2000], p. 95).

41 See Fichte, *The Science of Knowing*, p. 110.

42 See Christoph Asmuth, 'Wie viele Welten braucht die Welt? Goodman, Cassirer, Fichte', *Fichte-Studien*, 35 (2010): 63–83.

43 On this aim in the *Phenomenology of Spirit*, see Markus Gabriel, 'A very hetero-dox reading of the lord-servant allegory in Hegel's *Phenomenology of Spirit*', in Markus Gabriel and Anders Moe Rasmussen (eds), *German Idealism Today* (Berlin: de Gruyter, 2017), pp. 95–120, and Gabriel, 'What kind of an idealist (if any) is Hegel?', *Hegel Bulletin*, 27/2 (2016): 181–208.

44 G. W. F. Hegel, *Phenomenology of Spirit*, trans. A. V. Miller (Oxford: Oxford University Press, 2010), p. 46.

45 Manfred Frank, Der unendliche Mangel an Sein: Schellings Hegelkritik und die Anfänge der Marxschen Dialektik (Munich: Fink, 1992).

46 See Arthur Schopenhauer, *The World as Will and Representation*, vol. 2, trans. Judith Norman, Alistair Welchman and Christopher Janaway (Cambridge: Cambridge University Press, 2018), p. 299, where Schopenhauer attributes his variety of idealism to a 'brain phenomenon', and especially also the explicit reference on p. 272 to the brain as the 'subject of all cognition'.

47 For an example, see Peter Carruthers, *The Centred Mind: What the Science of Working Memory Shows Us about the Nature of Human Thought* (Oxford: Oxford University Press, 2015).

48 See Hogrebe, *Duplex: Strukturen der Intelligibilität* (Frankfurt: Klostermann, 2018).

49 See the *locus classicus* Manfred Frank, *'Unendliche Annäherung': Die Anfänge der philosophischen Frühromantik* (Frankfurt: Suhrkamp, 1997).

50 For an ironic view, with corresponding passages from Fichte that articulate his failure to deal with embodiment, see Markus Gabriel, 'Anstoss, Widerstand, Gegenstand – Erwin Wurm zwischen Fichte und Neuem Realismus', in Ralf Beil (ed.), *Erwin Wurm: Fichte* (Baden-Baden: Kunstmuseum Wolfsburg, 2015), pp. 98–109.

51 Wolfram Hogrebe, *Riskante Lebensnähe: Die szenische Existenz des Menschen* (Berlin: Akademie, 2009), p. 40.

52 See Dasgupta, 'Realism and the absence of value', *Philosophical Review*, 127/3

(2018): 279–322, in opposition to Theodore Sider, *Writing the Book of the World* (Oxford: Oxford University Press, 2013).
53 See Gabriel, *Why the World Does Not Exist*, pp. 127–37.
54 The recent *locus classicus* is David Lewis, 'New work for a theory of universals', *Australasian Journal of Philosophy*, 61/4 (1983): 343–77. Admittedly, the idea is at least as old as Plato's theory of forms, to which the common metaphor of the joints of nature – 'carving nature at its joints' – refers. See Plato, *Phaedrus*, 265e1–3.
55 Dasgupta, 'Realism and the absence of values', p. 289.
56 See, paradigmatically, Graham Harman, *Object-Oriented Ontology: A New Theory of Everything* (London: Penguin, 2018), and *Immaterialism: Objects and Social Theory* (Cambridge: Polity, 2016). See also Stephen Mulhall, 'How complex is a lemon?', *London Review of Books*, 40/18 (2018): 27–30. Similarly, see Gabriel, 'Tatsachen statt Fossilien – Neuer vs. Spekulativer Realismus', *Zeitschrift für Medien und Kulturforschung*, 7/2 (2016): 187–204.

Part III Social Realism

1 The counterpart of this concept of dissent is that of 'aesthetic difference', which is used by Josef Simon to describe the indissoluble individuality of our respective factual mental situation. See Josef Simon, *Kant: Die fremde Vernunft und die Sprache der Philosophie* (Berlin: de Gruyter, 2003), pp. 20–30 and *passim*. See also Gabriel, 'Dissens und Gegenstand', in Gabriel (ed.), *Skeptizismus und Metaphysik* (Berlin: Akademie, 2011), pp. 73–92.
2 Of course, this does not mean that all substances of thought are explicitly social, much less that all objects of thought are social (which would be absurd). What we think does not always refer directly or indirectly to action coordination. The fact that thinking is socially produced and its orientation embedded in relations of dissent does not, moreover, mean that objectivity is replaced or explicable by intersubjectivity. Someone who thinks that p can do so only in contexts that are in part socially conditioned, which does not constitute a fundamental obstacle to the objectivity of thoughts.
3 As a number of other, non-human beings are also social thinkers, sociality is not a *differentia specifica* of humans in any case and is therefore not automatically suitable for the demarcation of anthropological difference.
4 Of course, this no longer applies without qualifications to the place and impulse of elementary particles, and the possibility that the emergence of social production in the universe causally modifies its architecture should not be dismissed. See George Ellis and Markus Gabriel: 'Physical, logical, and mental top-down effects', in Markus Gabriel and Jan Voosholz (eds), *Top-Down Causation and Emergence* (Dordrecht: Springer, 2021). The ontological architecture of the universe changes fundamentally as soon as social beings that practise science exist.
5 It should be noted that the now widespread opinion that there is no difference between nature and culture, as argued in Philippe Descola, *Beyond Nature and*

Culture, trans. Janet Lloyd (Chicago: University of Chicago Press, 2013), does not exceed the frame of this problem. This point at best overcomes the opposition between nature and culture in an analysis of human life forms, but it does not show that there is or was no anonymous nature. It would be outlandish if cultural studies could prove that all natural-scientific statements about the pre-social conditions of the universe are wrong – which is admittedly not Descola's aim.

6 One particularly unambiguous example of the connection between emergentism and social constructivism has been presented by Maurizio Ferraris, in *Emergenza* (Turin: Einaudi, 2016), drawing on his earlier work *Documentality: Why it is Necessary to Leave Traces*, trans. Richard Davies (New York: Fordham University Press, 2013). He refers explicitly to Derrida's famous dictum that nothing is outside the text and writes: 'writing is the condition of possibility of social objects, which include science as a social event that begins with the subdivision, fixation and transmission of documents. In science, nothing exists outside of the text, just as there is generally nothing social that exists outside the text' (p. 60). Ferraris even goes so far as to make the case for a general alethic anti-realism: 'truth *as an epistemological function* depends on registration, as there would be no true propositions without registration' (ibid.). Thus the entire set-up descends into the very constructivism that Ferraris, drawing on an 'ontological correspondentism' (p. 61), claims to reject. But how can this succeed if truth is constitutively tied to registrations – if no truth would have existed if no one had registered it? If p would not have been true without registration, p would not have existed without registration either; what follows from Ferraris's explanation is thus a metaphysical constructivism à la Latour.

7 See, paradigmatically, John McDowell, *Mind and World* (Cambridge, MA: Harvard University Press, 1996), and, building on this, Michael Thompson, *Life and Action: Elementary Structures of Practice and Practical Thought* (Cambridge, MA: Harvard University Press, 2008). For a critical discussion of the concept of second nature in proximity to contemporary so-called neo-Aristotelianism, see Christoph Menke, *Autonomie und Befreiung: Studien zu Hegel* (Berlin: Suhrkamp, 2018), pp. 119–48; Thomas Khurana, *Das Leben der Freiheit: Form und Wirklichkeit der Autonomie* (Berlin: Suhrkamp, 2017), pp. 389–409. For a critical overview, see also Jens Rometsch, 'Neues aus Pittsburgh', *Philosophische Rundschau*, 56/4 (2009): 335–42.

8 Kant, *Groundwork of the Metaphysics of Morals* (Cambridge: Cambridge University Press, 1996), p. 41.

9 See the essays in Andrea Kern and Christian Kietzmann (eds), *Selbstbewusstes Leben: Texte zu einer transformativen Theorie der menschlichen Subjektivität* (Berlin: Suhrkamp, 2017).

10 See Gabriel, *The Limits of Epistemology* (Cambridge: Polity, 2020), §15. This belongs to an entirely different discursive landscape from the original idea in Peter L. Berger and Thomas Luckmann, *The Social Construction of Reality: A Treatise in the Sociology of Knowledge* (London: Penguin, 1991). For these authors dispute neither the 'objective facticity' nor the 'subjectively meant sense' of the social, viewing it rather as a reality *sui generis*. What they consider

constructed (in this case, a historically variable result of the dual structure of society as objective facticity and the subjective reception of its existence) is the natural, pre-theoretical attitude whereby sequences of actions appear self-evident to us. This assumption is socio-ontologically harmless and even ideology-theoretically recommendable, since it unmasks the concept of a singular lifeworld from the outset as an artefact of a hypostatization of the natural attitude.

11 See Adrian Johnston, *Prolegomena to Any Future Materialism*, vol. 2: *A Weak Nature Alone* (Evanston, IL: Northwestern University Press, 2910), which addresses this exact problem.

12 This line of argumentation is familiar from Jürgen Habermas, *Postmetaphysical Thinking: Between Metaphysics and the Critique of Reason*, trans. William Mark Hohengarten (Cambridge, MA: MIT Press, 1992), *Postmetaphysical Thinking II*, trans. Ciaran Cronin (Cambridge: Polity, 2017), and *Between Naturalism and Religion: Philosophical Essays*, trans. Ciaran Cronin (Cambridge: Polity, 2008). Habermas employs the distinction between nature and social construction when, for example, he states: 'The "I" is a social construct (which is why the search by neurobiology for a central instance in the midst of decentrally networked brain waves is also condemned to failure)' (*Postmetaphysical Thinking II*, p. 233, n. 8). In *Between Naturalism and Religion*, he writes: '. . . the "I" can indeed be understood as a social construction – but it is not therefore an illusion' (p. 179). However, he does not comment any further on the distinction he employs between *construction* and *illusion*. Habermas himself refers to the introduction, co-authored by himself, to Rainer Döbert et al. (eds), *Entwicklung des Ichs* (Königstein: Athenäum, Hain, Scriptor & Hanstein, 1980), pp. 9–30, in which the authors are concerned with the sociological concept of identity. They state: 'A person simultaneously claims an identity for themselves and in relation to others; self-identification, the differentiation from others, must also be recognized by these others. The reflexive relation of the self-identifying individual depends on intersubjective relationships that they enter with other persons who identify them' (p. 10). But what does 'must' mean here? In which sense 'must' my self-identification be recognized by others? It would be incoherent, at any rate, to claim that one only gains an identity at all by having it ascribed to one by others. At best, it can apply that the fact that others react to my self-differentiation influences my self-descriptions, which influences the process of socialization. But this thesis is far removed from an ontological insight into the relation between identity and identity ascription from which one might develop the idea of the social construction of the self.

13 This concept of social construction is described particularly clearly in Heinrich Popitz, *Soziale Normen* (Frankfurt: Suhrkamp, 2006), for example, pp. 76–80.

14 See the overview of standard positions in Hans Bernhard Schmid and David P. Schweikard, *Kollektive Intentionalität: Eine Debatte über die Grundlagen des Sozialen* (Frankfurt: Suhrkamp, 2009). The irreparable flaws of this model have been pointed out by Stephan Zimmermann in his habilitation thesis for the University of Bonn, drawing, among other things, on the foundational socio-

logical debates; see *Vorgängige Gemeinsamkeit: Studie zur Ontologie des Sozialen*. I do not, however, follow him in his suggestion to ground collective intentionality in the concept of life experience and identify the latter as the source of the social. See also his preliminary study 'Is society built on collective intentions? A response to Searle', *Rivista di Estetica*, 57 (2014): 121–41 [special issue: *Social Objects: From Intentionality to Documentality*].

15 One can find a recent example of this argumentation as a contribution to the political 'post-truth' debate in Steve Fuller, *Post-Truth: Knowledge as a Power Game* (London: Anthem Press, 2018).

16 See, paradigmatically, Axel Honneth, *The Struggle for Recognition: The Moral Grammar of Social Conflicts*, trans. Joel Anderson (Cambridge: Polity, 1995). Admittedly, Honneth offers different strategies for solving the problem mentioned in the main text; I do not address it in detail here, since New Realism operates outside of the recognition paradigm for the socio-ontological reasons described in the following.

17 The concepts of first and second nature prove invalid in the framework of a neo-realist natural philosophy.

18 See the concept of society as an organization of coexistence in Hannah Arendt, *The Human Condition* (Chicago: University of Chicago Press, 2019), p. 46: 'Society is the form in which the fact of mutual dependence for the sake of life and nothing else assumes public significance and where the activities connected with sheer survival are permitted to appear in public.'

19 Some of the social sciences, as well as psychology, are located at the intersection between human self-studies in the natural sciences and the humanities, in so far as they apply methods from natural science in order to predict genuinely human behaviour and make it manipulable.

20 See Gabriel, *Moral Progress in Dark Times*.

21 Dennett famously distinguishes between 'intentional', 'functional (design)' and 'physicalist stance', although the distinction can be interpreted in different ways, as Dennett never adequately clarifies its ontological foundations. See Dennett, *The Intentional Stance* (Cambridge, MA: MIT Press, 1987). The main problem always facing his thesis that intentionality can be reduced to (idealizing) ascription practices is that one cannot ascribe intentional states to another person without being in corresponding states oneself. Regarding this frequent objection, see Galen Strawson, 'The consciousness deniers', *New York Review of Books*, 13 March 2018, www.nybooks.com/daily/2018/03/13/the-consc iousness-deniers/.

22 See, for example, Friedrich Nietzsche, *The Will to Power*, trans. R. Kevin Hill and Michael A. Scarpitti (London: Penguin, 2017).

23 See the impressive study by Florian Klinger, *Urteilen* (Zurich: Diaphanes, 2011), to which Sepp Gumbrecht drew my attention.

24 Gabriel, 'Dissens und Gegenstand'.

25 From this perspective, the current postmodern theorist *par excellence* is Francis Fukuyama, who went from diagnosing the end of history to thinking in social identities. See Francis Fukuyama, *Identity: The Demand for Dignity and the Politics of Resentment* (New York: Farrar, Straus & Giroux, 2018).

26 See more comprehensively Gabriel, *The Meaning of Thought* Cambridge: Polity, 2020).

27 Immanuel Kant, 'Idea for a universal history with a cosmopolitan purpose', in *Political Writings*, ed. H. S. Reiss, trans. H. B. Nisbet (Cambridge: Cambridge University Press, 1991), p. 44.

28 Rather, one should recall an insight expressed by Karl Mannheim in *Ideology and Utopia* (London: Routledge, 2013): 'The more consistently one probes the preconditions for thought in the interests of true empiricism, however, the more apparent it is that this empirical procedure (in the historical sciences, at least) is only possible on the basis of certain meta-empirical, ontological, and metaphysical judgments and the expectations and hypotheses that follow from them' (p. 79, translation modified). I agree with Tony Lawson when he also states that social change guided by ideals cannot be undertaken if one operates in an ontologically blind manner: 'ontological reasoning is always effectively required at some level if we are to intervene anywhere in anything at all competently. . . . Simply put, capable successful intervention into the social realm likely necessitates, and always stands to benefit from, explicit social ontological reasoning' (*The Nature of Social Reality* [Abingdon: Routledge, 2019], p. 4). I do not agree with the details of Lawson's socio-ontological analysis, but that is a different matter.

29 See the exemplary reconstruction of the role of repeating the exemplary in Axel Hutter, *Narrative Ontologie* (Tübingen: Mohr Siebeck, 2017).

30 For a study of arguments against overblown views of autonomy geared towards self-constitution, see Charles Larmore, *The Autonomy of Morality* (Cambridge: Cambridge University Press, 2008), as well as the literature survey in Rainer Schäfer, 'Gegenwärtige Freiheit', *Philosophische Rundschau*, 65/4 (2018): 311–25.

31 G. W. F. Hegel, *Elements of the Philosophy of Right*, trans. H. B. Nisbet (Cambridge: Cambridge University Press, 1991), p. 57.

32 Bourdieu, *Pascalian Meditations* (Cambridge: Polity, 2000), p. 108: 'And one may in any case doubt the reality of a resistance which ignores the resistance of "reality".'

33 See my earlier studies Gabriel, *Der Mensch im Mythos* (Berlin: de Gruyter, 2006); Markus Gabriel and Slavoj Žižek, *Mythology, Madness and Laughter: Subjectivity in German Idealism* (London: Continuum, 2009); Markus Gabriel, 'Aarhus Lectures: Schelling and contemporary philosophy – Fourth Lecture: The very idea of a philosophy of mythology in contemporary philosophy', *SATS: Northern European Journal of Philosophy*, 17/2 (2016): 115–44. See also Hans Blumenberg, *Work on Myth* (Cambridge, MA: MIT Press, 1988), and 'Wirklichkeitsbegriff und Wirkungspotential des Mythos', in Manfred Fuhrmann (ed.), *Terror und Spiel: Probleme der Mythenrezeption* (Munich: Fink, 1971), pp. 11–66.

34 My reservation about Sloterdijk's much discussed analysis of anthropotechnics is that he does not locate the emergence of such techniques at a sufficiently deep ontological level. As minded beings, humans are social animals whose conditions of production, since their inception, have located them in the human park. The error lies in ontically simplifying anthropotechnics as a

specifically modern phenomenon or a consequence of alphabetization, which may work against Heidegger (though I would dispute this) but falls conceptually short of the socio-ontological insight that humans are essentially socially produced. See of course Peter Sloterdijk, 'Rules for the human park: a response to Heidegger's "Letter on humanism"', in *Not Saved: Essays After Heidegger*, trans. Ian Alexander Moore and Christopher Turner (Cambridge: Polity, 2017), pp. 193–216.

35 At the time of writing, a paradigmatic example of ideology is the Twitter account of Donald Trump.

36 For an identification of some of the manifold mereological fallacies circulating throughout the neurophilosophical discourse of the cognitive neurosciences, see Maxwell R. Hacker and Peter M. Bennett, *Philosophical Foundations of Neuroscience* (Oxford: Wiley, 2022). As Karl Mannheim already recognized in *Ideology and Utopia*: 'In actuality it is far from correct to assume that an individual of more or less fixed absolute capacities confronts the world and in striving for the truth constructs a world-view out of the data of his experience' (p. 26). This same assumption, however, is continuing its successful career in the form of neurophilosophy.

§12 The Nature of Social Facts

1 Berger and Luckmann, *The Social Construction of Reality*; John R. Searle, *The Construction of Social Reality* (New York: Simon & Schuster, 1995), and *Making the Social World: The Structure of Human Civilization* (Oxford: Oxford University Press, 2010); Judith Butler, *Gender Trouble: Feminism and the Subversion of Identity* (New York: Routledge, 1990); Sally Haslanger, *Resisting Reality* (Oxford: Oxford University Press, 2012).

2 Searle, *Making the Social World*, p. 3. Opposing Searle, Lawson – in part correctly – argues that Searle's notion of emergence, causation and, especially, the metaphysics of particle physics is unacceptably simplified in this context and suggests corresponding socio-ontological revisions in *The Nature of Social Reality*, pp. 33–46. This does not go far enough, however, as Lawson overlooks the option that a strong emergence of models of top-down causation can be supported, such that the already questionable assumption of a 'causal closure of the universe' as the foundation of a metaphysical naturalism also collapses for physical reasons. See also the essays in Gabriel and Voosholz (eds), *Top-Down Causation and Emergence*.

3 This already appears in John R. Searle, *Speech Acts: An Essay in the Philosophy of Language* (Cambridge: Cambridge University Press, 1969), pp. 35ff.

4 See for example Searle, *Making the Social World*, p. 109.

5 See of course John R. Searle, *Intentionality: An Essay in the Philosophy of Mind* (Cambridge: Cambridge University Press, 1983), esp. pp. 262–72. For a critical inspection of the background to the naturalization programme in Searle, see Philip Freytag, *Die Rahmung des Hintergrunds* (Frankfurt: Klostermann, 2019), pp. 157–69.

6 From a philosophical perspective, with references to the underlying epigenetic research on the plasticity of the brain, see Catherine Malabou, *What Should We Do with Our Brain?*, trans. Sebastian Rand (New York: Fordham University Press, 2008), and *Morphing Intelligence* (New York: Columbia University Press, 2019), pp. 59–68.

7 To be sure, human beings evolved from other life forms through step-by-step processes of mutation, selection, and so forth. These processes had long been social, since the beings that existed before the human species developed were already social. Thus humans emerged neither diachronically nor synchronically from the disposition of non-living matter but under conditions that are themselves social. As far as we know, cooperation within the framework of consciously shared goals with the aim of enabling offspring to survive successfully already existed in the animal kingdom long before there were humans.

8 See Aristotle, *Metaphysics*, 1032a25, 1033b32, 1070a8.

9 Even so-called cerebral organoids – that is, neuronal tissue cultivated by scientists outside of organisms – are socially produced – by people who produce, nurture and cherish them in laboratories. This does not, of course, answer the question of whether cerebral organoids can be conscious, since this depends on whether consciousness still needs an organism outside the social production of suitable neuronal architectures. Thomas Fuchs makes a well-grounded case for this in *Ecology of the Brain: The Phenomenology and Biology of the Embodied Mind* (Oxford: Oxford University Press, 2018). I will leave aside this question, which cannot be empirically answered at present, since it has no bearing on the argument in the main text and cerebral organoids are clearly socially produced. I am grateful to Christof Koch for explaining the current state of research to me during my flying visit to the Allen Brain Institute in March 2019.

10 See, for example, John R. Searle, *Mind, Language and Society: Philosophy in the Real World* (New York: Basic Books, 1998), pp. 54f.

11 The universe is difficult to know because, among other things, every epistemic interaction with the object area of the natural sciences rests on an intervention; this means that only some things can be known, since others are excluded as part of the modelling framework.

12 This poses many problems, such as that the logical form of declarative speech acts can at best explain the presence of basic institutional conditions for the existence of social facts but scarcely the existence of an individual social fact – for example that *this* 5 euro note has this or that exchange value – since there is no adequately specific representation (be it individually or collectively reconstructable) that allows this individual fact to come into existence and remain there.

13 For a philosophy-friendly discussion, see Niklas Luhmann, 'Cognition as construction', trans. Hans-Georg Moeller, in Hans-Georg Moeller, *Luhmann Explained: From Souls to Systems* (Chicago: Open Court, 2006), pp. 241–60. Luhmann considers the following an 'empirical assertion': 'Cognition is only possible *because* it has no access to the reality external to it' (p. 242), which he sees as the point of departure for radical constructivism. It does not become clear, however, why this 'position' is specifically sociological – indeed, in what

sense it is a coherently articulable position at all. Luhmann makes no attempt to clarify the concept of construction, merely stating: 'Cognition remains unique as a construction based on distinction. As such it does not know anything external to it which would correspond to itself' (pp. 255f.). This situation probably results from a mixing of two logically independent assumptions: (1) we cannot cognize anything without reference to distinctions that would not exist in the absence of an epistemic system; (2) the reality that is external to cognition fundamentally cannot intrinsically display the distinctions that we use to cognize it. (2) does not follow directly or indirectly from (1) through the addition of a few assumptions; it is an entire supplementary metaphysical package. Luhmann gives no reasons for (2) that would make a convincing case for a radical constructivism based on the given facts.

14 Ferraris, *Emergenza*.
15 Friedrich A. Kittler, *Aufschreibesysteme* (Munich: Fink, 1987).
16 Richard Rorty, *Philosophy and the Mirror of Nature* (Princeton, NJ: Princeton University Press, 2009).
17 See the now canonical discussion of the weaknesses of coherentism in McDowell, *Mind and World*.
18 This requires no deeper reason, such as the adaptation of a discriminating being to its natural environment, or a discursive norm that would require us to speak the truth to others in order to be understood. The foundation of the practice of judgement is the already true or false holding-to-be-true. Admittedly, this is embedded in practices that are socially produced, since humans cannot believe anything to be true without belonging to a community that has produced them. This does not at all mean that the content of the judgement is socially produced. The concept of social construction comes from the idea that there are contents of judgements that are socially produced, since the acts of judgement that refer to them are what initially create the social facts with which those judgements deal.
19 Sebastian Rödl, *Self-Consciousness and Objectivity* (Cambridge, MA: Harvard University Press, 2018).
20 See the impressively precise elaborations in Charles Tarvis, *Objectivity and the Parochial* (Oxford: Oxford University Press, 2011). See also my analysis of the consequences of the private language issue for the objectivity of thought in Gabriel, *The Limits of Epistemology*.
21 See the reading of Wittgenstein, ibid.
22 See the *locus classicus* for a blending of Hegel and Wittgenstein in Michael N. Forster, *Hegel's Idea of a Phenomenology of Spirit* (Chicago: University of Chicago Press, 1998), and Terry Pinkard, *Hegel's Phenomenology: The Sociality of Reason* (Cambridge: Cambridge University Press, 1994).
23 See Klinger's innovative discussion of judgement in Klinger, *Urteilen*, especially pp. 66–8. His suggestion for overcoming the tension between the universal predictability of the judgement (which the term 'proposition', common since Russell's appropriation thereof from Frege, attempts to capture) leads to a 'thinking of the *respective*' [*Denken des Jeweiligen*] (p. 38) that attempts to circumvent ad hoc the distinction between the context-free content of a judgement

and the context-bound act of judgement. 'That the judgement essentially posits something, justifies a position, creates a commitment or certainty, must no longer conceal the fact that it ultimately does this without invoking criteria, that this commitment is temporary: only this respective time, only in the respective case' (pp. 20f.). However, Klinger overlooks the option, developed in particular by Jocelyn Benoist, that the judgement is criterially, normatively saturated *because of* its embeddedness in a factually existing context: we do not decide haphazardly but in the face of the facts that motivate (but do not force) us to make a judgement. Those facts that do not take the form of judgments still have a bearing on our judgements because they play a substantial part in answering the question of what is the case. Yet this role does not absolve us of the context-sensitivity of all acts of judgement.

24 I am grateful to Clemens Albrecht for the valuable observation that one can distinguish between the social and society. 'Society' is a name for a modern situation of irritation for the social resulting from the fact that it no longer appears as nature but as something completely different that is chaotic and adaptable. The human community responds to this with the introduction of society as an explicit form of sociality that is meant to allow the formation of a bond which seems to have been lost. Then society is a variety of socialization that comes about specifically because the individuals, who are in fact already socialized, attempt to decipher this circumstance through the explicit formulation of a constitution. Thus sociology emerged in the wake of the French Revolution as part of the attempt to heal the cracks that had suddenly opened. This process is still not finished, and one cannot tell what it would mean to complete it. See Peter Sloterdijk's reflections on this in Sloterdijk, *Die schrecklichen Kinder der Neuzeit: Über das anti-genealogische Experiment der Moderne* (Berlin: Suhrkamp, 2014).

25 On the concept of the criterion of publicity, see Gabriel, *The Limits of Epistemology*, §§2–3.

26 Wittgenstein, *Philosophical Investigations* (Oxford: Wiley-Blackwell, 2010), p. 94 (§242).

27 Ibid.

28 Ibid.

29 This does not even touch on the question, paradigmatically discussed by Max Weber, of the conditions under which a given action is classifiable as social, and hence as an object of sociology. See the famous introductory deliberations in Max Weber, *Economy and Society*, ed. and trans. Keith Tribe (Cambridge, MA: Harvard University Press, 2019), pp. 77ff.

30 From this perspective, see Gabriel, 'Dissens und Gegenstand'.

31 Kant, *Critique of Pure Reason* (Cambridge: Cambridge University Press, 1998), A820/B848.

32 Ibid.

33 Ibid., A821/B849.

34 Ibid.

35 Ibid., A820/B848.

36 At this point I would like to thank the Käte Hamburger Centre for Advanced

Study in the Humanities 'Law as Culture' in Bonn for a fellowship in 2011/12, during which I researched the non-normative foundations of normativity. This ultimately provided a decisive impulse for my contribution to New Realism, as documented at the international conference 'Prospects for a New Realism', which was held at the University of Bonn together with the Käte Hamburger Centre. See Gabriel (ed.), *Der Neue Realismus* (Berlin: Suhrkamp, 2016).

37 Arguing from a different direction, Charles Travis arrives at a similar result: 'Thought's social nature means: *I* think things to be some given way only where some extendible range of thinkers would agree (and agree with me) sufficiently as to what would count as things *being* that way; only where, so to speak, there is a (potential) community of agreement (or of ones who agree)' (Travis, *Objectivity and the Parochial*, p. 304). The emphasis on agreement, which goes back to Wittgenstein, is based here on the idea that there can only be a contradiction if the party that believes p true and the one that believes not-p is true agree on the conditions of application for the terms they use to articulate their thought. Unlike this train of thought, the dissent theory of truth proposed here emphasizes the idea that our thinking has a need for correction without which we could not maintain any explicable contact with the real. In this sense, the reality of dissent precedes the establishment of consensus-sensitive norms of meaning. The normalization of language always follows Babylonian confusion. On this note, see Jacques Derrida, 'Des tours de Babel', in Gil Anidjar (ed.), *Acts of Religion* (London: Routledge, 2002), pp. 104–34.

38 Here one should undertake a close examination of the 'whistleblower' concept. In a case of success, whistleblowers are democratic dissidents who point out legal flaws in constitutional democracy that are incompatible with the ideal of democracy as an emancipatory social fabric, and which can therefore only be made visible through an act of martyrdom.

39 This does not mean that this fallacy is an instance of what has been defined as a fallacy since G. E. Moore. See the *locus classicus* G. E. Moore, *Principia Ethica* (Mineola, NY: Dover, 2004), pp. 9–15. Rather, it refers to the idea that social facts can be placed within a natural-scientific worldview, in so far as it consists in the assumption that all entities are 'brute facts' – an error already pointed out by Searle in *Speech Acts*.

40 Haslanger, *Resisting Reality*.

41 Ibid., p. 21, n. 9. In fact, Haslanger does not shy away from circularity, as in the following passage (ibid., p. 41, n. 11): 'At this point, in saying that the relations are "social" I mean simply to indicate that they concern certain relations that hold between individuals by virtue of their place in a social system.'

42 Ibid., p. 7, n. 3.

43 However, what Haslanger means by an 'analysis, strictly speaking' is probably the naming of necessary and collectively sufficient conditions for the existence of a state of affairs that can be described with a word such as 'social'. She does not expand on this, admittedly, and in the passage quoted she does not offer any argument to support her opinion that the 'social' is undefinable in this sense.

44 Haslanger, *Resisting Reality*, p. 7, n. 3.

45 Ibid., pp. 13–15.
46 Ibid., p. 15: 'an externalist bias towards the natural sciences is not warranted, for social kinds are no less real for being social.'
47 Ibid., pp. 86–90.
48 Ibid., p. 86.
49 Ibid., p. 85.
50 Ibid., pp. 85f.: 'In addition to straightforward artifacts like washing machines and power drills, there is a clear sense in which, for example, the Supreme Court of the United States and chess games are artifacts, as are languages, literature, and scientific inquiry.'
51 Haslanger frequently withdraws to an unrewarding pragmatism, for example when she tersely states: 'it isn't useful to try to determine what social construction "really is" because it is many different things, and the discourse of social construction functions differently in different contexts' (ibid., p. 113). On the failure of such a discourse analysis as a starting point for effective destruction, see the accurate analysis in Bourdieu, *Pascalian Meditations*.
52 See Haslanger, *Resisting Reality*, pp. 4f., 112 and *passim*.
53 Ibid., p. 88: 'I'd say that there is no doubt that in this sense you and I are socially constructed. We are the individuals we are today at least partly as a result of what has been attributed (and self-attributed) to us. In other words, there is a sense in which adult human beings are a special kind of artifact.'
54 In *The Meaning of Thought* I tried to analyse the discursive formation associated with so-called digitalization in such a way as to make this area of phenomena accessible to a Marxist analysis. For the products of digitalization (social networks, smartphones, AI systems, and so on) are textbook examples of the diagnosis of commodity fetishism.
55 Jean Baudrillard, *Forget Foucault*, trans. Nicolas Dufresne (Los Angeles: Semiotext(e), 2007). Latour senses in 'Why has critique run out of steam?' (*Critical Inquiry*, 30/2 [2004]: 225–48), p. 230, that the concept of the social is poorly constructed if defined via the incoherent concept of social construction. Unfortunately, he draws the absurd conclusion from this that we should abandon the concept of the social. See Bruno Latour, 'Gabriel Tarde and the end of the social', www.bruno-latour.fr/sites/default/files/82-TARDE-JOYCE-SOCIAL-GB.pdf. The fact that a given theoretical basis for social ontology is incoherent does not, of course, mean that nothing social exists. That Latour concludes this is an unmistakable sign of his continuing entanglement in constructivism.
56 Baudrillard, *Forget Foucault*, p. 37. On the concept of the production, see ibid., pp. 36–8.
57 See Searle, *Making the Social World*, pp. 28ff. See the formulation of the book's central thesis: 'The claim that I will be expounding and defending in this book is that all human institutional reality is created and maintained in existence by (representations that have the same logical form as) SF Declarations, including the cases that are not speech acts in the explicit form of Declarations' (ibid., p. 13). But he also states: 'Prelinguistic intentional states cannot create facts in the world by representing those facts as already existing. This remarkable

feat requires a language' (ibid., p. 69). The incoherence of this framework of premises becomes explicit in a footnote directly after this, in which Searle immediately retracts what he had previously claimed with unqualified generality: 'There are some odd apparent exceptions to this. Descartes' thinking that he is thinking can create the fact that he is thinking' (ibid., n. 5).

58 See, for greater detail, Searle, *Intentionality*, as well as the bold statement in *Making the Social World*, p. 43: 'Intentionality is already naturalized because, for example, thinking is as natural as digesting.'

59 See the detailed analysis of this problem in Freytag, *Die Rahmung des Hintergrunds*, pp. 129–204.

60 This problem cannot be solved by incorporating additional reflexive loops or by rejecting this form of critique *ad hominem* and attempting to provincialize the position of such metacritique as 'Christian', 'Platonic', 'metaphysical', 'ahistorical', or whatever else. This is one of the points of Derrida's critique of Foucault, incidentally, to which Foucault responded in polemical fashion. On this constellation, see Benoît Peeters, *Derrida: A Biography*, trans. Andrew Brown (Cambridge: Polity, 2013), pp. 131–33, as well as p. 240.

61 I am indebted to Cem Kömürcü for pointing out that one can read Marx and Baudrillard as critics of the constellation of social construction.

62 Mind manifests itself in the form of what Popits aptly refers to as 'human self-ascertainment', from which he infers 'various universally valid traits of social norm-boundness', especially the 'fact of society'; because we are social beings, our self-constitution is an *ascertaining-one-another*. See Popitz, *Soziale Normen*, p. 64.

63 Clearly, then, there is mental causation that consists not only in an incorporeal mind interacting with the epiphysis or some other organ of our body. Rather, the real 'mental' and hence social causation lies in the mereological structures of the mind, which offers production relations of new facts on the model of top-down causation. For a definition of retroactive causality proceeding from Kant, see Catherine Malabou, *Before Tomorrow: Epigenesis and Rationality*, trans. Carolyn Shread (Cambridge: Polity, 2016), as well as the systematic, interdisciplinary contributions in Gabriel and Voosholz (eds), *Top-Down Causation and Emergence*.

§13 Our Survival Form

1 It would be an unfounded exaggeration, however, to argue – as sociologists from a constructivist background sometimes do when they are insufficiently cautious about introducing this valid point – that the 'material' of our thinking therefore comprises 'the contents and meaningful referential structures of a social and cultural nature' (Armin Nassehi, *Muster: Theorie der digitalen Gesellschaft* (Munich: C. H. Beck, 2019), p. 259). Contrary to Nassehi's belief, there are natural components of human intelligence without which we would have no causal contact with an environment and, hence, be incapable of survival. On these partly subliminal conditions for objectivity, see Tyler Burge,

Origins of Objectivity (Oxford: Oxford University Press, 2010). As stated above, neither all substances [*Gehalte*] nor all objects of our thinking, perception, and so forth, are social, which does not mean that thinking, perception, and so forth, are not socially produced. There are also various objects one might not consider socially produced (such as neuronal tissue) that are certainly partially social.

2 Hegel, *Phenomenology of Spirit* (Oxford: Oxford University Press, 2010), p. 119.

3 See Markus Gabriel, *The Limits of Epistemology*, §8.

4 Ludwig Wittgenstein, *Zettel*, ed. G. E. M. Anscombe and G. H. von Wright, trans. G. E. M. Anscombe (Oxford: Blackwell, 1967), p. 31e (§173).

5 See Tononi and Koch, 'Consciousness: here, there and everywhere?', p. 6: 'Consciousness is *definite*, in content and spatio-temporal grain: each experience has the set of phenomenal distinctions it has, neither less (a subset) nor more (a superset), and it flows at the speed it flows, neither faster nor slower.'

6 See Klinger, *Urteilen*, pp. 38f.

7 Of course, an occasion can become a reason if one refers to it. If someone denies that my car is outside the door, a pointer from me will set them straight. The position of my car can be confirmed with reference to an occasion.

8 See Durs Grünbein, 'Ein Kaff bei Ulm', in *Vom Schnee* (Frankfurt: Suhrkamp, 2003), pp. 19–21.

9 The concept of reason I employ here avoids the weakness of the concept of a good reason found in the idealized analytical theory of action, as accurately shown by Christoph Möllers. I completely agree with him when he ties the idea of opposition to the legitimacy of holding a different opinion, something that should be taken up into the theory of normativity. 'Crucial features of democratic orders, particularly the institutionalization of an opposition whose role is to oppose, regardless of content, the opinion of the majority, cannot be reconciled with a conception of democracy that is fixated on good reasons alone' (Möllers, *The Possibility of Norms* (Oxford: Oxford University Press, 2020), p. 37).

10 See the striking shift from the concept of the enemy to that of the stranger in Carl Schmitt, *The Concept of the Political*, trans. George Schwab (Chicago: University of Chicago Press, 2008), pp. 26f. There (p. 27) he writes:

> The political enemy need not be morally evil or aesthetically ugly; he need not appear as an economic competitor, and it may even be advantageous to engage with him in business transactions. But he is, nevertheless, the other, the stranger; and it is sufficient for his nature that he is, in a specially intense way, existentially something different and alien, so that in the extreme case conflicts with him are possible. These can neither be decided by a previously determined general norm nor by the judgement of a 'disinterested' and therefore 'neutral' third party.

11 This means that humans are born the same but are individually different owing to causal biological circumstances, which is why some people have faculties that others do not. That humans are biologically different does not reduce their

humanity, of course, which knows no degrees; something or someone either is a hominid or not. The simple characteristic of a hominid is minimal survival capability as a result of social, sexual reproduction that is, of course, possible *in vitro* through advances in medical knowledge. A human being produces a human being. Social reproduction of the human survival form, then, does not necessarily require sexual intercourse. Based on the current state of knowledge, however, it is no coincidence that human embryos grow into human animals capable of survival only in the womb, since this leads to the development of specific faculties. Be that as it may, the formation conditions of human beings are no less social if certain elements of the reproductive process take place *in vitro*. The statistically averaged universal has ethical potential because the vast majority of people are born with the ability to experience social situations as morally charged. As a social creature, the human being is normative and thus moral; this means that one can, in principle, name several anthropological constants through a self-exploration of our survival form, which is a factual source of universal self-determination (human rights). For more detail, see Gabriel, *Wer wir sind und wer wir sein wollen.*

12 Nassehi, *Muster: Theorie der digitalen Gesellschaft*, p. 261. Nassehi convincingly argues (pp. 259–62 and *passim*) that natural intelligence is always constitutively intransparent and, thus, no different in this respect from a black box; from this, he draws the necessary conclusions for a philosophy of AI.

13 Ibid., p. 277.

14 On this topos, see Hans Blumenberg, *The Laughter of the Thracian Woman: A Protohistory of Theory*, trans. Spencer Hawkins (New York: Bloomsbury, 2015).

15 By contrast, see George Ellis and Mark Solms, *Beyond Evolutionary Psychology: How and Why Neuropsychological Modules Arise* (Cambridge: Cambridge University Press, 2018), and Raymond Tallis, *Aping Mankind* (London: Routledge, 2011).

16 This nonsense was already debunked by Nietzsche in his critique of Darwinist explanatory patterns, where he points out that characteristic activities of humans (and other animals) should be understood not on the model of the will to life but the will to power – that is, the increase without which one cannot explain the ascetic values that he sees as the foundation for the scientific view of objectivity. See Friedrich Nietzsche, *Beyond Good and Evil*, ed. Rolf-Peter Horstmann and Judith Norman, trans. Judith Norman (Cambridge: Cambridge University Press, 2002), pp. 144f. (§253, translation modified), where Darwin, John Stuart Mill and Herbert Spencer are referred to as 'worthy but mediocre Englishmen'. He sees an appropriate subjectivity in this, 'a certain narrowness, aridity, and diligent, painstaking care' that 'may bestow a favourable disposition' when it comes to making 'scientific discoveries of a Darwinian type'. On the connection between self-discipline and objectivity, see the science-historical study by Lorraine Daston and Peter Galison, *Objectivity* (New York: Zone Books, 2007). On the incoherence of the perspectivism in the background here, see especially the subtle reconstruction in James F. Conant, 'The dialectic of perspectivism I', *SATS: Nordic Journal of Philosophy*, 6/2 (2005): 5–50, and 'The dialectic of perspectivism II', *SATS: Nordic Journal of Philosophy*, 7/1 (2006): 6–57.

See also James F. Conant, 'Zur Möglichkeit eines sowohl subjektiven als auch objektiven Gedankens', in Thomas Hilgers et al. (eds), *Perspektive und Fiktion* (Paderborn: Brill, 2017), pp. 17–35. Biologistic interpretations of Nietzsche overlook his critique of science. A paradigmatic example is Markus Wild, 'Nietzsches Perspektivismus', in Hartmut von Sass (ed.), *Perspektivismus: Neue Beiträge aus der Erkenntnistheorie, Hermeneutik und Ethik* (Hamburg: Meiner, 2019), pp. 37–59, which deliberately ignores Conant's texts as well as the subtle manoeuvres for developing a non-banal alethic perspectivism. For a rejection of the standard rebuttals of relativism (which Wild uncritically employs), see the impressive study by Dorothee Schmidt, *Das Selbstaufhebungsargument: Der Relativismus in der gegenwärtigen philosophischen Debatte* (Berlin: de Gruyter, 2018).

17 See Gabriel, *Why the World Does Not Exist* (Cambridge: Polity, 2015), pp. 154ff.

18 There was a long tradition of viewing the raised head of the upright gait as proof of this. See the overview in Kurt Bayertz, *Der aufrechte Gang: Eine Geschichte des anthropologischen Denkens* (Munich: C. H. Beck, 2012).

19 Vitalism is described with particular analytical acumen in Hans Driesch, *Die Maschine und der Organismus* (Leipzig: J. A. Barth, 1935), in which Driesch defends himself specifically against Schlick (pp. 69–75) and Carnap (pp. 75f.). On the state of the debate around Bergson, which gave rise to the myth that he had been made scientifically obsolete, see the historically informed reconstruction of the facts in Jimena Carter, *The Physicist and the Philosopher: Einstein, Bergson, and the Debate that Changed Our Understanding of Time* (Princeton, NJ: Princeton University Press, 2015). Contrary to widespread legend, Driesch and Bergson by no means argue for the existence of an *élan vital* that, as a causal factor, constitutes a form of vital energy that cannot be grasped mechanically or, in the modern sense, via molecular biology. Rather, they both espouse a view that must be understood in the contemporary context as a mereology, stating that life employs formats of top-down causation and can therefore not be reconstructed purely from the bottom up. For a contemporary view on this, see Denis Noble, 'Biological relativity: developments and concepts a decade on', in Gabriel and Voosholz (eds), *Top-Down Causation and Emergence*.

20 Gabriel, *The Meaning of Thought*, p. 23 and passim.

21 Yuval Noah Harari, *Sapiens: A Brief History of Humankind* (New York: Random House, 2014).

22 See the compelling objections to this distinction from the milieu of symmetrical anthropology, especially in Latour, *We Have Never Been Modern* (Cambridge, MA: Harvard University Press, 2012), as well as Eduardo Viveiros de Castro, *The Inconstancy of the Indian Soul* (Chicago: Prickly Paradigm Press, 2011). I am indebted to Castro for valuable insights into the striking parallels between sense field ontology and what he calls 'Amazonian perspectivism' – that is, an ontology he found among so-called Indians. We were able to discuss this at a conference in October 2012 in Porto Alegre on the ontological turn, as well as during my visiting professorships at PUC Rio de Janeiro. For an overview in the ethnological context, see Martin Holbraad and Morten Axel Pedersen, *The Ontological Turn* (Cambridge: Cambridge University Press, 2017).

23 In this regard, I continue to follow Schelling as I read him in Gabriel, *Der Mensch im Mythos*.

24 An appropriate title for his follow-up book *Homo Deus* would have been *Go West*.

25 Yuval Noah Harari, 'The myth of freedom', *The Guardian*, 14 September 2018 (www.theguardian.com/books/2018/sep/14/yuval-noah-harari-the-new-threat -to-liberal-democracy).

26 Helmuth Plessner, *Levels of Organic Life and the Human: An Introduction to Philosophical Anthropology*, trans. Millay Hyatt (New York: Fordham University Press, 2019), p. 267 and *passim*.

27 Schopenhauer, *The World as Will and Representation* (Cambridge: Cambridge University Press, 2018), vol. 2, p. 6.

28 Ibid.

29 Carnap, with his Schopenhauer- and Nietzsche-inspired post-metaphysical expressivism, is absolutely right here. Schopenhauer's metaphysics is not a theory but a normatively charged self-disclosure, which, on closer inspection, he admits (like Nietzsche). It is a matter not of describing facts but of human self-determination, in which Schopenhauer searches for an anti-Christian path to salvation.

30 See Ian Hacking, *The Social Construction of What?* (Cambridge, MA: Harvard University Press, 1999), pp. 32, 59, 103–7 and *passim*.

31 For a discussion of this, see Gabriel, 'Der Neue Realismus zwischen Konstruktion und Wirklichkeit', in Ekkehard Felder and Andreas Gardt (eds), *Wirklichkeit oder Konstruktion?* (Berlin: de Gruyter, 2018), pp. 45–65.

32 This does not, of course, mean that every social system has founders, only that it is possible to found social systems explicitly. This does not eliminate intransparency, however, but only transfers it to the configuration of the social system that follows its foundation.

33 See the incisive formulation of the ubiquitous systems-theoretical principle of the blind spot in Luhmann, 'Cognition as construction', p. 247: '. . . the distinction with which cognizing systems respectively observe are their "blind spots" or their latent structure – because this distinction can itself not be distinguished; if it could, then another distinction, namely this one, would itself be blindly applied as a guiding distinction.' For a philosophical reconstruction of the benefits of the theory of the blind spot for meta-epistemology, see Gabriel, *The Limits of Epistemology*.

34 Lewis R. Gordon, *Disciplinary Decadence: Living Thought in Trying Times* (London: Routledge, 2006), and 'Der Realität zuliebe: teleologische Suspensionen disziplinärer Dekadenz', in Gabriel (ed.), *Der Neue Realismus*, pp. 244–67).

35 On the distinction between 'ontological truth' and 'ontological commitment', see Willard Van Orman Quine, 'Ontology and ideology', *Philosophical Studies*, 2/1 (1951): 11–15.

36 Willard Van Orman Quine, 'Two dogmas of empiricism', in *Quintessence: Basic Readings from the Philosophy of W. V. Quine*, ed. Roger F. Gibson (Cambridge, MA: Harvard University Press, 2008), pp. 31–53.

37 Quine, *Word and Object* (Cambridge, MA: MIT Press, 2013), p. 20.

38 For more detail, see Gabriel, *Der Sinn des Denkens*, pp. 221–7.
39 See Willard Van Orman Quine, 'Ontological relativity', in *Ontological Relativity and Other Essays* (New York: Columbia University Press, 1969), pp. 26–68.
40 For more detail, see Cornelius Castoriadis, *The Imaginary Institution of Society* (Cambridge, MA: MIT Press, 1997).
41 For a discussion of this version of 'knowledge first' epistemology, see Patrick Greenough and Duncan Pritchard (eds), *Williamson on Knowledge* (Oxford: Oxford University Press, 2009), as well as Gabriel, *Die Erkenntnis der Welt* (Freiburg: Alber, 2012), pp. 85–94.
42 Concerning Plato's objection to a standard analysis of knowledge, see ibid., pp. 38–64.
43 Andrea Kern is absolutely right that the condition of non-coincidence is sufficient to rule out Gettier cases, which is why adducing Gettier cases is not a counterargument to the classical conception of knowledge, merely a distrustful misunderstanding. The result of the Gettier discussion is quite simply this: *not everything that is performed by a subject via the application of a logical truth to given premises can be accepted in epistemic contexts as a justification.* See Kern, *Sources of Knowledge* (Cambridge, MA: Harvard University Press, 2017).
44 See, following on from Foucault and thus visibly under the influence of Nietzsche, Daston and Galison, *Objectivity*.
45 See Hans-Jörg Rheinberger, *Historische Epistemologie zur Einführung* (Hamburg: Junius, 2007).
46 This triggered the disjunctivism debate; see, paradigmatically, John McDowell, *Perception as a Capacity for Knowledge: Aquinas Lecture* (Milwaukee: Marquette University Press, 2011); Rödl, *Self-Consciousness and Objectivity*.
47 See Gabriel, *Propos réalistes* (Paris: Librairie Philosophique J. Vrin, 2019), ch. 6.
48 Thus also Jens Rometsch, *Freiheit zur Wahrheit* (Frankfurt: Klostermann, 2018), ch. 4.
49 Gabriel, *Propos réalistes*, pp. 205f. Here I act on a conversational remark by Michael Forster about Hegel's pun *begriffene Geschichte* [grasped history] (Hegel, *Phenomenology of Spirit*, p. 493). In the course of their articulation, the individual forms of consciousness in the *Phenomenology of Spirit* becomes modules of mind, such that they retroactively, from the perspective of their elevation, appear necessary and complete – which does not mean that one can predict a priori how the mind develops. See Forster's attempt to bring historicity and necessity together, in Forster, *Hegel's Idea of a Phenomenology of Spirit*.
50 See Markus Gabriel, 'The meaning of existence and the contingency of sense', *Frontiers of Philosophy in China*, 9/1 (2014): 109–29, here pp. 123–6.
51 This corresponds to the second of the five tropes in Sextus' portrayal of Agrippa's trilemma; see, with references, Markus Gabriel, 'Die metaphysische Wahrheit des Skeptizismus bei Schelling und Hegel', *Internationales Jahrbuch des Deutschen Idealismus*, 5 (2007): 126–56.
52 The position outlined here is therefore resolutely hermeneutical, as Anton Friedrich Koch points out in his review of *The Limits of Epistemology*. See Anton F. Koch, 'Buchnotiz zu Markus Gabriel: An den Grenzen der Erkenntnistheorie', *Philosophische Rundschau*, 59/2 (2012): 185–9. See also Koch's characterization

of hermeutical finitude in Koch, *Hermeneutischer Realismus* (Tübingen: Mohr Siebeck, 2016).

53 See the argumentation in Gabriel, *Neo-Existentialism* (Cambridge: Polity, 2018).

54 Anyone who finds this example dubious on account of its ontology of unobservable entities can replace it with some other example involving an error about natural species. In any scenario, something is considered a natural species because it does not vary when our opinions about it change. According to this view, even simple ideas in Berkeley's idealism are natural species, which is why Berkeley rightly believed that he could develop a philosophy of nature based on his epistemological deliberations, something that is usually ignored. See the extensive description of his natural philosophy in George Berkeley, *Siris: A Chain of Philosophical Reflexions and Inquiries Concerning the Virtues of Tar Water: And Divers Other Subjects Connected Together and Arising One from Another* (London: Forgotten Books, [1744] 2017).

55 Normativity is realized exclusively in practices of normalization. Foucault is right in this respect, though he is of course influenced by Canguilhem, who pointed out that normality has innate conditions for implantation in our survival form. See Georges Canguilhem, *On the Normal and the Pathological*, trans. Carolyn R. Fawcett (Dordrecht: D. Reidel, 1978).

56 See Wittgenstein, *Philosophical Investigations*, p. 44 (§85).

57 Bourdieu, *Pascalian Meditations*, p. 9.

58 Möllers, *The Possibility of Norms*, p. 125.

59 Ibid., p. 73.

60 Ibid.

61 Ibid., p. 125. Canguilhem makes a similar point in *On the Normal and the Pathological* when he argues that regulation begins with the violation of norms, such that 'the condition of the possibility of rules is but one with the condition of the possibility of the experience of rules' (p. 148).

62 The invented name 'Kripkenstein' is a portmanteau of 'Kripke' and 'Wittgenstein' (Trans.).

63 Möllers considers this problem unproductive (*The Possibility of Norms*, pp. 121ff.), yet consistently remains trapped in it with the remarks that follow this rejection, such as the following passage, where he poses exactly the same question as Kripke, namely 'why something from the past can justify current restrictions. Methodologically, we face the problem of whether any application inevitably represents an actualization, which brings about something completely different from the supposedly "original" norm' (ibid., p. 210, translation modified). This is a concise formulation of Kripke's problem.

64 See his reconstruction of the dialectic of theories of command and recognition of the normative, ibid., pp. 56–9: 'the more successful a norm is by corresponding to the course of events, the less clear it becomes what *noticeably* distinguishes this norm from said course of events' (ibid., p. 59). Note that Möllers rejects the idea of a 'predominant ontology of the social' (p. 156) that 'conceives of norms as products of coordinating or cooperating individual subjects' (ibid.). He rightly sees its weakness in describing the social 'as if every normative practice were a perpetuated foundational situation' (ibid.).

65 Ibid., p. 152. Quoted from Blumenberg, *Theorie der Unbegrifflichkeit* (Frankfurt: Suhrkamp, 2007), p. 76.

66 This is one of Frege's main reasons for keeping objectivity away from representations, since he universally considers the latter logically private, which unfortunately opens a divide between thinking and thoughts. See Gabriel, *Sinn und Existenz* (Berlin: Suhrkamp, 2016), §§2b and 12.

67 Here I am taking up Nassehi's concept of complexity, under which he subsumes the idea that 'nothing can be understood any longer without the idea that things actually look different from different perspectives' (*Muster: Theorie der digitalen Gesellschaft*, p. 284). OFS is a complex theory of complexity, which explains a socio-ontological family resemblance to systems theory. Of course, the *differentia specifica* to this lies in neutral realism and the critique of constructivism: the concept of construction is not a condition for complexity but, rather, an ontologically and epistemologically questionable form of complexity reduction.

68 This is also the tenor of Searle's answer to the question of the objectivity of the social sciences in *Making the Social World*.

69 See Möllers, *The Possibility of Norms*, pp. 25ff.

70 Ibid., p. 25, n. 81 (translation modified).

71 Ibid., p. 25.

72 Infants clearly assent to the execution of language as something that is normative for them before they are able to communicate this in the execution of language, which happens only later once they become aware that there are other languages which they do not understand. Then they can decide on their native language(s) as something that is binding in a certain situation, and even tell adults to use a particular language.

73 See Dave Elder-Vass, *The Reality of Social Construction* (Cambridge: Cambridge University Press, 2012).

74 Wittgenstein, *Philosophical Investigations*, pp. 94f. (§242).

75 This was the spirit of an objection to Joseph Raz's intentionalist concept of action made by Paul Boghossian during a lecture at NYU in the autumn of 2015.

76 Quassim Cassam, *Conspiracy Theories* (Cambridge: Polity, 2019).

77 Möllers, *The Possibility of Norms*, p. 101.

78 Ibid., p. 126. See ibid., p. 89: 'Since the real is possible, norms can also refer to that which is real. It is the case that norms refer to the real when they are observed. The affirmation of an existing condition or an established practice is a common application of norms. Such an affirmation can become socially relevant in two ways. For one, by giving the affirmed condition a new meaning through the norm. It conforms with the norm, is made explicit by the norm, and is explicitly affirmed.'

79 Ibid., p. 75.

80 The theological undertone returns in a number of passages, such as the examination of the 'relationship between transcendence and normativity' (ibid., p. 259). Of course, Möllers himself does not espouse any theological justification for norms but, rather, points in his outline of a genealogy of modern normative orders to a transitional theological stage; however, this is the origin

of the concept of a 'counter-world' (p. 259) and of transcendence, which Möllers does not entirely jettison.

81 Kant likewise introduces heautonomy in the context of a knowability problem, albeit in relation to the position of the power of judgement vis-à-vis nature as the object area of empirical judgements. See Immanuel Kant, *Critique of the Power of Judgment*, trans. Paul Guyer and Eric Matthews (Cambridge: Cambridge University Press, 2000), p. 72:

> The power of judgment thus also has in itself an *a priori* principle for the possibility of nature, though only in a subjective respect, by means of which it prescribes a law, not to nature (as autonomy), but to itself (as heautonomy) for reflection on nature, which one could call the law of the specification of nature with regard to its empirical laws, which it does not cognize in nature *a priori* but rather assumes in behalf of an order of nature cognizable for our understanding in the division that it makes of its universal laws when it would subordinate a manifold of particular laws to these.

82 For characteristic examples, see Robert B. Pippin, *Idealism as Modernism: Hegelian Variations* (Cambridge: Cambridge University Press, 1997), and *Hegel's Practical Philosophy: Rational Agency as Ethical Life* (Cambridge: Cambridge University Press, 2008); Robert B. Brandom, *Tales of the Mighty Dead: Historical Essays in the Metaphysics of Intentionality* (Cambridge, MA: Harvard University Press, 2002), as well as his recent masterpiece *A Spirit of Trust: A Reading of Hegel's Phenomenology* (Cambridge, MA: Harvard University Press, 2019). For a critical view of Pippin, see Markus Gabriel, 'Robert B. Pippin a) Hegel's Practical Philosophy and b) Hegel on Self-Consciousness', *Internationales Jahrbuch des Deutschen Idealismus*, 8 (2010): 362–70, as well as Markus Gabriel, 'Transcendental ontology and apperceptive idealism', *Australasian Philosophical Review*, 2/4 (2018): 383–92.

§14 Rule-Following, Realistically Conceived

1 Saul A. Kripke, *Wittgenstein on Rules and Private Language: An Elementary Exposition* (Cambridge, MA: Harvard University Press, 1982).

2 See the classification of Kripke's problem as a variety of Kantian scepticism in James F. Conant, 'Spielarten des Skeptizismus', *Deutsche Zeitschrift für Philosophie*, 28: 21–72 [special issue: *Skeptizismus und Metaphysik*].

3 This is argued by Kwame Anthony Appiah in *The Ethics of Identity* (Princeton, NJ: Princeton University Press, 2005) and *The Lies that Bind* (London: Profile Books, 2018), in contrast to Fukuyama, *Identity*. See also the much discussed standard work Benedict Anderson, *Imagined Communities: Reflections on the Origin and Spread of Nationalism* (London: Verso, 2006).

4 Here I am following a point made by Marius Bartmann, who, in his 2018 dissertation for the University of Bonn entitled *Beyond Realism and Idealism: On a*

Leitmotif in Early and Late Wittgenstein, examines the option that deviation from a given rule always consists in following a different rule, which means that application errors are not without rules.

5 For more detail, see Gabriel, *Propos réalistes*, pp. 135–64.

6 Admittedly, Wittgenstein rejects the description of his thinking as pragmatism on several occasions, for example in *Remarks on the Philosophy of Psychology*, vol. 1, ed. G. E. M. Anscombe and G. H. von Wright, trans. G. E. M. Anscombe (Chicago: University of Chicago Press, 1988), p. 54: 'But you aren't a pragmatist? No. For I am not saying that a proposition is true if it is useful.' See also Ludwig Wittgenstein, *On Certainty*, ed. G. E. M. Anscombe and G. H. von Wright, trans. Denis Paul and G. E. M. Anscombe (Oxford: Blackwell, 1974), p. 54: 'So I am trying to say something that sounds like pragmatism. Here I am being thwarted by a kind of *Weltanschauung*.'

7 Kripke, *Wittgenstein on Rules and Private Language*, pp. 63–8.

8 Ibid., p. 22.

9 Ibid., p. 21.

10 Ibid., p. 13.

11 See, paradigmatically, Wolfgang Wieland, *Platon und die Formen des Wissens* (Göttingen: Vandenhoeck & Ruprecht, 1999), esp. §13. Wieland shows that propositional knowledge presupposes non-propositional utility knowledge that is 'not capable of errors' (p. 233) and hence not infallible.

> In all cases one is dealing with forms of a knowledge that is, in a strict sense, neither objectifiable nor communicable; that does not directly intend any object and is therefore not capable of errors; that is always tied to the authority of a bearer, and precisely therefore discloses reality for its bearer in untenable fashion. There can be no reasonable doubt that by far the largest part of knowledge at the disposal of humans belongs to the non-propositional type. Familiarity with the world is only imparted to humans in small measure through the knowledge of true statements about them. (Ibid.)

12 On the relationship between education and scepticism, see the comprehensive study by Andreas Gelhard, *Skeptische Bildung: Prüfungsprozesse als philosophisches Problem* (Zurich: Diaphanes, 2018).

13 See Kripke, *Wittgenstein on Rules and Private Language*, p. 12:

> So I am supposing that the sceptic, provisionally, is not questioning my *present* use of the word 'plus'; he agrees that, according to my *present* usage, '68 plus 57' denotes 125. Not only does he agree with me on this, he conducts the entire debate with me in my language as I *presently* use it. He merely questions whether my present usage agrees with my past usage, whether I am *presently* conforming to my *previous* linguistic intentions.

14 Möllers, *The Possibility of Norms*, p. 121. By contrast, see Kripke, *Wittgenstein on Rules and Private Language*, p. 21: 'So formulated, the problem may appear

to be epistemological – how can anyone know which of these I meant? Given, however, that everything in my mental history is compatible both with the conclusion that I meant plus and with the conclusion that I meant quus, it is clear that the sceptical challenge is not really an epistemological one.'

15 In one regard not mentioned by Kripke, incidentally, the answer is open anyway, since '125' is not the only possible value for x and there are really an infinite number of possibilities that are compatible with the 'a + b = x' function in a given formal system, such as '66 + 59', '57 + 68', '69 + 56', and so on. Kripke commits an error when he presents the rule of addition as if the '+' in '68 + 57' required supplying the outcome '125'. But we will leave aside this *smikron ti* [something small] – which is actually far from insignificant – in Kripke's favour. The upshot of the idea only hinted at here is that the choice of a formal system for determining what one should do is grounded in a social context that co-determines the overall conditions of our normatively relevant decisions. The exercising of mathematical abilities takes place in social contexts and is not restricted to some inherent ingenuity in finding the correct answers to the more or less difficult assignments set by the teacher.

16 See Dave Elder-Vass, *The Reality of Social Construction* (Cambridge: Cambridge University Press, 2012), pp. 15–34. The concept is introduced as follows: 'A norm circle is the group of people who are committed to endorsing and enforcing a particular norm. Such groups are social entities with people as their parts, and because of the ways in which the members of such groups interact (a *mechanism*) they have the causal power to produce a tendency in individuals to follows standardized practices' (p. 23). Elder-Vass advocates a social realism that ascribes causal forces to social structures, though he ultimately reduces these powers to the material dimension of human beings in order to develop a 'materialist account of social structure and indeed of culture, language, discourse, and knowledge' (p. 21). In doing so, however, he confuses realism (as well as causality) with naturalism (and thus a view of causality tied to particular entities). By contrast, see Gabriel, 'Für einen nicht-naturalistischen Realismus', in Magdalena Marszałek and Dieter Mersch (eds), *Seien wir realistisch* (Zurich: Diaphanes, 2016), pp. 59–8. On the theory of causality in Elder-Vass, see his book *The Causal Power of Social Structures: Emergence, Structure and Agency* (Cambridge: Cambridge University Press, 2010).

17 As an aside, this is a central subject of the classical theory of friendship canonically laid out in Aristotle's *Nicomachean Ethics*. It holds that a community which possesses some form of collective intentionality is thus logically deficient if it is limited to the fact that several human animals are 'grazing in the same place (*en to auto nemesthai*')' (*Nicomachean Ethics*, 9.1170b14). The norm (the *nomos*) differs *categorially*, not *summatively*, from the spatiotemporal contiguity of many who are doing the same thing (grazing, *nemesthai*).

18 In opposition to any form of mental finitism, see David Deutsch, *The Beginning of Infinity: Explanations that Transform the World* (London: Penguin, 2011). Rejecting Kripke's experimental design, Margaret Gilbert also argues that we can grasp concepts, and hence infinite chains of application, without this assumption being successfully undermined by the sceptic introduced

by Kripke. See Margaret Gilbert, *On Social Facts* (Princeton, NJ: Princeton University Press, 1989), pp. 112–24.

19 Kripke, *Wittgenstein on Rules and Private Language*, p. 17.

20 Wittgenstein, *Philosophical Investigations*, p. 91.

21 See Wieland, *Platon und die Formen des Wissens*, §13.

22 Wittgenstein, *Philosophical Investigations*, p. 351.

23 Ibid., pp. 91f.

24 This is a result of the thought in *Philosophical Investigations*, §201, which points out that 'there is a way of grasping a rule that is *not* an interpretation' (ibid., p. 88).

25 This is paradigmatically represented by the so-called strong programme in the sociology of science, which explicitly invokes Wittgenstein and interprets him through Kripke's lens. See David Bloor, *Wittgenstein, Rules and Institutions* (London: Routledge, 1997), as well as the attempt at a philosophical justification of this set-up in Martin Kusch, *A Sceptical Guide to Meaning and Rules: Defending Kripke's Wittgenstein* (Montreal: Acumen, 2006).

26 Möllers, *The Possibility of Norms*, p. 231. For the tie example, see pp. 230f.

27 Ibid., p. 231.

28 Ibid.

29 In explicit opposition to Kant, or Patricia Kitcher's reading of Kant, see ibid., p. 228.

30 Gabriel, 'A very heterodox reading of the lord-servant allegory in Hegel's *Phenomenology of Spirit*', in Markus Gabriel and Anders Moe Rasmussen (eds), *German Idealism Today* (Berlin: de Gruyter, 2017), pp. 95–120.

31 Scott Hershovitz, 'Wittgenstein on rules: the phantom menace', *Oxford Journal of Legal Studies*, 22 (2002): 619–40, here p. 628.

32 Wittgenstein, on the other hand, falls prey to a naturalization of intransparency. See Gabriel, *The Limits of Epistemology*, §9.

33 See the useful overview in Helen Beebee et al. (eds), *Making a Difference: Essays on the Philosophy of Causation* (Oxford: Oxford University Press, 2017).

§15 Mythology, Ideology, Fiction

1 See Bourdieu, *Distinction* (Cambridge, MA: Harvard University Press, 1984), and *The Rules of Art* (Stanford, CA: Stanford University Press, 1996).

2 This difference is overlooked by Jason Stanley, *How Propaganda Works* (Princeton, NJ: Princeton University Press, 2015).

3 See the elaborated critical concept of ideology in John B. Thompson, *Ideology and Modern Culture: Critical Theory in the Era of Mass Communication* (Cambridge: Polity, 1990), esp. pp. 52–73.

4 Science can also assume the function of mythology, for example by 'explaining' current human behaviour with recourse to a factually epistemically inaccessible deep, paleoanthropological past. There are many possible (and real) ways for science to be placed in the ideological service of a mythology without the actors being aware of it. Abandoning one particular myth is no guarantee that

one has not taken on a different one. See Wolfram Hogrebe, '"Wer im Mythos lebt . . ."', in *Echo des Nichtwissens* (Berlin: Akademie, 2006), pp. 330–41.

5 See Gabriel, *The Power of Art* (Cambridge, Polity, 2020). Art is essentially ambivalent, and its ontological status makes it fluctuate between a self-illumination of our form of life and kitsch – a well-known problem since Adorno's writings on the issue.

6 See Gabriel, *Der Mensch im Mythos*, as well as Gabriel and Žižek, *Mythology, Madness and Laughter*.

7 This is famously one of the central insights in Max Horkheimer and Theodor W. Adorno, *Dialectic of Enlightenment: Philosophical Fragments*, trans. Edmund Jephcott (Stanford, CA: Stanford University Press, 2002).

8 By contrast, see Gabriel, *Der Sinn des Denkens*, pp. 221–7, as well as Hubert Dreyfus and Charles Taylor, *Retrieving Realism* (Cambridge, MA: Harvard University Press, 2015).

9 For a critique of this type of mythology, see Tallis, *Aping Mankind*.

10 Stanislas Dehaene et al., 'What is consciousness, and could machines have it?', *Science* 358 (2017): 486–92).

11 Ibid., p. 486.

12 In response to my explicit question at a conference held at the Vatican by the Papal Academy of Sciences (16–17 April 2019), Stanislas Dehaene did not supply any natural-scientific evidence or argument, instead resorting to defensive rhetoric and systematic avoidance of dialogue; more recently he unleashed a 'shitstorm' on Twitter (www.youtube.com/watch?v=hPsrQAZF d6Q&t=1537s). I read this unscientific behaviour as a sociological indication that my criticism is entirely accurate and his research programme is hopelessly doomed to failure because of an arbitrary choice of meaning for 'consciousness'. If one cannot state what one is actually looking for when looking for the neuronal correlate of 'consciousness' (in what sense of the word?), then one is simply not looking for anything.

13 Dehaene et al., 'What is consciousness, and could machines have it?'.

14 Ibid.

15 Ibid.

16 Ibid., p. 487.

17 See this empirically empty, purely metaphysical promise (ibid.):

> The computations implemented by current deep-learning networks correspond mostly to nonconscious operations in the human brain. However, much like artificial neural networks took their inspiration from neurobiology, artificial consciousness may progress by investigating the architectures that allow the human brain to generate consciousness, then transferring those insights into computer algorithms. Our aim is to foster such progress by reviewing aspects of the cognitive neuroscience of consciousness that may be pertinent for machines.

18 An undoubtedly significant difficulty that I cannot deal with here stems from the fact that, ever since humans have been informed about their

self-representations, they have given information about their conception of non-human mental life. This particularly includes the divine, the gods, or God in the eminent singular. Therefore, New Realism would here require a comprehensive philosophy of religion that could not be evaded by anti-naturalism based on the convenient, yet verifiably misguided claim of God's allegedly proven non-existence. See Markus Gabriel, 'Der Sinn der Religion', in Michael Meyer-Blanck (ed.), *Geschichte und Gott: XV. Europäischer Kongress für Theologie (14.–18. September 2014 in Berlin)* (Leipzig: Evangelische Verlagsanstalt, 2016), pp. 58–75, and '"Niemand hat Gott je gesehen" – Eine philosophische Tischrede', in Wolfram Kinzig and Julia Winnebeck (eds), *Glaube und Theologie: Reformatorische Grundeinsichten in der ökumenischen Diskussion* (Leipzig: Evangelische Verlagsanstalt, 2019), pp. 329–41.

19 For a critical account, see Stephen Cave, *Immortality: The Quest to Live Forever and How it Drives Civilization* (New York: Crown, 2012).

20 On the other hand, compare the dawning consciousness in earlier phases of cybernetics in Norbert Wiener, *God & Golem, Inc.: A Comment on Certain Points Where Cybernetics Impinges on Religion* (Cambridge, MA: MIT Press, 1964).

21 This was shown especially clearly by Schelling in his writings on natural philosophy, incidentally; he was the first to deal with the question of what a metaphysics should look like that allows mind to be understood as something that has become. He formulated the decisive insight that a philosophy which seeks to address the having-become of mind must work with two lines of inquiry: one leads conceptually from nature to mind, while the other leads conceptually from mind to nature and accepts that mind can never be fully grasped through concepts that exclusively suppose non-conscious forces and anonymous processes.

22 The body of transhumanist literature is (unfortunately) extensive. For paradigmatic examples, see Raymond Kurzweil, *The Age of Intelligent Machines* (Cambridge, MA: MIT Press, 1990); *The Singularity Is Near: When Humans Transcend Biology* (New York: Penguin, 2004); *How to Create a Mind: The Secret of Human Thought Revealed* (New York: Penguin, 2012); also Max Tegmark, *Our Mathematical Universe* (New York: Knopf, 2014).

23 If one considers the universe as a whole, it is questionable whether such facts exist in the universe, since we, as minded beings, interact causally with the universe, so it is affected in its totality by the fact that we exist in it. However, whether the universe is a whole that is ontologically open towards the future is a question for natural philosophy that cannot be answered here. If the universe exists as a whole and we occur in it, then the universe does not contain any maximally objective facts, since every fact is causally intertwined with the circumstance that we know something about some non-human areas of the universe through knowledge exchange.

24 Quine, *Word and Object*, p. 275.

25 'Character is destiny': Heraclitus, DK 22 B 119.

26 See again Hutter, *Narrative Ontologie*.

27 One example is the much discussed thought experiment in which we can replace one neuron at a time in our brain with a silicon copy without causing

our consciousness to disappear entirely, since it would gradually be replaced by an artificial one. This idea relies on the *locus classicus* in David Chalmers, *The Conscious Mind: In Search of a Fundamental Theory* (Oxford: Oxford University Press, 1997), ch. III.7. To show that this thought experiment goes against the medical facts of being-human – that is, it enacts something impossible – it is sufficient to point out that we cannot even accomplish organ transplants without extremely fragile immunosuppressants. Foreign organs are rejected and lead sooner or later to death. The idea that one could even remotely work on replacing a brain with silicon (however small the steps) contradicts the neurobiological facts. The thought experiment leads nowhere empirically and should on no account be used to support the misguided 'intuition' that it must be possible to realize consciousness by non-biological means.

28 For a discussion, see Michael Hampe, *Die Dritte Aufklärung* (Berlin: NP & I, 2018).

§16 The Ontology of Social Networks

1 See the impressive and wide-ranging groundwork in Thomas S. Hoffmann, *Philosophische Physiologie: Eine Systematik des Begriffs der Natur im Spiegel der Geschichte der Philosophie* (Stuttgart-Bad Cannstatt: frommann-holzboog, 2003). According to Hoffmann, the 'basic concept of nature' is 'the directly broken centre, *inequality*: not an inequality "of" and "for something", but rather an inequality in relation to the equal itself, to the *totality* of identity, from which also follows its inhomogeneity in relation to the form of the world' (p. 109).

2 Koch provides a wealth of arguments against transparentism in *Versuch über Wahrheit und Zeit* (Paderborn: Brill, 2006) and *Hermeneutischer Realismus*, as well as in *Die Evolution des logischen Raums* (Tübingen: Mohr Siebeck, 2014).

3 See Shoshana Zuboff, *The Age of Surveillance Capitalism: The Fight for a Human Future at the New Frontier of Power* (London: Profile Books, 2019).

4 As Nassehi shows in *Muster: Theorie der digitalen Gesellschaft*, modernity is from the outset the project of a digital society that has now found a suitable media format to objectify itself. Similarly, see Dirk Baeker, *4.0 oder Die Lücke die der Rechner lässt* (Leipzig: Merve, 2018), showing that information is the 'form of reflection in the next society' (p. 192).

5 Gabriel, *Der Sinn des Denkens*, pp. 143–93.

6 See the accurate remarks in Nassehi, *Muster: Theorie der digitalen Gesellschaft*, p. 279:

> Crudely put, free-floating online communication is subject to little selection pressure, since the promise that everyone essentially has free rein also leads to a disabling of community-stabilizing forms of selection. If someone can say what they want, they will do so – and when that occurs, communication processes will more probably take polemogenic than community-forming directions. Anyone who considers this a diagnosis of a crisis must have had unrealistic, even naive expectations.

7 Ibid., p. 280.
8 See the overview in Franklin Foer, *World Without Mind: The Existential Threat of Big Tech* (New York: Penguin, 2017). For a critical analysis of the AI discourse, see also Luc Julia, *L'intelligence artificielle n'existe pas* (Paris: First éditions, 2019). One should note that Julia is one of the inventors of Siri. See also Jean-Gabriel Ganascia, *Le mythe de la singularité: faut-il craindre l'intelligence artificielle?* (Paris: Éditions Points, 2019).
9 See Natasha Dow Schüll, *Addiction by Design: Machine Gambling in Las Vegas* (Princeton, NJ: Princeton University Press, 2012).
10 Against the myth of an essentially inexplicable yet intelligent black box of deep learning, see Julia, *L'intelligence artificielle n'existe pas*, pp. 169–81. For a euphoric promotion of the same that more or less shares the ontological diagnosis presented in the main text, yet draws different social conclusions from it, see Alex Pentland, *Social Physics: How Social Networks Can Make Us Smarter* (New York: Penguin, 2014). I do not know if he changed his opinion after Trump's election success.
11 See my interview with *El País* of 1 May 2019 – published exactly on Labor Day.
12 See the overview in Yvonne Hofstetter, *Das Ende der Demokratie: wie die künstliche Intelligenz die Politik übernimmt und uns entmündigt* (Munich: C. Bertelsmann 2016), and 'Soziale Medien: Wer Newsfeeds auf Werbeplattformen liest, kann Propaganda erwarten, aber nicht die Wahrheit', in Jakob Augstein (ed.), *Reclaim Autonomy: Selbstermächtigung in der digitalen Weltordnung* (Berlin: Suhrkamp, 2017), pp. 25–38. I am grateful to Yvonne Hofstetter for further explanations of her reflections during the economic summit in the *Süddeutsche Zeitung* on 17 November 2016 and at the phil.cologne on 10 July 2017.
13 See Luciano Floridi, *The Fourth Revolution: How the Infosphere is Reshaping Human Reality* (Oxford: Oxford University Press, 2014); regarding the echoes of the mythologeme of the noosphere, see Oliver Krüger, 'Gaia, God, and the internet – revisited: the history of evolution and the utopia of community in media society', *Heidelberg Journal for Religions on the Internet*, 8 (2015): 56–87, and more recently also *Virtual Immortality – God, Evolution, and the Singularity in Post- and Transhumanism* (Bielefeld: transcript, 2019). Floridi has metaphysical ambitions, as becomes apparent when he defines reality as the 'totality of information' and devotes his groundwork for a philosophy of information to this idea in *The Philosophy of Information* (Oxford: Oxford University Press, 2013).
14 See the now-canonical theory of ideology in Slavoj Žižek, *For They Know Not What They Do: Enjoyment as a Political Factor* (London: Verso, 2008).

§17 The Public Sphere of Mind

1 Jürgen Habermas, *The Structural Transformation of the Public Sphere: An Inquiry into a Category of Bourgeois Society*, trans. Thomas Burger (Cambridge, MA: MIT Press, 1991).
2 Jürgen Habermas, 'Further reflections on the public sphere', in Craig Calhoun

(ed.), *Habermas and the Public Sphere* (Cambridge, MA: MIT Press, 1993), p. 457.

3 Ibid., p. 456.
4 Ibid.
5 Ibid., p. 457.
6 Ibid.
7 In his foreword to the second edition, Habermas introduces the concept of a 'public sphere infiltrated by power' (p. 437) [*vermachtete Öffentlichkeit*] resulting from the mass media. With these emerged

> a new sort of influence, i.e., media power, which, used for purposes of manipulation, once and for all took care of the innocence of the principle of publicity. The public sphere, simultaneously prestructured and dominated by the mass media, developed into an arena infiltrated by power in which, by means of topic selection and topical contributions, a battle is fought not only over influence but over the control of communication flows that affect behaviour while their strategic intentions are kept hidden as much as possible. (Ibid.)

8 Habermas, *The Structural Transformation of the Public Sphere*, p. 276, n. 147.
9 Ibid., p. 85.
10 Ibid.:

> The public sphere of civil society stood or fell with the principle of universal access. A public sphere from which specific groups would be *eo ipso* excluded was less than merely incomplete; it was not a public sphere at all. Accordingly, the public that might be considered the subject of the bourgeois constitutional state viewed its sphere as a public one in this strict sense; in its deliberations it anticipated in principle that all human beings belong to it. The private person too was simply a human being, that is, a moral person. We have designated the historical and social location in which this self-interpretation developed. The consciousness of this, if you will, formless humanity grew up in the patriarchal conjugal family's intimate sphere that was oriented to a public.

11 On the concept of ideology, see ibid., p. 88.
12 Ibid.
13 See the relevant first fragment by Heraclitus, DK 22 B 1.
14 In DK 22 B 2, Heraclitus contrasts the public or universal (*xynon*) with private opinion (*idia phronesis*).
15 This is how one can read Derrida's rebuttal of Levinas in Derrida, 'Violence and metaphysics', in *Writing and Difference*, trans. Alan Bass (Chicago: University of Chicago Press, 1978), pp. 79–153. From this perspective, Derrida's project from the beginning until *The Politics of Friendship* is a defence of a universal – a far better reading than the one (circulated especially by Habermas and Manfred Frank) which consigns Derrida, of all people, to the realm of particularist,

anti-reason sophistry and claims that, 'all denials notwithstanding', he 'remains close to Jewish mysticism' (Jürgen Habermas, *The Philosophical Discourse of Modernity: Twelve Lectures*, trans. Frederick Lawrence [Cambridge: Polity, 2018], p. 182). See the lengthy and famously shocking misreading of Derrida, ibid., pp. 161–210, and Manfred Frank, *What Is Neostructuralism?*, trans. Sabine Wilke and Richard T. Gray (Minneapolis: University of Minnesota Press, 1989). The sometimes crude misunderstandings and distortions in these readings have been extensively noted. By contrast, productive applications of Derrida in the context of critical theory can be found in Christoph Menke, *The Sovereignty of Art: Aesthetic Negativity in Adorno and Derrida*, trans. Neil Solomon (Cambridge, MA: MIT Press, 1998); Andrea Kern and Christoph Menke (eds), *Philosophie der Dekonstruktion* (Frankfurt: Suhrkamp, 2002); Raoul Moati, *Derrida/Searle: Deconstruction and Ordinary Language*, trans. Timothy Attanucci and Maureen Chun (New York: Columbia University Press, 2014), and *Derrida et le langage ordinaire* (Paris: Hermann, 2014); Freytag, *Die Rahmung des Hintergrunds*.

16 On the debate around Jaspers's concept of an Axial Age, see Jan Assmann, *Achsenzeit: Eine Archäologie der Moderne* (Munich: C. H. Beck, 2018).

17 See Habermas, *The Structural Transformation of the Public Sphere*.

18 Ibid., p. 153.

19 Dave Eggers, *The Circle* (New York: Knopf Doubleday, 2013).

20 Habermas, *The Structural Transformation of the Public Sphere*, p. 170.

21 Ibid., p. 171.

22 For an appropriately deluded expression of this constellation, see of course Nick Bostrom, *Superintelligence: Paths, Dangers, Strategies* (Oxford: Oxford University Press, 2014), as well as the following influential works by Yuval Noah Harari: *Sapiens: A Brief History of Humankind*; *Homo Deus: A Brief History of Tomorrow* (New York: Random House, 2016); *21 Lessons for the 21st Century* (New York: Random House, 2018). Bostrom and Harari do not realize that superintelligence has already existed for a long time, namely in the media formats of the internet that control our behaviour. Strictly speaking, of course, superintelligence is not intelligence, since it pursues no specific intention except those installed by its creators: software engineers, the ruling class of the digital world.

23 See, with various socioeconomic and contemporary historical details, Foer, *World Without Mind*, and, regarding social media, Roger McNamee, *Zucked: Waking up to the Facebook Catastrophe* (New York: Penguin, 2019).

24 Daniel Suarez, 'Wie die Technik unser Denken verändert: Unser Geist in den sozialen Medien', in Augstein (ed.), *Reclaim Autonomy*, pp. 155–65, reminds us that this mirror structure is connected to adverts that are displayed independently of whether a virtual avatar is telling the truth or not. 'Let us not forget: the hall of mirrors in social media was constructed solely for the purpose of inducing us to share and like posts. Why? So that one can do better advertising, or so that the number of users on the platforms increase, to the joy of investors. It turns out, however, that this architecture considerably privileges emotions over reality – which is a problem' (ibid., p. 162). Regarding the subject of

mirrors in this context, see also the contribution to the same volume by Yvonne Hofstetter, 'Soziale Medien: Wer Newsfeeds auf Werbeplattformen liest, kann Propaganda erwarten, aber nicht die Wahrheit', pp. 25–37.

25 This is paradigmatically connected to the work of Heidegger, Herbert Dreyfus and Searle. For a modern update of these arguments, see Gabriel, *Der Sinn des Denkens.*

26 See McNamee, *Zucked.*

27 See ibid., p. 159.

On a Final Note

1 Jean Baudrillard, *Simulacra and Simulation*, trans. Sheila Faria Glase (Ann Arbor: University of Michigan Press, 1994).

2 See also his 'travelogue': Jean Baudrillard, *America*, trans. Chris Turner (London: Verso, 1988).

3 In this context, there is a remarkable essay by Baudrillard on Artificial Intelligence whose diagnoses I would unreservedly support in several respects. See Jean Baudrillard, 'Videowelt und fraktales Subjekt', in Ars Electronica (ed.), *Philosophien der neuen Technologie* (Berlin: Merve, 1989), pp. 113–31. He accurately describes the fantasy structure of the digital age, which reduces the subject to a 'spectacle of the brain' (p. 118). On the fantasy structure of AI, see especially pp. 126f.

4 Which, importantly, does not apply to Derrida (or Lyotard), who is usually the object of similar blanket accusations. On Derrida, see again Freytag, *Die Rahmung des Hintergrunds*. For an analytical reconstruction of Lyotard in the light of the challenges posed by 'post-truth' accusations, see the sketches by Mathew Congdon, 'Wronged beyond words: on the publicity and repression of moral injury', *Philosophy and Social Criticism*, 42/8 (2016): 815–34, as well as Matthew McLennan, 'Differend and "post-truth"', *French Journal for Media Research*, 9 (2018): 1–13.

5 This is masterfully staged in the Broadway musical *Hadestown*, which received eight Tony Awards. It embeds the destructive powers of global production chains and their constitutive socioeconomic asymmetries in the mythological parameters of Orphic mythemes. It ends by replacing political revolt with the insuperability of the self-destruction and self-renewal of Gaia (represented by the pairing of Hades and Persephone), which offers food for thought.

Index

absolute idealism 102–3
absolute metaphors 112
absolute nothingness 80–1
absolutism and pluralism 183
abstract objects 28
action coordination 206, 216
    and rule-following 263
    and social construction 235–6
adaptive behaviour 245
adaptive disorders 255
adiaphoron (the concept of the neutral)
    214, 297
Adorno, Theodor 196
adumbration 13, 111, 143, 147
aesthetic experience
    of art works 6, 10, 18, 21–5, 36–42,
        43–5, 51, 60, 77, 78–9
AI *see* Artificial Intelligence (AI)
the Aleph 12, 30, 82–9, 90–1, 93, 103,
    195
alethic transparency principle 35
algorithms 287, 289
American society
    as a hyperreality 301
anonymous nature
    and social realism 208–10, 211,
        212
anthropology, higher-order 247
anti-realism 96–7, 101
archaic thinking 218
Aristotle 27, 51, 120, 126, 170, 178, 190,
    234

art works
    aesthetic experience of 6, 10, 18,
        21–5, 36–42, 43–5, 51, 60, 77, 78–9
    composition of 36–7, 44–5
    conceptual dimensions of 38–45
    effective history of 42–3
    existence and non-existence in 11,
        76–7
    fiction and reality 76–7
    fictive and fictional objects in 1–2,
        46–55, 60, 77, 78–80
    and hermeneutical objects 10, 37, 48
    production of 38–9
    readings of 10, 24–5, 77
    reception of 39–42, 45
    work aesthetics of 38, 42–5
    see also scores (of art works)
Artificial Intelligence (AI) 281, 282,
    291
    and the public sphere 299
artistic representation
    and the non-existent 34
astrophysical objects 166
astrophysics 247
atomic bomb 3
atomism
    socio-ontological 215
Austin, John L. 155
    speech act theory 236
autonomy
    and social normativity 217
Axial Age 296

axioms of foundation 85–6
Ayer, Alfred J. 155
Azzouni, Jodi 34–5, 55–6, 57

Badiou, Alain 72, 92, 182
Baud, Jean 42
Baudrillard, Jean 237
    Forget Foucault 236
    Simulacra and Simulation 301–2,
        302–3
behavioural science 213
being and semblance 1–2, 4, 7, 18, 39
Benoist, Jocelyn 69, 163, 165, 187, 192
Bergson, Henri 246
    Creative Evolution 70–1
Berkeley, George 44, 113–14, 172
Bible 76
Big Data 287
blind fictional realism 100–2
Blumenberg, Hans 23, 112, 218, 256
    Theory of Nonconceptuality 78–9
Borges, Jorge Luis
    The Aleph 12, 30, 82–9, 90–1, 93, 176,
        178
    On Rigour in Science 90–1
    'The yellow rose' 87
Bourdieu, Pierre 16, 217, 255, 276
brain
    and consciousness 118–19, 121–2,
        222, 237
    and ideology 218
    and the mind 13
    and realism 115
Brandom, Robert 257, 260
Bredekamp, Horst 173
broad realism 102
Brock, Stuart 54, 55
Bubner, Rüdiger 21
Buddhism 116
Butler, Judith 221, 236

Campbell, John 115, 147
Cantor, Georg 71, 92
Carnap, Rudolf 191
Cartesianism 3
Caruso, Gregg D. 174

Cassam, Quassim 115, 147
causality
    and the indispensability of mind
        134–5
    Kant on reasons and causes 148
    paradigms of 13
    and phenomenology 111
Cavell, Stanley 5
censorship 242
CERN 292
Chalmers, David 36
Cohen, G. A. 91
coherence formation
    and aesthetic experience 37
collective intentionality 210
communitization 244
computer science
    and neuroscience 284
confrontation
    and representation 77–8
consciousness 2, 9, 12, 105–6, 109–10,
        111, 242
    'artificial consciousness' 280–1
    conscious-independence and
        metaphysical realism 201
    false image of 16
    and fictionalism 119–20
    first-order object-consciousness
        126
    and global availability 280
    ideology and mythology of
        consciousness 218, 278–85
    and the imagination 172, 173, 175
    and the indispensability of mind
        126–7
    and intentional objects 188
    and ipsundrum 118–19
    and metaphysical imagination 193
    and naïve ontological realism 57
    and naturalism 200
    as an optical illusion 120, 124
    perceptual consciousness and the
        speck-star problem 155–6
    as a projection 118
    and secondary qualities 119
    self-consciousness 114, 126, 127, 190

consciousness (*cont.*)
  and senselessness 174
  and social facts 222, 223, 231–2
  and subjective idealism 116
  synthetic unity of 121
  theories of phenomenal
    consciousness 114–15
  user illusion of 117
  see also illusions/illusionism
conspiracy theories 259
constitutive opacity 189
constructivism 14
content
  of objects of perception 144–5
contradiction
  judgement and social facts 228–9
convictions
  maximum objectivity/subjectivity of
    283
cooperation 243–4
corporations
  and the public sphere 298
Crane, Tim 76
critical social philosophy 16
cultural differences and norms 259

Daneri, Carlos 82, 83, 84, 87
Dante Alighieri 82, 87
Dasein 142
Dasgupta, Shamik 201–2
Death in Venice (Mann) 24, 46, 48
Dehaene, Stanislas 279
democratic states
  and norms 259
  and the public sphere 294, 297
Dennett, Daniel 106, 114, 116, 117, 122,
    200, 213
deontological difference
  and social construction 209–10
deontological model
  of mental representations 147–8
Derrida, Jacques 192
Descartes, René 97, 131–2, 147, 172
  and the imagination 172, 173
Detel, Wolfgang 145–6
dialetheism 81

dictatorships
  and social networks 290–1
  totalitarian 243
digital media
  fantasy and reality 23
  and self-images 7
digital proletariat 17, 288, 290
digital revolution 3, 214
digital surveillance 247
digitalization
  and intransparency zones 302
  mythology and ideology of 281,
    284–5
  and the public sphere 296–7,
    298–9
  self-digitalization 7
  and social networks 286, 289, 292
disagreement 16, 17
disciplinary fallacy 249
discourses
  and social realism 215–16
discursive violence 295
dissent 207, 214, 215, 248, 257
  communities of dissenters 16
  and the intransparency of society
    260–1
  and norm circles 272
  and social facts 207, 227, 231, 232
  and social networks 288
Dostoyevsky, Fyodor 56
Doyle, Arthur Conan 100, 101
Driesch, Hans 246

ecological destruction 304
Eggers, David 298
Elder-Vass, Dave 268
Eleatic puzzle/paradox of non-
    existence 7–8, 11, 30–1, 73–5, 94
election forecasts 276–7
eliminative materialism 121
eliminative physicalism 138
emergentism 224–5
empirical regress blockers 253
empiricism
  classical 44, 171
  and the imagination 172

and objective phenomenology 171
and subjective idealism 114
emptiness of fictional objects 57–8
epiphenomenalism 13, 128–30
epistemic realism 125, 126, 127–8
epistemic self-consciousness 126
error, norms arising from 273–4
Eurocentrism 237
Everett, Anthony 54, 55, 59
evolution
    and the mind 244–5
    and natural history 281
evolutionary humanism 199
existent objects
    and FOS (ontology of fields of sense)
        8, 61–3
existentialism 106, 174
    neo-existentialism 282–3
experimental philosophy
    and social networks 291–2

facets
    in perception of objects 144
fact-perception 154
facticity, argument from 63–4, 115, 158
facts
    factual disagreement 14–15
    FOS and objects 62
fake news 300
fallibility
    and factual dissent 14
    and human thought 244
    and the imagination 172, 181
    and judgements 229, 242
    and knowledge claims 250–3
    and normalization 240
    and objectivity 166–7
    and perceptual knowledge 170
    and self-regulation 238
    and social theory 249
fallibility environment 184
fantasy and reality 5
Fargo (TV series) 39–40
Faust (Goethe)
    artistic representation and
        semblance 22–3

existence and non-existence in 8, 11,
    34–5, 74
fictional and fictive objects in 6, 10,
    11, 19–20, 22, 42, 46, 50, 52–3, 57
and fictional realism 10, 11, 33
and metaphysical fictionalism 175–6
production of 38
Ferraris, Maurizio 14, 224, 225
Fichte, Johann Gottlieb 97–8, 126, 189
    and metaphysical intentionalism
        195, 197, 199
fiction 16, 218, 276–85
    Vaihinger on fiction and hypothesis
        161
    see also ideology
fictional irrealism 33, 53, 58–9
fictional objects 5–6, 19–25
    emptiness of 57–8
    and fictional irrealism 33
    and fictional realism 10, 33
    and fictive objects 1–2, 6, 19–23,
        33–4, 46–55
    fields of sense 10, 35–6, 75–6
    hermeneutical and meta-
        hermeneutical 10, 20–2, 46
    imaginary objects 6
    incoherence of 57, 58–9
    interpretation of 51
    isolation thesis 22–3
    in literary art works 1–2
    and Meinongianism 94
    non-existence of 46–60, 74–5, 79–81
    polysemy of 57, 59–60
    see also art works; fictive objects
Fictional Objects (Brock and Everett)
    54, 55
fictional places 1
fictional realism 9–12, 19–104
    blind fictional realism 100–2
    and hermeneutical objects 10
    interpretation and reading 33–45
    and meta-hermeneutical objects 10
    and naïve ontological realism 55–7
    see also fictional objects; fictive
        objects; FOS (ontology of fields of
        sense)

fictional times 1
fictionalism 119–20, 121–2
    metaphysical fictionalism 30, 175–8,
        191–2
fictions 5
    and ideology 218
    and norms 273–4
fictive objects 6, 10, 14, 18, 22–3, 46–60,
        190–1
    and facts 11
    fictional need for supplementation
        52
    and fictional objects 1–2, 6, 19–23,
        33–4, 46–55, 60
    fictive fictive objects 50
    FOS (ontology of fields of sense) 8,
        10, 11, 22, 85, 200–1
    and imaginary objects 112, 187
    and the imagination 172
    in literary texts 24–5
    and mental realism 14, 187
    and meta-hermeneutical objects 77
    and metaphysical fictionalism 191–2
    and metaphysical intentionalism
        197
    and metaphysical realism 200–1,
        202, 203
    and non-existent objects 34–7
    performance-dependence of 6
    the Terminator 304
    and virtual reality 299–300
fields of sense *see* FOS (ontology of
    fields of sense)
Fields of Sense [*Sinn und Existenz*]
    (Gabriel) 8, 89
Flanagan, Owen 174
flat formal theory of objects 95–6
Floridi, Luciano 292
focal analysis 234
FOS (ontology of fields of sense) 8, 61,
        62–4
    appearing in themselves 89
    argument from facticity 63–4
    and existence 11, 61–2, 69–71, 72,
        180–1
    and existent objects 8, 61–3

fictional objects 10, 35–6, 75–6
fictive objects 8, 10, 11, 22, 85,
        200–1
    and the imagination 173, 174,
        178–82, 184, 186
    and the indispensability of mind
        125, 139–40
    and the lifeworld 13, 141–51
    Meinongian ontology of 69, 74–5
    meontology of 8, 11, 26, 28–9, 64,
        67–81
    and metaphysical fictionalism
        175–8, 191–2
    and metaphysical imagination
        192–5
    and metaphysical intentionalism
        195–6, 197, 199–200
    and metaphysical realism 200–1,
        203
    and models of objects 189
    and neo-Meinongian object theory
        12, 30–1, 94–104
    neutral realism of 12, 63
    no-world view of 11–12, 67, 91, 92
    and non-existence 11
    and object-perception theory 154
    objects in a field of sense 61–4, 71,
        73, 163–4, 190–1, 241
    ontological realism of 98–9, 186
    and ontological relationism 70, 71,
        75–6
    ordering function of 61–2
    and perceptual realism 13, 158–70
    Priest's model of the Mehlich–Koch
        objection 11–12, 30, 82–93
    realistic 188
    rejection of the argument from
        annihilation 80
    and round squares 178–80
    and social facts 226
    and social realism 211–12
    and 'the world' 112
    in the universe 108
    and worldviews 91
Foucault, Michel 236, 237, 296
    and Eurocentrism 237

Frankish, Keith 116, 117, 118–19, 120–1, 121–2
free will 213
  and digitalization 247
  in Hegel 217
freedom
  and disagreement 14, 17
  and normativity 256
  and sociality 291
Frege, Gottlob 96, 156, 163–4

Gadamer, Hans-Georg 26, 42–3, 78, 79
  Truth and Method 43
Galileo Galilei 147
game theory 213, 216, 274
Garay, Juan de 82
Geist (human mindedness) 8–9, 13, 17, 18, 107, 174
generic social construction
  Haslanger on 234–5
German Idealism 198, 199
Giordano Bruno Foundation 199
global observables 193
Gödel, Kurt 72–3, 91
Goethe, Johann Wolfgang von 10, 27
  see also Faust
Goodman, Nelson 201
Gordon, Lewis 249
Greco-Roman subjectivity theory 280
Greek philosophers
  and non-existence 7–8, 74
Grim, Patrick 182
Gründgens, Gustaf 34, 42

Habermas, Jürgen
  on the public sphere 7, 294–6, 298
Hacking, Ian 248
hallucinations
  existence of 8
  and FOS (ontology of fields of sense) 8
  and naïve ontological realism 56, 57
Hamlet (Shakespeare) 83–4

handshakes 255
Harari, Yuval Noah
  Sapiens: A Brief History of Humankind 246–7
Harman, Graham 203
Haslanger, Sally
  concept of social construction 14, 221, 233–5
heautonomy model of normativity 260, 274
Hegel, G. W. F. 23, 106, 217
  'idea of the will' 217
  on norms in modernity 260
  Phenomenology of Spirit 137, 197–8
  Science of Logic 123
  on 'self-will' 241
Heidegger, Martin 3, 146, 174
  Being and Time 142–3
  Contributions to Philosophy 9
hermeneutical objects 10, 20–2, 24, 25, 37–8, 46, 52, 54, 60
  and the aesthetic experience 44–5
  see also fictive objects
hermeneutical realism 25, 184–6
Hesiod 55
heterophenomenology 114
Hill, James T. 178–9, 180, 181–2
Hobbes, Thomas 84
Hölderlin, Friedrich 304
holding-to-be-true 14, 15, 207, 215, 226–31, 238
  and knowledge claims 250, 251
  and objectivity 240–1
  and the public sphere 295
  and rule-following 217, 273–4
  and social facts 228–31, 232
  and social networks 288–9
  and social theory 242
holism
  socio-ontological 215
Holmes, Sherlock
  and fictional realism 24, 53, 54, 100–1
Homer 7–8, 87, 249
  Iliad 77
homunculi 107, 109, 122

Houellebecq, Michel
  The Map and the Territory 1, 20, 22,
      24, 26, 52, 76, 79–80, 175, 176, 177
human beings
  animality of 246, 304
  minded form of life 303–4
  and modellism 278, 280
  myth-making 247
  mythology and ideology of 280–5
  and social construction 235, 243–4
  and social reproduction 14, 216,
      222–3, 231–2, 238–9
  survival form 212, 245–7
human mindedness *see Geist* (human
      mindedness)
human self-portraits 17, 18
human standpoint 4, 111, 125
  and the indispensability of mind
      134–5, 137
human thought 244–5
humanism 282
humanistic irreducibility thesis 3–4,
      12–13
humanities 2, 3, 4, 10, 107, 285
  and rule-following 263
  and social realism 212
Hume, David 44, 172, 264
Humphrey, Nicholas 118–19
Husserl, Edmund 99, 111, 146, 156,
      161
  and the lifeworld 111, 141–3
  The Crisis of European Sciences 13,
      141, 142, 150
Hutter, Axel 284
hypotheses
  sceptical 259, 265
  Vaihinger on fiction and hypothesis
      161

ideal objects 97, 98
idealism
  absolute 102–3
  German Idealism 198, 199
  ontic 196–7
  ontological 12, 97, 99
  subjective 113–14, 115, 116

idealistic transparency thesis 126
identity
  and existence 68
ideology 16, 218, 277–8
  of consciousness 278–85
  and implicit norms 256
  and the public sphere 295
  and social networks 293
Iliad (Homer) 77
illusions/illusionism 12, 110–11,
      116–24
  and epiphenomenalism 129
  and imaginary objects 187
  and the indispensability of mind
      125, 127, 128
  optical illusions 120, 125, 164, 167–8
  and qualia 116, 118, 119
  and realism 241
  and the speck-star problem 162–70
  UFOs and God 120–1
  see also consciousness
imaginary objects 6, 14, 112, 187,
      190–1
  and intentional objects 187–8, 189
  and metaphysical imagination 193
  and metaphysical intentionalism
      197
  and metaphysical realism 200, 202,
      203
imagination 13–14, 172–86
  and fallibility 172
  and fictive objects 6
  and hermeneutical realism 184–6
  and the manifestation of the world
      13–14
  and metaphysical fictionalism 30,
      175–8
  metaphysical imagination 192–5
  and metaphysical objects 111–12
  and the no-world view 11
  and self-determination 7
imaginative abstraction 185
implicit norms 255–6, 257, 259, 260,
      261
incoherence of fictional objects 57,
      58–9

indispensability thesis 111
individual autobiographies 6
inductive world-appropriation 111
industrial feudalism 298
inferentialist pseudology 171
infinite regress 252–3
institutions
    dismantling of 254
    and social realism 214
intelligibility of the mind 138–40
intentional consciousness 123
intentional objects 6, 14, 31, 69, 112,
        187–8, 189, 190–1, 195
    and metaphysical realism 200, 202,
        203
intentionalism
    metaphysical 195–200
intentionality 2, 12, 31, 49, 240
    and consciousness 279
    and language 222
    and metaphysical realism 201
    and the naturalization of the social
        254
    norms and intentional actions 258
    and rule-following 267
    and social construction 237
    and social realism 205–6, 210
interpretations
    of art works 25
    and fictive objects 6, 25
interpretive space 22
intrafictional truth 70
intransparency 260–1, 273, 276
    and digitalization 302
    and the public sphere 296
introspection 117, 118, 121, 122
intuition
    of objects 66, 188, 189
ipsundrum 118–19
irradiation 13, 111
    and perception theory 147
irrealism
    and FOS (ontology of fields of sense)
        63–4
    and the imagination 172
irreducibility thesis 3–4, 12–13

isolation thesis 22–3
iterativity thesis 126

James, William 183–4
judgements
    about the social 15, 214–15
    and corrections 230–1, 243
    and dissent 207, 257
    equation with existential statements
        68
    and fallibility 229, 242
    and the indispensability of mind
        133–4
    and knowledge claims 252
    measuring norms 258–9
    self-referential 284
    and social facts 226, 228–31, 232,
        238
    subjective and objective 283–4

Kant, Immanuel 21, 65, 94, 100, 121–2,
        188
    Critique of Pure Reason 214
    *Groundwork of the Metaphysics of
        Morals* 148–9
    on judgement 231
    on mathematical judgements
        264–5
    and metaphysical intentionalism
        106
    Refutation of Idealism 44
    and self-determination 233
Kant–Vaihinger tradition 30
Kantian physicalism 146
Kehlmann, Daniel
    F 40–1
Kierkegaard, Søren 174
Kittler, Friedrich 225
Kleist, Heinrich von 194
knowledge
    and epiphenomenalism 129–30
    fallibility and knowledge claims
        250–3
    and social networks 291–2
Koch, Anton Friedrich 29, 175
    hermeneutical realism 184–6

Koudier, Sid 279
Kripke, Saul A. 15, 47, 155, 262
    on rule-following 264, 265, 266–7,
        268, 269, 271
Kripkenstein rule problem 256, 262,
        268, 270

language
    acquisition 51, 222–3
    linguistic references 225–6
    norms 257–8
language-independence
    and naïve ontological realism 55–6,
        56–7, 62
Laplace's demon 110
The Last Unicorn (film) 11, 36–7, 69–70
Lau, Hakwan 279
Leibniz, Gottfried 84–5, 101, 114, 121
Lewis, David 71
liberal democracy 247
lifeworlds
    and fictional realism 78
    and mental realism 13, 111, 141–3,
        149–50
    and science 175
The Limits of Epistemology (Gabriel) 56
literary art works *see* art works
local observables 193–4
Locke, John 172
logos 250
luminosity argument (Williams) 130–3

Man, Paul de 84
Mann, Thomas
    Death in Venice 24, 46, 48
manners as social norms 255
Marino, Giambattista 87
mathematics 72–3, 179
Matravers, Derek
    Fiction and Narrative 77, 78
The Matrix 302
Max, Karl 235–6, 237
media
    mass media and the public sphere
        298
    reporting 276–7

medicine
    and human survival 246–7
Mehlich, Julia 29, 175
Mehlich–Koch objection 11–12, 29–31,
        30, 82, 82–93
Meillassoux, Quentin 71–2, 91, 92, 195,
        196
Meinong, Alexius 8, 30, 31, 88, 99
    see also neo-Meinongian object
        theory
memory
    and fictional realism 56
mental life 138–9
    and survival form 244
mental realism 12–14, 105–203
    and ideology 218
    imagination 13–14, 172–86
    the indispensability of mind 125–40
    and lifeworlds 13, 111, 141–51
    and metaphysical realism 27, 125,
        127–8, 184, 200–3
    naïve realism 12, 55–8, 110–11,
        113–16
    see also consciousness; illusions/
        illusionism; intentional objects;
        perception
mental states 241
meontological isolationism 10, 26,
        35–6, 50
meontological realism 64–5
meontological relationism 28–9
meontology 5
    of FOS (ontology of fields of sense)
        8, 11, 28–9, 67–81
Mephistopheles
    as a fictive object 8, 27, 49
    non-existence of 27
metacognition 280
metadata 287
metafictional narratives 54
metafictional truth 70
meta-hermeneutical objects 10, 20, 22,
        24, 43–4, 46, 54, 56, 60, 77
meta-ontological realism 63
metaphors
    absolute 112

metaphysical fictionalism 30, 175–8, 191–2
metaphysical idealism 194–5
metaphysical imagination 192–5
metaphysical intentionalism 195–200
  and naturalism 198–9
metaphysical mereology
  and Priest's model of the Mehlich–Koch objection 86–7
metaphysical naturalism 212, 303
metaphysical realism 27, 125, 127–8, 184, 200–3
metaphysics 26–7, 30
  critique of 16
  and the imagination 174–5
mind 2
  and the brain 13
  and evolution 244–5
  Geist (human mindedness) 8–9, 13, 17, 18, 107
  indispensability of 125–40, 141, 150–1
  living a minded life 284
  and nature 255
  public sphere of the mind 17–18, 219–20
  and social realism 213, 238–9
mind-independence 105, 110–11, 126
  and naïve realism 55–6, 56–7, 62, 115, 116
  and perception 168
modal realism 71
modellism 278, 280
models of objects 188–9
  self-modelling 189–90
modernity 247
  and the intransparency of society 260
Möllers, Christopher
  concept of norms 255–8, 259–60, 273–4
money
  and Searle on social constructivism 224
monopolization 219
moral progress 4–5, 17

Müller–Lyer illusion 120, 124, 164
myth-making 247
mythology 16, 218, 277–81
  of consciousness 278–85
  and implicit norms 256
  of modellism 278
  and scientific paradigms 249
  and social networks 293

naïve realism 12, 55–8, 110–11, 113–16
  argument from facticity 113, 158
narrative ontology 284
narratology
  metafictional narratives 54
Nassehi, Armin 244, 288
nationalism 243
natural and social species 253–4
natural facts 223–4
  and social facts 230
natural history
  and evolution 281
natural philosophy
  and metaphysical intentionalism 198
  and social constructivism 210
  and social facts 225
natural properties
  of metaphysical realism 201–2
natural sciences
  and anonymous nature 209–10, 212
  and consciousness 110
  and rule-following 263, 272–3
  and social facts 224, 225, 233
naturalism 16, 18
  and human survival 246
  and Husserl's phenomenology 141, 145–6
  and the indispensability of mind 138–9, 140
  and metaphysical intentionalism 198–9
  and realism 135
  and rule-following 272–3
naturalistic fallacy 233
naturalistic worldviews 9

naturalization of the social 254
negation
  Bergson on negation of existence
    70–1
  and holding-to-be-true 242
neo-existentialism 106, 281
neo-Meinongian object theory 8, 12,
    14, 30–1, 94–104, 176
  characterization principle (CP) 95
neo-Platonism 178
neo-realism
  and perception theory 147, 156
neurocentrism 16, 129
neuroexistentialism 174
neuroscience 4, 7, 174
  and computer science 284
neutral monism 169
neutral realism 63
'Neutral Realism' (Gabriel) 56
New Realism 14, 126, 268, 299
newspaper hoaxes 300
Nietzsche, Friedrich 174, 191, 192, 199,
    237, 247, 296
no-world view 11–12, 28, 30, 67, 147
  and absolute nothingness 81
  and fields of sense 180
  Hill's objection from inexpressibility
    to 178–9
  and intentional objects 69
  and the Mehlich–Koch objection
    11–12, 82, 85, 91, 92
  and objects 98–9
Noble, Denis 107–8
non-existence 9, 11, 27–8
  Eleatic puzzle/paradox of 7–8, 11,
    30–1, 73–5, 94
  existing and non-existing objects
    34–7
  of fictional objects 46–60
  see also meontology
non-existent objects
  and FOS (ontology of fields of sense)
    8
non-intentional objects
  and metaphysical intentionalism
    197, 199–200

and metaphysical realism 200–1,
    202, 203
non-natural properties
  of metaphysical realism 201–2
norm circles 271, 272, 273
normalization
  and fallibility 240
norms/normativity 255–60
  affirmation and negation of 259–60
  and fictions 273–4
  heautonomy model of normativity
    260, 274
  implicit 255–6, 257, 259, 260, 261
  intransparent 258
  manners as social norms 255
  of mental representations 147–8
  Möller's concept of 255–8
  as a realizing marker 255
  and rule-following 15, 217, 218,
    258–9, 267–9, 271–4
  and social facts 232, 233, 276
  and social realism 208, 210–11, 212,
    213, 214, 215, 217
nothingness 12
  absolute 80–1

object-perception theory 153–5
object-theoretical contingentism 102
object-theoretical necessitism 102
objective mind 206–7
objective perceptual fields 5
objective phenomenology 13, 111, 149,
    152–71
  the speck-star problem 155–7,
    155–8, 160, 162–70
objectivity
  and error 3–4
  and the mind 240–1
  of scientific and technological
    knowledge 2–3
  and subjectivity 252
objects
  abstract objects 188
  the Aleph 12, 30, 82–9, 90–1, 93, 103,
    195
  being objects 81

existence of 66–7
existing objects 81, 183
factivity link in perception of 152–3
in a field of sense 61–4, 71, 73,
   163–4, 190–1, 241
and hermeneutical realism 184–5
ideal objects 97–8
intentional objects 6, 14, 31, 69, 112,
   187–8, 189, 190–1, 195
Meinongian theory of 30, 31, 88
and mental realism 146–7
merely imagined 19
meta-hermeneutical objects 10, 20,
   22, 24, 43–4, 46, 54, 56, 60, 77
and metaphysical imagination 194
and metaphysical realism 202–3
models of 188–9
neo-Meinongian theory of 8, 12, 14,
   30–1, 94–104, 176
non-existence of 7–8, 11, 30–1, 68,
   73–4
non-intentional 197, 199–200, 200–1
perception of 5, 6, 143–5, 153–5,
   162–71
physical and non-physical 158–9
pre-ontological experience of 65
real objects 97–8, 188
and social facts 221, 226
see also fictional objects; fictive
   objects; imaginary objects;
   intentional objects
occasions and stimuli 241
Olam
   and metaphysical fictionalism 176–8
ontic idealism 196–7
ontological idealism 12, 97, 99
ontological irrealism 64
ontological pluralism 67, 125, 183–4,
   203
ontological realism 64, 67, 97, 98, 179,
   180, 186
ontological relationism 70, 71, 75–6, 80
ontology
   and meontology 61
   of social networks 17
opacity of the social 15, 16, 215, 216

optical illusions 120, 124, 125, 164,
   167–8
otherness of the social 15

Parfit, Derek 66
Parmenides 27, 55, 61, 64, 65
perception 3–4, 5, 6, 13
   Aristotelian tradition of 170
   and causation 13
   concept of 65–6
   condition theory of 156–7
   factivity of 150, 152–3, 170
   and fictional objects 5
   and intentional objects 6, 187–8
   and metaphysical imagination
      193–4
   and naïve realism 114, 158
   neo-realist theory of 111
   object-perception theory 153–5
   and objective phenomenology 111,
      152–71
   perceptual realism 158–70
   and the phenomenological
      argument 142–51, 152, 154–8
   and sensation 136
   as a social product 240
   and the speck-star problem 155–8,
      162–70
Pessoa, Fernando
   The Book of Disquiet 41
phantom pain 105, 123
phenomenal consciousness
   and illusionism 116–24
   theories of 114–15
   see also consciousness
phenomenological argument
   and perception 142–51, 152, 154–8
phenomenology
   in Husserl 141–5
   indispensability of phenomenality
      127–33
   see also objective phenomenology
physicalism
   eliminative 138
physics 3
   and imagination 173

physics (*cont.*)
  and the lifeworld 141
  and neuroscience 174
  and physical and non-physical
    objects 158–9
  and social ontology 226
  see also quantum theory
Pippin, Robert B. 260
Plato 22, 27, 61, 178, 250
  Apology 214
  Republic 55
  and rule-following 265, 268
  Symposium 181
pluralism, ontological 67, 125, 183–4,
  203
political autonomy 232–3
polysemy of 'fictional object' 57, 59–60
postmodernity 2, 301
post-truth era 299, 301–2, 303, 304
power relations 16
  Foucault on 236, 237
predication theory 182
predictive policing 214
Price, Huw 115
Priest, Graham 179
  on absolute nothingness 80–1
  and neo-Meinongian object theory
    8, 12, 94–7, 100, 101, 102
  reconstruction of the Mehlich–Koch
    objection 11–12, 30–1, 84–9, 93
primate research 213
prisoner's dilemmas 274
privacy
  and social realism 214
private sphere 297–8, 299
production
  of social facts 235–6, 237–8
projectivism 118
Proust, Marcel
  In Search of Lost Time 48–9
public sphere 294–300
  digitalized 296–7
  and ideology 295
  and the intransparency of society
    260
  of the mind 17–18, 219–20

  and the private sphere 297–8, 299
  and self-digitalization 7
  and social networks 297–8
  and social realism 214
Putnam, Hilary 184, 191

Quakers 255
qualia (feeling) 116, 118
quantum theory
  and the indispensability of mind
    134–8, 139–40
  and intentional objects 188
  and metaphysical imagination 193,
    194
  and perception 166, 168, 170
Quine, W. V. O. 64–5, 249, 250, 257
  Word and Object 195

radical social constructivism 207, 224
readings of art works 10, 24–5, 77
the real
  and rule-following 217
real objects 97–8, 188
realism
  anti-realism 96–7, 101
  broad realism 102
  FOS and perceptual realism 158–70
  hermeneutical realism 25, 184–6
  and idealism 115
  and illusionism 241
  meta-ontological 63
  metaphysical realism 27, 125, 127–8,
    184, 200–3
  neutral realism 63
  old realism 27
  ontological 64, 67, 97, 98, 179, 180,
    186
  perceptual 169
  realist social philosophy 16
  and rule-following 268
  see also fictional realism; mental
    realism; naïve realism; New
    Realism; social realism
reality
  in art works 78–80
  being and semblance 1

and fantasy 5
and fictive objects 6, 50
resistance of 16
reason, sociality of 228
reasons 241–2
recognition 14
recursive complexity 274
recursive self-determination 233
reflexive autonomy 260
registration-independent thought 113
relativity theory 166
religion
and human survival 246
representation
and confrontation 77–8
Rilke, Rainer Maria 9
Rodin, Auguste
The Thinker 41–2
Rödl, Sebastian 134
Römer, Hartmann 193
Rometsch, Jens 79, 131
Rorty, Richard 84, 225
'round squares' manoeuvre 178–80
Rousseau, Jean-Jacques 192
Rovelli, Carlo 134–8, 139, 159–60
rule-following 15–16, 216–17, 262–75, 276
context of delusion 271
correct and deviant actions 263
and learning behaviour 265–6
and miscalculation 267
norms 15, 217, 218, 258–9, 267–9, 271–2
and self-regulation 263
and social facts 15, 262–3
sociologism 271
in Wittgenstein 262, 263, 269–70
Russell, Bertrand 87, 156, 169, 171
Ryle, Gilbert 29

Sartre, Jean-Paul 174
sceptical hypotheses 259, 265, 266
Schelling, Friedrich 198
Schiller, Friedrich 21
Schmitt, Carl 243
Schopenhauer, Arthur 199, 247

Schwarzenegger, Arnold 304
science
and the imagination 173
and the lifeworld 142
and philosophy 303
science fiction 18, 76–7
scientific and technological knowledge
cooperation and moral progress 4–5
and FOS (ontology of fields of sense) 107–8
and the human standpoint 111
and naturalism 139
objectivity and subjectivity of 2–3
scientism 66
scores (of art works) 42–3, 77
aesthetic experience of 10, 21, 23–5, 36–8
meta-hermeneutics of 52
performance of 37–8
Searle, John 258
consciousness theory 119, 222, 237
and social facts 14, 221–2, 223, 224, 225, 226, 236–7
self-awareness 190
self-conceptions 106–7
and the indispensability thesis 111
self-consciousness 114, 126, 127, 190, 242
self-delusion 253–4, 283
self-determination 232–3, 247, 254–5
and consciousness 280, 282
self-images
and human mindedness 8–9, 107, 108–9, 110, 239
self-referential judgements 284
semblance
artistic representation as 22–3
and being 1–2, 4, 6–7, 18, 39
post-truth 303
sensation
and perception 136
senselessness and the imagination 173–4
set theory 98, 182
Sider, Theodore 201
simplicity, argument of 158

The Simpsons 301
social and natural species 253–4
social autonomy 233
social constructivism 14, 16, 18,
    207–14, 215–16, 224–5, 233–6,
    243–4, 248, 276
  and anonymous nature 208–10
  and coordinated activity 235–6
  and deontological difference 209–10
  and free will 217
  moderate 209
  and normativity 210–11
  radical 207, 209, 224
  and rule-following 274
  and speech acts 236–7
social facts 205–7, 214, 221–39, 243
  and actions 206, 216
  construction of 207–11
  and dissent 207, 227, 231, 232
  and emergentism 224–5
  existence of 206
  and fictions 276
  humans as socially produced beings
    205–6
  the implicit in 236
  and judgements 226, 228–31, 232,
    238
  and language 222–3
  and natural facts 223–4
  and non-social facts 205, 224
  and norms 232, 233, 276
  and rule-following 15, 262–3, 266,
    274
  Searle on 221
  and social networks 290
  see also holding-to-be-true; social
    constructivism
social identity 8
  and rule-following 262
social media *see* social networks
social networks 17, 214, 219, 286–93
  algorithms 289
  and analogue communication
    289–90, 291
  biases in 287
  defining 286

and dissent 288
and experimental philosophy 291–2
externalization of experiences 287
and the intransparency of society
  260
and knowledge claims 291–2
and the public sphere 297–8
self-images 286–7, 292
and the virtual 289, 292
social ontology 14, 18
social opacity 215
social realism 14–18, 205–300
  and anonymous nature 208–10, 211,
    212
  and FOS (ontology of fields of sense)
    211–12
  judgement about the social 214–15
  and mind 213
  and normativity 208, 210–11, 212,
    213, 214
  and objective mind 206–7
  and philosophical theory-building
    248–50
  and predictive policing 214
  see also social facts
social sciences 2, 4, 10, 107, 212
  ideology 277, 285
  and norms 257, 258–9, 260, 273
  and rule-following 263, 272, 274–5
social systems, production of 248
sociality 18, 244
  and disagreement 16
  and human neural networks 238
  of minded beings 245–6
  of thinking and speaking 237
  and truth 17, 290–1
  virtual 292–3
socio-ontological atomism 215
socio-ontological holism 215
sociologism and rule-following 271
Socrates 55
Solon 55
Sophism 295
speck-star problem 155–8, 160, 162–70
speculative realism 202–3
speech acts 236–7

stars
  and metaphysical realism 201–2
  speck-star problem 155–8, 160,
    162–70
states, totalitarian 243
stimuli and occasions 241
strict ontological irrealism 64
subjective idealism 113–14, 115, 116
subjective perceptual fields 5
subjectivity 106
  and consciousness 280
  Koch's subjectivity thesis 185–6
  Nietzsche on 237
  and objectivity 252
  of scientific and technological
    knowledge 2–3
suchness
  and neo-Meinongian object theory
    101, 103–4
  of social facts 206
the sun
  perception of 147, 148–9, 156, 164–6,
    169–70
supervenience 105
surveillance 242
  and social networks 290
survival form
  and mental life form 244
sustainability 304
systems theory 242

technology
  and fictional realism 78
  see also scientific and technological
    knowledge
Terminator films 304
totalitarian dictators 243
trace model of mental representations
    156–7
transcendental argument (TA)
  and metaphysical intentionalism
    195–6
transcendental imagination 185
transhumanism 247, 281
transparentism 185
Travis, Charles 182–3, 187

Trump, Donald 301
truth
  and disagreement 14, 17
  and the disciplinary fallacy 249
  metafictional and intrafictional 70
  post-truth era 299, 301–2, 303, 304
  and the social 15
  and social networks 288–9
  and sociality 17, 290–1
  of statements 98–9
  see also holding-to-be-true
truth-apt 6, 44
  intentional attitudes 239
  and non-existence 7
  and objects of knowledge 99–100
  and perception 3–4

unicorns 11, 36–7, 69–70
unity and sociality 15
the universe 108, 110
  and emergentism 224–5
  and human animality 246
  and the imagination 173–4, 175
  and the indispensability of mind
    134–8, 139–40
  pluralistic 183–4
  and social facts 224
unsocial sociability 215
the urtext 25, 43
utility, objects of 38

Vaihinger, Hans 161, 191, 192
  The Philosophy of 'As If' 90
van Inwagen, Peter 42
vicious infinite regress 252–3
Vienna Circle 111
violence, discursive 295
virtual reality 299–300
vitalism 246
Viterbo, Beatriz 82, 83, 84

Walton, Kendall 34, 47
War and Peace (Tolstoy) 47, 58–9
Wigner, Eugene 194
Williamson, Timothy 250
  luminosity argument 130–3

witches 28
Wittgenstein, Ludwig 110, 227, 230,
    255, 259
  On Certainty 263
  Philosophical Investigations 258, 262,
    263, 269–70
  Tractatus 163

world objects
    and absolute nothingness 80–1

Xenophanes 55

the *zeitgeist* 1, 3, 174, 303
zones of opacity 15, 16